SRA ART Connections

Arts Education for the 21st Century

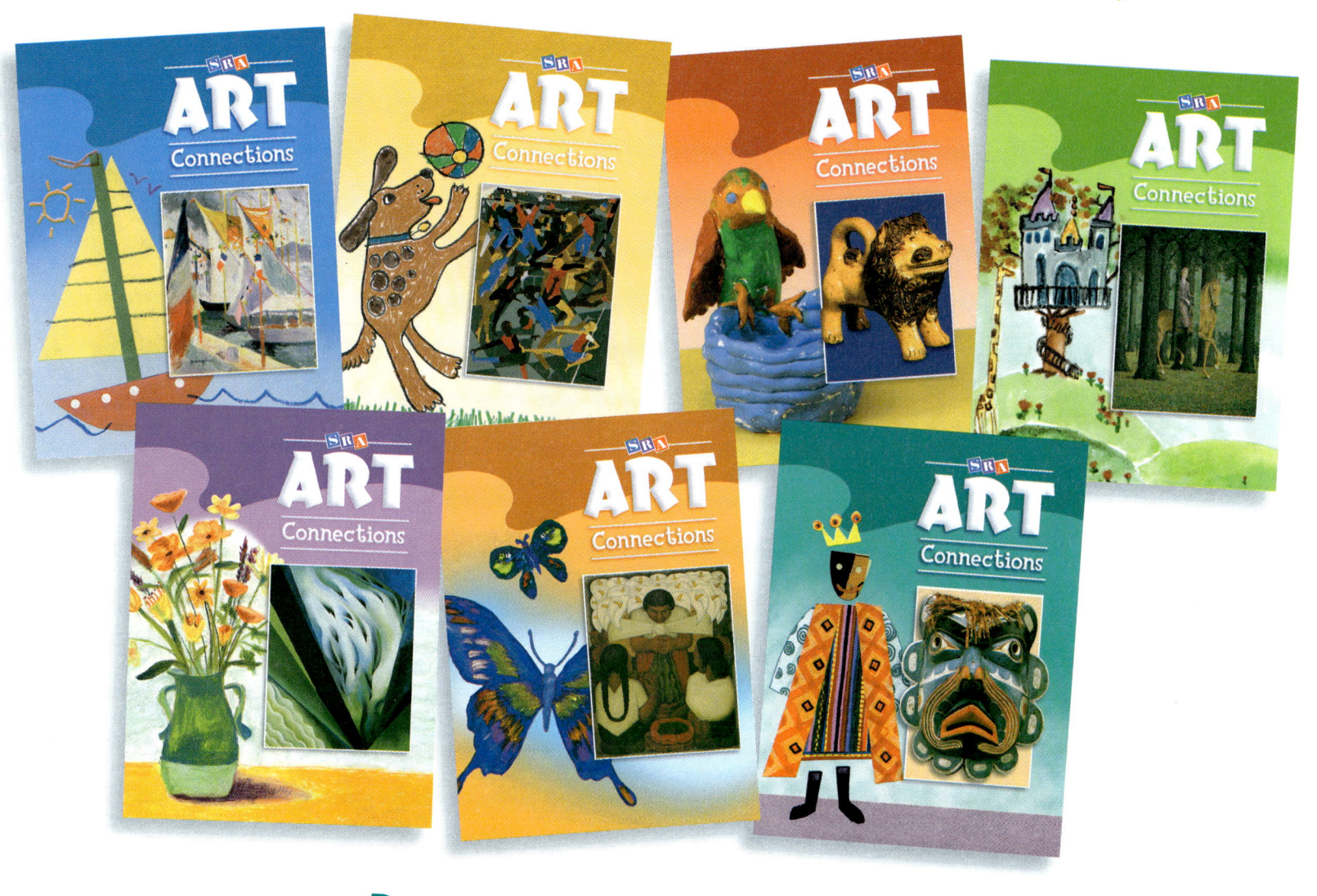

Culture   **Personal Expression**   **Creativity**

History   **Beauty**   **Critical Thinking**

Art encourages different ways of learning, knowing, and communicating.

i

SRA ART Connections

All the Resources you Need for Great Art Teaching!

Art Connections provides everything teachers need to offer meaningful art education.

Student Edition K-6

Comprehensive student materials in two formats:

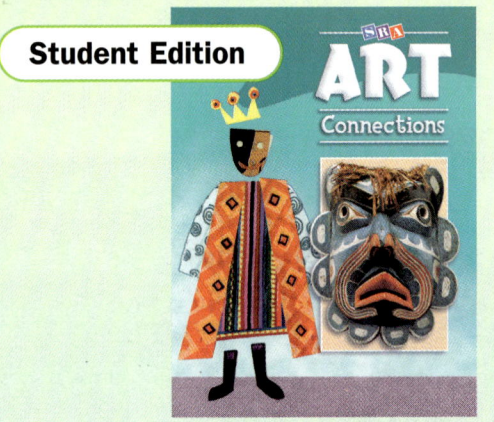

- Student Edition
- Big Book

LEVEL 6

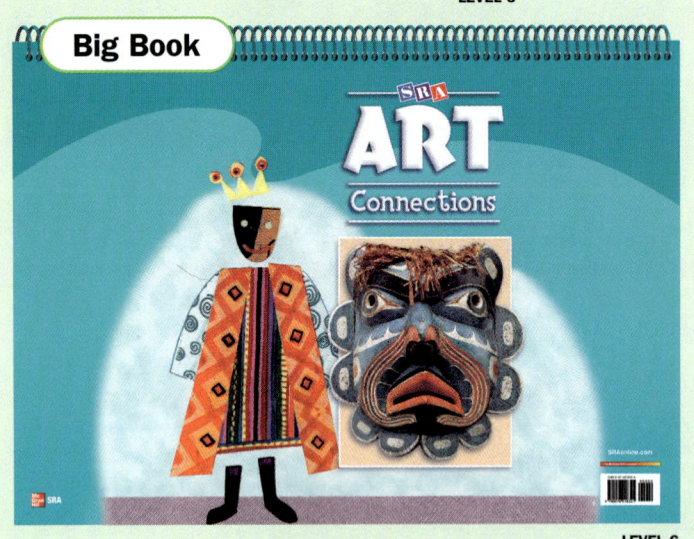

Teacher Edition

Everything classroom and art teachers need to teach art effectively

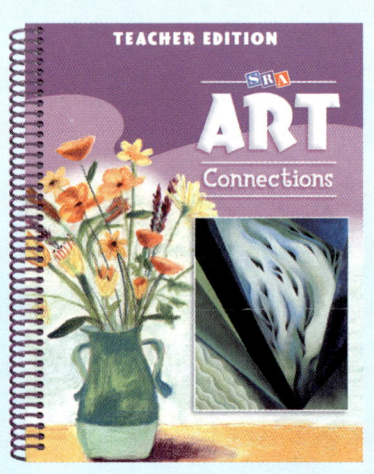

LEVEL 4

- Complete lesson plans to teach
  - elements and principles of art
  - art history and culture
  - art criticism
  - art production
- Art background
- Cross-curricular connections
- Program resources guide

Technology Components

e-Presentation for students and teachers

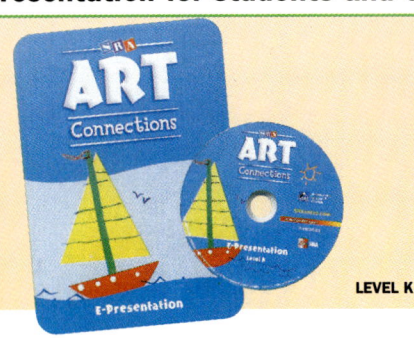

LEVEL K

e-Presentation offers the complete Student Edition as a presentation tool for teachers, complete with multimedia experiences, assessments, teacher materials, and a gallery of all artworks in the entire program.

This electronic gallery allows immediate access to all the artwork in the *Art Connections* program.

Teacher Resources

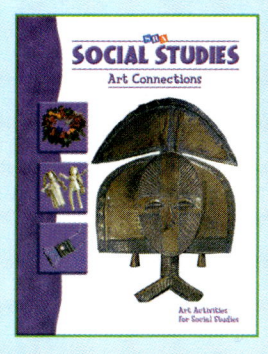

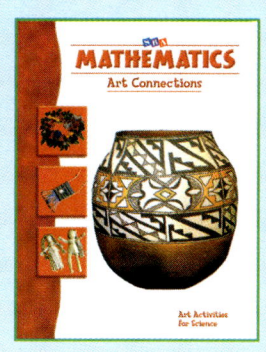

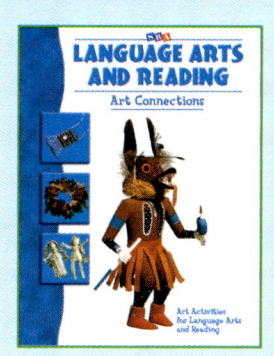

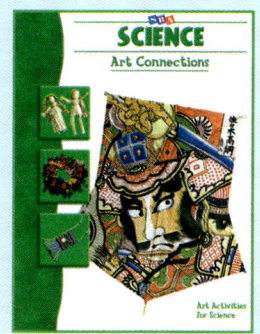

Cross-Curricular Art Connections include practical art projects for the classroom to help meet subject-area guidelines in
- Social Studies
- Mathematics
- Language Arts and Reading
- Science

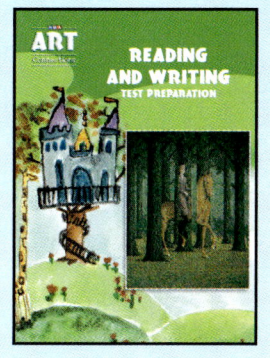

Reading and Writing Test Preparation that reinforces art content

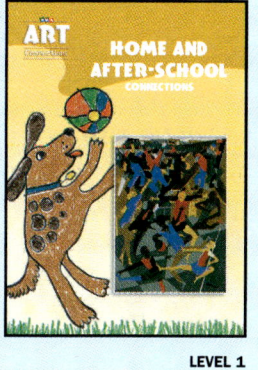

LEVEL 3

Home and After-School Connections for every unit, in English and Spanish

LEVEL 1

Professional Development Guide for both classroom teachers and art specialists

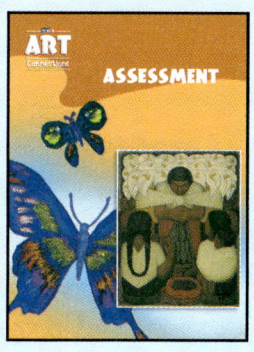

Assessment with tests in English and Spanish for every lesson

LEVEL 5

Art Around the World CD-ROM includes 150 works of art from the *Art Around the World Collection,* representing a variety of thought-provoking perspectives and activities.

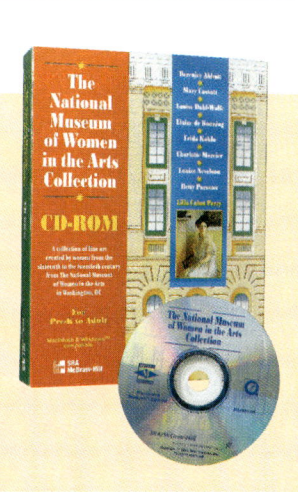

The National Museum of Women in the Arts Collection CD-ROM dynamically explores the 200-print collection to introduce students to key women artists.

SRA ART Connections

Enrich students' lives with exposure to the great masters and cultures of the world.

Fine-Art Resources

Transparencies Overhead transparency study prints for all lesson artwork allow for up-close examination.

LEVEL 5

Large Prints for each unit provide exemplary artwork to develop unit concepts.

LEVEL 2

Artist Profiles Pictures, background information, and profiles for every artist in the program provide valuable historical and cultural information at your fingertips.

LEVEL 1

Literature and Art Videos and DVD develop art connections to literature.

The Polar Express

Art Around the World 150-print resource explores the art of the world's cultures.

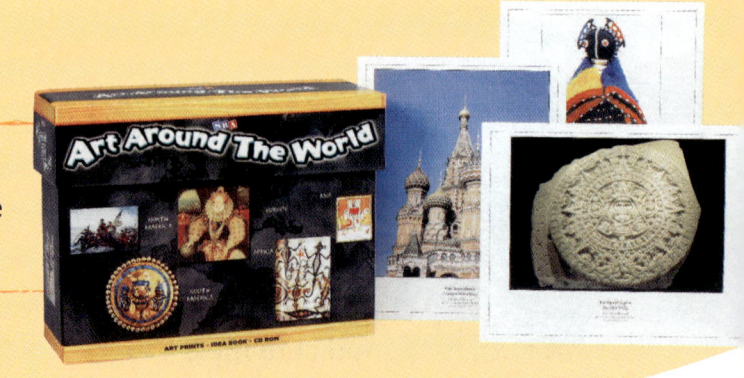

iv

Artsource® Performing Arts Resource Package (Video and DVD) integrates the performing arts of dance, music, and theatre.

LEVEL 3

The National Museum of Women in the Arts Collection This 200-print resource provides famous artwork from famous women artists.

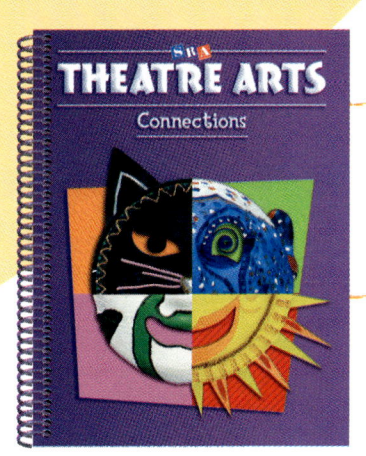

Theatre Arts Connections is a complete dramatic arts program that ties to *Art Connections*.

LEVEL 4

Elements and Principles of Art Teaching Resources

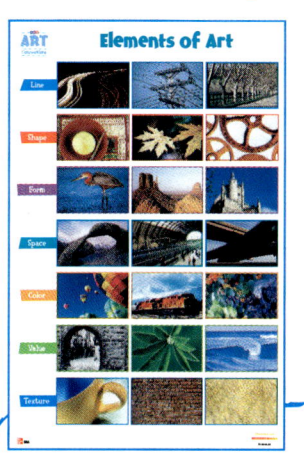

Elements of Art poster reinforces line, shape, color, value, form, space, and texture.

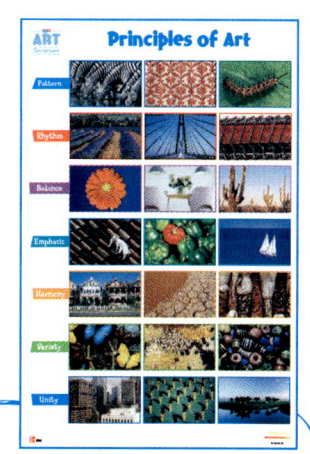

Principles of Art poster develops concepts of rhythm, balance, movement, harmony, variety, emphasis, and unity.

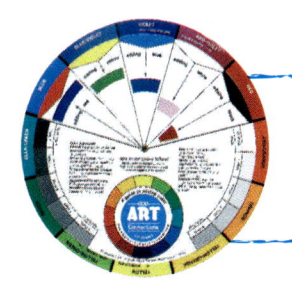

Use the *Color Wheel* to explore color concepts.

Flash Cards provide a quick review of the elements and principles of art.

v

SRA ART Connections

Build a foundation in the elements and principles of art.

36 Lessons at every grade level develop the elements and principles of art in six-lesson units.

Unit Openers introduce students to unit concepts and master artists.

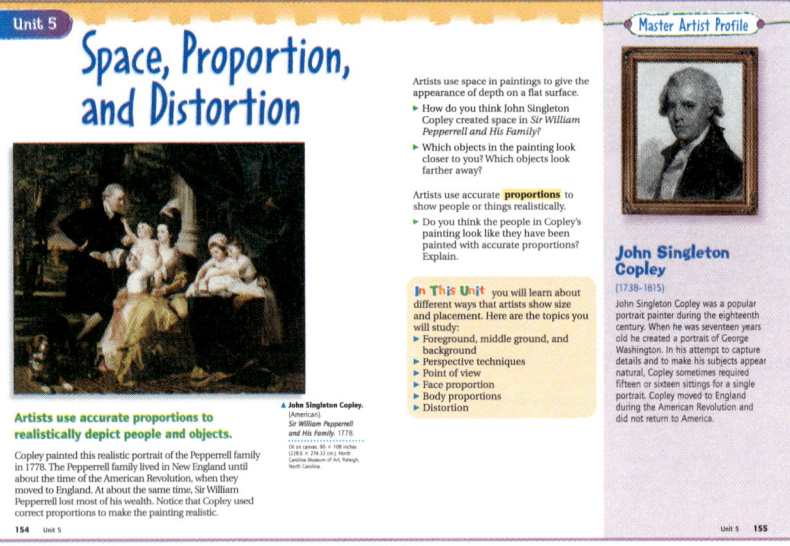

Unit Wrap-Ups review concepts, explore Art Museums or Art Careers and allow students to experience Artsource® connections to dance, theatre, and music.

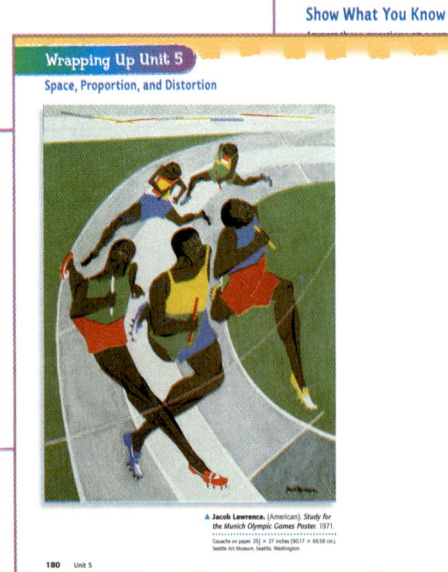

Integrate the four disciplines of art into every lesson for well-rounded exposure to all the dimensions of art.

Art History and Culture
Explore the great art, artists, and cultures of the world.

Aesthetic Perception
Develop an understanding and appreciation for art.

Creative Expression
Encounter a broad range of art media in a variety of hands-on art activities that give students an avenue for self-expression and self-esteem.

Art Criticism
Enrich critical-thinking skills as students learn about the elements and principles of art by examining their own and others' artwork.

SRA ART Connections

Add dimension to all subjects with meaningful art connections.

Connect Art to Mathematics, Social Studies, Science, Language Arts and Reading.

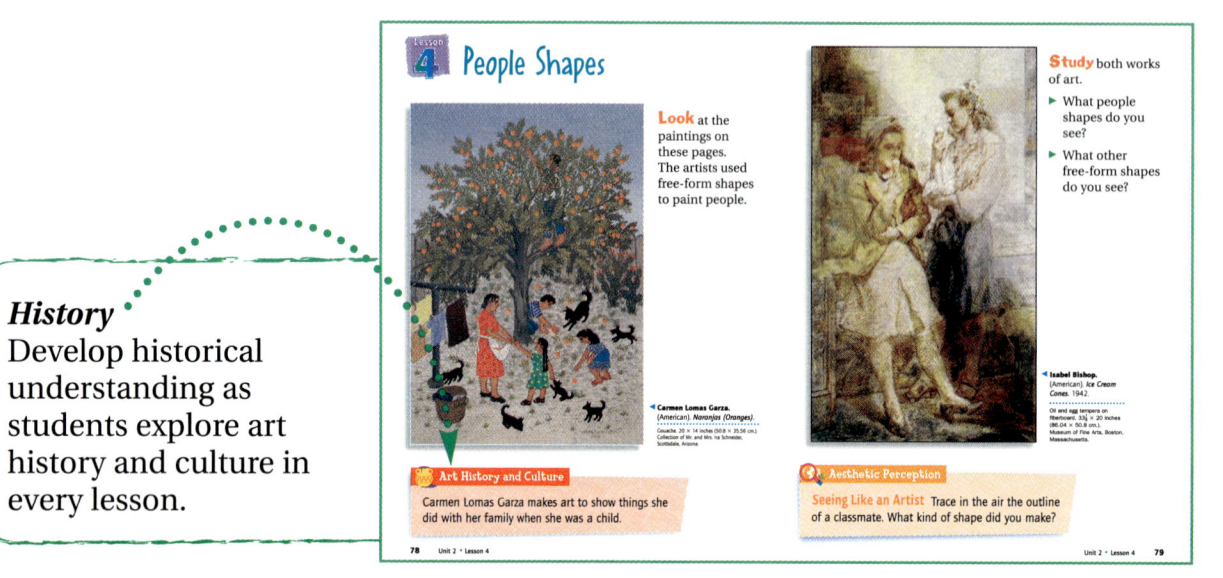

LEVEL 1

History
Develop historical understanding as students explore art history and culture in every lesson.

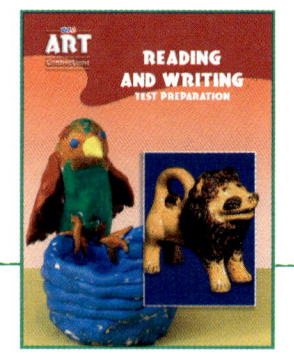

LEVEL 2

Reading and Writing Test Preparation
Use art content, information about artists, art concepts, and art history to practice reading and writing skills in every unit.

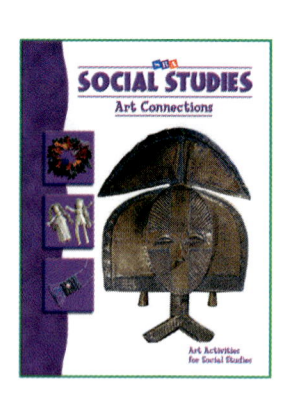

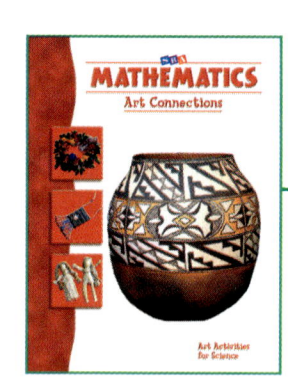

Cross-Curricular Art Connections
These books provide a wealth of exciting art activities designed specifically to support subject-area studies in Science, Mathematics, Social Studies, Language Arts and Reading as they reinforce art concepts.

viii

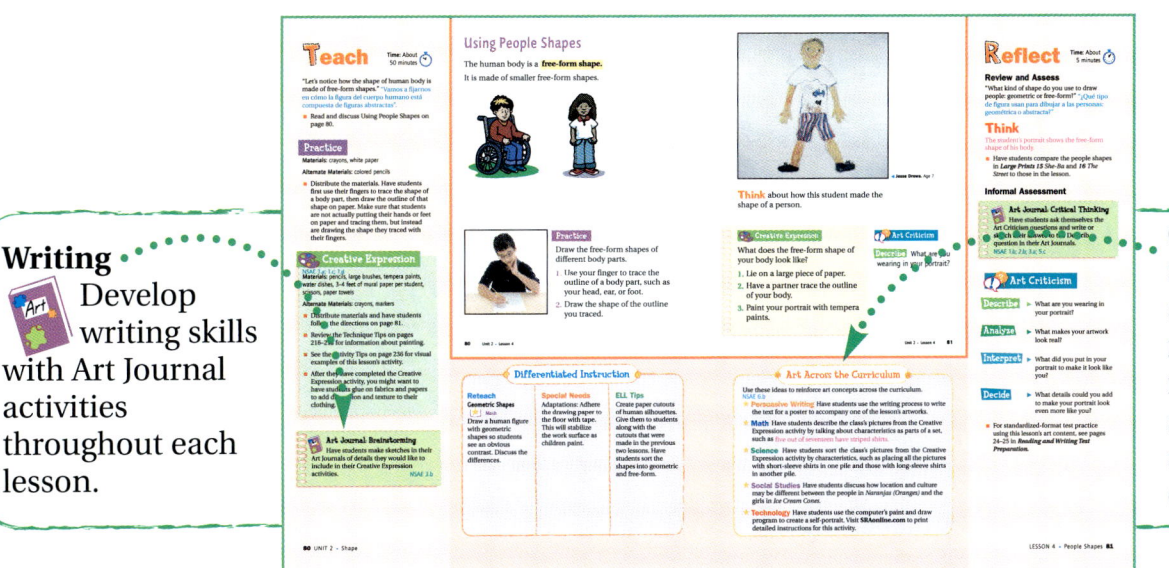

Writing Develop writing skills with Art Journal activities throughout each lesson.

Cross-Curricular Ideas Show students how artwork and concepts relate to science, mathematics, social studies, reading/language arts, and technology in every lesson.

LEVEL 1

Cross-Curricular Integration Integrate language arts and reading, math, science, and social studies concepts naturally as students work through each art lesson.

LEVEL 2

Vocabulary Development Key vocabulary terms are highlighted, defined, and reviewed to develop the language of art.

LEVEL 4

Literature Integration Integrate literature with Illustrator Profiles and Literature and Art video experiences at the beginning of every unit.

LEVEL 3

Research has shown that incorporating the arts into core curriculum areas in a way that actively involves students in the learning process produces "significant positive effects on student achievement, motivation, and engagement in learning, and notable changes in classroom practices" ("Different Ways of Knowing: 1991-94 National Longitudinal Study Final Report" in Schools, Communities, and the Arts: A Research Compendium).

ix

SRA ART Connections

Integrate all the Performing Arts for a complete Art education.

Expose children to music, dance, and theatre as they explore the visual arts.

Music

LEVEL 2

LEVEL 5

Music Connections in every Unit Opener translate the visual arts elements and principles into music.

Music Experiences in every lesson from Macmillan/McGraw-Hill's *Spotlight on Music* expand creativity and develop music appreciation.

Artsource® music performances on video and DVD explore the elements and principles of art through the performing arts.

LEVEL 4

x

Dance

Artsource® dance performances on video and DVD explore the elements and principles of art through the performing arts.

LEVEL 3

Case studies have indicated that students perceive "that the arts facilitate their personal and social development." It also appears that to gain the full benefit of arts education, students should be exposed to all of the arts, including fine arts, dance, theatre, and music ("Arts Education in Secondary School: Effects and Effectiveness" in Critical Links, p. 76).

Theatre

Artsource® theatre performances on video and DVD explore the elements and principles of art through the performing arts.

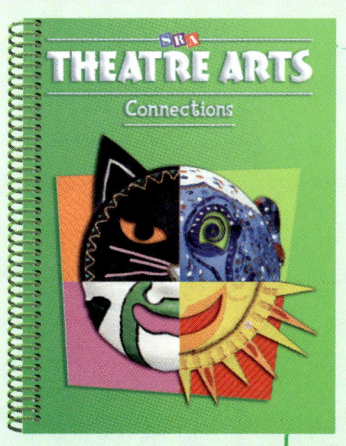

LEVEL 5

Theatre Arts Connections for grades K–6 lessons explore the elements and principles of theatre arts as students develop the elements and principles of visual arts.

LEVEL 3

xi

SRA Art Connections

Meet Today's Standards for Art Education.

Art Connections exceeds the national standards for art education.

National Standards for Arts Education

Content Standard #1:
Understanding and applying media, techniques, and processes

The Creative Expression activity in every lesson of *Art Connections* develops understanding and experience with a wide variety of media, techniques, and processes. Practice activities in every lesson focus specifically on techniques.

Content Standard #2:
Using knowledge of structures and functions

Art Connections develops the elements and principles of art in every grade level, K–6. Units and lessons are organized to explore the elements and principles in exemplary art and then to practice techniques and create works of art that employ specific structures and functions of art.

Content Standard #3:
Choosing and evaluating a range of subject matter, symbols, and ideas

Art Connections introduces students to subject matter and symbols at the beginning of every grade level and then uses that knowledge throughout every lesson in the Aesthetic Perception questions and Creative Expression activities as students explore content to develop meaning in artwork.

Ali M. Forbes. Age 7.

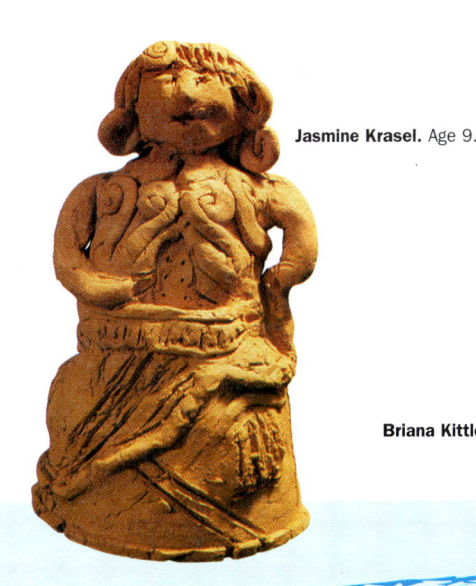

Jasmine Krasel. Age 9.

Briana Kittle. Age 6.

Content Standard #4:
Understanding the visual arts in relation to history and cultures

Every lesson in *Art Connections* has a specific objective related to the understanding of art history and culture. These objectives are met as students analyze and interpret exemplary artwork and develop their own artwork.

Content Standard #5:
Reflecting upon and assessing the characteristics and merits of one's own work and the work of others

The four steps of art criticism are explored in every lesson throughout the program as students analyze their own artwork and the work of others.

Content Standard #6:
Making connections between visual arts and other disciplines

Theatre, Dance, and Music are integrated into every unit of *Art Connections*. The elements and principles of visual art are translated into Dance, Theater, and Music through the Artsource® lessons and experiences. In addition, *Theatre Arts Connections* lessons and Music connections throughout the program develop a comprehensive understanding of the connections between visual arts and the performing arts.

Cross-curricular connections are built into every lesson through teaching strategies and ideas that integrate language arts and reading, math, science, and social studies concepts. Art Projects for each of the different subject areas are also included in the program.

SRA Art Connections

Let the experts bring the best practices to your classroom.

Rosalind Ragans, Ph.D., Senior Author
Artist, Associate Professor Emerita
Georgia Southern University

Authors

Willis "Bing" Davis
Artist, Art Consultant
Associate Professor Emeritus,
Central State University, Ohio

Tina Farrell
Assisstant Superintendant, Curriculum and Instruction
Clear Creek Independent School District, Texas

Jane Rhoades Hudak, Ph.D.
Professor of Art
Georgia Southern University

Gloria McCoy
Former President, Texas Art Education Association
K–12 Art Director
Spring Branch Independent School District, Texas

Bunyan Morris
Art Teacher
Effingham County School System
Springfield, Georgia

Nan Yoshida
Art Education Consultant
Los Angeles, California

Contributors

Jackie Ellet
Elementary Art Teacher
Duncan Creek Elementary School
Georgia

Artsource® Music, Dance, and Theatre Lessons
Education Division
The Music Center of Los Angeles County

National Museum of Women in the Arts Collection
National Museum of Women in the Arts
Washington, D.C.

Your Fine-Arts Partner for K–12 Art, Theatre, Dance and Music

McGraw-Hill offers textbook programs to build, support, and extend an enriching fine-arts curriculum from kindergarten through high school.

Senior Author Rosalind Ragans

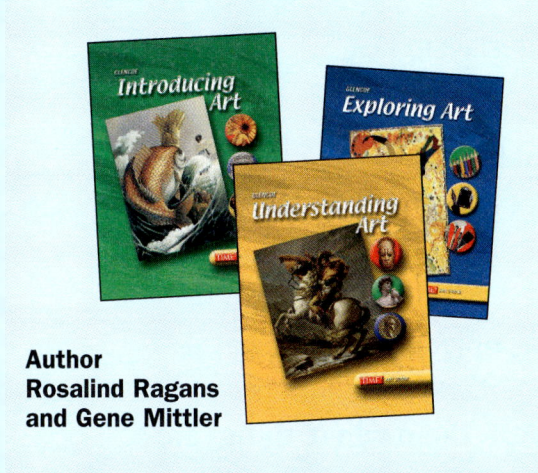

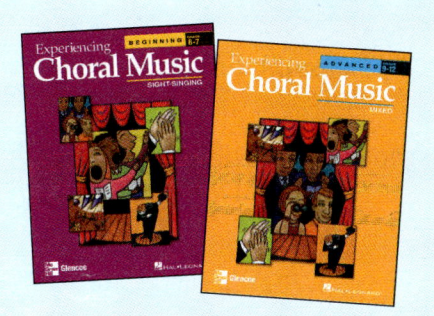

Start with Art — McGraw-Hill SRA

SRA/McGraw-Hill presents *Art Connections* for Grades K–6. *Art Connections* builds the foundations of the elements and principles of art across the grade levels as the program integrates art history and culture, aesthetic perception, creative expression in art production, and art criticism into every lesson.

Art Connections also develops strong cross-curricular connections and integrates the arts with literature, *Theatre Arts Connections* lessons, *Artsource*® experiences, and integrated music selections from Macmillan/McGraw-Hill's *Spotlight on Music*.

Author Rosalind Ragans and Gene Mittler

Author Rosalind Ragans

Integrate with Art — McGraw-Hill Glencoe

Glencoe/McGraw-Hill offers comprehensive middle and high school art programs that encourage students to make art a part of their lifelong learning. All Glencoe art programs interweave the elements and principles of art to help students build perceptual skills, promote creative expression, explore historical and cultural heritage, and evaluate artwork.

- Introduce students to the many themes artists express.
- Explore the media, techniques, and processes of art.
- Understand the historical and cultural contexts of art.

ArtTalk offers high school students opportunities to perceive, create, appreciate, and evaluate art as it develops the elements and principles of art.

Motivate with Music — Macmillan McGraw-Hill

Macmillan/McGraw-Hill's *Spotlight on Music* offers an exiting and comprehensive exposure to music foundations and appreciation.

Sing with Style — McGraw-Hill Glencoe

Glencoe/McGraw-Hill introduces *Experiencing Choral Music* for Grades 6–12. This multilevel choral music program includes instruction in the basic skills of vocal production and music literacy, and provides expertly recorded music selections in many different styles and from various periods of history.

SRA ART Connections

Getting Started
The very basics...

Here are some tips for Getting Started with Art Connections.

Before School Begins

1. Explore the components you have (student materials, **Overhead Transparencies**, **Large Prints**, and so on). Consider uses and alternative uses for each of the components.

2. Plan your year.
   - Consider how often you meet with students.
   - Decide how many lessons you can present.
   - Examine your curriculum requirements.
   - Select the lessons that best meet your curriculum requirements.

3. Organize art materials.
   - Identify the *Creative Expression* activities you will have students develop.
   - Determine how you will budget materials to last the entire year.
   - Compile a list of materials and order them.
   - Arrange classroom space to store materials.

4. Arrange classroom space to create and store student artwork.

The First Day of School

1. Give an overview of your expectations, objectives, and what you want students to accomplish.

2. Introduce the artroom to students. Show them where things are kept.

3. Establish and communicate:
   - rules for behavior.
   - rules for handling art materials.
   - rules for cleaning up.

4. Begin the **Art Connections** introductory lessons, including *What Is Art?*, *About Art Criticism*, *About Aesthetic Perception*, and *About Art History and Culture*.

Planning a Lesson

1. Review the lesson in the *Teacher's Edition*, including lesson objectives, in-text questions, *Practice*, and *Creative Expression* activities.

2. Assemble program components, such as **Transparencies, Large Prints,** and the **Big Book**.

3. Make any copies of activities or assessments that will be needed for the lesson.

4. Assemble art materials.

5. Determine how you will assess the lesson.

"I am enough of an artist to draw freely upon my imagination. Imagination is more important than knowledge. Knowledge is limited. Imagination encircles the world."

—Albert Einstein
(1879–1955)
physicist

TEACHER'S EDITION

SRA
ART
Connections

Level 6

Authors

Rosalind Ragans, Ph.D., Senior Author

Willis "Bing" Davis   Jane Rhoades Hudak, Ph.D.   Bunyan Morris
Tina Farrell   Gloria McCoy   Nan Yoshida

Contributing Author

Jackie Ellett

Education Division
The Music Center of Los Angeles County

SRA
Columbus, OH

The McGraw·Hill Companies

Authors

Senior Author
Dr. Rosalind Ragans, Ph.D.
Associate Professor Emerita
Georgia Southern University

Willis "Bing" Davis
Associate Professor Emeritus
Central State University - Ohio
President & Founder of SHANGO:
The Center for the Study of
African American
Art & Culture

Tina Farrell
Assistant Superintendent,
Curriculum and Instruction
Clear Creek Independent School
District,
League City, Texas

Jane Rhoades Hudak, Ph.D.
Professor of Art
Georgia Southern University

Gloria McCoy
Former President,
Texas Art Education Association
Spring Branch Independent
School District, Texas

Bunyan Morris
Art Teacher
Effingham County School System,
Springfield, Georgia

Nan Yoshida
Art Education Consultant
Retired Art Supervisor,
Los Angeles Unified School
District
Los Angeles, California

Photo Credit Cover, Unknown artist from Kwakwaka'wakw tribe, *Face Mask of K̲umugwē.* Seattle Art Museum, Gift of John H. Hauberg. Photograph by Paul Macapia.

SRAonline.com

McGraw Hill SRA

Copyright © 2005 by SRA/McGraw-Hill.

All rights reserved. Except as permitted under the United States Copyright Act, no part of this publication may be reproduced or distributed in any form or by any means, or stored in a database or retrieval system, without the prior written permission of the publisher, unless otherwise indicated.

Send all inquiries to:
SRA/McGraw-Hill
8787 Orion Place
Columbus, OH 43240-4027

Printed in the United States of America.

ISBN 0-07-600396-5

2 3 4 5 6 7 8 9 BCM 10 09 08 07 06 05

The McGraw-Hill Companies

Contributors

Contributing Author
Jackie Ellett, Ed.S
Elementary Art Teacher
Duncan Creek Elementary School
Hoschton, Georgia

Contributing Writer
Lynda Kerr, NBCT
Ed. D. Candidate, Art Teacher
Henry County, Georgia

Artsource® Music, Dance, Theatre Lessons
Mark Slavkin, Vice President for Education
The Music Center of Los Angeles County
Michael Solomon, Managing Director
Music Center Education Division
Melinda Williams, Concept Originator and Project Director
Susan Cambigue-Tracey, Project Coordinator and Writer
Madeleine Dahm, Movement and Dance Connection Writer
Keith Wyffels, Staff Assistance
Maureen Erbe, Logo Design

Music Connections
Kathy Mitchell
Music Teacher
Eagan, Minnesota

More about Aesthetics
Richard W. Burrows, Executive Director
Institute for Arts Education
San Diego, California

Art History
Gene A. Mittler, Ph.D.
Professor Emeritus
Texas Tech University

Resources for Students with Disabilities
Mandy Yeager
Ph.D. Candidate
The University of North Texas
Denton, Texas

Brain-Based Learning in the Arts
Jamye Ivey
K-12 Art Supervisor
Dougherty County School System, Georgia

Safe Use of Art Materials
Mary Ann Boykin
Director, The Art School for Children and Young Adults
University of Houston—Clear Lake
Houston, Texas

Integrating the Four Art Forms
Susan Cambigue-Tracey
The Music Center of Los Angeles County

Using Writing to Enhance Your Art Curriculum
Mary Lazzari, EdS
Elementary Art Teacher
Clarke County School District
Athens, Georgia

Museum Education
Marilyn J. S. Goodman
Director of Education
Solomon R. Guggenheim Museum
New York, New York

Displaying Student Artwork
Jackie Ellett
Duncan Creek Elementary School
Hoschton, Georgia

Student Activities

Cassie Appleby
Glen Oaks Elementary School
McKinney, Texas

Maureen Banks
Kester Magnet School
Van Nuys, California

Christina Barnes
Webb Bridge Middle School
Alpharetta, Georgia

Beth Benning
Willis Jepson Middle School
Vacaville, California

Chad Buice
Craig Elementary School
Snellville, Georgia

Beverly Broughton
Gwinn Oaks Elementary School
Snellville, Georgia

Missy Burgess
Jefferson Elementary School
Jefferson, Georgia

Marcy Cincotta-Smith
Benefield Elementary School
Lawrenceville, Georgia

Joanne Cox
Kittredge Magnet School
Atlanta, Georgia

Carolyn Y. Craine
McCracken County Schools
Paducah, Kentucky

Jackie Ellett
Duncan Creek Elementary School
Hoschton, Georgia

Tracie Flynn
Home School
Rushville, Indiana

Phyllis Glenn
Malcom Bridge Elementary
Bogart, Georgia

Dallas Gillespie
Dacula Middle School
Dacula, Georgia

Dr. Donald Gruber
Clinton Junior High School
Clinton, Illinois

Karen Heid
Rock Springs Elementary School
Lawrenceville, Georgia

Alisa Hyde
Southwest Elementary
Savannah, Georgia

Kie Johnson
Oconee Primary School
Watkinsville, Georgia

Sallie Keith, NBCT
West Side Magnet School
LaGrange, Georgia

Letha Kelly
Grayson Elementary School
Grayson, Georgia

Diana Kimura
Amestoy Elementary School
Gardena, California

Desiree LaOrange
Barkley Elementary School
Fort Campbell, Kentucky

Deborah Lackey-Wilson
Roswell North Elementary
Roswell, Georgia

Dawn Laird
Goforth Elementary School
Clear Creek, Texas

Mary Lazzari
Timothy Road Elementary School
Athens, Georgia

Michelle Leonard
Webb Bridge Middle School
Alpharetta, Georgia

Lynn Ludlam
Spring Branch ISD
Houston, Texas

Mark Mitchell
Fort Daniel Elementary School
Dacula, Georgia

Martha Moore
Freeman's Mill Elementary School
Dacula, Georgia

Connie Niedenthal
Rushville Elementary
Rushville, Indiana

Barbara Patisaul
Oconee County Elementary School
Watkinsville, Georgia

Elizabeth Paulos-Krasle
Social Circle Elementary
Social Circle, Georgia

Jane Pinneau
Rocky Branch Elementary School
Watkinsville, Georgia

Marilyn Polin
Cutler Ridge Middle School
Miami, Florida

Michael Ramsey
Graves County Schools
Mayfield, Kentucky

Rosemarie Sells
Social Circle Elementary
Social Circle, Georgia

Jean Neelen-Siegel
Baldwin School
Alhambra, California

Debra Smith
McIntosh County School System
Darien, Georgia

Patricia Spencer
Harmony Elementary School
Buford, Georgia

Melanie Stokes
Smiley Elementary School
Ludowici, Georgia

Rosanne Stutts
Davidson Fine Arts School
Augusta, Georgia

Fran Sullivan
South Jackson Elementary School
Athens, Georgia

Kathy Valentine
Home School
Burkburnett, Texas

Debi West
Rock Springs Elementary School
Lawrenceville, Georgia

Sherry White
Bauerschlag Elementary School
League City, Texas

Patricia Wiesen
Cutler Ridge Middle School
Miami, Florida

Deayna Woodruff
Loveland Middle School
Loveland, Ohio

Gil Young
El Rodeo School
Beverly Hills, California

Larry A. Young
Dacula Elementary School
Dacula, Georgia

Table of Contents

What Is Art?
Introduction 12
Subject Matter 16
Elements of Art 22
Principles of Art 23

About Art
Art History and Culture 24
Aesthetic Perception 26
Art Criticism 28
Creative Expression 30
Safety 32

◀ **Gustav Klimt.** *Fulfillment.*

Unit 1 Line, Shape, Form, and Space

An Introduction to Line, Shape, Form, and Space 34

Lesson	Activity	Medium	
●◆ ❶ **Line and Qualities of Line**	Contour Drawing	Marker	36
●◆ ❷ **Geometric and Free-Form Shapes**	Pictorial Square	Felt, Yarn	40
❸ **Geometric Forms**	Sculpture	Wood, Acrylic Paint	44
❹ **Free-Form Form**	Sculpture	Wire, Tissue Paper	48
●◆ ❺ **Space and Perspective**	Perspective Drawing	Watercolors, Color Pencil	52
❻ **Positive and Negative Space**	Assemblage	Construction Paper, Acrylic Paint	56

Wrapping Up Line, Shape, Form, and Space 60

Artsource® Lesson
Line, Shape, Form, and Space in Music and Storytelling 63

●◆ indicates Core Lessons

Reading Comprehension Skills and Strategies

❶ Vocabulary, Using Literature, Comparing and Contrasting
❷ Vocabulary, Using Literature, Comparing and Contrasting
❸ Vocabulary, Using Literature
❹ Vocabulary, Using Literature, Artist's Purpose
❺ Vocabulary, Using Literature
❻ Vocabulary, Using Literature

▲ **Auguste Renior.**
Young Spanish Woman with a Guitar.

Unit 2 Color and Texture

An Introduction to Color and Texture 64

Lesson	Activity	Medium	
❶ Hue	Color Wheel	Tempera	66
❷ Value	Landscape	Tempera	70
❸ Intensity	Portrait	Oil Pastel	74
❹ Color Schemes	Landscape	Tempera	78
❺ Visual Texture	Textural Drawing	Computer	82
❻ Tactile Texture	Textured Hat	Mixed Media	86

Wrapping Up Color and Texture 90

Artsource® Lesson
Color and Texture in Dance 93

6   ⊷ indicates Core Lessons

Reading Comprehension Skills and Strategies
❶ Vocabulary, Using Literature
❷ Vocabulary, Using Literature
❸ Vocabulary, Using Literature, Thematic Connection: Feelings
❹ Vocabulary, Using Literature
❺ Vocabulary, Using Literature, Editing
❻ Vocabulary, Using Literature

▲ **Max Weber.**
Chinese Restaurant.

Unit 3 Rhythm, Movement, and Pattern

An Introduction to Rhythm, Movement, Pattern 94

Lesson	Activity	Medium
❶ **Motif and Pattern**	Costume Design	Marker, Color Pencil 96
◆❷ **Two-Dimensional Pattern**	Nonobjective Design	Marker, Color Pencil 100
◆❸ **Three-Dimensional Pattern**	Animal Sculpture	Clay 104
◆❹ **Rhythm**	Nonobjective Design	Color Pencil 108
❺ **Visual Movement**	Jungle Painting	Tempera 112
❻ **Kinetic Movement**	Mobile	Wire, Matboard 116

Wrapping Up Rhythm, Movement, Pattern 120

Artsource® Lesson
Pattern, Rhythm, and Movement in Dance 123

◆ indicates Core Lessons

Reading Comprehension Skills and Strategies
❶ Vocabulary, Using Literature
❷ Vocabulary, Using Literature
❸ Vocabulary
❹ Vocabulary, Using Literature
❺ Vocabulary, Using Literature
❻ Vocabulary, Using Literature

◀ **Rembrandt van Rijn.** *Portrait of Rembrandt.*

Unit 4 Balance and Emphasis

An Introduction to Balance and Emphasis 124

Lesson	Activity	Medium
❶ Formal Balance and Symmetry	Drawing of a Building	Watercolors 126
❷ Approximate Symmetry	Computer-Generated Design	Computer 130
❸ Informal Balance	Still-Life Drawing	Chalk 134
❹ Radial Balance	Radial Design	Color Pencils, Markers 138
❺ Emphasis of an Element	Collograph Print	Crayon 142
❻ Emphasis of Area	Group Sculpture	Foil, Wire 146

Wrapping Up Balance and Emphasis 150

Artsource® Lesson
Balance in Dance 153

8   ●○ indicates Core Lessons

Reading Comprehension Skills and Strategies
❶ Vocabulary, Using Literature, Summarizing
❷ Vocabulary, Using Literature, Logical Reasoning
❸ Vocabulary, Using Literature, Comparing and Contrasting
❹ Vocabulary, Using Literature
❺ Vocabulary, Using Literature, Thematic Connection: Things That Stand Out
❻ Vocabulary, Using Literature

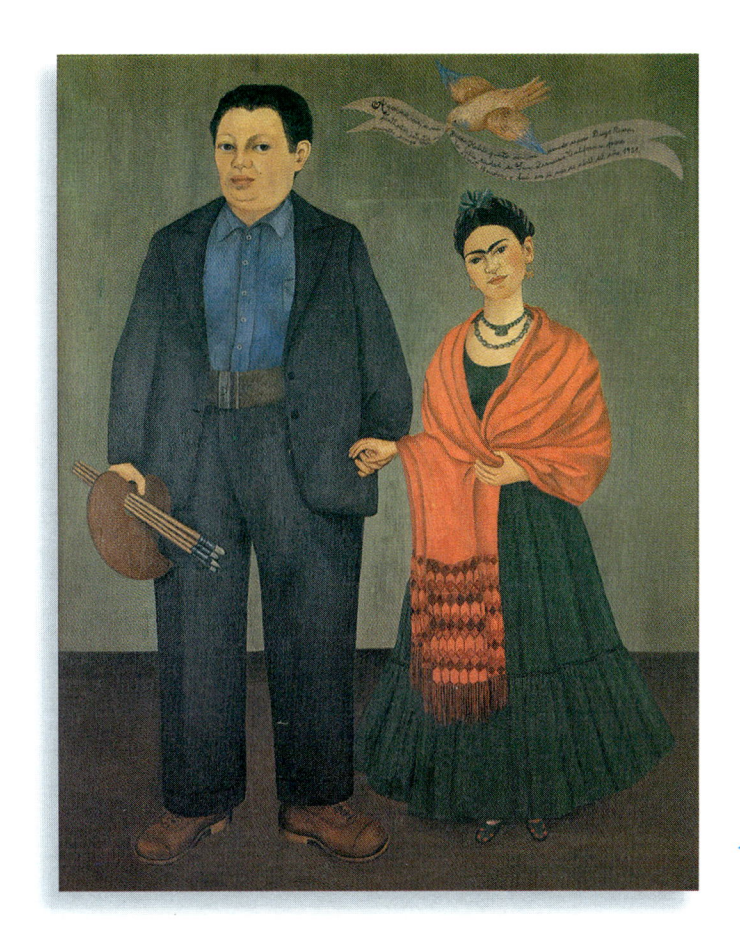

◀ **Frida Kahlo.**
Frida y Diego Rivera.

Unit 5 Proportion, Distortion, and Scale

An Introduction to Proportion, Distortion, and Scale 154

Lesson	Activity	Medium
❶ **Facial Proportions**	Self-Portrait	Oil Pastel 156
❷ **Figure Proportion**	Line Drawing	Marker 160
❸ **Facial Distortion**	Face Jug	Clay 164
❹ **Figure Distortion**	Photograph Distortion	Computer 168
❺ **Realistic Scale**	Chair Design	Color Pencil 172
❻ **Unrealistic Scale**	Surrealistic Collage	Mixed Media 176

Wrapping Up Proportion, Distortion, and Scale 180

Artsource® Lesson
Proportion and Distortion in Theatre 183

◆ indicates Core Lessons

9

Reading Comprehension Skills and Strategies
❶ Vocabulary, Using Literature, Looking at Details
❷ Vocabulary, Using Literature
❸ Vocabulary, Using Literature, Artist's Purpose
❹ Vocabulary, Using Literature
❺ Vocabulary, Using Literature
❻ Vocabulary, Using Literature

9

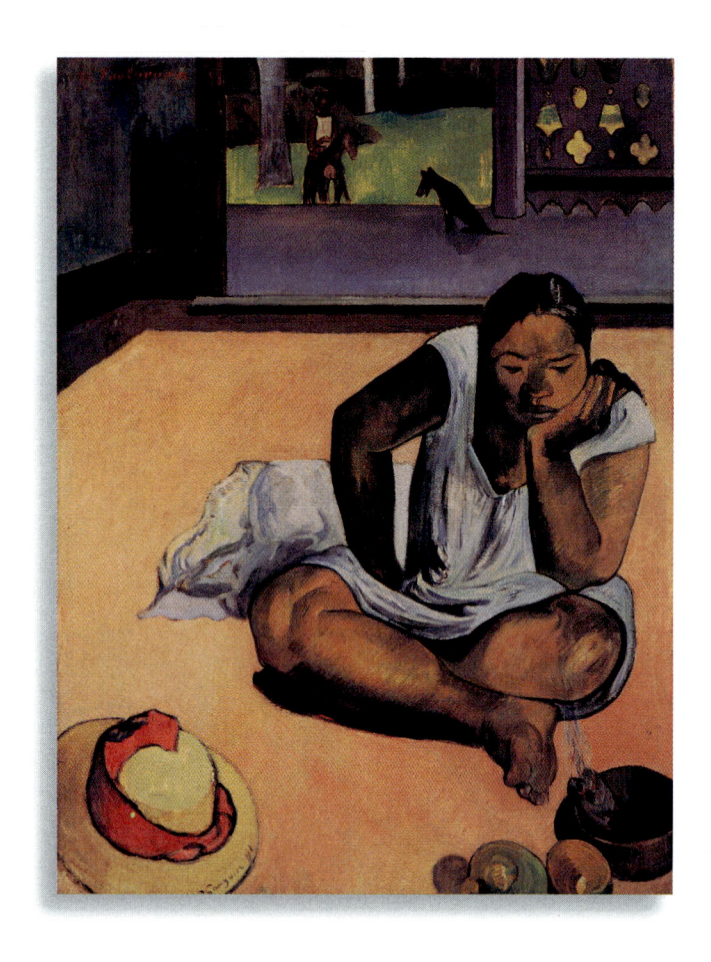

◀ **Paul Gauguin.**
The Brooding Woman.

Unit 6 Variety, Harmony, and Unity

An Introduction to Variety, Harmony, and Unity 184

Lesson	Activity	Medium	
❶ Variety through Line, Shape, and Color	Collage	Mixed Media	186
❷ Variety through Contrast	Hand-Colored Photograph	Black-and-White Film	190
❸ Harmony in Two-Dimensional Art	Embroidery	Yarn, Burlap	194
❹ Harmony in Three-Dimensional Art	Group Assemblage	Mixed Media	198
❺ Unity in Weaving	Weaving	Yarn, Cardboard	202
❻ Unity in Three-Dimensional Art	Sculpture	Mixed Media	206

Wrapping Up Variety, Harmony, and Unity 210

Artsource® Lesson
Variety, Harmony, and Unity in Animation 213

10

•❖ indicates Core Lessons

Reading Comprehension Skills and Strategies
❶ Vocabulary, Using Literature, Looking at Details
❷ Vocabulary, Using Literature, Thematic Connection: Communication
❸ Vocabulary, Using Literature
❹ Vocabulary, Using Literature
❺ Vocabulary, Using Literature
❻ Vocabulary, Using Literature, Thematic Connection: A Question of Value

Technique Tips

Embroidery 214
Drawing 215
Painting 220
Collograph Print 223
Handcoloring a Photograph 224
Mobile 225
Collage 226
Weaving 227
Sculpting 228

Activity Tips

Unit 1 230
Unit 2 233
Unit 3 236
Unit 4 239
Unit 5 242
Unit 6 245

Visual Index 248
Glossary 258
Index 266

11

Teacher Handbook T1

Overview

The purpose of these pages is to open students' minds to the idea that visual arts include many components and take many forms. The arts satisfy the human need for display, celebration, personal expression, and communication. We use the visual arts to enhance our innermost feelings and to communicate ideas. Art is made by people. Even people who are not professional artists can enjoy the creative process.

Activating Prior Knowledge

- Ask students what they think art is. Encourage creative, divergent thinking. In visual art, there are many answers to a question.

Questions to Discuss

- Have students look at the images on pages 12 and 13 and name the things that are visual art. Then ask the following questions.
  - ▶ Which of these things could you hold in your hands?
  - ▶ Which one could you walk inside?
  - ▶ Which ones would you hang on a wall?
  - ▶ Which ones could you wear?
- Encourage students to think about things they have at home that fit the categories on these pages. The building they live in is architecture. They have dishes and other containers. Many of them have things hanging on the walls to enhance their visual environments. A few may have sculpture in the home. Many will have seen sculptures in and around public buildings.

What Is Art?

Art is . . .

Painting is color applied to a flat surface.

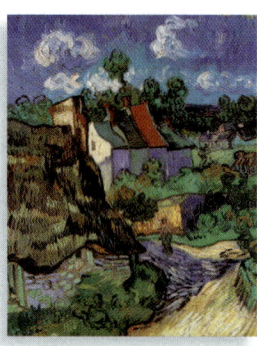

▲ **Vincent Van Gogh.** (French). *Houses at Auvers.* 1890.
Oil on canvas. $29\frac{3}{4} \times 24\frac{3}{8}$ inches (75.56 × 61.93 cm.). Museum of Fine Arts, Boston, Massachusetts.

Drawing is the process of making art with lines.

▲ **Pablo Picasso.** (Spanish). *Portrait of Dora Maar.* 1938.
Pencil on paper mounted on fiberboard. $30\frac{9}{16} \times 22\frac{7}{16}$ inches (77.62 × 57 cm.). Hirshhorn Museum and Sculpture Garden, Smithsonian Institution, Washington, D.C.

Sculpture is art that fills up space.

▲ **David Bates.** (American). *Seated Man #4.* 1995.
Painted wood. $88 \times 37\frac{1}{2} \times 45\frac{1}{2}$ inches (223.52 × 95.25 × 115.57 cm.). Dallas Museum of Art, Dallas, Texas.

Architecture is the art of designing and constructing buildings.

▲ **Jørn Oberg Utzon.** (Danish). *Opera House.* 1957–1973.
Sydney, Australia.

12   What Is Art?

Printmaking is the process of transferring an original image from one prepared surface to another.

▲ **Katsushika Hokusai.** (Japanese.) *Winter Loneliness,* from *One Hundred Poems Explained by the Nurse.* 1839.
Woodcut. 10 1/8 × 14 1/2 inches (25.5 × 36.8 cm.). Honolulu Academy of Art, Honolulu, Hawaii

Photography is the act of capturing an image on film.

◀ **Eliot Elisofon.** (American). *Asante Paramount Chief Nana Akyanfuo Akowuah Dateh II, Akwamuhene of Kumase.* 1970.
Photograph. National Museum of African Art, Smithsonian Institution, Washington, D.C.

Ceramics is the art of making objects with clay.

▲ **Artist Unknown.** (Kongo peoples, Congo and Democratic Republic of Congo.) **Bowl.** Late-nineteenth to early-twentieth century.
Ceramic and resin. 5 7/8 × 4 1/8 × 5 7/8 inches (14.9 × 10.49 × 14.94 cm.). National Museum of African Art, Smithsonian Institution, Washington, D.C.

A mask is a covering for the face to be used in ceremonies and other events.

▲ **Charlie James.** (Southern Kwakiutl.) *Sun Tranformation Mask.* Early nineteenth century.
Royal British Columbia Museum, British Columbia, Canada.

Art is created by people

▶ to communicate ideas.
▶ to express feelings.
▶ to give us well-designed objects.

Using the Credit Line

The credit line is a list of important facts about the work of art that appears below or next to the work. For example, you can help students understand the size of an artwork and how it relates to their own size. Most credit lines contain the following information.

- Name of the artist.
- Title of the work. This always appears in italics. If the word *detail* follows the title, it means that the image is part of a larger work of art.
- Year the work was created. A *c* before the date indicates that the piece was made around the year given.
- Medium used by the artist.
- Size of the work. The first number is the height, the second is the width, and a third number indicates depth for three-dimensional works.
- Location of the work. This tells the museum, gallery, or collection in which the work is housed.

Art Studios, Galleries, and Museums

Works of art are created in ***studios.*** A studio is an artist's workplace, much like a classroom is a studio for students. Almost everything an artist needs to create an artwork will be found in his or her studio. It is possible for people to visit artist studios, but an invitation from the artist is usually required.

Art galleries are private businesses where art dealers display and sell works of art. Art galleries are typically open to the public, and the works of art may be viewed even if the patrons do not intend to buy anything.

A ***museum*** is a public or private building where valuable and important artwork is cared for and displayed for the public to view. *Curators* are people who supervise the museum and organize exhibitions. *Docents* are special tour directors who help explain the art to visitors.

Overview

These pages introduce students to the three components that define a work of art: the subject, the composition, and the content.

Subject

The subject is the image that the viewer can easily identify in a work of art. The subject may be one person or many people. It may be a thing. It can be an event, such as a party. In recent years, some artists have chosen to create nonobjective art. This is art that has no recognizable subject matter. In this type of art, the elements of art become the subject.

Composition

The composition is the way the principles of art are used to organize the elements of art. Notice how Benny Andrews uses color and shape to portray the image of a family dinner.

Content

The content is the message the work communicates to the viewer. The message may be an idea, such as family unity, or an emotion or feeling, such as joy or loneliness. If the work of art is functional, such as *Habitat,* then the function is the meaning. Does the work of art look like it could perform the function it is supposed to?

What Is Art?

Every work of art has three parts.

Subject

The objects you can recognize are the subject matter of a work of art. When a work has no recognizable objects, the elements of art such as lines, shapes, colors, and so on become the subject of the work.

Composition

The composition of the work is the way the artist has used the principles to organize the elements of art.

Content

The content is the message the artwork communicates. Content is the meaning of the work. If the work is functional, such as a chair or clothing, then the content is the function of the object.

- ▶ In which work of art do you think the subject matter is very important?
- ▶ In which artwork do you think composition is most important?
- ▶ Which work seems to have the strongest message? Explain.
- ▶ Which artwork's meaning relates to its function?

▲ **Benny Andrews.** (American). *Grandmother's Dinner.* 1992.
Oil on canvas. 72 × 52 inches (182.88 × 132.08 cm.). Ogden Museum of Southern Art, New Orleans, Louisiana.

▲ **William Sharp.** (English/American). *Great Water Lily of America.* 1854.
Chromolithograph on woven white paper. $21\frac{1}{4}$ × 27 inches (53.98 × 68.58 cm.). Amon Carter Museum, Fort Worth, Texas.

▲ **Artist Unknown.** (Maya/Huipil). *Huipil Weaving.* c. 1950.
Backstrap woven plain weave with supplementary-weft pattern, silk on cotton. 50 × $14\frac{1}{2}$ inches (127 × 36.83 cm.). Museum of International Folk Art, Santa Fe, New Mexico.

▲ **Mosche Safdie.** (Israeli). *Habitat.* 1967.
Concrete. Montreal, Canada.

What Is Art? **15**

Activating Prior Knowledge
■ Ask students to say the first thing they look for when they look at a work of art. Students may say they look at color, size, or what the work is about. Some may say they look for the feeling or message they get from the artwork. Give students time to explore this question. It will provide a good context for the discussion on these pages.

Questions to Discuss
■ Read with students the text on page 14 and look at the images on page 15. Share with them some of the information above. Encourage students to think about their responses during the Activating Prior Knowledge discussion as they look at these images and think about the information you have shared with them.

▶ Read the questions on page 14 and discuss the answers. The subject matter is important in *Grandmother's Dinner* and *Great Water Lily of America.* Composition is important in *Huipil Weaving. Huipil Weaving* and *Habitat* are works in which the meaning relates to function. Most students will think that *Grandmother's Dinner* has the strongest message. However, it is important to point out that the function of a work is an important message *(Huipil Weaving* and *Habitat).*

What Is Art? **15**

Overview

In art, subject means something an artist has depicted or represented in an artwork. For example, the subject matter of Paul Cézanne's painting of fruit is called a still life. Some subject matter, like the objects in Cézanne's still life, is easy to identify. Others are more difficult because the artwork may be symbolic or nonobjective. Artists create works of art on a variety of subjects: the natural world, literature, religion, the constructed world, history, and so on. These pages deal with several of the most common subject-matter topics—people, objects, everyday life, stories, things outside, colors and shapes, and things that have a deeper meaning.

Talk with students about each subject-matter topic description below. Encourage them to look for examples of different subject matter in the lessons. By helping them to look at each subject in greater detail and by asking thoughtful questions, your students will begin to develop an understanding for differences among subject matter in art.

Still Life

Artists create works of art that show a variety of objects. Traditional still lifes are bowls, vases, bottles, pitchers, fruit, flowers, food on a table, and/or musical instruments (among other things) that are artfully arranged.

▶ **Question:** What are the objects in this still life?

What Is Art?
Subject Matter

Artists make art about many subjects. *Subject matter* is the content of an artist's work. For example, the subject of a painting can be a vase of flowers or a self-portrait. This subject matter is easy to see. The subject matter is harder to understand when the artwork stands for something beyond itself. Look at the artwork on these pages. Notice the different kinds of subject matter.

Still Life

▲ **Paul Cézanne.** (French). *Still Life with Basket of Apples.* 1895.
Oil on canvas. 23⅝ × 31½ inches (60 × 80 cm.). The Art Institute of Chicago, Chicago, Illinois.

Landscape

▲ **Z. Vanessa Helder.** (American). *Rocks and Concrete.* c. 1940.
Watercolor on paper. 19 × 15⅞ inches (48.26 × 40.34 cm.). Cheney Cowles Museum, Spokane, Washington.

Landscape

This area includes the natural world—plants, animals, or other things outside. The suffix *-scape* means "a view of." For example, a *cityscape* is buildings and city life seen in an artwork. A *seascape* is a scene of the sea.

▶ **Question:** What objects do you see in this landscape?

Genre

In art, the term *genre* is used to indicate subjects that have to do with ordinary people engaged in everyday activities.

▶ **Question:** What everyday activities is this boy doing?

What Is Art?

Genre

▲ **Winslow Homer.** (American.) *Nooning.* c. 1872.
Oil on canvas. 13 3/16 × 19 3/8 inches (33.02 × 48.26 cm.). Wadsworth Atheneum, Hartford, Connecticut.

Nonobjective

◀ **Natalya Goncharova.** (Russian). *Maquillage.* 1913.
Gouache on paper. 4⅜ × 6⅜ inches (11.13 × 16.21 cm.). Dallas Museum of Art, Dallas, Texas.

Portrait

◀ **Elizabeth Catlett.** (American). *Sharecropper.* 1970.
Color linocut. 26 × 22 inches (66.04 × 55.88 cm.). Smithsonian American Art Museum, Washington, D.C.

Nonobjective

Sometimes artwork is nonobjective. It does not have an identifiable subject matter—no familiar subjects are shown. People respond to the way the artwork has been organized and designed. Nonobjective art focuses specifically on the elements and principles of art: line, shape, color, and so on.

▶ **Question:** The artwork does not use a subject we can identify. What are some of the lines, shapes, and colors you see in this picture?

Portrait

This category includes portraits, self-portraits, and group portraits. Portraits are one of the oldest subjects in art history. Artists try to present both an accurate depiction and also other aspects of a person's character in a portrait.

▶ **Question:** What do you think the artist is telling us about this person?

Stories

A story is an account of some incident from a real person's life, a historic event, or from a myth, legend, or other piece of symbolic literature.

▶ **Question:** What story do you think is being told in this artwork?

What Is Art?

Allegory

▲ **Jan van Eyck.** (Flemish.) *Portrait of Giovanni Arnolfini and His wife Giovanna Cenami.* 1434. Oil on wood panel. 32 x 23 inches. The National Gallery, London, England.

Symbolism

Artist Unknown. (Huichol People/Mexico). *Mother of the Eagles.* 1991. Braided yarn embedded in vegetable wax on wood. 15¾ × 19½ inches (40 × 49.53 cm.). Private collection.

Symbols

Sometimes works of art contain symbols—visual signs of something invisible. For example, a dove can be a symbol of peace, or an hourglass may represent the passing of time. Symbols represent a broader idea or sometimes have a secret meaning.

▶ **Question:** What symbols do you see in this work? What do you think they mean?

What Is Art? **21**

Overview

Each language has its own system of words and rules of grammar. To learn a new language, you need to learn new words and a new set of rules for putting the words together. The language of visual art also has its own system. The words of the language are the **elements** of art. They are the basic visual symbols in the language of art. Just as there are basic kinds of words such as nouns, verbs, adjectives, and adverbs, there are basic kinds of art elements. These are line, shape, color, value, space, form, and texture. These elements are the visual building blocks that the artist puts together to create a work of art. No matter what materials are used, the artwork will contain all of the visual elements. Sometimes one element will be more important than the others.

Visual images are organized according to rules. In language, these are the rules of grammar. In visual art, the rules for organizing the elements of art are called the **principles** of art. These principles include pattern, rhythm, balance, emphasis, harmony, variety, and unity.

Activating Prior Knowledge

- Ask students what they think of when they hear each of the following words: *line, shape, color*. Encourage them to look around the classroom for examples.

Questions to Discuss

- Have students examine the images on pages 22 and 23. Ask them what they can tell about each photo. What stands out in each image? How does each image help explain the element or principle?

What Is Art?

Elements of Art

Art is a language. The words of the language are the elements of art.

Principles of Art

Artists organize their artwork using the principles of art.

Pattern

Rhythm

Balance

Emphasis

Harmony

Variety

Unity

The Language of Art

The elements and principles of art are the concepts or ideas that artists use to organize their artwork. Artists use a variety of media and materials to make art. *Media* are types of art such as photography, watercolor, and so on. *Materials* are the things used to make the art, such as markers, paint, paper, clay, fabric, wood, metal, or glass.

There are specific techniques and processes that artists use to manipulate the materials. For example, the proper way to hold a brush to create a thin line with watercolor paint is a specific technique unique to watercolor painting. The process of creating a finished watercolor painting consists of many interwoven steps, such as thinking about what to paint, sketching several ideas, deciding which elements and principles will enhance the work, choosing the best sketch, deciding which watercolor techniques to use, and finally, producing the finished work.

Special techniques and procedures are used with each material. You will need to learn different techniques and follow different procedures for modeling clay than you will for creating paper sculpture. Drawing with crayons requires different techniques and procedures from drawing with oil pastels or chalk. Using the computer to make original art requires that you learn how to use specific computer hardware and software.

Overview

Art History and Culture

Art history is the record of art from the past to the present. By looking at art from the past, we learn what the people who lived before us were like—their feelings and beliefs, clothes, food, houses, and how they viewed the world around them.

Questions to Discuss:

Knowledge
- Who created the artwork?
- When was the artwork created?
- What is the artwork's title?
- Have you ever seen an artwork like this? Where?

Comprehension
- Is this artwork useful? How is it used?
- Compare this artwork with another work from a similar time period. How are the works alike and different?
- What interests you most about this artwork?
- What is the major theme of this artwork?

Application
- What types of materials were used to create this artwork?
- Demonstrate how the artwork was created.
- Explain how this artwork could have a different use today.

Analysis
- What are the main elements in this artwork?
- Compare this painting with another painting in this book. How are they alike? How are they different?
- What does this artwork mean?

About Art

▲ **Frida Kahlo.** (Mexican). *Frida y Diego Rivera.* 1931.
Oil on canvas. 39 3/8 × 31 inches (100.01 × 78.74 cm.). San Francisco Museum of Modern Art, San Francisco, California.

Art History and Culture

Look at the artwork.
- What people or objects do you see?
- Do they look like people and objects you see around you today? Explain.

Look at the caption.
- When was the artwork created?
- What can you learn about the artist?

Learn more.
- Do some research to find out more about the artist, the artwork, and the time period.

Synthesis
- How many titles can you create for this artwork? Name them.
- Name a person you would like to give this artwork to as a gift. Why?
- Imagine that two people in this room are having a conversation. What would they say to each other? Why?

Evaluation
- Do you think this artwork is interesting? Why?
- Summarize this artwork's unique qualities.

What to Do
- Have students research to find out information about the life and times of Frida Kahlo. Students may write a biography of the artist or dress up as the artist and tell the artist's story to classmates.
- Have students research Kahlo and another artist who lived at the same time. Students should research information about the media, styles, techniques, and procedures the artists used. Have pairs of students role-play a discussion between the two artists about media, style, and personal beliefs about art.
- Have students work in groups to act out this painting. They should write a script for what happened before, during, and after the moment shown in the painting.

Overview

Aesthetic Perception

Aesthetic perception encourages students to make choices rather than give "correct answers." By understanding the process of aesthetic perception, students can see something from a new perspective and ultimately realize that art is all around them.

Journal writing is an integral part of aesthetic perception. It is an ongoing record of what a student does, notices, and thinks. Journals track the evolution of thoughts and experiences over time. Through this recorded journey, the student has the ability to reflect on where one has been and where one is going. Writing thoughts, reactions, perceptions, new information, and questions intensifies each student's life experiences.

Guidelines for Aesthetic Perception

Students like to know what is important about a work of art and what was important to the artist. They are fascinated with information, questions, and descriptions. There are some guiding principles in the development of aesthetic perception at this level that can profoundly influence teaching practice.

1. All aesthetic perception actively involves the learner.
2. All aesthetic perception involves reflection.
3. The works of art have substance. Their tools and a working vocabulary are vital to empower the learner.
4. Aesthetic perception is a process based upon examination of the artist's choices and the choices in response made by the viewer.
5. All responses are valid. Right and wrong are irrelevant issues when viewing works of art.
6. All works of art relate to each other, and each relates to all other areas of life.

About Art

▲ **Frida Kahlo.** (Mexican). *Frida y Diego Rivera.* 1931.
Oil on canvas. 39 3/8 × 31 inches (100.01 × 78.74 cm.). San Francisco Museum of Modern Art, San Francisco, California.

Aesthetic Perception

Look
- Look at the work of art. What sounds, smells, or feelings are in this work of art?
- What happened just before and just after in this work of art?
- What kind of music would be playing in this work of art?

Look Inside
- Imagine you are one of these people. Who are you? What are you thinking? How do you feel?
- If you could add yourself to the painting, what would you look like? What would you be doing?
- Act out or tell the story in this work of art with a beginning, a middle, and an end.
- Draw what you can't see in this work of art. Are there hidden images that should be revealed?

Look Outside
- How is this like or different from your own world?
- What does the artist want you to know or think about in this work of art?
- Describe your journey in viewing this work of art. Include your thoughts, ideas, and changes in thinking.
- What will you remember about this work?

Questions to Discuss
- What is happening in this work of art?
- What is this work of art about?
- What is your favorite part of this work of art?
- What is most important in this artwork?
- What happened just before and just after in this work of art?
- If you were in this work of art, what would you be doing?
- What have you learned about the work of art?
- What does the artist want you to know or think about in this work of art?
- How do you feel about the work of art? What does it make you feel?
- What will you remember about this work of art?
- Has this work of art changed your thinking?

Things to Do
- Draw yourself into the work of art.
- Draw what you can't see in the work of art.
- Act out or show the story in the work of art.
- Collect objects that are similar to the objects in the work of art and make aesthetic judgments about them.
- Role-play an interview with the artist about how the work of art was made.

Overview

Art Criticism

Art criticism is an organized system for looking at and talking about art. The purpose of art criticism is to get the viewer involved in a perception process that delays judgment until all aspects of the image have been studied. Learning art criticism also gives each viewer the confidence to discuss a work of art without worrying what other people might think.

Describe What do I see?

During this step, the viewer lists all the obvious things in the artwork. Objectivity is important.

Questions to Discuss

- List and describe everything you see in the artwork. Answers may include: We see the full figures of a man and a woman standing on a plain, brown floor. Above Frida's head flies a tan dove with blue-tipped wings. Frida looks tiny. She is wearing a floor-length, ruffled, dark blue-green skirt and a red scarf that is trimmed with diamond shapes and fringe. Diego is wearing a plain, dark blue suit (and so on).

Analyze How is the work organized?

During this step the viewer examines how the elements and principles of art are used in the artwork.

Questions to Discuss

- Describe the elements of art that you see. Answers may include: **Line**—There are horizontal lines where the floor meets the wall, on the wall, and in the rug. **Shape**—The tabletops, bookcase, lamp, doilies, and picture frames are geometric. The chairs, vase, flowers, leaves, and pitchers are free-form shapes (and so on).

- How has the artist used the principles of design? Answers may include: **Balance**—Informal balance; the large, plain shape of Diego is balanced by the small, busy shape and bright color of Frida. **Emphasis**—The bright red scarf leads our eyes to the clasped hands (and so on).

About Art

▲ **Frida Kahlo.** (Mexican). *Frida y Diego Rivera.* 1931.
Oil on canvas. 39⅜ × 31 inches (100.01 × 78.74 cm.). San Francisco Museum of Modern Art, San Francisco, California.

Art Criticism

Describe
- List everything you see in this painting. Be sure to describe the people and their clothing.

Analyze
- How has the artist used line, shape, color, value, space, and texture?
- What kind of balance has the artist used?
- Has the artist used emphasis to make us notice one thing more than others?

Interpret
- What is happening?
- What is the artist telling us about these two people?

Decide
- Have you ever seen another artwork like this?
- Is it successful because it is realistic?
- Is it successful because it is well-organized?
- Is it successful because you have strong feelings when you study it?

Interpret — What is the artist saying to me?

During interpretation, viewers will make inferences about the message in the work of art. Each interpretation can be different because each is based upon the feelings and life experiences of the viewer.

Questions to Discuss
- What do I think about this work?
- What is the artist trying to tell us about these people and their lives? The clasped hands of these two people represent the link between them. They are married, and this is their wedding portrait. She leans toward him, but he turns away from her to the outside world. She shows her need for him; he shows his independence.

Decide

This is when the viewer decides whether or not the work is successful. There are two levels of judgment to be made. The first is personal: do you like the work?

The second level is also subjective, but it uses aesthetic theories to help the viewer decide whether the work is successful. More than one theory may be used to judge a work.

- Some critics think that the most important thing about a work of art is the realistic presentation of the subject matter. This aesthetic theory is called **imitationalism** or **realism.**
- Other critics think that composition is the most important factor in a work of art. This aesthetic theory, called **formalism** or **composition,** emphasizes the design qualities and the arrangement of the elements of art using the principles of art.
- Some critics claim that no object should be considered art if it fails to arouse an emotional response in the viewer. **Emotionalism** or **expressionism** is a theory concerned with the content or the meaning of the work of art.

Questions to Discuss
- Have you seen any works in this book that look similar to the style of this artist?
- Which aesthetic theories would you use to judge the success of this work? The two people and the objects are realistic. The artist has used informal balance to organize the work, and has used the red scarf as a point of emphasis. The artist has shown the feelings of these two people.

More About Aesthetic Judging

You can use art criticism to make aesthetic judgments about functional objects such as cars or shoes. Follow the first two steps (**Describe** and **Analyze**) as described. During **Interpret,** consider the purpose of the object as its meaning. (Does a pitcher look like it will pour liquid without spilling?) As you **Decide,** consider whether the object works when it is used. (If a chair is not comfortable to sit in, it is not functioning properly and is not successful as a chair.)

Overview

Creative Expression

The creative process, like the writing process or the scientific method, is an organized approach to creative problem solving that can be used by professional artists and students alike. Throughout *Art Connections,* the Creative Expression activities are presented as problems to be solved. Remind students of the steps in the creative process as they work on the activities.

Get an idea.

- Inspiration can come from many places. In the *Art Connections* Creative Expression activities, the idea comes from the activity instructions. Professional artists may get ideas from a client who has commissioned a piece of art from nature, from a historical event, from everyday life, or from the available media and materials.

- Try the following to help students when they have trouble getting an idea.

    1. As a class, brainstorm about where to get ideas for artwork: works by other artists, personal experiences, stories students have read, and so on.
    2. Encourage students to write ideas in the Ideas section of their Art Journals. Remind students that they can make notes for ideas anytime, not just in art class.
    3. Pair students who are having trouble thinking of ideas with students who have many ideas. One student can model getting ideas for the other student.

Plan your work.

- Once students have an idea, they must decide the best way to execute that idea. Would a two-dimensional or three-dimensional artwork best convey the idea that students are trying to show? Should students use watercolor or pencil?

Make a sketch.

- Just like professional writers, professional artists do not make a perfect work on the first try. They may make several sketches, evaluate those sketches, and revise them before deciding on a final vision for the artwork.

- Encourage students to make sketches in the Ideas section of their Art Journals.

About Art

▲ **Frida Kahlo.** (Mexican). *Frida y Diego Rivera.* 1931.
Oil on canvas. 39 3/8 × 31 inches (100.01 × 78.74 cm.). San Francisco Museum of Modern Art, San Francisco, California.

Creative Expression

How does an artist create a work of art?

Art is a process. You can follow the same steps to create your own work of art.

1. Get an idea.
   - Artists get inspiration from many places. Look around you. People, objects, and scenes may provide inspiration for a work of art.
2. Plan your work.
   - Do you want your artwork to be two-dimensional or three-dimensional?
   - Decide what media you want to use.
   - What materials will you need?
3. Make a sketch.
   - Think about how you want your artwork to look. Sketch several ideas.
   - If your artwork will be three-dimensional, sketch it from different points of view.
   - Then choose the best idea.
4. Use the media.
   - Make an artwork based on your best idea. You may want to practice using the materials first.
   - When making your composition, remember the elements and principles of art. How can you use them to make your artwork say what you want it to say?
5. Share your final work.
   - Evaluate your work using the four steps of art criticism. What do you like best about your work? What would you do differently next time?

Use the media.
- In this stage of the creative process, students make their artwork based on their plans. Encourage students to practice using unfamiliar media, and to try new techniques on a small practice piece before using those techniques on their artwork.
- Even during this stage of the process, students may get new ideas. Encourage them to be flexible.

Share your final work.
- Art is meant to be shared with and viewed by others. Encourage students to share their artwork with family or friends, display it in the classroom, or display it in the school display area. This is also a good time for students to self-evaluate their work using the four steps of art criticism.

More About Art Journals
- Art Journals are a wonderful way to work through ideas. At the beginning of the school year, help students set up an Art Journal. This can be a spiral notebook or a three-ring binder with pages for writing and sketching. The Art Journal will be divided into sections for Concepts, Ideas, Critical Thinking (Art Criticism), Vocabulary.

  1. Encourage students to use the Concepts section of their journals for summarizing unit and lesson concepts, writing questions they have, and listing other things they want to learn.
  2. Students can use the Ideas section of their Art Journals for brainstorming, organizing, planning, and sketching. Remind students that they can write ideas in their journals any time; they do not need to wait until a designated time in art class.
  3. Students can use the Critical Thinking section of their journals to self-evaluate their work using the four steps of Art Criticism. In *Art Connections,* students are asked to self-evaluate after each Creative Expression activity. This can be a valuable tool to help students review art concepts and get ideas for their next work.
  4. Encourage students to use the Vocabulary section of their Art Journals to record unfamiliar words, summarize or explain definitions, and so on. Developing vocabulary is an important step in being able to think about and communicate about art.

Overview

Elementary teachers are responsible for the safety of their students. Specific guidelines have been established by the Center for Safety in the Arts, and these guidelines should be followed to ensure that both students and teachers use art materials safely. Following are some general tips for using art materials safely. For more detailed information, see "Safe Use of Art Materials" on page T12 of this book.

Safe Art Materials

- Use only water-soluble AP- or CP-designated markers. Never use permanent or scented markers.
- Use only dustless chalk.
- Make sure that crayons have the AP or CP label to ensure that they do not contain lead.
- When using tempera paint, use only liquid tempera, not powdered tempera. Do not use any spray paints or fixatives.
- Use only water-soluble printers' inks.
- Use pencils to carve into soft surfaces for printing blocks. Do not use mat knives or other sharp instruments.
- Do not allow young children to use sharp scissors; blunt points are safe.
- Do not use rubber cement unless it bears the AP or CP label. Do not use solvent-based glues.

About Art

Safety

- Use art materials only on your artwork.
- Keep art materials out of your mouth, eyes and ears.
- Use scissors and other sharp tools carefully. Keep your fingers away from the cutting blades.
- Wash your hands after using the art materials.
- Wear an art shirt or smock to protect your clothes.
- Use only art materials with a "nontoxic" label.

- Return art materials to their proper storage place.
- Be careful not to breathe chalk or clay dust.
- Use only new and clean foam trays.
- Do not walk around the room with sharp tools in your hand.
- Be aware of others in your work space.
- Always follow your teacher's directions when using the art materials.

General Safety Precautions

- Read the labels on all materials used in the art room. Look carefully for the AP/CP labels. If these are not present, be suspicious. Imported art materials should be looked upon with extreme caution. Other countries have not developed the rigid safety codes adopted by the United States.
- Do not accept or use old art materials that may have been left in the school or donated by some well-meaning adult. If the materials do not bear the current safety codes, toss them out.
- Never allow food or drink in the room where art activities are being conducted. Dust and even fibers float freely in the air and can readily contaminate food or drink.
- Practice cleanliness. Have children wash their hands thoroughly with soap after using art materials.
- Use absolutely no permanent markers or solvent-based materials in the art room. If a material stains the clothes or hands and does not clean up with simple soap and water, it is not appropriate or safe for young children to use.
- Use plastic containers for washing paintbrushes; glass is dangerous in the hands of young children.
- Paper cutters should not be used by elementary-school children. The paper cutter should be kept out of the students' reach, and left in a locked position always with the blade turned to the wall.
- Do not use commercial dyes around children; use vegetable or natural dyes (flowers, teas, onion skins).
- Do not allow children in a room where a kiln is firing; both the heat and the fumes are dangerous.

Unit 1 Planning Guide

	Lesson Title	Suggested Pacing	Creative Expression Activity
Lesson 1	Line and Qualities of Line	1 hour	Create a contour drawing.
Lesson 2	Geometric and Free-Form Shapes	1 hour	Make a pictorial quilt square.
Lesson 3	Geometric Forms	1 hour	Make a wooden sculpture.
Lesson 4	Free-Form Form	1 hour	Create a model of an outdoor sculpture.
Lesson 5	Space and Perspective	1 hour	Create a perspective drawing.
Lesson 6	Positive and Negative Space	1 hour	Create an assemblage using positive and negative space.
ARTSOURCE	Line, Shape, Form, and Space in Music and Storytelling	35 minutes	Describe sounds in the environment.

34A UNIT 1 • Line, Shape, Form, and Space

Materials	Program Resources	Fine Art Resources	Literature Resources
markers, pencils, white paper	*Assessment,* pp. 9–10 *Reading and Writing Test Preparation,* pp. 6–7 *Home and After-School Connections* *Flash Cards* 1–6	Transparency 1 *Artist Profiles,* pp. 40, 73 *Large Prints* 73 and 74 *The National Museum of Women in the Arts Collection*	*Homer Price* by Robert McCloskey
felt, yarn, chalk, cotton fabric, scissors, needles, embroidery floss	*Assessment,* pp. 11–12 *Reading and Writing Test Preparation,* pp. 8–9 *Flash Cards* 7–8	Transparency 2 *Artist Profiles,* pp. 49, 80 *Large Prints* 73 and 74 *Art Around the World Collection*	*The Keeping Quilt* by Patricia Polacco and *Tar Beach* by Faith Ringgold
wood, acrylic paint, tape, paintbrushes, wood glue, paper towels, mixing palettes, water containers	*Assessment,* pp. 13–14 *Reading and Writing Test Preparation,* pp. 10–11	Transparency 3 *Artist Profiles,* pp. 29, 61 *Large Prints* 73 and 74 *The National Museum of Women in the Arts Collection*	*The Secret Garden* by Frances Hodgson Burnett
wire, tissue paper, white paper, scissors, tape, markers, chenille sticks, glue, polystyrene foam, acrylic paints, paper towels, newspaper, mixing palettes	*Assessment,* pp. 15–16 *Reading and Writing Test Preparation,* pp. 12–13	Transparency 4 *Artist Profiles,* pp. 4, 66 *Large Prints* 73 and 74 *Art Around the World Collection*	*The Music of Dolphins* by Karen Hesse
watercolors, color pencils, white paper, markers, paintbrushes, water containers, mixing palettes, paper towels, newspaper, pencils, erasers	*Assessment,* pp. 17–18 *Reading and Writing Test Preparation,* pp. 14–15	Transparency 5 *Artist Profiles,* pp. 47, 64 *Large Prints* 73 and 74 *Art Around the World Collection*	*Silverwing* by Kenneth Oppel
pencils, white paper, acrylic paint, paintbrushes, water containers, mixing palettes, paper towels, newspaper, cardboard, scissors, glue, fine-line black markers	*Assessment,* pp. 19–20 *Reading and Writing Test Preparation,* pp. 16–17 *Flash Card* 20	Transparency 6 *Artist Profiles,* pp. 5, 48 *Large Prints* 73 and 74 *The National Museum of Women in the Arts Collection*	*Treasure of Green Knowe* by L. M. Boston
"The Boy Who Wanted to Talk to Whales"			

Unit Overview

1 Line, Shape, Form, and Space

Lesson 1: Line is the pathway made through space by a moving point.

Lesson 2: Shape is a two-dimensional area that is measured by height and width.

Lesson 3: Geometric forms are precise and can be measured by height, width, and depth.

Lesson 4: Free-form forms are irregular and can have straight or curved edges.

Lesson 5: Perspective is used to create the illusion of space or depth.

Lesson 6: Positive space refers to any object, shape, or form. **Negative space** is the empty space that surrounds objects, shapes, and forms.

Introduce Unit Concepts

"Artists use the art elements of line, shape, form, and space to create a variety." "Los artistas usan los elementos artísticos de línea, figura, forma, y espacio para crear variedad."

Line and Shape
- What types of lines are used every day? Have students come up with some examples. Ask students to brainstorm and list on the board as many kinds of shapes as they can think of.

Form and Space
- Have students name different types of forms. Explain that forms are similar to shapes; however, they are also measured by depth.
- Ask students to explain what the word *space* means. In art, it is the air or area around and between objects.

Cross-Curricular Projects
- See the *Language Arts and Reading, Mathematics, Science,* and *Social Studies Art Connections* books for activities that further develop line, shape, space, and form concepts.

34 UNIT 1 • Line, Shape, Form, and Space

Unit 1
Line, Shape, Form, and Space

Artists use line, shape, form, and space to create a variety of works of art.

Gustav Klimt's use of line, shape, form, and space in *Fulfillment* makes it an eye-catching work of art. Each time a viewer looks at this piece, he or she will notice something new. Klimt is known for creating lively portraits and colorful landscapes.

◀ **Gustav Klimt.** (Austrian). *Die Erfüllung (Fulfillment).* 1905–1909.
Mixed media with gold leaf on paper. $76\frac{3}{8} \times 47\frac{5}{8}$ inches (194 × 121 cm.). Österreichisches Museum für angewandte Kunst, Vienna, Austria.

Fine Art Prints

Display **Large Prints 73** *Qualicraft Shoes/Chinese Lady* and **74** *The Wedding Banquet.* Refer to the prints throughout the unit as students learn about line, shape, form, and space.

Large Print 73

Large Print 74

Artists use **lines** to create two-dimensional works of art.
- What types of lines do you see in the background?

Artists use **shapes** to represent objects found in nature and made by people.
- What types of shapes do you see on the clothes?

Forms are used by artists to create three-dimensional sculptures and architectural structures.
- Are there any forms in this work of art? Explain.

Artists use **space** to create two- and three-dimensional works of art.
- Do the people in the painting look like they are standing far from the wall? Explain.

In This Unit you will learn about different types of lines and shapes and how artists use them in different kinds of art. You will also learn about three-dimensional forms and about techniques used to create space. Here are the topics you will study:
- Line
- Shape
- Form
- Space
- Depth
- Perspective
- Positive and Negative Space

Master Artist Profile

Gustav Klimt
(1862–1918)

Gustav Klimt was born near Vienna, Austria, and was part of an artistic family. His father was an engraver of gold and silver. One of his brothers was a goldsmith, and another brother was a painter. At the age of fourteen, Klimt enrolled in art school. He did not gain worldwide fame until the mid-twentieth century and was known only in the European art community up to that time. He preferred his art to speak for itself, rather than for him to talk about it.

Unit 1   **35**

Art History and Culture

Gustav Klimt

Gustav Klimt's (goos´ täv klimt) (1862–1918) technique was fairly classical, but his subjects were often criticized. The use of ornamentation in his work was apparent. He used a variety of colors (often mixed with gold leaf) and abstract figures, which made his art very distinctive. Klimt created his works of art not only on canvases but also in places like theatres and homes. *Fulfillment* is part of *The Stoclet Frieze,* which has four distinct sections. The final product was located in the dining room of Adolphe Stoclet in Brussels, and included semiprecious stones.

See pages 24–25 and 16–21 for more about art history and the subject matter.

Artist Profiles, p. 35

Examine the Artwork

"Let's look closely at this artwork by Gustav Klimt." "Vamos a observar detalladamente esta obra de arte de Gustav Klimt."

- Have students study *Fulfillment.* Ask them to describe what they see.
- Have students answer the questions about line, shape, form, and space on page 35.
  ▶ Curved lines make up the majority of the background. There are also diagonal and horizontal lines in some of the images. Students may say that some of the lines look like zigzags.
  ▶ There are circles, ovals, squares, triangles, and rectangles in various colors. There are also free-form shapes such as birds and fish.
  ▶ There are no true forms in this piece, but the people are based on real forms.
  ▶ The people look like they are rather close to the wall. The way the wall and floor meet near the bottom of the drawing and the location of the people on the floor indicate that they are not standing next to the wall.

Unit Pretest

Display **Transparency 43** as a pretest.
Answers: 1. B, 2. A, 3. A, 4. C, 5. C

Home Connection

- See *Home and After-School Connections* for family newsletters and activities for this unit.

UNIT 1 • Line, Shape, Form, and Space   **35**

Unit 1 Arts Integration

ILLUSTRATOR PROFILE
William Steig
(1907–2003)

William Steig was born into an artistic family in Brooklyn, New York. Both of his parents experimented with art, and his older brother Irwin gave Steig his first lessons in painting. As a teenager, Steig created cartoons for his high school's newspaper. He later attended the National Academy of Design.

Steig began working as an artist to support his parents and a younger sibling during the Great Depression. In 1930 he sold his first of more than 1,600 cartoons to *The New Yorker;* he also created 117 covers for the magazine.

In 1968 Steig wrote and illustrated his first children's book, *C D B!,* at the suggestion of a friend in the publishing industry. Although many people might be reluctant to launch a new career at age 61, Steig was enthusiastic. His third book, *Sylvester and the Magic Pebble,* was awarded the Caldecott Medal in 1970, and *The Amazing Bone* was named a Caldecott Honor book. Another of Steig's notable works is the picture book *Shrek!,* which provided the basis for the popular animated film by the same name.

In his books, Steig managed to combine a bit of wisdom with a sense of wide-eyed wonder. In the journal *Children's Literature in Education,* James E. Higgins captured the nature of Steig's work with the following statement: "He writes not out of a remembrance of childhood, but out of the essence of childhood . . ."

Throughout Unit 1, share Steig's illustrations with the class and discuss the use of line, shape, form, and space in his books. Which types of lines does he use? Which illustrations would be forms in real life?

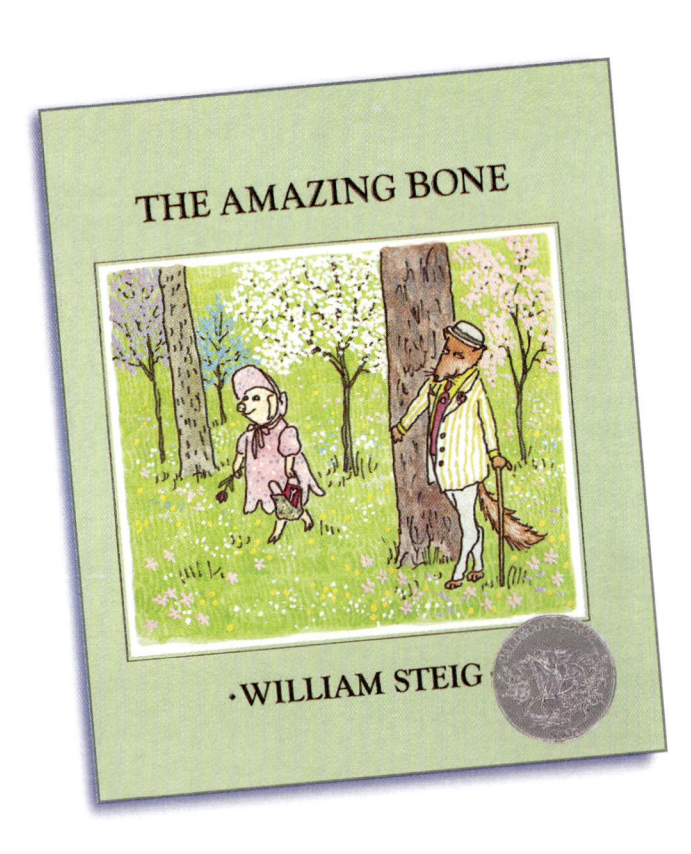

Music
Form in music relates to how music is organized. Many traditional songs, such as "Oh, Susannah," are in AB form, in which the second section sounds different from the first section.

Literature
Show the video *Call It Courage* to introduce the concepts of line, shape, form, and space. Pause the video and have students identify these concepts.

Literature and Art

Performing Arts
Show "The Boy Who Wanted to Talk to Whales." Point out how sounds can represent lines and shapes.

Artsource®

35A UNIT 1 • Line, Shape, Form, and Space

Lesson 1 Overview: Line and Line Qualities

Lesson 1 introduces the element of line and line qualities in two-dimensional art. A line will have different expressive qualities based on its direction and type.

Objectives

Art History and Culture
To demonstrate knowledge of Henri Matisse and Indonesian art

Creative Expression
To create a contour drawing using different types and qualities of line

Aesthetic Perception
To distinguish different lines in two-dimensional art and to understand how artists use line in their work

Art Criticism
To evaluate own work using the four steps of art criticism

Lesson Materials
- pencils
- 9" × 12" paper
- felt-tip markers

Alternate Materials:
- crayons
- ballpoint pens

Program Resources
- *Reading and Writing Test Prep.,* pp. 6–7
- *Transparency* 1
- *Flash Cards* 1–6
- *Artist Profiles,* pp. 40, 73
- *Animals Through History Time Line*
- *Assessment,* pp. 9–10
- *Large Prints 73* Qualicraft Shoes/Chinese Lady and **74** *The Wedding Banquet*
- *The National Museum of Women in the Arts Collection*

Concept Trace
Line
Introduced: Level 5, Unit 1, Lesson 1
Reinforced: Level 7, Chapter 2, Lesson 2

Vocabulary — Reading
Review the following vocabulary words with students before beginning the lesson.

line *línea*—the path of a moving point through space

directional lines *líneas de dirección*—how a line moves: diagonally, vertically, or horizontally

See page 59B for additional vocabulary and Spanish vocabulary resources.

Art Journal: Vocabulary
Have students add these words to the Vocabulary section of their Art Journals.

Lesson 1 Arts Integration

Theatre
Complete Unit 1, Lesson 1, on pages 18–19 of *Theatre Arts Connections.*

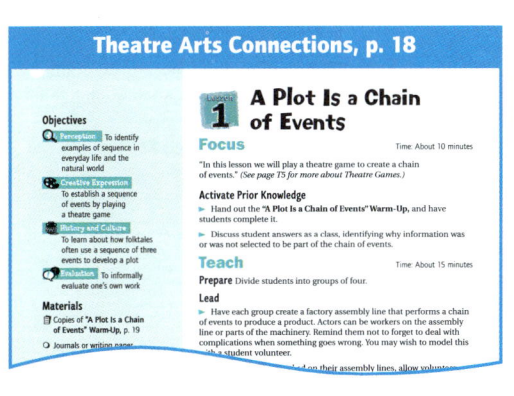

Music
Brandenburg Concerto No. 5. J.S. Bach.

Line in music refers to the way a melody moves higher and lower (up, down, or the same). To relate the concept of line in music to line in visual art, play Bach's *Brandenburg Concerto,* which includes a wide range of musical lines. Have students draw the vertical, horizontal, diagonal, zigzag, curved, thick, thin, and broken lines that they think go with the music.

Movement & Dance
Have students spread out and stand in separate spaces of the room. Have each person hold the end of a string, representing a line, observing how the points connect. Can students identify the type of angles created when lines meet at a corner? Ask selected students to go from standing to sitting, still holding the string. Lastly, have students walk slowly, still holding the string taut, to a new place in the room.

LESSON 1 • Line and Line Qualities 35B

Focus

Time: About 5 minutes

Activate Prior Knowledge

"When creating a personal piece of art, do the lines sometimes reflect how you are feeling?"

"Cuando hacen una obra de arte personal, ¿Las líneas a veces reflejan lo que sienten?"

- As a class, discuss students' responses. Explain that artists often use lines to help express a feeling or emotion in their work.

Using Literature ⭐ Reading

- Have students look at the cover illustration of *Homer Price* by Robert McCloskey. Discuss the various lines used in the illustration. Have students notice the use of contour lines and how they are used to communicate the various parts of the machinery.

Thematic Connection ⭐ Social Studies

- **Water:** Have students share different stories about voyages that take place across bodies of water. Have them identify any animals that were encountered, especially those that live or swim in the water.

Introduce the Art

Look

"Look closely at both *Ceremonial Skirt* and *Plate 24.*" "Miren de cerca las obras *Ceremonial Skirt* y *Plato 24.*"

Comparing and Contrasting ⭐ Reading

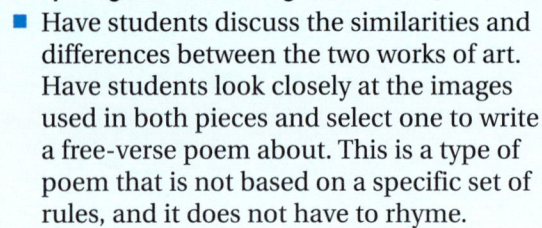

- Have students discuss the similarities and differences between the two works of art. Have students look closely at the images used in both pieces and select one to write a free-verse poem about. This is a type of poem that is not based on a specific set of rules, and it does not have to rhyme.

Art History and Culture

Make sure students know that the years included in the nineteenth century are 1800–1899. The twentieth century includes 1900–1999. Point out that they are living in the twenty-first century.

💻 Web Connection

Visit www.loc.gov/rr/rarebook/guide/illusbk.html for more information about illustrated books.

36 UNIT 1 • Line, Shape, Form, and Space

Lesson 1: Line and Qualities of Line

Look at *Plate 24* and *Ceremonial Skirt* on these pages. Matisse created the illustration of the swan for a book of poems titled *Poésies*, by Stéphane Mallarmé. Matisse incorporated the curved lines of the lettering into his illustration. He also used line to communicate the shape of the swan. *Ceremonial Skirt* is from Indonesia. The decorative design is applied to the top of the tapestry using **embroidery** techniques. The swan illustration and the figures in the cloth both include straight and curved lines. Notice that although the same types of lines are used in both works, they are used differently.

▲ **Henri Matisse.** (French). *Plate 24* from *Poésies* by Stéphane Mallarmé. 1932. Etching. 13 × 9¾ inches (33.02 × 24.76 cm.). Museum of Modern Art, New York, New York.

Art History and Culture

What years are included in the nineteenth and twentieth centuries?

36 Unit 1 • Lesson 1

Art History and Culture

Henri Matisse

Henri Matisse (än´ rē ma tēs´) (1869–1954) was an accomplished painter, sculptor, and graphic designer. Matisse was the leader of an art movement called fauvism. Members of this movement were called *fauves*, meaning "wild beasts," because they rejected traditional styles and painted with brilliant colors and bold distortions of reality. Matisse experimented with color and line throughout his art career. He is considered one of the most influential artists of the 1900s.

See pages 24–25 and 16–21 for more about art history and the subject matter.

Artist Profiles, p. 40

Artist Profile
Henri Matisse
1869–1954

Henri Matisse (än´ rē ma tēs´) was the son of a middle-class couple in the north of France. He was not interested in art while he was in school. After high school his father sent him to law school in Paris. When he was 21 an appendicitis attack changed his life. Because he had to spend a long time in the hospital, his mother brought him a paint box to help him pass the time. Matisse eventually convinced his father to let him drop out of law school and study art. Matisse married and started a family soon after. His paintings were not selling, so he worked for a decorator and his wife opened a hat shop. During the last years of his life he suffered from arthritis. Unable to hold a brush in his hands, he devoted his efforts to

Study both works of art to discover more about lines and how they can be used.

- What types of lines do you recognize? What type of line is used most often in both works?
- How are the lines in *Ceremonial Skirt* different from those in *Plate 24*? How are they the same?
- Describe the edges of the swan figure by Matisse.
- How were lines used to fill in the details of the swan figure?

◀ **Artist unknown.** (Flores/Indonesia). *Ceremonial Skirt.* Nineteenth century.
Cotton, glass beads, shell, and metal. $68\frac{1}{2} \times 31\frac{1}{4}$ inches (173.99 × 79.38 cm.). Dallas Museum of Art, Dallas, Texas.

Aesthetic Perception

Design Awareness Look around the classroom and notice the shapes of objects. What types of lines do you see most often?

Unit 1 • Lesson 1   37

Art History and Culture

Indonesian Artisans

Ceremonial Skirt is a sarong, or long tubular skirt. The sarong is worn by both men and women, though the men usually wear a wider and shorter version. The human figures, the boat, and the spiderlike designs are made of glass beads stitched onto the background cloth. Glass beads were used by people of high social status. The beaded skirts are symbolic of prosperity and abundance and were worn only on important ceremonial occasions. Birth, marriage, house building, and death were considered important events.

See pages 24–25 and 16–21 for more about art history and the subject matter.

Artist Profiles, p. 73

Ceremonial Skirt
This skirt, also called a *tapis*, was crafted by an unknown Indonesian artist. Indonesia is a republic of more than 13,000 islands situated between the Pacific Ocean, the Indian Ocean, and the South China Sea. Indonesia is a densely populated nation of many different cultures and ethnic groups. While the capital city of Jakarta has some of the tallest, most spectacular high-rise buildings and advanced technologies in the world, there are other areas where primitive rain forest-dwelling peoples live much like their ancestors have for centuries.

◀ **Artist unknown.** (Flores/Indonesian). *Ceremonial Skirt.* Nineteenth century.
Cotton, glass beads, shell, and metal.

Study

- In *Plate 24,* straight lines were used to indicate the longer feathers in the swan's wings, and curved lines complete the rest of the image. In *Ceremonial Skirt,* curved and straight lines were used in the human and spiderlike figures. Straight and zigzag lines were used in the boat shapes.
- In *Ceremonial Skirt,* the lines are more linear or straight. In *Plate 24,* there are very few straight lines in the swan. Those few lines that may be considered straight are in the wings.
- The figure of the swan has few details. The head, neck, and body are an outline of the swan. These are all made of continuous, curved lines.
- The only details are in the face and wings. These are minimal.
- For more examples of utilitarian art, see ***The National Museum of Women in the Arts Collection.***

Art Journal: Writing
Have students think about a decorative fabric they own or have seen. Encourage students to write a description of this fabric and how line is used. What else do they want to know about line?

Aesthetic Perception

Design Awareness Some of the lines in the classroom move up and down (vertical); others move side to side (horizontal). The vertical lines found in plants give the feeling of stability. A tree whose roots are visible and slanted gives the feeling of instability; it looks like it may soon fall.

Developing Visual Literacy Discuss the use of symbols in each artwork. How did the artists use the element of line to communicate their ideas? Ask students to share personal experiences that contribute to their interpretations. NSAE 5a

Web Connection
Visit www.dm-art.org for more information about the Dallas Museum of Art.

LESSON 1 • Line and Line Qualities   37

Teach

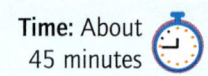

Time: About 45 minutes

"Can you practice using different types of lines and line qualities?" *"¿Pueden practicar el uso de diferentes tipos de líneas y cualidades lineales?"*

- Read and discuss "Using Formal Balance" on page 38.

Practice

Materials: pencil, 9" × 12" paper

Alternate Materials: crayons

- Distribute the materials and have students follow the directions on page 38.
- Explain to students that for blind contour drawings, they should not look at their papers or lift their pencils.

Creative Expression

Materials: 9" × 12" paper, felt-tip markers

Alternate Materials: ballpoint pen

- Distribute the materials and have students follow the directions on page 39.
- Have students demonstrate their technical skills by using a variety of art media and materials in their contour drawings. NSAE 1a; 1b
- Review the Activity Tips on page 230 for visual examples of techniques.

Art Journal: Researching

Have students write directions on how to make a contour drawing after their practice activity. Ask students to list any questions and observations they may have. Have students keep their directions and notes in their Art Journals. Students can look over their directions prior to starting the Creative Expression activity.

38 UNIT 1 • Line, Shape, Form, and Space

Types of Lines

Artists use lines to lead the eyes through a work of art. A **line** is the path of a moving point through space. When looking at a line, a person's eyes will follow the path of its direction. Lines can look different. They can be thick or thin, short or long, and rough or smooth. A **contour line** defines the edges and surface ridges of an object. Artists use various types of lines and line qualities when creating contour drawings.

Vertical lines move up and down and are inactive. They appear to be at rest and give the feeling of stability. Artists use vertical lines to show pride and stiffness in their work.

Horizontal lines move from side to side. They too are inactive and give the feeling of stability, calm, and quiet. They make us feel relaxed and content.

Diagonal lines move on a slant. They are active and express a feeling of instability. Artists use them to show excitement, instability, and activity. These lines often make us feel uncomfortable or tense.

Zigzag lines are made by joining diagonal lines. They are very active and express feelings of confusion and excitement.

Curved lines bend and change gradually or turn inward to form spirals. They express calm flowing activity. A spiral curves around, leading your eye toward a central point.

Practice

Use different types of lines to create blind contour drawings.

1. Look at your hand. Study its outline, or contours. Use a pencil, and draw a blind contour drawing of your hand.
2. Find an object in the room and create another blind contour drawing.
3. What type of lines did you use in each drawing? Describe how your eyes moved when you created your contours.

38   Unit 1 • Lesson 1

Differentiated Instruction

Reteach

Ask students to look through their books for examples of works of art that best illustrate each of the five types of lines. Have students see how many different line qualities they can find in each example.

Special Needs

Students may have difficulty letting their eyes follow the contour lines of subjects. The teacher may facilitate this ability by standing near the subjects and slowly air-tracing the contour lines for students to observe.

ELL

Students may find it helpful if you pantomime stiffness and stability when describing vertical lines, calm and relaxed for horizontal lines, excited and slanted for diagonal and zigzag lines, gradually turning for curved lines.

◀ Laura Lynch. Age 12.

Think about what lines and line qualities this student artist used in the contour drawing.

Creative Expression

Find an object, or objects, and create a contour drawing using different types of lines.

1. Look over the directions you wrote in your Art Journal on how to make a contour drawing. Make a practice drawing of your object, or objects, following your directions.
2. Using a marker, make a second drawing of the same object.
3. Make some lines thick and some lines thin. You may pick up your marker and look at your paper to make the thick and thin lines. Always concentrate on the contours of your object.
4. Look at your first contour drawing and compare it to your second one.

Art Criticism

Describe What object did you select?

Analyze List the lines and line qualities you used in your contour drawings. What type of line did you use most often?

Interpret Give your completed work a title. What did you notice when you compared your first drawing with your second?

Decide Do you feel your contour drawing was a success? Explain.

Unit 1 • Lesson 1   **39**

Reflect

Time: About 10 minutes

Review and Assess
"How would you explain the differences and similarities between the different lines?"
"¿Cómo explicarían las diferencias y las semejanzas entre las diferentes líneas?"

Think

The artist used all five types of lines. Most of the objects appear calm, except the hair on the doll.

- Use **Large Prints 73** *Qualicraft Shoes/Chinese Lady* and **74** *The Wedding Banquet* to have students identify the different types of lines and line qualities. Do they see any contour lines?

Informal Assessment

- For standardized-format test practice using this lesson's art content, see pages 6–7 in *Reading and Writing Test Preparation*.

Art Journal: Critical Thinking

Have students answer the four art criticism questions—Describe, Analyze, Interpret, and Decide—in their Art Journals. Within groups, have students discuss the different types of lines they used in their contour drawings. Have them compare how they used different types of lines and line qualities depending on the objects they drew.

Art Across the Curriculum

Use these simple ideas to reinforce art concepts across the curriculum.

★ **Narrative Writing** Have students pretend to take a line for a walk with them through their classes on a typical day.

★ **Math** Have students create a class graph on types of lines and line qualities used in their works of art.

★ **Science** Have students study lines up close in both natural and humanmade objects with the help of a microscope.

★ **Social Studies** Have students think of other pieces of art from various cultures that use the same symbols and line types as *Ceremonial Skirt*.

★ **Technology** Have students use the computer's paint or draw program to create a nonobjective design. Use the different types of lines. Have them use a variety of tools to add various line qualities. Visit **SRAonline.com** to print detailed instructions for this activity.
NSAE 6b

LESSON 1 • Line and Line Qualities   **39**

Lesson 1 Wrap-Up: Line and Line Qualities

Extra! For the Art Specialist
Time: About 45 minutes

Focus
Have students study **Large Print 73** *Qualicraft Shoes/Chinese Lady* and discuss how the artist used line. How does the use of line affect the mood of the artwork? Is it calm or active? Have students explain their responses.

Teach
Have students collect images of cities. Ask students to create several sketches from a selected image. Explain that they should include a variety of lines in their sketches but emphasize one type to create a mood. Then have them complete the alternate activity.

Reflect
Have students use the four steps of art criticism to evaluate their work. Did they effectively use a variety of lines in their cityscapes?

Alternate Activity

Materials:
- collected city images, sketchbook
- pencils, erasers, rulers
- white drawing paper
- fine-line permanent black marker
- watercolor paints, brushes (optional)

1. Ask students to select their best sketch and transfer their drawing onto their paper. They should draw the basic shapes first, then the details. Explain that the drawing does not have to be exactly like the image they selected.
2. Have students use a marker to outline the drawing.
3. As an option, students can add color to their cityscape using washes of watercolor.

Research in Art Education

Research continues to try to answer the questions of if and how the arts impact student learning in other subject areas. Some researchers suggest that the relationship between the arts and other subject areas "may not be as unidirectional—from the arts to other disciplines—as other studies have implied. Rather, the relationship may be more dynamic and interactive" ("Learning In and Through the Arts: Curriculum Implications" in *Champions of Change*, p. 43).

Assessment
Use the following rubric to evaluate the artwork students made in the Creative Expression activity and to assess students' understanding of how line and line qualities are used in two-dimensional works of art.

Have students complete page 9 or 10 in their *Assessment* books.

	Art History and Culture	Aesthetic Perception	Creative Expression	Art Criticism
3 POINTS	The student demonstrates knowledge of Henri Matisse and Indonesian art.	The student accurately identifies line types and qualities in a work of art.	The student's contour drawing demonstrates how to use line and line qualities.	The student thoughtfully and honestly evaluates own work using the four steps of art criticism.
2 POINTS	The student's knowledge of Henri Matisse and Indonesian art is weak or incomplete.	The student shows emerging awareness of line types and qualities, but cannot consistently identify them.	The student's contour drawing shows some awareness of how to use line and line qualities.	The student attempts to evaluate own work but shows an incomplete understanding of evaluation criteria.
1 POINT	The student cannot demonstrate knowledge of Henri Matisse or Indonesian art.	The student cannot identify line types and qualities.	The student's contour drawing shows no understanding of how to use line and line qualities.	The student makes no attempt to evaluate own work.

UNIT 1 • Line, Shape, Form, and Space

Lesson 2 Overview: Geometric and Free-Form Shapes

Lesson 2 introduces the element of shape. A shape is a two-dimensional area that is measured by height and width. Geometric shapes are precise shapes having mathematical measurements. Free-form shapes are irregular or uneven shapes made of straight or curved lines or a combination of both.

Objectives

Art History and Culture
To demonstrate knowledge of North American quiltmaking

Creative Expression
To design and create a quilt square that effectively illustrates a selected story using two-dimensional shapes

Aesthetic Perception
To identify geometric and free-form shapes in two-dimensional works of art

Art Criticism
To evaluate own work using the four steps of art criticism

Vocabulary — Reading

Review the following vocabulary words with students before beginning the lesson.

shapes *figuras*—a two-dimensional area that is measured by height and width

appliqué *aplicación*—decoration made from cloth cutouts and applied, usually through embroidery, onto a background cloth

See page 59B for additional vocabulary and Spanish vocabulary resources.

Art Journal: Vocabulary
Have students add these words to the Vocabulary section of their Art Journals.

Lesson Materials
- colored construction paper
- plastic sandwich bags
- scissors
- craft glue
- $9\frac{1}{2}''$ to $10\frac{1}{2}''$ squares colored cotton fabric
- various colors of felt
- light-colored chalk
- pencils
- sewing needles, embroidery floss

Alternate Materials:
- drawing or sketch paper
- envelopes
- school glue
- colored construction paper
- felt
- fine-line marker

Program Resources
- *Reading and Writing Test Prep.*, pp. 8–9
- *Transparency 2*
- *Flash Cards* 7–8
- *Artist Profiles,* pp. 40, 80
- *Animals Through History Time Line*
- *Assessment,* pp. 11–12
- *Large Prints 73* Qualicraft Shoes/Chinese Lady and *74* The Wedding Banquet
- *Art Around the World Collection*

Concept Trace
Geometric and Free-Form Shapes
Introduced: Level 5, Unit 1, Lesson 3
Reinforced: Level 7, Chapter 2, Lesson 5

Lesson 2 Arts Integration

Theatre
Complete Unit 1, Lesson 2, on pages 20–21 of *Theatre Arts Connection.*

Music
Lakota Flute Song from Heartbeat/Voices of First Nations Women. Georgia Wettlin-Larsen.

Geometric shapes have mathematical measurements, like triangles, circles, and squares. Free-form shapes are irregular. Play Georgia Wettlin-Larsen's *Lakota Flute Song* as students complete the Practice activity. Have students draw geometric and free form shapes that represent the music.

Movement & Dance
Mark off an area on the floor, outlining it with string or tape. Have three students walk in, arrange themselves separately in the space, and each create three geometric shapes. Have three more students enter, arranging themselves around the first group, but not touching them, and create free-form shapes. Have a third group enter and through touch, find a way to connect each free-form shape to a geometric shape.

LESSON 2 • Geometric and Free-Form Shapes **39B**

Focus

Time: About 10 minutes

Activate Prior Knowledge

"Have you ever slept under a quilt or seen a quilt?" "¿Alguna vez han dormido bajo una colcha o han visto una colcha?"

- As a class, discuss student responses. Explain that shapes are used by artists to imitate things we see. Shapes can also be used to express feelings or emotions.

Using Literature ⭐ Reading

- Have students look at the illustrations in *The Keeping Quilt* by Patricia Palacco and *Tar Beach* by Faith Ringgold. Discuss and compare the various uses of quilts and the different quilt styles.

Thematic Connection ⭐ Math

- **Shapes:** Have students give examples of any geometric or free-form shapes that they associate with a certain feeling or emotion.

Introduce the Art

Look

"Study the details in both the *Pictorial Quilt* by Harriet Powers and *Quilt*." "Estudien los detalles de *Pictorial Quilt* de Harriet Powers y *Quilt*."

Comparing and Contrasting ⭐ Reading

- Have students create a list of the similarities and differences between the two quilts. Both pieces use different types of fabrics and have geometric shapes. *Pictorial Quilt* has images of people and animals at solar events. Repeated geometric shapes are what make up the design of *Quilt*.

Art History and Culture

Possible answer: Pictorial quilts often depict a certain time in history and can be regarded as a piece of history. Quilts that do not necessarily tell a story through pictures often have their own history of how they were kept in a family.

💻 Web Connection

Visit www.moifa.org for more information about the International Folk Art Museum.

40 UNIT 1 • Line, Shape, Form, and Space

Lesson 2: Geometric and Free-Form Shape

Look at both of the quilts on these pages. The design for *Quilt* is called a "fan." Each circle is made of four fans, or quilt squares, which are sewn together by hand. *Pictorial Quilt* is an **appliqué**; it was made with cloth cutouts made from fabric scraps. The shapes were arranged to tell a story.

▲ **Artist unknown.** (American). *Quilt*. c. 1885.
Pieced and embroidered silk, velvet, velveteen, and cotton sateen. 69¼ × 68¼ inches (175.9 × 173.4 cm.). Museum of International Folk Art, Santa Fe, New Mexico.

Art History and Culture

Why might a quilt be kept in a family for many years?

40 Unit 1 • Lesson 2

Art History and Culture

Quilt was created during the late 1800s in upstate New York. In the Victorian era, there was a great fascination with optical illusions. It was very popular at that time to use a variety of leftover scraps of materials to create quilts. A circular illusion was created by placing four units of the fan design together. This is similar to the designs created by a kaleidoscope—a favorite optical toy at the time. The arched, alternating dark and light fabric pieces surrounding the circles add to the illusion by creating a star shape that seems to stand out from the quilt. Unfortunately many Victorian quilts have not survived as intact as is *Quilt*. This is because the popular fabrics of that time period were silks, velvets, and satins, all of which are fragile materials and disintegrate at a faster rate than fabrics such as cotton.

See pages 24–25 and 16–21 for more about art history and the subject matter.

Artist Profiles, p. 80

Artist Profile
Quilt
This American quilt was made in upstate New York during the late 1800s. Although it is not known who created the quilt, it may be assumed that the artist was a woman, or several women, from a relatively prosperous American family. During the Victorian era when this quilt was made, nearly all quiltmakers were women. Considering the amount of time needed to design, cut, assemble, and sew a quilt, the maker would have to be someone who had significant time to spend on these tasks, free from other work. The quilt may have been made by a group of women, perhaps at a quilting bee or quilting party, but the process would still have been time-consuming.

Artist unknown. (American). *Quilt*. c. 1885.

Study both quilts to become aware of how the artists used a variety of shapes.

▶ Can you find any rectangles, squares, circles, triangles, or diamonds in either quilt?
▶ Do you see any free-form shapes in the quilts?
▶ Do you recognize any objects in either of the quilts? Explain.
▶ What shapes are repeated in both quilts? How do you think the artists made these shapes?

▲ **Harriet Powers.** (American). *Pictorial Quilt.* c. 1895–98.
Cotton with cotton and metallic yarns. 68⅞ × 105 inches (174.96 × 266.7 cm.). Museum of Fine Arts, Boston, Massachusetts.

Aesthetic Perception

Design Awareness Pick up your textbook and look at it from different angles. What shapes do you see? Now think of a leaf. How is the shape of the leaf different from that of the textbook?

Unit 1 • Lesson 2   41

Art History and Culture

Harriet Powers

Harriet Powers (ha´ rē ət pou´ ərz) (1837–1911) lived her whole life in Athens, Georgia. Her works are considered to be the best existing examples of African American pictorial quilts. Powers made her first quilt soon after the Civil War. It was displayed during the cotton fair in 1887. *Pictorial Quilt* is the second of two quilts made by Harriet Powers. Both quilts depict scenes from the Bible; however, *Pictorial Quilt* also documents local history in four of the fifteen panels. One scene is an eclipse (second panel, May 19, 1779), and another is a meteor shower (center panel, November 13, 1833).

See pages 24–25 and 16–21 for more about art history and the subject matter.

Artist Profiles, p. 49

Artist Profile
Harriet Powers
1837–1911

Harriet Powers (ha´ rē ət pou´ ərz) was born in Athens, Georgia. She and her husband bought a small farm where they raised 11 children. Powers earned money by raising chickens, working as a seamstress, and making patchwork quilts until she died in 1911. Although she did not gain fame as a quilt artist in her lifetime (everything she owned at her death was worth a total of $70), her exquisite quilts now are appreciated by visitors to the Smithsonian Institution, and the Museum of Fine Arts in Boston, Massachusetts.

▲ **Harriet Powers.** (American). *Pictorial Quilt.* c. 1895–98.
Cotton with cotton and metallic yarns. 68⅞ × 105 inches (174.96 × 266.7 cm.). Museum of Fine Arts, Boston, Massachusetts.

Study

▶ Geometric shapes: rectangles, squares, and circles in *Pictorial Quilt*; rectangles, squares, circles, and quarter circles in *Quilt*.
▶ Free-form shapes: human figures, animals, shooting stars, and sun in *Pictorial Quilt*; curved triangular shapes around each circle in *Quilt*; fan shapes in *Quilt*.
▶ Shooting stars, fish, men, women, angels, sun, snake, birds, animals, and moon in *Pictorial Quilt*; fans in *Quilt*.
▶ Large square panels and circles. In *Pictorial Quilt*, the circles were cut as one piece and appliquéd onto the squares. In *Quilt*, the circles are part of the square panels and were made by sewing together separate shapes.
■ For more examples of art from North America, see the *Art Around the World Collection*.

Art Journal: Writing

Have students create a list of places they have seen shapes. Ask them to describe what they think are the differences between geometric and free-form shapes in the Concepts section of their Art Journals. What else do they want to know about shapes?

Aesthetic Perception

Design Awareness Discuss how humanmade objects are often geometric, especially if they must be uniform, such as a series of books or architectural elements, like windows. If you look at your shadow you will notice a free-form shape, but the shadow of a building is more likely to be made of geometric shapes.

Developing Visual Literacy Discuss the use of shapes in each artwork. How did the artists use shapes to communicate their ideas and designs? Ask students to share direct observations that contribute to their interpretations. NSAE 5c

Web Connection

Visit **www.mfa.org** for more information about the Boston Museum of Art.

LESSON 2 • Geometric and Free-Form Shapes   41

Teach

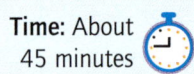

Time: About 45 minutes

"How can you use shapes in your artwork?"
"¿Como pueden usar las figuras en sus obras de arte?"

- Have students read and discuss the use of geometric and free-form shapes on page 42.
- Have students analyze the interdependence of art elements such as line and shape.

Practice

Materials: $9\frac{1}{2}"$ to $10\frac{1}{2}"$ squares and smaller pieces of colored construction paper, pencils, scissors, plastic sandwich bags

Alternate Materials: white drawing or sketch paper, envelopes

- Distribute the materials and have students follow the directions on page 42.

Creative Expression

Materials: $9\frac{1}{2}"$ to $10\frac{1}{2}"$ squares colored cotton fabric, various colors of felt squares, light-colored chalk, embroidery floss, scissors, sewing needles

Alternate Materials: glue and felt; or glue, construction paper and fine-line marker to create "stitches"

- Distribute the materials and have students follow the directions on page 43.
- Have students demonstrate their technical skills, using a variety of art media and materials to produce their pictorial quilt squares. NSAE 1a; 1b
- Review the Activity Tips on page 230 for visual examples of techniques.

Art Journal: Researching

Have students research modern-day pictorial or story quilts on the Internet or in the school media center. Students can take notes and compare the differences and similarities between the researched quilt and Harriet Powers' quilt in their Art Journals. Have students look over their notes prior to completing the Creative Expression activity.

Types of Shapes: Geometric and Free-Form

A **shape** is a two-dimensional area that is measured by height and width. Shapes can be solid, like a painted square, or outlined, like a drawing of a square. All shapes can be categorized as being either geometric or free-form.

Geometric shapes are exact and have mathematical measurements. Road signs, architecture, and many pieces of furniture are made of geometric shapes. There are three basic types of geometric shapes: circle, square, and triangle. By combining these shapes, artists can create **complex geometric shapes.** These combinations include an oval, rectangle, diamond, parallelogram, trapezoid, pentagon, hexagon, and octagon.

Trapezoid   Parallelogram   Pentagon   Hexagon   Octagon

Free-form shapes are irregular or uneven. Artists often use free-form shapes to represent things found in nature. Your shadow is an example of a free-form shape.

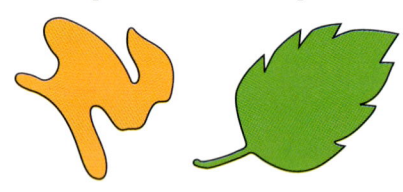

Practice

Design a pattern for a pictorial quilt square using geometric and free-form shapes.

1. Select one piece of colored construction paper as a background. Select contrasting pieces of paper to cut into a variety of shapes. Include at least one geometric and one free-form shape in the design. Try making complex geometric shapes.
2. Arrange your shapes on the background paper. Try overlapping smaller shapes onto larger shapes. Place your pattern pieces in a plastic sandwich bag to be used later.

Differentiated Instruction

Reteach
Ask students to look through the book or *Large Prints* for examples of works of art that best illustrate geometric and free-form shapes. Ask them to describe the different shapes that they find.

Special Needs
Students with lack of fine motor control or low vision may benefit from larger plastic needles and the use of thicker, more visible thread such as yarn.

ELL
Students may benefit from seeing a variety of free-form and geometric shapes. Prepare free-form and geometric shapes on flash cards so students can practice identifying different shapes.

◀ Savannah Ankerich.
Age 12.

Think about the types of shapes this student artist used in the pictorial quilt square.

🎨 Creative Expression

What scene from a story would you like to illustrate? Use both geometric and free-form shapes to design a pictorial quilt square.

1. Collect your pattern pieces from the Practice activity. Select a background square in the color that best depicts the time or place of your scene. Select various colors of felt for each of your pattern pieces.
2. Use a piece of chalk or a pencil to outline the paper shapes onto the felt pieces. Cut out the felt shapes and arrange them on the background square. Secure your shapes with either straight pins or a dot of craft glue.
3. Thread your needle and stitch the cut shapes into place on the background. Look at the embroidery Technique Tips on page 214 to get ideas for different stitches to use.

💬 Art Criticism

Describe What scene did you select? Describe the scene you depicted.

Analyze Create two columns labeled *Geometric shapes* and *Free-form shapes*. List all of the objects in your quilt square under the appropriate shape. What type of shape did you use most often? Did you use any complex geometric shapes in your final design?

Interpret What mood or emotions are depicted in your square?

Decide Do you feel your quilt square successfully tells this part of the story? Explain.

Unit 1 • Lesson 2   43

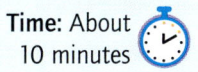

Reflect
Time: About 10 minutes

Review and Assess
"Describe the differences between geometric and free-form shapes. How are they similar? How did you use these shapes in your quilt square?" "Describan las diferencias entre las figuras geométricas y las abstractas. ¿En qué se parecen? ¿Cómo usaron estas figuras en sus cuadrados para la colcha?"

Think
The artist used triangular and round shapes to create tree shapes and free-form shapes.

- Use **Large Prints 73** *Qualicraft Shoes/Chinese Lady* and **74** *The Wedding Banquet* to have students identify and categorize the different shapes as either geometric, free-form, or complex geometric shapes.

- Have students analyze the quilt exhibition to form conclusions about formal properties and historical and cultural contexts used by their peers.
NSAE 4a

Informal Assessment
- For standardized-format test practice using this lesson's art content, see pages 8–9 in ***Reading and Writing Test Preparation.***

Art Journal: Critical Thinking
Have students answer the four art criticism questions—Describe, Analyze, Interpret, and Decide—in their Art Journals. As a class, have students discuss the different types of shapes used in the class quilt compared to their individual squares. Ask them to compare how similar objects were represented differently by different people. Discuss the impact of the quilt as a whole versus the individual panels.

Art Across the Curriculum

Use these simple ideas to reinforce art concepts across the curriculum.

★ **Narrative Writing** Have students write a story based on their portion of the class pictorial quilt.

★ **Math** Have students use mathematics to learn more about geometric shapes.

★ **Science** Have students identify free-form shapes in different ecosystems.

★ **Social Studies** Discuss the impact African American quilts had on the Underground Railroad during the nineteenth century.

★ **Technology** Have students use the computer's paint or draw program to plan a quilt with a geometric design. Select the shape icon to make various geometric shapes. Add color to your design by selecting the paint icon. Visit **SRAonline.com** for directions to print detailed instructions for this activity.
NSAE 6b

LESSON 2 • Geometric and Free-Form Shapes   **43**

Lesson 2 Wrap-Up: Geometric and Free-Form Shapes

Extra! For the Art Specialist
Time: About 45 minutes

Focus
Have students study **Large Print 73** *Qualicraft Shoes/Chinese Lady* and discuss how the artist used two-dimensional shapes. How are geometric and free-form shapes used together? Explain.

Teach
Have students create a quilt square based on a personal event or literary theme. Have them write a brief description of this event or story. Then complete the steps in the alternate activity to construct the quilt square.

Reflect
Have students use the four steps of art criticism to evaluate their work. Were they successful in creating a story quilt square? What story was selected?

Alternate Activity

Materials:
- sketchbook
- pencils, erasers
- fabric, felt
- embroidery needles and floss
- scissors
- fine-line permanent black marker

1. Have students create several sketches based on the written story and select one as a plan for the quilt.
2. Have students create the quilt square and embellish it using a variety of embroidery stitches.
3. Have students attach a piece of fabric to the completed square and use a felt-tip permanent marker to write their stories.
4. Quilt squares can be completed with a contrasting fabric border.

Research in Art Education

"The purposes of Art Education are to build awareness of the aesthetic components in human experience: the feeling of kinship between the young 'artist-analyst' and the traditions of artistic creation and comprehension of the language of visual form as embodied and as experienced through the visual impact of everyday objects." (*Report of the Commission on Art Education,* 1965, NAEA.)

Assessment
Use the following rubric to evaluate the artwork students make in the Creative Expression activity and to assess students' understanding of geometric and free-form shapes.

	Art History and Culture	Aesthetic Perception	Creative Expression	Art Criticism
3 POINTS	The student demonstrates knowledge of North American quiltmaking.	The student accurately identifies geometric and free-form shapes in a work of art.	The student's quilt square clearly demonstrates the use of geometric and free-form shapes.	The student thoughtfully and honestly evaluates own work using the four steps of art criticism.
2 POINTS	The student's knowledge of North American quiltmaking is weak or incomplete.	The student shows an emerging awareness of geometric and free-form shapes, but cannot consistently identify them.	The student's quilt square shows some awareness of geometric or free-form shapes.	The student attempts to evaluate own work but shows an incomplete understanding of evaluation criteria.
1 POINT	The student cannot demonstrate knowledge of North American quiltmaking.	The student cannot identify geometric and free-form shapes.	The student's quilt square shows no understanding of geometric or free-form shapes.	The student makes no attempt to evaluate own work.

Have students complete page 11 or 12 in their *Assessment* books.

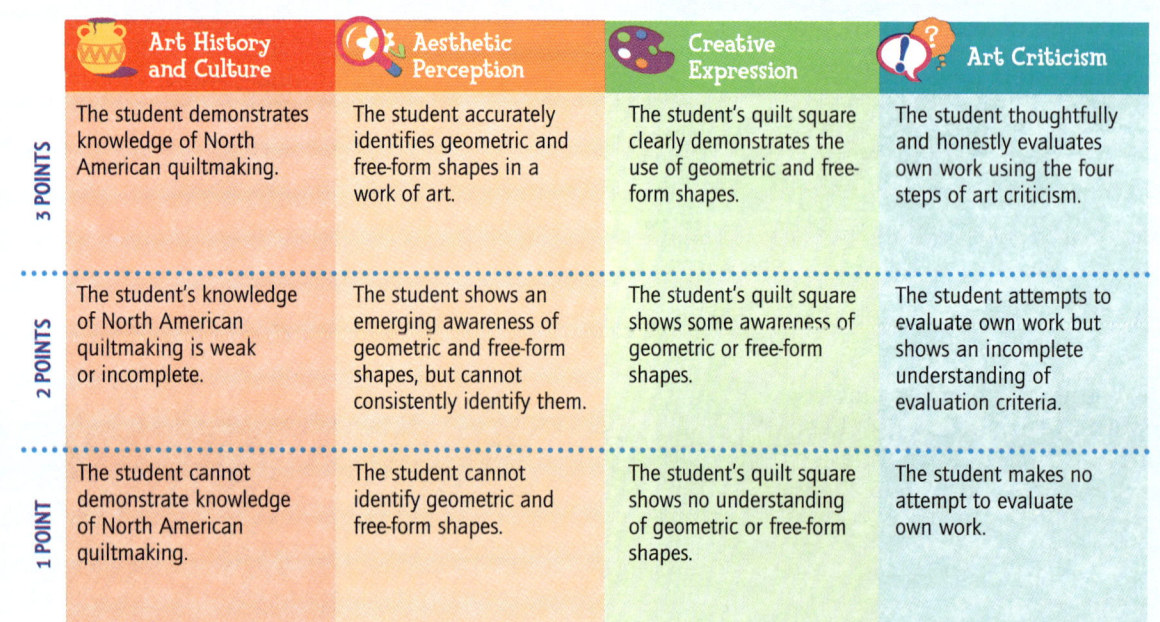

Assessment, p. 11

Geometric and Free-Form Shapes — Lesson 2, UNIT 1

A. Matching
Match the words in Column 1 to the definitions in Column 2.

Column 1	Column 2
___ 1. geometric shapes	a. a combination of geometric shapes
___ 2. free-form shapes	b. are exact and have mathematical measurements
___ 3. complex geometric shape	c. are irregular or uneven
___ 4. shape	d. two-dimensional area measured by height and width

B. Drawing
Draw and label three geometric shapes and two free-form shapes.

C. Writing
Examine the shapes in the quilt created by Harriet Powers. Write a paragraph about the free-form shapes that are repeated.

Level 6 — Unit 1 • Line, Shape, Form, and Space — 11

43A UNIT 1 • Line, Shape, Form, and Space

Lesson 3 Overview: Geometric Forms

Lesson 3 introduces the element of form and focuses on geometric forms in sculpture. Geometric forms are precise forms based on mathematical measurements, such as a circle, square, and triangle. The basic geometric forms are a sphere, cube, and pyramid.

Objectives

Art History and Culture
To demonstrate knowledge of the lives and work of David Smith and George W. Hart

Creative Expression
To design and create a freestanding three-dimensional sculpture using three or five geometric forms

Aesthetic Perception
To identify forms in three-dimensional art and understand how artists use geometric forms in freestanding sculpture

Art Criticism
To evaluate own work using the four steps of art criticism

Vocabulary [Reading]

Review the following vocabulary words with students before beginning the lesson.

freestanding sculpture *escultura autoestable*—a three-dimensional work of art that can be viewed on all sides because it is surrounded by space

monumental sculptures *esculturas monumentales*—sculptures that are larger than human forms

See page 59B for additional vocabulary and Spanish vocabulary resources.

Art Journal: Vocabulary
Have students add these words to the Vocabulary section of their Art Journals.

Lesson Materials

- various wood scraps, no larger than 8" × 8"
- hot glue gun and sticks, wood, or craft glue
- tape
- various sizes of brushes
- acrylic paint
- water container
- paper towels
- mixing palettes

Alternate Materials:
- small cardboard boxes and food boxes
- white school glue
- watercolor or tempera paint
- paper plates

Program Resources

- *Reading and Writing Test Prep.*, pp. 10–11
- *Transparency 3*
- *Artist Profiles*, pp. 29, 61
- *Animals Through History Time Line*
- *Assessment*, pp. 13–14
- *Large Prints 73 Qualicraft Shoes/Chinese Lady* and *74 The Wedding Banquet*
- *The National Museum of Women in the Arts Collection*

Concept Trace
Geometric Forms
Introduced: Level 5, Unit 2, Lesson 5
Reinforced: Level 7, Chapter 2, Lesson 5

Lesson 3 Arts Integration

Theatre
Complete Unit 1, Lesson 3, on pages 22–23 of *Theatre Arts Connection*.

Music
If I Had a Hammer. Lee Hays and Pete Seeger.

Geometric forms, like cylinders, cubes, cones, pyramids, and spheres, are based on mathematical formulas. Form in music relates to a way a composition is organized. To reinforce the precision of geometric forms, play and/or have students sing *If I Had a Hammer* and discuss the parts that are the same in each verse.

Movement & Dance
Working with a partner, have students select an object such as a chair that combines geometric form and shape. When they look closely at the object, they can see it also has geometric shapes like a square seat. Have partners work together to create three different geometric forms that show geometric shapes.

LESSON 3 • Geometric Forms **43B**

Focus

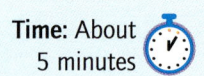

Time: About 5 minutes

Activate Prior Knowledge

"Have you ever seen a sculpture before? Where was it? What did it look like?" "¿Alguna vez han visto una escultura? ¿Dónde estaba? ¿Cómo era?"

- As a class, discuss the student responses. Explain that all types of forms are used by artists to create three-dimensional works of art. Geometric forms, which are based on exact measurements, are most often used in architecture and furniture design.

Using Literature ⭐ Reading

- In *The Secret Garden* by Frances Hodgson Burnett, look at the illustrations of the garden sculpture and identify which vegetation would be considered geometric forms in the real world.

Thematic Connection ⭐ Math

- **Math:** Have students identify as many geometric shapes and forms in both sculptures.

Introduce the Art

Look

"Look closely at the forms in *Cubi XVII* and *Roads Untaken*." "Miren de cerca las formas en *Cubi XVII* y *Roads Untaken*."

Measurement ⭐ Math Skill

- Have students create a list of things that are approximately the same size as the sculptures in this lesson. *Cubi XVII* is approximately nine feet tall. A stegosaurus, ceilings in a house, and the tallest human being ever, are all about nine feet tall. *Roads Untaken* is 17 inches in diameter. A computer monitor, an open textbook, and three dollar bills are close to 17 inches.

Art History and Culture

Both pieces in this lesson belong to the modern period. The modern period encompasses the nineteenth and twentieth centuries.

💻 Web Connection

Visit www.dm-art.org for more information about the Dallas Museum of Art.

44 UNIT 1 • Line, Shape, Form, and Space

Lesson 3: Geometric Forms

Look at the two sculptures on these pages. *Cubi XVII* is made of several simple metal forms that have been welded together. David Smith intended for this sculpture to be viewed in an outdoor landscape. He finished the surface to reflect the natural light and the colors surrounding the sculpture. George Hart also used a simple form to create his sculpture. The surface design that makes up *Roads Untaken* is based on a mathematical formula. Hart created his form by combining four different types of wood.

◀ **David Smith.** (American). *Cubi XVII.* 1963.
Polished stainless steel. 107⅞ × 64⅜ × 30¼ inches (273.69 × 163.53 × 96.83 cm.). Dallas Museum of Art, Texas.

Art History and Culture

Both *Cubi XVII* and *Roads Untaken* belong to the modern art period.

44 Unit 1 • Lesson 3

Art History and Culture

David Smith

David Smith (dā´ vəd smith) (1906–1965) worked at an automobile plant, where he learned welding. Smith studied painting at the Art Student League in New York (1927–1932), where he became fascinated with Picasso's welded-steel sculptures. During the 1930s he began experimenting with constructing welded sculptures of his own. Smith, along with many other sculptors, turned to new materials and methods of sculpture construction that were reflective of the industrial and scientific age. Smith worked on numerous series in a variety of styles. His "Cubi" series, which Smith worked on from 1961 to 1965, was his last.

See pages 24–25 and 16–21 for more about art history and the subject matter.

Artist Profiles, p. 61

Artist Profile
David Smith
1906-1965

David Smith (dā´ vəd smith) was born in Decatur, Indiana. He studied art during high school through a correspondence course with the Cleveland Art School in Cleveland, Ohio. He then attended Ohio University in Athens, Ohio, and the University of Notre Dame in South Bend, Indiana. In 1926, Smith studied at the Art Students League in New York. He taught art at many colleges, including Sarah Lawrence College in New York, and Bennington College in Vermont. Smith became interested in the welded-steel sculptures of Picasso while studying in New York. Drawing on skills learned while employed in a car factory one summer, he used his welding experience to construct welded steel sculptures. He was the first

Study how the two artists used geometric forms in the works of art.

▶ What do the forms in each sculpture remind you of?

▶ Describe the shapes used in the design of *Roads Untaken*. Are any of these shapes used in *Cubi XVII*? Explain.

▶ How many surfaces do you think are in each of the square and rectangular forms in *Cubi XVII*? What about the form in *Roads Untaken*?

▲ **George Hart.** (American). *Roads Untaken.* 1998.
Exotic hardwoods with walnut grout. 17-inch diameter (43.18 cm.). Private Collection.

Aesthetic Perception

Design Awareness Look around the classroom for an eraser, a small ball, a small box, and a pencil container. Place these objects on an overhead projector. Project their shadows onto a screen or wall. What shapes do you see?

Unit 1 • Lesson 3   **45**

Art History and Culture

George W. Hart

George Hart (jorj härt) (twentieth century) is a mathematician, an artist, and a teacher. Hart works with constructive geometric forms and uses a variety of materials, from wood to compact discs. These forms are made of polygons, which are flat shapes made of straight lines such as triangles, hexagons, and squares. By attaching these shapes together, Hart creates three-dimensional forms called *polyhedra*. Hart began constructing polyhedra forms from hundreds of toothpicks when he was in his teens. Though his degrees are in mathematics, linguistics, electrical engineering, and computer science, he also considers himself a sculptor.

See pages 24–25 and 16–21 for more about art history and the subject matter.

Artist Profiles, p. 29

Study

▶ Shapes and forms: rectangles, squares, boxes, blocks in *Cubi XVII;* circle, or sphere ball, or globe, in *Roads Untaken*. On the surface of *Roads Untaken,* the square is used as a part of the design.

▶ Geometric shapes: In *Roads Untaken,* Hart uses squares, triangles, rectangles, and hexagons. In *Cubi XVII,* the forms are made of rectangles and squares.

▶ Geometric forms: *Cubi XVII* has rectangles and squares that each have six surfaces: top, bottom, both sides, front, and back. The cylinder form has three surfaces: the top and bottom and the continuous curved tube.

■ For more examples of abstract/nonobjective art, see *The National Museum of Women in the Arts Collection.*

Art Journal: Writing

Have students write two descriptions, one for *Cubi XVII,* the other for *Roads Untaken,* in the Concepts section of their Art Journals. Ask students to share their descriptions with a classmate to check for clarity. Any necessary changes can then be made.

Aesthetic Perception

Design Awareness Ask students to think about other three-dimensional geometric forms they have seen. Explain why it is important to use geometric forms in architecture. Geometric forms allow architects to design a building with precise measurements that are easily followed by others.

Developing Visual Literacy Discuss the use of geometric forms in each artwork. How did the artists use shapes to communicate their ideas and designs? How did both artists use geometric forms? Ask students to share their personal experiences with sculpture.

Web Connection

Visit **www.georgehart.com** for more information about the art of George Hart.

LESSON 3 • Geometric Forms   **45**

Teach

Time: About 45 minutes

"How can you use three-dimensional geometric forms in an artwork?" "¿Cómo pueden usar formas geométricas tridimensionales en una obra de arte?"

- Have students read and discuss forms and geometric forms on page 46.

Practice

Materials: collected wood scraps in various sizes, no larger than 8" × 8" (geometric forms)

Alternate Materials: small cardboard boxes, tubes, food boxes/containers

- Wood scraps can be found at home improvement and lumber stores. Ask a few days ahead of time and they will save them for you.
- Have students demonstrate their technical skills, using a variety of art media and materials to produce their sculptures. NSAE 1a; 1b
- Distribute the materials and have students follow the directions on page 46.

Creative Expression

Materials: collected wood scraps in various sizes, no larger than 8" × 8" (geometric forms), tape, wood or craft glue, acrylic paint, various sizes of brushes, water container, paper towels, mixing palettes, hot glue gun and sticks (for teacher use)

Alternate Materials: cardboard boxes, tubes, food boxes/containers, white school glue, watercolors, tempera paint, paper plates

- Distribute the materials and have students follow the directions on page 47.
- Review the Activity Tips on page 231 for visual examples of techniques.

Art Journal: Planning

Have students select either three or five geometric forms from the box of wood scraps. In their Art Journals, have them design two sculptures using the geometric forms they selected. Have students select one idea for their Creative Expression activity.

46 UNIT 1 • Line, Shape, Form, and Space

Using Forms

Forms are three-dimensional objects that are measured by height, width, and depth. They have a thickness and can be viewed from more than two sides. Humans are forms. The chair you are sitting on and the building you are in are examples of forms. The type of forms used most often in objects made by people are called geometric forms.

Geometric forms, like geometric shapes, are based on mathematical formulas with precise measurements. For example the end of a cylinder is a circle, and a sphere is circular. Think about a square box. Because it is three-dimensional, it is called a cube. It is based on the geometric shape called a square. The three-dimensional form of a rectangle is called a rectangular solid. A cone or pyramid is the three-dimensional form of a triangle.

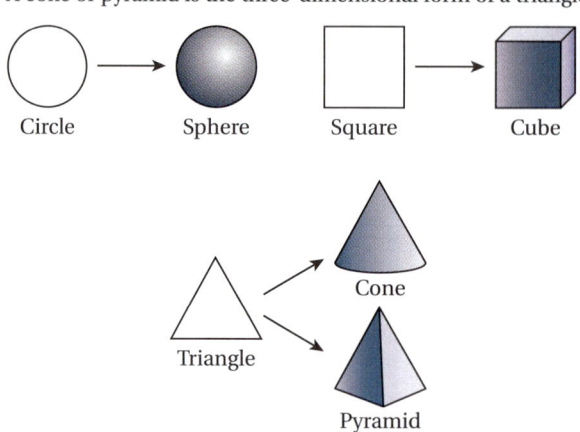

Circle → Sphere   Square → Cube

Triangle → Cone
Triangle → Pyramid

Practice

Design a nonobjective sculpture based upon geometric forms.

1. Select either three or five geometric forms from the box of wood scraps. Look at them carefully from different directions and different angles.
2. Stack the forms in different arrangements. Look at the stacked sculpture from different angles.
3. How do the forms look from different angles? What would they look like if they were made from another material, such as steel?

46 Unit 1 • Lesson 3

Differentiated Instruction

Reteach
Ask students to look through the book or *Large Prints* for examples of works of art that best illustrate sculptural geometric forms. Have them describe the different geometric forms that they find. Is more than one type of geometric form used in any one work of art?

Special Needs
Allow students to arrange their shapes in a variety of ways before beginning to glue them. Encouraging students to do this will increase their confidence in art making.

ELL
Students may benefit from seeing everyday objects that are considered geometric forms. Point to the different shapes that make up each form as well as what is considered the width, height, and depth.

◀ Calvin Banks. Age 11.

Think about the geometric forms used by this student artist to construct the sculpture.

Creative Expression

Use three or five geometric forms to construct a nonobjective sculpture.

1. Look at the sketches in your Art Journal and collect the wooden forms you will need.
2. Use either wood glue or craft glue to put your sculpture together. You may need to use a hot-glue gun and sticks for those pieces that will not hold together. Ask your teacher for assistance with this.
3. As you glue your pieces together, see if your sculpture will stand on its own. You may need to make adjustments to your sculpture as you work.
4. Apply acrylic paint to your sculpture once the glue has dried completely. You may want to test colors on a scrap piece of paper before using it on the wood.

Art Criticism

Describe What materials did you use to create your sculpture? How many forms did you use?

Analyze What types of geometric forms did you use? Which form was used as your base? Why? What color or colors did you use to finish your sculpture?

Interpret Give your finished sculpture a title. Explain why you chose this title.

Decide Would you have liked to use another material for your sculpture? Where would you like to have it displayed? Why?

Unit 1 • Lesson 3   **47**

Reflect

Time: About 10 minutes

Review and Assess

"Can you explain how an artist uses geometric forms to create freestanding sculptures?" "¿Pueden explicar cómo un artista usa las formas geometricas para crear esculturas autoestables?"

Think

The artist used cylinders and cubes.

- Use **Large Prints 73** *Qualicraft Shoes/Chinese Lady* and **74** *The Wedding Banquet* to have students identify the different geometric forms.

Informal Assessment

- For standardized-format test practice using this lesson's art content, see pages 10–11 in *Reading and Writing Test Preparation*.

Art Journal: Critical Thinking

Have students answer the four art criticism questions—Describe, Analyze, Interpret, and Decide—in their Art Journals. Within small groups, have students discuss the different types of geometric forms they chose for their individual sculptures and how they used them. Then have students analyze other students' artwork to form conclusions about formal properties.
NSAE 6a

Art Across the Curriculum

Use these simple ideas to reinforce art concepts across the curriculum.

★ **Expository Writing** Have students use the writing process to write step-by-step directions on how to create a freestanding sculpture using wooden geometric forms.

★ **Math** Have students use the mathematical terms when describing geometric forms.

★ **Science** Explain to students that planets are examples of geometric forms.

★ **Social Studies** Have students describe vehicles in the space program that look like geometric forms.

★ **Technology** Have students use the computer's paint or draw program and use geometric forms to plan a sculpture. Select the shape tool to make various geometric shapes. Add color to your design by selecting the paint tool. Visit **SRAonline.com** for directions to print detailed instructions for this activity.
NSAE 6b

LESSON 3 • Geometric Forms   **47**

Lesson 3 Wrap-Up: Geometric Forms

Extra! For the Art Specialist

Time: About 45 minutes

Focus
Study **Large Print 73** *Qualicraft Shoes/Chinese Lady* and discuss how the artist used geometric forms. How are the geometric forms arranged? Explain how the artist created open areas in this sculpture.

Teach
Have students create a freestanding sculpture using papier-mâché. Begin by having the students collect cardboard boxes in a variety of sizes. Encourage them to find boxes that have unique shapes. Then have them complete the alternate activity.

Reflect
Have students use the four steps of art criticism to evaluate their work. Were they successful in creating a freestanding sculpture using geometric forms? Describe the forms selected.

Alternate Activity

Materials:
- variety of cardboard boxes (student-collected)
- masking tape
- newspaper, wheat paste
- acrylic paints (all colors)
- brushes, water container

1. Using masking tape, have students stack and arrange the boxes so that they are not stacked directly on top of one another. Have them use no more than five boxes.
2. Have students use papier mâché to cover the forms once they are secure with tape.
3. Using acrylic paint, have students add one unifying color to the sculpture.
4. Have students name their sculptures and put them on display in the room to create an art show.

Research in Art Education

Research has indicated that one important outcome of integrating arts into other curriculum areas is an increased level of classroom discussions and more time spent on problem solving. The level of teacher dedication and experience seems to influence these outcomes ("Different Ways of Knowing: 1991–94 National Longitudinal Study Final Report" in *Schools, Communities, and the Arts: A Research Compendium*). If teachers are excited to discuss art history and culture of sculptors, students will be interested in learning more on their own.

Assessment

Use the following rubric to evaluate the artwork students make in the Creative Expression activity and to assess students' understanding of geometric forms.

Have students complete page 13 or 14 in their *Assessment* books.

	Art History and Culture	Aesthetic Perception	Creative Expression	Art Criticism
3 POINTS	The student demonstrates knowledge of the lives and work of David Smith and George Hart.	The student accurately identifies geometric forms in a work of art.	The student's freestanding sculpture clearly demonstrates using geometric forms.	The student thoughtfully and honestly evaluates own work using the four steps of art criticism.
2 POINTS	The student's knowledge of David Smith and George Hart is weak or incomplete.	The student shows emerging awareness of geometric forms, but cannot consistently identify them.	The student's freestanding sculpture shows some awareness of geometric forms.	The student attempts to evaluate own work but shows an incomplete understanding of evaluation criteria.
1 POINT	The student cannot demonstrate knowledge of David Smith or George Hart.	The student cannot identify geometric forms.	The student's freestanding sculpture shows no understanding of geometric forms.	The student makes no attempt to evaluate own work.

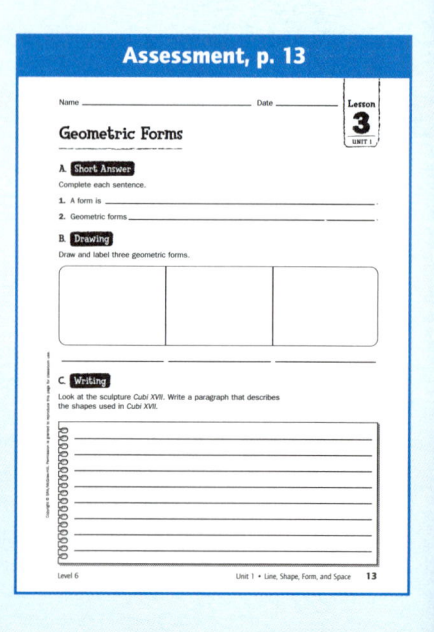

Assessment, p. 13

Geometric Forms

A. Short Answer — Complete each sentence.
1. A form is
2. Geometric forms

B. Drawing — Draw and label three geometric forms.

C. Writing — Look at the sculpture *Cubi XVII*. Write a paragraph that describes the shapes used in *Cubi XVII*.

Level 6 • Unit 1 • Line, Shape, Form, and Space • 13

47A UNIT 1 • Line, Shape, Form, and Space

Lesson 4 Overview: Free-Form Form

Lesson 4 further explains the element of form and focuses on free-form forms used in sculpture. Unlike geometric forms, they are not based on mathematical measurements; instead they are based on forms found in nature. A cloud and a rock formation are examples of free-form forms.

Objectives

Art History and Culture
To demonstrate knowledge of the lives and work of Paul Baliker and John Warren

Creative Expression
To design and create a model for an outdoor sculpture based on three or more free-form shapes and forms

Aesthetic Perception
To identify free-form forms and to understand how an artist uses free-form forms in sculpture

Art Criticism
To evaluate own work using the four steps of art criticism

Vocabulary — Reading

Review the following vocabulary word with students before beginning the lesson.

sculpture model *escultura modelo*—the study or detailed example of what the sculpture will look like when completed

See page 59B for additional vocabulary and Spanish vocabulary resources.

Art Journal: Vocabulary
Have students add this word to the Vocabulary section of their Art Journals.

Lesson Materials

- notebook paper, pencils, erasers
- sketch paper, thin wire
- fine-line permanent black marker
- scissors, tape
- large paintbrushes
- white glue, chenille sticks
- 9" × 12" sheets of tissue paper in various colors
- polystyrene foam, water containers
- acrylic paints, paper towels
- newspaper, mixing palettes

Alternate Materials:
- copier or drawing paper
- dry-erase board and dry-erase markers
- plastic foam meat trays or cardboard boxes
- construction paper
- paper plates

Program Resources

- *Reading and Writing Test Prep.*, pp. 12–13
- *Transparency 4, 66*
- *Artist Profiles*, p. 4
- *Animals Through History Time Line*
- *Assessment*, pp. 15–16
- *Large Prints 73* Qualicraft Shoes/Chinese Lady and *74 The Wedding Banquet*
- *Art Around the World Collection*

Concept Trace
Free-Form Forms
Introduced: Level 5, Unit 2, Lesson 6
Reinforced: Level 7, Chapter 2, Lesson 5

Lesson 4 Arts Integration

Theatre
Complete Unit 1, Lesson 4, on pages 24–25 of *Theatre Arts Connection*.

Theatre Arts Connections, p. 24

Music
Spotlight on Music
Belhadawa Walla Belshaawa. Hossam Ramzy.

Free-form forms are three-dimensional with uneven or irregular edges. Play Ramzy's *Belhadawa Walla Belshaawa,* which features a wide range of rhythms from the Middle East. As students listen to the music, have them sketch the free-form shapes and forms from nature that come to mind.

Movement & Dance
Have students find an object that is free form. Have them translate it into movement, interpreting its mass, weight, and shape. Have students explore four ways to move with the free-form object and organize the movements into a sequence. Students should take four counts for each idea and four counts to transition.

LESSON 4 • Free-Form Form **47B**

Focus

Time: About 10 minutes

Activate Prior Knowledge

"Have you seen a sculpture outside before? Where was it? What did it look like?" "¿Alguna vez han visto una escultura al aire libre? ¿Dónde estaba? ¿Cómo era?"

- As a class, discuss the student responses. Explain that different types of forms are used to create sculptures. Free-form forms, which are based on forms in nature, are most often used in sculptures to represent living things.

Using Literature ⭐ Reading

- Have students read *The Music of Dolphins* by Karen Hesse. Discuss the use of free-form shapes in the illustrations and the natural sea life free-form forms written about in the book.

Thematic Connection ⭐ Science

- **Ocean Life:** Have students discuss animals they have seen that live in the ocean and what they look like.

Introduce the Art

Look

"Let's take a closer look at the forms used in the two works of art." "Vamos a observar detalladamente las formas usadas en las dos obras de arte."

Artist's Purpose ⭐ Reading

- Have students list reasons they think these two artists created both of these sculptures. Both artists grew up near the ocean and aquatic life. The forms these sculptures take are from personal experience. Baliker is making a play on the phrase "a fish story" in his sculpture titled *Fish Story*. *Dark Snapper* is a decorative piece that portrays the fish Warren has seen on his many diving trips.

Art History and Culture

Fish Story and *Dark Snapper* are from the modern art period. They were completed in the twentieth century.

💻 Web Connection

Visit www.paulbaliker.com for more information about the Baliker Gallery.

48 UNIT 1 • Line, Shape, Form, and Space

Lesson 4: Free-Form Form

▲ Paul A. Baliker. (American). *Fish Story*. Bronze. Coles Garden, Northwest Territory. Oklahoma City, Oklahoma.

Look at the sculptures on these pages. Artists often look to nature for inspiration and ideas when creating sculptural forms. Paul Baliker is the sculptor who created *Fish Story*. He works with wood and bronze, creating sculptures that reflect the wildlife of Florida. *Dark Snapper*, by John Warren, was inspired by the aquatic life of California where he lives. Both artists use free-form forms that they find in nature.

Art History and Culture

Do both of these pieces belong in the same period? Look at the dates in the captions to give you a clue.

48 Unit 1 • Lesson 4

Art History and Culture

Paul Baliker

Paul Baliker (pôl bälik kər) (1970–) lives in Florida near the aquatic creatures that inspire his work. Baliker researches and studies his subject matter before he even begins planning his sculptures. Baliker uses the lost wax process of bronze casting. He begins by making a carving from wood; then he makes a mold of the carving out of rubber. The mold is taken to a foundry, where it is put in plaster. The rubber is burned out, leaving open spaces in the mold. Hot bronze is poured into the plaster mold, which is opened once the bronze cools. Baliker then finishes the work by cleaning and adding small details to the bronze pieces.

See pages 24–25 and 16–21 for more about art history and the subject matter.

Artist Profiles, p. 4

Artist Profile
Paul Baliker
b. 1970

Paul Baliker (pôl bä'li kər) created his first sculpture at the age of eight. To earn money during his college years, he collected driftwood from beaches and rivers and whittled simple images into it. Since then sculpting has been his passion and livelihood. Baliker is a self-taught artist, and his interest in nature has drawn him to the water. He can often be found fishing or surfing. Spending so much time near the water has provided him with an intense respect for nature.

Study both sculptures to see the use of free-form forms.

▶ What forms do you see in both sculptures?
▶ Describe the shapes in *Dark Snapper*. Are any of these shapes repeated in *Fish Story*? Explain.
▶ Where do you think *Dark Snapper* would best be displayed? Do you think *Fish Story* belongs outdoors? Why?

▲ John Warren.
(American). *Dark Snapper.*
Steel and lava rock. 31 inches long (78.74 cm.).

Aesthetic Perception

Design Awareness Think about outdoor sculptures you may have seen. Where were they? What were they? Did they look like they were part of their environment?

Unit 1 • Lesson 4   49

Art History and Culture

John Warren

John Warren (jän wär´ ən) (1946–) grew up near the ocean, fishing, diving, and surfing. The ocean is a constant theme in his work. He studied both marine biology and art at San Diego State College, working primarily in scientific illustration. Inspired by his natural surroundings, Warren began his *Rockfish* series, combining both natural and humanmade forms. *Dark Snapper* is part of the *Rockfish* series and is made of steel and lava rock.

See pages 24–25 and 16–21 for more about art history and the subject matter.

Artist Profiles, p. 66

Artist Profile
John Warren
b. 1946

Born in Corona Del Mar, California, John Warren (jän wôr´ ən) grew up near the ocean where fishing, surfing, and diving were predominant sources of entertainment and occupation. He had a natural artistic ability that he began cultivating in high school, where he used painting and drawing to express his observations of the natural environment. The sea played an integral role in his compositions and continues to be a driving force in his studies and creations.

Study

▶ *Fish Story:* A fish, driftwood, a man, a boy, and a fishing pole. *Dark Snapper:* A fish form with an oval stone as its body.

▶ Geometric shapes: Oval body made from stone, cut circles in the fins and tail, repeated triangular shapes in the fins. Free-form shapes: Mouth, fins, and body shape. Yes. Triangular shapes in the fin and circle in the eyes, free-form forms of the fish, driftwood, and people.

▶ Student responses will vary. Because of its size, *Dark Snapper* might look best as part of a display in an aquarium, on a rock in a pond, or in a garden. *Fish Story* was made specifically to be displayed outdoors. It may look best in a park or at the entrance to an aquarium or fishing store.

■ For more examples of art from North America, see the ***Art Around the World Collection.***

Art Journal: Writing

Encourage students to write their own explanations of free-form forms in the Concepts section of their Art Journals. What else do they want to know about free-form forms?

Aesthetic Perception

Design Awareness Often sculptors will create several sketches of the place where their sculpture will be displayed so that it looks more natural in its setting. If an artist is commissioned to create a sculpture for a specific place, the sculpture usually reflects the forms found most often in and around that environment.

Developing Visual Literacy Discuss how the two sculptures communicate the artists' ideas and experiences. Invite students to share their personal experiences with outdoor sculptures that contribute to their understanding of the sculptures.

Web Connection

Visit **www.rockfish.com** for more information about John Warren's art.

LESSON 4 • Free-Form Form   49

Teach

Time: About 45 minutes

"How can you use three-dimensional free-form forms in an outdoor sculpture?"

"¿Cómo pueden usar formas abstractas tridimensionales en una escultura al aire libre?"

- Have students read and discuss where free-form forms are found and how they are used in art on page 50.
- Have students form generalizations about the interdependence of art elements such as form and shape. NSAE 1a; 1b

Practice

Materials: notebook paper and pencils

Alternate Materials: copier or drawing paper, dry-erase board, dry-erase markers

- Distribute the materials and have students follow the directions on page 50.

Creative Expression

Materials: sketch paper, pencil, eraser, fine-line permanent black marker, thin wire, scissors, tape, white glue, 9" × 12" sheets of tissue paper in various colors, chenille sticks, polystyrene foam (hardware stores), acrylic paints, large paintbrushes, water containers, paper towels, newspaper, mixing palettes

Alternate Materials: plastic-foam meat trays or cardboard boxes for the base, construction paper, and paper plates for mixing paint

- Distribute the materials and have students follow the directions on page 51.
- Review the Activity Tips on page 231 for visual examples of techniques.

Art Journal: Sketching

Have students review the list they created during the Practice activity. In their Art Journals, have them design two outdoor sculptures based on free-form forms. Have them make their designs fit the environment. Have students select one sketch for their Creative Expression activity.

50 UNIT 1 • Line, Shape, Form, and Space

Using Free-Form Forms

Forms are three-dimensional objects measured by height, width, and depth. All forms can be placed into one of two categories: geometric or free-form. **Geometric forms** are forms based on mathematical measurements. **Free-form forms** are three-dimensional; however, they have uneven or irregular edges, like clouds, trees, or rocks have. All human and animal forms are examples of free-form forms. Because free-form forms occur most often in nature, they are sometimes referred to as natural or organic forms.

Practice

Make a list of free-form forms.

1. In a small group, brainstorm a list of free-form forms you have seen.
2. Next to each object on your list, write either an *N* or an *H* (*N* for forms found in nature or *H* for forms made by human hands). There may be some items that fit both categories.
3. Share your list with the class. Add any new ideas to the list.

50   Unit 1 • Lesson 4

Differentiated Instruction

Reteach
Have each student name a living object or thing found in nature. Explain that all living objects and most things found in nature are free-form forms.

Special Needs
The use of thicker gauge wire will help students with poor vision or fine-motor control successfully create their sculptures.

ELL
In order to differentiate between a free-form form and a geometric form, students may benefit from seeing examples of geometric forms in contrast to free-form forms.

◀ Amelia Ankerich.
Age 11.

Think about how this student artist used free-form forms to create this sculpture model.

Creative Expression

Create a model for an outdoor sculpture using free-form forms.

1. Look at the sketches you drew in your Art Journal and select one. On sketch paper, make simple contour line drawings of the main forms for your model.
2. Cut a piece of thin wire so that it is about three inches longer than the contour of your drawing. Start at the bottom of the drawing and trace around the object using the wire. Leave about 1½ inches of extra wire at the beginning. As you bend your wire around the line, tape it in place. When you reach the bottom where you started, twist the two ends together so that you form a stake, or stick.
3. Cover your wire shapes with tissue paper.
4. Color your base with acrylic paints. Construct your model by pushing the wire stakes or sticks into the base.

Art Criticism

Describe What materials and forms did you use to create your sculpture? What place or environment did you design your model for?

Analyze Did you use mostly straight or curved lines in the contours of your free-form shapes?

Interpret Based on its subject matter, create a list of all the places your sculpture could be displayed.

Decide Were you able to successfully create a sculpture using free-form shapes and forms for a specific environment? Explain.

Unit 1 • Lesson 4   51

Reflect

Time: About 10 minutes

Review and Assess

"Can you explain how an artist uses free-form forms to create outdoor sculptures?"

"¿Pueden explicar cómo un artista usa las formas abstractas para hacer esculturas al aire libre?"

Think

The artist used butterfly forms to surround flower forms.

- Use **Large Prints 73** *Qualicraft Shoes/Chinese Lady* and **74** *The Wedding Banquet* to have students identify the different free-form forms.

Informal Assessment

- For standardized-format test practice using this lesson's art content, see pages 12–13 in ***Reading and Writing Test Preparation***.

Art Journal: Critical Thinking

Have students answer the four art criticism questions—Describe, Analyze, Interpret, and Decide—in their Art Journals. Lead a class discussion on how different types of free-form shapes and forms were used in the individual sculptures by the students.

Art Across the Curriculum

Use these simple ideas to reinforce art concepts across the curriculum.

★ **Narrative Writing** Ask students to write a narrative based on their sculpture models.

★ **Math** Have students write out proportioned measurements for each form in their model as if it were going to be made into a real outdoor sculpture.

★ **Science** Have students explain the habitats of the forms in their sculptures.

★ **Social Studies** Discuss outdoor sculptures in your region versus other areas of the nation or another culture.

★ **Technology** Have students use the computer's paint or draw program to plan an outdoor sculpture in an environment using free-form forms. Visit **SRAonline.com** for directions to print detailed instructions for this activity.
NSAE 6b

LESSON 4 • Free-Form Form   51

Lesson 4 Wrap-Up: Free-Form Form

Extra! For the Art Specialist

Time: About 45 minutes

Focus
Have students study **Large Print 74** *The Wedding Banquet* and discuss how the artist used free-form forms. How are the forms arranged? Describe the edges of these forms as compared to those of geometric forms.

Teach
Have students create a freestanding wire sculpture. Begin by having the students make a series of sketches of objects or people from various points of view. Have students look closely at their sketches before starting the alternate activity.

Reflect
Have students use the four steps of art criticism to evaluate their work. Were the students successful in creating a freestanding wire sculpture? Describe the sculpture and how it was made.

Alternate Activity

Materials:
- sketchbook, pencil, eraser
- needle-nose pliers
- wire cutter, wire that is thin enough to bend
- scrap pieces of wood, sandpaper
- acrylic paint, brushes
- staple gun, staples

1. Have students begin bending and twisting their wire to create the image in their sketches. Several pieces of wire may be joined together to give the sculpture depth. Encourage students to work their sculptures from all sides.

2. Next have students prepare the base by sanding a selected block of wood. They can use paint to add color to the base.

3. Attach the completed sculpture to the base using staples. (Stapling is to be done by the teacher.)

4. Have students name their sculptures and put them on display in the room to create an art show.

Research in Art Education

"Art is a biological phenomenon that has been present as a characteristic of the human race ever since Homo sapiens emerged from prehistory. Since art is the skill man uses to give meaningful form to his intuitions and perceptions, art was one of the chief agencies of man's emergence." (Herbert Read, *Education Through Art*. Random House, 1974.)

Assessment

Use the following rubric to evaluate the artwork students make in the Creative Expression activity and to assess students' understanding of geometric forms.

Have students complete page 15 or 16 in their *Assessment* books.

	Art History and Culture	Aesthetic Perception	Creative Expression	Art Criticism
3 POINTS	The student demonstrates knowledge of the lives and work of Paul Baliker and John Warren.	The student accurately identifies free-form forms in three-dimensional sculpture.	The student's sculpture model clearly demonstrates using free-form forms.	The student thoughtfully and honestly evaluates own work using the four steps of art criticism.
2 POINTS	The student's knowledge of Paul Baliker and John Warren is weak or incomplete.	The student shows an emerging awareness of free-form forms in three-dimensional sculpture, but cannot consistently identify them.	The student's sculpture model shows some awareness of free-form forms.	The student attempts to evaluate own work but shows an incomplete understanding of evaluation criteria.
1 POINT	The student cannot demonstrate knowledge of Paul Baliker and John Warren.	The student cannot identify free-form forms.	The student's sculpture model shows no understanding of free-form forms.	The student makes no attempt to evaluate own work.

Assessment, p. 15

Free-Form Forms — Lesson 4, UNIT 1

A. Short Answer — Complete each sentence.
1. A free-form form is
2. A free-form form is also called a

B. Drawing — Draw and label three free-form forms.

C. Writing — Look at the sculpture by Paul Baliker. Write a paragraph that describes the forms used in *Fish Story*.

Level 6 — Unit 1 • Line, Shape, Form, and Space — 15

51A UNIT 1 • Line, Shape, Form, and Space

Lesson 5 Overview

Space and Perspective

Lesson 5 introduces the elements of space and perspective techniques used in two-dimensional art. Space refers to the areas above, below, between, within, and around an object. Perspective is a system used to create the illusion of space or depth.

Objectives

Art History and Culture
To demonstrate knowledge of the lives and work of Giovanni Pannini and Vincent van Gogh

Creative Expression
To create a hallway drawing using linear perspective

Aesthetic Perception
To understand how artists use space to create the illusion of depth in two-dimensional art

Art Criticism
To evaluate own work using the four steps of art criticism

Vocabulary — Reading

Review the following vocabulary words with students before beginning the lesson.

atmospheric perspective *perspectiva aérea*—the effects air and light have on how we perceive an object

one-point linear perspective *perspectiva lineal en un punto*—a system used to create the illusion of depth on a flat surface where all receding lines meet at one point

See page 59B for additional vocabulary and Spanish vocabulary resources.

Art Journal: Vocabulary
Have students add these words to the Vocabulary section of their Art Journals.

Lesson Materials
- notebook paper, pencils, erasers
- sketch paper, acrylic paints
- fine-line permanent black marker
- large paintbrushes, newspaper
- water containers, paper towels
- mixing palettes

Alternate Materials:
- copier or drawing paper
- dry-erase board and dry-erase markers
- construction paper
- paper plates for mixing paint

Program Resources
- *Reading and Writing Test Prep.,* pp. 14–15
- *Transparency 5*
- *Artist Profiles,* pp. 47, 64
- *Animals Through History Time Line*
- *Assessment,* pp. 17–18
- *Large Prints 73* Qualicraft Shoes/Chinese Lady and *74* The Wedding Banquet
- *Art Around the World Collection*

Concept Trace
Perspective
Introduced: Level 5, Unit 2, Lessons 2–3
Reinforced: Level 7, Chapter 2, Lesson 5

Lesson 5 Arts Integration

Theatre
Complete Unit 1, Lesson 5, on pages 26–27 of *Theatre Arts Connection.*

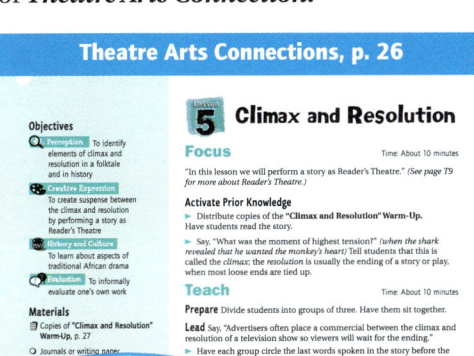

Music
Concerto Grosso Op.6 No. 11 in A, Movement 1. George Frideric Handel.

Play Handel's *Concerto Grosso* to give students a sense of eighteenth-century music that was composed at the same time as the Pannini painting in this lesson. Have students research and discuss the differences between Pannini's neoclassical work and Handel's baroque composition.

Movement & Dance
Each of us has a personal perspective. Have students pick one object in the classroom to look at. Have them view the object from different angles. They can look over their shoulder, through their legs, from a seated or standing position, or as they lie down. How is their perspective altered with each position?

LESSON 5 • Space and Perspective **51B**

Focus

Time: About 10 minutes

Activate Prior Knowledge

"Can you think of places that have long hallways or corridors?" "¿Puedan pensar en lugares que tienen pasillos o corredores largos?"

- Create a list on the board of the students' answers. Discuss the different places listed. Explain that artists use techniques in their work to create the illusion of depth. These techniques are based on how we as people see space.

Using Literature ⭐ Reading

- Read *Silverwing* by Kenneth Oppel. Look at the cover and discuss the use of space in the illustration.

Thematic Connection ⭐ Social Studies

- **Buildings:** Have students describe the interiors of buildings that they think are interesting.

Introduce the Art

Look

"Let's take a closer look at the way space is used in the two paintings." "Vamos a observar detalladamente la manera en que se usa el espacio en las dos pinturas."

Places and Regions ⭐ Social Studies

Have students discuss if the two paintings look like any outdoor café or museum they have visited. The café looks typical except for the fact that it does not look like many people are eating or drinking. Most American museums do not look like the gallery depicted by Pannini, but students may have seen something like it overseas.
NSAE 4b

Art History and Culture

Pannini was part of the neoclassical movement, which focused on the revival of classical thought. Van Gogh was part of postimpressionism, which was influenced by impressionism but with no single well-defined style.

💻 Web Connection

Visit www.wadsworthatheneum.org for more information about the Wadsworth Atheneum.

52 UNIT 1 • Line, Shape, Form, and Space

Lesson 5: Space and Perspective

▲ **Giovanni Paolo Pannini.** (Italian). *The Picture Gallery of Cardinal Silvio Valenti Gonzaga.* 1749.

Oil on canvas. $78\frac{3}{8} \times 105\frac{3}{8}$ inches (198.6 × 267.67 cm.). Wadsworth Atheneum. Hartford, Connecticut.

Look at how space was created in these paintings by giving the illusion of moving back into the canvas. Giovanni Paolo Pannini was the first artist to specialize in painting architectural ruins. In *The Picture Gallery of Cardinal Silvio Valenti Gonzaga*, Pannini allows us to view the cardinal's large collection of art. Vincent van Gogh's *The Café Terrace* was the first work in a trilogy of paintings that had a starlit sky. *Starry Night* and *Portrait of Eugene Boch* were the other two works in the trilogy. This yellow café is still open for business in Arles, France, but it has been renamed Café van Gogh.

Art History and Culture

Are these paintings from the same art movement?

52 Unit 1 • Lesson 5

Art History and Culture

Giovanni Pannini

Giovanni Pannini (jō vän´ nē pä nē´ n´ē) (1691–1765) is best known for his view paintings known as *vedute*. These works are precise representations of architecture, cities, and landscapes. Pannini produced two types of vedute: accurate views of actual places and imaginary views based on combinations of real buildings and monuments. Many of his views of ancient and modern Rome were of the most famous sights of the city and have aided in documenting the history of Rome. Cardinal Silvio Valenti Gonzaga was a supporter of the arts and established many regulations to protect the artwork of Rome.

See pages 24–25 and 16–21 for more about art history and the subject matter.

Artist Profiles, p. 47

Artist Profile
Giovanni Pannini
1691–1765

Giovanni Pannini (jō vän´ nē pä nē´ nē) was born in 1691 in Piacenza, Italy. As a child Pannini planned to pursue a religious career, but his education in perspective and architectural painting navigated him toward a life in architecture and painting. He first trained in illusionistic painting under a stage designer in Piacenza and then moved to Rome to study figure drawing. Though he created portraits, decorative frescoes and stage designs, he specialized in decorations and *vedute*, or view, paintings. Pannini also designed buildings, carvings, festival decorations, and furnishing for churches.

Study both paintings to see how depth is used.

▶ Use your fingers to trace the top of the buildings in van Gogh's painting. Follow the diagonal lines above the arches in Pannini's work. Where do they meet in each painting?

▶ Look at the shapes on the walls and the arched hallway in Pannini's painting. What happens to these shapes the farther away they become? What do you notice about the buildings and tables in van Gogh's painting?

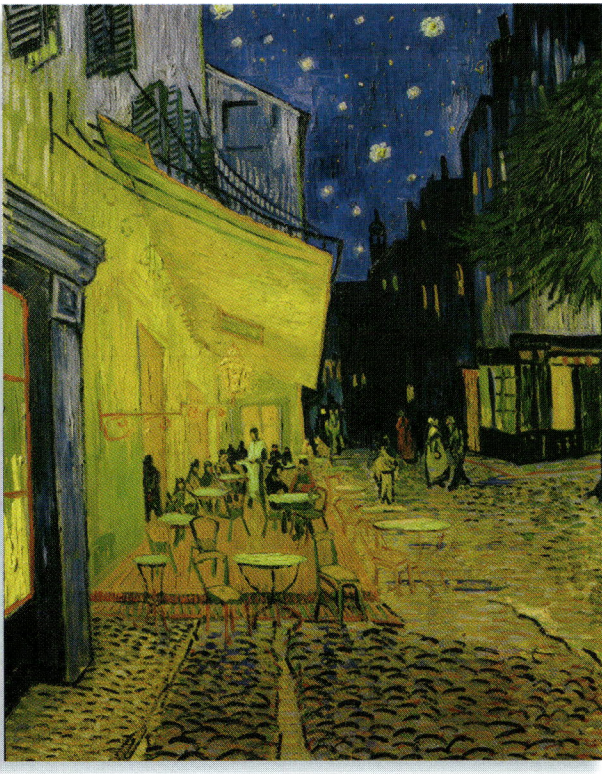

▲ **Vincent van Gogh.** (Dutch). *Café Terrace at Night.* 1888. Oil on canvas. 31⅞ × 25 13/16 inches (81 × 65.54 cm). Kröller-Müller Museum, Otterlo, Netherlands.

Aesthetic Perception

Design Awareness Stand in a long hallway. Look at the lines formed where the walls meet the floor and ceiling on either side of you. As you look down the hallway, what do you notice about these lines?

Study

▶ In *The Picture Gallery of Cardinal Silvio Valenti Gonzaga*, the lines meet behind the low painting of a woman in a dark dress beside the left column. In *Café Terrace at Night*, the lines meet at the top of the middle ground.

▶ The shapes of the paintings on the wall become smaller with less detail and the color becomes dull as the objects move farther away. The shapes on the arched ceiling and widths of the arches become smaller as they move farther away from the viewer. The details become fuzzy. In van Gogh's painting the tables and buildings become smaller. The details become less noticeable as the images enter the middle ground.

■ For more examples of art from Europe, see the *Art Around the World Collection.*

Art Journal: Writing

Ask students to continue working in their groups and to create a list of the techniques they think artists use to create the illusion of space in two-dimensional works of art. Have them write their lists in the Concepts section of their Art Journals.

Aesthetic Perception

Design Awareness Discuss how the human eye sees dimension. Each eye sees things from a slightly different angle. Our brain merges these two images, so we see in three dimensions. When looking down a road, it appears to become narrower. Have students close one eye and look at an object. Next, close that eye and open the other eye without moving the pointing finger. Discuss that the object appears to have moved.

Developing Visual Literacy Art historians often use artwork to learn more about a time, place, culture, or person. What would these two paintings tell an art historian? Invite students to share their thoughts.

Art History and Culture

Vincent van Gogh

Vincent van Gogh (vin´ sənt van gō´) (1853–1890) was one of the first artists to use brightly colored canvases and thick paint to express his feelings. Van Gogh wrote almost daily to his brother Theo, who supported him with paints and canvas. He wrote about his thoughts, feelings, and motivations. Because of these extensive letters, historians have a detailed account of the working mind of the artist. Suffering from mental illness, van Gogh would periodically register himself into the monastery hospital near his home. Dr. Salle, on the hospital staff, became a good friend and encouraged van Gogh to continue his painting.

See pages 24–25 and 16–21 for more about art history and the subject matter.

Artist Profiles, p. 64

Vincent van Gogh
1853–1890

Even as a boy in the Netherlands, Vincent van Gogh (vin´ sənt van gō´) cared about other people very much. He tried many jobs, including being a teacher, minister, and social worker. However, he had problems getting along with nearly everyone except his younger brother, Theo. At the age of 28, van Gogh decided that the best way he could serve others was through art. He expressed his deep feelings about people through his paintings. As he moved from place to place, he left many of his works behind. Some were burned in fireplaces for heat, and some were even used to patch holes in walls. Van Gogh was poor his entire life and often went hungry so that he could buy painting supplies. He died at age 37.

Web Connection

Visit **www.kmm.nl** for more information about the Kröller-Müller Museum.

Teach

Time: About 45 minutes

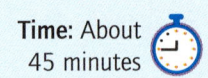

"How do you think you might be able to show space on a flat surface?" "¿Cómo creen que podrían mostrar el espacio en una superficie plana?"

- Read and discuss using space and perspective techniques in two-dimensional art on page 54.

Practice

Materials: *Art Connections* Grade 6 textbook, strips of scrap paper, notebook paper, pencils

Alternate Materials: magazines or illustrated children's books, self-sticking notes, dry-erase board, dry-erase markers

- Select a reproduction and demonstrate for students how to recognize the perspective techniques.
- Distribute the materials and have students follow the directions on page 54.

Creative Expression

Materials: sketch paper, pencil, eraser, fine-line permanent black marker, 9" × 12" or larger white drawing paper, watercolor paint sets, medium and small paintbrushes, water containers, paper towels, newspaper, mixing palettes, colored pencils

Alternate materials: colored markers, crayons

- Distribute the materials and have students follow the directions on page 55.
- Have students demonstrate their technical skills, using a variety of art media and materials to produce their perspective drawings. NSAE 1a; 1b
- Review the Activity Tips on page 232 for visual examples of techniques.

Art Journal: Brainstorming

Have students brainstorm in their Art Journals ideas for items they have seen in school hallways. They may wish to sketch a picture of them. Then have students select two to three items that they will include in the Creative Expression activity. NSAE 2c

---

54 UNIT 1 • Line, Shape, Form, and Space

Space in Two-Dimensional Art

Space is the art element that refers to the areas above, below, between, within, and around an object. In drawings and paintings, artists use perspective techniques to create the illusion of space. **Perspective** is a system used to create the illusion of depth and volume on a flat surface. There are six perspective techniques.

Overlapping: One object covers a portion of another object. The first object appears to be closer and larger.

Size: Objects that are closer look larger than objects that are farther away.

Placement: Objects placed lower in a picture appear to be closer than those placed near eye level. There are three areas on a picture surface: the **foreground,** the area that is closest to the viewer; the **middle ground,** usually toward the center of the picture plane; and the **background,** the area farthest from the viewer.

Detail: Objects with fuzzy, blurred edges appear farther away than those with clear sharp edges.

Color: Bright-colored objects seem closer, while dull or pale objects appear farther away. This is also known as **atmospheric perspective** because the air or atmosphere has an effect on how we see an object.

Converging lines: Parallel lines seem to converge or move toward the same point as they move away from the viewer. This is also known as **linear perspective.**

Practice

Which perspective techniques do you recognize?

1. Look through this book and find eight images you like. Use strips of paper numbered 1 through 8 to mark each image.
2. List the six perspective techniques on a piece of paper.
3. Study each image selected and mark the image number next to each technique that is used. Which technique was used most often?

54 Unit 1 • Lesson 5

Differentiated Instruction

Reteach
Ask three students of approximately the same size to stand in the hallway as follows: one in front of the group, one halfway down the hall, the third toward the end of the hall.

Special Needs
Students who have difficulty understanding the concept of one-point linear perspective may benefit from a guided-drawing practice activity using a photograph of one-point perspective in architecture with a transparency placed over it.

ELL
Have pairs of students look for three examples and three non-examples of one-point linear perspective in magazines.

◀ Nicole Yackley. Age 11.

Think about the perspective techniques used in this student's work.

Creative Expression

Create a **one-point linear perspective** drawing of a hallway in your school.

1. Using a pencil, draw a horizontal or vertical rectangle in the center of your paper, no larger than three inches. This will be the end of the hall. Draw very lightly.
2. Mark a point near the center of your box—the vanishing point. Draw four lines with a ruler coming out from that point toward each corner of your paper. These lines will create the walls of your hallway. Add guide lines for the top and bottom of doors or objects on the walls or in the hall.
3. Outline your drawing with a marker. Erase any unnecessary guide lines. Use watercolor or color pencils, to complete your drawing.

Art Criticism

Describe What objects did you place in your hallway?

Analyze Explain how you used linear perspective.

Interpret Give your work a descriptive title.

Decide Do you feel your linear-perspective drawing was a success? Explain.

Unit 1 • Lesson 5 **55**

Reflect
Time: About 10 minutes

Review and Assess
"Can you explain how artists use perspective techniques to create depth in paintings?"
"¿Pueden explicar cómo los artistas usan las técnicas de perspectiva para crear profundidad en las pinturas?"

Think
The artist used all six perspective techniques.

- Use **Large Prints 73** *Qualicraft Shoes/Chinese Lady* and **74** *The Wedding Banquet* to have students identify the perspective techniques used.

Informal Assessment

- For standardized-format test practice using this lesson's art content, see pages 14–15 in **Reading and Writing Test Preparation**.

Art Journal: Critical Thinking
Have students answer the four art criticism questions—Describe, Analyze, Interpret, and Decide—in their Art Journals. Lead a class discussion on how different perspective techniques were used in the drawings made by the students.

Art Across the Curriculum

Use these simple ideas to reinforce art concepts across the curriculum.

★ **Persuasive Writing** Have students write a paragraph about how they would like to redesign the school. Have them state the reasons their design would be the best choice.

★ **Math** Have students look for parallel lines in the classroom.

★ **Science** Discuss how telescopes make distant objects appear closer and larger.

★ **Social Studies** Have students explain how objects appear from the tops of hills or mountains.

★ **Technology** Using the line tool and the paintbrush tool in a paint or draw program, have students create a one-point linear perspective of a road. Visit **SRAonline.com** for directions to print detailed instructions for this activity.
NSAE 6b

LESSON 5 • Space and Perspective **55**

Lesson 5 Wrap-Up: Space and Perspective

Extra! For the Art Specialist

Time: About 45 minutes

Focus
Have students look closely at **Large Print 74** *The Wedding Banquet* and point out how the artist used one-point perspective. What techniques did the artist use to achieve this perspective?

Teach
Have students sketch a simple room using one-point linear perspective. Demonstrate and discuss how some objects, such as signs or banners, will be sticking out from the walls, and some objects may be hanging from the ceiling. Then have them complete the alternate activity.

Reflect
Have students evaluate their work using the four steps of art criticism. Did they effectively use one-point perspective in their gallery designs?

Alternate Activity

Materials:
- 12" × 18" white drawing paper
- pencils
- erasers
- pens

1. Challenge students to design the interior of an art gallery using one-point linear perspective. Have students brainstorm ideas by sketching in their Art Journals. Ask them to select their best sketches to transfer.
2. Have students complete their designs, using pen and ink. Encourage them to add details that further emphasize one-point perspective.
3. If students prefer, they may complete their designs by painting on canvas instead of using pen and ink.

Research in Art Education

An ideal art curriculum would be "one that offers in-depth, carefully sequenced teaching in several art forms for the entire span of young people's schooling." It is also beneficial to have extended times of learning in which students may visit museums and concert halls ("Learning In and Through the Arts: Curriculum Implications" in *Champions of Change*, p. 44). These trips expose students to places they may never have had a chance to see—places educators take for granted that all students have visited.

Assessment

Use the following rubric to evaluate the artwork students make in the Creative Expression activity and to assess students' understanding of how space and perspective techniques are used in two-dimensional art.

	Art History and Culture	Aesthetic Perception	Creative Expression	Art Criticism
3 POINTS	The student demonstrates knowledge of the lives and work of Giovanni Pannini and Vincent van Gogh.	The student accurately identifies the use of space in two-dimensional works of art.	The student's one-point linear perspective drawing clearly demonstrates using perspective techniques to create space.	The student thoughtfully and honestly evaluates own work using the four steps of art criticism.
2 POINTS	The student's knowledge of Giovanni Pannini and Vincent van Gogh is weak or incomplete.	The student shows an emerging awareness of space in two-dimensional works of art but cannot consistently identify it.	The student's one-point linear perspective drawing shows some awareness of perspective techniques used to create space and depth.	The student attempts to evaluate own work but shows an incomplete understanding of evaluation criteria.
1 POINT	The student cannot demonstrate knowledge of Giovanni Pannini or Vincent van Gogh.	The student cannot identify how space is used.	The student's one-point linear perspective drawing shows no understanding of how to create space and depth.	The student makes no attempt to evaluate own work.

Have students complete page 17 or 18 in their *Assessment* books.

55A UNIT 1 • Line, Shape, Form, and Space

Lesson 6 Overview: Positive and Negative Space

Lesson 6 further explores how space is used in sculpture. **Positive space** refers to any object, shape, or form in two- and three-dimensional art. It is also referred to as the figure. **Negative space** is the empty space that surrounds objects, shapes, and forms. It is also known as the ground.

Objectives

Art History and Culture
To demonstrate knowledge of the lives and work of Pablo Picasso and David Bates

Creative Expression
To create an assemblage using positive and negative space

Aesthetic Perception
To understand how artists use positive and negative space in three-dimensional art

Art Criticism
To evaluate own work using the four steps of art criticism

Vocabulary — Reading

Review the following vocabulary words with students before beginning the lesson.

assemblage *ensamblaje*—a sculpture technique in which a variety of objects is assembled to create one complete piece

maquette *maqueta*—a small model for a larger sculpture

See page 59B for additional vocabulary and Spanish vocabulary resources.

Art Journal: Vocabulary
Have students add these words to the Vocabulary section of their Art Journals.

Lesson Materials
- pencils, erasers
- acrylic paints
- 9" × 12" construction paper, any color
- 12" × 18" construction paper in a contrasting color
- scissors, white school glue
- scraps of thin cardboard
- fine-line permanent black marker
- 9" × 12" or larger mat board
- medium and small paintbrushes
- water containers, paper towels
- newspaper, mixing palettes

Alternate Materials:
- 12" × 18" white paper or pre-cut shapes
- posterboard
- watercolors or colored markers
- shoe box lids for a base

Program Resources
- *Reading and Writing Test Prep.*, pp. 16–17
- *Transparency 6*
- *Flash Card* 20
- *Artist Profiles*, pp. 5, 48
- *Animals Through History Time Line*
- *Assessment*, pp. 19–20
- *Large Prints 73 Qualicraft Shoes/Chinese Lady* and *74 The Wedding Banquet*
- *The National Museum of Women in the Arts Collection*

Concept Trace
Positive and negative space
Introduced: Level 5, Unit 2, Lesson 1
Reinforced: Level 7, Chapter 2, Lesson 5

Lesson 6 Arts Integration

Theatre
Complete Unit 1, Lesson 6, on pages 28–33 of *Theatre Arts Connections*.

Music
Slap That Bass George Gershwin and *It Don't Mean a Thing*. Duke Ellington and Irving Mills

Play Gershwin's *Slap That Bass* and *It Don't Mean a Thing* to give students a sense of the type of American music that was composed at the same time as Pablo Picasso's work in this lesson.

Movement & Dance
Have students explore shaping negative space between their bodies and parts of the room. How can negative space be shaped using the wall and their bodies? How can negative space be shaped using the floor and their bodies? Now have students stand back to back with a partner, so there is no negative space. Have them take four counts to transition into a new position, so there is negative space between them.

LESSON 6 • Positive and Negative Space **55B**

Focus

Time: About 15 minutes

Activate Prior Knowledge

"Have you ever walked through a tunnel or under a bridge?" "¿Alguna vez han caminado por un túnel o bajo un puente?"

- Discuss the students' comments and explain that we, as people, constantly negotiate space. It is so much a part of the way we move that we often do not think about it unless the objects we encounter are very large. Artists use their personal experiences with space when constructing and creating sculptures.

Using Literature ⭐ Reading

- Have students look at the cover of the book *Treasure of Green Know* by L. M. Boston. Discuss the use of negative space between the boy and the branches of the tree.

Thematic Connection ⭐ Science

- **Imagination:** Have students give examples of when they had to use their imaginations to create something.

Introduce the Art

Look

"Let's take a closer look at the way space is used in the two sculptures." "Vamos a observar detalladamente la manera en que se usa el espacio en las dos esculturas."

Hypothesizing ⭐ Science

- Have students decide what kinds of materials would make a sculpture feel heavy. Materials like marble, stone, solid metals, and clay will make a sculpture heavy. Using wire, hollow metals, and paper will make a sculpture lighter.

Art History and Culture

Both of these sculptures are from the twentieth century. Students may be familiar with sculptures such as *David*, *The Thinker*, and the *Statue of Liberty*.

Web Connection

Visit www.moma.com for more information about the Museum of Modern Art.

56 UNIT 1 • Line, Shape, Form, and Space

Lesson 6: Positive and Negative Space

Look at the open areas used in these two sculptures. David Bates assembled various pieces of wood to create *Seated Man #4*. He uses the materials that are available to him from his environment. Spanish artist Pablo Picasso is best known for his cubist paintings and collages of distorted faces and objects. In *Proposal for a Monument to Apollinaire*, Picasso pays tribute to the famous French poet, Guillaume Apollinaire. The completed sculpture in memory of Apollinaire, located in the gardens of the Metropolitan Museum, stands nineteen feet tall.

◀ **David Bates.** (American). *Seated Man #4*. 1995.
Painted wood. 88 × 37½ × 45½ inches (223.52 × 95.25 × 115.57 cm.).
Dallas Museum of Art, Dallas, Texas.

Art History and Culture

What famous sculptures from before the twentieth century are you familiar with?

56 Unit 1 • Lesson 6

Art History and Culture

David Bates

David Bates (dā´ vəd bāts) (1952–) was born in Dallas, Texas. Bates's love of the Southwest and his knowledge of art history and folk art are all inspirational components of his work. His work is regional. He spent a year studying at the Whitney Museum in New York City. There he became friends with Red Grooms, who encouraged Bates to paint realistic figures during a time when expressionism was being explored. During the late 1970s Bates began experimenting with wood reliefs. These reliefs led to his working with abstract sculptures made of painted wood and painted bronze.

See pages 24–25 and 16–21 for more about art history and the subject matter.

Artist Profiles, p. 5

Artist Profile
David Bates
b. 1952

David Bates (dā´ vid bāts) was born in Goshen, Indiana. He received a bachelor of fine arts degree from Southern Methodist University (SMU) in Dallas, Texas. He then became part of the Whitney Museum's independent study program and later returned to SMU to complete his master of fine arts degree.

◀ **Pablo Picasso.** (Spanish). *Proposal for a Monument to Apollinaire.* 1928.
Iron and sheet metal. 19⅞ × 7⁵⁄₁₆ × 16¹⁄₁₆ inches (50.5 × 18.5 × 40.8 cm.). Musée Picasso, Paris, France.

Study how space is used in three-dimensional sculptures.
- Where do you see a large oval in Picasso's sculpture? Describe this oval.
- Look at the lines Picasso used to form the sculpture that honors Apollinaire. Describe the open spaces between these lines.
- What types of shapes do you see in *Seated Man #4*? Describe the area around these shapes.
- Describe the materials used by both artists.

Aesthetic Perception

Seeing Like an Artist Think about a tree with bare branches during the winter. Describe the empty spaces between, around, above, below, and within the tree.

Unit 1 • Lesson 6   57

Art History and Culture

Pablo Picasso

Pablo Picasso (pä´ blō pi kä´ sō) (1881–1973) is widely acknowledged as one of the most important artists of the twentieth century. He made major contributions to the field of art by developing the art movement known as cubism and inventing both collage and assemblage. He created both two- and three-dimensional art, working in the mediums of painting, collage, sculpture, ceramics, and printmaking. *Apollinaire* is a model that was created for a monument to be made in honor of the French poet Guillaume Apollinaire. Apollinaire had written an art criticism titled *The Cubist Painter* in 1949 that helped the world understand Picasso and other modern artists.

See pages 24–25 and 16–21 for more about art history and the subject matter.

Artist Profiles, p. 48

Artist Profile
Pablo Picasso
1881–1973

Pablo Picasso (pä´ blō pi kä´ sō) was born in Málaga, Spain. He did poorly in school but his father, an art teacher, taught him to draw and paint. Picasso learned quickly. When he was only 14 he had a painting accepted for an exhibition. Picasso moved to Paris, France when he was 18. At the time he was very poor. Thieves stole what little he had, yet they left his now valuable drawings. In time the outgoing Picasso made many friends. Among them were the American writers Ernest Hemingway and Gertrude Stein and the Russian composer Igor Stravinsky. Picasso painted at night and slept late most mornings. He worked hard his entire life. He completed 200 paintings the year he turned 90.

Study

▶ This is negative space. The oval is toward the center of Picasso's *Apollinaire*. It is open, or empty, and was formed by the steel rods. Lines are moving through it, breaking it down into smaller, open geometric shapes.

▶ This is negative space. In *Apollinaire*, the open spaces form geometric shapes. Some of the geometric shapes are ovals, triangles, trapezoids, rectangles, and half circles. They would look the same on both sides but different from the front.

▶ Rectangles, triangles, and a trapezoid form the ankle. The seat of the chair could possibly be a square. Geometric shapes are formed in the spaces around and between the sculpture.

▶ *Apollinaire*: Steel rods that have been painted and soldered onto a rectangular steel-and-wood base. *Seated Man #4*: Various types of wood that have been painted. The wood is cut into different thicknesses and looks as if it is composed of scraps left over from different projects.

■ For more examples of abstract/nonobjective art, see **The National Museum of Women in the Arts Collection.**

Art Journal: Writing

Encourage students to write their explanations of positive and negative space in the Concepts section of their Art Journals. What else do they want to know about positive and negative space?

Aesthetic Perception

Design Awareness Explain to students that the openings between the bare branches of a tree are the negative spaces. A good way to remember negative space is to consider any place that has air a negative space.

Developing Visual Literacy Discuss what each artwork tells us. What meaning was the artist trying to communicate? Invite students to share personal experiences that contribute to their understanding of the works of art.

Web Connection

Visit **www.dm-art.org** for more information about the Dallas Museum of Art.

LESSON 6 • Positive and Negative Space   57

Teach

Time: About 45 minutes

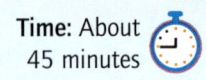

"How do you think you might be able to create positive and negative space in a sculpture?"
"¿Cómo creen que podrían crear un espacio positivo o negativo en una escultura?"

- Read and discuss using positive and negative space in three-dimensional art on page 58.

Practice

Materials: 9" × 12" construction paper any color, 12" × 18" construction paper in a contrasting color, scissors, glue

Alternate Materials: 12" × 18" white paper or pre-cut shapes

- Demonstrate cutting the 9" × 12" construction paper using four cuts to make five shapes.
- Distribute the materials and have students follow the directions on page 58.

Creative Expression

Materials: pencils, erasers, scraps of thin cardboard and/or mat board, scissors, white school glue, fine-line permanent black marker, 9" × 12" or larger mat board for base, acrylic paints, medium and small paintbrushes, water containers, paper towels, newspaper, mixing palettes

Alternate Materials: posterboard, watercolors or color markers, shoe box lids for a base

- Distribute the materials and have students follow the directions on page 59.
- Have students demonstrate their technical skills, using a variety of art media and materials to produce their assemblages.
  NSAE 1a; 1b
- Review the Activity Tips on page 232 for visual examples of techniques.

Art Journal: Sketching

Have students make several sketches of an assemblage of an animal or a person. Have them look at the Creative Expression activity to see how the sculpture will be assembled to help them create their sketches.

58 UNIT 1 • Line, Shape, Form, and Space

Using Positive and Negative Space in Three-Dimensional Art

Space refers to the areas above, below, between, within, and around an object. Space is taken up by all objects. Objects are defined by the area around and within them. In both two- and three-dimensional art, the shapes and forms are called **positive space,** or the figures. The area of empty space between the shapes or forms is called **negative space,** or the ground. In sculpture, both positive and negative spaces are important to understanding the work. Open negative spaces help artists communicate thoughts or feelings in their sculptures. Large negative spaces within a sculpture make it appear to be light and can create feelings of isolation or freedom. The use of little negative space in a sculpture makes it appear to be heavy. It may also make the sculpture appear to be stable and give the feeling of strength or togetherness.

Positive space

Negative space

Practice

Use cut shapes to create positive and negative spaces.

1. Cut a sheet of paper into five separate pieces. Each piece should be an ant shape in a different size.
2. On background paper, arrange the cut shapes several times so that you have open spaces between your shapes. Study each of your arrangements.
3. Glue down your best arrangement.

58   Unit 1 • Lesson 6

Differentiated Instruction

Reteach
Have five students stand together to create a living sculpture. They can connect arms and legs to make negative spaces within the "sculpture."

Special Needs
To reinforce lesson objectives for students with disabilities, have them create a drawing of their completed sculptures, shading in the negative spaces.

ELL
Have students come up with a list of synonyms for *positive* and *negative*. The list may also include words from other languages.

◂ **Galilee Denard.**
Age 12.
Joshua Swift.
Age 11.
Jonathan Tanner.
Age 12.

Think about how these students used both positive and negative space in the sculpture.

Creative Expression

Construct an **assemblage** using positive and negative space.

1. Look over your selected sketch in your Art Journal. Begin cutting the geometric and free-form shapes for your sculpture. Cut slots and tabs in the shapes to construct your assemblage. Add your features separately, such as eyes, ears, nose, and mouth. Try to create a distinct personality with the facial features.
2. Arrange your shapes on your base as you work. Be sure to include negative space within your sculpture. Glue your sculpture to the base.
3. Use acrylic paints and a marker to add color and details. Glue your collected items to your sculpture to embellish it. Give your completed sculpture a descriptive title.

Art Criticism

Describe How did you create your assemblage? What objects did you add?

Analyze Explain how you arranged your shapes to create positive and negative space in your sculpture.

Interpret Does your sculpture have a personality? Explain.

Decide Do you feel you successfully used positive and negative space in your sculpture? Explain.

Unit 1 • Lesson 6

Reflect

Time: About 10 minutes

Review and Assess

"How is positive and negative space used by artists in their sculptures?" "¿Cómo usan los artistas el espacio positivo y negativo en sus esculturas?"

Think

The artist used little negative space; therefore, the assemblage looks heavy.

- Use **Large Prints 73** *Qualicraft Shoes/Chinese Lady* and **74** *The Wedding Banquet* to have students identify how positive and negative space is used.

Informal Assessment

- For standardized-format test practice using this lesson's art content, see pages 16–17 in *Reading and Writing Test Preparation*.

Art Journal: Critical Thinking

Have students answer the four art criticism questions—Describe, Analyze, Interpret, and Decide—in their Art Journals. Lead a class discussion on how positive and negative space was used differently in the sculptures by the students.

Art Across the Curriculum

Use these simple ideas to reinforce art concepts across the curriculum.

★ **Descriptive Writing** Have students write a paragraph about one of the sculptures in this lesson for a person who is not able to see.

★ **Math** Explain the difference between metric and customary measurement.

★ **Science** Discuss with students the idea of continental drift.

★ **Social Studies** Have students look at the map of the world and examine the positive and negative space.

★ **Technology** Using a photo-editing program, have students convert a photo to a negative to emphasize positive and negative space. Visit **SRAonline.com** for directions to print detailed instructions for this activity.
NSAE 6b

LESSON 6 • Positive and Negative Space

Lesson 6 Wrap-Up: Positive and Negative Space

Extra! For the Art Specialist
Time: About 45 minutes

Focus
Have students look closely again at *Seated Man #4* by David Bates. Talk about how the positive and negative space contributes to communicating the natural and relaxed sitting arrangement of the figure.

Teach
Have students create a sketch of their assemblage from the Creative Expression activity, reversing the positive and negative spaces. Using the student artwork in this lesson as an example, demonstrate how to reverse the positive and negative spaces. Then have students complete the alternate activity.

Reflect
Have students evaluate their work using the four steps of art criticism. Did they effectively reverse the positive and negative space in the sketches of their assemblages?

Alternate Activity
Materials:
- wood scraps
- other student-collected objects
- wire, medium-sized nails
- wood glue
- acrylic paints
- cloth

1. Have students collect a variety of wood scraps and found objects. Explain to your students that they will be creating a sculpture of a real or an imaginary person.

2. Have students select five to seven wood scraps to start experimenting with arrangements for their figures. Suggest using wire to dangle forms within open spaces, such as eyes within an open face.

3. Students can use wood glue and/or medium-sized nails to help in constructing the figures once an arrangement has been decided upon. Acrylic paints, cloth, and collected accessories can be added to complete the sculpture.

Research in Art Education
There is a link between "arts education and creative thinking, academic self-concept, and school climate" ("Learning In and Through the Arts: The Question of Transfer" in *Critical Links,* p. 66). Students in schools with quality arts programs tend to use more creativity, take more risks, and view themselves as academically competent. As students plan their assemblages, encourage them to stretch their imaginations by thinking of different ways they can create positive and negative spaces in sculptures.

Assessment
Use the following rubric to evaluate the artwork students make in the Creative Expression activity and to assess students' understanding of how positive and negative spaces are used in three-dimensional art.

	Art History and Culture	Aesthetic Perception	Creative Expression	Art Criticism
3 POINTS	The student demonstrates knowledge of the lives and work of Pablo Picasso and David Bates.	The student accurately identifies the use of positive and negative space in three-dimensional works of art.	The student's assemblage clearly demonstrates the use of positive and negative space.	The student thoughtfully and honestly evaluates own work using the four steps of art criticism.
2 POINTS	The student's knowledge of Pablo Picasso and David Bates is weak or incomplete.	The student shows an emerging awareness of positive and negative space in three-dimensional art, but cannot consistently identify them.	The student's assemblage shows some awareness of positive and negative space.	The student attempts to evaluate own work but shows an incomplete understanding of evaluation criteria.
1 POINT	The student cannot demonstrate knowledge of Pablo Picasso or David Bates.	The student cannot identify how positive and negative space is used.	The student's assemblage shows no understanding of positive and negative space.	The student makes no attempt to evaluate own work.

Have students complete page 19 or 20 in their *Assessment* books.

59A UNIT 1 • Line, Shape, Form, and Space

Unit 1 Vocabulary Review

appliqué—decoration made from cloth cutouts and applied, usually through embroidery, onto a background cloth **aplicación**—decoración hecha de recortes de tela y aplicado, generalmente bordando, en una tela de fondo

assemblage—a sculpture technique in which a variety of objects is assembled to create one complete piece **ensamblaje**—una técnica de escultura en la cual se juntan una variedad de objetos para crear una obra completa

atmospheric perspective—the effects air and light have on how we perceive an object **perspectiva atmosférica**—los efectos del aire y la luz sobre la manera en que percibimos un objeto

complex geometric shapes—combined basic geometric shapes: a pentagon or hexagon **figuras geométricas complejas**—combinación de figuras geométricas básicas: un pentágono o un hexágono

contour line—defines the edges and surface ridges of an object **línea de contorno**—define los bordes y los surcos de la superficie de un objeto

converging lines—Parallel lines seem to converge or move towards the same point as they move away from you. **líneas convergentes**—líneas paralelas que parecen converger o moverse hacia el mismo punto a medida que se alejan del espectador

curved—lines that bend and change gradually or turn inward to form spirals **curva**—líneas que se doblan y cambian gradualmente o dan la vuelta hacia adentro para formar espirales

diagonal—lines that move from angle to angle **diagonal**—líneas que se mueven del ángulo al ángulo

directional lines—the movement of a line: diagonal, vertical, or horizontal **líneas direccionales**—el movimiento de una línea: diagonal, vertical u horizontal

embroidery—the art of decorating designs with needle and thread **bordado**—el arte de decorar diseños con aguja e hilo

focal point—the point which the receding lines meet. It is the first part of a composition to attract the viewer's attention **punto focal**—el punto en el cual se encuentran las líneas. Es la primera parte de una composición para atraer la atención del espectador

form—a three-dimensional object that is measured by height, width, and depth **forma**—un objeto tridimensional que se mide según su altura, ancho y profundidad

free-form forms—three-dimensional forms with irregular edges often found in nature **formas abstractas**—formas tridimensionales con bordes irregulares que a menudo se hallan en la naturaleza

free-form shapes—made of straight or curved lines or a combination of both **figuras abstractas**—se forman con líneas rectas o curvas o una combinación de ambas

freestanding sculpture—a three-dimensional work of art that can be viewed on all sides because it is surrounded by space **escultura autoestable**—una obra de arte tridimensional que se puede ver desde todos los lados porque está rodeada de espacio

geometric forms—mathematically precise forms based on geometric shapes: sphere, cube, and pyramid **formas geométricas**—formas matemáticas precisas basadas en figuras geométricas: esfera, cubo y pirámide

geometric shapes—mathematically precise shapes: circle, square, and triangle **figuras geométricas**—figuras matemáticas precisas: esfera, cubo y pirámide

horizontal—lines that move from side to side **horizontal**—líneas que se mueven de lado a lado

line—the path of a moving point through space **línea**—la ruta de un punto en movimiento a través del espacio

linear perspective—a system used to create the illusion of depth on a flat surface **perspectiva lineal**—un sistema usado para crear la ilusión de profundidad en una superficie plana

maquette—a small model for a larger sculpture **maqueta**—un pequeño modelo para una escultura más grande

monumental sculptures—sculptures that are larger than human forms **esculturas monumentales**—esculturas que son más grandes que las formas humanas

negative space—the empty space that surrounds objects, shapes, and forms **espacio negativo**—el espacio vacío que rodea los objetos, las figuras y las formas

one-point linear perspective—a system used to create the illusion of depth on a flat surface where all receding lines meet at one point **perspectiva lineal de un punto**—un sistema usado para crear la ilusión de profundidad en una superficie plana donde todas las líneas inclinadas se encuentran en un punto

overlapping—one object covers a portion of another object **superposición**—un objeto cubre una porción de otro

perspective techniques—the six techniques an artist uses to create the illusion of depth in two-dimensional art: overlapping, size, placement, detail, color, converging lines **técnicas de perspectiva**—las seis técnicas que un artista usa para crear la ilusión de profundidad en el arte bidimensional: superposición, tamaño, colocación, detalle, color, líneas convergentes

placement—objects placed lower in the picture appear to be closer than those placed near eye level. There are three areas on a picture surface: 1. **foreground,** the area that is closest to you; 2. **middle ground,** usually towards the center of the picture plane; 3. **background,** the area farthest from you. **colocación**—objetos colocados más abajo en la pintura parecen estar más cerca que los que están cerca del nivel de la vista. Hay tres áreas en la superficie de una pintura: 1. **primer plano,** el área que está más cerca del espectador; 2. **medio fondo,** por lo general está hacia el centro del plano de la pintura; 3. **fondo** o **trasfondo,** el área que está más lejos del espectador.

positive space—refers to any object, shape, or form in two- and three-dimensional art **espacio positivo**—se refiere a cualquier objeto, figura o forma en el arte bidimensional y tridimensional

sculpture model—the study or detailed example of what the sculpture will look like when completed **modelo de escultura**—el estudio o el ejemplo detallado de cómo se verá la escultura cuando se complete

shape—a two-dimensional area that is measured by height and width **figura**—un área bidimensional que se mide según su altura y ancho

space—the art element that refers to the areas above, below, between, within, and around an object **espacio**—el elemento artístico que se refiere a las áreas arriba de, entre, dentro de y alrededor de un objeto

vertical—lines that move from top to bottom **vertical**—líneas que se mueven de arriba a abajo

zigzag—lines that are made by joining diagonal lines **en zigzag**—líneas que se forman al unir líneas diagonales

UNIT 1 • Line, Shape, Form, and Space

Wrapping Up Unit 1

Line, Shape, Form, and Space

Art Criticism

Critical Thinking Art criticism is an organized system for looking at and talking about art. You can criticize art without being an expert. The purpose of art criticism is to get the viewer involved in a perception process that delays judgment until all aspects of the artwork have been studied. Push the students to expand beyond the art criticism questions.

- See pages 28–29 for more about art criticism.

Describe

▶ Possible answers may include the following: There are three large apartment buildings. A fruit stand or fruit cart appears on the left side. There is a group of children on the left who look like they are playing leap frog. In the lower-right corner there is a store window. In front of it, there are two women wearing long black dresses. In the center of the foreground is a woman with long red hair.

Analyze

▶ Possible answers may include the following: **Diagonal:** Clotheslines, the balconies, and fire escapes. **Vertical:** The edges of the buildings and the trolley windows. **Horizontal:** The roof of the building at the end of the street. **Curved:** All the people.

▶ **Free-form:** All the living things. **Geometric:** All the manufactured things.

▶ Possible answers may include the following: **Overlapping:** The three large buildings overlap those in the background. **Size:** People in the foreground are larger than those in the distance. **Detail:** Features and hairstyles can be seen in the people in the foreground.

▶ This painting is a shape because it has only two dimensions: height and width.

60 UNIT 1 • Line, Shape, Form, and Space

Wrapping Up Unit 1

Line, Shape, Form, and Space

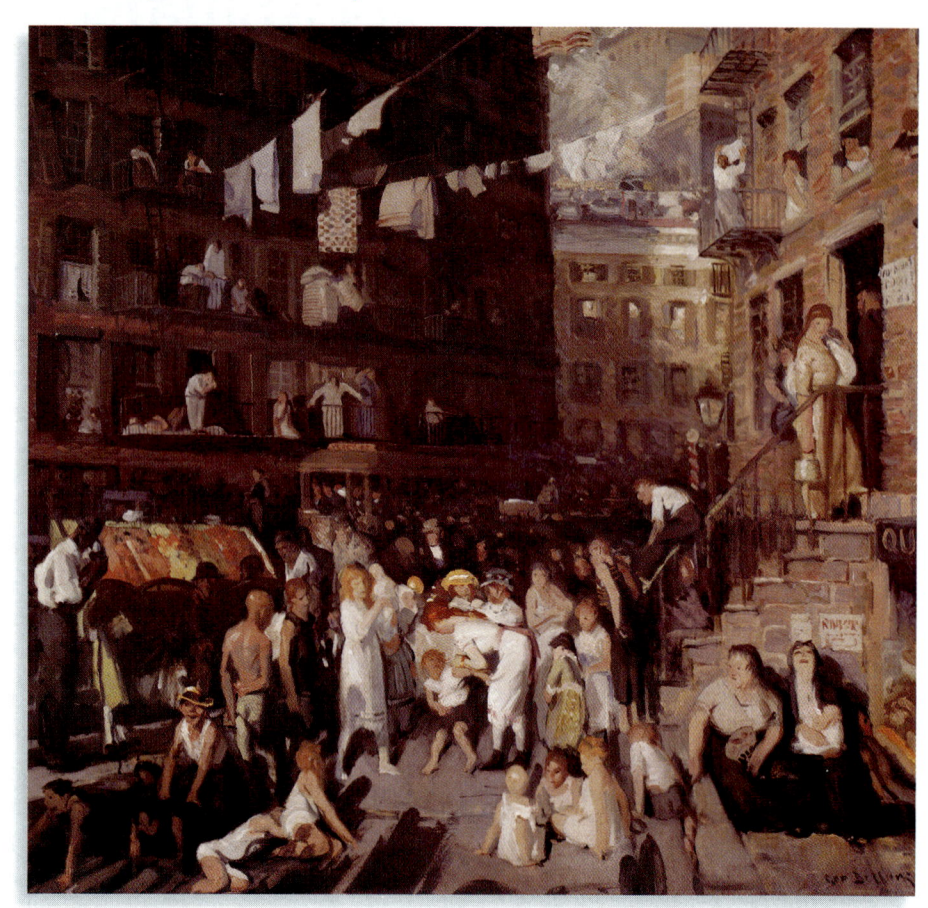

▲ **George Bellows.** (American). *Cliff Dwellers.* 1913.
Oil on canvas. $40\frac{3}{16} \times 42\frac{1}{8} \times 12$ inches ($102.08 \times 106.83 \times 30.48$ cm.). Los Angeles County Museum of Art, Los Angeles, California.

60   Unit 1

Art History and Culture

George Bellows

George Bellows (jorj be′ lōz) (1882–1925) was born in Ohio and was an outstanding athlete. His background in sports led to a desire to capture the strength and grace of athletes in action in his work. In 1904 Bellows moved to New York where he studied with American realist painter Robert Henri. Henri advocated the depiction of contemporary, urban subjects. A whole group of artists were influenced by Henri, and in 1908 they had a group exhibition under the name "The Eight." Although not officially part of the group, Bellows is associated with them because of his bold, vibrant style and his interest in subjects like the city's streets, the boxing ring, the piers, and the bars.

See pages 24–25 and 16–21 for more about art history and the subject matter.

Artist Profiles, p. 6

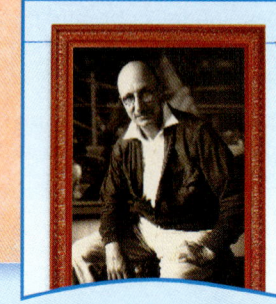

Artist Profile

George Bellows
1882–1925

George Bellows (jorj bel′ lōz), a native of Columbus, Ohio, showed an early talent for both drawing and athletics. After several years at The Ohio State University, where he made sketches for the yearbook and the student newspaper, Bellows left college to play semiprofessional baseball. His baseball earnings, plus the sale of several drawings enabled him to go to New York and study art. He lived in an apartment across the street from Sharkey's, a prizefighting club that became the setting of his famous painting *Stag at Sharkey's*. Restless and ambitious, he was always ready to try new projects and techniques. By the time he was 28, he was selling his paintings, and later his lithographs, to top collectors. Bellows

Art Criticism — Critical Thinking

Describe What do you see?
During this step you will collect information about the subject of the work.
- Describe the objects, the people, and their clothing.

Analyze How is this work organized?
Think about how the artist used the elements and principles of art.
- Locate and list the different types of lines.
- Where do you see free-form shapes? Where do you see geometric shapes?
- How did Bellows show depth?
- Is this painting a shape or a form? Explain.

Interpret What is the artist trying to say?
Combine clues you collected during Describe and Analyze with your personal experiences to find out what this painting is about.
- Is this a calm or an active picture? Which elements create that feeling?
- What did you observe about the time, place, and season in this painting?

Decide What do you think about the work?
Use all the information you have gathered to decide whether this is a successful work of art.
- Is this painting successful because it is realistic or well organized? Does it send a message? Explain.

Unit 1   61

Interpret

- This is an active picture because of the way the artist used the elements of line, shape, and space.
- **Historical time:** Explain to the students that, judging by the style of clothing that the people are wearing, it looks like it is the turn of the twentieth century. **Place:** This is a scene of a city. There are apartment buildings, crowds of people, and no trees. This is a painting depicting the lower eastside of Manhattan. **Season:** Several people are wearing sleeveless or short-sleeved shirts and shorts; one boy has no shirt. People are outside trying to cool off; it may be summer.

Decide

- Each student will answer this question differently based on their personal experiences. There is no one right answer, but make sure that the student's explanation is reasonable.

Art Journal: Writing
Have students write answers to Aesthetic Perception in their Art Journals. Have them discuss their answers in small groups.

Aesthetic Perception

Critical Thinking Ask students to think about a city they have visited or in which they have lived. Ask students to share their experiences and compare them with *City Dwellers*. NSAE 5c

Describe
- List and describe everything in the area.

Analyze
- Where do you see line, shape, space, and form in the area?
- How do these elements contribute to the look of the city?

Interpret
- How does the city make you feel? Why?

Decide
- Do you have strong feelings when you look at the city?

UNIT 1 • Line, Shape, Form, and Space   61

"Artists use variations of line, shape, form, and space to create different moods or feelings in pieces of art." "Los artistas usan variaciones de línea, figura, forma y espacio para crear diferentes estados de ánimo o sentimientos en las obras de arte."

T Review unit vocabulary with students using *Transparency 37*.

Art Journal: Writing
Have students answer the questions on page 62 in their Art Journals or on a separate sheet of paper. **Answers 1. A, 2. C, 3. B, 4. B, 5. A**

T For further assessment, have students complete the unit test on *Transparency 43*.

CAREERS IN ART
Animation
► Have students compare the career and vocational opportunities in animation.

► Explain what a storyboard artist does. A storyboard artist interprets scripts to create storyboards. This includes visualizing the story before drawing it, planning shots, and being careful to maintain continuity among the shots. This line of work involves a lot of cutting and pasting, drawing and sketching, working with perspective, composition, story development, and interpretation.

"Art strives for form and hopes for beauty."
— George Bellows

62 UNIT 1 • Line, Shape, Form, and Space

Wrapping Up Unit 1
Line, Shape, Form, and Space, continued

Show What You Know
Answer these questions on a separate sheet of paper.

1. A _____ is a two-dimensional area that is measured by height and width.
   A. shape
   B. space
   C. form

2. The shapes and forms in a work of art represent _____.
   A. geometric forms
   B. converging lines
   C. positive space

3. The area above, below, between, within, and around an object is called _____.
   A. shape
   B. space
   C. form

4. A _____ is the pathway made through space by a moving point.
   A. shape
   B. line
   C. form

5. A chair and a person are examples of _____.
   A. form
   B. perspective
   C. space

62   Unit 1

Unit Assessment Options

Aesthetic Perception
Practice Have students select one of the concepts in the Show What You Know Section on page 62 and find examples of each concept in the classroom.

Creative Expression
Student Portfolio Have students review all the artwork they have created during this unit and select the pieces they wish to keep in their portfolios.

Art Criticism
Activity Have students select an artwork from this unit and study it using the four steps of art criticism. (See pages 28–29 for more information about art criticism.) Have students work alone or in pairs and present their findings aloud or in writing.

CAREERS IN ART
Animation

Think about what cartoons you like. Have you ever wondered how artists get the characters to move? Traditionally, animators created cartoons for movies and television, but now they have more job choices.

Storyboard artists read a movie script and create a storyboard. They visualize the story before they draw it.

Special-effects technicians often work in the movie industry. They work with ordinary images and add computer-generated elements that change the images into fantastic designs.

Layout artists create backgrounds for each scene, usually referring to storyboards and additional research materials. These do not appear in the final product, but are critical for the positioning and perspective of the animation.

▲ Storyboard Artist

Line, Shape, Form, and Space in Music and Storytelling

The Robert Minden Ensemble performs musical stories. They turn ordinary objects into musical instruments. In telling the story "The Boy Who Wanted to Talk to Whales," the group uses a carpenter's saw, empty tin cans, wood, vacuum-cleaner hoses, and a spring toy. Conch shells and a microtonal waterphone create a magical ocean sound.

What to Do Listen to and describe ordinary sounds in your environment.

1. Close your eyes. Listen to the sounds in the classroom. Try to visualize the sounds.
2. Write some words or thoughts that describe what you hear when the room is quiet.
3. Take turns reading the descriptions. Discuss what sounds you heard. Did other people hear different sounds? Explain.
4. Repeat the exercise, having different people add sounds to the silence, such as keys jingling, a ruler tapping, or the pages of a book rustling. Listen very carefully. Make a new list of all the sounds you heard.

▲ Robert Minden Ensemble. "The Boy Who Wanted to Talk to Whales."

Art Criticism

Describe Can you describe the sounds in terms of line or shape?

Analyze Explain how the quality, length, and rhythm of the sounds varied.

Interpret How were the sounds alike? How were they different?

Decide Decide whether you were successful in hearing and identifying all the sounds.

Unit 1   63

Art History and Culture

Storytelling

Two separate influences inspired "The Boy Who Wanted to Talk to Whales." Robert Minden met Richard Waters, the inventor of the waterphone, and became interested in experimenting with the instrument's sound. Coupled with that interest was a concern for the fragile ecology of the U.S. West Coast region. The story expresses a desire to connect with the landscape, soundscape, and species of our world. Sound can add so much to a story, especially when it is created with odd, yet ordinary objects. Each of us draws upon our imagination, cultural background, and past experiences when we listen to a story, watch actors bring it to life, or hear it enhanced with sound and music.

Line, Shape, Form, and Space in Music and Storytelling

Objective: To listen for sounds in the environment and create line and shape words that describe them

Materials: "The Boy Who Wanted to Talk to Whales," performed by the Robert Minden Ensemble. Running time: 6:05

Focus
Time: About 5 minutes

- Discuss the information on page 63.

Art History and Culture

- Have students brainstorm sounds they might hear in their environment to prepare them for the listening experience. Encourage them to think of words that might describe these sounds and think about lines or shapes these sounds evoke.

Teach
Time: About 20 minutes

Aesthetic Perception

- Have students close their eyes and concentrate on listening to sounds in the room for three minutes. Which sounds cannot be heard unless it is quiet?

Creative Expression

- When the time is up, have students write down the sounds and types of lines and shapes they envisioned.
- Repeat the activity, but add a variety of sounds, such as keys jingling, paper tearing, or footsteps.
- **Informal Assessment** When students share their lists, comment positively on the sounds they describe.

Reflect
Time: About 10 minutes

Art Criticism

- Have students answer the four art criticism questions on page 63 aloud or in writing.
- Did students effectively observe the sounds and identify the words that related to images, lines, and shapes?

UNIT 1 • Line, Shape, Form, and Space   63

Unit 2 Planning Guide

	Lesson Title	Suggested Pacing	Creative Expression Activity
Lesson 1	Hue	1 hour	Design a color wheel.
Lesson 2	Value	1 hour	Paint a monochromatic landscape.
Lesson 3	Intensity	1 hour	Make an oil pastel portrait.
Lesson 4	Color Schemes	1 hour	Create four similar landscapes.
Lesson 5	Visual Texture	1 hour	Create a textural drawing using a computer.
Lesson 6	Tactile Texture	1 hour	Create a textured hat.
ARTSOURCE	Color and Texture in Dance	35 minutes	Create a musical hand rattle.

64A UNIT 2 • Color and Texture

Materials	Program Resources	Fine Art Resources	Literature Resources
paper, pencils, tagboard, white paper, black or white mat or posterboard, scissors, glue, fine-line permanent black marker, tempera paints, paintbrushes, water containers, paper towels, newspaper, mixing palettes	*Assessment,* pp. 21–22 *Reading and Writing Test Preparation,* pp. 18–19 *Home and After-School Connections* *Flash Cards* 1–8	*Transparency 7* *Artist Profiles,* pp. 38, 57 *Large Prints 75* and *76* *The National Museum of Women in the Arts Collection*	*Absolutely Normal Chaos* by Sharon Creech
landscape sketch, pencils, erasers, white paper, tempera paints in all colors plus black and white, paintbrushes, water containers, paper towels, newspaper, mixing palettes	*Assessment,* pp. 23–24 *Reading and Writing Test Preparation,* pp. 20–21 *Flash Cards* 1–8	*Transparency 8* *Artist Profiles,* pp. 63–64 *Large Prints 75* and *76* *Art Around the World Collection*	*When My Name Was Keoko* by Linda Sue Park
portrait sketch, pencils, erasers, white paper, oil pastels, paper towels, newspaper, various tools for scraping, mat board strips	*Assessment,* pp. 25–26 *Reading and Writing Test Preparation,* pp. 22–23 *Flash Cards* 7–10	*Transparency 9* *Artist Profiles,* pp. 21, 58 *Large Prints 75* and *76* *The National Museum of Women in the Arts Collection*	*By the Great Horn Spoon* by Sid Fleishman
landscape sketch, pencils, erasers, white paper, tempera paints, all colors and black and white, paintbrushes in various sizes, water containers, paper towels, newspaper, mixing palettes	*Assessment,* pp. 27–28 *Reading and Writing Test Preparation,* pp. 24–25 *Flash Cards* 11–13	*Transparency 10* *Artist Profiles,* pp. 12, 24 *Large Prints 75* and *76* *Art Around the World Collection*	*Joe Pigza Loses Control* by Jack Gantos
computer, draw, paint or word-processing program, printer, paper	*Assessment,* pp. 29–30 *Reading and Writing Test Preparation,* pp. 26–27 *Flash Card* 19	*Transparency 11* *Artist Profiles,* pp. 17, 36 *Large Prints 75* and *76* *The National Museum of Women in the Arts Collection*	*Fever 1793* by Laurie Halse Anderson
pencils, erasers, scissors, needles, thread, wire, glue, scrap material, paper towels, newspaper, fabric, student- and teacher-collected objects	*Assessment,* pp. 31–32 *Reading and Writing Test Preparation,* pp. 28–29 *Flash Card* 19	*Transparency 12* *Artist Profiles,* pp. 74, 79 *Large Prints 75* and *76* *Art Around the World Collection*	*Casey at the Bat* by Ernest Lawrence Thayer, illustrated by Christopher Bing
"Sarve Kashmir," bottle caps, sticks, raffia, beads			

UNIT 2 • Color and Texture **64B**

Unit Overview

2 Color and Texture

Lesson 1: Hue is the art element that is derived from reflective light.

Lesson 2: Value is the art element that describes the lightness or darkness of a color.

Lesson 3: Intensity is the brightness or dullness of a hue.

Lesson 4: A **color scheme** is a plan for organizing colors. There are many types of color schemes.

Lesson 5: Texture is the art element that refers to the way something feels. **Visual texture** imitates real texture.

Lesson 6: Tactile texture, or actual texture, is texture that can be felt.

Introduce Unit Concepts

"Artists use the elements of color and texture to create different types of art." *"Los artistas usan los elementos de color y textura para crear diferentes tipos de arte."*

Color
- "What types of colors do you see every day?" Have students brainstorm a list of objects that are most often a particular color. Why would it be difficult to describe color to a person who cannot see?

Texture
- Have students name different types of textures, both tactile and visual. Explain that textures are perceived by both touch and sight. Objects and surfaces can actually be rough or smooth, matte or shiny, or they can appear to look that way.

Cross-Curricular Projects
- See the *Language Arts and Reading, Mathematics, Science,* and *Social Studies Art Connections* books for activities that further develop color and texture concepts.

64 UNIT 2 • Color and Texture

Unit 2
Color and Texture

Artists use color and texture to create both two- and three-dimensional works of art.

The impressionist artist Auguste Renoir is best known for his paintings of children, outdoor scenes, and beautiful women. His use of color and texture make the people in his portraits seem alive.

▲ **Auguste Renoir.** (French). *Young Spanish Woman with a Guitar.* 1898.
Oil on canvas. $21\frac{7}{8} \times 25\frac{5}{8}$ inches (55.6×65.2 cm.). National Gallery of Art, Washington, D.C.

64   Unit 2

Fine Art Prints

Display **Large Prints 75** *Ermine Skin Shirt* and **76** *Violet Persian Set with Red Lip Wraps.* Refer to the prints throughout the unit as students learn about color and texture.

Large Print 75

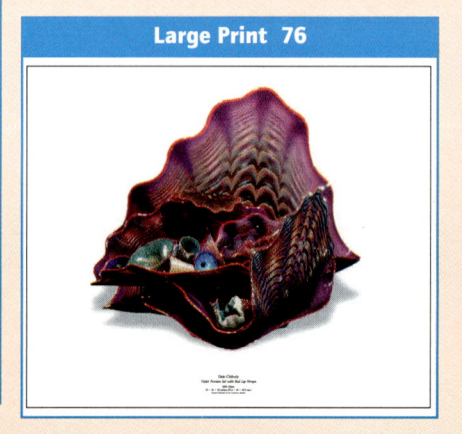

Large Print 76

Artists use color in all types of artwork.
- What colors do you see?
- Where are the darkest and lightest colors in this painting?

Artists imitate textures in two-dimensional artwork and use real textures in three-dimensional artwork.
- Where do you see rough textures in this painting?
- Where do you see smooth textures in this painting?

In This Unit you will learn how artists use color. You will use different color media and processes to create personal works of art. You will also learn about texture you can see and texture you can touch. Here are the topics you will study:
- Color spectrum
- Color value
- Color intensity
- Color schemes
- Visual texture
- Tactile texture

Master Artist Profile

Auguste Renoir
(1841–1919)

Auguste Renoir was born in Limoges, France. He started his career at the age of thirteen as an artist in a porcelain factory. His job was to copy famous paintings of beautiful women onto porcelain plates. This experience taught him how to use color to paint portraits. He later belonged to a group of artists known as impressionists. They were concerned with capturing the impression of light and color in everyday scenes.

Unit 2   **65**

Examine the Artwork

"Let's closely examine this painting by Auguste Renoir." "Vamos a examinar de cerca esta pintura de Auguste Renoir."

- Have students study Auguste Renoir's painting and ask them to describe what they see.
- Have students answer the questions about color and texture on page 65.
   - Red, yellow, orange, brown, and black
   - Darkest: hat, guitar fret, opening in the guitar, background behind the girl. Lightest: the girl's skin.
   - Rough textures: the girl's jacket, the red scarf, and the guitar fret
   - Smooth textures: the guitar, the girl's skin, and the hat

Unit Pretest

Display **Transparency 44** as a pretest. Have students write their answers on a separate piece of paper.
Answers: 1. B, 2. C, 3. A, 4. C, 5. A

Home Connection

- See *Home and After-School Connections* for family newsletters and activities for this unit.

Art History and Culture

Auguste Renoir

Auguste Renoir (o gūst´ ren´ wär) (1841–1919), along with Claude Monet, was one of the founding members of the impressionist movement. The impressionists were the first to take their canvases out of doors to paint in natural sunlight. Their goal was to give objects a shimmering, sunlit quality. At first their works were scorned by critics. Today they are among the most admired painters in the history of art.

See pages 24–25 and 16–21 for more about art history and the subject matter.

Artist Profiles, p. 51

UNIT 2 • Color and Texture   **65**

Unit 2 Arts Integration

ILLUSTRATOR PROFILE
David Macaulay
(1946–)

David Macaulay was born in England, but moved to New Jersey with his family when he was 11. As a child he was interested in both drawing and problem solving, and combined these interests by studying architecture at the Rhode Island School of Design. After graduation, he began working as a freelance illustrator. His first book, *Cathedral: The Story of Its Construction,* was a Caldecott Honor book in 1973.

Since then, Macaulay has written and illustrated nearly 20 more books, many of which deal with architecture or design. Macaulay's pen-and-ink illustrations are full of detail; his book *The Way Things Work* took nearly three years to produce. Macaulay has said he considers himself an illustrator "in the broadest sense, someone who makes things clear through pictures and teaches through pictures."

Throughout Unit 2, share Macaulay's illustrations with the class and discuss the use of color and texture. What kinds of color schemes does Macaulay use? Where do students see visual texture?

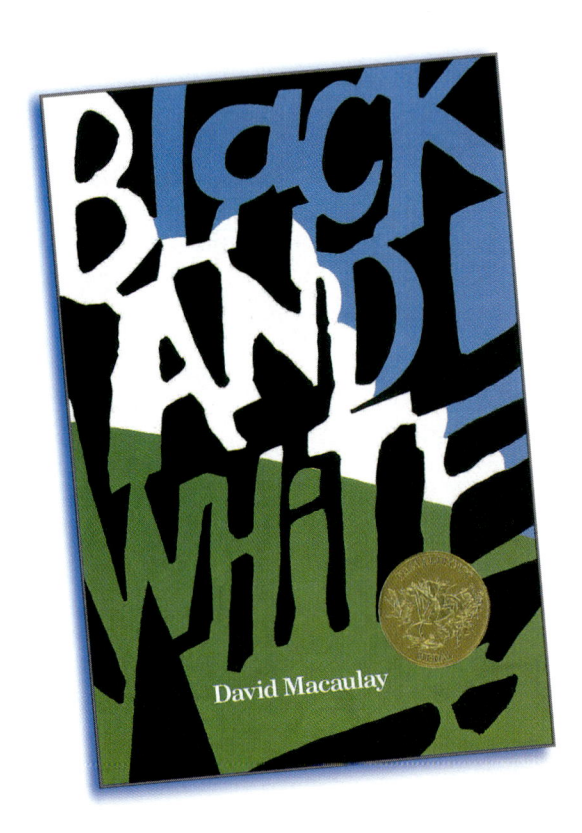

Music
In music, *color* refers to the distinctive tone qualities, or timbre, of different instruments and voices. *Value* is the ability of performers to create differences in tone, sometimes characterized as "warm" or "cool." Have students choose instruments to represent warm and cool colors. Then point to warm and cool colors and have students play their instruments.

Literature
Show the video *Bridge to Terabithia* to introduce the concepts of color and texture. Pause the video and have students describe the colors and textures they see.

Literature and Art

Performing Arts
Show *Sarve Kashmir*. Point out the color and textures of the costumes.

Artsource®

65A UNIT 2 • Color and Texture

Lesson 1 Overview: Hue

Lesson 1 introduces the art element of color. Color is the element of art that is derived from reflected light. Color appears in both two-dimensional and three-dimensional works of art. There are twelve spectral colors, which include the primary, secondary, and intermediate colors.

Objectives

Art History and Culture
To demonstrate knowledge of the lives and work of Miriam Shapiro and Stanton MacDonald-Wright

Creative Expression
To create a unique color wheel using only the primary colors to mix the secondary and intermediate colors

Aesthetic Perception
To identify the twelve spectral colors in both two-dimensional and three-dimensional works of art

Art Criticism
To evaluate own work using the four steps of art criticism

Vocabulary

Review the following vocabulary word with students before beginning the lesson.

color spectrum *espectro del color*—the effect that occurs when light passes through a prism and separates into a band of colors in the order of red, orange, yellow, green, blue, and violet

See page 89B for additional vocabulary and Spanish vocabulary resources.

Art Journal: Vocabulary
Have students add this word to the Vocabulary section of their Art Journals.

Lesson Materials
- pencils, erasers, fine-line permanent black marker
- construction paper in spectral colors
- 12" × 18" heavy white drawing paper
- 3" × 3" tagboard
- black or white posterboard
- scissors, school glue
- Art Journal
- tempera paints
- medium and small paintbrushes
- water containers, paper towels
- newspaper, mixing palettes

Alternate Materials:
- objects around the room or swatches of fabric that represent spectral colors
- manila folders for the tagboard
- 12" × 18" construction paper in black or white
- crayons in place of paint

Program Resources
- *Reading and Writing Test Prep.,* pp. 18-19
- *Transparency 7*
- *Flash Cards* 1-8
- *Artist Profiles,* pp. 38, 57
- *Animals Through History Time Line*
- *Assessment,* pp. 21-22
- *Large Prints 75 Ermine Skin Shirt* and *76 Violet Persian Set with Red Lip Wraps*

Concept Trace
Hue
Introduced: Level 5, Unit 3, Lesson 1
Reinforced: Level 7, Chapter 2, Lesson 3

Lesson 1 Arts Integration

Theatre
Complete Unit 2, Lesson 1, on pages 36–37 of *Theatre Arts Connections.*

Theatre Arts Connections, p. 36

Music
Have students imagine that music research has discovered most people associate certain instrumental sounds with the same colors. To learn to identify the sounds of the orchestral families, have students listen to "Theme and Variations" from *The Young Person's Guide to the Orchestra.*

Movement & Dance
Have students create a color wheel. Assign each person a color from the color wheel. Once students are in place, call each of the colors to the center of the wheel. Have students take four counts to create a shape together and return to place.

LESSON 1 • Hue 65B

Focus

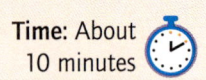

Time: About 10 minutes

Activate Prior Knowledge

"Have you ever seen people in a performance such as a dance?" "¿Alguna vez han visto a personas en una presentación, como un baile?"

- As a class, discuss the students' responses. Explain that performers often dress in bright clothing that they might not wear if they were going on an everyday outing such as going to a movie. Explain that the bright colors often worn by performers are the same colors that artists use in their work. These same colors appear in the color wheel.

Using Literature ⭐ Reading

- Have students look at the cover illustration of *Absolutely Normal Chaos* by Sharon Creech. Discuss the colors used in the cover illustration.

Thematic Connection ⭐ Science

- **Colors:** Ask students what their favorite colors are and write their answers on the board. Then have students explain why these are their favorites.

Introduce the Art

Look

"Look closely at how color is used in the *Anna and David* sculpture and the painting *Conception Synchromy*." "Miren detalladamente cómo se usa el color en la escultura *Anna and David* y la pintura *Conception Synchromy*."

Graphing ⭐ Math

- Using the information on the board about students' favorite colors, have students decide what type of graph would be the best to show the data collected.

Art History and Culture

Anna and David is considered abstract because it is an abstraction of something real. *Conception Synchromy* is nonobjective because it is composed only of shapes on a canvas that do not represent real objects.

💻 Web Connection

Visit www.arlingtonarts.org/cultural_affairs/public_art.html for more information about Arlington Public Arts, which includes *Anna and David*.

66 UNIT 2 • Color and Texture

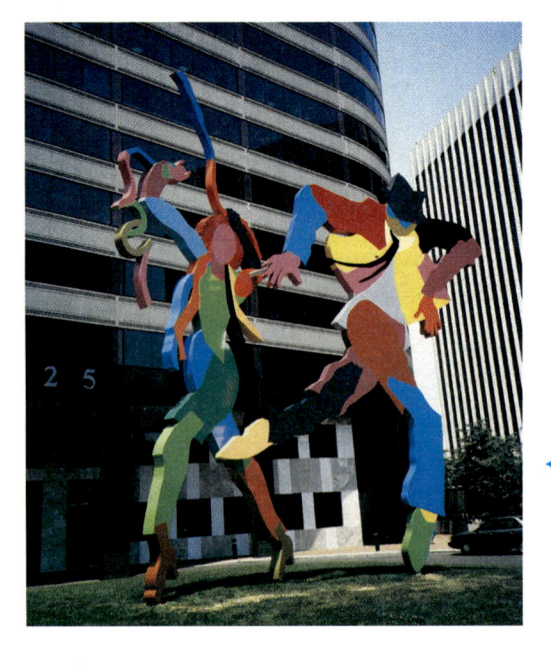

Lesson 1 — Hue

◀ **Miriam Schapiro.** (Canadian/American). *Anna and David.* 1987.
Stainless steel and painted aluminum. 35 × 31 feet × 6 inches (10.7 × 9.5 meters × 15.24 cm.). Rosslyn Metro Station, Arlington, Virginia.

Look at the two works of art on these pages. Miriam Schapiro made the sculpture *Anna and David* out of cut steel and aluminum. These two dancing figures were the subject of a fabric-and-paint collage created a year earlier. Notice how the colors look bright against the dark buildings. In *Conception Synchromy*, Stanton MacDonald-Wright used both primary and secondary colors. He was interested in exploring how colors react together. The word *synchromy* means "with color."

Art History and Culture

What is the subject matter of each work of art?

66 Unit 2 • Lesson 1

Art History and Culture

Miriam Schapiro

Miriam Schapiro (mir´ē əm shə pir´ ō) (1923–) was an active leader in the feminist art movement and a spokesperson for women artists. Schapiro coined the term *femmage* for the images she created, which combine hand-sewn work by women with canvas and acrylic paint. In 1984 she completed a femmage based on a dance called *I'm Dancin' as Fast as I Can*. *Anna and David* was constructed after the femmage titled *Pas de Deux* in 1987.

See pages 24–25 and 16–21 for more about art history and the subject matter.

Artist Profiles, p. 57

Artist Profile

Miriam Schapiro
b. 1923

Miriam Schapiro (mir´ē əm shə pir´ō) is an American artist who was born in Toronto, Canada. She grew up in the Flatbush section of Brooklyn, New York. Her parents encouraged her pursuit of a career in art and sent her to art classes at the Museum of Modern Art. She met her husband, artist Paul Brach, while attending college. They married in 1946 and have a son who is a writer. Schapiro organizes her home life so that art is woven into it. She can move from baking in the kitchen to painting in her studio and back to the kitchen without feeling interrupted. Her husband says that she has learned to live a "seamless life."

Study both pieces of art to discover more about how artists use color.

▶ What colors do you recognize in both pieces of artwork?
▶ Which color do you see repeated most often in *Anna and David*?
▶ What bright areas of color are next to dark areas in *Anna and David*?

▲ **Stanton MacDonald-Wright.** (American). *Conception Synchromy.* 1914.
Oil on canvas. 36 × 30⅛ inches (91.44 × 76.51 cm.). Hirshhorn Museum and Sculpture Garden, Washington, D.C.

Aesthetic Perception

Design Awareness We are surrounded by different colors. Think about where you have seen a range of colors. Have you seen a rainbow or a prism? What did you notice about the colors?

Unit 2 • Lesson 1   67

Art History and Culture

Stanton MacDonald-Wright

In 1907 Stanton MacDonald-Wright (stan´ tən mək dä´ nəld rīt) (1890–1973) went to Paris to study painting. MacDonald-Wright felt the schools stifled his creativity, and he began exploring cubism, fauvism, futurism, and orphism. He met American painter Morgan Russell, and they developed a style of abstraction called the *synchronism movement.* They believed that color, like sound, could be organized in a painting similar to the way a composer arranges notes in a musical composition. They developed a system of painting based on "color scales." Their synchromies were some of the first abstract nonobjective paintings in American art.

See pages 24–25 and 16–21 for more about art history and the subject matter.

Artist Profiles, p. 38

Artist Profile
Stanton Macdonald-Wright
1890–1973

Stanton Macdonald-Wright (stan´ tən mak dä´ nəld rit) was born in Charlottesville, Virginia. He ran away from home at the age of 11 to Los Angeles, California. He studied at the Art Students League and later attended art school in Paris, France, where he developed a painting style called synchromism. Upon returning to the United States, Macdonald-Wright settled in New York and California to focus on his new avant-garde methods, which spanned a career of more than six decades. Later in life he studied Eastern philosophy and painted in an Asian-influenced style. He lived in California and Kyoto, Japan.

Study

▶ In both works of art, the primary colors are red, yellow, and blue; the secondary colors are orange, green, and violet. *Anna and David* also has the intermediate colors yellow-green and yellow-orange. *Conception Synchromy* has the intermediate colors blue-violet and red-violet. Both works of art have the neutral colors black and white.

▶ In *Anna and David,* the color red appears most often. In *Conception Synchromy,* the blues and violets appear the most.

▶ On the man, there are areas of yellow-orange (the jacket) next to red (the arm) and yellow next to purple. There are yellow-orange and black ribbons or a scarf on the woman's shoulder.

■ For more examples of abstract/nonobjective art, see *The National Museum of Women in the Arts Collection.*

Art Journal: Writing

Have students describe what they know about light and color in the Concepts section of their Art Journals. What else do they want to know about color?

Aesthetic Perception

Seeing Like an Artist Discuss how after it rains and a bright sun comes out, the moisture in the air causes the light to bend and separate, showing us a rainbow. What we are actually looking at is a natural color spectrum. Another way to see a natural color spectrum is to let sunlight pass through a prism.

Developing Visual Literacy Discuss the use of spectral colors in each artwork. How did the artists use color to communicate their ideas? Ask students to share direct observations that contribute to their interpretations. For example, have they seen similar images or uses of bright spectral colors in their neighborhood or elsewhere in their environment?

Web Connection

Visit **www.hirshhorn.si.edu** for more information about the Hirshhorn Museum of Art.

LESSON 1 • Hue **67**

Teach

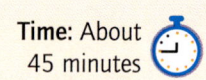

Time: About 45 minutes

"How can you create a color spectrum?"
"¿Cómo pueden crear un espectro de color?"

- Read and discuss color and the color spectrum on page 68.
- Have students analyze and form generalizations about the interdependence of the art elements, such as color, using art vocabulary appropriately. **NSAE 2.b**

Practice

Materials: construction paper in spectral colors, any size

Alternate Materials: objects around the room or swatches of fabric that represent spectral colors

- Distribute the materials and have students follow the directions on page 68.

Creative Expression

Materials: paper, pencils, 3" × 3" tagboard, 12" × 18" heavy white drawing paper, 18" × 18" black or white posterboard, scissors, school glue, fine-line permanent black markers, tempera paints, medium and small paintbrushes, water containers, paper towels, newspaper, mixing palettes

Alternate Materials: objects around the room or swatches of fabric that represent spectral colors, manila folders for the tagboard, 12" × 18" construction paper in black or white, crayons in place of paint

- Distribute the materials and have students follow the directions on page 69.
- Review the Activity Tips on page 233 for visual examples of techniques, if needed.

Art Journal: Planning

In their Art Journals, have students draw several sketches of shapes and contours of objects to be used for the color wheel. Then have students select one shape to be used in the Creative Expression activity.

Using Color

Color is derived from reflected light. Light from the sun is a combination of all colors. When light hits an object, like an apple, you see the color red. The apple absorbs the other colors and reflects the red waves of light, which our brain reads as the hue "red." **Hue** is another name for color. A wedge-shaped piece of glass called a **prism** bends light as it passes through. When light bends, the colors separate, creating the **color spectrum.** The hues in the spectrum always appear in the same order: red, orange, yellow, green, blue, and violet. The **color wheel** below shows the spectrum bent into a circle.

The **primary hues**—red, yellow, and blue—are used to create the other hues on the color wheel. The primary hues are considered pure colors because they cannot be made by mixing other hues together. When you mix two primary hues you get the **secondary hues**—orange, green, and violet. When a primary is mixed with an equal amount of a secondary hue an **intermediate color** is made. For example, yellow and green make yellow-green. Intermediate colors are also called *tertiary colors*.

Practice

As a class, create a color spectrum by lining up students in color order.

1. Look at your clothing and at your classmates' clothing. Begin by finding someone who is wearing the color red. That person will be first in line. Now find the color orange, then yellow, green, blue, and violet.
2. If you are missing a color, have a student hold a piece of construction paper in that color.
3. See if you can come up with ideas on how to create the intermediate colors.

Differentiated Instruction

Reteach
Ask students to look through their textbooks for examples of works of art that best illustrate the spectral colors: primary, secondary, and intermediate.

Special Needs
For this lesson activity, have visual reminders for students of the primary, secondary, and intermediate colors.

ELL
When discussing a color, point to an object in the classroom that has the same color so students can attach a visual image to the color.

◀ Ansley Axelberg.
Age 11.

Think about how this student artist shows the correct color relationships in the color wheel.

Creative Expression

Select any shape or object to create a unique color wheel.

1. Make a pattern of your selected shape or object and trace it twelve times on white paper. Outline your shapes using a permanent marker.
2. Mix only primary colors to make secondary and intermediate colors. Paint your first three shapes the primary colors. Paint the next three shapes the secondary colors. Paint the last shapes the intermediate colors.
3. Once your shapes are dry, cut them out. Arrange them to show the correct color relationships. Your color wheel does not have to be perfectly round, nor does it have to be a wheel. Glue your shapes onto a black or white background once you have your idea.

Art Criticism

Describe What shape or object did you use? How did you arrange your color wheel?

Analyze Describe how you made each of your intermediate colors.

Interpret Describe how someone would read your color wheel.

Decide Do you feel you were able to create a unique color wheel that shows the correct color relationships? Explain.

Unit 2 • Lesson 1   **69**

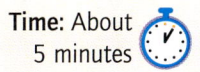

Reflect
Time: About 5 minutes

Review and Assess
"Describe how secondary and intermediate colors are mixed." "Describan cómo se mezclan los colores secundarios e intermedios."

Think
The artist created 12 circular shapes with rough edges that were placed side-by-side to form the color wheel.

- Use **Large Prints 75** *Ermine Skin Shirt* and **76** *Violet Persian Set with Red Lip Wraps* to have students identify the different spectral colors.

Informal Assessment
- For standardized-format test practice using this lesson's art content, see pages 18–19 in *Reading and Writing Test Preparation*.

Art Journal: Critical Thinking
Have students answer the four art criticism questions—Describe, Analyze, Interpret, and Decide—in their Art Journals. Within their table groups, have students discuss the differences among the spectral colors and how they mixed their secondary and intermediate colors. Have students compare the different shapes and objects used within their group.

Art Across the Curriculum

Use these simple ideas to reinforce art concepts across the curriculum.

★ **Poetry Writing** Have students write a haiku about a primary or secondary color.

★ **Math** Have students create a graph of the class's favorite colors.

★ **Science** Show students where visible light falls on the electromagnetic spectrum.

★ **Social Studies** Show students some flags from different countries and have them note which colors are used most often.

★ **Technology** Using a paint or draw program, have students draw three circles and color them the primary colors. Then have them label each circle. **Visit SRAonline.com** to print detailed instructions for this activity.
NSAE 6.b

LESSON 1 • Hue **69**

Lesson 1 Wrap-Up: Hue

Extra! For the Art Specialist
Time: About 45 minutes

Focus
Have students look closely at **Large Print 76** *Violet Persian Set with Red Lip Wraps* and discuss how the artist used color. What spectral colors are most dominant?

Teach
Explain to students that they will be creating a nonobjective painting using all of the spectral colors. Review with students the different spectral colors. Then have them complete the Alternate Activity.

Reflect
Have students use the four steps of art criticism to evaluate their work. Did they effectively mix their secondary and intermediate colors? Did they use all of the spectral colors?

Alternate Activity

Materials:
- paper, pencils
- 12" × 18" heavy white drawing paper
- fine-line permanent black markers
- tempera paints, medium and small paintbrushes
- water containers, paper towels
- newspaper, mixing palettes
- acrylic paints
- canvas

1. Have students begin by using markers to divide their sheets of paper with five lines—two in one direction—and three intersecting in the opposite direction. The lines can be straight, curved, zigzag, or a combination.
2. Have students use a palette to mix both secondary and intermediate colors.
3. Students may prefer to complete their designs using acrylic paints and canvas instead of tempera and paper.

Research in Art Education

Research has shown that incorporating the arts into core curriculum areas in a way that actively involves students in the learning process produces "significant positive effects on student achievement, motivation, and engagement in learning, and notable changes in classroom practices" ("Different Ways of Knowing: 1991–94 National Longitudinal Study Final Report" in *Schools, Communities, and the Arts: A Research Compendium*).

Assessment
Use the following rubric to evaluate the artwork students make in the Creative Expression activity and to assess students' understanding of how color is used in two- and three-dimensional works of art.

Have students complete page 21 or 22 in their *Assessment* books.

	Art History and Culture	Aesthetic Perception	Creative Expression	Art Criticism
3 POINTS	The student demonstrates knowledge of the lives and work of Miriam Shapiro and Stanton MacDonald-Wright.	The student accurately identifies the use of spectral colors in two- and three-dimensional works of art.	The student's color wheel clearly demonstrates how to mix and organize the color spectrum.	The student thoughtfully and honestly evaluates own work using the four steps of art criticism.
2 POINTS	The student's knowledge of the lives and work of Miriam Shapiro and Stanton MacDonald-Wright is weak or incomplete.	The student shows an emerging awareness of spectral colors in two- and three-dimensional art, but cannot consistently identify them.	The student's color wheel shows some awareness of how to mix and organize the color spectrum.	The student attempts to evaluate own work, but shows an incomplete understanding of evaluation criteria.
1 POINT	The student cannot demonstrate knowledge of Miriam Shapiro or Stanton MacDonald-Wright.	The student cannot identify how spectral colors are used.	The student's color wheel shows no understanding of how to mix or organize the color spectrum.	The student makes no attempt to evaluate own work.

Assessment, p. 21

Lesson 1 UNIT 2

Hue

A. Matching
Match the words in Column 1 to the definitions in Column 2.

Column 1
___ 1. hue
___ 2. color spectrum
___ 3. primary hue
___ 4. secondary hue
___ 5. intermediate hue

Column 2
a. red, yellow, and blue
b. when light bends and separates into colors
c. the mixture of two primary hues
d. the mixture of a primary hue and a secondary hue
e. another name for color

B. Short Answer
Label each color as primary or secondary.
1. red
2. orange
3. violet
4. yellow

C. Writing
Look at *Anna and David* and *Conception Synchromy*. Write a paragraph about the colors in both pieces of artwork.

Level 6 — Unit 2 • Color and Texture — 21

69A UNIT 2 • Color and Texture

Lesson 2 Overview: Value

Lesson 2 further explores the art element of color and focuses on value and value techniques. Value is the lightness or darkness of a hue. Neutral colors such as black, white, and gray give hues a range of values. Value techniques of blending, hatching, cross-hatching, and stippling are also reviewed.

Objectives

Art History and Culture
To demonstrate knowledge of the lives and work of van Gogh and Twachtman

Creative Expression
To experiment with value techniques while painting a monochromatic landscape

Aesthetic Perception
To identify and understand value and how an artist uses different value techniques in a two-dimensional artwork

Art Criticism
To evaluate own work using the four steps of art criticism

Lesson Materials
- notebook paper, pencils, erasers
- 9" × 12" white paper
- fine-line permanent black markers
- 12" × 18" heavy white drawing paper
- tempera paints: red, yellow, blue, black, and white (green is optional)
- paintbrushes in various sizes
- water containers, paper towels
- newspaper, mixing palettes

Alternate Materials:
- oil pastels or crayons
- paper plates for mixing paint

Program Resources
- *Reading and Writing Test Prep.,* pp. 20–21
- *Transparency 8*
- *Flash Cards* 1–8
- *Artist Profiles,* pp. 63–64
- *Animals Through History Time Line*
- *Assessment,* pp. 23–24
- *Large Prints 75 Ermine Skin Shirt* and *76 Violet Persian Set with Red Lip Wraps*

Concept Trace
Value
Introduced: Level 5, Unit 1, Lessons 4–6
Reinforced: Level 7, Chapter 2, Lesson 3

Vocabulary

Review the following vocabulary words with students before beginning the lesson.

monochromatic *monocromático*—a color scheme that has one hue and the tints and shade of that hue

shade *sombra*—any hue blended with black

tint *tinte*—any hue blended with white

See page 89B for additional vocabulary and Spanish vocabulary resources.

Art Journal: Vocabulary
Have students add these words to the Vocabulary section of their Art Journals.

Lesson 2 Arts Integration

Theatre
Complete Unit 2, Lesson 2, on pages 38–39 of *Theatre Arts Connections.*

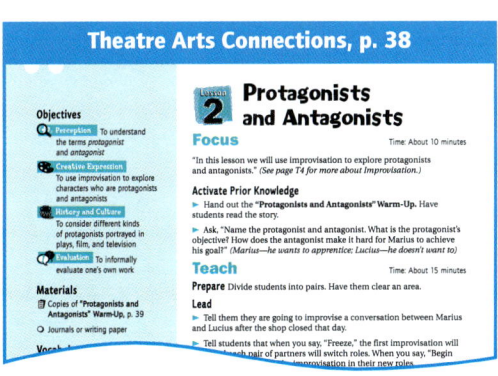

Music
Listen to "Cuckoo in the Woods" from *Carnival of the Animals.* The sound of the bird is brighter than the background instruments. What kind of feelings would music have if there were only bright colors? Would students get tired of it?

Movement & Dance
Have students make a large circle and divide into primary and neutral colors. Have the red group run to the center and freeze in a shape together. Have the black group enter next, making the hue darker. When the black group reaches the center, the red group should take four counts to contract their shape closer to the black group. Repeat this process with the remaining primary and neutral colors.

LESSON 2 • Value **69B**

Focus

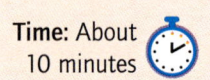

Time: About 10 minutes

Activate Prior Knowledge

"Have you ever seen a drawing or painting that had shadows and light or bright areas?"

"¿Alguna vez han visto un dibujo o una pintura con sombras y áreas claras o brillantes?"

- As a class, discuss the students' responses. Explain that artists use shadows and highlights or lighted areas in their artwork to give the feeling of depth and to portray a certain time of day.

Using Literature — Reading

- Read *When My Name Was Keoko* by Linda Sue Park. Discuss the use of color value in the cover illustration.

Thematic Connection — Science

- **Shadows:** See if students can explain how to create a shadow. If they cannot explain it verbally, have them demonstrate, if possible.

Introduce the Art

Look

"Let's take a closer look at the shadows and highlights used in the two works of art."

"Vamos a observar detalladamente las sombras y toques de luz usados en las dos obras de arte."

Variables — Math

- Ask students if they know what a variable is in a math problem. A variable is part of an algebraic expression. It is a symbol, usually a letter of the alphabet, that stands for an unknown number. The variable needs to be isolated to determine its value.

Art History and Culture

Possible answers: Other artists who painted portraits include Leonardo da Vinci *(Mona Lisa)* and Hans Holbein *(Henry VIII)*. Camille Pissarro and Joseph Mallord William Turner both were known for painting landscapes.

Web Connection

Visit www.getty.edu for more information about the Getty Museum.

70 UNIT 2 • Color and Texture

Lesson 2 — Value

▲ **Vincent van Gogh.** (Dutch). *Portrait of Joseph Roulin.* 1888.
Reed and quill pen, brown ink, and black chalk. $12\frac{5}{8} \times 9\frac{5}{8}$ inches (32.06 × 24.44 cm). The J. Paul Getty Museum, Los Angeles, California.

Look at the two works of art on these pages. Vincent van Gogh drew *Portrait of Joseph Roulin,* an image of the local postmaster. Van Gogh wrote almost daily to his brother, and so he became friends with Roulin. He created many drawings and paintings of the Roulin family. John Henry Twachtman painted images that reflected the changing seasons at his home in Greenwich, Connecticut. He is considered an American impressionist painter. The landscape *Snow Scene* captures the effects of light and atmosphere on a common subject. Notice how shadows and highlights are created differently in both works of art.

Art History and Culture

Which other artists created portraits or landscapes?

70   Unit 2 • Lesson 2

Art History and Culture

Vincent van Gogh

Vincent van Gogh (vin´sənt van gō´) (1853–1890) completed more than 1,600 drawings and 750 paintings before his death at the age of 37. In 1886 van Gogh went to Paris to live with his brother Theo, who was an art dealer. There he was exposed to the brightly colored impressionist paintings and Japanese prints. In 1888 van Gogh left Paris for Arles. Joseph Roulin was one of the people van Gogh painted while in Arles.

See pages 24–25 and 16–21 for more about art history and the subject matter.

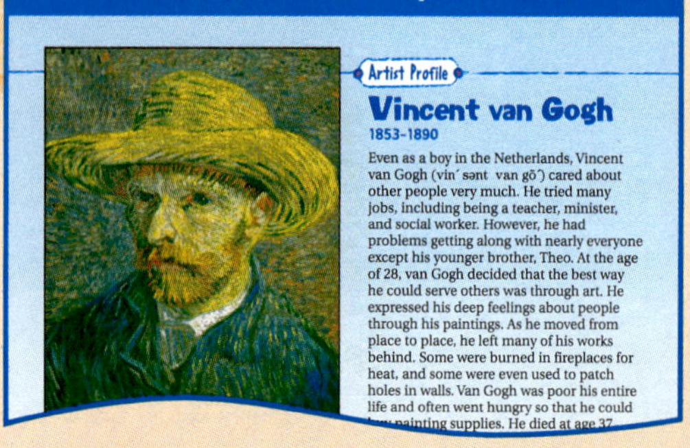

Artist Profiles, p. 64

▲ **John Henry Twachtman.** (American). *Snow Scene.* 1882.
Oil on canvas. 12 1/8 × 16 1/8 inches (30.63 × 40.79 cm.). Cincinnati Art Museum, Cincinnati, Ohio.

Study both works of art to see how the artists used shadow and light in their artwork.

▶ Find the light and dark areas in *Snow Scene*. Do you see a gradual change in the painting from light to dark?
▶ Describe how Vincent van Gogh depicted dark and light areas in his drawing of Joseph Roulin.
▶ What direction are the light sources coming from in these two pieces of art?
▶ What mood is created by the light and shadows in each work of art?

Aesthetic Perception

Design Awareness Think about the shadows you see in the early morning or at the end of the day. How are they different from the shadows at noon or midday? How do the shadows differ on a sunny day versus a cloudy day?

Unit 2 • Lesson 2   71

Art History and Culture

John Henry Twachtman

John Henry Twachtman (jän hen´ rē twäkt´ mən) (1853–1902) studied art at the Ohio Mechanics Institute and the McMicken School of Design. In 1875 he traveled to Munich to study and quickly adopted the dark palette and quick, open brushwork of the Munich artists. During his lifetime, Twachtman did not achieve the status of a great artist that he yearned for. His work had an abstract quality that people were not interested in. Around 1889 Twachtman moved his family to a seventeen-acre estate in Greenwich, Connecticut. This property was the leading subject matter for his art and is where he painted *Snow Scene*.

See pages 24–25 and 16–21 for more about art history and the subject matter.

Artist Profiles, p. 63

Artist Profile
John Henry Twachtman
1853–1902

Born in Cincinnati, Ohio, John Henry Twachtman (jän hen´ rē twäkt´ mən) began studying art when he was 18. As his artistic style evolved, he moved from harsh, radical impressionist compositions to a calmer style. Near the end of his career, when he was painting some of his most famous works on his country farm, he came to believe that a person is most true and content in the solitude of nature.

Study

▶ Students' answers will include some of the following. The left side of the painting has more lighted areas than the right side. There are dark values/shades in the area between the first tree in the front and the stand of trees in the middle and background. A gradual change in value occurs on the right side of the middle ground.

▶ Cross-hatching appears under the hat and the collar of the jacket, the cheeks, and the area behind Roulin. Hatching is located on the side of the face, the temple, areas of the cheek, around the eyes, in the lighter areas of the jacket, the edges of the background, and in the beard and hat. Stippling is the repeated dots on the left side of the face.

▶ In both works the light source is coming from the right side.

▶ *Snow Scene* is quiet and calm. There is the feeling of a sunny day in van Gogh's portrait.

■ For more examples of art from North America, see the *Art Around the World Collection.*

Art Journal: Writing

Have students write what *value* means to them in the Concepts section of their Art Journals. Do they see a connection between their definition of *value* and how it is used by artists?

Aesthetic Perception

Seeing Like an Artist Explain that both the direction from which the sun is shining and the atmosphere or dampness/dryness of the air all have an effect on the shadows we see.

Developing Visual Literacy Discuss how the two works of art communicate the artists' ideas and personal experiences with their subject matter. What meaning did each artist try to convey in his work of art?

Web Connection

Visit **www.cincinnatiartmuseum.com** for more information about the Cincinnati Art Museum.

LESSON 2 • Value **71**

Teach

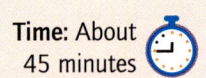

Time: About 45 minutes

"How do you create values in a painting? How do you create values in a drawing?" "¿Cómo crean valores en una pintura? ¿Cómo crean valores en un dibujo?"

- Read and discuss value and how it is used in two-dimensional art on page 72.

Practice

Materials: 9" × 12" paper, pencils, tempera paints in the primary colors and in black and white, medium paintbrushes, water containers, paper towels, newspaper, mixing palettes, fine-line permanent black markers

Alternate Materials: oil pastels or crayons, color markers, paper plates for palettes

- Distribute the materials and have students follow the directions on page 72.

Creative Expression

Materials: landscape sketch in Art Journal, pencils and erasers, 12" × 18" heavy white drawing paper, tempera paints in all colors plus black and white, paintbrushes in various sizes, water containers, paper towels, newspaper, mixing palettes

Alternate Materials: oil pastels or crayons, paper plates for mixing paint

- Distribute the materials and have students follow the directions on page 73.
- Have students demonstrate their technical skills, using a variety of art media and materials to produce their paintings.
  NSAE 1.a; 1.b
- Have students conduct in-progress analyses and critiques of their paintings.
  NSAE 1.b
- Review the Activity Tips on page 233 for visual examples of techniques, if needed.

Art Journal: Researching

Have students collect several images of landscapes. In their Art Journals, have students create several sketches of landscapes from the collected images. Ask students to select one sketch for the Creative Expression activity.

72 UNIT 2 • Color and Texture

Using Value

Value refers to the darkness or lightness of a hue. Not all hues have the same value; yellow has the lightest value and violet has the darkest. **Neutral colors**—black, gray, and white—can be added to any hue to change its value. The more black that is added to a color, the darker the hue; the more white, the lighter the hue.

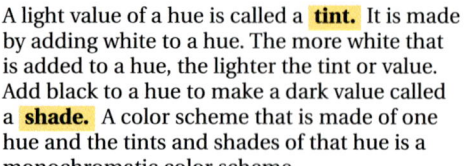

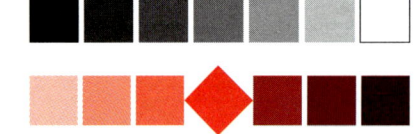

A light value of a hue is called a **tint.** It is made by adding white to a hue. The more white that is added to a hue, the lighter the tint or value. Add black to a hue to make a dark value called a **shade.** A color scheme that is made of one hue and the tints and shades of that hue is a monochromatic color scheme.

Hatching    Cross-Hatching

Blending    Stippling

When drawing, artists often use the shading techniques hatching, cross-hatching, blending, and stippling. **Hatching** is a series of parallel lines. **Cross-hatching** is sets of parallel lines that cross or intersect. **Blending** is a gradual change from light to dark or dark to light. **Stippling** uses dots; the closer the dots, the darker the value.

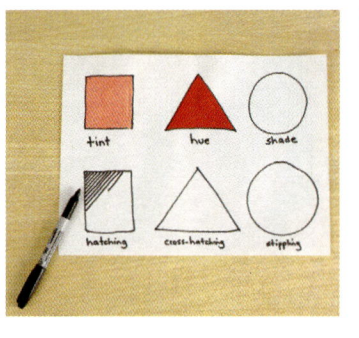

Practice

Practice shading techniques. Use tempera paint and a fine-tipped marker.

1. Draw two horizontal rows of three shapes each. Label the shapes on the first row *tint, hue,* and *shade*. Label the remaining shapes *hatching, cross-hatching,* and *stippling*.
2. Choose a primary color and paint in the "hue" shape. Mix white with your hue to create a tint. Next, mix black to create a shade of your hue.
3. Look at the figure above and imitate the shading techniques to complete the second row of shapes.

72 Unit 2 • Lesson 2

Differentiated Instruction

Reteach
Have students with shirts from the same color family stand up together. Have them line up by clothing color, from lightest to darkest. Explain that value is the lightness or darkness of a color. Have students brainstorm other examples of values of a color they have seen.

Special Needs
If students have difficulty grasping small paintbrushes, place a foam rubber cylinder around the brush using tape or a rubber band. This will make it easier for the student to grasp the paintbrush.

ELL
Ask students to point to an object that has a certain hue. Then have them point to another object that is a tint or a shade of that hue.

◀ Alexx Diera.
Age 13.

Think about this painting. What monochromatic colors did the student artist use?

Creative Expression

Paint a landscape using monochromatic colors to show value.

1. Look over your planned sketch in your Art Journal. Lightly transfer your sketch onto your paper, filling the whole page.
2. Select any one color from the color wheel. From your paint palette, mix tints and shades and try them out on a scrap sheet of paper.
3. Paint your landscapes. Using tints and shades of your selected color, make gradual changes in value in some areas of your painting. Show a wide range of values from almost-white highlights to dark shadows.

Art Criticism

Describe What is in your landscape?

Analyze Describe your monochromatic color scheme. Explain how you created a range of values.

Interpret How does the value change affect the mood?

Decide Were you successful in creating a monochromatic painting with a wide range of values? Explain.

Unit 2 • Lesson 2   73

Reflect

Time: About 5 minutes

Review and Assess

"Can you explain how to create a monochromatic color scheme with a range of values?" "¿Pueden explicar cómo crear un esquema de color monocromático con un rango de valores?"

Think

The artist used tints and shades of blue to create the landscape.

- Use **Large Print 76** *Violet Persian Set with Red Lip Wraps* to have students identify different values.

Informal Assessment

- For standardized-format test practice using this lesson's art content, see pages 20–21 in *Reading and Writing Test Preparation.*

Art Journal: Critical Thinking

Have students answer the four art criticism questions—Describe, Analyze, Interpret, and Decide—in their Art Journals. Lead a class discussion on why the landscapes are all very different, even though everyone used a monochromatic color scheme. Talk about how some students used similar colors but chose to use more tints or shades in their paintings.

Art Across the Curriculum

Use these simple ideas to reinforce art concepts across the curriculum.

★ **Expository Writing** Have students write an explanation of the difference between hatching and cross-hatching and why an artist would use either technique.

★ **Math** Have students draw different geometric shapes, incorporating shading techniques.

★ **Science** Explain to students how Earth creates a shadow during a lunar eclipse.

★ **Social Studies** Have students discuss what they know about the U.S. Postal Service.

★ **Technology** Using a paint or draw program and different shading techniques, have students each draw a tree. Visit **SRAonline.com** to print detailed instructions for this activity.
NSAE 6.b

LESSON 2 • Value   **73**

Lesson 2 Wrap-Up: Value

Extra! For the Art Specialist
Time: About 45 minutes

Focus
As a class, study **Large Print 76** *Violet Persian Set with Red Lip Wraps* and discuss how the artist used value. "What mood is created by the values used in this work?"

Teach
Explain to students that they will be creating landscape paintings. Have students select a landscape, cityscape, or seascape as their subject matter. Ask them to draw several sketches with little details and to select the sketch they like best. Then have students complete the Alternate Activity.

Reflect
Have students use the four steps of art criticism to evaluate their work. Did they effectively mix tints and shades to create a range of values in their landscape paintings? Was one color used predominantly?

Alternate Activity

Materials:
- pencils, erasers
- sketchbooks
- canvases
- acrylic paints
- paintbrushes

1. Have students recreate their sketches on canvas. Students should experiment with mixing tints and shades of colors before using them on the canvas.

2. When painting their scenes, students should use tints and shades to show value, making one color predominant. Have students use quick brushstrokes, imitating Twachtman's technique.

Research in Art Education

"The making of art is an essential activity for elementary children. They need and want hands-on experiences in this 'other language.' Art lessons must include cycles of experiences with basic media and techniques, allowing students to acquire and then build upon skills fundamental to creative expression." (Kay Alexander, "Art Curricula by and for Art Educators," in *Art Education: Elementary* ed. Andra Johnson. 1992.)

Assessment
Use the following rubric to evaluate the artwork students make in the Creative Expression activity and to assess students' understanding of value and monochromatic color.

Have students complete page 23 or 24 in their *Assessment* books.

	Art History and Culture	Aesthetic Perception	Creative Expression	Art Criticism
3 POINTS	The student demonstrates knowledge of the lives and work of Vincent van Gogh and John Henry Twachtman.	The student accurately identifies use of value in drawings and paintings.	The student's monochromatic landscape clearly demonstrates use of value, tints, and shades.	The student thoughtfully and honestly evaluates own work using the four steps of art criticism.
2 POINTS	The student's knowledge of Vincent van Gogh and John Henry Twachtman is weak or incomplete.	The student shows an emerging awareness of value in drawings and paintings, but cannot identify it consistently.	The student's monochromatic landscape shows some use of value, tints, and shades.	The student attempts to evaluate own work but shows an incomplete understanding of evaluation criteria.
1 POINT	The student cannot demonstrate knowledge of Vincent van Gogh or John Henry Twachtman.	The student cannot identify uses of value.	The student's monochromatic landscape shows no understanding of value, tints, or shades.	The student makes no attempt to evaluate own work.

73A UNIT 2 • Color and Texture

Lesson 3 Overview: Intensity

Lesson 3 concentrates on color intensity and the use of complementary colors. Intensity is the brightness or dullness of a color. High-intensity colors are bright and pure. Low-intensity colors are dull or muted. Complementary colors are opposite each other on the color wheel.

Objectives

Art History and Culture
To demonstrate knowledge of the lives and work of Andre Derain and Karl Schmidt-Rottluff

Creative Expression
To create an oil-pastel portrait using intensity and complementary colors to create a mood

Aesthetic Perception
To identify and understand how artists use intensity in two-dimensional artwork

Art Criticism
To evaluate own work using the four steps of art criticism

Lesson Materials
- sketchbooks, pencils, erasers
- 9" × 12" white paper
- 12" × 18" heavy white drawing paper
- tempera paints: red, yellow, blue, orange, green, violet
- medium-sized paintbrushes
- water containers, paper towels
- newspaper, mixing palettes
- oil pastels, scrap paper

Alternate Materials:
- oil pastels
- paper plates for mixing paint
- chalk pastels, color pencils, or crayons

Program Resources
- *Reading and Writing Test Prep.*, pp. 22–23
- *Transparency* 9
- *Flash Cards* 7–10
- *Artist Profiles*, pp. 21, 58
- *Animals Through History Time Line*
- *Assessment*, pp. 25–26
- *Large Prints 75 Ermine Skin Shirt* and *76 Violet Persian Set with Red Lip Wraps*

Concept Trace
Intensity
Introduced: Level 4, Unit 3, Lesson 4
Reinforced: Level 7, Chapter 2, Lesson 3

Vocabulary

Review the following vocabulary words with students before beginning the lesson.

complementary colors *colores complementarios*—colors that are opposite each other on the color wheel

intensity *intensidad*—the brightness or dullness of a color

See page 89B for additional vocabulary and Spanish vocabulary resources.

Art Journal: Vocabulary
Have students add these words to the Vocabulary section of their Art Journals.

Lesson 3 Arts Integration

Theatre
Complete Unit 2, Lesson 3, on pages 40–41 of *Theatre Arts Connections.*

Music
Listen to "Russian Sailors Dance" by Reinhold Gliere. The main melody repeats many times with variations to keep the listener's interest. When is the melody most intense? Why? Discuss the instrumentation of the variations.

Movement & Dance
Have students create simple actions, such as pull and push. Students should explore each action with high-intensity energy. For example, have students imagine pulling large sandbags and pushing against a train rolling down a hill. Then have students explore the same actions with low-intensity energy, for example, pulling a thread or pushing objects aside to clear a table.

LESSON 3 • Intensity **73B**

Focus

Time: About 10 minutes

Activate Prior Knowledge

"Have you ever seen a drawing or painting that has dull, muted colors or bright colors?" "¿Alguna vez han visto un dibujo o una pintura con colores opacos y apagados o colores vivos?"

- As a class, discuss students' responses. Explain that artists use dull, muted colors and bright, contrasting colors to communicate an idea or feeling.

Using Literature ⭐ Reading

- Have students read *By the Great Horn Spoon* by Sid Fleishman. Discuss the use of color intensity on the cover illustration. The use of high-intensity colors in the cover illustration causes excitement and energy.

Thematic Connection ⭐ Reading

- **Feelings:** Have students create a list of different feelings. What kinds of words do students associate with these feelings?

Introduce the Art

Look

"Let's take a closer look at how intensity is used in the two paintings." "Vamos a observar detalladamente cómo se usa la intensidad en las dos pinturas."

Light Intensity ⭐ Science

- Ask students what they know about the brightness of a light relative to the distance of the viewer. The brightness of a light seems to decrease as a person moves away from the light; however, doubling the distance from a light source does not halve the amount of light, as many people believe. As a person moves away from a light, the brightness decreases by the square of the distance.

Art History and Culture

Andre Derain (1880–1954) lived in France, and Karl Schmidt-Rottluff (1884–1976) lived in Germany. Students will learn how two artists who lived during the same time period had very different styles of painting.

💻 Web Connection

Visit www.hermitagemuseum.org for more information about the Hermitage Museum.

74 UNIT 2 • Color and Texture

Lesson 3: Intensity

▲ **André Derain.** (French). *Portrait of a Young Girl in Black.* 1914.
Oil on canvas. 45 × 34½ inches (114.3 × 87.63 cm).
State Hermitage Museum, St. Petersburg, Russia.

Look at how both portraits were painted using color intensity. Derain used a range of values when painting *Portrait of a Young Girl in Black*. He is best known for creating brightly colored landscapes and cityscapes. Schmidt-Rottluff was interested in the simple shapes and distorted features of African masks. He helped form a group that he named *Die Brücke*, or "The Bridge." The group believed that they were the bridge between traditional and modern art. In *Portrait of Emy*, Schmidt-Rottluff uses the bright colors characteristic of *Die Brücke*. Emy was his wife.

Art History and Culture

Were Derain and Schmidt-Rotluff contemporaries?

74 Unit 2 • Lesson 3

Art History and Culture

André Derain

André Derain (än drā´ də ran´) (1880–1954) was born in Chatou, near Paris, France. His father was a successful pastry chef and town councillor, so Derain was given a good education. He studied engineering for a short time, which he abandoned to pursue painting. Most of Derain's paintings are landscapes and cityscapes. He also illustrated books, was commissioned to paint ballet and theatre sets, and painted numerous portraits.

See pages 24–25 and 16–21 for more about art history and the subject matter.

Artist Profiles, p. 21

Artist Profile
André Derain
1880-1954

André Derain (än drā´ də ran´) was a French artist who studied engineering before deciding to become a painter. After attending art school in Paris, he served three years in the military, painting in his free time. Derain's friend Matisse encouraged him to exhibit his paintings. Soon Derain was considered part of Matisse's *fauves*, a group of painters who used brilliant, almost violent, colors in their artworks. Derain also began to sculpt, first in wood and then in stone. He liked to try different artistic styles and did not hesitate to return to traditional approaches. During Derain's lifetime, some people rejected his work when it no longer seemed to be on the cutting edge of modern … His work is greatly admired today.

▲ **Karl Schmidt-Rottluff.** (German). *Portrait of Emy.* 1919. Oil on canvas. 28 5/16 × 25 3/4 inches (71.91 × 65.41 cm.). North Carolina Museum of Art, Raleigh, North Carolina.

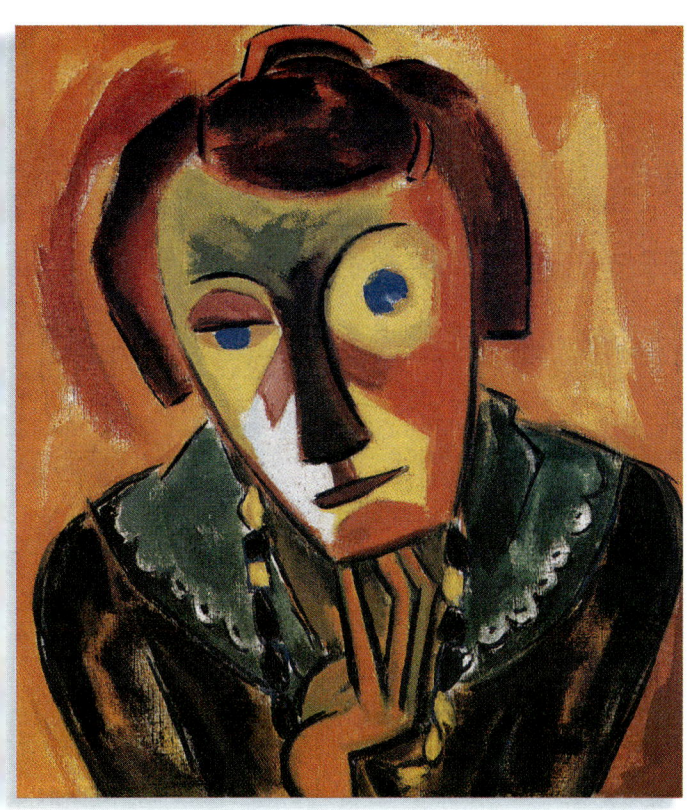

Study both portraits on these pages. How did the artists use color in their paintings?
- What colors do you see?
- Describe the different values used in each painting.
- Which color dominates the painting *Portrait of a Young Girl in Black*? Why do you think Derain chose this color?
- How was contrast used in *Portrait of Emy* by Karl Schmidt-Rottluff?

Aesthetic Perception

Seeing Like an Artist What colors do you think of when you imagine the bark of a tree?

Unit 2 • Lesson 3   75

Art History and Culture

Karl Schmidt-Rottluff

Karl Schmidt-Rottluff (kärl shmit rot´ loof) (1884–1976) began studying architecture in Dresden in 1905. While at the university he met Fritz Bleye and Ernst Ludwig Kirchner and founded a small association, which he named *Die Brücke* (The Bridge). In 1906 he stopped studying architecture to devote himself solely to his painting. From 1912 onward, Rottluff was influenced by cubism, futurism, and African tribal art. For several years he produced only woodcuts and sculptures. In 1918 Schmidt-Rottluff married Emy Frisch, whom he painted in the portrait illustrated above.

See pages 24–25 and 16–21 for more about art history and the subject matter.

Artist Profiles, p. 58

Artist Profile
Karl Schmidt-Rottluff
1884–1976
Karl Schmidt-Rottluff (kärl shmit rot´ loof) was born in Germany, and began his education as a student of architecture in Dresden. As a young man he abandoned his studies of architecture for painting and became an active self-taught German expressionist painter. With his passion for expressionism Schmidt-Rottluff became a co-founder of the avant-garde group of painters known as *Die Brücke* (The Bridge) in 1906.

Karl Schmidt-Rottluff. (German). *Self-Portrait.* 1968.

Study

▶ Derain: Complementary colors: blue and orange. Low-intensity colors: mostly blues and muted oranges. Schmidt-Rottluff: Complementary colors: blue and orange in the eye; red and green in the lower right of the canvas. High-intensity colors: yellow, orange, green, blue, and white. Low-intensity colors: brown; yellow-orange in the hand and upper-right background; areas of the black dress.

▶ Possible answers: Derain: Tints: blue-and-orange striped pattern in the back of the chair; a tint of orange mixed into the black of the dress; the girl's skin has muted oranges. Shades: dark areas are shaded on the face and neck; the dress has areas of dark solid black for shadows; background has medium shades of blue. Schmidt-Rottluff: Tint: the hand; white in the face is a highlighted area. Shade: low-intensity oranges and browns in the hair and the nose.

▶ Blue takes up the entire background and is used in the chair. Student responses will vary based on personal experiences.

▶ Contrasts: dark dress against yellow background; green and red are close to each other; muted hair color against the bright yellows; white area of color on the face next to the dark green shawl and dark nose.

■ For more examples of portraits, see *The National Museum of Women in the Arts Collection.*

Art Journal: Writing
Have students describe what it means to be *intense* in the Concepts section of their Art Journals. What else do they want to know about intensity in art?

Aesthetic Perception

Design Awareness Discuss how trees are not really brown. They reflect a variety of light and dark low-intensity grays. Our eyes naturally blend the colors together.

Developing Visual Literacy Discuss what each artwork "says." Invite students to share personal experiences that contribute to their understanding of the artwork.

Web Connection
Visit **www.ncmoa.org** for more information about the North Carolina Museum of Art.

LESSON 3 • Intensity   75

Teach

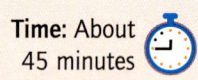

Time: About 45 minutes

"How do you create low- and high-intensity colors in a painting?" *"¿Cómo crean colores débiles y muy intensos en una pintura?"*

- Read and discuss using low- and high-intensity and complementary colors in two-dimensional art on page 76.

Practice

Materials: 9" × 12" paper, pencils, tempera paint in the primary and secondary colors, medium paintbrushes, water containers, paper towels, newspaper, mixing palettes

Alternate Materials: oil pastels or crayons, paper plates for palettes

- Demonstrate adding equal amounts of the complements for the center shape. Also show students that only a brushload of paint is needed per color to mix.
- Distribute the materials and have students follow the directions on page 76.

Creative Expression

Materials: Art Journals, pencils and erasers, 12" × 18" heavy white drawing paper, oil pastels, paper towels, newspaper, various tools for scraping: nails, dull tapestry needles, matboard strips

Alternate Materials: chalk pastels or crayons, paper plates for mixing paint

- Distribute the materials and have students follow the directions on page 77.
- Review the Activity Tips on page 234 for visual examples of techniques, if needed.

Art Journal: Brainstorming

As a class, have students brainstorm a list of people they could use as models for a portrait. Have students transfer the class list into their Art Journals and create several sketches of one of the people from their list. Ask students to select one sketch for the Creative Expression activity.

76 UNIT 2 • Color and Texture

Using Intensity

Intensity is the brightness or dullness of a color. A pure hue is called a high-intensity color. Dull hues are called low-intensity colors. One way to create a low-intensity color is to mix a color with its complement.

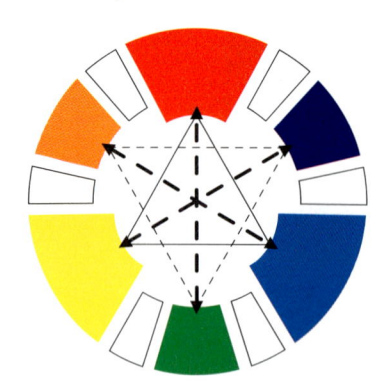

Complementary colors are colors that are opposite each other on the color wheel. For example, blue and orange are complementary colors. The complement of a hue absorbs all the light waves that the hue reflects. It is the strongest contrast to that color. For example, orange absorbs blue waves and reflects yellow and red waves. Yellow and red combine to make orange.

Mixing a hue with its complementary color dulls it. It lowers the intensity. The more of the complement you add, the duller the hue becomes. Eventually the hue will lose its own color and become a neutral gray or brownish color.

Practice

Practice mixing low-intensity colors.

1. Draw a rectangle large enough to fill your paper. Divide it into five sections.
2. Look at the color wheel, and select one set of complementary colors.
3. Look at the intensity scale. Begin by coloring your first shape one hue and the last shape its complement. Color the next shape in from both sides the pure hue and mix a little of its complement. The center shape will have equal amounts of both complementary colors, creating a neutral gray or brown.

76   Unit 2 • Lesson 3

Differentiated Instruction

Reteach
Have students look at the color wheel as you review the concept that complementary colors are opposite each other on the color wheel. One way for students to remember complementary colors is to remember the three primary colors.

Special Needs
Demonstrate for students how to blend oil pastels, providing them with an opportunity to practice this skill before they begin adding color to their pictures.

ELL
Make sure students understand the difference between the words *compliment* and *complement*. Then have them give examples of each.

◀ **Chandler Verner.**
Age 11.

Think about the portrait created by the student artist. Can you tell what complements were used to create the high- and low-intensity colors?

Creative Expression

Make an oil pastel portrait using bright and dull colors to create a mood.

1. Choose your best sketch from your Art Journal. Transfer it onto your paper, touching three edges to fill your page.
2. Select any one complementary color set. On a scrap sheet of paper, practice blending colors and creating textures.
3. Color in your portrait with oil pastels. Overlap and blend colors in some areas of your work; use bright colors in other areas. Show both high- and low-intensity colors. Keep your background simple so that it does not distract from the portrait.

Art Criticism

Describe Who is the person in your drawing? What oil pastel techniques did you use?

Analyze Describe your complementary color scheme. How did you create low- and high-intensity colors?

Interpret How do the colors affect the mood?

Decide Were you successful in creating a portrait using low- and high-intensity colors? Explain.

Unit 2 • Lesson 3   77

Reflect

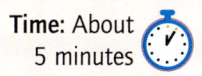

Time: About 5 minutes

Review and Assess

"Explain how you created a portrait using low- and/or high-intensity colors."

"Expliquen cómo crearon un retrato usando colores débiles e intensos."

Think

The artist mixed green and red to create a low-intensity brown color.

- Use **Large Prints 75** *Ermine Skin Shirt* and **76** *Violet Persian Set with Red Lip Wraps* to have students identify the use of color intensity in each artwork.

Informal Assessment

- For standardized-format test practice using this lesson's art content, see pages 22–23 in *Reading and Writing Test Preparation*.

Art Journal: Critical Thinking

Have students answer the four art criticism questions—Describe, Analyze, Interpret, and Decide—in their Art Journals. Ask students to think about how they used color intensity in their artwork. What problems did they have to overcome, if any, and how did they solve them?

Art Across the Curriculum

Use these simple ideas to reinforce art concepts across the curriculum.

★ **Descriptive Writing** Have students write a paragraph describing how a specific color makes them feel.

★ **Math** Explain that complementary angles are two angles whose sum is 90°.

★ **Science** Have students discuss intensity and earthquakes.

★ **Social Studies** Have students list places where they have seen portraits of U.S. presidents.

★ **Technology** In a paint or draw program, have students draw a visual example of how a low-intensity color is created by mixing two complementary colors together. Visit **SRAonline.com** to print detailed instructions for this activity.
NSAE 6.b

LESSON 3 • Intensity   **77**

Lesson 3 Wrap-Up: Intensity

Extra! For the Art Specialist
Time: About 45 minutes

Focus
As a class, study **Large Print 76** *Violet Persian Set with Red Lip Wraps* and discuss how color intensity is used by the artist. What mood is created by the use of color in this work?

Teach
Have students take turns posing for one another for five-minute portrait drawings in their Art Journals. Encourage students to create the portraits from various points of view: looking up toward the model, from a three-quarters view, and so forth. Then have students complete the Alternate Activity.

Reflect
Have students use the four steps of art criticism to evaluate their work. Did they effectively use color intensity in their artwork? Was one color used predominantly?

Alternate Activity

Materials:
- 12" × 18" heavy white drawing paper
- tempera paints
- oil pastels
- crayons
- paintbrushes
- canvases

1. Ask students to re-create their best sketch on paper or canvas and to make sure it touches three edges.
2. Have students decide whether they want to use paints, pastels, crayons, or a combination for their portraits.
3. Students can complete the portraits using the media selected to show color intensity.

Research in Art Education

Students are challenged by the comprehensive nature of big art projects, and "in doing so, [they] master an enormous number of artistic skills, direct a myriad of aesthetic and expressive qualities toward given ends, and symbolize human behaviors and emotions in a great variety of ways" (*Gaining the Arts Advantage: Lessons from School Districts that Value Arts Education*). Art projects can also provide students with the opportunity to learn time-management skills.

Assessment

Use the following rubric to evaluate the artwork students make in the Creative Expression activity and to assess students' understanding of color intensity and monochromatic color.

Have students complete page 25 or 26 in their *Assessment* books.

	Art History and Culture	Aesthetic Perception	Creative Expression	Art Criticism
3 POINTS	The student can demonstrate knowledge of the lives and work of Andre Derain and Karl Schmidt-Rottluff.	The student accurately identifies use of color intensity in two-dimensional art.	The student's portrait demonstrates uses of color intensity.	The student thoughtfully and honestly evaluates own work using the four steps of art criticism.
2 POINTS	The student's knowledge of Andre Derain and Karl Schmidt-Rottluff is weak or incomplete.	The student shows an emerging awareness of color intensity in two-dimensional art, but cannot identify it consistently.	The student's portrait shows some use of color intensity.	The student attempts to evaluate own work, but shows an incomplete understanding of evaluation criteria.
1 POINT	The student cannot demonstrate knowledge of Andre Derain or Karl Schmidt-Rottluff.	The student cannot identify uses of color intensity.	The student's portrait shows no understanding of color intensity.	The student makes no attempt to evaluate own work.

Assessment, p. 25

77A UNIT 2 • Color and Texture

Lesson 4 Overview: Color Schemes

Lesson 4 is about color schemes. Analogous, warm, and cool colors are the color schemes discussed and studied. A color scheme is a plan for organizing the colors used in an artwork.

Objectives

Art History and Culture
To demonstrate knowledge of the lives and work of James Ensor and Georges Braque

Creative Expression
To experiment with color schemes by creating a series of four similar landscapes using different color schemes

Aesthetic Perception
To identify and understand color schemes and how artists use them in two-dimensional artwork

Art Criticism
To evaluate own work using the four steps of art criticism

Vocabulary

Review the following vocabulary word with students before beginning the lesson.

color scheme esquema del color—a plan for organizing the colors used in an artwork

See page 89B for additional vocabulary and Spanish vocabulary resources.

Art Journal: Vocabulary
Have students add this word to the Vocabulary section of their Art Journals.

Lesson Materials

- sketchbooks, pencils, erasers
- self-adhesive notes, magazines
- fine-line permanent black markers
- $4\frac{1}{2}" \times 6"$ sketch paper
- $12" \times 18"$ heavy white drawing paper
- tempera paints in primary and secondary colors plus black and white
- paintbrushes in various sizes
- water containers, paper towels
- newspaper, mixing palettes

Alternate Materials:
- scrap pieces of paper to mark color schemes
- oil pastels
- paper plates for mixing paint

Program Resources

- *Reading and Writing Test Prep.*, pp. 24–25
- *Transparency 10*
- *Flash Cards* 11–13
- *Artist Profiles*, pp. 12, 24
- *Animals Through History Time Line*
- *Assessment*, pp. 27–28
- *Large Prints 75 Ermine Skin Shirt* and *76 Violet Persian Set with Red Lip Wraps*

Concept Trace
Color Schemes
Introduced: Level 5, Unit 3, Lesson 2
Reinforced: Level 7, Chapter 2, Lesson 3

Lesson 4 Arts Integration

Theatre
Complete Unit 2, Lesson 4, on pages 42–43 of *Theatre Arts Connections*.

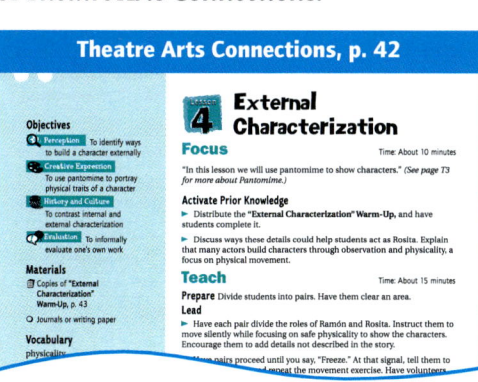

Music
Listen to "Variations on the Theme Pop! Goes the Weasel" by Lucien Caillet. When orchestration changes, so does the tone color. How many different tone colors do students hear in the variations? The possibilities are infinite.

Movement & Dance
Color schemes are used in dance to emphasize theme, character, and sometimes the historical or geographical setting. In small groups, have students sketch costumes and sets for a dance piece, such as *The Nutcracker*. Students need to create a color scheme for each scene and each main character.

Focus

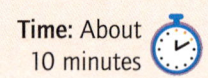

Time: About 10 minutes

Activate Prior Knowledge

"Have you ever seen a display of fireworks in the night sky?" "¿Alguna vez han visto un espectáculo de fuegos artificiales en el cielo nocturno?"

- As a class, discuss students' responses. Explain that artists use bright colors against cool colors to create contrast and to show excitement.

Using Literature ★ Reading

- Have students read *Joe Pigza Loses Control* by Jack Gantos. Have them study the cover illustration and discuss the use of warm and cool colors. Warm colors can create a feeling of excitement and come toward the viewer, while cool colors are calm and recede.

Thematic Connection ★ Science

- **Organization:** Have students discuss ways in which they could organize the classroom.

Introduce the Art

Look

"Let's take a closer look at the use of color in the two paintings." "Vamos a observar detalladamente el uso del color en las dos pinturas."

U.S. Government ★ Social Studies

- Have students explain how the U.S. government is organized. The U.S. government is organized into three branches: executive, judicial, and legislative. The executive branch is headed by the president. The judicial branch is headed by the Supreme Court. The legislative branch is Congress, which includes the Senate and the House of Representatives.

Art History and Culture

Les XX (The Twenty) was a group of artists who sought to reform society and the arts. Along with Picasso, Braque co-founded the cubism movement, which redefined art in the twentieth century.

Web Connection

Visit www.albrightknox.org for more information about the Albright Knox Museum.

78 UNIT 2 • Color and Texture

Lesson 4: Color Schemes

▲ **James Ensor.** (Belgian). *Fireworks.* 1887.
Oil and encaustic on canvas. 40¼ × 44¼ inches (102.24 × 112.4 cm). Albright-Knox Art Gallery, Buffalo, New York.

Look at how Ensor used complementary colors to draw your attention away from the dark ground in *Fireworks*. By applying pigment to wash, he created a thick paint called *impasto*. This paint adds to the texture of his painting. Georges Braque used low-intensity and neutral colors in *Fishing Boats*. Braque and Pablo Picasso invented the style of art called *cubism*. This style emphasizes structure and design. Notice how the objects are shown from different points of view at the same time.

Art History and Culture

Did you know that Ensor was a founding member of the group *Les XX*, and that Braque co-founded cubism?

78 Unit 2 • Lesson 4

Art History and Culture

James Ensor

James Ensor (jāmz en´ sor) (1860–1949) was born in Ostend, Belgium, where his parents sold masks, shells, puppets, and other curio items in their souvenir shop. Many of the items in his parents' shop later became subject matter for Ensor's paintings. From 1877 to 1880 he studied at the Brussels Beaux-Arts. A mask theme is used in much of his artwork. He created fantasies, dreams, and visions. It is this subject matter that put Ensor in the movement called *symbolism*. Ensor's art was a precursor of expressionism. His fantasy paintings also foreshadow surrealism.

See pages 24–25 and 16–21 for more about art history and the subject matter.

Artist Profiles, p. 24

Artist Profile

James Ensor
1860-1949

James Ensor (jāmz en´ sor) was born in Ostend, Belgium. Except for three years when he studied at the Brussels Academy, he lived in Ostend his entire life. A member of a group of progressive artists called *Les Vingt* (*The Twenty*), Ensor was considered to be a master by the time he was only 20 years old. He was interested in masks and portraying the nature of people in Belgium in a sometimes carnivalesque manner. As he grew older the negative criticism he received for his art caused him to become cynical and reclusive.

▲ **Georges Braque.** (French). *Fishing Boats.* 1909. Oil on canvas. 36¼ × 28⅞ inches (92.08 × 73.36 cm.). Museum of Fine Arts, Houston, Texas.

Study and compare how the artists used different color schemes in their paintings.

▶ List the objects you see in each painting.

▶ What colors are used in *Fireworks?* What colors are used in *Fishing Boats?*

▶ Which color do you notice first in *Fireworks?* Why do you think this happens?

▶ Which areas are the lightest and darkest in each painting?

Aesthetic Perception

Design Awareness Look at the clothing you and your classmates are wearing. Which colors would "go together" or look good? Which colors would contrast?

Unit 2 • Lesson 4   79

Art History and Culture

Georges Braque

Georges Braque (zhorzh bräk) (1882–1963) was impressed by the bold style of fauvism. (*Fauves* is French for "wild beasts.") Braque began painting in the style of fauvism, using bold, brilliant colors and creating compositions that were not in perspective. However, in 1908, Braque saw the paintings of Paul Cézanne, who distorted forms and used unconventional perspectives. This led Braque to paint in the style that became known as cubism. In his paintings he experimented with the effects of light and perspective. Braque worked closely with Picasso, and together they established cubism as an art style and collage as an art form.

See pages 24–25 and 16–21 for more about art history and the subject matter.

Artist Profiles, p. 12

Georges Braque
1882-1963

Georges Braque (zhorzh bräk) was born in Argenteuil-sur-Seine, France. Helping his father, a house decorator, taught him much about painting. In 1900 he moved to Paris to study under a master decorator. He then spent several years painting at the Académie Humbert. Braque worked with Pablo Picasso in creating cubism, but after fighting in World War I, he ended his work with Picasso. His style constantly evolved until his death in 1963.

Study

▶ *Fireworks:* large sky; giant fire in the sky; small, dark figures. *Fishing Boats:* buildings, boats, sail masts, geometric shapes.

▶ Complementary colors: blue and orange in the sky. Shades: yellow mixed with black on the ground. Cool color: blue. Warm colors: yellow and orange. Neutral colors: black, white, and gray. Low-intensity color: a brownish gray color.

▶ Yellow: when placed next to the blue, the yellow and then the orange come forward, causing the blue to recede. The yellow also takes up the largest area in the painting and is in the center.

▶ *Fireworks:* Lightest: yellow in the giant fire in the sky. Darkest: small, black figures and dark areas in the foreground. *Fishing Boats:* Lightest: rooftops to the right; white areas inside the boats and on the ground in the very front of the painting. Darkest: center building in the back; both top corners of the painting; side of the building on the right side, center area behind the boats; under the boats in the foreground.

■ For more examples of art from Europe, see *Art Around the World Collection.*

Art Journal: Writing

Have students list examples of color schemes in the Concepts section of their Art Journals. What else do they want to know about color schemes?

Aesthetic Perception

Design Awareness Discuss how artists organize colors according to a plan called a color scheme. Many designers use color schemes to create clothing.

Developing Visual Literacy Invite students to share personal experiences that contribute to their understanding of the artwork; for example, have they been to a fireworks display, to a marina, or to a boat dock?

Web Connection

Visit **www.mfah.org** for more information about the Museum of Fine Art, Houston.

LESSON 4 • Color Schemes   79

Teach

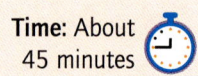

Time: About 45 minutes

"What colors do you like to use in an outdoor painting?" "¿Qué colores les gusta usar en una pintura de una escena al aire libre?"

- Read and discuss color schemes in two-dimensional artwork on page 80.

Practice

Materials: self-adhesive notes, magazines

Alternate Materials: scrap paper strips or folded pieces of paper

- Distribute the materials and have students follow the directions on page 80.

Creative Expression

Materials: landscape sketch in Art Journal, pencils and erasers, 12" × 18" heavy white drawing paper, tempera paints of all colors plus black and white, paintbrushes in various sizes, water containers, paper towels, newspaper, mixing palettes

Alternate Materials: oil pastels or crayons, paper plates for mixing paint

- Distribute the materials and have students follow the directions on page 81.
- Have students demonstrate their technical skills, using a variety of art media and materials to produce their paintings.
  NSAE 1.a; 1.b
- Review the Activity Tips on page 234 for visual examples of techniques, if needed.

Art Journal: Planning

Have students collect several images of landscapes and keep them in the Ideas section of their Art Journals. Also in their Art Journals, have students create several sketches of simple line drawings of landscapes from the collected images. Limit them to no more than five landforms. Ask students to each select one sketch for the Creative Expression activity.

80 UNIT 2 • Color and Texture

Using Color Schemes

A **color scheme** is a plan for organizing the colors used in an artwork. When two colors come into contact, their differences increase. Some colors look good together, while others clash. Artists use color schemes to help them organize colors so that they can communicate an idea or an emotion. Primary, secondary, intermediate, monochromatic, and complementary colors are color schemes that have already been discussed in this unit, but there are two other color schemes that are used frequently.

Analogous colors are colors that sit side by side on the color wheel and have a common hue. Violet, blue-violet, blue, blue-green, and green all have blue in common. You can narrow this related scheme by limiting it to only three colors, such as violet, blue-violet, and blue.

The color spectrum is divided into two groups—warm colors and cool colors, which are associated with temperature. **Warm colors** are red, yellow, and orange and suggest warmth. **Cool colors** are violet, blue, and green and suggest coolness. Warm colors seem to move toward the viewer, and cool colors seem to recede or go back from the viewer.

Analogous colors    Warm colors / Cool colors

Practice

Look through magazines to find pictures that illustrate different color schemes.

1. As a table group, find at least one example of each color scheme in your magazines.
2. On self-adhesive notes write each of the color scheme names as you find them to label your examples. Tag the pages with the adhesive notes.
3. Do not tear out the pages. See how many examples you can find.

80   Unit 2 • Lesson 4

Differentiated Instruction

Reteach
Have students look through their textbooks and/or the *Large Prints* with a partner to find examples of artwork that use each of the color schemes studied.

Special Needs
Sequence instruction for students with disabilities by providing a list of directions and visual prompts showing each stage of this project.

ELL
Explain the definitions of the words *analogous* and *scheme* to students and have them create a list of synonyms for each word.

Think about the landscape created by the student artist. Do you recognize the four color schemes used?

Creative Expression

Use different color schemes to paint a series of four similar landscapes.

1. Divide your paper into four equal sections. Fold the paper in half, open it, and fold it in half in the opposite direction.
2. Using your sketch, make a simple line drawing on a small piece of paper. Transfer your line drawing onto each of the rectangles on your drawing paper.
3. Look at the color schemes in this unit, and select any four. Paint each of your four small landscapes, using a different color scheme.
4. Use the primary and secondary colors to mix your intermediate colors. Using a small brush, paint the shapes by outlining them with a color. Then use a medium-sized brush to fill them in.

Art Criticism

Describe List all the objects in your landscapes.

Analyze Describe the four different color schemes you used.

Interpret Compare how the different color schemes affect the mood in each landscape.

Decide Were you successful in creating a series of four landscapes using different color schemes? Explain.

Reflect

Time: About 5 minutes

Review and Assess

"Can you explain the differences and similarities among the color schemes you used?" "¿Pueden explicar las diferencias y las semejanzas entre los esquemas del color que usaron?"

Think

The artist used a neutral color scheme, a monochromatic/cool color scheme, a complementary color scheme, and a warm color scheme.

- Use **Large Prints 75** *Ermine Skin Shirt* and **76** *Violet Persian Set with Red Lip Wraps* to have students identify different color schemes used in each artwork.

Informal Assessment

- For standardized-format test practice using this lesson's art content, see pages 24–25 in *Reading and Writing Test Preparation.*

Art Journal: Critical Thinking

Have students answer the four art criticism questions—Describe, Analyze, Interpret, and Decide—in their Art Journals. Lead a class discussion on the differences and similarities among the color schemes. Explain that students who used the same color schemes may have used different values and intensities based on the proportion of mixed colors.

Art Across the Curriculum

Use these simple ideas to reinforce art concepts across the curriculum.

★ **Persuasive Writing** Have students write a letter to an adult stating why they should go to a fireworks display or take a fishing trip.

★ **Math** Have students discuss ways they can organize data in charts and graphs.

★ **Science** Explain that stars have different colors and temperatures associated with them.

★ **Social Studies** Have students discuss where there are warm and cool climates in the world.

★ **Technology** Using a paint or draw program, have students create a diagram of three analogous colors. Visit **SRAonline.com** to print detailed instructions for this activity.
NSAE 6.b

Lesson 4 Wrap-Up: Color Schemes

Extra! For the Art Specialist

Time: About 45 minutes

Focus
As a class, study **Large Print 75** *Ermine Skin Shirt* and discuss how the artist used color. Did the color scheme create a mood? Have students explain their answer.

Teach
Have students collect interesting objects from around the classroom. Using boxes and cloth, create a base of varying heights to display the collected objects. Arrange the objects so that the view is interesting from all sides. Then have students complete the Alternate Activity.

Reflect
Have students use the four steps of art criticism to evaluate their work. Did they effectively blend hues in their still-life drawing? What color scheme was used? Why?

Alternate Activity

Materials:
- color pastels, vine charcoal
- kneaded eraser
- blending stump or towel
- variety of colors of drawing paper

1. Have students use vine charcoal to create quick sketches from different angles.
2. Students should each select one sketch to be re-created on the drawing paper.
3. Have students use black, white, and gray pastels to draw in the objects.
4. Students should each select a color scheme and layer the colors, blending with a stump or towel as needed to complete the drawing.

Research in Art Education

There are several possible reasons for the academic achievement associated with student involvement in arts organizations. Arts organizations tend to place high expectations for achievement on participating students; they give students a chance to perform school-related tasks (such as reading, calculating, and planning); and they value and encourage risk-taking ("Living the Arts Through Language and Learning" in *Critical Links*, p. 78).

Assessment

Use the following rubric to evaluate the artwork students make in the Creative Expression activity and to assess students' understanding of color schemes.

Have students complete page 27 or 28 in their *Assessment* books.

	Art History and Culture	Aesthetic Perception	Creative Expression	Art Criticism
3 POINTS	The student demonstrates knowledge of the lives and work of James Ensor and Georges Braque.	The student accurately identifies use of color schemes in two-dimensional art.	The student's landscape series demonstrates a good understanding of how to use different color schemes.	The student thoughtfully and honestly evaluates own work using the four steps of art criticism.
2 POINTS	The student's knowledge of the lives and work of James Ensor and Georges Braque is weak or incomplete.	The student shows an emerging awareness of color schemes in two-dimensional art, but cannot identify it consistently.	The student's landscape series shows some use and understanding of different color schemes.	The student attempts to evaluate own work, but shows an incomplete understanding of evaluation criteria.
1 POINT	The student cannot demonstrate knowledge of the lives and work of James Ensor or Georges Braque.	The student cannot identify use of color schemes.	The student's landscape series shows no understanding of color schemes.	The student makes no attempt to evaluate own work.

Assessment, p. 27

Lesson 5 Overview: Visual Texture

Lesson 5 introduces the art element of texture and focuses on visual texture. Texture is the art element that refers to the way something feels. Visual texture, or simulated texture, imitates real texture.

Objectives

Art History and Culture
To demonstrate knowledge of the lives and work of Jean-Baptiste Simeon Chardin and Susan LeVan

Creative Expression
To explore using the computer as an art tool for creating textural drawings

Aesthetic Perception
To identify how artists use texture to create the illusion of realism in two-dimensional art

Art Criticism
To evaluate own work using the four steps of art criticism

Lesson Materials
- sketchbooks, pencils, erasers
- computer
- draw, paint, or word-processing program

Alternate Materials:
- copier or drawing paper
- crayons

Program Resources
- *Reading and Writing Test Prep.*, pp. 26–27
- *Transparency* 11
- *Flash Card* 19
- *Artist Profiles*, pp. 17, 36
- *Animals Through History Time Line*
- *Assessment*, pp. 29–30
- *Large Prints* 75 *Ermine Skin Shirt* and 76 *Violet Persian Set with Red Lip Wraps*

Concept Trace
Visual Texture
Introduced: Level 5, Unit 5, Lesson 1
Reinforced: Level 7, Chapter 2, Lesson 7

Vocabulary

Review the following vocabulary words with students before beginning the lesson.

texture *textura*—the art element that refers to the way something feels

simulated texture *textura simulada*—another word for visual texture

See page 89B for additional vocabulary and Spanish vocabulary resources.

Art Journal: Vocabulary
Have students add these words to the Vocabulary section of their Art Journals.

Lesson 5 Arts Integration

Theatre
Complete Unit 2, Lesson 5, on pages 44–45 of *Theatre Arts Connections.*

Music
SPOTLIGHT on MUSIC Listen to "The Moldau" by Bedrich Smetana. The Moldau is a river in his native Czechoslovakia. The piece starts with a small flow of melody from two flutes, depicting two streams coming out of the mountains. Have students listen for how the texture changes as the music continues and instruments are added.

Movement & Dance
Have students select three objects of different weight, texture, and color. Have three students participate while others sit as an audience. Each student should take one of the objects and explore how to express it in movement for twelve counts. Ask the audience how the weight and texture effect the movements of each object.

Focus

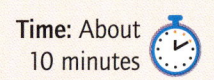

Time: About 10 minutes

Activate Prior Knowledge

"Have you ever seen a still life before?"
"¿Alguna vez han visto una naturaleza muerta?"

- Explain that artists use techniques to imitate the real textures of objects in paintings and drawings.

Using Literature ⭐ Reading

- Have students read *Fever 1793* by Laurie Halse Anderson. Notice how the repeated lines and use of value in the cover illustration imitate textures in a realistic manner.

Thematic Connection ⭐ Science

- **Look Again:** Have students describe times when they have had to take a second look at something to see whether it was real or not. When they looked closer at the object, what did they notice?

Introduce the Art

Look

"Let's take a closer look at the way texture is portrayed in these two works of art." "Vamos a observar más detalladamente la manera en que se representa la textura en estas dos obras de arte."

Editing ⭐ Language Arts

- Have students read a page of text from their Art Journals and ask them what kinds of mistakes they see now that they have had a chance to look at their writing again. Some students may encounter misspellings, capitalization and punctuation errors, problems with clarity or incorrect use of words or phrases.

Art History and Culture

The work by Susan LeVan was created in the twentieth century. The painting by Chardin was done in 1766, the eighteenth century.

💻 Web Connection

Visit www.oakton.edu/acad/dept/grd/STUDENT_ART.html?40,31 for more examples of computer-generated art. This Web site is for the teachers use only.

82 UNIT 2 • Color and Texture

Lesson 5: Visual Texture

▲ **Susan LeVan.** (American). *Two Birds in Hand.*
Digital media. Bruck & Moss Gallery, New York, New York.

Look closely at the works of art by LeVan and Chardin. Notice how these artists used lines and value to show smooth and bumpy areas. Chardin used thick layers of color and thin glazes to create the feeling of smooth, rough, matte, and shiny surfaces. *Still Life with the Attributes of the Arts* has objects that represent the arts. The paintbrushes represent painting, and the statue is of Mercury, the god of the arts. Susan LeVan created *Two Birds in Hand* on a computer. She uses a program that allows her to alter colors so that she can imitate rough and smooth surfaces. Though these artists are from two different centuries, they both understood how to imitate different surfaces.

Art History and Culture

Which of these two works of art was created in the twentieth century?

82   Unit 2 • Lesson 5

Art History and Culture

Susan LeVan

Susan LeVan (sōō´ zən luh vân´) (1947–) was a mixed-media collage artist, but since 1991 she has worked primarily on the computer. Sometimes she starts an image on the computer, prints it, collages it, and then scans it back into the computer to work on it some more. She works on a computer with a pressure-sensitive graphics tablet and uses a program that imitates natural mediums, such as watercolor, chalk, and pencil. The tablet and software allow her to start from scratch on the computer and work exactly the same way that she would using regular paints and brushes.

See pages 24–25 and 16–21 for more about art history and the subject matter.

Artist Profiles, p. 36

Artist Profile
Susan LeVan
b. 1947

Computer artist Susan LeVan (sōō´ zən luh vân´) was born and raised in Michigan. She received a bachelor of arts degree in anthropology from the University of Michigan and a master of fine arts degree in printmaking from the Cranbrook Academy of Art. Her background in printmaking filters into her current work with digital imaging. It also influenced her earlier work with mixed media. In 1991 LeVan shifted from an emphasis in mixed-media collage to a focus on computer graphics using this technique. She continues to create her vividly colored computer paintings today.

Study both works of art to see how visual texture is used.

- Where do you see a bumpy surface?
- Look closely at the painting by Chardin. List the objects that are rough, smooth, matte, or shiny.
- Which area in LeVan's picture looks smooth?
- Describe the surface area of the shirt in LeVan's picture.

▲ **Jean-Baptiste Simeon Chardin.** (French). *Still Life with the Attributes of the Arts.* 1766.

Oil on canvas. 44 × 55 inches (111.76 × 139.7 cm). State Hermitage Museum, St. Petersburg, Russia.

Aesthetic Perception

Design Awareness Think about the following items: an egg, a feather, a leather coat, and the chrome on a car. How does light reflect or shine on these surfaces?

Unit 2 • Lesson 5   **83**

Art History and Culture

Jean-Baptiste Simeon Chardin

Jean-Baptiste Simeon Chardin (zhä[n] ba tēst´ si´ mā´ ən shär da[n]´) (1699–1779) was mostly self-taught, but on the basis of two still lifes he produced in 1728, he was admitted to the Royal Academy of Painting and Sculpture in Paris. Chardin's technical skill gave his paintings a realistic texture. He portrayed forms by using thick, layered brushstrokes and thin, luminous glazes to create lights and shadows. He was called "the grand magician" by critics because of his ability to realistically render textures. As he aged, his eyesight began to fail and he turned to pastels, abandoning painting.

See pages 24–25 and 16–21 for more about art history and the subject matter.

Artist Profiles, p. 17

Artist Profile

Jean-Baptiste Siméon Chardin
1699–1779

John Baptiste Siméon Chardin (zhä[n] ba tēst´ si´ mā´ an shär dan´), a French painter of the eighteenth century, was born in Paris in 1699. His early artistic skills were self-taught, and he was strongly influenced by seventeenth-century painters like Metsu. After an independent beginning, Chardin attended the Royal Academy of Painting and Sculpture, and in the 1730s, painted scenes of Parisian bourgeois life. The majority of his paintings were commissioned or supported by wealthy aristocrats, including King Louis XV. Chardin was primarily a still-life painter, and he is still regarded as a master of realism and form.

▲ **Jean-Baptiste Siméon Chardin.** (French). *Still Life with the Attributes of the Arts.* 1766.

Study

▶ **Bumpy:** In Chardin's painting the brass medal has a bumpy surface, and the urn has bumpy areas around the neck and handle. LeVan's drawing has no bumpy surfaces.

▶ **Rough:** The covers of the red and cream-colored books behind the urn look like rough cloth. **Smooth:** the wooden table; the soft-covered blue book; the rolled and spread-out papers; the metal and bristles of the paintbrushes and the body of the urn. **Matte:** the background wall. **Shiny:** the urn; brass medal; metal thimble shape near the brush and palette.

▶ The green in the hat; the area of red in the background; the ovals of the trees.

▶ Rough, made up of alternating overlapping vertical and horizontal lines of various thicknesses. The colors of the lines also vary in intensity.

■ For more examples of still lifes, see *The National Museum of Women in the Arts Collection.*

Art Journal: Writing

Have students write what they know about texture in the Concepts section of their Art Journals. What else do they want to know about texture?

Aesthetic Perception

Design Awareness Discuss how the lights and shadows on the objects create surface patterns that show the textures. Artists study the way objects reflect light and cast shadows and imitate these through lines and values to create visual texture. By doing this, artists are able to create the illusion of a three-dimensional surface.

Developing Visual Literacy Have students compare the two works of art. Can they identify the influence of historical or political events?
NSAE 4.a; 4.b; 4.c

Web Connection

Visit **www.hermitagemuseum.org** for more information about the Hermitage Museum.

LESSON 5 • Visual Texture   **83**

Teach

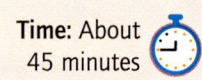

Time: About 45 minutes

"How can you use a computer to create visual textures?" "¿Cómo pueden usar una computadora para crear texturas visuales?"

- Read and discuss visual texture in two-dimensional art on page 84.

Practice

Materials: computer and either a draw, paint or word processing program, printer paper

Alternate Materials: crayons and white paper

- As an alternative to using the computer, students can make crayon rubbings from objects around the classroom.
- Distribute the materials and have students follow the directions on page 84.

Creative Expression

Materials: computer and either a draw, paint or word processing program, printer paper

Alternate Materials: crayons and white paper

- Distribute the materials and have students follow the directions on page 85.
- Have students demonstrate their technical skills, using a variety of art media and materials to produce their computer drawings. NSAE 1.a; 1.b
- Have students express a variety of ideas based on personal experience and direct observations. NSAE 2.a; 2.c
- Review the Activity Tips on page 235 for visual examples of techniques, if needed.

Art Journal: Researching

Look through a variety of visual resources such as photographs, magazines, books, and calendar images. Have students select one or two images that they would like to base their drawings on and place them in their Art Journals. Ask students to plan their compositions for the Creative Expression activity.

84 UNIT 2 • Color and Texture

Using Visual Texture

Everything has texture. **Texture** refers to how things feel, or how things look as if they might feel if touched.

You perceive texture with two of your senses: touch and sight. When you look at a surface, you can guess how it would feel. This is based on prior experiences of touching that surface or a similar surface. Your eyes communicate with your brain how an object would feel if you were to touch it.

When you look at photographs of objects, the lights and shadows create surface patterns that imitate texture. This is called **visual texture,** or the illusion of a three-dimensional surface. Another name for visual texture is *simulated texture*. **Simulated texture** imitates real textures. Plastic surfaces that look like real wood, and material made to look like real leather are examples of simulated textures. Artists use simulated textures to imitate textures that are rough, smooth, matte, or shiny.

Simulated textures    Real textures

Practice

Use a computer to experiment with visual texture.

1. Use a photo-editing program to explore textures.
2. Open the document your teacher has prepared. Select the menu to see the choices you have. Fill in the shapes with textures that interest you.
3. Print a copy of the textures and label them to use for reference.

84   Unit 2 • Lesson 5

Differentiated Instruction

Reteach
Have students work in small groups and look through magazines to find examples of rough, smooth, matte, and shiny textures.

Special Needs
Students with visual impairments may benefit from having the computer's display settings changed so that images and fonts are larger.

ELL
Give groups of students an object with a simulated texture. Have students take turns describing what the real texture would feel like.

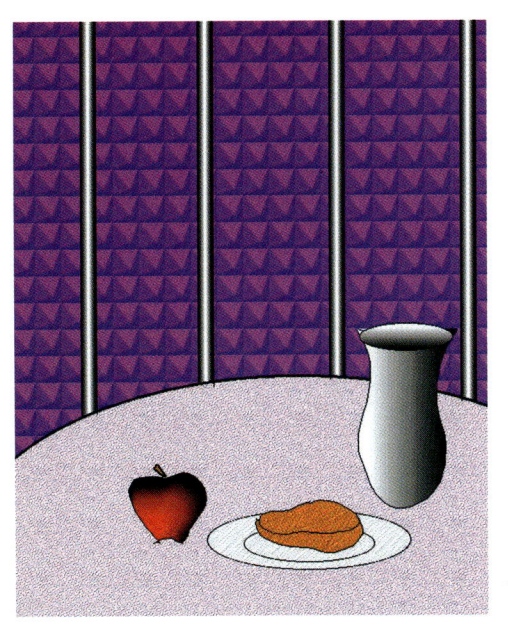

◀ Katie C. Fetzer.
Age 10.

Think about the types of textures you recognize in this student's work.

Creative Expression

Explore using the computer as an art tool for creating textured drawings.

1. Look over your sketch and draw your image using a computer program. Use any tools or options available on your software to resize and manipulate the image. When your image is completed to your satisfaction, save it as "Original Image."
2. Copy your image and save it as "Drawing 1." Use the fill bucket and other tools to add and create textures.
3. Copy several images and explore a variety of textures for each one. Label and save each drawing as you complete it.
4. Select your three best images to print.

Art Criticism

Describe Describe your original image. Describe your favorite image.

Analyze List the different textures you were able to create.

Interpret Compare how the various textures used in your drawings alter the images.

Decide Which of your computer drawings do you feel best portrays visual texture? Explain.

Unit 2 • Lesson 5   85

Reflect
Time: About 5 minutes

Review and Assess
"Can you explain how an artist uses visual texture to imitate real textures in two-dimensional art?" "¿Pueden explicar cómo un artista usa la textura visual para imitar texturas verdaderas en obras de arte bidimensionales?"

Think
The student artist used a rough texture for the wall and smooth texture for the vase and apple.

- Use **Large Print 75** *Ermine Skin Shirt* and **76** *Violet Persian Set with Red Lip Wraps* to have students identify the types of textures used.

Informal Assessment
- For standardized-format test practice using this lesson's art content, see pages 26–27 in ***Reading and Writing Test Preparation.***

Art Journal: Critical Thinking
Have students answer the four art criticism questions—Describe, Analyze, Interpret, and Decide—in their Art Journals. Lead a class discussion on how textures were used in the drawings created by the students.

Art Across the Curriculum

Use these simple ideas to reinforce art concepts across the curriculum.

★ **Descriptive Writing** Have students look at a picture of something they have never seen, and write a paragraph about how they think it feels.

★ **Math** Have students approximate the actual size of the statue in Chardin's painting.

★ **Science** Have students explain the difference between real wood and a flat surface that looks like wood.

★ **Social Studies** Explain to students that many marble statues from ancient Greece and Rome survive today.

★ **Technology** Using a desktop publishing program, have students create a flyer with a textured background for a school open house. Visit **SRAonline.com** to print detailed instructions for this activity.
NSAE 6.b

LESSON 5 • Visual Texture   **85**

Lesson 5 Wrap-Up: Visual Texture

Extra! For the Art Specialist
Time: About 45 minutes

Focus
As a class, study **Large Print 76** *Violet Persian Set with Red Lip Wraps* and discuss how the artist used texture. "How do you think the artist imitated the texture in this work?" Explain.

Teach
Discuss with students how objects look different when they are examined with a microscope or viewfinder. Then provide each student with a black-and-white photograph and have them complete the Alternate Activity.

Reflect
Have students use the four steps of art criticism to evaluate their work. Did they effectively blend values and use lines to create visual textures? Do they feel they were successful at imitating texture? Why or why not?

Alternate Activity
Materials:
- pencils
- paper
- viewfinder
- black-and-white photographs

1. Have students use a black-and-white image with a range of values to copy.
2. Using a viewfinder, have students focus in on one section of the image. Then have them begin to lightly pencil-in what they see.
3. Make sure students try to imitate the selected section as closely as possible. They should carefully study the lines and value changes while drawing.

Research in Art Education
Research has shown that the "looking and reasoning skills" learned during visual art training can also be applied to scientific images ("Investigating the Educational Impact and Potential of the Museum of Modern Art's Visual Thinking Curriculum" in *Critical Links*, p. 142). Students involved in visual-arts training showed less circular reasoning and more evidential reasoning when evaluating both fine-art images and scientific images.

Assessment
Use the following rubric to evaluate the artwork students make in the Creative Expression activity and to assess students' understanding of how texture is used in two-dimensional art.

Have students complete page 29 or 30 in their *Assessment* books.

	Art History and Culture	Aesthetic Perception	Creative Expression	Art Criticism
3 POINTS	The student demonstrates knowledge of the lives and work of Jean-Baptiste Simeon Chardin and Susan LeVan.	The student accurately identifies the use of texture in two-dimensional works of art.	The student's computer drawing clearly demonstrates the use of visual texture.	The student thoughtfully and honestly evaluates own work using the four steps of art criticism.
2 POINTS	The student's knowledge of Jean-Baptiste Simeon Chardin and Susan LeVan is weak or incomplete.	The student shows an emerging awareness of texture in two-dimensional artwork, but cannot consistently identify them.	The student's computer drawing shows some awareness of visual texture.	The student attempts to evaluate own work but shows an incomplete understanding of evaluation criteria.
1 POINT	The student cannot demonstrate knowledge of the lives and work of Jean-Baptiste Simeon Chardin or Susan LeVan.	The student cannot identify how texture is used.	The student's computer drawing shows no understanding of how to create visual texture.	The student makes no attempt to evaluate own work.

Lesson 6 Overview: Tactile Texture

Lesson 6 further explores how tactile texture is used in three-dimensional objects. Tactile textures, or *actual textures,* are textures that can be felt.

Objectives

Art History and Culture
To demonstrate knowledge of African and Chinese headpieces

Creative Expression
To create a mixed-media celebratory hat using tactile textures

Aesthetic Perception
To identify how artists use tactile texture in three-dimensional forms

Art Criticism
To evaluate own work using the four steps of art criticism

Vocabulary

Review the following vocabulary words with students before beginning the lesson.

mixed-media medios mezclados—an art object that has been created from an assortment of media or materials

tactile texture textura táctil—actual texture, texture that can be felt

See page 89B for additional vocabulary and Spanish vocabulary resources.

Art Journal: Vocabulary
Have students add these words to the Vocabulary section of their Art Journals.

Lesson Materials
- pencils, erasers
- Art Journal
- scissors, sewing needles, thread
- embroidery floss
- wire, glue
- scrap material
- paper towels, newspaper

Alternate Materials:
- 12" × 18" construction paper
- stapler and staples
- markers and/or crayons

Program Resources
- *Reading and Writing Test Prep.,* pp. 28–29
- *Transparency* 12
- *Flash Card* 19
- *Artist Profiles,* pp. 74, 79
- *Animals Through History Time Line*
- *Assessment,* pp. 31–32
- *Large Prints 75 Ermine Skin Shirt* and *76 Violet Persian Set with Red Lip Wraps*

Concept Trace
Tactile Texture
Introduced: Level 5, Unit 5, Lesson 1
Reinforced: Level 7, Chapter 2, Lesson 7

Lesson 6 Arts Integration

Theatre
Complete Unit 2, Lesson 6, on pages 46–51 of *Theatre Arts Connections.*

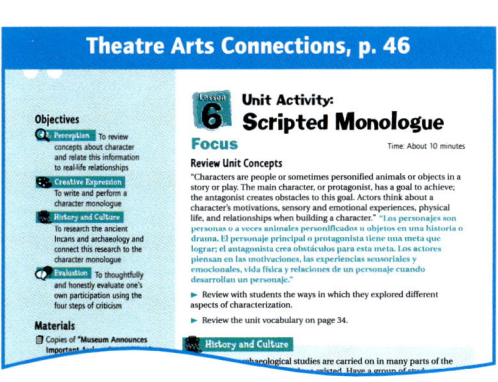

Music
SPOTLIGHT ON MUSIC Listen to Aaron Copeland's "Variations on Simple Gifts" from *Appalachian Spring*. He created the ballet *Appalachian Spring* for the dancer Martha Graham in 1944. His textures are open and transparent. One of the ways he created this open sound is by grouping few instruments together.

Movement & Dance
Place four objects of different textures in front of the students. With a partner, have students close their eyes and reach into the bag to select an object. The student should explore the object through touch and describe how it feels, while his or her partner writes down the description.

Focus

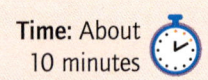

Time: About 10 minutes

Activate Prior Knowledge

"Have you been to a birthday party where you or someone else wore a birthday hat?" "¿Alguna vez han ido a una fiesta de cumpleaños donde ustedes u otra persona se han puesto un sombrero?"

- Discuss the students' comments and explain that this is a common custom in the United States as well as in other cultures. Have students discuss some other events that are celebrated.

Using Literature ⭐ Reading

- Have students look at the scanned images in *Casey at the Bat* by Ernest Lawrence Thayer, illustrated by Christopher Bing. Have students describe how the images might feel if they were touched.

Thematic Connection ⭐ Social Studies

- **Ancient Civilizations:** Have students share stories they have heard about ancient civilizations. Do they know anything about ancient China or Africa?

Introduce the Art

Look

"Let's take a closer look at the way the artists created the two headpieces." "Vamos a observar detalladamente la manera en que los artistas crearon las dos prendas para la cabeza."

Geography ⭐ Social Studies

- Have students locate China and one country in Africa on a map or globe. Can they identify the capitals? Make sure students know that Africa is a continent, not a country. The capital of China is Beijing. Some countries and their capitals in Africa are Egypt (Cairo), and Uganda (Kampala).

Art History and Culture

There is historical evidence that primitive humans used some form of head covering for protection against the elements.

💻 Web Connection

Visit www.slam.org for more information about the Saint Louis Museum of Art.

86 UNIT 2 • Color and Texture

Lesson 6 Tactile Texture

Look at the two headpieces on these pages. *King's Crown* is an image of a headpiece worn during a ceremony to celebrate a new king. The long beads are not to keep people from looking at the new chief, but to partially block the chief's view so that he is forced to look within himself. This keeps him from being distracted by what is going on around him during the time of this ceremony. *Coming of Age Hat* was also created for the purpose of ceremony. It is given to a boy when he turns twelve. It represents leaving childhood and becoming a young adult. The objects attached all have personal meaning for the young boy who receives the hat. If you look closely at the circle in the center of the brim you will see an embroidered image of the boy who owned this hat. Both of these headpieces are made of a variety of textured materials and objects.

◀ **Artist unknown.** (Yoruba). *King's Crown*. c. 1930.
Bamboo framework, beads, cloth, leather. 12-inch diameter (30.48 cm.). Saint Louis Museum of Art, Saint Louis, Missouri.

Art History and Culture

Did you know that the origin of hats can be traced back to primitive humans?

86 Unit 2 • Lesson 6

Art History and Culture

King's Crown

King's Crown (c. 1930) is from West Africa and was made by an artist of the Yoruba people. This object is called an *adenla,* which is a ceremonial headdress used for rites of passage. This object is worn only by royalty. The top of the headpiece has a birdlike figure on it. Many of the adenla are decorated with woodpeckers, which is symbolic of the "pecking order" in the Yoruban culture. The long-beaded fringe is used to shield the face of the new king. This is not done to hide his face from spectators, but to shield distractions so that he can look inward.

See pages 24–25 and 16–21 for more about art history and the subject matter.

Artist Profiles, p. 79

Artist Profile

King's Crown

This crown was made by an unknown artist of the Yoruban culture of west Africa. Yoruba-speaking people are among the most numerous in Africa, with an estimated population of more than 25 million today. They live in Benin and Nigeria. Yoruban artisans are experts at creating pottery and in weaving, beadworking, and metalsmithing.

◀ **Artist unknown.** (Yoruba). *King's Crown*. c. 1930.
Bamboo framework, beads, cloth, leather.

Study how tactile texture is used in these three-dimensional forms.

- Where do you see a face? Describe the materials used.
- Look closely at both headpieces. List the objects that are rough, smooth, matte, or shiny.
- List the materials used by both artists.

▲ **Artist unknown.** (Chinese). *Coming of Age Hat.* Twentieth century.
Mixed media, embroidery. 12 × 15 inches (30.48 × 38.1 cm.). Private Collection.

Aesthetic Perception

Design Awareness Think about hats that you or someone you know may have worn to celebrate an event. What were they like? Can you think of any cultures today that use headpieces for ceremonies or celebrations?

Unit 2 • Lesson 6   **87**

Art History and Culture

Coming of Age Hat

Coming of Age Hat (twentieth century) Many cultures celebrate the time of puberty as the "coming of age." This is the time when children pass from childhood to adulthood, learning to accept the responsibilities that adults face. *Coming of Age Hat* was made in China and is part of the tradition of wearing a hat to mark the transition into adulthood. The hat contains a detailed embroidered image of the young boy for whom it was made. Good-luck charms and wishes are attached to the brim and top of the hat. In China, a coming of age hat is made individually for each boy. Girls in China have rites of passage that are different.

See pages 24–25 and 16–21 for more about art history and the subject matter.

Artist Profiles, p. 74

Coming of Age Hat

This hat was made in China sometime during the twentieth century. The identity of the artist or artists who designed, sewed, and skillfully embroidered this spectacular hat is not known, but it is a typical example of the Coming-of-Age hats created in the twentieth century.

▲ **Artist unknown.** (Chinese). *Coming of Age Hat.* Twentieth century.
Mixed media, embroidery. 12 × 15 inches (30.48 × 38.1 cm.). Private Collection.

Study

▶ *Coming of Age Hat:* In the circle on the brim of the headpiece is a portrait of a boy. It looks smooth, but it was embroidered, most likely with silk. There are also small dolls on either side of the portrait that have faces. They are made of cloth. *King's Crown:* There are six masklike faces that are made from beads.

▶ *Coming of Age Hat:* Rough: raised areas on the top; the red and green areas; the beads hanging on either side of the hat. Smooth: dark blue area of the brim; golden forms on either side of the hat. Matte: the dark vertical rows of material. Shiny: the golden fabric and tassels. *King's Crown:* Rough: the beaded strands hanging from the brim. Smooth: the strips around the brim. Matte: small dark-blue area at the base. Shiny: the beadwork.

▶ *Coming of Age Hat:* Mixed media, embroidery, fabric, beads; *King's Crown:* Bamboo framework, beads, cloth, and leather.

■ For more examples of Asian art, see the *Art Around the World Collection.*

Art Journal: Writing

Have students describe different types of textures in the Concepts section of their Art Journals. What else do students want to know about using texture in three-dimensional objects?

Aesthetic Perception

Design Awareness Headdresses, or headpieces, are a part of different rituals and ceremonies in many cultures. A bride often wears a veil when getting married, and some children wear birthday hats or crowns.

Developing Visual Literacy Discuss what each headdress represents. Do the students notice any similarities? What items did the artist use to communicate its function?
NSAE 4.a; 4.b; 4.c

Web Connection

Visit www.textilesocietyofhk.org/aboutus.asp for more information about Chinese textiles. This Web site is for teachers use only.

LESSON 6 • Tactile Texture **87**

Teach

Time: About 45 minutes

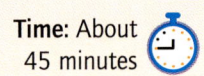

"How do you think you may be able to use real or tactile textures in an artwork?"

"¿Cómo creen que podrían usar la textura verdadera o la táctil en una obra de arte?"

- Read and discuss tactile textures on page 88.

Practice

Materials: pencils and erasers, 9" × 12" construction paper, scissors, magazines, glue

Alternate Materials: copier paper

- Distribute the materials and have students follow the directions on page 88.

Creative Expression

Materials: pencils, erasers, scissors, needles, thread, embroidery floss, wire, glue, scrap material, paper towels, newspaper, fabric, student- and teacher-collected objects

Alternate Materials: 12" × 18" construction paper, glue, stapler, staples, markers and/or crayons, fabric scraps, ribbon, yarn

- Distribute the materials and have students follow the directions on page 89.
- Students should express a variety of ideas based on their personal experiences.
  NSAE 1.a; 1.b
- Have students demonstrate their technical skills using a variety of art media and materials to incorporate photographic imagery into their headpieces.
- Review the Activity Tips on page 235 for visual examples of techniques, if needed.

Art Journal: Planning

Ask students to select an event or celebration and to write it in the Ideas section of their Art Journals. On the same page, have them create a list of items that could represent that event.

88 UNIT 2 • Color and Texture

Using Tactile Texture

Tactile textures, or actual textures, are textures you can touch and feel. When light reflects off a surface, it displays a pattern of light and dark values. From this pattern we can make a judgment about the texture of a surface or object, even if we cannot touch it.

There are four basic types of texture: rough, smooth, shiny, and matte. Sometimes these textures are combined, such as shiny-smooth or matte-smooth.

Rough-textured surfaces reflect light unevenly. They show irregular patterns of light and dark.

Smooth-textured surfaces reflect light evenly. They have no dents and so no patterns of light or shadows appear.

Shiny-textured surfaces reflect bright light. They have highlights and sometimes reflect bright sunlight that makes you squint your eyes.

Matte-textured surfaces reflect light that is soft, with an almost dull look.

Artists often use a variety of tactile textures when creating three-dimensional forms. They sometimes combine more than one material or medium, such as beads, fabric, wood, and metal. This type of art, in which an art object is created from an assortment of media, is called **mixed-media.**

Practice

Look in magazines for images of the four textures: smooth, rough, shiny, and matte.

1. Fold a sheet of paper into four sections.
2. Label each section with one of the four textures.
3. Look through a magazine for examples of each texture and cut them out. Glue each example in its proper box.

88 Unit 2 • Lesson 6

Differentiated Instruction

Reteach
Have students look around the classroom to find examples of actual textures. See if they can find an example of a smooth, rough, shiny, and matte texture.

Special Needs
Use this activity as an opportunity to foster self-esteem in students with disabilities. Have students identify and discuss things about themselves that they are proud of, and help them choose items that convey these ideas.

ELL
Show students an object that is considered mixed-media. Have them identify the different media and describe how the objects feel.

◀ Paden Janney.
Age 10.

Think about how this student artist used tactile textures in the celebratory hat.

Creative Expression

Create a mixed-media celebratory hat using tactile textures.

1. Look over your ideas in your Art Journal. Bring in an old hat to decorate, or make a headpiece from decorated paper. Place collected textured items in a central location to be shared. Keep your personal objects in a separate envelope or bag.
2. Begin by decorating your hat with various real textures, such as beads, ribbon, lace, and fabric. Overlap some of the material, and use thread, yarn, and glue to attach it to your hat base.
3. Next think about how your personal objects will be arranged to convey the theme of your chosen event or memory. Use thread, yarn, and glue to attach your items to your hat.

Art Criticism

Describe How did you create your hat? What objects did you add?

Analyze Describe the different textures you used in your celebratory hat.

Interpret What event or memory does your hat represent?

Decide Do you feel you successfully used tactile textures in your celebratory hat? Explain why or why not.

Unit 2 • Lesson 6   **89**

Art Across the Curriculum

Use these simple ideas to reinforce art concepts across the curriculum.

★ **Descriptive Writing** Have students write a description of an object with a rough or smooth texture, but tell them they cannot use the name of the object in the description.

★ **Math** Have students convert the size of one of the hats to millimeters.

★ **Science** Have students give examples of rocks with different textures.

★ **Social Studies** Ask students if they are familiar with any traditions from China or Africa.

★ **Technology** Using a word processing program, have students create an advertisement for a hat company featuring clip art that includes a hat. Visit **SRAonline.com** to print detailed instructions for this activity.
NSAE 6.b

Reflect
Time: About 5 minutes

Review and Assess
"Describe how tactile textures were used by the artists in their headpieces." "Describan cómo los artistas usaron las texturas táctiles en sus prendas para la cabeza."

Think
The artist used construction paper for the majority of the hat, which has a matte surface. The garland is soft to the touch, but looks like it would feel rough.

■ Use **Large Prints 75** *Ermine Skin Shirt* and **76** *Violet Persian Set with Red Lip Wraps* to have students identify how textures are used.

Informal Assessment

■ Have students describe in detail a variety of practical applications for their design ideas.

■ Have students evaluate their portfolios. Have them exchange their portfolios with classmates so they can form conclusions about historical and cultural contexts.
NSAE 4.b; 4.c

■ For standardized-format test practice using this lesson's art content, see pages 28–29 in **Reading and Writing Test Preparation**.

Art Journal: Critical Thinking
Have students answer the four art criticism questions—Describe, Analyze, Interpret, and Decide—in their Art Journals. Lead a class discussion on the variety of textures used by students.

LESSON 6 • Tactile Texture **89**

Lesson 6 Wrap-Up: Tactile Texture

Extra! For the Art Specialist
Time: About 45 minutes

Focus
As a class, study **Large Print 75** *Ermine Skin Shirt* and discuss how the artist used tactile textures. On the board, list the real or tactile textures used, and have students describe them.

Teach
Have students begin by collecting a variety of textural materials. Explain to the students that they will create a wall hanging. The wall hangings will be based on an approved image. Once the images have been approved, have students complete the Alternate Activity.

Reflect
Have students use the four steps of art criticism to evaluate their work. Did they effectively combine a variety of tactile textures in their wall hangings? What images did they choose to reproduce?

Alternate Activity

Materials:
- various fabrics in a variety of textures
- dowel, three inches longer than the width of the background fabric
- needles, thread, embroidery floss
- craft glue, hot-glue gun, glue sticks (for teacher use)

1. Have students create a simple sketch of the selected image as a guide.
2. Designate a size for the wall hangings, and have students select and cut the background material three inches longer. Have students fold over the top three inches and sew or glue it in place to create a sleeve.
3. Have students begin reproducing their drawing using a variety of textural materials. The materials can be glued down or sewn in place. Embroidery techniques can be used to embellish the images.
4. Students can slide a dowel rod through the sleeve for hanging.

Research in Art Education
"The general goal of art criticism is to try to understand mankind and the human condition. But beyond that, it seeks to discover and communicate the 'meaning' of art— usually of modern or contemporary art because it can be examined in the context of the present." (Risatti, H. "Art Criticism in Discipline-Based Art Education." *Journal of Aesthetic Education* 21, 1987.)

Assessment
Use the following rubric to evaluate the artwork students make in the Creative Expression activity and to assess students' understanding of how tactile textures are used in three-dimensional forms.

	Art History and Culture	Aesthetic Perception	Creative Expression	Art Criticism
3 POINTS	The student demonstrates knowledge of African and Chinese headpieces.	The student accurately identifies the use of tactile textures in three-dimensional forms.	The student's celebratory hat clearly demonstrates use of tactile texture.	The student thoughtfully and honestly evaluates own work using the four steps of art criticism.
2 POINTS	The student's knowledge of African and Chinese headpieces is weak or incomplete.	The student shows an emerging awareness of tactile textures in three-dimensional forms, but cannot consistently identify them.	The student's celebratory hat shows some awareness of tactile texture.	The student attempts to evaluate own work but shows an incomplete understanding of evaluation criteria.
1 POINT	The student cannot demonstrate knowledge of African or Chinese headpieces.	The student cannot identify how tactile texture is used in three-dimensional forms.	The student's celebratory hat shows no understanding of how to create tactile texture.	The student makes no attempt to evaluate own work.

Have students complete page 31 or 32 in their *Assessment* books.

Unit 2 Vocabulary Review

analogous colors—colors that are side by side on the color wheel and have a common hue **colores análogos**—colores lado a lado en la rueda de color y tengan un matiz común

blending—a gradual change from light to dark or dark to light **mezclado**—un cambio gradual de colores claros a oscuros u oscuros a claros

color scheme—a plan for organizing the colors used in an artwork **esquema del color**—un plan para organizar los colores usado en obra de arte

color spectrum—the effect that occurs when light passes through a prism and separates into a band of colors in the order of red, orange, yellow, green, blue and violet **espectro del color**—el efecto que ocurre cuando la luz en una banda de colores en el orden de rojo, anaranjado, amarillo, verde, azúl, y violeta

color wheel—shows the spectrum bent into a circle **rueda de color**—demuestra el espectro doblado en un círculo

complementary colors—colors that are opposite each other on the color wheel **colores complementarios**—colores que son opuesto a cada uno en la rueda de color

cross-hatching—when sets of parallel lines cross or intersect **sombreado con rayas entrecruzadas**—cuando un grupo de líneas paralelas se cruzan

hatching—a series of parallel lines **sombreado con rayas**—serie de líneas paralelas

hue—another name for color **matiz**—otro nombre para color

intensity—the brightness or dullness of a color **intensidad**—la brillantez o matidez de un color

intermediate colors—yellow-green, red-orange, blue-green; made by combining a primary color with either of the secondary colors that are adjacent on the color wheel **colores intermedios**—amarillo-verde, rojo-anaranjado, azúl-verde; hecho combinando un primario, con cualquier color que está al lado de la rueda de color

neutral colors—black, white, and gray give hues a range of values **colores neutros**—negro, blanco, y gris dan un rango de valores a matices

primary hues—red, yellow, and blue used to mix the other hues on the color wheel **matices primarios**—rojo, amarillo, y azul se usan para mezclar los otros matices en el círculo cromático

secondary hues—orange, green and violet the result of mixing two primary hues **matices secundarios**—anaranjado, verde, y violeta el resultado de mezclar dos matices primarios

shade—any hue blended with black **tono**—cualquier matiz mezclado con negro

stippling—uses dots to show value **punteado**—usa puntos para demostrar valor

tactile texture—or actual texture, texture that can be felt **textura táctil**—o textura actual, textura que se puede sentir

texture—the art element that refers to the way something feels **textura**—el elemento de arte que refiere como algo se siente

tint—any hue blended with white **tinte**—cualquier matiz mezclado con blanco

value—the lightness or darkness of a hue **valor**—la brillantez u oscuridad de un matiz

visual texture—or simulated texture, imitates real texture **textura visual**—una textura simulada, imita textura verdadera

Vocabulary Practice

T Display *Transparency 38* to review unit vocabulary words.

Compare and Contrast ⭐ Vocabulary
Have students compare and contrast the unit vocabulary words. Ask students which words are related.

Analogies ⭐ Vocabulary
Have volunteers select a vocabulary word, such as *shade*, and create an analogy. Repeat for other unit vocabulary words.

Phonetic Spellings ⭐ Vocabulary
Have students locate the phonetic spelling for the word *value*. Repeat the process for other unit vocabulary words.

Wrapping Up Unit 2
Color and Texture

Art Criticism

Critical Thinking Art criticism is an organized system for looking at and talking about art. You can criticize art without being an expert. The purpose of art criticism is to get the viewer involved in a perception process that delays judgment until all aspects of the artwork have been studied.

- See pages 28–29 for more about art criticism.

Describe

▶ There is a woman sitting in a chair holding a child on her lap. The child is resting on her shoulder, gently touching the woman's face with one hand. The woman is wearing a long, peach-colored dress covered with a pink and light-blue flower design. Her eyes are looking down at the child. The child has blond hair and dark eyes that are staring into the distance. The child is wearing a short-sleeved white outfit.

▶ There is an open window with wooden shutters. There is a painted wall, possibly made of wood.

Analyze

▶ The primary hues: light red on the dress; blue on the dress, the pitcher and basin, in the shadow of the child's outfit, and the cloth behind the child; yellow in the child's hair, the background, and the shutters

▶ The lightest values are on the child's outfit and the spot on the pitcher behind the woman's head. The darkest values are the bottom of the dress, the areas behind the child's feet and behind the child's raised arm, and in the window at the top of the painting.

▶ The textures around the heads are painted in a realistic manner. Below the heads, the tactile texture of the brushstrokes of paint take over.

Wrapping Up Unit 2
Color and Texture

▲ **Mary Cassatt.** (American). *Mother and Child.* c. 1890.
Oil on canvas. $35\frac{3}{8} \times 25\frac{3}{8}$ inches (89.87 × 64.47 cm.). Wichita Museum, Wichita, Kansas.

Art History and Culture

Mary Cassatt

Mary Cassatt (mâr´ ē kə sat´) (1845–1926) was an American who worked in Paris with the French impressionists. She created prints based on one theme: the relationship between mother and child. Cassatt had no children of her own. She presented the mother and child in everyday settings without making them look sentimental. Her mothers protectively embrace their children. The children sit comfortably on their mothers' laps, hands gently touching. They express a sense of belonging together. During her career, Cassatt produced 225 prints, 300 oil paintings, 400 pastels, and many watercolors and drawings.

See pages 24–25 and 16–21 for more about art history and the subject matter.

Artist Profiles, p. 15

Artist Profile

Mary Cassatt
1845–1926

Mary Cassatt (mer´ ē kə sat´) was born into an upper middle-class family in western Pennsylvania in 1844. She was enrolled at the Pennsylvania Academy of the Fine Arts from 1861 to 1865. She later studied in Paris, France, in the studios of Gérôme and Couture. In 1874, she settled permanently in Paris, where she regularly submitted work to the yearly Salon exhibitions. The painter and sculptor Edgar Degas saw her work at the Salon and invited Cassatt to join the Impressionists in 1877. She was the only American ever to exhibit in the group's shows. During her lifetime, Cassatt's work was more popular in Europe than in the United States. In her spare time, she loved to entertain friends and ride her

Art Criticism Critical Thinking

Describe What do you see?
During this step you will collect information about the subject of the work.
- List and describe the people, their posture, and their clothing.
- Describe what you see in the background.

Analyze How is this work organized?
Think about how the artist used the elements and principles of art.
- Which hues do you see? Where are they?
- Where are the darkest values? Where are the lightest values?
- Where do you see realistic visual texture? Where do you see tactile texture?

Interpret What is the artist trying to say?
Combine clues you collected during description and analysis with your personal experiences to find out what this painting is about.
- What does this work tell you about the relationship between the woman and the child?
- What do the clothing and background tell you about the time this was painted?
- What emotion does this work convey?

Decide What do you think about the work?
Use all the information you have gathered to decide why this is a successful work of art.
- Is this painting successful because it is realistic, well organized, and conveys a message? Explain.

Unit 2   **91**

Interpret

- Answers will vary. Some students may see the tenderness between the woman and child and guess that they are mother and child.
- Responses will vary. Some students might say this was painted a long time ago because of the clothing the people are wearing, and because the pitcher and washbasin place this prior to indoor plumbing.
- Answers will vary. Most students will say "love."

Decide

- Students' answers will vary based on individual experiences. They may use more than one aesthetic theory to explain the success of this work. There is no one correct answer, but make sure that students' explanations are reasonable.

Art Journal: Writing
Have students write answers to the Aesthetic Perception questions in their Art Journals. Have them discuss their answers in small groups.

Aesthetic Perception

Critical Thinking Ask students to describe common everyday activities they share with their families. Does *Mother and Child* remind them of their own families?

Describe
- List and describe common everyday activities that you share with your family.

Analyze
- What colors do you associate with these activities?
- Can the colors change depending on the day?

Interpret
- How do the activities make you feel? Why?

Decide
- Do you have strong feelings when you think about your family?

UNIT 2 • Color and Texture   **91**

"Artists use color and texture to create both two- and three-dimensional artwork." "Los artistas usan el color y la textura para crear obras de arte bidimensionales y tridimensionales."

T Review unit vocabulary with students using **Transparency 38**.

Art Journal: Writing
Have students answer the questions on page 92 in their Art Journals or on a separate sheet of paper. **Answers: 1. C, 2. A, 3. B, 4. C, 5. A**

T For further assessment, have students complete the unit test on **Transparency 44**.

VISIT A MUSEUM
The Whitney Museum
▶ In addition to Mrs. Whitney's donations, the museum's holdings have been greatly enriched through the generous gifts of other major collectors. Today, the Whitney holds the world's largest collection of Edward Hopper's art and has the largest body of work by Alexander Calder in any museum, which includes *Calder's Circus*.

"To make a great collection it is necessary to have the modern note in it, and to be a great painter, you must be classic as well as modern."

—Mary Cassatt

92 UNIT 2 • Color and Texture

Wrapping Up Unit 2
Color and Texture, continued

Show What You Know
Answer these questions on a separate sheet of paper.

1. _____ is the brightness or dullness of a color.
   A. Tint
   B. Stippling
   C. Intensity

2. _____ refers to how things feel, or how they look as they might feel, if touched.
   A. Texture
   B. Hue
   C. Color wheel

3. Red, blue, and yellow are _____.
   A. intermediate colors
   B. primary colors
   C. secondary colors

4. _____ refers to the darkness and lightness of a hue.
   A. Shade
   B. Hatching
   C. Value

5. A _____ is a plan for organizing the colors used in an artwork.
   A. color scheme
   B. visual texture
   C. neutral color

92 Unit 2

VISIT A MUSEUM
The Whitney Museum

The Whitney Museum in New York, New York, is home to one of the world's best collections of twentieth-century American art. The permanent collection at the Whitney contains about 12,000 works, including paintings, sculptures, prints, drawings, and photographs. The museum was founded in 1931 with 700 pieces, many of them from the personal collection of founder Gertrude Vanderbilt Whitney. Today, the Whitney has works of art by nearly 2,000 artists and holds the world's largest collection of works by Edward Hopper, Alexander Calder, and Reginald Marsh. The museum also has major holdings by Marsden Hartley, Georgia O'Keeffe, Charles Burchfield, Gaston Lachaise, Louise Nevelson, and Agnes Martin.

Unit Assessment Options

Aesthetic Perception
Practice Have students select one of the concepts in the Show What You Know section on page 92, and then have them find examples of each concept in the classroom.

Creative Expression
Student Portfolio Have students review all the artwork they have created during this unit and select the pieces they want to keep in their portfolios.

Art Criticism
Activity Have students select an artwork from this unit and study it using the four steps of art criticism. (See pages 28–29 for more information about art criticism.) Have students work alone or in pairs and present their findings aloud or in writing.

Color and Texture in Dance

"Sarve Kashmir" is a joyous Persian dance. The dancer's jewelry add rhythmic texture to the music. The intense colors and shiny texture of the costumes are similar to those found in the deserts of Northern Africa. The women wear open veils over their heads to shield them from the hot sun.

What to Do Create a musical hand-rattle from simple found materials.

1. Collect bottle caps (about ten per person). Make a hole in the center of each one that is larger than the width of an unsharpened pencil.
2. Thread two, back to back bottle caps, onto a stick until you have five sets. After they are on the stick, bind each end of the stick. Leave enough space for them to rattle against each other. You need enough room for the caps to move up and down so they can make noise. Make sure you leave enough room on one end to hold it as you shake.
3. Use masking tape or raffia to bind the end or glue a large wooden bead on each end. Decorate your hand rattle with pieces of colored raffia or other decorative material.
4. Put on a lively piece of music and use your rattle to emphasize the basic beat or create a rhythm pattern that works well musically.

▲ Djanbazian Dance Company. "Sarve Kashmir."

Art Criticism

Describe Can you describe the texture of the rattle sounds?

Analyze Explain how the sharp, percussive sounds of the music could be shown visually using texture and color.

Interpret Is there a variety in the pitch of the sounds of different instruments or do they all sound the same? How could this be used with dance?

Decide Decide whether you were successful making a musical rattle.

Unit 2   93

Art History and Culture

Persian Dance

Persia (known today as Iran) was an ancient culture with unique customs and a rich cultural heritage. "Sarve Kashmir" is a dance with quick, percussive gestures done by the hands, shoulders, and feet, producing sounds from the women's jewelry. It is choreographed in the style of dances found in the deserts of Northern Africa. Anna Djanbazian is the daughter of a Persian mother and an Armenian father. She earned a degree in classical ballet and Armenian folk dance in Russia. Although she returned to Iran, she and her family left because of the 1979 Iranian Revolution. She moved to Southern California, studied modern dance at UCLA, and then formed her own company.

Color and Texture in Dance

Objective: To create a musical hand rattle from everyday materials

Materials: "Sarve Kashmir," performed by the Anna Djanbazian Dance Company. Running time: 3:38

Focus
Time: About 5 minutes

- Discuss the information on page 93.

Art History and Culture

- Have students think of instruments that dancers from different cultures might use to add sounds to their movement.

Teach
Time: About 20 minutes

Aesthetic Perception

- Have students observe people. Have them notice the different types of gestures people have.

Creative Expression

- Help students create holes in the bottle caps. You may need to use a nail and hammer. Provide various selections of music so students visualize different textures and colors.

- **Informal Assessment** Comment positively on students' rattles. Encourage them if they have a difficult time emphasizing the beat.

Reflect
Time: About 10 minutes

Art Criticism

- Have students answer the four art criticism questions on page 93 aloud or in writing.
- Did students successfully make a hand rattle that could make musical sounds that could accompany dance?

UNIT 2 • Color and Texture   93

Unit 3 Planning Guide

	Lesson Title	Suggested Pacing	Creative Expression Activity
Lesson 1	Motif and Pattern	1 hour	Design a costume.
Lesson 2	Two-Dimensional Pattern	1 hour	Create a non-objective design.
Lesson 3	Three-Dimensional Pattern	1 hour	Make an animal sculpture.
Lesson 4	Rhythm	1 hour	Create rhythm in a non-objective design.
Lesson 5	Visual Movement	1 hour	Create a jungle painting.
Lesson 6	Kinetic Movement	1 hour	Create a moving mobile.
ARTSOURCE	Pattern, Rhythm, and Movement in Dance	35 minutes	Create rhythmic patterns using movement.

94A UNIT 3 • Rhythm, Movement, and Pattern

Materials	Program Resources	Fine Art Resources	Literature Resources
pencils, white paper, fine-line permanent black marker, color pencils, color markers	*Assessment,* pp. 33–34 *Reading and Writing Test Preparation,* pp. 30–31 *Home and After-School Connections*	*Transparency 13* *Artist Profiles,* pp. 76, 78 *Large Prints 77* and *78* *Art Around the World Collection*	*Nzingha: Warrior Queen of Matamba* by Patricia McKissack
pencils, white paper, color pencils, color markers	*Assessment,* pp. 35–36 *Reading and Writing Test Preparation,* pp. 32–33	*Transparency 14* *Artist Profiles,* pp. 25, 30 *Large Prints 77* and *78* *Art Around the World Collection*	*Where the Sidewalk Ends* by Shel Silverstein
self-hardening clay, acrylic paints, paper plates to mix colors, paintbrushes, paper towels, newspaper	*Assessment,* pp. 37–38 *Reading and Writing Test Preparation,* pp. 34–35	*Transparency 15* *Artist Profiles,* pp. 9, 71 *Large Prints 77* and *78* *Art Around the World Collection*	*Dave at Night* by Gail Carson Levine
pencils, erasers, white paper, felt-tipped black markers, color pencils	*Assessment,* pp. 39–40 *Reading and Writing Test Preparation,* pp. 36–37 *Flash Card* 18	*Transparency 16* *Artist Profiles,* pp. 39, 48 *Large Prints 77* and *78* *The National Museum of Women in the Arts Collection*	*Fair Weather* by Richard Peck
Art Journal, pencils, erasers, white paper, tempera paints, mixing trays, water containers, paintbrushes, paper towels, newspaper	*Assessment,* pp. 41–42 *Reading and Writing Test Preparation,* pp. 38–39 *Flash Cards* 6, 9	*Transparency 17* *Artist Profiles,* pp. 16, 54 *Large Prints 77* and *78* *The National Museum of Women in the Arts Collection*	*Henri Rousseau* by Susanne Pfleger
Art Journal, pencils, erasers, scissors, string, hole punch, pliable wire, pliers, matboard, fine sandpaper, acrylic paints, paintbrushes, mixing trays, water containers, paper towels, newspaper	*Assessment,* pp. 43–44 *Reading and Writing Test Preparation,* pp. 40–41	*Transparency 18* *Artist Profiles,* pp. 14, 52 *Large Prints 77* and *78* *The National Museum of Women in the Arts Collection*	*Call It Courage* by Armstrong Sperry
Isicathulo			

UNIT 3 • Rhythm, Movement, and Pattern

Unit Overview

3 Rhythm, Movement, and Pattern

Lesson 1: Pattern is a repeated surface decoration. **Motif** is a unit that is made of objects or art elements and is repeated.

Lesson 2: There are three types of pattern: random, alternating, and regular.

Lesson 3: Three-dimensional pattern has depth and is formed on the surface of a form.

Lesson 4: Rhythm is the principle of design that organizes the elements in a work of art by repeating elements and/or objects.

Lesson 5: Movement is the principle of art that leads a viewer's eyes throughout a work of art.

Lesson 6: Kinetic movement is actual or real movement.

Introduce Unit Concepts

"Artists use the art principles of pattern, rhythm, and movement to organize the art elements in works of art." "Los artistas usan el principio de patrón, ritmo y movimiento para organizar los elementos artísticos en obras de arte."

Pattern
- Ask the class to create a list of patterns that they see. These can be patterns in their clothing, patterns in architectural forms, or patterns in nature.

Rhythm and Movement
- Explain that rhythm is created by repeated positive shapes, separated by negative spaces.
- Think about the word *movement*. As a class, come up with a definition for the term *movement*. Write it on the board.

Cross-Curricular Projects
- See the *Language Arts and Reading, Mathematics, Science,* and *Social Studies Art Connections* books for activities that further develop rhythm, movement, and pattern concepts.

94 UNIT 3 • Rhythm, Movement, and Pattern

Unit 3

Rhythm, Movement, and Pattern

▲ **Max Weber.** (American). *Chinese Restaurant.* 1915.
Oil on canvas. 40 × 48 inches (101.6 × 121.92 cm.). Whitney Museum of American Art, New York, New York.

Artists use pattern, rhythm, and movement to arrange the art elements in all kinds of artwork.

American artist Max Weber was best known for introducing cubism and modern art to the United States. Cubism was developed by Pablo Picasso and Georges Braque. This style of art broke down three-dimensional objects into flat shapes which were arranged so that all sides could be seen at once. In *Chinese Restaurant,* Weber uses the elements of cubism. The top and side of the table can be seen at the same time.

94 Unit 3

Fine Art Prints

Display **Large Prints 77** *Jubilee: Ghana Harvest Festival* and **78** *The Horse Fair.* Refer to the prints throughout the unit as students learn about pattern, rhythm, and movement.

Large Print 77

Large Print 78

Artists use **pattern** in all types of artwork.
- What repeated lines and shapes do you see? Describe these lines.

Artists use **rhythm** in two-dimensional artwork to organize the art elements and objects.
- What art elements do you see repeated?
- Which element attracts your eye most: line, shape, or color? Explain.

Movement is used to move the viewer's eyes in an artwork by placing the art elements or objects in a certain order.
- Which elements or objects are pulling your eyes through the artwork?

In This Unit you will learn about how artists create and use pattern. Art elements and objects create a motif that, when repeated, create different types of patterns. You will also learn about rhythm, the illusion of movement, and movement that you actually can see.

Here are the topics you will study:
- Pattern
- Motif
- Random pattern
- Regular pattern
- Alternating pattern
- Three-dimensional pattern
- Rhythm
- Movement
- Visual movement
- Kinetic movement

Master Artist Profile

Max Weber
(1881–1961)

Max Weber was born in Bialystok, Russia, and came to the United States at the age of ten. In 1909 he went to Paris to study art. There he met Pablo Picasso, Georges Braque, Paul Cézanne, and Henri Matisse. The works of these artists all shaped Weber's style and influenced his subject matter. He worked in the style of cubism, breaking down objects into their basic shapes in the manner of Picasso and Braque. Weber used bright colors in his work, like Matisse, and created space through overlapping of shapes, like Cézanne. After 1920 Weber developed a more realistic style.

Unit 3   95

Art History and Culture

Max Weber

Max Weber (maks weˊbər) (Russian/Ukranian, 1881–1961) was born in Bialystok, Russia, and came to the United States at the age of ten. He was one of the first Americans to bring modernism to the United States, and he introduced the style of cubism. Though critics did not like this approach, many artists were excited by it. After 1920 Weber developed a more realistic style. Throughout his artistic career he was influenced by Henri Matisse and his use of color, Paul Cézanne's use of space, and Pablo Picasso's cubist style.

See pages 24–25 and 16–21 for more about art history and subject matter.

Artist Profiles, p. 67

Examine the Artwork

"Let's closely examine this painting by Max Weber." "Vamos a mirar detalladamente a esta pintura de Max Weber."

- Have students study the painting *Chinese Restaurant* by Max Weber. Ask them to describe what they see.
- Have students answer the questions about pattern, rhythm, and movement on page 95.
  - Students answers may include the following: Lines: The straight lines are repeated in the top right as vertical green lines that turn to pink; horizontal blue lines that move from long to short. Shapes: Squares are repeated in a checkerboard; rectangles are repeated vertically in the upper right; half circles are repeated in a row forming a scalloped edge; two begin in a regular order but then change direction.
  - Line, shape, and color.
  - This answer may vary, but students may say shapes. The repeated checkerboard pattern takes up a large area of the canvas, and the black and tan contrast of color attracts the eye. Some students may say color, particularly the white, which jumps out at the viewer.
  - The white angle leads the eye to the black angle, to the repeated vertical zigzag lines, up into the overlapping shapes and fragments of faces to the upper dark areas, back through the large white shape, and down the black angle again.

Unit Pretest

Display **Transparency 45** as a pretest. Have students write their answers on a separate piece of paper.
Answers: 1. A, 2. A, 3. B, 4. C, 5. B

Home Connection

- See *Home and After-School Connections* for family newsletters and activities for this unit.

UNIT 3 • Rhythm, Movement, and Pattern   95

Unit 3 Arts Integration

ILLUSTRATOR PROFILE
Faith Ringgold
(1930–)

Faith Ringgold is best known for her painted story quilts that combine painting, quilted fabric, and storytelling. Her mother taught her to sew fabrics and her great-great-grandmother taught her to make quilts. Ringgold and her mother began to sew fabric borders around her paintings, instead of stretching the canvas over wooden stretchers. In time, she and her mother produced a quilt together which contained thirty portraits of Harlem residents. When her mother died, Ringgold decided to continue the family tradition of storytelling and history through writing.

She began to write stories for children, like *Tar Beach,* which told the story of when her family ate and played cards on the roof on hot evenings in Harlem. She first told this story in a quilt/painting in 1988, and a publisher saw it and suggested that she tell the story in a book. This was her first of many children's books. Her stories of fictional heroines encourage children to "take flight" and follow their dreams. They are often painted in a folk style with no indications of perspective.

Ringgold has a motto on her website: "If One Can Anyone Can, All You Gotta Do Is Try." Her work deals with serious issues in society, but the final analysis is connected to following personal dreams and overcoming all obstacles, with a soaring and unstoppable spirit.

Throughout Unit 3, share Ringgold's illustrations with the class and discuss her use of rhythm, movement, and pattern. What kind of objects have patterns on them? Where are there examples of rhythm? Where and how does Ringgold create visual movement?

Music
Rhythm in music comes from the pattern of strong and weak beats, and shorter and longer note values over a steady pulse. A pattern is created when a rhythm is repeated. Quick, fast sounds in a rhythm pattern give a feeling of movement.

Literature
Show the video *The Girl Who Loved Wild Horses* to introduce the concepts of rhythm, movement, and pattern. Pause the video and have students describe different patterns and rhythms they see.

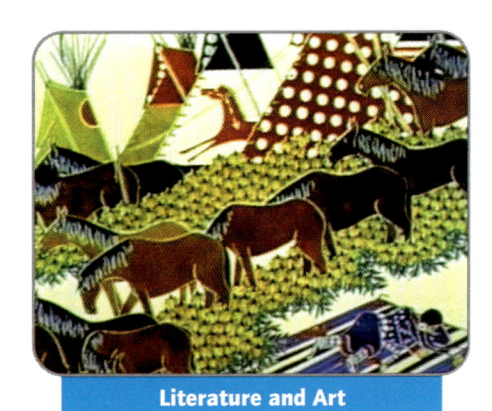

Literature and Art

Performing Arts
Show *Isicathulo*. Have students watch the rhythm of the dancers.

Artsource®

95A UNIT 3 • Rhythm, Movement, and Pattern

Lesson 1 Overview

Motif and Pattern

Lesson 1 introduces the art principle of pattern and the concept of motif. **Pattern** is a repeated surface decoration. **Motif** is a unit that is made of objects or art elements that is repeated. Motif and pattern work together.

Objectives

Art History and Culture
To demonstrate knowledge of the Kwakwaka'wakw and the Yoruba

Creative Expression
To use two or more motifs to create patterns for a costume design for an event

Aesthetic Perception
To identify the use of motif and pattern as surface design in two- and three-dimensional works of art

Art Criticism
To evaluate their own work using the four steps of art criticism

Lesson Materials
- pencils, erasers
- Art Journal
- 9" × 12" drawing paper
- 12" × 18" heavy white drawing paper
- fine-tipped permanent black marker
- color pencils, color markers

Alternate Materials:
- copier paper
- white construction paper
- crayons

Program Resources
- *Reading and Writing Test Prep.,* pp. 30–31
- *Transparency 13*
- *Artist Profiles,* pp. 76, 78
- *Animals Through History Time Line*
- *Assessment,* pp. 33–34
- *Large Prints 77 Jubilee: Ghana Harvest Festival* and *78 The Horse Fair*
- *Art Around the World Collection*

Concept Trace
Motif/Pattern
Introduced: Level 5, Unit 3, Lesson 5
Reinforced: Level 7, Chapter 3, Lesson 5

Vocabulary

Review the following vocabulary words with students before beginning the lesson.

motif *motivo*—a unit that is made of objects or art elements that is repeated

pattern *patrón*—a repeated surface decoration

See page 119B for additional vocabulary and Spanish vocabulary resources.

Art Journal: Vocabulary
Have students add these words to the Vocabulary section of their Art Journals.

Lesson 1 Arts Integration

Theatre
Complete Unit 3, Lesson 1, on pages 54–55 of *Theatre Arts Connections.*

Theatre Arts Connections, p. 54

Music
Keeping a steady pulse, have students clap the rhythm to the lyrics "the power of the dream" from the song "The Power of the Dream" as sung by Celine Dion. This short pattern has what is called an upbeat in music because the strong pulse does not fall on the first word, but the second word. Have students listen to the song and find the strong pulse in the words and in the instruments.

Movement & Dance
In small groups, have students create a visual pattern using levels (high, medium, and low). Have them create four different patterns that can be repeated using a free-form shape. Possible patterns could be high, middle, high, low or low, low, middle, high.

LESSON 1 • Motif and Pattern **95B**

Focus

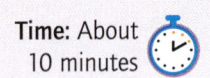

Time: About 10 minutes

Activate Prior Knowledge

"Have you seen a mask or costume from a different culture before?" "¿Han visto una máscara o vestuario de una cultura diferente?"

- As a class, discuss the student responses. Explain that in many cultures the traditions of ceremonial dance are still used to honor ancestors, tell a story, or celebrate an event. Explain that the patterns are often those that have been passed down though the years.

Using Literature ⭐ Reading

- Look at the cover illustration of *Nzingha: Warrior Queen of Matamba* by Patricia McKissack. Discuss the patterns used in the border around the cover illustration.

Thematic Connection ⭐ Social Studies

- **Costumes:** Have students describe different opportunities for someone to wear a costume. Answers should include holidays, plays, and parties.

Introduce the Art

Look

"Look closely at how repeated lines, shapes, and colors are used in the works of art."

"Miren detalladamente como líneas repetidas, figuras, y colores son usados en obras de arte."

Geography ⭐ Social Studies

- Have students locate British Columbia, Canada on a map. This is where the Kwakwaka'wakw people live. Have students locate Nigeria and the Republic of Benin, and tell them that this is where the Yoruba people live.

Art History and Culture

The mask and the costume are from two different cultures. The Kwakwaka'wakw people are from Canada, and the Yoruba people live in western Africa.

Web Connection

Visit www.seattleartmuseum.org for more information about the Seattle Museum of Art.

96 UNIT 3 • Rhythm, Movement, and Pattern

Lesson 1: Motif and Pattern

Look at the two works of art on these pages. *Face Mask of Ḵumugwe'* was carved from wood and painted in the traditional colors of blue, white, red, and black. This mask was used in a day-long ceremony and worn by a dancer who represented the chief of the undersea creatures. *Egungun from Ogbomoso* is part of a costume used to honor ancestors during the egungun ("powers concealed") ceremony. Each costume is made of layers of cloth in a variety of colors, textures, and patterns. The fabric strips are attached to a wood panel that is balanced on top of the head. Each year the family member who wears the costume adds new strips of valuable cloth. Notice how the colors and shapes are repeated in both works of art.

▲ **Artist unknown.** (Kwakwaka'wakw). *Face Mask of Ḵumugwe'.* c. 1880.
Alder, red cedar bark, cloth, paint. 19¼ × 17 × 6 inches (48.9 × 43.18 × 15.24 cm.). Hauberg Collection, Seattle Museum of Art, Seattle, Washington.

Art History and Culture

Do you think that these costumes are from the same culture?

96 Unit 3 • Lesson 1

Art History and Culture

Face Mask of Ḵumugwe'

Face Mask of Ḵumugwe' (c. 1880) was carved from wood and painted in the traditional colors of blue, white, red, and black. The Kwakwaka'wakw are a tribe of The First Nations of the Northwest Coast of British Columbia, Canada. *Face Mask of Ḵumugwe'* was used in a potlatch, or ceremony, held by all Northwest Coast native groups. It once lasted several days but is now a day-long festival. Feasting, dancing, singing, and storytelling are all part of the potlatch. This mask was worn during the potlatch by a dancer who represented the chief of the undersea creatures.

See pages 24–25 and 16–21 for more about art history and subject matter.

Artist Profiles, p. 78

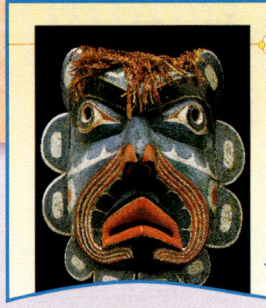

Artist Profile

Face Mask of 'Ḵumugwe'

This mask was carved and painted by an unknown artist of the Kwakwaka'wakw (or Kwakiutl, as they are also known) peoples of northwestern Canada. The term *Kwakiutl* is used to refer collectively to approximately 5,500 tribes of the Canadian First Nations, while *Kwakwaka'wakw* is used by the Kwakiutl people to describe themselves and their tribal affiliations with other members of the Kwakiutl.

◀ **Artist unknown** (Kwakwaka'wakw). (Canada). *Face Mask of 'Ḵumugwe'.* c. 1880.
Alder, red cedar bark, cloth, paint.

Study both pieces of art to discover more about how artists use motif and pattern.

- What colors, lines, and shapes do you recognize in both pieces of art?
- Which color, line, and shape are repeated most often in *Face Mask of Ḱumugwe'*?
- Look closely at *Egungun from Ogbomoso*. Describe any two strips of fabric that show repeated lines, shapes, and colors.

▲ **Artist unknown.** (Yoruba). *Egungun from Ogbomoso.* Twentieth century.

Cloth, wood, buttons. Approximately 60 inches (152.4 cm.). North Carolina Museum of Art, Raleigh, North Carolina.

Aesthetic Perception

Seeing Like an Artist We are surrounded by different patterns. Think about a tree or plant you have seen. What shape are the leaves? Are all the leaves on the tree or plant basically the same?

Unit 3 • Lesson 1   **97**

Study

- *Face Mask of Ḱumugwe'*: colors: red, blue, white, and black. Lines: straight and curved. Shapes: geometric such as ovals, circles, and half circles; free-form shapes such as the wavelike white shapes, curved shapes on the nose, and the repeated curved red shapes around the mouth. *Egungun Costume:* Colors: red, blue, white, and black. Lines: straight, curved, and zigzag. Shapes: geometric such as squares, triangles, rectangles, circles, and diamond; free-form shapes such as plants, flowers, and leaves.
- The color blue; the curved, rounded, squarelike blue shapes around the mouth and under the eyes.
- Student responses will vary, however, they may reply as follows. Motif: Any stripe can be described that repeats a color, line, and shape more than one time.

■ For more examples of art from Africa, see the *Art Around the World Collection.*

Art Journal: Writing

Have students describe what they know about motif and pattern in the Concepts section of their Art Journals. What else do they want to know about motif and pattern?

Aesthetic Perception

Design Awareness Discuss how patterns in nature have inspired designers to use them in such things as fabrics and papers. Have students look at their clothing for possible examples. Explain that a designer will create an image based on an object or the art elements and will repeat the image several times to create a pattern design.

Developing Visual Literacy Discuss the use of repeated lines, shapes, and colors in each artwork. How did the artists use these art elements to create patterns? Were the patterns created by the artists in both works? Ask students to explain their answers.

Art History and Culture

Egungun Costume

Egungun Costume (twentieth century) was made by the Yoruban people of Africa. It is part of a costume used to honor ancestors during the *egungun* ("powers concealed") ceremony. The fabric strips are attached to a wood panel that is balanced on top of the head. The dancer whirls around, causing the fabric strips to fan out and touch the spectators. The wind caused by the moving fabric panels is said to be the ancestors blessing the spectators. Each year the family member who wears the costume adds new strips of valuable cloth. The older costumes have multiple layers of cloth.

See pages 24–25 and 16–21 for more about art history and the subject matter.

Artist Profiles, p. 76

Web Connection

Visit www.ncmoa.org for more information about the North Carolina Museum of Art.

LESSON 1 • Motif and Pattern   **97**

Teach

Time: About 45 minutes

"How can you create a costume for an event?" "¿Cómo pueden crear un vestuario para un evento?"

- Read and discuss using motif and pattern on page 98.

Practice

Materials: 9" × 12" paper, color pencils

Alternate Materials: copier paper, crayons

- Distribute the materials and have students follow the directions on page 98.

Creative Expression

Materials: paper, pencils, 12" × 18" heavy white drawing paper, fine-line permanent black marker, color pencils and/or color markers

Alternate Materials: copier paper, white construction paper, crayons

- Distribute the materials and have students follow the directions on page 99.
- Review the Activity Tips on page 236 for visual examples of techniques, if needed.

Art Journal: Planning

Have students brainstorm a list of events where costumes are worn. Then have students sketch two to three costumes to be worn for an event in the Idea section of their Art Journals. Have them use one of their designs in their Creative Expression activity.

98 UNIT 3 • Rhythm, Movement, and Pattern

Using Motif and Pattern

When people think of a pattern they think of something that is repeated. In art this "something" is called a motif. A **motif** is an object or art element that is repeated. Each motif is an exact duplicate of the first. For example, in a striped shirt, the first set of stripes is a motif. When a motif, like the stripe on a shirt, is repeated, a pattern is created. A **pattern** is a repeated surface decoration. The motif is the unit of repetition in the pattern.

These are the motifs of the two patterns above.

Practice

Design a motif using color, line, and shape.

1. Fold a piece of paper into four sections. Using your pencil, draw a different motif in each section.
2. Draw one motif using only black and white, draw a second using straight lines, and use a free-form shape in the third. In your fourth section create a motif of your choice. Use color pencils to complete.

Unit 3 • Lesson 1

Differentiated Instruction

Reteach
Ask students to look through wallpaper or fabric books for examples of motifs and patterns. If these items are not available, magazines can be substituted.

Special Needs
Because students with disabilities learn best when multiple senses are engaged, have actual costumes or richly patterned fabrics available for students to examine prior to beginning this lesson.

ELL
Have students bring in a picture of a costume from their culture and point out any motifs and patterns.

◀ Tiffany Fauvre.
Age 11.

Think about and describe the motif and pattern this student artist used in the costume design.

Creative Expression

Use two or more motifs to create patterns for a costume design for an event.

1. Begin by lightly drawing two or more figures dressed in costume. Refer to your sketches and the student's art above.
2. Look at the motifs you created in the Practice activity. Select one of these to begin a pattern in part of one of the costumes or create a new one. Use a ruler to help you draw straight lines.
3. Continue creating patterns based on your motifs. You may use the same motif again, but change the color.
4. Once your drawing is complete, outline it using a fine-line black marker. Use either color pencils or markers to finish your work.

Art Criticism

Describe How many people are included in your drawing?

Analyze Describe how you made each of your patterns.

Interpret Could someone guess which event your costumed figures would be a part of based on the patterns? Explain.

Decide Do you feel you were able to successfully create patterns based on different motifs? Explain.

Unit 3 • Lesson 1   99

Art Across the Curriculum

Use these simple ideas to reinforce art concepts across the curriculum.

★ **Expository Writing** Have students write steps that explain how to make a mask.

★ **Math** Have students count the number of patterns used in *Egungun Costume*.

★ **Science** Ask students if they think the *Face Mask of Ḱumugwe'* is supposed to resemble any sea creature in particular.

★ **Social Studies** Have students discuss what other cultures have masks and costumes that look similar to the ones in the lesson.

★ **Technology** Using a paint or draw program, have students design patterns using squares and circles. Visit **SRAonline.com** to print detailed instructions for this activity.
NSAE 6.b

Reflect

Time: About 5 minutes

Review and Assess
"Describe how a motif is used to create a pattern." "Describa como un motivo es usado para crear un patrón."

Think
The artist used a variety of patterns in the costume design. Many of the motifs are made of vertical, horizontal, diagonal, and curved lines.

- Use **Large Print 77** *Jubilee: Ghana Harvest Festival* to have students identify the different patterns and motifs.

Informal Assessment

- Have students analyze their peers' costume designs to form conclusions about historical and cultural contexts. Do they think the costume designs belong in certain eras or cultures?
NSAE 4.b; 5.a
- For standardized-format test practice using this lesson's art content, see pages 30–31 in *Reading and Writing Test Preparation.*

Art Journal: Critical Thinking
Have students answer the four art criticism questions—Describe, Analyze, Interpret, and Decide—in their Art Journals. As a class, ask students to share how they created their patterns. Have them discuss how they came up with their motifs, and compare the similarities and differences.

LESSON 1 • Motif and Pattern   99

Lesson 1 Wrap-Up: Motif and Pattern

Extra! For the Art Specialist

Time: About 45 minutes

Focus
Study **Large Prints 77** *Jubilee: Ghana Harvest Festival,* and examine how the artist repeated a motif to create a pattern. Describe the patterns in the artwork, and list the motifs used to create these patterns.

Teach
Explain to the students that they will be designing a poster using colored markers. The poster will be based on a class-approved event, such as a class or school play or performance. Have students complete the alternate activity to create their posters.

Reflect
Have students use the four steps of art criticism to evaluate their work. Did they effectively create a motif based on the subject of the selected play or story? Describe the motif and how it was made into a pattern. What story or event was chosen to be used for the poster design?

Alternate Activity

Materials:
- sketchbook, pencils, erasers,
- rulers, fine-tipped black marker
- posterboard or drawing paper
- markers, color pencils

1. Begin by having students create several sketches based on the selected theme, including words. Have them choose the best sketch to be reproduced.
2. Have students design a motif to be repeated as a border for the poster. Have them use items in the motif that represent what the poster is advertising.
3. Have students sketch in an area to create their border.
4. Students should transfer the sketch and words inside the border area.
5. Have students use black marker to outline the design. Markers or color pencils can be used to complete the poster.

Research in Art Education

"If perception is basic to all learning, if selective viewing is a desirable kind of behavior, and if conceptualization comes after sensory experiences, then it becomes imperative that teachers provide paths for numerous visual and tactile explorations so as to keep all of the child's senses alive and active." (Herberholz, Barbara, and Lee Hanson. *Early Childhood Art.* New York: McGraw-Hill, 1994.)

Assessment
Use the following rubric to evaluate the artwork students make in the Creative Expression activity and to assess students' understanding of how a motif is used to create a pattern in works of art.

	Art History and Culture	Aesthetic Perception	Creative Expression	Art Criticism
3 POINTS	The student demonstrates knowledge of the Kwakwaka'wakw and the Yoruba.	The student accurately identifies the use of motif and pattern in two- and three-dimensional works of art.	The student's costume design clearly demonstrates how to use motif and pattern.	The student thoughtfully and honestly evaluates own work using the four steps of art criticism.
2 POINTS	The student's knowledge of the Kwakwaka'wakw and the Yoruba is weak or incomplete.	The student shows an emerging awareness of motif and pattern in two- and three-dimensional art but cannot consistently identify them.	The student's costume design shows some awareness of how to use motif and pattern.	The student attempts to evaluate own work but shows an incomplete understanding of evaluation criteria.
1 POINT	The student cannot demonstrate knowledge of the Kwakwaka'wakw and the Yoruba.	The student cannot identify how motif and pattern are used.	The student's costume design shows no understanding of how to use motif and pattern.	The student makes no attempt to evaluate own work.

Then have students complete pages 33 or 34 in their *Assessment* books.

Lesson 2 Overview: Two-Dimensional Pattern

Lesson 2 looks at the three pattern types. **Random Pattern** occurs when a repeated motif has no apparent order. **Alternating pattern** repeats a motif but changes position, alters spacing, or adds a new motif. **Regular pattern** occurs when identical motifs are repeated with an equal space between them.

Objectives

Art History and Culture
To demonstrate knowledge of the lives and work of Marsden Hartley and Minnie Evans

Creative Expression
To create a nonobjective design using the three pattern types

Aesthetic Perception
To identify and recognize the three types of pattern in two-dimensional art

Art Criticism
To evaluate own work using the four steps of art criticism

Lesson Materials
- pencils, erasers
- Art Journal
- 9" × 12" drawing paper
- 12" × 18" heavy white drawing paper
- color pencils, color markers

Alternate Materials:
- copier paper
- white construction paper
- crayons

Program Resources
- *Reading and Writing Test Prep.,* pp. 32–33
- *Transparency 14*
- *Artist Profiles,* pp. 25, 30
- *Animals Through History Time Line*
- *Assessment,* pp. 35–36
- *Large Prints 77* Jubilee: Ghana Harvest Festival and *78* The Horse Fair
- *Art Around the World Collection*

Concept Trace
Pattern Types
Introduced: Level 5, Unit 3, Lesson 6
Reinforced: Level 7, Chapter 4, Lesson 3

Vocabulary

Review the following vocabulary word with students before beginning the lesson.

nonobjective art *arte abstracto*—art that has no recognizable subject matter

See page 119B for additional vocabulary and Spanish vocabulary resources.

Art Journal: Vocabulary
Have students add this word to the Vocabulary section of their Art Journals.

Lesson 2 Arts Integration

Theatre
Complete Unit 3, Lesson 2, on pages 56–57 of *Theatre Arts Connections.*

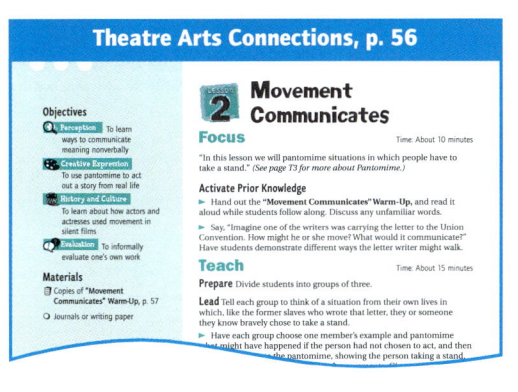

Music
In music, putting pulse in units of two, a strong beat plus a weak beat, is called duple meter. A march is in duple meter. Have students listen to "Walking the Dog" by George Gershwin. Before they even hear the piece can students guess if it is in duple or triple meter?

Movement & Dance
Have students look at pictures of Egyptian wall art. Discuss how the characters are painted and the kinds of postures they are in. Have the class create an Egyptian wall painting using their bodies. Everyone must flatten the shape of their body, as though it were on a two-dimensional plane. In slow motion, give twelve counts for students to slowly change their shapes.

LESSON 2 • Two-Dimensional Pattern **99B**

Focus

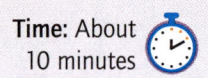

Time: About 10 minutes

Activate Prior Knowledge

"Have you seen repeated lines, shapes, colors, or objects organized like these paintings?" "¿Han visto líneas repetidas, figuras, colores u objetos organizados en estas pinturas?"

- As a class, discuss students' responses. Explain that in two-dimensional art the surface design is often organized in a particular pattern. This is also done in clothing, papers, and even everyday objects such as dishes.

Using Literature ⭐ Reading

- Look at the illustrations in *Where the Sidewalk Ends* by Shel Silverstein. Discuss the patterns used in the art. Have students read poems in the book and discuss how poems also have patterns.

Thematic Connection ⭐ Social Studies

- **Heritage:** Using direct observation, have students illustrate ways artists can share their heritage with others. Point out that works of art sometimes have nothing to do with a person's heritage; rather, the artist could have borrowed a culture's techniques.

Introduce the Art

Look

"Look closely at the two works of art." "Miren detalladamente las dos obras de arte."

Hypothesizing ⭐ Science

- Have students hypothesize the location of the scene in *Indian Fantasy* and of the ruler in *King*. Have students explain any clues that led them to their conclusion.

Art History and Culture

Students' answers will vary. Make sure students explain their answers. Minnie Evans is a self-taught artist.

💻 Web Connection

Visit www.ncmoa.org for more information about the North Carolina Museum of Art.

100 UNIT 3 • Rhythm, Movement, and Pattern

Lesson 2: Two-Dimensional Pattern

▲ **Marsden Hartley.** (American). *Indian Fantasy.* 1914. Oil on canvas. 46 11/16 × 39 5/16 inches (118.59 × 99.95 cm.). North Carolina Museum of Art, Raleigh, North Carolina.

Look at the two works of art on these pages. Marsden Hartley painted *Indian Fantasy* with oil paints. Hartley created a series of what he called "the idea of America" in 1914. This series consisted of four paintings showing his interpretations. Minnie Evans used color pencils to create *King*. Her drawings and paintings reflect her private dreams. It is believed that the floral motifs she uses in her artwork were inspired by the Airlie Gardens in North Carolina. She worked as a gatekeeper for more than 25 years at the gardens. Notice how the repeated patterns are created using colors, lines, and shapes.

Art History and Culture

Can you tell which of these artists was self-taught?

Art History and Culture

Marsden Hartley

Marsden Hartley (märz´ dən härt´ lē) (1877–1943) met Alfried Stieglitz in 1909. He also met numerous artists who were considered the most progressive in America and he became a part of the Stieglitz circle. The circle included Arthur Dove and Georgia O'Keeffe. Hartley's work was almost entirely abstract for a while. He was a painter, author, and poet and spent much of his life in Paris, Berlin, New York, and Mexico before returning to Maine. He is best known for his bright, bold colors and paintings of people, stilllifes, and landscape paintings of Maine.

See pages 24–25 and 16–21 for more about art history and the subject matter.

Artist Profiles, p. 30

Artist Profile

Marsden Hartley
1877-1943

Marsden Hartley (märz´ dən härt´ lē) was born Edmund Hartley in 1877 in Lewiston, Maine. His mother died when he was eight, and when he was 16 he went to live with his father and stepmother in Cleveland, Ohio. It was there that he began his formal art training. After winning an art scholarship, Hartley attended New York's National Academy of Design. In New York he became friends with Alfred Stieglitz who ran 291, a vanguard art gallery in the early 1900s where Hartley had his first solo exhibition. As he progressed as an artist his style constantly changed, yet he continued to address the importance of an individual's connection with nature.

Study both pieces of art to discover more about how artists use different types of patterns in their artwork.

- Which color, line, shape, or object is repeated most often in *Indian Fantasy*?
- Which color, line, shape, or object is repeated most often in *King*?
- Describe how the motifs are arranged in each artwork.

▲ **Minnie Evans.** (American). *King.* 1962.
Colored pencil on paper. 11⅞ × 8¾ inches (30.18 × 22.23 cm.). North Carolina Museum of Art, Raleigh, North Carolina.

Aesthetic Perception

Design Awareness Think about where you live. What does the outside of your home look like? What motif is used most often and how is it arranged?

Unit 3 • Lesson 2   **101**

Study

- Students' responses will vary, however, they may reply as follows: Color: yellow or black. Lines: straight. Shapes: triangles or rectangles. Objects: fish, teepees, or native Americans.
- Student's responses will vary; however, they may reply as follows: Color: yellow or red. Lines: curved. Shapes: free-form or organic. Objects: flowers or plants.
- Student answers may include: *Indian Fantasy:* Random pattern: the star motif in the teepee. Regular pattern: the stars in the sky; the shapes of the canoes. Alternating pattern: the fish; the designs on the canoes; the repeated teepees. *King:* Alternating pattern: in the breastplate; green grouping of shapes above yellow and orange flowers. Regular pattern: green curves with grouping of three red circles on blue background in the headdress, the repeated pattern on either side of the face.
- For more examples of art from North America, see the *Art Around the World Collection.*

Art Journal: Writing
Have students describe what kinds of patterns they like or find interesting in the Concepts section of their Art Journals. What else do they want to know about two-dimensional pattern?

Aesthetic Perception

Design Awareness Discuss with students that in architecture, as well as in other art forms, a motif can be arranged in a variety of ways. Have students discuss how they have seen windows, bricks, and wood siding arranged.

Developing Visual Literacy Discuss the use of repeated lines, shapes, colors, and objects in each artwork. Have students describe the patterns created by the artists in both works. Have they seen patterns used in a drawing or painting before? Ask students to share their answers.

Web Connection
Visit www.ncmoa.org for more information about the North Carolina Museum of Art.

LESSON 2 • Two-Dimensional Pattern   **101**

Art History and Culture

Minnie Evans

Minnie Evans (min´ ē e´ vənz) (1890–1987) was a self-taught artist whose dreams and visions, which she felt were messages from God, influenced her work. She used bright colors and patterns to spread the good news of salvation. Born in North Carolina, Evan spent almost 26 years working as a gatekeeper at the Airlie Gardens near Wilmington. The gardens were a source of inspiration for her motifs of flowers and leaves. Many of her works combine exotic faces and floral motifs and are often symmetrical. The faces are of the wise ancient people she has encountered in her dreams.

See pages 24–25 and 16–21 for more about art history and the subject matter.

Artist Profiles, p. 25

Artist Profile
Minnie Evans
1890-1987

Minnie Evans (min´ ē ev´ ənz) was born in North Carolina. She left the state only once in her life. She went to school through the sixth grade, and had no training in art. Yet she said, "Something told me to draw or die." She started drawing in 1925 and continued for the rest of her life. Evans first used crayons and later created collages. All of her work expressed her vision of the relationship between God, people, and nature. She worked as a maid and a gatekeeper at Airlie Gardens in Wilmington, North Carolina. Her art hangs in the permanent collections of museums as far away as Switzerland.

Teach

Time: About 45 minutes

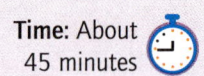

"How can you create a design using different types of patterns?" "¿Cómo pueden crear un diseño usando tipos de patrones diferentes?"

- Read and discuss using two-dimensional pattern types on page 102.
- Have students analyze and form generalizations about the interdependence of art elements, such as pattern, using appropriate vocabulary.

Practice

Materials: 9" × 12" paper, pencils

Alternate Materials: copier paper, crayons

- Distribute the materials and have students follow the directions on page 102.

Creative Expression

Materials: paper, pencils, 12" × 18" heavy white drawing paper, color pencils and/or color markers

Alternate Materials: copier paper, white construction paper, crayons

- Distribute the materials and have students follow the directions on page 103.
- Have students demonstrate their technical skills, using a variety of art media and material to produce their nonobjective designs.
- Review the Activity Tips on page 236 for visual example of techniques, if needed.

Art Journal: Planning

Have student look for examples of patterns in magazines, fabrics, and various papers. These can either be reproduced or cut and glued in the Idea section of their Art Journals. Students may use their collected patterns for their Creative Expression activity.

Using Pattern Types

You have learned that a **pattern** is a repeated surface decoration. The unit of repetition in the pattern is called a **motif.** Each motif is an exact duplicate of the first unit. When a motif is repeated, a pattern is created. How the motif is arranged can be grouped into one of three different types of patterns: random, alternating, and regular.

A **random pattern** occurs when the motif is repeated in no apparent order. For example, the leaves that cover the ground during autumn form a random pattern.

A **regular pattern** occurs when the motif is repeated with an equal amount of space between each unit. Regular patterns have a sense of order. For example, the lines indicating parking spaces and the windows in skyscrapers create regular patterns.

An **alternating pattern** can occur in three ways. It can repeat a motif but change position, alter spacing between motifs, or add a second motif. Bricks and stones are often laid in alternating patterns.

Practice

Practice the three pattern types. Use geometric shapes.

1. Look at the pattern types defined above. Fold your paper into four sections. Label each section with a pattern type. Leave the last section blank.
2. Using your pencil, draw simple geometric shapes to create random, regular, and alternating patterns in each section.
3. In the last section, combine two of the pattern types. Label this section with the two pattern types that you used.

102   Unit 3 • Lesson 2

Differentiated Instruction

Reteach

Ask students to look through newspapers and magazines for examples of random, regular, and alternating patterns.

Special Needs

Some students with cognitive disabilities may find it overwhelming to use all three of the pattern types. Assess the students' needs during the practice activity and make modifications as needed.

ELL

Have students manipulate different objects in the classroom to show their understanding of random, regular, and alternating patterns.

◀ **Alexandrea Brandl.**
Age 11.

Think about the types of patterns used by this student artist in the pattern design.

Creative Expression

Use all three pattern types to create a nonobjective design.

1. Begin by lightly drawing one large shape off center on your paper. Divide the rest of your paper using straight and curved lines. Have your lines go through your shape. You will have created a variety of shapes.
2. Look at the patterns you created in the Practice activity. Select one of these to begin a pattern in one of the shapes in your design or create a new one. Use a ruler to help you draw straight lines.
3. Continue creating patterns in each shape. Use random, regular, and alternating patterns.
4. Use either color pencils or markers to finish your patterns and complete your work.

Art Criticism

Describe What shape did you use to begin your design?

Analyze Describe the patterns and colors in your work.

Interpret If you could put a beat to your work, how would it sound?

Decide Do you feel you were able to successfully create the different types of patterns in a nonobjective drawing? Explain.

Unit 3 • Lesson 2   **103**

Reflect

Time: About 5 minutes

Review and Assess

"Describe how a motif was used to create the different pattern types." "Describan cómo un motivo fue usado para crear tipos de patrones diferentes."

Think

The artist used a variety of regular, alternating, and random patterns. Some of the patterns have geometric shapes, and others have lines.

- Use **Large Prints 77** *Jubilee: Ghana Harvest Festival* and **78** *The Horse Fair* to have students identify the different types of patterns used.

Informal Assessment

- For standardized-format test practice using this lesson's art content, see pages 32–33 in *Reading and Writing Test Preparation.*

Art Journal: Critical Thinking

Have students answer the four art criticism questions—Describe, Analyze, Interpret, and Decide—in their Art Journals. Have students share their completed nonobjective designs. Ask them to discuss the different pattern types and how they created them.

Art Across the Curriculum

Use these simple ideas to reinforce art concepts across the curriculum.

★ **Poetry Writing** Have students write a poem about a king and his land.

★ **Math** Have students measure the size of the angles in *Indian Fantasy.*

★ **Science** Have students describe the ecosystem depicted in *Indian Fantasy.*

★ **Social Studies** Have students name ancient artifacts that have decorative patterns.

★ **Technology** Using a paint or draw program, have students add a decorative pattern around a person's face in a photo. Visit SRAonline.com to print detailed instructions for this activity.
NSAE 6.b

LESSON 2 • Two-Dimensional Pattern   **103**

Lesson 2 Wrap-Up: Two-Dimensional Pattern

Extra! For the Art Specialist
Time: About 45 minutes

Focus
Study **Large Prints 77** *Jubilee: Ghana Harvest Festival* and examine how the artist repeated different motifs to create the three types of patterns. Describe the patterns used in the artwork.

Teach
Explain to the students that they will be creating a collage using patterned fabrics and papers. Their collages will be nonobjective, or will not have any subject matter in their compositions. Have students complete the alternate activity.

Reflect
Have students use the four steps of art criticism to evaluate their work. Did they effectively create a nonobjective collage combining fabric, papers and drawn pattern types? Did students include all three pattern types in their collages: random, regular, and alternating?

Alternate Activity

Materials:
- pencils, erasers, rulers
- 9" × 12" or larger mat board
- variety of fabrics and papers
- fine-tipped black markers
- color markers

1. Begin by collecting a variety of fabrics and papers. Have students look for examples of random, regular, and alternating patterns.
2. Explain that all three pattern types must be used in their collages. After fabric and papers have been glued onto the background paper, have students use black markers to create original patterns in the negative space. No empty white spaces should be left.
3. Have students use color markers to complete the patterns in the negative spaces.

Research in Art Education
"Just as culture shapes art, art shapes culture. Our convictions, our technology, and our imagination shape our images, and our images, in turn, shape our perception of the world." (Eisner, Elliot. *The Role of Disciplined-Based Art Education in America's Schools*. The Getty Center for Arts Education in the Arts, 1987.)

Assessment
Use the following rubric to evaluate the artwork students make in the Creative Expression activity and to assess students' understanding of different pattern types used in two-dimensional works of art and how to create them.

Then have students complete pages 35 or 36 in their *Assessment* books.

	Art History and Culture	Aesthetic Perception	Creative Expression	Art Criticism
3 POINTS	The student demonstrates knowledge of the lives and work of Marsden Hartley and Minnie Evans.	The student accurately identifies the use of different pattern types in two-dimensional works of art.	The student's nonobjective design clearly demonstrates how to use different pattern types.	The student thoughtfully and honestly evaluates own work using the four steps of art criticism.
2 POINTS	The student's knowledge of Marsden Hartley and Minnie Evans is weak or incomplete.	The student shows an emerging awareness of different pattern types in two-dimensional art but cannot consistently identify them.	The student's nonobjective design shows some awareness of how to use different pattern types.	The student attempts to evaluate own work but shows an incomplete understanding of evaluation criteria.
1 POINT	The student cannot demonstrate knowledge of Marsden Hartley or Minnie Evans.	The student cannot identify how different pattern types are used.	The student's nonobjective design shows no understanding of how to use different pattern types.	The student makes no attempt to evaluate own work.

Lesson 3 Overview

Three-Dimensional Pattern

Lesson 3 continues looking at the art principle of pattern but applies it to three-dimensional forms. **Pattern** is a repeated surface decoration. **Three-dimensional patterns** are patterns that have depth and are formed on the surface of a sculptural form.

Objectives

Art History and Culture
To demonstrate knowledge of Teodora Blanco and Oaxacan sculptors

Creative Expression
To create a clay animal using patterns as surface design

Aesthetic Perception
To identify and understand how artists use pattern on three-dimensional works of art

Art Criticism
To evaluate own work using the four steps of art criticism

Lesson Materials
- sketchbook, pencils, erasers
- oil pastels, toothpick
- $4\frac{1}{2}" \times 6"$ construction paper in a variety of colors
- self-hardening clay, acrylic paints
- small- and medium-size paintbrushes
- water containers, paper towels
- newspaper, paper plates
- paint pens

Alternate Materials:
- watercolor paints, color markers
- clay, kiln
- paper to draw an animal and add pattern with color markers

Program Resources
- *Reading and Writing Test Prep.*, pp. 34–35
- *Transparency 15*
- *Artist Profiles*, pp. 9, 71
- *Animals Through History Time Line*
- *Assessment*, pp. 37–38
- *Large Prints 77 Jubilee: Ghana Harvest Festival* and *78 The Horse Fair*
- *Art Around the World Collection*

Concept Trace
Three-dimensional pattern
Introduced: Level 5, Unit 3, Lesson 6
Reinforced: Level 7, Chapter 12, Lesson 4

Vocabulary

Review the following vocabulary words with students before beginning the lesson.

pattern patrón—a repeated surface decoration

three-dimensional patterns patrones tridimensionales—patterns that have depth and are formed on the surface of a sculptural form

See page 119B for additional vocabulary and Spanish vocabulary resources.

Art Journal: Vocabulary
Have students add these words to the Vocabulary section of their Art Journals.

Lesson 3 Arts Integration

Theatre
Complete Unit 3, Lesson 3, on pages 58–59 of *Theatre Arts Connections*.

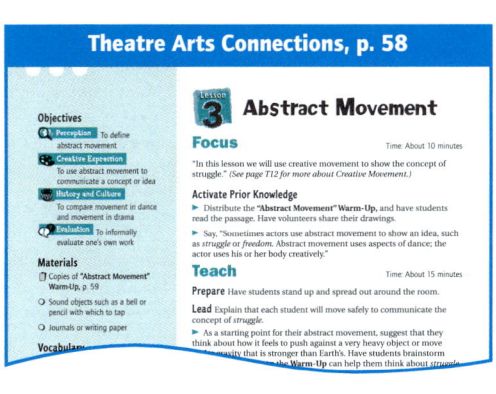

Music
In music, putting pulse in units of three, with one strong beat plus two weak beats is called triple meter. The most famous triple meter dance is a waltz. Have students listen to "Skater's Waltz" by Emile Waldteufel. Ask students how a skater would move to this waltz—on every pulse or just the strong pulses?

Movement & Dance
Teach students a short circle dance that moves on different planes. Take eight counts to walk in, going to the center, and eight counts out. REPEAT. Take eight counts to move the circle to the right, and eight counts to the left. REPEAT. Four counts to reach up, and four counts to reach down. REPEAT. Eight counts to jump in place. Eight counts to turn around.

LESSON 3 • Three-Dimensional Pattern 103B

Focus

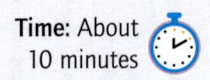

Time: About 10 minutes

Activate Prior Knowledge

"Have you ever seen a sculpture that was decorated with painted patterns or with raised patterns that you could feel?" "¿Han visto una escultura que fue decorada con patrones pintados o con patrones levantados que pudieron sentir?"

- As a class, discuss the student responses. Explain that artists use patterns as surface design on sculptural forms. Patterns can be painted by repeating lines, shapes, and colors; other times added objects or forms are used to create a pattern.

Using Literature — Reading

- Read *Dave at Night* by Gail Carson Levine. Look at the cover design. Though the objects are not three-dimensional in the drawing, they represent objects that are three-dimensional.

Thematic Connection — Science

- **Animals:** Have students identify the animal forms in the sculptures. Are any of the animals similar? How are they different?

Introduce the Art

Look

"Let's take a closer look at how pattern was applied to the sculptures shown on these pages." "Miren detalladamente cómo un patrón fue aplicado a las esculturas mostradas en estas páginas."

Classifying — Math

- Have groups classify the different patterns that each artist used in his or her sculptures. Then have the groups compare their findings.

Art History and Culture

Each culture has its own style of folk art. Folk art can be any type of everyday object, including paintings, sculptures, ceramics, metalwork, costume, and tools.

Web Connection

Visit samuseum.org for more information about the San Antonio Museum of Art.

104 UNIT 3 • Rhythm, Movement, and Pattern

Lesson 3 — Three-Dimensional Pattern

Look at the sculptures on these pages. Teodora Blanco is considered one of the most important folk artists of Mexico. She uses surface designs and patterns that make her sculptures unique. The Oaxacan sculptures are carved by the Zapotec people, who still live in the southern Mexican state of Oaxaca. The sculptures are hand-painted, then decorated with tiny detailed patterns. The most popular images are of animals, mystical beasts, and religious figures.

▲ **Teodora Blanco.** (Mexican). *Ceramic Figures.* 1978.
Single-fired earthenware. Average height 14 inches (35.56 cm.). Nelson A. Rockefeller Collection, San Antonio Museum of Art, Texas.

Art History and Culture

Folk artists usually use traditional techniques and styles of a particular region that have been used for many generations.

104 Unit 3 • Lesson 3

Art History and Culture

Teodora Blanco

Teodora Blanco (tā ō dor´ ä bläng´ kō) (1928–1980) was born in Atzompa, Mexico. This small rural village in the state of Oaxaca is famous for its potters, who create their clay vessels on a primitive potter's wheel. The wheel is created from a plate or saucer balanced on a round rock or overturned saucer. As they work, the potters turn the plate, which has a lump of clay on top. Blanco became inspired by the ceramics she saw when she visited the archaeological museums in Oaxaca. She invented the technique of adding small decorative clay designs to the pottery that is called *pastillaje*.

See pages 24–25 and 16–21 for more about art history and the subject matter.

Artist Profiles, p. 9

Study the sculptures on these pages. How did the artists use patterns in their work?
- What objects do you see in *Ceramic Figures*?
- Describe the art elements used most often to decorate the surface of the Oaxacan sculptures.
- Describe how the patterns were applied to the Oaxacan sculptures and *Ceramic Figures*.

▲ **Artist unknown.**
(Oaxacan, Mexican).
Carved Animals.
Private collection.

Aesthetic Perception

Design Awareness What patterns do you see in the clothing around you? What patterns do you see in the fur of an animal?

Unit 3 • Lesson 3   **105**

Art History and Culture

Carved Animals

The Zapotec, a Native American group, live in the Mexican state of Oaxaca. Oaxacan sculptors have carved toys and masks for hundreds of years. They have passed down the carving techniques from generation to generation. The wooden sculptures are hand-carved from the wood of the copal tree. Each piece is then hand-sanded, painted in bright bold colors, and finally embellished with patterns. The sculptures are often real and imaginary animals and religious figures, such as angels. There are approximately two hundred families of wood-carvers in the Oaxaca Valley. These are poor farming areas, but the popularity of the sculptures has enabled the Zapotec to live more comfortably.

See pages 24–25 and 16–21 for more about art history and the subject matter.

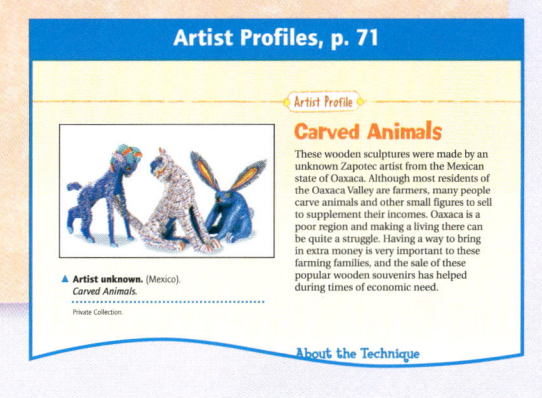

Artist Profiles, p. 71

Artist Profile
Carved Animals
These wooden sculptures were made by an unknown Zapotec artist from the Mexican state of Oaxaca. Although most residents of the Oaxaca Valley are farmers, many people carve animals and other small figures to sell to supplement their incomes. Oaxaca is a poor region and making a living there can be quite a struggle. Having a way to bring in extra money is very important to these farming families, and the sale of these popular wooden souvenirs has helped during times of economic need.

▲ **Artist unknown.** (Mexico).
Carved Animals.
Private Collection.

About the Technique

Study
▸ Animals such as birds, pigs, fish, and a lamb; four women; jewelry; braided hair; vines, leaves, and flowers.
▸ Tiny repeated lines that imitate fur; dotting of contrasting color; a red and white woven pattern repeated on the cat.
▸ *Carved Animals:* Some areas look carved, but they were mainly painted and overlapped on top of a solid color. Some patterns were created by lines painted on top of other lines, other patterns are repeated curved lines, and some look like flowers or stars that are randomly placed. *Ceramic Figures:* The patterns were drawn into the clay surface; others were attached to the surface, forming three-dimensional random patterns. The braided hair forms a regular pattern.
■ For more examples of art from North America, see the *Art Around the World Collection.*

Art Journal: Writing
Have students describe sculptures that have patterns in the Concepts section of their Art Journals. What else do they want to know about three-dimensional pattern?

Aesthetic Perception

Design Awareness Discuss with students how artists are all influenced by their environment. Artists are very aware of their environment. Some artists emphasize patterns; others colors, shapes, or common objects. Folk artists often study their surroundings and produce art from the materials, patterns, and textures around them.

Developing Visual Literacy Discuss the subject matter of each image. They are based on real forms. What did the artists do to transform ordinary people and animals? Invite students to share personal experiences that contribute to their understanding of the works of art.

Web Connection
Visit **www.manos-de-oaxaca.com** for more information about Oaxacan artists. Note: This Web site is for teacher use only.

LESSON 3 • Three-Dimensional Pattern   **105**

Teach

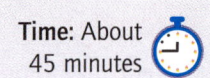

Time: About 45 minutes

"How do you create patterns on a three-dimensional form?" "¿Cómo pueden crear patrones en una forma tridimensional?"

- Read and discuss using three-dimensional pattern on sculptural forms on page 106.

Practice

Materials: oil pastels, $4\frac{1}{2}" \times 6"$ construction paper in a variety of colors

Alternate Materials: color markers, crayons, white paper

- Distribute the materials and have students follow the directions on page 106.

Creative Expression

Materials: self-hardening clay, acrylic paints in all colors, paper plates on which to mix colors, small and medium brushes, paper towels, newspaper, optional: paint pens

Alternate Materials: clay, kiln for firing the clay, paper on which to draw an animal and add pattern with color markers

- Distribute the materials and have students follow the directions on page 107.
- Have students demonstrate their technical skills using a variety of art media and materials to produce their figures as a hollow clay, or ceramic, sculpture.
- If available, use a kiln to fire students sculptures.
- Review the Activity Tips on page 237 for visual examples of techniques if needed.

Art Journal: Brainstorming

Ask students to brainstorm a list of animals. Ask them to choose one animal from the list to be used for a sculpture. Students can then create a list of characteristics that are unique to their animal in their Art Journals. Students can refer to their list for their Creative Expression activities.

106 UNIT 3 • Rhythm, Movement, and Pattern

Using Three-Dimensional Pattern

A **pattern** is a repeated surface decoration. There are three types of patterns: regular, random, and alternating. The motif is the unit of repetition in a pattern. In both two- and three-dimensional artwork, artists use the same types of patterns. They also create them the same way—by repeating a motif.

In three-dimensional art, there are different ways an artist can create a pattern on a form's surface. An artist can create a pattern on clay by gently pressing an object or stamp into the clay surface. Patterns can be drawn using a clay needle, pencil, or other sharp tool. Clay forms and coils can be used to create raised patterns. In all sculptural forms, patterns can be added by drawing and painting or by adding similar objects to the surface.

Practice

Practice drawing random, regular, and alternating patterns using oil pastels.

1. Select three different colors of construction paper.
2. Use oil pastels in a contrasting color to create a random pattern using a motif. On a second piece of construction paper, draw a regular pattern. Create an alternating pattern on a third piece of colored construction paper.
3. Look at the three pattern types you created. How could these be used on a three-dimensional form?

106 Unit 3 • Lesson 3

Differentiated Instruction

Reteach
Have students look around the room for examples of pattern on three-dimensional objects.

Special Needs
To reinforce student understanding of pattern types, create visual prompts that show examples of random, regular, and alternating patterns.

ELL
Have students look in their *Art Connections* book for good and bad examples of patterns of three-dimensional objects.

◀ **Harley Dean.**
Age 11.

Think about the types of designs that were applied to the surface of the animal form.

Creative Expression

Form a three-dimensional real or fantasy animal covered with patterns.

1. Begin by forming your clay animal.
2. Once you have your basic animal form, add ears. You can either pinch out or attach the ear forms.
3. Think about other details that are important for your particular animal, like eyes and feet. When you have finished forming your animal, use a toothpick or pencil to add details.
4. Paint your animal using one or two base colors. Once the base color has dried, add patterns using a thin brush or paint pen. Dots and lines can be layered on top of one another.

Art Criticism

Describe What animal did you create?

Analyze Describe the patterns and colors you used.

Interpret What effect do the pattern and color have on your animal sculpture?

Decide Were you successful in creating a three-dimensional real or fantasy animal covered with patterns? Explain.

Unit 3 • Lesson 3   **107**

Reflect
Time: About 5 minutes

Review and Assess
"Explain how you created the pattern on your animal sculpture." "Expliquen como crearon el patrón en sus esculturas de animales."

Think
The artist used random, regular, and alternating patterns to decorate the surface of this sculpture.

- Use **Large Prints 77** *Jubilee: Ghana Harvest Festival* and **78** *The Horse Fair* to have students identify if the artists applied patterns to each artwork.

Informal Assessment
- For standardized-format test practice using this lesson's art content, see pages 34–35 in ***Reading and Writing Test Preparation***.

Art Journal: Critical Thinking
Have students answer the four art criticism questions—Describe, Analyze, Interpret, and Decide—in their Art Journals. Ask students to think about how they applied pattern to their artwork. What problems did they have to overcome, if any, and how did they solve them?

Art Across the Curriculum

Use these simple ideas to reinforce art concepts across the curriculum.

★ **Narrative Writing** Have students write a short story about the figures in this lesson.

★ **Math** Have students create a graph showing the different animals used by the artists.

★ **Science** Explain to students that clay is a secondary mineral that is formed through the weathering and alteration of certain rocks and minerals.

★ **Social Studies** Explain to students that some cultures use gifts to improve communication with other cultures.

★ **Technology** Using a paint or draw program, have students create a pattern that could be transferred to a T-shirt. Visit **SRAonline.com** to print detailed instructions for this activity.
NSAE 6.b

LESSON 3 • Three-Dimensional Pattern **107**

Lesson 3 Wrap-Up: Three-Dimensional Pattern

Extra! For the Art Specialist

Time: About 45 minutes

Focus
Have students examine the sculptures in this lesson and discuss how pattern was used by the artists. Ask them what effect the applied patterns have.

Teach
Explain to students that they will be creating figures covered with three-dimensional patterns similar to those made by Teodora Blanco. They should make a sketch of the figure they would like to create. Have students complete the alternate activity.

Reflect
Have students use the four steps of art criticism to evaluate their sculptures. Did they effectively create a three-dimensional pattern in their figures? Which pattern types did the students use?

Alternate Activity

Materials:
- clay, acrylic paints in all colors
- paper plates to mix colors
- small and medium brushes
- paper towels, newspaper
- kiln for firing the clay, paint pens
- various glazes (optional)

1. Students should begin by forming the body. If making a female figure, start with a pinch pot, invert it, and attach a ball of clay for the body, a coil for the arms, then the head. If creating a male figure, use a large oval clay form and pinch out the head. Use a pencil or needle tool to cut half of the remaining oval to divide the clay into two legs. Pinch out the arms.
2. Have your students use the clay tools to add features with patterns.
3. After firing, figures can be left in the natural clay color, glazed, or painted.

Research in Art Education

Research has shown that "learning happens best when kids have fun, and the arts are fun for kids." It is important to remember that while the arts can act "as catalysts for learning other subject areas across the curriculum," they are also valuable in their own right ("Arts Literacy for Business" in *The Vision for Arts Education in the 21st Century*).

Assessment
Use the following rubric to evaluate the artwork students make in the Creative Expression activity and to assess students' understanding of patterns used on three-dimensional works of art.

	Art History and Culture	Aesthetic Perception	Creative Expression	Art Criticism
3 POINTS	The student demonstrates knowledge of the lives and work of Teodora Blanco and Oaxacan sculptors.	The student accurately identifies use of patterns on three-dimensional works of art.	The student's clay animal demonstrates using pattern.	The student thoughtfully and honestly evaluates own work using the four steps of art criticism.
2 POINTS	The student's knowledge of Teodora Blanco and Oaxacan sculptors is weak or incomplete.	The student shows an emerging awareness of patterns on three-dimensional works of art but cannot identify it consistently.	The student's clay animal shows some use of pattern.	The student attempts to evaluate own work but shows an incomplete understanding of evaluation criteria.
1 POINT	The student cannot demonstrate knowledge of Teodora Blanco Oaxacan sculptors.	The student cannot identify use of patterns on three-dimensional works of art.	The student's clay animal shows no understanding of pattern.	The student makes no attempt to evaluate own work.

Then have students complete pages 37 or 38 in their *Assessment* books.

Lesson 4 Overview: Rhythm

Lesson 4 is an introduction to rhythm. **Rhythm** is the principle of design that organizes the elements in a work of art by repeating elements and/or objects.

Objectives

Art History and Culture
To demonstrate knowledge of the lives and work of Franz Marc and Pablo Picasso

Creative Expression
To create rhythm using lines and/or shapes in a nonobjective design

Aesthetic Perception
To identify and understand how artists use visual rhythm in two-dimensional works of art

Art Criticism
To evaluate own work using the four steps of art criticism

Lesson Materials
- sketchbook, pencils, erasers
- fine-line permanent black marker
- 9" × 12" white drawing paper
- color pencils

Alternate Materials:
- crayons

Program Resources
- *Reading and Writing Test Prep.,* pp. 36–37
- *Transparency* 16
- *Flash Card* 18
- *Artist Profiles,* pp. 39, 48
- *Animals Through History Time Line*
- *Assessment,* pp. 39–40
- *Large Prints 77 Jubilee: Ghana Harvest Festival* and *78 The Horse Fair*
- *The National Museum of Women in the Arts Collection*

Concept Trace
Rhythm
Introduced: Level 5, Unit 5, Lesson 2
Reinforced: Level 7, Chapter 3, Lesson 5

Vocabulary

Review the following vocabulary word with students before beginning the lesson.

nonobjective art *arte abstracto*—art that has no recognizable subject matter

See page 119B for additional vocabulary and Spanish vocabulary resources.

Art Journal: Vocabulary
Have students add this word to the Vocabulary section of their Art Journals.

Lesson 4 Arts Integration

Theatre
Complete Unit 3, Lesson 4, on pages 60–61 of *Theatre Arts Connections.*

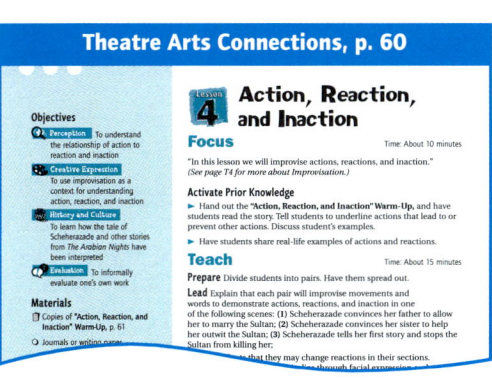

Music
Have students listen to "Badinerie" from *Orchestral Suite No.2 in B minor* by Johann Sebastian Bach. Have students clap to the main flute rhythm. Then have students use this rhythm to speak ordinary sentences.

Movement & Dance
Have students form a large circle. Have them stand in a neutral position and send their eye focus across the circle. When they make eye contact with someone, they should clap hands to signal recognition, run to the center, clasp hands, turn around each other, and exchange places. Several people will move at the same time, so a sense of group rhythm is essential to keep the flow continuous and smooth.

LESSON 4 • Rhythm **107B**

Focus

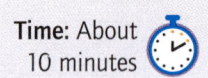

Time: About 10 minutes

Activate Prior Knowledge

"Have you ever been to a fair or amusement park?" "¿Han estado en una feria o parque de diversión?"

- As a class, discuss the student responses. Explain that artists repeat lines, shapes, and colors to lead a viewer's eyes through a work of art.

Using Literature ⭐ Reading

- Study the cover illustration of *Fair Weather* by Richard Peck and discuss the use of repeated line and shapes and the cool blue color. The repeated seats on the Ferris wheel and circular shape and the use of dark blue against light blue causes the viewer's eye to move around the illustration on the cover.

Thematic Connection ⭐ Math

- **Repetition:** Ask students what kind of activities they repeat on a weekly basis. Then have them explain why they repeat the activities.

Introduce the Art

Look

"Let's take a closer look at the use of visual rhythm in the two paintings." "Miren detalladamente al uso del ritmo visual en las dos pinturas."

Sound ⭐ Science

- Have students look at the two paintings in this lesson. What sounds do they associate with the colors that the artists used? Answers will vary, but for the Marc piece, students should give examples of louder sounds than for the Picasso piece.

Art History and Culture

Yes. Picasso was part of the cubism movement. Marc was part of *der Blaue Reiter*.

Web Connection

Visit www.the-artfile.com/uk/gallery/marc.htm for more information about Franz Marc.

108 UNIT 3 • Rhythm, Movement, and Pattern

Lesson 4 — Rhythm

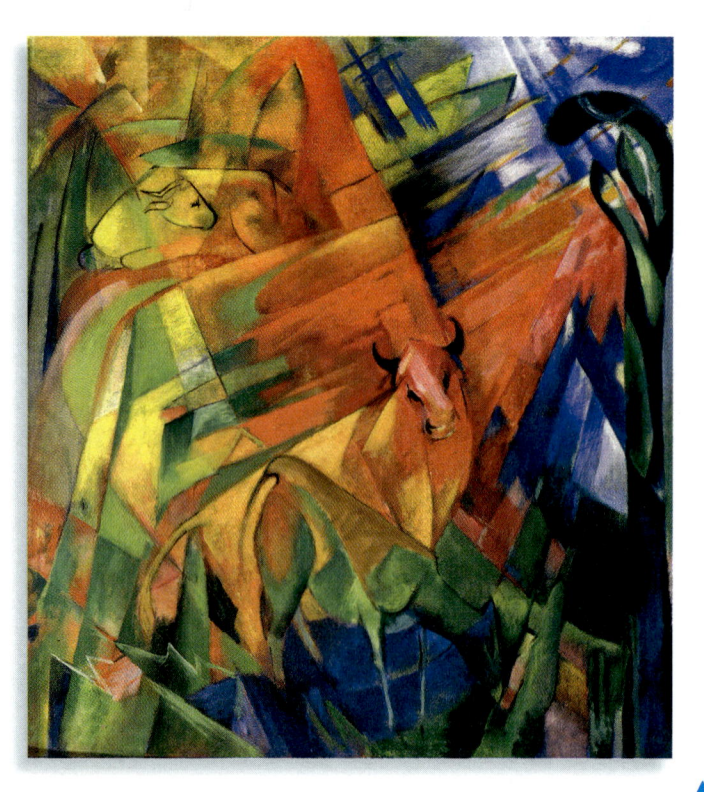

▲ **Franz Marc.** (German). *Animals in a Landscape.* 1914.
Oil on canvas. $43\frac{3}{8} \times 39\frac{1}{4}$ inches (110.2 × 99.7 cm.). Detroit Institute of Arts, Detroit, Michigan.

Look at the artwork on these pages. The repetition of shapes and colors create rhythm in *Animals in Landscape*. The blues pull the eye to the right side; the greens dance across the bottom. The warm colors pull the viewer's eyes down from the upper left and into the work. Pablo Picasso developed the style known as cubism. *Portrait of Dora Maar* is an example of cubism, which portrays a three-dimensional object from many viewpoints at once.

Art History and Culture

Are Pablo Picasso and Franz Marc part of the modern art movement?

108   Unit 3 • Lesson 4

Art History and Culture

Franz Marc

Franz Marc (fränts marc) (1880–1916) was born in Munich, Germany. He began his formal study of art at the Munich Art Academy but studied on his own as well. In 1911 he and the artist Wassily Kandinsky began a network of German and Russian abstract painters called *der Blaue Reiter,* often referred to as the "Blue Rider group." Marc was fascinated by the idea of mood and symbolism in color and with the natural forms of animals. Much of his work shows horses or cows in various bright, saturated colors.

See pages 24–25 and 16–21 for more about art history and the subject matter.

Artist Profiles, p. 39

Franz Marc
1880–1916

Franz Marc was born in Munich, Germany, in 1880. He began his formal studies of art at the Munich Art Academy, but studied on his own as well, traveling to Paris, France to see the works of Van Gogh, Gauguin, and the impressionists. In 1911, he and the artist Wassily Kandinsky began a network of German and Russian abstract painters called *Der Blaue Reiter,* or The Blue Rider, group. Marc was fascinated by the idea of mood and symbolism in color, as well as the natural forms of animals. Many of his works show horses or cows in various bright, saturated colors. Marc joined the military and served in World War I. In 1916, at the age of 36, he was killed in battle in France.

Study and compare how Marc and Picasso used rhythm in their paintings.

▶ What art element do you see repeated in each painting?

▶ Look at *Animals in a Landscape*. Which element most attracts your eye: line, shape, or color? Explain.

▶ Which painting seems active, and which seems calm?

▲ **Pablo Picasso.** (Spanish). *Portrait of Dora Maar.* 1938.
Pencil on paper mounted on fiberboard. 30 9/16 × 22 7/16 inches (77.62 × 57 cm.). Hirshhorn Museum and Sculpture Garden, Smithsonian Institution, Washington, D.C.

Aesthetic Perception

Design Awareness Think about a line of people or a row of books on a shelf. How do these two rows move? What if there is a break in the line, or a few of the books lie in a small stack?

Study

▶ *Animals in a Landscape:* Color: Bright colors seem to jump across the picture. Line: There are repeated diagonal and curved lines which help the viewer's eyes through the work. *Portrait of Dora Maar:* Line: Curved and straight lines that are repeated. The horizontal and vertical lines run parallel to one another in the background, the chair and the clothing. There are repeated curved lines in the hair and neck. Color: an overall neutral color scheme, black lines, even gray tone throughout the work and a white in the face, neck and hands.

▶ These answers will vary; however many may say *color* because Marc used bold primary and secondary colors.

▶ *Animals in a Landscape:* The movement is active because the large sections of color cause the viewer's eyes to jump around the landscape. The diagonal and curved lines also help add to the quick rhythm of the painting. *Portrait of Dora Maar* is calm because of the limited color; straight horizontal and vertical lines hold down the image. The arms are curved and resting; the stiff body is still.

■ For more examples of abstract and nonobjective artwork, see **The National Museum of Women in the Arts Collection.**

Art Journal: Writing

Have students describe what they know about rhythm in the Concepts section of their Art Journals. What else do they want to know about rhythm?

Art History and Culture

Pablo Picasso

As a boy, Pablo Picasso (pä´ blō pi kä´ sō) (1881–1973) never stopped drawing. In fact, his mother claimed that he could draw before he could talk. Everywhere Picasso went, his pad and pencil went with him. His father was a painter and a teacher. One day he came home to find that his son had finished a portrait. After examining Picasso's work, he gave the boy all of his art materials. Picasso's painting was so great that his father vowed never to paint again—and did not. For some time, he created the fractured images that were the hallmark of the cubist movement. *Portrait of Dora Maar* was a painting of the artist and photographer whom Picasso met in 1936.

See pages 24–25 and 16–21 for more about art history and the subject matter.

Artist Profiles, p. 48

Aesthetic Perception

Design Awareness The repeated objects, or positive shapes, carry our eyes along a line, or a row of books. When there is a break in this line, or a rest (negative space), our eyes pause momentarily.

Developing Visual Literacy Discuss what each work of art "says." What meaning were the two artists trying to communicate? Invite students to share personal experiences that contribute to their understanding of the works of art.

Web Connection

Visit **www.hirshhorn.si.edu** for more information about the Hirshhorn Museum.

Teach

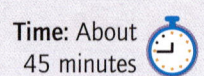

Time: About 45 minutes

"How can you create visual rhythm?" "¿Cómo pueden crear el ritmo visual?"

- Read and discuss using rhythm in two-dimensional works of art on page 110.
- Have students analyze and form generalizations about the interdependence of art elements, such as rhythm, using appropriate vocabulary.

Practice

Materials: only students are needed

- Have students follow the directions on page 110.

Creative Expression

Materials: pencils and erasers, 9" × 12" white drawing paper, felt-tipped black markers, color pencils

Alternate Materials: crayons

- Distribute the materials and have students follow the directions on page 111.
- Have students demonstrate their technical skills by using a variety of art media and materials to produce their nonobjective designs.
- Review the Activity Tips on page 237 for visual examples of techniques, if needed.

Art Journal: Collecting

In the Research section of their Art Journals, have students collect examples of parallel lines. These can be either drawn or collected from wallpaper, wrapping paper, or magazine images. These can be used later for their Creative Expression activity.

Using Rhythm

Rhythm is a principle of design. **Rhythm** organizes the elements of art in a work by repeating elements and objects. In music, rhythm is created by the pause or rest between musical sounds. There is a beat followed by a rest. In a piece of art, visual rhythm is created by repeated positive shapes separated by negative spaces. The shapes are the "beats"; the spaces that separate them are the "rests." Visual rhythm pulls the viewer's eyes through a work of art.

Visual rhythm can be found in nature and in objects made by people.

Practice

Act out visual rhythm in a group.

1. Form a group of four to five people. Within the group, plan two or three ways to arrange the people to create visual rhythm.
2. Present your visual rhythm to the class. See if they can clap the beat and rest between the forms (the people).
3. Take turns with other groups performing your visual rhythms.

110   Unit 3 • Lesson 4

Differentiated Instruction

Reteach
Have students look through this book to find other examples of visual rhythm.

Special Needs
Students who are artistically gifted may need a more challenging activity that addresses the same lesson objectives. Consider having students create a stamp from foam shapes or yarn affixed to a base. The stamp design can be repeated to form visual rhythm.

ELL
Have students listen to a song and clap along with the rhythm. Ask them if the rhythm of the song is similar to one of the paintings in the lesson.

110   UNIT 3 • Rhythm, Movement, and Pattern

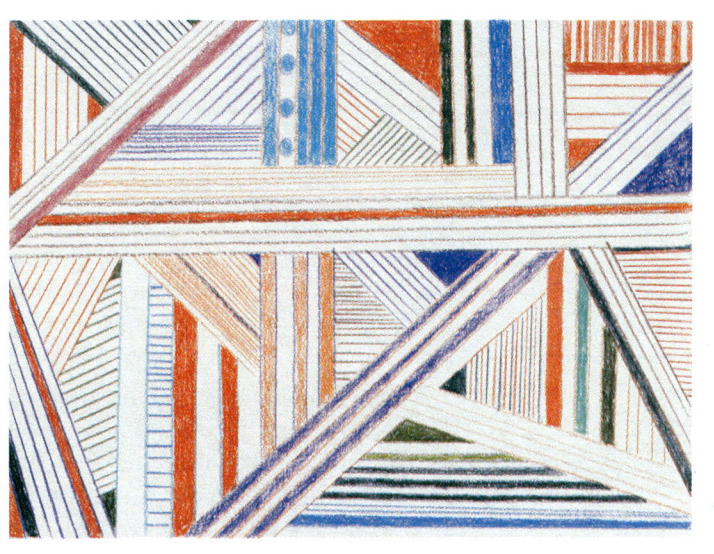

◀ John Gaston.
Age 11.

Think about how this student artist created rhythm in the design.

Creative Expression

Create rhythm using lines and shapes in a nonobjective design.

1. Select a shape and a line. Repeat parallel lines and shapes to create visual rhythm. Place them so that your entire paper is covered. Make your design nonobjective; there should be no recognizable objects in your composition.
2. Once your design is drawn to your satisfaction, use a felt-tip marker to trace over your lines.
3. Look at the color schemes in Unit 2. Select one color scheme to use in your nonobjective design. Use color pencils to add color to complete your design.

Art Criticism

Describe Describe your composition.

Analyze Which color scheme did you use in your design? How did you arrange your art elements to create rhythm?

Interpret Give your nonobjective design a title.

Decide Were you successful in creating a nonobjective design using lines and shapes to create rhythm? Explain.

Unit 3 • Lesson 4   **111**

Reflect

Time: About 5 minutes

Review and Assess

"How did you use rhythm in your nonobjective design?" "¿Cómo usaron el ritmo en su diseño abstracto?"

Think

The artist used a variety of diagonal, horizontal, and vertical lines to lead the viewer's eyes through the design.

- Use **Large Prints 77** *Jubilee: Ghana Harvest Festival* and **78** *The Horse Fair* to have students identify the different ways rhythm was used in each artwork.

Informal Assessment

- For standardized-format test practice using this lesson's art content, see pages 36–37 in *Reading and Writing Test Preparation*.

Art Journal: Critical Thinking

Have students answer the four art criticism questions—Describe, Analyze, Interpret, and Decide—in their Art Journals. Have students analyze the differences and similarities of the use of rhythm and other formal properties in their designs. Point out that even though lines and shapes were used in each work, rhythm was used differently.

Art Across the Curriculum

Use these simple ideas to reinforce art concepts across the curriculum.

★ **Personal Writing** Have students write a letter to one of the artists in this lesson.

★ **Math** Have students estimate the age of Dora Maar.

★ **Science** Ask students, "What kind of observable traits can you find in *Portrait of Dora Maar*?"

★ **Social Studies** Explain to students that societal issues can influence an artist's creative expression.

★ **Technology** Using a paint or draw program, have students create a picture of a landscape in the style of Franz Marc. Visit **SRAonline.com** to print detailed instructions for this activity.
NSAE 6.b

LESSON 4 • Rhythm **111**

Lesson 4 Wrap-Up: Rhythm

Extra! For the Art Specialist

Time: About 45 minutes

Focus
Study **Large Print 78** *The Horse Fair* and discuss how the artist used rhythm. What art elements were repeated to create visual rhythm?

Teach
Explain to students that they will be creating a nonobjective painting based on the art elements. They will use visual movement by repeating one or more of the art elements. Have students complete the alternate activity.

Reflect
Have students use the four steps of art criticism to evaluate their work. Did they effectively create a nonobjective painting showing visual rhythm? What color scheme was used?

Alternate Activity

Materials:
- Art Journals, pencils, erasers
- canvas (any size), acrylic paints
- mixing tray, various size brushes
- water container, paper towels, newspaper

1. Have students look at the work of Franz Marc and Pablo Picasso on pages 108–109. Discuss how rhythm was used in their paintings.

2. In their Art Journals, have students create several sketches using one or more of the art elements to create a nonobjective composition. Have them select their best sketch to transfer onto canvas.

3. Have students select a color scheme to complete the nonobjective paintings.

Research in Art Education

Some researchers suggest that studying art helps students develop critical-thinking and problem-solving skills. Certain aspects of art education may encourage these skills—"art history and art criticism . . . are probably more responsible than studio courses for producing measured improvements in vocabulary, writing, and critical thinking skills" ("Theories and Research That Support Art Instruction for Instrumental Outcomes" in *Schools, Communities, and the Arts: A Research Compendium*).

Assessment

Use the following rubric to evaluate the artwork students make in the Creative Expression activity and to assess students' understanding of visual rhythm.

	Art History and Culture	Aesthetic Perception	Creative Expression	Art Criticism
3 POINTS	The student demonstrates knowledge of the lives and work of Franz Marc and Pablo Picasso.	The student accurately identifies use of visual rhythm in two-dimensional art.	The student's nonobjective design demonstrates a good understanding of how to use visual rhythm.	The student thoughtfully and honestly evaluates own work using the four steps of art criticism.
2 POINTS	The student's knowledge of Franz Marc and Pablo Picasso is weak or incomplete.	The student shows an emerging awareness of visual rhythm in two-dimensional art but cannot identify it consistently.	The student's nonobjective design shows some use and understanding of visual rhythm.	The student attempts to evaluate own work but shows an incomplete understanding of evaluation criteria.
1 POINT	The student cannot demonstrate knowledge of Franz Marc and Pablo Picasso.	The student cannot identify use of visual rhythm.	The student's nonobjective design shows no understanding of visual rhythm.	The student makes no attempt to evaluate own work.

Then have students complete pages 39 or 40 in their *Assessment* books.

Lesson 5 Overview: Visual Movement

Lesson 5 introduces the art principle of movement and focuses on visual movement. **Movement** is the principle of art that leads a viewer's eyes through a work of art. **Visual movement** is created by repeating an art element or object in a work of art.

Objectives

Art History and Culture
To demonstrate knowledge of the lives and work of Henri Rousseau and Paul Cézanne

Creative Expression
To create a fantasy landscape using visual movement

Aesthetic Perception
To understand how artists use visual movement in two-dimensional art

Art Criticism
To evaluate own work using the four steps of art criticism

Lesson Materials
- sketchbook, pencils, erasers
- computer, Art Journal
- draw, paint, or word program
- pencils, erasers
- 9" × 12" heavy white drawing paper
- tempera paints, mixing trays
- water containers, paintbrushes
- paper towels, newspaper
- teacher-collected images of animals, birds, reptiles (optional)

Alternate materials:
- copier or drawing paper
- crayons, oil pastels
- watercolor paints

Program Resources
- *Reading and Writing Test Prep.*, pp. 38–39
- *Transparency 17*
- *Flash Cards* 6, 9
- *Artist Profiles*, pp. 16, 54
- *Animals Through History Time Line*
- *Assessment*, pp. 41–42
- *Large Prints 77* Jubilee: Ghana Harvest Festival and *78* The Horse Fair
- *The National Museum of Women in the Arts Collection*

Concept Trace
Movement
Introduced: Level 5, Unit 5, Lesson 3
Reinforced: Level 7, Chapter 3, Lesson 6

Vocabulary

Review the following vocabulary words with students before beginning the lesson.

movement *movimiento*—the principle of art that leads a viewer's eyes throughout a work of art

visual movement *movimiento visual*—created by repeating an art element or object in a work of art

See page 119B for additional vocabulary and Spanish vocabulary resources.

Art Journal: Vocabulary
Have students add these words to the Vocabulary section of their Art Journals.

Lesson 5 Arts Integration

Theatre
Complete Unit 3, Lesson 5, on pages 62–63 of *Theatre Arts Connection*.

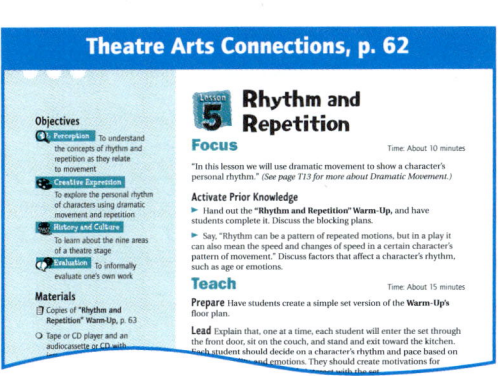

Music
Have students listen to "Spinning Wheel" by Blood Sweat and Tears. Ask students what patterns in the melody and rhythm seem to suggest a spinning wheel? When do the voices suggest movement, when does the accompaniment?

Movement & Dance
Working with groups of eight, have students make secret tableaux (frozen pictures). The first group decides on a theme and then creates and sequences three frozen pictures to show that idea. Have the rest of the class seated as an audience. The group creates their first tableau and holds it for eight counts, and then the audience closes their eyes for eight counts while the group creates the next tableau. Have students continue this sequence.

LESSON 5 • Visual Movement **111B**

Focus

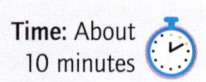

Time: About 10 minutes

Activate Prior Knowledge

"Have you ever seen a landscape where your eyes seemed to travel from one thing to the next?" "¿Han visto un paisaje en que sus ojos se mueven de una cosa a la otra?"

- Discuss students' answers. Explain that artists use techniques that cause the viewer to look at everything in a picture. They do this by repeating lines, shapes, colors, and objects in an organized manner.

Using Literature ⭐ Reading

- Read *Henri Rousseau* by Susanne Pfleger. Read about Rousseau and study the illustrations in the book for visual movement.

Thematic Connection ⭐ Science

- **Environment:** Have students describe different types of environments using as many senses as possible.

Introduce the Art

Look

"Let's take a closer look at the way visual movement is used in these two works of art." "Miren detalladamente cómo un movimiento visual es usado en estas dos obras de arte."

Laws ⭐ Social Studies

- What laws does the government have in place to protect the environment? Answers will vary, but discuss the Environmental Protection Agency. The agency's mission is "to protect human health and to safeguard the natural environment—air, water, and land—upon which life depends."

Art History and Culture

Both paintings are landscapes. *Exotic Landscape* looks like a jungle landscape; *Bottom of the Ravine* looks like a mountainous landscape.

Web Connection

Visit www.nortonsimon.org for more information about the Norton Simon Museum.

112 UNIT 3 • Rhythm, Movement, and Pattern

Lesson 5: Visual Movement

▲ **Henri Rousseau.** (French). *Exotic Landscape.* 1910.
Oil on canvas. 51¼ × 64 inches (130.18 × 162.56 cm.). Norton Simon Museum, Pasadena, California.

Look closely at the works of art by Rousseau and Cézanne. Henri Rousseau never lived in the exotic places his paintings depict. Instead, his paintings are based on his imagination and on images from books and personal sketches. He often visited the zoo and botanical garden, studying what he saw and creating detailed drawings. Rousseau was a self-taught artist and began painting after age forty. Paul Cézanne began his career with the impressionist painters in Paris. This group painted outdoors or from photographs. Although *Bottom of the Ravine* is a landscape, it was not painted outside or from a photograph. Instead, Cézanne created his landscape from several images in his sketchbooks, arranging them into one composition. Notice how the painted shapes and colors lead your eyes through both paintings.

Art History and Culture

Do both of the paintings have the same subject matter?

112 Unit 3 • Lesson 5

Art History and Culture

Henri Rousseau

Henri Rousseau (än rē ´rōō sō´) (1844–1910) is most famous for his painted images of exotic jungle scenes and animals. Rousseau never visited the places he painted. His images were composed from the numerous sketches he made in the Paris Botanical Gardens and Zoo. He also worked from postcards, photographs, and encyclopedias to create the animals in his paintings. Rousseau was a self-taught artist and did not begin painting until after he was 40. He was greatly admired by Pablo Picasso and Georges Braque.

See pages 24–25 and 16–21 for more about art history and the subject matter.

Artist Profiles, p. 54

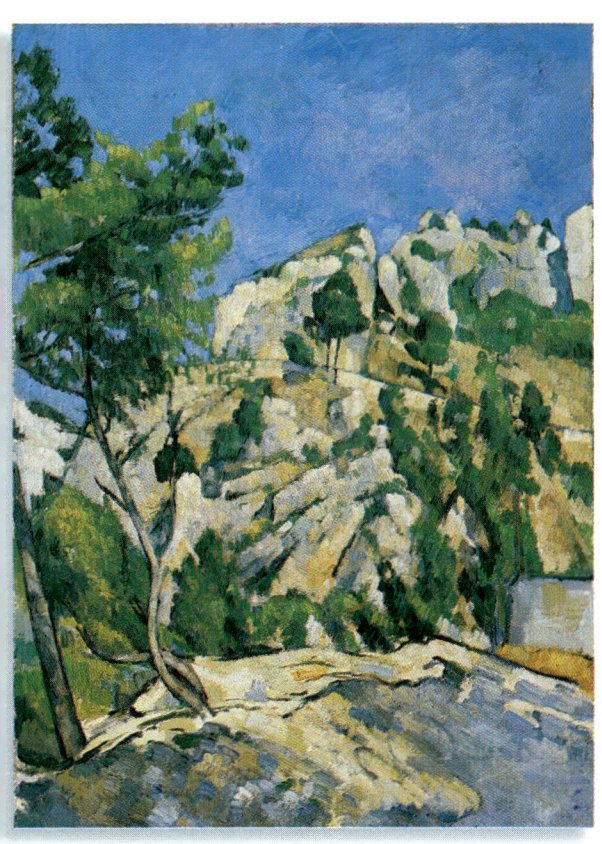

Study Both works of art to see how visual movement is used.

- Which elements or objects pull your eyes through each work?
- What object or area do you see first in Rousseau's painting? Describe the direction in which your eyes move when you look at *Exotic Landscape*.
- What object or area do you notice first in *Bottom of the Ravine*? Describe the direction in which your eyes move when you look at this painting.
- Which painting is the most active and which one is the most calm?

▲ **Paul Cézanne.** (French). *Bottom of the Ravine.* 1879.
Oil on canvas. 28¾ × 21¼ inches (73.03 × 53.98 cm.). Museum of Fine Arts, Houston, Texas.

Aesthetic Perception

Design Awareness Think about a street in a neighborhood. What are some of the objects that you would see? Are any of these objects repeated?

Unit 3 • Lesson 5   113

Study

- Possible answers are as follows. Rousseau: Color: The white shapes of the flowers on the left side draw your eye into the work; the repeated orange shapes and monkeys lead your eyes further into the work. Shapes: Across the repeated green leaf shapes back to the orange shapes and white flowers. Cézanne: Color: The greens that surround the blue gray central shapes pull your eyes in toward the center, the yellow-green leaves draw the eye through the painting. Shapes: The green shapes are created by the brush.
- Objects: The white flowers, then the oranges and white flowers to the right; the eyes move from left to right and up.
- Objects: The green tree on the upper left; the eyes move in a circular motion from the left down and around.
- Active: Rousseau: The color contrast of white, orange, and reds against the greens causes the eyes to jump around quickly. Calm: Cézanne: The cool, calm colors and a gradual value change of the blue-gray are calming.
- For more examples of landscapes, see *The National Museum of Women in the Arts Collection.*

Art Journal: Writing

Have students describe what they know about movement or motion in the Concepts section of their Art Journals. What else do they want to know about visual movement?

Art History and Culture

Paul Cézanne

Paul Cézanne (pôl sā zan´) (1839–1906) believed that he could not paint the human form properly and later in life painted only still lifes and landscapes, for which he is best known. Cézanne applied color in short brushstrokes or patches, creating a mosaic effect of equal intensity. His need for perfection often caused him to work on a painting for several years. Many of his works are unsigned because he did not consider them finished.

See pages 24–25 and 16–21 for more about art history and the subject matter.

Artist Profiles, p. 16

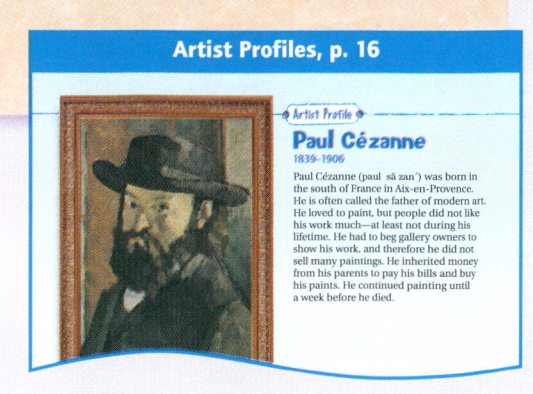

Paul Cézanne
1839–1906

Paul Cézanne (paul sā zan´) was born in the south of France in Aix-en-Provence. He is often called the father of modern art. He loved to paint, but people did not like his work much—at least not during his lifetime. He had to beg gallery owners to show his work, and therefore he did not sell many paintings. He inherited money from his parents to pay his bills and buy his paints. He continued painting until a week before he died.

Aesthetic Perception

Design Awareness Explain to students that in a neighborhood the structure of homes, whether they are brick apartment buildings or wooden homes, the structures are often similar. This arrangement is pleasing to the eye and causes the viewer to look along the street at the homes.

Developing Visual Literacy Compare the two works of art. What were the two artists trying to communicate? Encourage students to share personal experiences that contribute to their understanding of the works of art.

Web Connection

Visit www.mfah.org for more information on the Museum of Fine Arts, Houston.

LESSON 5 • Visual Movement   113

Teach

Time: About 45 minutes

"How can you use visual movement in your art?" "¿Cómo pueden usar el movimiento visual en su arte?"

- Read and discuss using visual movement in two-dimensional art on page 114.

Practice

Materials: pre-cut construction paper shapes in a variety of colors; 9" × 12" or larger black or white background paper; envelope to hold cut shapes (one per table group)

Alternate Materials: crayons

- Each group needs a minimum of fifteen pre-cut shapes, five each of any three shapes such as five free-form, five triangles, or five squares. Use a variety of colors.
- Distribute the materials and have students follow the directions on page 114.

Creative Expression

Materials: art journal, pencils and erasers, 9" × 12" heavy white drawing paper or bristol board (illustration board), tempera paints, mixing trays, water containers, thick and thin paintbrushes, paper towels, newspaper, optional: teacher-collected images of animals, birds, reptiles

Alternate Materials: crayons or oil pastels, watercolor paints and white drawing paper

- Distribute the materials and have students follow the directions on page 114.
- Review the Activity Tips on page 238 for visual examples of techniques if needed.

Art Journal: Research/Planning

Have students look through a variety of visual resources such as photographs, magazines, and books for animal images. Have students select one or two images to create several sketches in their Art Journals. Students can use the studies and sketches for the Creative Expression activity.

114 UNIT 3 • Rhythm, Movement, and Pattern

Using Visual Movement

Have you ever seen an image of repeated circles or curves on the surface of water? When a rock is thrown into a body of calm water, we see a rippling effect. In one ring after another, the circles move from where the rock landed. The photograph captures this effect. You do not see the actual movement: the repeated circles and curved lines cause your eyes to move away from the center. Repeated windows on a building make your eyes move across the building. While driving in a car, have you ever noticed fence or telephone poles? The repeated posts and poles pull your eyes along as you are driving by. These are all examples of movement. **Movement** is the principle of art that leads a viewer's eyes through a work of art.

Artists use **visual movement** in a work of art by repeating art elements or objects. Look at the photographs on this page. Notice how the repeated lines, shapes, colors, and objects lead your eyes through the images.

Practice

As a group, arrange cut shapes to create visual movement.

1. Look through the shapes you have been given by your teacher. Select a piece of paper as a background color. Do not glue any of your arrangements.
2. Make two arrangements. First, arrange all like shapes to create a path across your background color. Randomly add in two or three other shapes.
3. Make up your own design for your second arrangement.

114 Unit 3 • Lesson 5

Differentiated Instruction

Reteach
Have students work in small groups and look through magazines to find examples of visual movement by locating repeated shapes, lines, colors, and objects.

Special Needs
To ensure student success in this activity, give them an opportunity to practice creating visual movement by affixing cut-out objects onto a display board.

ELL
Have students create a list of words that they associate with movement.

◀ Soyeon Hwang.
Age 12.

Think about what art element or object was used to create visual movement in the student artist's work.

Creative Expression

Show visual movement in a fantasy jungle painting.

1. Look over your sketches and select several of your images to transfer onto your drawing paper. Choose at least one animal to include in your composition and lightly draw it in first. As you draw, fill in any open spaces with overlapping plant shapes.
2. Practice mixing a variety of greens and testing them on a scrap piece of paper. Do this with any color you mix before applying it to your painting.
3. Begin painting the objects in your drawing. First outline your shape with a small paintbrush, then fill it in.
4. Create an area of interest by using a lighter color or different shape.

Art Criticism

Describe Describe the objects in your painting.

Analyze List the colors, lines, shapes, and objects you used to create visual movement.

Interpret Does your work convey a particular feeling? Explain.

Decide Do you feel you were successful in creating visual movement in a fantasy jungle painting? Explain.

Unit 3 • Lesson 5   **115**

Reflect

Time: About 5 minutes

Review and Assess

"Can you explain how an artist uses visual movement in two-dimensional works of art?"
"¿Pueden explicar cómo un artista usa el movimiento visual en obras de arte bidimensionales?"

Think

The various tints and shades of green create visual movement, as well as the repeated leaf shapes.

- Use **Large Prints 77** *Jubilee: Ghana Harvest Festival* and **78** *The Horse Fair* to have students identify how visual movement was created.

Informal Assessment

- For standardized-format test practice using this lesson's art content, see pages 38–39 in *Reading and Writing Test Preparation*.

Art Journal: Critical Thinking

Have students answer the four art criticism questions—Describe, Analyze, Interpret, and Decide—in their Art Journals. Lead a class discussion on how visual movement was used in the fantasy jungle paintings by the students. Compare how the students used different art elements and objects to show movement in their work.

Art Across the Curriculum

Use these simple ideas to reinforce art concepts across the curriculum.

★ **Descriptive Writing** Have students write a description of a jungle at night.

★ **Math** Explain to students that in most countries distance is measured in kilometers, not miles.

★ **Science** Have students list what animals live in mountainous and jungle areas.

★ **Social Studies** Have students identify ways people have modified the environment.

★ **Technology** Using clip art in a word processing program, have students make a collage of things found in the jungle. Visit **SRAonline.com** to print detailed instructions for this activity.
NSAE 6.b

LESSON 5 • Visual Movement   **115**

Lesson 5 Wrap-Up: Visual Movement

Extra! For the Art Specialist

Time: About 45 minutes

Focus
Study **Large Print 78** *The Horse Fair*, and discuss how the artist used the art elements and objects to create visual movement. What elements or objects move your eyes through the artwork?

Teach
Have the students gather a variety of plants and leaves from around your classroom or from home. Also have students collect images of animals, birds, and reptiles. These can be real or imaginary animals. Then have students complete the alternate activity.

Reflect
Have students use the four steps of art criticism to evaluate their work. Did they effectively use the art elements and objects to create visual movement? Can they recognize what plants and animals their classmates used as models?

Alternate Activity

Materials:
- sketchbook, pencils, erasers
- heavy white drawing paper
- crayons or oil pastels, watercolor paints
- mixing trays, water containers
- paintbrushes
- paper towels, newspaper, real plants and/or leaves

1. Begin by having students look closely at the plants and create several sketches, directly observing the shapes, textures, and various colors of the leaves. Then have students add animals to their sketches. Emphasize filling the page.

2. Have students color the botanical forms and animals with crayons or oil pastels. Have them apply the color so that it is thick enough to resist the watercolor paint when it is applied.

3. Have students use watercolor washes in contrasting colors to help create visual movement.

Research in Art Education

Collaboration is an important benefit of the arts. In the visual arts, students may engage in "enterprises such as painting murals and scenery, producing books, and organizing exhibitions." They also often have the opportunity to learn to appropriately critique the work of others ("Learning in and Through the Arts: Curriculum Implications" in *Champions of Change*, p. 40).

Assessment

Use the following rubric to evaluate the artwork students make in the Creative Expression activity and to assess students' understanding of how visual movement is used in two-dimensional art.

Then have students complete pages 41 or 42 in their *Assessment* books.

	Art History and Culture	Aesthetic Perception	Creative Expression	Art Criticism
3 POINTS	The student demonstrates knowledge of the lives and work of Henri Rousseau and Paul Cézanne.	The student accurately identifies the use of visual movement in two-dimensional works of art.	The student's fantasy landscape clearly demonstrates using visual movement.	The student thoughtfully and honestly evaluates own work using the four steps of art criticism.
2 POINTS	The student's knowledge of Henri Rousseau and Paul Cézanne is weak or incomplete.	The student shows an emerging awareness of visual movement in two-dimensional works of art, but cannot consistently identify them.	The student's fantasy landscape shows some awareness of visual movement.	The student attempts to evaluate own work but shows an incomplete understanding of evaluation criteria.
1 POINT	The student cannot demonstrate knowledge of Henri Rousseau and Paul Cézanne.	The student cannot identify how visual movement is used.	The student's fantasy landscape shows no understanding of how to create visual movement.	The student makes no attempt to evaluate own work.

115A UNIT 3 • Rhythm, Movement, and Pattern

Lesson 6 Overview

Kinetic Movement

Lesson 6 closely looks at how kinetic movement is used in three-dimensional objects. **Kinetic movement** is actual or real movement. **Kinetic sculpture** is a sculpture that actually moves in space.

Objectives

Art History and Culture
To demonstrate knowledge of the lives and work of Alexander Calder and Timothy Rose

Creative Expression
To create a mobile based on kinetic movement

Aesthetic Perception
To understand how artists use kinetic movement in three-dimensional forms

Art Criticism
To evaluate own work using the four steps of art criticism

Lesson Materials
- $4\frac{1}{2}" \times 6"$ pieces of construction paper
- chenille sticks, paper clips
- string, hole punch
- pencils, erasers
- Art Journal, scissors
- pliable wire, pliers
- fine sandpaper, mat board
- acrylic paints, paintbrushes
- mixing trays, paper towels
- water containers
- newspaper, wire cutters

Alternate Materials:
- copier paper or notebook paper
- thin wire coat hangers
- posterboard, manila folders or paper plates
- tempera paint or color markers

Program Resources
- *Reading and Writing Test Prep.*, pp. 40–41
- *Transparency 18*
- *Artist Profiles,* pp. 14, 52
- *Animals Through History Time Line*
- *Assessment,* pp. 43-44
- *Large Prints 77 Jubilee: Ghana Harvest Festival* and *78 The Horse Fair*

Concept Trace
Kinetic Movement
Introduced: Level 6, Unit 3, Lesson 6
Reinforced: Level 7, Chapter 3, Lesson 6

Vocabulary

Review the following vocabulary words with students.

futurists *futuristas*—a group of Italian artists during the early twentieth-century who repeated and overlapped shapes and lines to create the illusion of movement

mobile *móvil*—a moving sculpture in which shapes are balanced and arranged on wire arms and suspended from the ceiling to move freely in the air currents

See page 119B for additional vocabulary and Spanish vocabulary resources.

Art Journal: Vocabulary
Have students add these words to the Vocabulary section of their Art Journals.

Lesson 6 Arts Integration

Theatre
Complete Unit 3, Lesson 6, on pages 64–69 of *Theatre Arts Connections.*

Music
Have students listen to "Five Step Waltz" by Edward Roland. Ask students what happens to the strong beats? Do the strong beats stay even? Ask students if it is possible to have five beats for a waltz? Do students enjoy listening to this music?

Movement & Dance
This activity explores the kinetic impact of wind. Place six people together. Four people will be various objects: trash cans, trees, paper, or clothes on a line. Two people will be the wind. The students should be in a shape that depicts their object, but they will remain still until the wind comes by and puts them in motion. Have students compare and contrast how each object moves.

LESSON 6 • Kinetic Movement **115B**

Focus

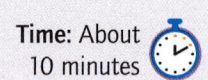

Time: About 10 minutes

Activate Prior Knowledge

"Have you ever seen a mobile or a wind sock hanging outside or from a ceiling?" "¿Han visto un móvil o una manga de aire colgado afuera o de un techo?"

- Discuss students' comments and explain that these objects are moved by air currents. There are many other objects that are moved by air currents, such as balloons and kites.

Using Literature ⭐ Reading

- Look at the cover illustration of *Call It Courage* by Armstrong Sperry. Notice how the waves are splashing up on the rocks and the waves are moving. Natural forces cause the ocean currents and formation of waves.

Thematic Connection ⭐ Science

- **Movement:** Have students describe different types of movement. Students can demonstrate or give examples of these movements if possible.

Introduce the Art

Look

"Let's take a closer look at the way Alexander Calder and Tim Rose created their mobiles."
"Miren detalladamente en la manera que Alexander Calder y Tim Rose crearon sus móviles."

Simple Machines ⭐ Science

- How are these mobiles like a simple machine? Answers will vary. Explain to students that simple machines are tools that make work easier. They have few or no moving parts and use energy to work. Some examples of simple machines are a lever, a pulley, a screw, and a wedge.

Art History and Culture

Rose was first influenced by Calder, but later he studied the work of Wassily Kandisky and combined the two influences in his mobiles.

💻 Web Connection

Visit www.calder.org for more information about the Calder Foundation.

116 UNIT 3 • Rhythm, Movement, and Pattern

Lesson 6: Kinetic Movement

▲ **Alexander Calder.** (American). *Lobster Trap and Fish Tail.* 1939. Painted steel, wire, and sheet aluminum. 8 feet 6 inches × 9 feet 6 inches (2.6 × 2.9 m.). Museum of Modern Art, New York, New York.

Look closely at the works of art by Alexander Calder and Timothy Rose. Both works are example of mobiles that hang from a ceiling. Alexander Calder invented the mobile in 1932. He named his works after they were installed in their settings. His last mobile, *Untitled,* was installed in the National Gallery of Art in Washington, D.C. after his death. You can see some similarities when you look at *Lobster Trap and Fish Tail* and *Double Pan Swoosh.* These mobiles contain painted cutout shapes connected by wires. Air currents set them in motion. Watching these mobiles move is like watching graceful dancers.

Art History and Culture

Do you think Alexander Calder's mobiles influenced the work of Timothy Rose?

116   Unit 3 • Lesson 6

Art History and Culture

Alexander Calder

In 1926 Alexander Calder (a lig zan´ dər kôl´ dər) (1898–1976) began creating small three-dimensional sculptures of circus figures. His work became more abstract and began taking the form of simple shapes. Eventually, he designed sculptures that moved mechanically and then created works that moved with the air. Calder had invented the mobile. These free-moving, hanging sculptures lead to "stabiles," which are sculptures that incorporate the mobiles with sculptural bases so that they stand on the ground. His mobiles were never named until they were installed.

See pages 24–25 and 16–21 for more about art history and the subject matter.

Artist Profiles, p. 14

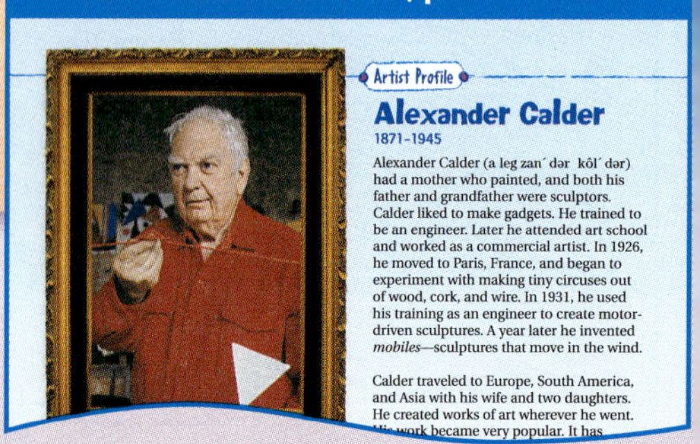

Artist Profile

Alexander Calder
1871-1945

Alexander Calder (a leg zan´ dər kôl´ dər) had a mother who painted, and both his father and grandfather were sculptors. Calder liked to make gadgets. He trained to be an engineer. Later he attended art school and worked as a commercial artist. In 1926, he moved to Paris, France, and began to experiment with making tiny circuses out of wood, cork, and wire. In 1931, he used his training as an engineer to create motor-driven sculptures. A year later he invented *mobiles*—sculptures that move in the wind.

Calder traveled to Europe, South America, and Asia with his wife and two daughters. He created works of art wherever he went. His work became very popular. It has

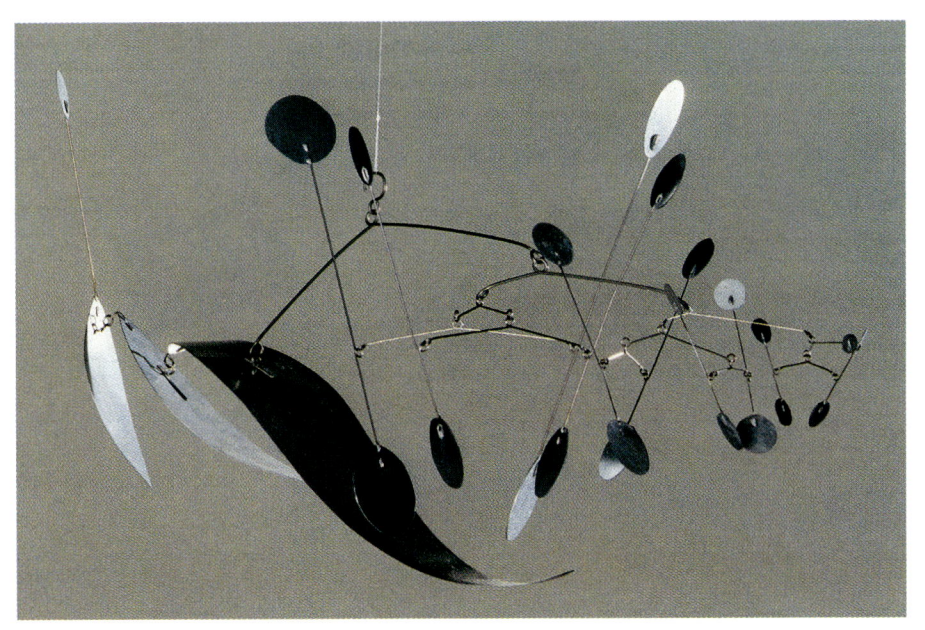

Study both works of art to see how kinetic movement is used.

- Which elements or objects do you see repeated in each artwork?
- Which lines or shapes appear to move in *Lobster Trap and Fish Tail*?
- Which lines or shapes appear to move in *Double Pan Swoosh*?
- Describe how you think both mobiles move.

▲ **Timothy Rose.** (American). *Double Pan Swoosh.* 2001. Stainless steel. 24 inches (60.96 cm.). Private Collection.

Aesthetic Perception

Design Awareness Think about banners or flags you have seen outdoors. What do they look like when they are hanging? What effect does a soft breeze have on them?

Unit 3 • Lesson 6 **117**

Art History and Culture

Timothy Rose

Timothy Rose (tiˊmə theˉ roˉz) (1941–) was born in Washington, D.C., and studied anthropology at San Francisco State University in California. His mobiles were first inspired by the work of Alexander Calder. Later, Kandinsky's drawings of overlapping layers of floating, outlined shapes influenced the way Rose created his sculptures. His sculptures changed from the Calderlike separated shapes to overlapping forms. Rose's works range in size from small sculptures to large installations that take up an entire ceiling. His works are often colorful, and many create the sensation of movement even while still. Rose has been creating mobile sculpture for more than 30 years.

See pages 24–25 and 16–21 for more about art history and the subject matter.

Artist Profiles, p. 52

Study

▶ *Lobster Trap and Fish Tail:* Flat organic or free-form shapes that move gradually from the smallest on the left to the largest on the right. *Double Pan Swoosh:* A series of 22 circles appear to move in diminishing size from the left to the right. Each set of circles is held by a straight vertical rod hung from horizontal hangers.

▶ Everything except the wires in the lobster trap seems to move.

▶ They all appear to move; however, the vertical rods with circles at each end appear to move the most because of their size and arrangement.

▶ *Lobster Trap and Fish Tail:* Flat organic or free-form shapes that are attached to horizontal wires appear to move up and down. The fish appears to move in a circular motion, and the lobster trap looks like it can move in any direction. *Double Pan Swoosh:* The long rods seem to move from side to side.

■ For more examples of abstract and nonobjective art, see **The National Museum of Women in the Arts Collection.**

Art Journal: Writing

Have students explain what they know about the word *kinetic* in the Concepts section of their Art Journals. What else do they want to know about kinetic movement?

Aesthetic Perception

Design Awareness Like mobiles, banners and flags move by air currents or wind. Discuss with students their experiences and knowledge of how air currents cause motion.

Developing Visual Literacy Discuss the subject matter of each mobile. Invite students to share personal experiences that contribute to their understanding of the works of art. For example, have they seen a fish swim before?

Web Connection

Visit www.mobilesculpture.com for more information about Timothy Rose.

LESSON 6 • Kinetic Movement **117**

Teach

Time: About 45 minutes

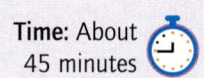

"How do you think you might be able to create a mobile to show how kinetic movement works?" "¿Cómo creen que pueden crear un móvil para demostrar como funciona el movimiento cinético?"

- Read and discuss using kinetic movement on page 118.

Practice

Materials: $4\frac{1}{2}" \times 6"$ pieces of construction paper, chenille sticks, paper clips, string, hole punch

Alternate Materials: notebook or copier paper

- Paper clips can be used with the "S" hook or in place of it. Demonstrate hooking two or more paper clips together to make a chain to hang the shapes.
- Distribute the materials and have students follow the directions on page 118.

Creative Expression

Materials: Art Journal, pencils and erasers, scissors, string, hole punch, scissors, pliable wire, pliers, mat board, fine sandpaper, acrylic paints, paintbrushes, mixing trays, water containers, paper towels, newspaper

Alternate Materials: thin wire coat hangers, posterboard, manila folders or paper plates, tempera paint or color markers

- Distribute the materials and have students follow the directions on page 119.
- Review the Activity Tips on page 238 for visual examples of techniques, if needed.

Art Journal: Brainstorming

Have students work in groups to generate a list of ideas that could be used as the subject matter of a mobile like Calder's. Ask students to write their lists in the Idea section of their Art Journals. Have each group share their ideas, and encourage students to add any ideas, that they did not have listed. Students can select an idea for their Creative Expression activity.

118 UNIT 3 • Rhythm, Movement, and Pattern

Using Kinetic Movement

Kinetic movement is actual or real movement. Artists can sometimes control the way their sculpture moves by limiting the amount of motion. A pendulum on a clock swings back and forth and only at a controlled distance. In other sculptural forms, such as a mobile, movement is unpredictable. The wind or air currents may move the objects on a mobile slightly or not at all.

It is difficult to capture kinetic movement in a painting or drawing. A group of artists known as the "futurists" portrayed the idea of movement in their paintings. They used overlapping and slanting lines and shapes to make painted surfaces seem as if they were moving. Alexander Calder believed in what the futurists were doing. In his work he repeated shapes, but unlike the futurists, his shapes really moved. He used the natural forces of gravity and air currents to put his sculptures into real motion. Calder's creation of the mobile is called a "kinetic sculpture" because it actually moves in space.

Practice

Experiment with kinetic movement.
1. Cut four equal-sized shapes of paper.
2. Punch a hole at the top and bottom of each shape.
3. Use paper clips to connect the shapes together. Try different configurations.

118 Unit 3 • Lesson 6

Differentiated Instruction

Reteach
Have students hold a long strip of paper away from their body. Ask them to move their arms slowly forward, then back, then come to rest until the paper stops moving. Ask the students to explain what happened to the paper when the arm was moving and then still.

Special Needs
Reinforce the concept of kinetic movement by engaging students' sense of hearing. Create a mobile whose parts make sounds as they touch (or bring in a windchime). Have students note the effect that air movement has upon the sculpture.

ELL
Have students explain in their own words the difference between visual and kinetic movement.

◀ **Courtney Davis.**
Age 11.

Think about what shapes or objects the student artist used in the mobile.

Creative Expression

Create a graceful moving mobile using wire and mat board.

1. Look over your list in the Ideas section of your Art Journal. Select one subject and begin by sketching simple shapes or objects.
2. Select five or seven of your images to transfer onto your pieces of mat board. Punch a hole in the top of each shape. Use sandpaper to smooth out the cut edges of your board by sanding in one direction.
3. Use acrylic paints to paint your shapes.
4. Lay out your shapes on a large piece of newspaper. Draw the wire lines showing how the pieces will connect. Begin at the bottom and work your way up.
5. Follow the Mobile Technique Tip, and connect your mobile. Attach the top bar last.

Art Criticism

Describe Describe the subject of your mobile.

Analyze List the colors, lines, shapes, and objects you used to create your mobile.

Interpret Does your mobile communicate your subject matter? Explain.

Decide Do you feel you were successful in creating a mobile using kinetic movement? Explain.

Unit 3 • Lesson 6   **119**

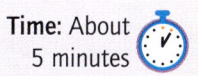

Reflect
Time: About 5 minutes

Review and Assess
"Describe how kinetic movement was used by the artists in their mobiles." "Describan como el movimiento cinético fue usado por los artistas en sus móviles."

Think
The artist used free-form shapes that include a moon, a star, and a sun.

- Use **Large Prints 77** *Jubilee: Ghana Harvest Festival* and **78** *The Horse Fair* to have students identify why these are not examples of kinetic movement.

Informal Assessment

- Have students compare career and avocational opportunities for people who create mobiles. What types of businesses might be interested in their artwork?

- For standardized-format test practice using this lesson's art content, see pages 40–41 in *Reading and Writing Test Preparation*.

Art Journal: Critical Thinking
Have students answer the four art criticism questions—Describe, Analyze, Interpret, and Decide—in their Art Journals. Lead a class discussion on how each mobile uses kinetic movement.

Art Across the Curriculum

Use these simple ideas to reinforce art concepts across the curriculum.

★ **Persuasive Writing** Have students write a paragraph about the best place to display one of the mobiles in this lesson.

★ **Math** Have students describe what kind of geometric shapes they could use to create a mobile.

★ **Science** Explain to students that an object at rest tends to stay at rest and can be changed only if force is applied to it.

★ **Social Studies** Discuss the movement of the Tower of Pisa.

★ **Technology** Using a paint or draw program, have students create geometric and free-form shapes that will be cut out and used for a mobile. Visit **SRAonline.com** to print detailed instructions for this activity.
NSAE 6.b

LESSON 6 • Kinetic Movement **119**

Lesson 6 Wrap-Up: Kinetic Movement

Extra! For the Art Specialist
Time: About 45 minutes

Focus
Study the works of art in this lesson and discuss how the artist used kinetic movement in the making of the mobile. Have students discuss the use of simple shapes in the mobile structure.

Teach
Explain to the students that they will be creating a mobile using various materials. Begin by having students brainstorm a list of materials that can be used to create a mobile. These items can be store-bought or recyclable. Give students the option of using the materials you will provide or materials they bring from home.

Reflect
Have students use the four steps of art criticism to evaluate their work. Did they effectively create a mobile that uses kinetic movement? What objects did they use? What subject matter did they choose?

Alternate Activity

Materials:
- thin aluminum
- cooper tooling or mat board for shapes
- wire cutters, pliers, pliable wire
- metal hole punch, sandpaper, scissors
- paper clips can be used in place of the "S" hook (optional)

1. Have students come up with an individual theme, such as fish or a school. Ask them to look at the materials collected and then create a simple sketch of the layout of their mobile.
2. Using scissors, have students cut their shapes from their selected materials and use the sandpaper to smooth out any rough edges.
3. Demonstrate and review the Mobile Technique Tip to form mobile wires.
4. Display the completed mobiles for class evaluation and discussion.

Research in Art Education

"The arts help students develop their abilities to appreciate and interpret art of other cultures and to learn about people of the past through exposure to reproductions, to art works in museums and galleries, or through discussions about contemporary artists and art works." (Andra Nyman, "Cultural Content, Identity, and Program Development: Approaches to Art Education for Elementary Educators," in *Contemporary Issues in Art Education*, edited by Y. Gaudelius and P. Speirs, 61–69. New Jersey: Prentice Hall, 2002.)

Assessment
Use the following rubric to evaluate the artwork students make in the Creative Expression activity and to assess students' understanding of how kinetic movement is used in mobiles.

	Art History and Culture	Aesthetic Perception	Creative Expression	Art Criticism
3 POINTS	The student demonstrates knowledge of the lives and work of Alexander Calder and Tim Rose.	The student accurately identifies the use of kinetic movement in three-dimensional objects.	The student's mobile demonstrates using kinetic movement.	The student thoughtfully and honestly evaluates own work using the four steps of art criticism.
2 POINTS	The student's knowledge of Alexander Calder and Tim Rose is weak or incomplete.	The student shows an emerging awareness of kinetic movement in three-dimensional objects, but cannot consistently identify them.	The student's mobile shows some awareness of kinetic movement.	The student attempts to evaluate own work but shows an incomplete understanding of evaluation criteria.
1 POINT	The student cannot demonstrate knowledge of Alexander Calder and Tim Rose.	The student cannot identify how kinetic movement is used.	The student's mobile shows no understanding of how to use kinetic movement.	The student makes no attempt to evaluate own work.

Have students complete pages 43 or 44 in their *Assessment* books.

Unit 3 Vocabulary Review

alternating pattern can repeat a motif but change position; alter spacing between motifs or add a second motif **patrón alternante**—puede repetir un motivo pero cambia de posición; cambiando espacio entre motivos o añadir un segundo motivo

futurists—a group of Italian artists during the early twentieth-century who repeated and overlapped shapes and lines to create the illusion of movement **futuristas**—un grupo de artistas italianos durante el principio del vigésimo siglo que repitieron y traslaparon figuras y líneas para crear la ilusión de movimiento

kinetic movement—actual or real movement **movimiento cinético**—movimiento actual o real

kinetic sculpture—a three-dimensional form that actually moves in space **escultura cinética**—una forma tridimensional que realmente se mueve en el espacio

mobile—a moving sculpture in which shapes are balanced and arranged on wire arms and suspended from the ceiling to move freely in the air currents **móvile**—una escultura movible en que figuras están balanceadas y arregladas en brazos de alambres y suspendidas del techo para moverse libremente en las corrientes de aire

motif—a unit that is made of objects or art elements which is repeated **motivo**—una unidad hecha de objetos o elementos del arte en que se repiten

movement—the principle of art that leads a viewer's eyes throughout a work of art **movimiento**—el principio artístico que guía a los ojos del observador en toda la obra de arte

nonobjective—art that has no recognizable subject matter **abstracto**—arte que no tiene materia de sujeto reconocido

parallel lines—lines that move in the same direction and always stay the same distance apart **líneas paralelas**—líneas que se mueven en la misma dirección y siempre se quedan a misma distancia

pattern—a repeated surface decoration **patrón**—una decoración de superficie que se repite

random pattern—occurs when the motif is repeated in no apparent order **patrón al azar**—ocurre cuando un motivo se repite en ningún orden aparente

regular pattern—occurs when identical motifs are repeated with an equal amount of space between them **patrón regular**—cuando motivos idénticos son repetidos con un espacio igual entre ellos

rhythm—the principle of design that organizes the elements in a work of art by repeating elements and/or objects **ritmo**—el principio del diseño que organiza los elementos en una obra de arte por elementos que se repiten y/u objetos

three-dimensional patterns—patterns that have depth and are formed on the surface of a sculptural form **patrones tridimensionales**—patrones que tienen profundidad y se forman en la superficie de una forma de escultura

visual movement—created by repeating an art element or object in a work of art **movimiento visual**—creado repitiendo un elemento de arte u objeto en una obra de arte

Vocabulary Practice

Display **Transparency 42** to review unit vocabulary words.

Similes — Vocabulary
Have students create a simile for the word pattern. Repeat the process for other unit vocabulary words.

Prefixes and Suffixes — Vocabulary
Have students identify prefixes and suffixes using the unit vocabulary words. Then have them discuss what these word parts mean.

Word Origins — Vocabulary
Have a volunteer look up the word *rhythm* in a dictionary and explain where the word originated. Repeat the process for other unit vocabulary words.

UNIT 3 • Rhythm, Movement, and Pattern **119B**

Wrapping Up Unit 3
Rhythm, Movement, and Pattern

Art Criticism

Critical Thinking Art criticism is an organized system of looking at and talking about art. You can criticize art without being an expert. The purpose of art criticism is to get the viewer involved in a perception process that delays judgment until all aspects of the artwork have been studied. Push the students to expand beyond the art criticism questions.

- See page 28–29 for more about art criticism.

Describe

- Students' answers may include the following: In the foreground there is a building. In the center of the painting is a four-lane highway with cars and a yellow bus. To the right of the highway, in the middle ground, are more buildings, some tall and some short.
- The land goes uphill. Things get smaller; the roads get narrower.

Analyze

- Straight diagonals: road and sidewalks. Two curving pathways moving vertically. Throughout the painting there are repeated vertical and horizontal lines in the buildings. A zigzag line is created by the connected rooftops.
- Cool greens, blues, and violets
- The floors and windows on the tall buildings, the repeated parallel lines on the roads
- Students' answers may include the following: There is rhythmic repetition in the repeated buildings, repeated tree shapes, and repeated lamps along the pathways.
- Visual movement is created through repeated lines, shapes, and colors and the converging lines as they move up the hill.

120 UNIT 3 • Rhythm, Movement, and Pattern

Wrapping Up Unit 3
Rhythm, Movement, and Pattern

▲ **Wayne Thiebaud.** (American). *Down Eighteenth Street.* 1980. Oil and charcoal on canvas. 48 × 35$\frac{7}{8}$ inches (121.92 × 91.14 cm.). The Hirshhorn Museum and Sculpture Garden, Smithsonian Institution, Washington, D.C.

120   Unit 3

Art History and Culture

Wayne Thiebaud

Wayne Thiebaud (wān tē´ bō) (1920–) became interested in drawing in high school and later worked as a freelance cartoonist and illustrator. During military service in World War II, he drew cartoons for the military-based newspaper. In 1949, he became a painter. His first one-person show in New York was received with praise. His subject matter was images of mass-produced consumer goods, particularly junk food, and he was considered a pop artist. Later he became classified as an American realist. Since the 1970s, he concentrated on urban landscapes of San Francisco.

See pages 24–25 and 16–21 for more about art history and the subject matter.

Artist Profiles, p. 62

Art Criticism Critical Thinking

Describe What do you see?
During this step you will collect information about the subject of the work.
- List all of the things you see.
- Describe how the environment changes from the foreground to the background.

Analyze How is this work organized?
Think about how the artist has used the elements and principles of art.
- What types of lines do you see?
- What is the main color scheme?
- Where do you see patterns?
- Where do you see rhythmic repetition?
- How does the artist create visual movement?

Interpret What does the artwork say?
Combine clues you collected during description and analysis with your personal experiences to find out what this painting is about.
- What season and what time of day does this work express?
- How does the artist's use of elements and principles affect the expressive quality of this work?
- Has the artist made this a place you would like to visit? Why or why not?

Decide What do you think about the work?
Use all the information you have gathered to decide why this is a successful work of art.
- Is this work successful because it is realistic? Because it is well organized? Because it conveys a message? Explain.

Interpret

▶ Answers will vary. Most will say springtime because of the yellow-green grass and the pinks and lavenders on the trees and bushes. The long, dark blue shadows indicate late afternoon. Very little traffic indicates late day.

▶ Answers will vary. Some students may comment on his use of line giving the painting a calm and stable quality to the painting. Others may comment on the colors, which also add to the calmness.

▶ Student answers will vary based on individual experiences. There is no one right answer, but make sure that the student's explanation is reasonable.

Decide

▶ Student answers will vary based on individual experiences. They may use more than one aesthetic theory to explain the success of this work. There is no one right answer, but make sure that the student's explanation is reasonable.

Art Journal: Writing
Have students write answers to Aesthetic Perception in their Art Journals. Have them discuss their answers in small groups.

Aesthetic Perception

Seeing Like an Artist Think about your favorite community. What types of patterns and rhythms would you see there? Compare and contrast this community to *Down Eighteenth Street*.

Describe
- List and describe common items in their community.

Analyze
- Which items have patterns?
- What kinds of rhythms do these items create?

Interpret
- How do patterns and rhythms in the community make you feel? Why?

Decide
- Do you have strong feelings when you think about this community?

"Artists use pattern, rhythm, and movement to organize art elements in both two- and three-dimensional works of art."

"Los artistas usan patrón, ritmo, y movimiento para organizar los elementos artísticos en obras de arte bi y tridimensionales."

T Review unit vocabulary with students, using **Transparency 39**.

Art Journal: Writing
Have students answer the questions on page 122 in their Art Journals or on a separate sheet of paper. **Answers: 1. B, 2. C, 3. B, 4. C, 5. A**

T For further assessment, have students complete the unit test on **Transparency 45**.

CAREERS IN ART
Archivist
▶ Explain what an archivist does.
Archivists save records on a variety of media, including paper, film, videotape, audiotape, electronic disk, and computer. They also may be copied onto some other format to protect the original, and to make them more accessible to researchers who use the records.

". . . painting I think is a kind of x-ray of the visual world. It looks under, around, through, develops different species, different configurations."
—Wayne Thiebaud

122 UNIT 3 • Rhythm, Movement, and Pattern

Wrapping Up Unit 3
Pattern, Rhythm, and Movement continued

Show What You Know
Answer these questions on a separate sheet of paper.

1. In a piece of art, _____ is created by repeated positive shapes separated by negative spaces.
   A. texture
   B. visual rhythm
   C. color scheme

2. A _____ is a repeated surface decoration.
   A. motif
   B. space
   C. pattern

3. _____ movement is actual or real movement.
   A. Visual
   B. Kinetic
   C. Active

4. _____ is the principle of art that leads a viewer's eyes through a work of art.
   A. Pattern
   B. Rhythm
   C. Movement

5. A _____ pattern occurs when the motif is repeated in no apparent order.
   A. random
   B. alternating
   C. regular

122   Unit 3

Unit Assessment Options

Aesthetic Perception
Practice Have students select one of concepts in the Show What You Know section on page 122, then find examples of each concept in the classroom.

Creative Expression
Student Portfolio Have students review all the artwork they have created during this unit and select the pieces they wish to keep in their portfolios.

Art Criticism
Activity Have students select an artwork from this unit and study it using the four steps of art criticism. (See pages 28–29 for more information about art criticism.) Have students work alone or in pairs and present their findings aloud or in writing.

CAREERS IN ART
Art Historian

People who study art history have many career options. They can work for organizations and businesses, but many art historians choose to work in museums.

Archivists determine what portion of the records maintained by various groups should be made part of permanent historical holdings and which of these records should be put on exhibit.

Curators oversee collections in museums and historic sites. They also plan and prepare exhibits. Most curators use computer databases to catalogue and organize their collections.

Conservators document, treat, and preserve works of art. They examine objects and determine their condition. They then document their findings and treat items to minimize deterioration or restore them to their original state.

▲ Conservator

Pattern, Rhythm, and Movement in Dance

Isicathulo is a Zulu step dance from South Africa. Zulu dock workers and gold miners perform clever, syncopated routines accompanied by a guitar and whistle. They create rhythmic dances by organizing their well-rehearsed patterns of movements. They discovered that they could make great sounds by slapping and clicking their rubber boots together.

What to Do Make rhythmic patterns of sounds that can be organized different ways to create dances.

Work in small groups to create three or four rhythmic patterns that can be repeated. Give each pattern or routine a name. Choose one of the following or create your own: "bicycle," "salute," or "jump." Following each other or shoulder to shoulder, each rhythmic pattern must be well rehearsed and performed in unison. Dancers do a stamping walk in place until the leader calls out the name of a pattern, which they perform together.

1. Create a rhythmic movement that can be repeated. Include slapping your legs, stamping, clicking fingers, clapping, jumping, or hopping. Give your pattern a name.
2. Get into groups of three or four. Each person shares one pattern and teaches it to the others.
3. Practice all of the patterns in a line formation and perform in unison.
4. Choose a leader to call out the name of each pattern to be performed.

▲ African American Dance Ensemble. "Isicathulo."

Art Criticism

Describe What patterns did your group learn?

Analyze Does the name of each pattern provide a clue for the movement?

Interpret Did the rhythmic patterns "feel" right? Did you change them to work better?

Decide Were you successful in making the rhythm and movements work together?

Unit 3 **123**

Art History and Culture

Zulu Dance

It is said that this dance was created by Zulu students attending a mission school where the authorities had banned the local country dances. When the students began wearing shoes, the sharp sound of their boots gave the movements a distinctive character in comparison with the muffled thud of bare feet. They liked this development and began adding clicking of the heels for a new sound. The dance evolved further when the Zulu men became dock laborers at the Port of Durban in South Africa and were issued Wellington gum boots to protect their feet while handling cargoes of chemical fertilizers. They found that they could enlarge the sounds of the dance as they slapped the boots or stamped them. From this time on the dance has been called *Isicathulo,* meaning *boots*.

Pattern, Rhythm, and Movement in Dance

Objective: To create rhythmic patterns using movement

Materials: *Isicathulo,* performed by the African American Dance Ensemble, Running time: 4:37.

Focus
Time: About 5 minutes

- Discuss the information on page 123.

Art History and Culture
- Have students create a list of dances that are associated with particular cultures.

Teach
Time: About 20 minutes

Aesthetic Perception
- Have students visit the playground or gymnasium to notice the movement of people and objects.

Creative Expression
- Have each group use different body parts to create their movements.
- **Informal Assessment** When the groups demonstrate their patterns, comment positively on their use of pattern.

Reflect
Time: About 10 minutes

Art Criticism
- Have students answer the four art criticism questions on page 123 aloud or in writing.
- Were students able to successfully create rhythmic patterns?

UNIT 3 • Rhythm, Movement, and Pattern **123**

Unit 4 Planning Guide

	Lesson Title	Suggested Pacing	Creative Expression Activity
Lesson 1	Formal Balance and Symmetry	1 hour	Design a building.
Lesson 2	Approximate Symmetry	1 hour	Create an computer-generated design.
Lesson 3	Informal Balance	1 hour	Make a still-life drawing.
Lesson 4	Radial Balance	1 hour	Create a radial design.
Lesson 5	Emphasis of an Element	1 hour	Make a collograph print.
Lesson 6	Emphasis of an Area	1 hour	Create a foil group sculpture.
ARTSOURCE	Balance and Emphasis in Dance	35 minutes	Create counterbalance designs.

124A UNIT 4 • Balance and Emphasis

Materials	Program Resources	Fine Art Resources	Literature Resources
pencils, erasers, Art Journal, white paper, fine-line permanent black marker, watercolor paints, water container, paintbrushes, paper towels, newspaper	*Assessment,* pp. 45–46 *Reading and Writing Test Preparation,* pp. 42–43 *Home and After-School Connections* *Flash Card* 12	*Transparency 19* *Artist Profiles,* pp. 22, 81 *Large Prints 79* and *80* *Art Around the World Collection*	*The Wright Brothers for Kids: How They Invented the Airplane with 21 Activities Exploring the Science and History of Flight* by Mary Kay Carson, Laura D'Argo
practice image, computer, draw or paint software, printer, paper	*Assessment,* pp. 47–48 *Reading and Writing Test Preparation,* pp. 44–45	*Transparency 20* *Artist Profiles,* pp. 31, 45 *Large Prints 79* and *80* *The National Museum of Women in the Arts Collection*	*Toning the Sweep* by Angela Johnson
pencils, erasers, Art Journal, various objects in different sizes, shapes and textures, black paper, white and color chalk, damp sponges or washcloths, newspaper	*Assessment,* pp. 49–50 *Reading and Writing Test Preparation,* pp. 46–47 *Flash Card* 13	*Transparency 21* *Artist Profiles,* pp. 15, 32 *Large Prints 79* and *80* *The National Museum of Women in the Arts Collection*	*Littlejim's Dreams* by Thomas B. Allen
pencils, erasers, white paper, ruler, fine-tipped black permanent marker, color pencil, markers, circle patterns	*Assessment,* pp. 51–52 *Reading and Writing Test Preparation,* pp. 48–49 *Flash Card* 14	*Transparency 22* *Artist Profiles,* pp. 6, 38 *Large Prints 79* and *80* *Art Around the World Collection*	*Fair Weather* by Richard Peck
Art Journal, pencils, erasers, $4\frac{1}{2}$" × 6" tagboard, glue, construction paper, printing ink, brayer, sponge or washcloth, paper towels, newspaper, plate or tray to hold ink	*Assessment,* pp. 53–54 *Reading and Writing Test Preparation,* pp. 50–51 *Flash Card* 15	*Transparency 23* *Artist Profiles,* pp. 53, 60 *Large Prints 79* and *80* *The National Museum of Women in the Arts Collection*	*A Mouse Called Wolf* by Dick King-Smith
gesture drawings, pliable wire, scissors or wire cutters, aluminum foil, small scraps of wood	*Assessment,* pp. 55–56 *Reading and Writing Test Preparation,* pp. 52–53 *Flash Card* 15	*Transparency 24* *Artist Profiles,* pp. 42, 59 *Large Prints 79* and *80* *Art Around the World Collection*	*Coroline* by Neil Gaiman
"The Brass Ring"			

UNIT 4 • Balance and Emphasis **124B**

Unit Overview

4 Balance and Emphasis

Lesson 1: Symmetry is a type of formal balance in which two halves of a balanced artwork are identical.

Lesson 2: Approximate symmetry is almost symmetrical, but small differences in the artwork make it more interesting.

Lesson 3: Informal Balance allows unlike objects to have equal visual weight.

Lesson 4: Radial balance occurs when the art elements radiate from a central point.

Lesson 5: Emphasis is the principle of design that stresses one area in an artwork over another.

Lesson 6: Emphasis is examined further in this lesson.

Introduce Unit Concepts

"Artists use the art principles of balance and emphasis to help organize the art elements in two- and three-dimensional works of art."

"Los artistas usan los principios artísticos de equilibrio y énfasis para organizar los elementos artísticos en obras de arte bi y tridimensionales."

Balance
- What does the word *balance* mean to you? Have students create a class definition of *balance* and then look up the definition in the dictionary.

Emphasis
- What does it mean to emphasize something? Ask students to form small groups and to come up with one interpretation of the word *emphasis*.

Cross-Curricular Projects
- See the *Language Arts and Reading, Mathematics, Science,* and *Social Studies Art Connections* books for activities that further develop balance and emphasis concepts.

124 UNIT 4 • Balance and Emphasis

Unit 4

Balance and Emphasis

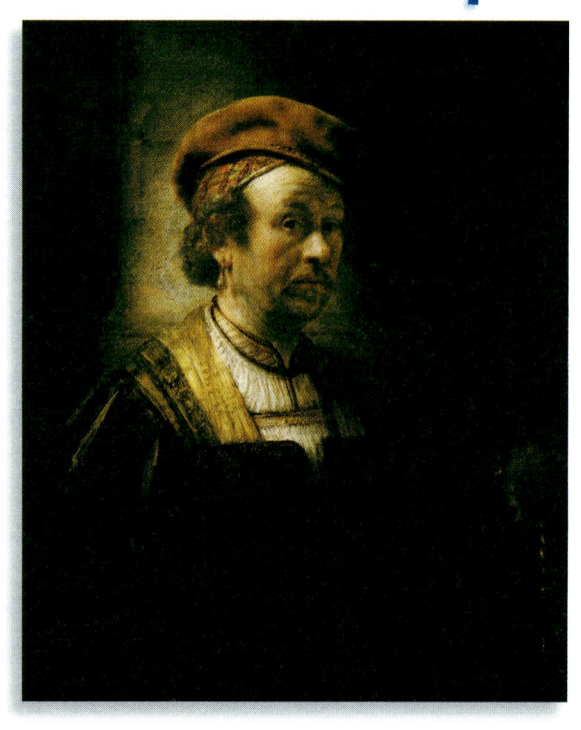

◀ **Rembrandt van Rijn.** (Dutch). *Portrait of Rembrandt.* 1650.
Oil on canvas. $36\frac{1}{4} \times 29\frac{3}{4}$ inches (92.08 × 75.57 cm.). National Gallery of Art, Washington, D.C.

Artists use balance and emphasis to arrange the art elements in a variety of artwork.

The Dutch artist Rembrandt van Rijn is best known for his portraits and paintings of everyday events. He used a technique called *chiaroscuro,* or bright light against a dark area, in his paintings. His ability to paint anything made him one of the most popular artists of his time.

124   Unit 4

Fine Art Prints

Display **Large Prints 79** *Long May Our Land Be Bright* and **80** *The Night Watch.* Refer to the prints throughout this unit as students learn about balance and emphasis.

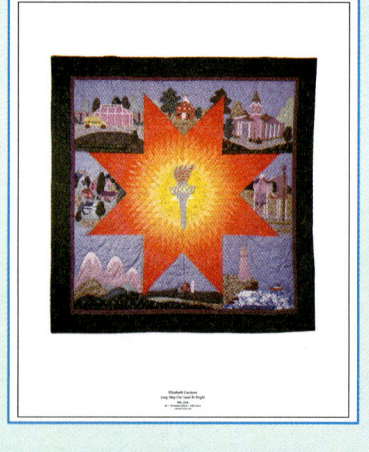

Large Print 79

Large Print 80

Artists use different types of balance in all types of artwork.
- What objects do you see?
- Pretend there is an imaginary line down the center of the painting. Describe how each half is arranged.

Artists can make the viewer look at certain areas in an artwork by using emphasis.
- What art element does Rembrandt van Rijn use to make you look at his self-portrait?
- Look at the painting. Close your eyes and then open them. What is the first area you see in this painting?

In This Unit you will learn how artists use balance. You will create personal works of art using a variety of media based on formal, informal, and radial balance. You also will learn about emphasis of an art element and how to emphasize an area.

Here are the topics you will study:
- Formal balance
- Symmetry
- Approximate symmetry
- Informal balance
- Asymmetry
- Radial balance
- Emphasis
- Focal point

Master Artist Profile

Self-portrait

Rembrandt van Rijn
(1606–1669)

Rembrandt was born in Leiden, in the Netherlands. He was the youngest of ten children and was given the opportunity to study art at a young age. He began teaching drawing and painting at the age of twenty-two. He is often referred to as the greatest Dutch painter of his era. Rembrandt painted portraits, everyday events, historical subjects, and landscapes. Wealthy citizens of Amsterdam were pleased with his style because he could paint the fine details of their clothing without detracting from the subject. Rembrandt was also skilled in the technique of chiaroscuro, which resulted in powerful and impressive portraits. It is believed he painted between fifty and sixty self-portraits.

Unit 4   **125**

Art History and Culture

Rembrandt van Rijn
Rembrandt van Rijn (rem´ brandt vän rīn´) (1606–1669) is often referred to as the greatest Dutch painter of his era. Wealthy citizens of Amsterdam were pleased with his style because he could paint the fine details of their clothing without detracting from the subject. Rembrandt also was skilled in the technique of *chiaroscuro,* which resulted in powerful and impressive portraits. Art historians believe that Rembrandt produced between 50 and 60 self-portraits. He created approximately 600 paintings, 300 etchings, and 1,400 drawings.

See pages 24–25 and 16–21 for more about art history and the subject matter.

Artist Profiles, p. 65

Examine the Artwork

"Let's study this self-portrait by Rembrandt van Rijn." *"Vamos a estudiar este autorretrato de Rembrant van Rijn."*

- Have students study Rembrandt van Rijn's self-portrait; then ask them to describe how the principles of balance and emphasis are used.
- Have students answer the questions about balance and emphasis on page 125.
  - Rembrandt, his hat, an earring in his ear, his shirt, a dark shape to the bottom right of the painting, a wall behind him.
  - On the left side are the back of Rembrandt's head, his hair, half of his hat, his ear, most of the light area of the wall, his right shoulder, and his shirt. On the right side are the front of his hat, his face including eyes, the shadowed area of his shirt, the dark shape to the bottom right of the painting, and a dark area of wall.
  - The art element of color. He uses warm colors in the face surrounded by dark values.
  - The face of Rembrandt van Rijn.

Unit Pretest

Display **Transparency 46** as a pretest. Have students write their answers on a separate piece of paper. Answers: 1. B, 2. C, 3. A, 4. A, 5. B

Home Connection

- See **Home and After-School Connections** for family newsletters and activities for this unit.

UNIT 4 • Balance and Emphasis   **125**

Unit 4 Arts Integration

ILLUSTRATOR PROFILE
N. C. Wyeth
(1882–1945)

Newell Convers Wyeth was born in Needham, Masachusetts. The farm where his family lived gave him a love of nature that lasted throughout his life. As a child, Wyeth sketched many scenes and animals that he found on the farm.

As a young man, Wyeth attended the Howard Pyle School of Art. Pyle stressed realism in illustration, and insisted that his students have a thorough art education. Wyeth thrived at the school, and began receiving commissions for magazine illustrations. His first book illustrations were completed in 1911, for *Treasure Island*, and are considered some of his best work.

When deciding whether to accept illustration work, Wyeth would look for an emotional connection to the story. He then researched the subject, often traveling to the location of the story. Next he created charcoal sketches, often using friends or family members as models. The final paintings were usually done in oil on canvas.

Throughout Unit 4, share Wyeth's illustrations with the class and discuss his use of balance and emphasis. What kind of balance does Wyeth use most often? Where are there examples of emphasis?

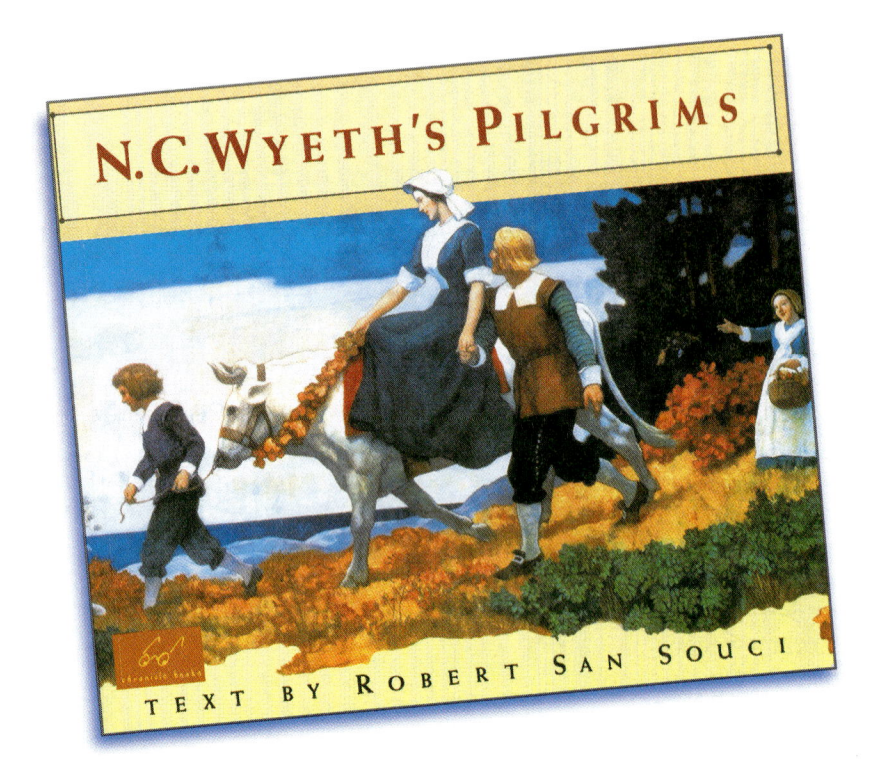

Music
Emphasis is a way of making a part of the music stand out. Balance in music is usually associated with symmetrical forms. For example, ABA form has three sections with the middle one different from the two outer sections. Have students sing an example of this by singing "Au Clair de la Lune." Students can also sing a round, such as "Frere Jacques," and try to balance the sound between parts.

Literature
Show the video *Tuesday* to introduce the concepts of balance and emphasis. Pause the video and have students identify symmetry, radial balance, and emphasis.

Literature and Art

Performing Arts
Show "The Brass Ring." Point out how balance is used.

Artsource®

125A UNIT 4 • Balance and Emphasis

Lesson 1 Overview

Formal Balance and Symmetry

Lesson 1 introduces the art principle of balance and symmetry. Balance is the principle of design that deals with visual weight in an artwork. Symmetry is a type of formal balance in which two halves of a balanced artwork are identical, mirror images of each other.

Objectives

Art History and Culture
To demonstrate knowledge of the United States Capitol and the Eiffel Tower

Creative Expression
To design a public building using symmetrical balance

Aesthetic Perception
To identify how formal balance, or symmetry, is used in architectural forms

Art Criticism
To evaluate own work using the four steps of art criticism

Vocabulary

Review the following vocabulary words with students before beginning the lesson.

central axis *eje central*—a real or imaginary dividing line that can run in two directions: vertically and horizontally

symmetry *simetría*—a type of formal balance in which two halves of a balanced artwork are identical, mirror images of each other

See page 149B for additional vocabulary and Spanish vocabulary resources.

Art Journal: Vocabulary
Have students add these words to the Vocabulary section of their Art Journals.

Lesson Materials
- objects of same size and shape
- pencils, erasers
- Art Journal
- 12" × 18" heavy white drawing paper
- fine-line permanent black marker
- watercolor paints
- water container, paintbrushes
- paper towels, newspaper

Alternate Materials
- cut pieces of paper of equal size and shape
- copier paper
- white construction paper
- crayons, colored markers, or colored pencils

Program Resources
- *Reading and Writing Test Prep.,* pp. 42–43
- *Transparency 19*
- *Flash Card* 12
- *Artist Profiles,* pp. 22, 81
- *Animals Through History Time Line*
- *Assessment,* pp. 45–46
- *Large Prints 79 Long May Our Land Be Bright* and *80 The Night Watch*
- *Art Around the World Collection*

Concept Trace
Symmetry
Introduced: Level 5, Unit 5, Lesson 4
Reinforced: Level 7, Chapter 3, Lesson 1

Lesson 1 Arts Integration

Theatre
Complete Unit 4, Lesson 1, on pages 72–73 of *Theatre Arts Connection.*

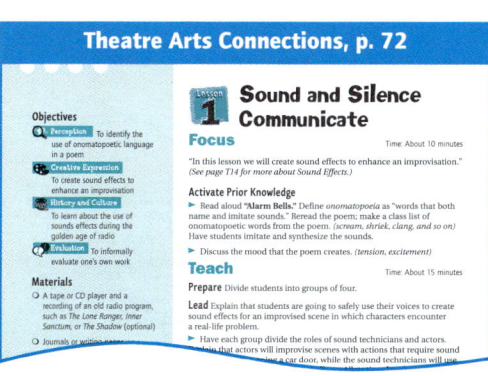

Music
Have students sing or listen to "This Land is Your Land." This song has a verse and a refrain, but it is in AA form. Ask students what they think this says about the music in the verse as compared to the refrain.

Movement & Dance
Have students look around the room and identify places that would be considered symmetrical. Color code index cards and place them in the symmetrical area. Have students make asymmetrical areas of the room symmetrical by adding or taking away objects.

LESSON 1 • Formal Balance and Symmetry **125B**

Focus

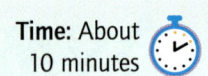

Time: About 10 minutes

Activate Prior Knowledge

"Have you ever seen a building that, if divided down the center, was identical on each half?" "¿Han visto alguna vez a un edificio que si dividido en el centro, era idéntico en cada mitad?"

- As a class, discuss the student responses. Explain that this type of balance derived from the Greeks and Romans, who used symmetrical balance in their important government buildings and temples.

Using Literature ⭐ Reading

- Have students read some passages from *The Wright Brothers for Kids: How They Invented the Airplane with 21 Activities Exploring the Science and History of Flight.* Then identify objects that are symmetrically balanced.

Thematic Connection ⭐ Social Studies

- **Architecture:** Have students describe different types of buildings they think are interesting.

Introduce the Art

Look

"Look closely at how repeated lines, shapes, and forms are arranged in these two architectural structures." "Observen detalladamente cómo líneas repetidas, figuras y formas son arregladas en estas dos estructuras arquitectónicas."

Summarizing ⭐ Reading

Have students locate a historical document that discusses either the Eiffel Tower or the United States Capitol. Then have them summarize their findings.

Art History and Culture

Possible answers: the Washington Monument, the White House, and the Lincoln Memorial in Washington, D.C. The Cathedral of Notre Dame, the Louvre, and the Arc de Triomphe in Paris, France. Show students photographs of these landmarks if possible.

💻 Web Connection

Visit www.aoc.gov/cc/capitol/capitol_overview.htm for more information about the United States Capitol.

126 UNIT 4 • Balance and Emphasis

Lesson 1: Formal Balance and Symmetry

▲ **United States Capitol.** 1793–1830; 1851–1863.
Stone-bearing masonry and cast-iron dome. Washington, D.C.

Look at the architectural structures on these two pages. The United States Capitol is one of the most important buildings in the world. It was originally built in three sections, under the supervision of six different architects and United States presidents. Over the course of two centuries, it has endured a fire and been rebuilt, extended, and restored. The Eiffel Tower of Paris was designed by French engineer Alexandre-Gustave Eiffel. He designed the tower for the 1889 world's fair; it was intended to last for only twenty years. It is an early example of large-scale, wrought-iron construction. The lower level has a restaurant, and elevators and a stairway take visitors to the top of the tower.

Art History and Culture

What other historic landmarks are located in Washington, D.C., and in Paris, France?

126 Unit 4 • Lesson 1

Art History and Culture

The United States Capitol

Construction of the United States Capitol began in 1791 as a competition, and it took 34 years to complete the original structure. In 1793 William Thornton's plan was accepted. In 1803 Benjamin Latrobe was summoned to Washington to complete the Capitol. In 1818 Charles Bulfinch succeeded Latrobe as the architect for the U.S. Capitol, which had been burned by the British in 1814. The cast-iron dome was designed by Thomas Ustick Walter in the 1850s. The Capitol covers an area of about 4 acres, and the five floors span approximately $16\frac{1}{2}$ acres. The Capitol has 540 rooms, 658 windows (108 in the dome alone), and 850 doorways.

See pages 24–25 and 16–21 for more about art history and the subject matter.

Artist Profiles, p. 81

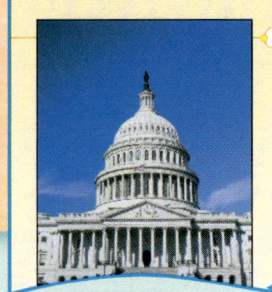

Artist Profile

United States Capitol

In 1792 a competition was held to decide who would design and build the United States Capitol building. The winner of this competition was amateur architect Dr. William Thornton. Thornton devised a plan for a central rotunda with north wings off to its sides that would house the Senate and the House of Representatives. When building began in 1793, President George Washington laid the cornerstone. Construction of the United States Capitol was completed 1830.

United States Capitol. 1793–1830; 1851–1863.

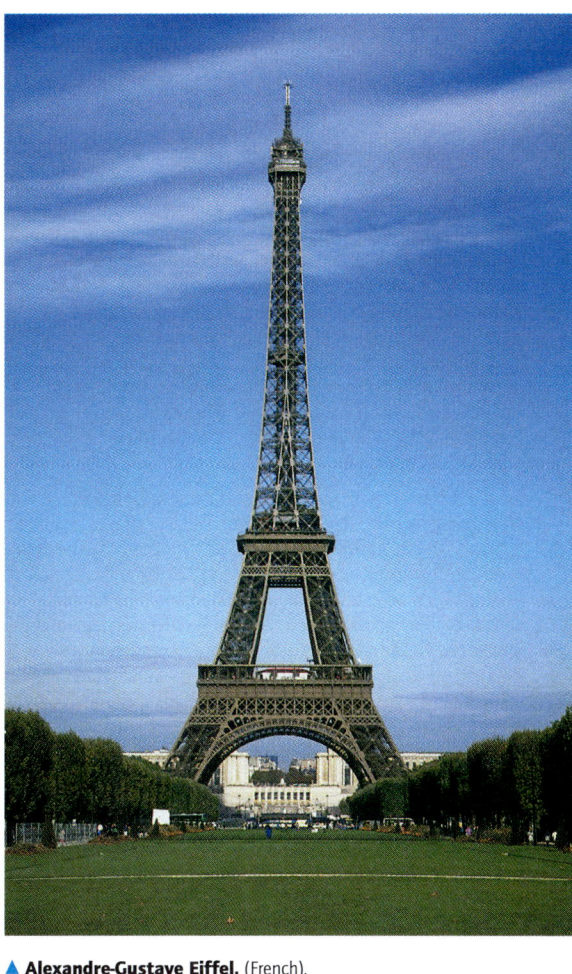

Study how formal balance is used by looking closely at both architectural structures.

▶ Describe how the shapes are arranged in the *United States Capitol*.
▶ How are lines and shapes repeated and arranged in the *Eiffel Tower*?
▶ Imagine a line drawn down the center of each structure. Describe what you see on either side of the center line.
▶ Think about the type of feeling you get when you look at each of these structures. Is it calm or uneasy? Explain.

▲ **Alexandre-Gustave Eiffel.** (French). *Eiffel Tower*. 1887–1889.
Exposed iron. 985 feet high (300.23 meters). Paris, France.

Aesthetic Perception

Design Awareness We are surrounded by architectural structures in our community that are available to everyone. Think about a public structure that is identical on each side.

Unit 4 • Lesson 1   **127**

Art History and Culture

Alexandre-Gustave Eiffel

The Eiffel Tower rises high above Paris. It was built for the World's Fair in 1889 by French engineer Alexandre-Gustave Eiffel (ä lek sän´ dr gue täv ī´ fəl) (1832–1923). Eiffel built hundreds of metal structures around the world. Bridges, and in particular railway bridges, were his favorite, but he also won renown for his metal structural work and industrial installations. Equally outstanding are certain other structures in which the pure inventiveness of Eiffel's company was allowed free rein. These structures include the "portable" bridges sold around the world in "kits."

See pages 24–25 and 16–21 for more about art history and the subject matter.

Artist Profiles, p. 22

Artist Profile
Gustave Eiffel
1832–1923

French architect Gustave Eiffel (gōōs´ tä v ī´ fəl) was born in Dijon, France, to a prosperous family. His mother was the reason for their prosperity, because she had started a coal business to ensure that Gustave received a good upbringing and education. She was a strong, intelligent woman and passed her work ethic down to her son. After graduating from college, Eiffel worked for a metal construction company, where he learned many architectural techniques. He began his building career at the early age of 26 when he was given his first independent assignment to build a bridge. Among his more famous creations are the Eiffel Tower and the framework for the Statue of Liberty. By the end of his life Gustave Eiffel moved

---

Study

▶ Possible answers include: The shapes are arranged as a long set of five rectangles. The central rectangular building form has a set of horizontal steps leading up to the front of the structure. There are two squares in front of two rectangular shapes, and a line of eight columns supports a rectangle on which a triangular shape sits.

▶ The lines are repeated in a regular pattern, crossing horizontally, vertically, and diagonally to form geometric shapes. The bottom is made of two identical rectangles that are joined by a curved arch. A band of repeated horizontal lines forms a trapezoid on which a thin rectangular shape of equal length rests.

▶ United States Capitol: The right side is a mirror image of the left side. Eiffel Tower: The right side is a mirror image of the left side.

▶ Responses may vary, but students will most likely say *calm* because the equal balance gives a feeling of security.

■ For more examples of art from Europe, see the *Art Around the World Collection*.

Art Journal: Writing
Have students explain in the Concepts section of their Art Journals what it means to say that something is symmetrical. What else do they want to know about symmetry?

Aesthetic Perception

Design Awareness Have the students discuss the various public structures in their community. Explain that public structures, are often arranged symmetrically. This is a calming and predictable arrangement that people feel very comfortable with because it is reliable and stable.

Developing Visual Literacy Discuss the use of repeated shapes and objects in each structure. Look closely at how the two architectural structures were arranged. Why do the students think these buildings were designed this way?

Web Connection
Visit www.tour-eiffel.fr/teiffel/uk/ for more information about the Eiffel Tower.

LESSON 1 • Formal Balance and Symmetry **127**

Teach

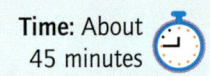

Time: About 45 minutes

"What type of public building will you design?" "¿Qué tipo de edificio público diseñarán?"

- Read and discuss using formal balance on page 128.

Practice

Materials: Objects of same size and shape: paper clips, new pencils, erasers, crayons, markers, etc.

Alternate Materials: Cut pieces of paper of equal size and shape, copier paper

- Distribute the materials and have students follow the directions on page 128.

Creative Expression

Objective: To create a public building using symmetrical balance

Materials: pencils, erasers, Art Journal, 12" × 18" heavy white drawing paper, fine-line permanent black marker, watercolor paints, water container, various sizes of paintbrushes, paper towels, newspaper

Alternate Materials: white construction paper, crayons, color markers or color pencils

- Distribute the materials and have students follow the directions on page 129.
- Have students demonstrate their technical skills, using a variety of art media and materials to produce their watercolor paintings. NSAE 1.a
- Review the Activity Tips on page 239 for visual examples of techniques if needed.

Art Journal: Researching

Ask students to look through magazines for examples of architectural details, such as windows, doors, dormers, brick, and stone. Have students cut out and place their items in their Art Journals. Students will use these collected architectural details in their Creative Expression activity designs.

128 UNIT 4 • Balance and Emphasis

Using Formal Balance and Symmetry

Look around you. You are looking at examples of balance and may not even be aware of it. Examine your chair, a table, and your clothes; consider your walk—all of these are balanced. We live with balance daily. A work of art must contain balance. **Balance** is the principle of design that relates to visual weight in an artwork. Visual balance causes the viewer to feel that the elements have been arranged just right. Artists often balance the art elements along an imaginary dividing line. This imaginary line is called the **central axis.** The central axis can run in two directions: vertically and horizontally.

Formal balance is one type of balance. **Formal balance** occurs when equal or similar elements are placed on opposite sides of a central axis. The central axis can be imaginary or real. **Symmetry** is a type of formal balance in which two halves of a balanced artwork are mirror images of each other. Symmetry gives the feeling of dignity, endurance, and stability. Furniture and clothing are usually symmetrical. Too much symmetry, however, can be dull because it is so predictable.

Notice the location of the central axes of these two symmetrical images.

Practice

Arrange five similar objects to show formal balance.

1. Look around your classroom for objects that are similar in size and shape, such as markers, pencils, paper clips, or crayons.
2. At your table and with a group, arrange the five items in a way that shows formal balance.
3. See how many different arrangements you can make. Discuss the differences and similarities that you notice.

128 Unit 4 • Lesson 1

Differentiated Instruction

Reteach
Have students find an example of symmetry in the classroom. Ask them to create a sketch of the object and describe how they drew it.

Special Needs
To help students achieve lesson objectives, ask them to think of a building that does not exist but should be located in their city. Ask them who the building is for and how it will be used.

ELL
Demonstrate the concept of symmetry using a volunteer and classroom objects. Have students pass items to the volunteer to create different examples of symmetry.

◀ **Allison Keeling.**
Age 11.

Think about how the student artist used symmetrical balance in this public-building design.

Creative Expression

Use symmetrical balance to design a public building.

1. Use one of the ideas in your Art Journal to create two sketches. Use basic shapes and architectural elements. Look at the architectural details that you collected in your Art Journal for ideas.
2. Look over your two sketches and decide which one you like best. Lightly transfer your sketch onto drawing paper. Use a ruler to help you draw straight lines.
3. Add architectural textures such as wood or stone to make your design more interesting. Decide where your building will be located and add a background.
4. After your drawing is complete, outline it using a fine-tip black marker. Use watercolor paints to complete your design.

Art Criticism

Describe Describe your public building.

Analyze Describe how you created symmetrical balance in your design.

Interpret What details did you use to communicate the type of public building you designed?

Decide Do you feel you successfully designed a public building using symmetrical balance? Explain.

Unit 4 • Lesson 1   **129**

Reflect

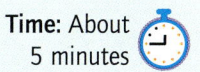

Time: About 5 minutes

Review and Assess

"How was formal or symmetrical balance used?" "¿Cómo usaron el equilibrio formal o simétrico?"

Think

The artist created a painting of the Eiffel Tower, which has two sides that are mirror images.

- Use **Large Prints 79** *Long May Our Land Be Bright* and **80** *The Night Watch* and ask students to compare how the two images used formal balance.

Informal Assessment

- For standardized-format test practice using this lesson's art content, see page 42–43 in *Reading and Writing Test Preparation.*

Art Journal: Critical Thinking
Have students answer the four art criticism questions—Describe, Analyze, Interpret, and Decide—in their Art Journals. Have students discuss within groups how they used formal balance. Ask them to notice the similarities and differences and form conclusions about historical and cultural contexts. Have the groups share their findings with the class.
NSAE 4.b

Art Across the Curriculum

Use these simple ideas to reinforce art concepts across the curriculum.

★ **Personal Writing** Have students write a letter to a member of Congress.

★ **Math** Have students convert the weight of the Eiffel Tower's metal structure—7,300 tons—to pounds.

★ **Science** Explain to students that wind causes the Eiffel Tower to sway a maximum of 4.72 inches.

★ **Social Studies** Discuss with students the purpose of the United States Capitol.

★ **Technology** Use a computer paint or draw program to create a design that is symmetrical. Visit **SRAonline.com** to print out detailed instructions for this activity.
NSAE 6.b

LESSON 1 • Formal Balance and Symmetry **129**

Lesson 1 Wrap-Up: Formal Balance and Symmetry

Extra! For the Art Specialist

Time: About 45 minutes

Focus
Study **Large Prints 79** *Long May Our Land Be Bright* and discuss how formal balance was used. What art elements are repeated? How are these elements and forms arranged?

Teach
Explain to the students that they will be designing a home, church, theater, or museum. Ask them to begin by collecting images of the following architectural details: domes, columns, doors, windows, turrets, pediments, and dormers. These images can be found in books, in magazines, and on the Internet, or sketches can be made from within the community. Then have them complete the Alternate Activity.

Reflect
Have students use the four steps of art criticism to evaluate their work. Describe the forms and details used and how they are arranged. What type of building was designed?

Alternate Activity

Materials:
- sketchbook, pencils
- erasers, rulers
- 9" × 12" or 12" × 18" drawing paper
- fine-line permanent black marker
- color pencils (optional)

1. Have students choose a building type to design using formal balance. Have them begin their design by drawing the door to their building. Using their collected images, have students build out from the door. Explain that they must use at least four of the architectural details in their final drawing.

2. Have students use the fine-line permanent black marker to outline the design. Then have them add textures with the marker, using stippling and hatching as well.

3. As an option, students can choose to keep the designs as black-and-white pen drawings or they can use color pencils to add color.

Research in Art Education

It has been shown that "elementary [art] programs establish a foundation in the arts for all students, not just for those in specialized programs or those who choose an arts course of study in high school." Providing consistent, quality instruction in the arts in elementary school also ensures that students have the time to foster skills in the arts. Many of these skills take time to develop (*Gaining the Arts Advantage: Lessons from School Districts that Value Arts Education*).

Assessment

Use the following rubric to evaluate the artwork students make in the Creative Expression activity and to assess students' understanding of how symmetry is used in architecture.

	Art History and Culture	Aesthetic Perception	Creative Expression	Art Criticism
3 POINTS	The student demonstrates knowledge of the United States Capitol and Eiffel Tower.	The student accurately identifies the use of formal or symmetrical balance in architectural structures.	The student's public building design demonstrates how to use formal or symmetrical balance.	The student thoughtfully and honestly evaluates own work using the four steps of art criticism.
2 POINTS	The student's knowledge of the United States Capitol and Eiffel Tower is weak or incomplete.	The student shows an emerging awareness of formal or symmetrical balance in architectural structures, but cannot consistently identify them.	The student's public building design shows some awareness of how to use formal or symmetrical balance.	The student attempts to evaluate own work but shows an incomplete understanding of evaluation criteria.
1 POINT	The student cannot demonstrate knowledge of the United States Capitol and Eiffel Tower.	The student cannot identify how formal or symmetrical balance is used in architectural structures.	The student's public building design shows no understanding of how to use formal or symmetrical balance.	The student makes no attempt to evaluate own work.

Have students complete page 45 or 46 in their *Assessment* books.

Assessment, p. 45

Formal Balance and Symmetry

A. Matching
Match each word in Column 1 to its definition in Column 2.

Column 1
1. balance
2. formal balance
3. central axis
4. symmetry

Column 2
a. the real or imaginary line that divides a design in half
b. the principle of design that relates to visual weight in a work of art
c. a type of formal balance in which the two halves are exactly the same
d. occurs when equal, or very similar, elements are placed on opposite sides of a central axis

B. Drawing
Draw a design that shows formal balance. Lightly draw the central axis.

C. Writing
Study the United States Capitol and write about paragraph about its symmetry.

Level 6 — Unit 4 • Balance and Emphasis — 45

Lesson 2 Overview

Approximate Symmetry

Lesson 2 continues the concept of the art principle of formal balance and helps students better understand approximate symmetry. **Approximate symmetry** is a type of balance that is almost symmetrical, but small differences in the artwork make it more interesting.

Objectives

Art History and Culture
To demonstrate knowledge of the lives and work of Georgia O'Keeffe and Ferdinand Hodler

Creative Expression
To use approximate symmetry to create a computer generated design

Aesthetic Perception
To identify how formal balance, or approximate symmetry, is used in two-dimensional works of art

Art Criticism
To evaluate own work using the four steps of art criticism

Vocabulary

Review the following vocabulary word with students before beginning the lesson.

approximate symmetry simetría aproximada—a type of balance that is almost symmetrical, but small differences in the artwork make it more interesting

See page 149B for additional vocabulary and Spanish vocabulary resources.

Art Journal: Vocabulary
Have students add this word to the Vocabulary section of their Art Journals.

Lesson Materials
- variety of objects that have approximate symmetry
- pencil and eraser
- 9" × 12" drawing paper
- practice image, computer monitor
- draw or paint software
- printer, paper

Alternate Materials
- magazine images of objects with approximate symmetry
- word processing program
- white drawing paper
- pencils, erasers
- crayons, color markers, color pencils

Program Resources
- *Reading and Writing Test Prep.,* pp. 44–45
- *Transparency 20*
- *Artist Profiles,* pp. 31, 45
- *Animals Through History Time Line*
- *Assessment,* pp. 47–48
- *Large Prints 79 Long May Our Land Be Bright* and *80 The Night Watch*
- *The National Museum of Women in the Arts Collection*

Concept Trace
Approximate Symmetry
Introduced: Level 6, Unit 4, Lesson 2
Reinforced: Level 7, Chapter 3, Lesson 1

Lesson 2 Arts Integration

Theatre
Complete Unit 4, Lesson 2, on pages 74–75 of *Theatre Arts Connection.*

Music
Balance in the form of a composition is the most readily apparent in the ABA form. Have students listen to "Minuet" from *Eine Kleine Nacht Musik* by Wolfgang Amadeus Mozart. Have students raise their hands when they hear the entrance of the B section and then again at the return of A. The second return of A might be played a bit differently.

Movement & Dance
Working in groups of three, have students explore balance. Have one student stand still to create a vertical line. Have the other students stand on either side of the center student. The student on the right side should create a shape with his or her body and freeze. The student on the left should copy the shape, but alter it to show approximate symmetry

LESSON 2 • Approximate Symmetry **129B**

Focus

Time: About 10 minutes

Activate Prior Knowledge

"Have you ever seen a formal painted portrait?"
"¿Han visto alguna vez un retrato formal pintado?"

- Discuss students' responses. Explain that in many formal portraits that were done prior to the 1900s, the people sat perfectly still and faced forward.

Using Literature — Reading

- Look at the cover illustration of *Toning the Sweep* by Angela Johnson. Discuss how approximate symmetry is used. The halves of the picture are not exactly the same.

Thematic Connection — Math

- **Not Quite:** Have students describe objects that they have seen that appeared to be perfect at first glance. However when they looked more carefully, they noticed that the object was not quite perfect. Have them explain how they felt after their discovery.

Introduce the Art

Look

"Look closely at how the artists placed their subjects within their compositions."
"Observen detalladamente cómo los artistas colocan sus sujetos dentro de sus composiciones."

Logical Reasoning — Reading

Have students analyze the nature of art, using the works of art in this lesson and debate the issue of beauty. Some students should argue that art does not have to show a beautiful image. Others should argue that the paintings in this lesson should not be considered art because they do not portray beauty.

Art History and Culture

Possible answers: *Fireworks* by James Esnor, *The Portrait of Joseph Roulin* by Vincent van Gogh, and the *Face Mask of Ḵumigwē'*. Make sure students explain why their choices are not symmetrical.

Web Connection

Visit www.metmuseum.org for more information about the Metropolitan Museum of Art.

130 UNIT 4 • Balance and Emphasis

Lesson 2: Approximate Symmetry

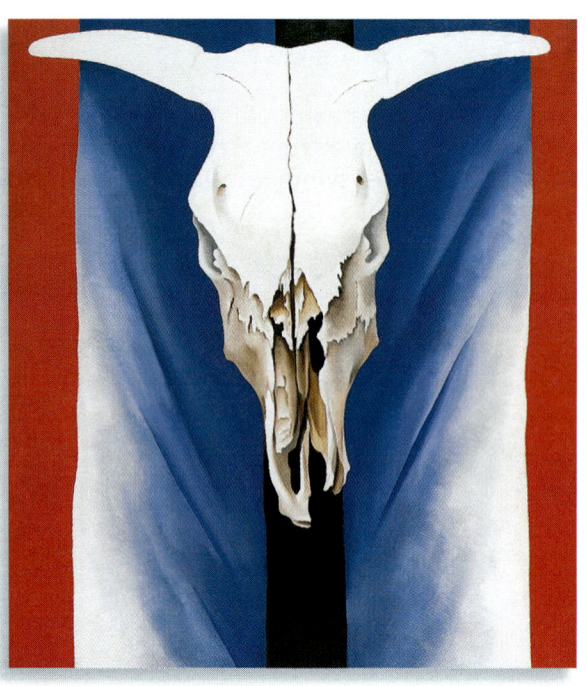

Look closely at the two paintings on these pages. Both works of art show a head-on view of the subject matter. In *Cow's Skull: Red White and Blue*, Georgia O'Keeffe placed the skull almost in the center of the painting. She is best known for her close-up views of flowers and animal bones. Most of her famous images were painted in New Mexico. Ferdinand Hodler painted *James Vibert, Sculptor* so large that the subject's shoulders barely fit within the canvas frame. Vilbert was a friend of Hodler's. In both paintings, the two sides are almost mirror images of each other. Both paintings illustrate approximate symmetry.

▲ **Georgia O'Keeffe.** (American). *Cow's Skull: Red White and Blue.* 1931.
Oil on canvas. 39⅞ × 37⅞ inches (101.3 × 96.22 cm.). Metropolitan Museum of Art, New York, New York.

Art History and Culture

What other paintings have you studied that look symmetrical but really are not?

130 Unit 4 • Lesson 2

Art History and Culture

Georgia O'Keeffe

As a child, Georgia O'Keeffe (jôr´jə ō´kēf´) (1887–1986) received art lessons at home, where her abilities were quickly recognized. Shortly thereafter, however, O'Keeffe quit making art, saying later that she knew then that she could never achieve distinction working within this tradition. Her interest in art was rekindled when she was introduced to Arthur Wesley Dow. Dow believed the goal of art was the expression of the artist's personal ideas and feelings and that such subject matter was best realized through harmonious arrangements. As early as the mid-1920s, O'Keeffe began painting large-scale depictions of flowers.

See pages 24–25 and 16–21 for more about art history and the subject matter.

Artist Profiles, p. 45

Study how approximate symmetry is used in the paintings by O'Keeffe and Hodler.

- Describe where the objects are placed in the compositions.
- Look at Hodler's painting. Why does it not show perfect symmetry?
- Imagine a line drawn down the center of *Cow's Skull: Red White and Blue*. Describe what happens on each side of the central axis.
- Think about the type of feeling you get when you look at each of these paintings. How does this type of balance affect those feelings?

▲ **Ferdinand Hodler.** (Swiss). *James Vibert, Sculptor.* 1907.
Oil on canvas. 25¾ × 26⅛ inches (65.41 × 66.35 cm.). Art Institute of Chicago, Chicago, Illinois.

Aesthetic Perception

Seeing Like an Artist Can you think of any objects in nature that are almost, but not quite, identical on both sides?

Unit 4 • Lesson 2   **131**

Study

- *Cow's Skull: Red White and Blue:* The skull is placed slightly to the left of the central axis. *James Vibert, Sculptor:* The figure of Vibert is placed in the center of the picture plane, taking up almost half of the canvas.

- The part on the viewer's left side, the thickness of Vibert's hair on the right, the pocket on the right side of the jacket, and the added wrinkles on the left sleeve contribute to this not being perfectly symmetrical.

- Answers may include: *Cow's Skull: Red White and Blue* looks to be exactly centered, but the left half of the skull is slightly larger than the right side. The left also has a complete nose opening where it has been broken off on the right.

- Student interpretations will vary based upon personal experiences. *Cow's Skull: Red White and Blue:* Some may say that the skull is scary. *James Vibert, Sculptor:* Some may say that Vibert appears to be important because he is wearing a suit.

■ For more examples of portraits, see **The National Museum of Women in the Arts Collection.**

Art Journal: Writing
Have students explain what approximate symmetry means in their Art Journals. What else do they want to know about approximate symmetry?

Art History and Culture

Ferdinand Hodler
Ferdinand Hodler (fer´ də nənd hō´ dlər) (1853–1918) worked in an ornamental style similar to art nouveau. In 1897, Hodler lectured to a group about art. By this time he had developed a personal artistic theory centered around what he called *parallelism,* or the representation of universals. Parallelism consisted of strong rhythmic patterns and a tight linear structure; it is an element of order. He pointed out examples from daily life that demonstrated the principle of parallelism, such as people walking in the same direction or people gathered around a speaker who represents an idea. He believed that what unites people is stronger than what divides them.

See pages 24–25 and 16–21 for more about art history and the subject matter.

Artist Profiles, p. 31

Aesthetic Perception

Seeing Like an Artist Explain to students that many of the plant forms that grow in nature have an approximate symmetrical balance. A tree does not have identical branches growing from it, nor is the trunk identical all the way around.

Developing Visual Literacy Discuss the use of placement and balance in each painting. They are balanced formally but are not mirror images.

Web Connection
Visit www.artic.edu for more information about the Art Institute of Chicago.

LESSON 2 • Approximate Symmetry   **131**

Teach

Time: About 45 minutes

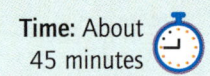

"How can you create an artwork using approximate symmetry?" "¿Cómo pueden crear una obra de arte usando simetría aproximada?"

- Read and discuss using formal balance on page 132.

Practice

Materials: variety of objects that have approximate symmetry, pencil, eraser, 9" × 12" drawing paper

Alternate Materials: magazine images of objects with approximate symmetry

- Distribute the materials and have students follow the directions on page 132.

Creative Expression

Materials: practice image, computer monitor, draw or paint software, printer, paper

Alternate Materials: word document program, white drawing paper, pencils, erasers, crayons, color markers, color pencils

- Distribute the materials and have students follow the directions on page 133.
- Have students demonstrate their technical skills, using a variety of art media and materials to produce their computer designs. NSAE 1.a; 1.b
- Students should conduct in-progress analyses and critiques of their computer designs. NSAE 1.a; 2.a
- Review the Activity Tips on page 239 for visual examples of techniques if needed.

Art Journal: Brainstorming

Ask students to work with a partner and locate five examples each of approximate symmetry in advertisements, magazines, or newspapers. Have them place their collected images in their Art Journals. Their collected images will be used in their designs for their Creative Expression activity.

132 UNIT 4 • Balance and Emphasis

Using Approximate Symmetry

Sometimes artists choose a balance for an artwork based on a feeling it expresses. Formal balance can sometimes be too stiff and formal, so artists will use another type of formal balance called *approximate symmetry* that has a calm feeling. **Approximate symmetry** is a type of balance that is almost symmetrical, but small differences in the artwork make it more interesting.

To avoid boring the viewer, artists often use approximate symmetry. Like symmetry, it is stable, but small differences make the arrangement more interesting. Your face is an example of approximate symmetry. If you look in a mirror you will notice that the two halves of your face are not exactly identical.

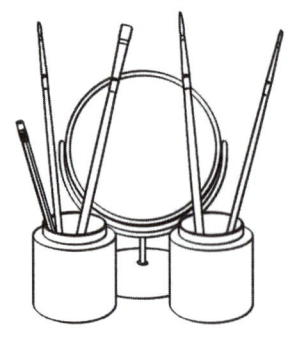

Notice how approximate symmetry can be found in nature and in objects made by people.

Practice

Draw a common object to show approximate symmetry.

1. Look around your classroom for objects that are almost symmetrical.
2. Create a line drawing showing the shape of your selected item. Look closely at the details.
3. Arrange your composition so that your object is large and is almost in the center. Save your drawing. What about the object makes it an example of approximate symmetry?

132 Unit 4 • Lesson 2

Differentiated Instruction

Reteach
Have students identify approximate symmetry as it appears in nature.

Special Needs
Use this project as an opportunity for cooperative learning among students of different abilities. Establish group norms of acceptance and collaboration by carefully pairing students and clearly defining individual responsibilities.

ELL
Have the students pose in a scene that portrays approximate symmetry.

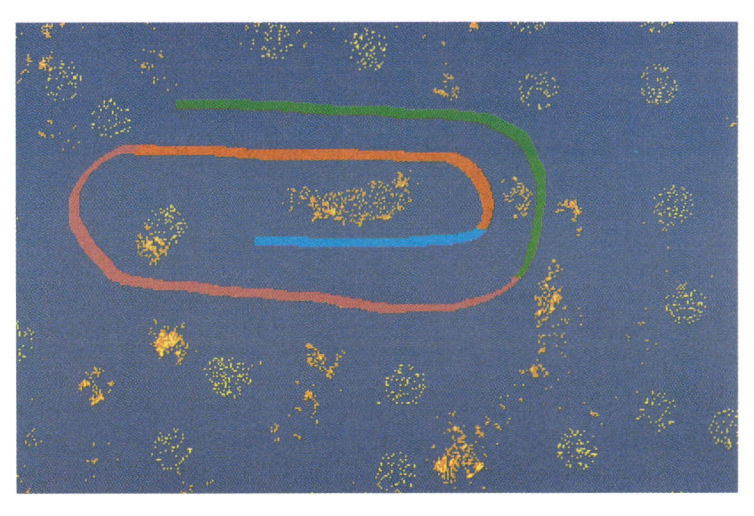

◀ Sam Sheffield.
Age 12.

Think about how this student artist used approximate symmetry in the design.

Creative Expression

Use approximate symmetry to create a computer-generated design.

1. Look at your collected images in your Art Journal. Choose one or two images.
2. Use a computer draw or paint program and the mouse to draw your interpretation of the selected images. Do not include anything from the images' background.
3. Create a copy of your images and save them. Use a variety of tools on the menu to create a design using approximate symmetry.
4. After your drawing is complete, select either a warm or cool color for your background. Create interest by using a contrasting color to complete your design. Title and save your work.

Art Criticism

Describe What object(s) did you select to use?

Analyze Describe how you created approximate symmetry in your design.

Interpret How does your selected color scheme affect the mood of your artwork? Is it calm or active?

Decide Do you think you were successful in creating a computer-generated design using approximate symmetry? Explain.

Unit 4 • Lesson 2   **133**

Reflect

Time: About 5 minutes

Review and Assess

"How was approximate symmetry used?"
"¿Cómo usaron la simetría aproximada?"

Think

The artist arranged the spiral design more on the left side than the right side of the screen.

- Use **Large Prints 79** *Long May Our Land Be Bright* and **80** *The Night Watch* and ask students to compare how approximate symmetry was used in the two images. Explain the differences and similarities.

Informal Assessment

- Have students describe in detail a variety of practical applications for their computer designs. NSAE 5.a

- For standardized-format test practice using this lesson's art content, see pages 44–45 in *Reading and Writing Test Preparation*.

Art Journal: Critical Thinking

Have students answer the four art criticism questions—Describe, Analyze, Interpret, and Decide—in their Art Journals. Have students explain as a class how they created approximate symmetry in their computer design. What is something new that they learned while working on this project?

Art Across the Curriculum

Use these simple ideas to reinforce art concepts across the curriculum.

★ **Narrative Writing** Have students write a short story from the point of view of *James Vibert, Sculptor*.

★ **Math** Have students round the dimensions of the paintings to the nearest ten.

★ **Science** Have students describe large animal fossils they have seen in museums.

★ **Social Studies** Have students share any information they know about Switzerland.

★ **Technology** Using a paint or draw program, have students draw a figure that demonstrates the concept of approximate symmetry. Visit **SRAonline.com** to print detailed instructions for this activity.
NSAE 6.b

LESSON 2 • Approximate Symmetry   **133**

Lesson 2 Wrap-Up: Approximate Symmetry

Extra! For the Art Specialist

Time: About 45 minutes

Focus
Study the works of art in this lesson and discuss how approximate symmetry was used. What art elements or objects are used? How are these elements and forms arranged?

Teach
Tell students they will be creating a portrait of a person or animal using approximate symmetry on the computer. Ask them to begin by collecting images of their selected subject matter. These can be photographs, digital images, or magazine images. Then have them create several sketches of the subject matter and complete the Alternate Activity.

Reflect
Have students use the four steps of art criticism to evaluate their work. Did the students successfully create a portrait on the computer showing approximate symmetry?

Alternate Activity

Materials:
- sketchbook, pencils, erasers
- computer monitor, printer
- printing paper or textured papers
- draw or paint program
- scanner

1. Using a draw or paint program, have students transfer their best sketch into the program. This can be done with a scanner.
2. Have students create a copy of the images and save them. Have them use a variety of tools in the program to create a drawing using approximate symmetry.
3. Students may also have the option of trying different painting techniques on their images, such as impressionism. See if your program has this capability.
4. Have students print the completed portrait. NSAE 1.a; 1.b

Research in Art Education

"Talk about art, or art criticism, is probably one of the ways we share the contents of our inner lives without embarrassment. Art criticism is very much like teaching: it is the sharing of discoveries about art, or in some cases about life, where art has its ultimate source." (Hurwitz, Al, and Stanley Madeja. *The Joyous Vision*. New Jersey: Prentice Hall, 1997.)

Assessment

Use the following rubric to evaluate the artwork students made in the Creative Expression activity and to assess students' understanding of how approximate symmetry is used in works of art.

	Art History and Culture	Aesthetic Perception	Creative Expression	Art Criticism
3 POINTS	The student demonstrates knowledge of the lives and work of Georgia O'Keeffe and Ferdinand Hodler.	The student accurately identifies the use of approximate symmetry in two-dimensional works of art.	The student's computer design demonstrates how to use approximate symmetry.	The student thoughtfully and honestly evaluates own work using the four steps of art criticism.
2 POINTS	The student's knowledge of the lives and work of Georgia O'Keeffe and Ferdinand Hodler is weak or incomplete.	The student shows an emerging awareness of approximate symmetry in two-dimensional art, but cannot consistently identify it.	The student's computer design shows some awareness of how to use approximate symmetry.	The student attempts to evaluate own work but shows an incomplete understanding of evaluation criteria.
1 POINT	The student cannot demonstrate knowledge of the lives and work of Georgia O'Keeffe and Ferdinand Hodler.	The student cannot identify how approximate symmetry used.	The student's computer design shows no understanding of how to use approximate symmetry.	The student makes no attempt to evaluate own work.

Have students complete page 47 or 48 in their *Assessment* books.

Lesson 3 Overview: Informal Balance

Lesson 3 introduces another type of balance known as informal, or asymmetrical, balance. **Informal balance** is a way of organizing parts of a design so that unlike objects have equal visual weight. **Asymmetry** is another name for informal balance.

Objectives

Art History and Culture
To demonstrate knowledge of the lives and work of Katsushika Hokusai and Mary Cassatt

Creative Expression
To create a color chalk still life using informal balance

Aesthetic Perception
To identify how informal balance, asymmetry, is used in two-dimensional works of art

Art Criticism
To evaluate own work using the four steps of art criticism

Lesson Materials
- magazines, scissors
- 9" × 12" paper any color and type
- medium-point black marker
- glue, Art Journals
- pencils, erasers
- various objects in different sizes, shapes, and textures
- 12" × 18" black paper
- white and color chalk
- damp sponges or washcloths
- newspaper

Alternate Materials:
- textbook
- white paper
- color pencils, markers, crayons

Program Resources
- *Reading and Writing Test Prep.,* pp. 46–47
- *Transparency* 21
- *Flash Card* 13
- *Artist Profiles,* pp. 15, 32
- *Animals Through History Time Line*
- *Assessment,* pp. 49–50
- *Large Prints* 79 *Long May Our Land Be Bright* and 80 *The Night Watch*
- *The National Museum of Women in the Arts Collection*

Vocabulary

Review the following vocabulary words with students before beginning the lesson.

asymmetrical balance *equilibrio asimétrico*—another name for informal balance

still life *naturaleza muerta*—the arrangement of common inanimate objects artists draw or paint

See page 149B for additional vocabulary and Spanish vocabulary resources.

Art Journal: Vocabulary
Have students add these words to the Vocabulary section of their Art Journals.

Concept Trace
Informal balance
Introduced: Level 5, Unit 5, Lesson 5
Reinforced: Level 7, Chapter 3, Lesson 1

Lesson 3 Arts Integration

Theatre
Complete Unit 4, Lesson 3, on pages 76–77 of *Theatre Arts Connection.*

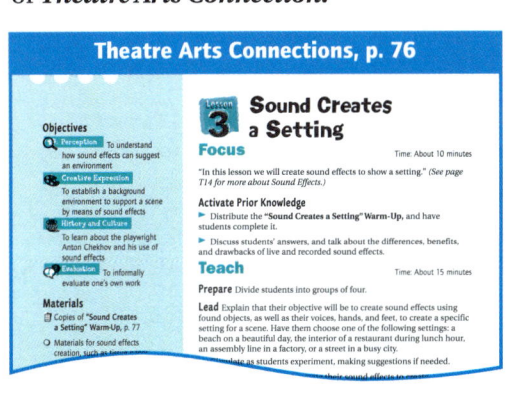

Music
Balance in music can describe how evenly different parts are performed at the same time to make the desired blend. Have students listen to "Akinla," from *African Suite,* by Fela Sowande. Discuss whether all parts are equal in dynamics at all times.

Movement & Dance
Mark off a canvas on the floor, outlining it with string or tape. Have ten students find a way to arrange themselves on the canvas, looking at the space as if it were a painting. Have students who are observing rearrange the students to create different varieties of informal balance.

Focus

Time: About 10 minutes

Activate Prior Knowledge

"Have you ever seen a photograph where more people or objects were on one side than the other?" "¿Han visto alguna vez fotografías donde había más personas u objetos en un lado que el otro?"

- As a class, discuss the student responses. Explain that in many photographs and images, people and objects are not arranged symmetrically.

Using Literature ⭐ Reading

- Look at the cover illustration of *Littlejim's Dreams* by Thomas B. Allen. Discuss how informal balance is used.

Thematic Connection ⭐ Science

- **Imbalance:** Have students give examples of things that can be imbalanced. After students offer an example, have them explain whether the imbalance can be easily corrected.

Introduce the Art

Look

"Look closely at how objects and colors are arranged in these two works of art."
"Observen detalladamente cómo los objetos y colores son arreglados en estas dos obras de arte."

Comparing and Contrasting ⭐ Reading

- Have students describe and compare a variety of individual responses to the works of art in this lesson. Answers will vary. Make sure answers include comments about other Japanese and American art they have seen or learned about in school.

Art History and Culture

Possible answer: An older man and two girls are depicted in these works of art. Hokusai and Cassatt preferred to depict everyday people in their paintings. Have students discuss whether or not they accomplished that here.

💻 Web Connection

Visit www.honoluluacademy.org for more information about the Honolulu Academy of Arts.

134 UNIT 4 • Balance and Emphasis

Lesson 3 — Informal Balance

Look closely at the two works of art on these pages. Katsushika Hokusai was raised by a family of craftsmen who taught him how to engrave the back of mirrors. He later applied what he had learned to carving woodblocks and became a successful printmaker. Mary Cassatt was the only American artist to join the French impressionists. She created many paintings like *The Tea*, in which she captured a moment of everyday life. The impressionists were influenced by photography and Japanese prints. Both of these mediums allowed artists to crop the image and capture the moment. Look at *The Tea*. Notice how a portion of the fireplace is off the canvas. This technique is called *cropping*. Notice the arrangement of the objects in both of these works.

◀ **Katsushika Hokusai.** (Japanese). *Li Bai.* 1834.
Woodblock print. $20\frac{1}{2} \times 9\frac{1}{8}$ inches (52.1 × 23.2 cm.). Honolulu Academy of Arts, Honolulu, Hawaii.

Art History and Culture

Look at the dates and titles of these works of art. What kinds of people are depicted by these artists?

134   Unit 4 • Lesson 3

Art History and Culture

Katsushika Hokusai

Katsushika Hokusai (kät soo´ shē kä hō´ koo sī) (1760–1849) was an outstanding artist of the Ukiyo-e, or "pictures of the floating world" school which specialized in depictions of everyday life. Hokusai was a thoroughly Bohemian artist. Hokusai learned from observing Dutch and French pastoral landscapes. More importantly, he introduced the serenity of nature and the unity of man and his surroundings into Japanese popular art. Instead of shoguns, samurai, and geishas, Hokusai placed the common man into his woodblocks, moving the emphasis from the aristocrats to the rest of humanity.

See pages 24–25 and 16–21 for more about art history and the subject matter.

Artist Profiles, p. 32

▲ **Mary Cassatt.** (American). *The Tea.* 1879.

Oil on canvas. 25½ × 36½ inches (64.77 × 92.71 cm.). Museum of Fine Arts, Boston, Massachusetts.

Study both works of art to better understand informal balance.
- List the objects in both works of art.
- How are the objects arranged in *The Tea*?
- Which are the largest objects in both works of art? Where are they placed?
- Imagine a line drawn down the center of each work of art. Describe what happens on either side of the center line.

Aesthetic Perception

Design Awareness Think about photographs you have seen. How are the people usually arranged? Are they always in the center of the photograph or to one side?

Unit 4 • Lesson 3   **135**

Art History and Culture

Mary Cassatt

The early years in Paris were a particularly happy time for Mary Cassatt (mâr´ē kə sat´) (1844–1926), and this gaiety is reflected in the subject matter she chose for her paintings. She depicted young girls sitting in the loge at the opera, women taking tea, knitting and reading. Many of her models were drawn from close family and friends. On the whole, Cassatt preferred to paint peasant women who took care of their own children; rather than the more affluent mothers who delegated the task to nannies or nursemaids. While in America, Cassatt decided to concentrate on pastels alone.

See pages 24–25 and 16–21 for more about art history and the subject matter.

Artist Profiles, p. 15

Artist Profile
Mary Cassatt
1845–1926

Mary Cassatt (mer´ē kə sat´) was born into an upper middle-class family in western Pennsylvania in 1844. She was enrolled at the Pennsylvania Academy of the Fine Arts from 1861 to 1865. She later studied in Paris, France, in the studios of Gérôme and Couture. In 1874, she settled permanently in Paris, where she regularly submitted work to the yearly Salon exhibitions. The painter and sculptor Edgar Degas saw her work at the Salon and invited Cassatt to join the Impressionists in 1887. She was the only American ever to exhibit in the group's shows. During her lifetime, Cassatt's work was more popular in Europe than in the United States. In her spare time, she loved to entertain friends and ride her...

Study

▶ Possible answers: *Imagery of the Poets:* a cliff with bushes and trees; a man holding a stick; two children; a waterfall. *The Tea:* two women; silver tea set; couch; table; a painting over the fireplace.

▶ Possible answer: The two women are sitting on the left side of the painting on a red and white couch. In front of them is the top of a red table and a silver tea set. To the far right is half of a mantle and a white fireplace.

▶ *Imagery of the Poets:* The largest objects are the two cliffs. The cliffs take up the same amount of space. *The Tea:* The largest objects are the two women sitting on the couch. They are placed on the left side of the painting, taking up a little more than half of the painting.

▶ Possible answer: *Imagery of the Poets:* The left edge of the waterfall is almost the center of the print. The right half contains mostly the waterfall. *The Tea:* On the left side of the painting, there are two women. The body of one of the women is partially on the right side of the painting.

■ For more examples of landscapes, see *The National Museum of Women in the Arts Collection.*

Art Journal: Writing

Have students explain what informal balance means in the Concepts section of their Art Journals. What else do they want to know about informal balance and asymmetry?

Aesthetic Perception

Design Awareness Most photographs have a portion of the person cropped. The image is not symmetrically balanced.

Developing Visual Literacy Discuss the arrangement of objects in each work of art. Have students explain why the artist might have wanted to use informal balance.

Web Connection

Visit **www.mfa.org** for more information about the Museum of Fine Arts, Boston.

LESSON 3 • Informal Balance   **135**

Teach

Time: About 45 minutes

"How will you use informal balance to arrange your objects for a still-life drawing?"

"¿Cómo usaran el equilibrio informal para arreglar sus objetos para un dibujo de la naturaleza muerta?"

- Read and discuss using informal balance on page 136.

Practice

Materials: magazines, scissors, 9" × 12" paper of any color and type, medium-point black marker, glue, Art Journals

Alternate Materials: textbooks

- Distribute the materials and have students follow the directions on page 136.

Creative Expression

Materials: pencils, erasers, Art Journal, various objects in different sizes, shapes and textures, 12" × 18" black paper, white and color chalk, damp sponges or washcloths, newspaper

Alternate materials: white paper, color pencils, markers or crayons

- Demonstrate "drawing" with the glue in a steady stream. Show students how they can use a pencil point or a toothpick to connect the glue that separates into dots. Scratch through the glue lines where the breaks are in the lines with a tooth pick or pencil, as if drawing.
- Distribute the materials and have students follow the directions on page 137.
- Review the Activity Tips on page 240 for visual examples of techniques if needed.

Art Journal: Discussing

After discussing how artists use informal balance, ask students to come up with one question for each of the ways informal balance is created. Have students place the questions in their Art Journals. Once the students have completed the Practice activity, ask them to see if their questions apply to the three images they collected.

136 UNIT 4 • Balance and Emphasis

Using Informal Balance

Think about riding in a car. A road divides your view in half and is symmetrically balanced. The objects on either side are probably not the same, but they take up the same amount of space. **Informal balance** is a way of organizing parts of a design so that unlike objects have equal visual weight. *Asymmetry* is another name for informal balance. The negative space, or the areas around the object or group of objects, is often larger on one side of an asymmetrical piece than on the other side. Artists create asymmetrical balance in several ways.

Size: A large shape or form appears to be heavier than a small shape. Several small shapes can balance one large shape. To create informal balance, artists place large shapes closer to the center and small shapes farther away.

Color: A bright color has more visual weight than a dull color.

Texture: A rough texture has an uneven pattern of highlights and shadows. For this reason, a rough surface attracts the viewer's eyes more easily than a smooth, even surface.

Position: A larger, positive shape and a small, negative space can be balanced by a small, positive shape and a large, negative space.

Practice

Collect images that have asymmetrical balance from a magazine.

1. Find three examples of asymmetrical balance based on size, color, texture, or position.
2. Cut out the images and fold them in half. Using a marker, outline the objects on each side of the folded line.
3. Notice how the objects are arranged, and discuss this with your table group. Glue your collected images onto a piece of paper. Below each image, list how balance was achieved by size, color, texture, or position. Place this in your Art Journal.

136   Unit 4 • Lesson 3

Differentiated Instruction

Reteach
Have students identify free-form shapes in the classroom. Then have them explain why they are asymmetrical.

Special Needs
Increase interest in the still life assignment by asking each student to contribute a favorite possession to include in the still life arrangement.

ELL
Have students look at photographs of activities around the school. View the images in the classroom and discuss how balance was created.

◀ **Sussy Pelaez.** Age 11.

Think about how this student artist used asymmetrical balance in the still-life drawing.

Creative Expression

Use asymmetrical balance to create a still-life drawing using color chalk.

1. Arrange a variety of objects to create a still life. Include tall and short objects, and items with various patterns and colors.
2. Create two quick sketches from different viewpoints using asymmetrical balance. Select the one you like best.
3. Use white chalk to transfer your sketch onto black paper. Use white glue to outline your drawing. Let it dry.
4. Use color chalk to add color to your still-life drawing.
5. Give your completed work a title.

Art Criticism

Describe Describe the objects in your still life.

Analyze How did you create asymmetrical balance in your still life?

Interpret How did your choice of colors affect the mood of your still life?

Decide Do you feel you successfully created a color-chalk still life using asymmetrical balance? Explain.

Unit 4 • Lesson 3   **137**

Reflect

Time: About 5 minutes

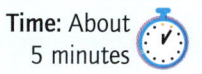

Review and Assess
"How was informal, or asymmetrical, balance used?" "¿Cómo fue usado el equilibrio informal o asimétrico?"

Think
The artist placed a stringed instrument and leaves on the left side of the drawing. There is a large flower vase that is almost in the center, but it is actully more on the right side than the left side.

- Use **Large Prints 79** *Long May Our Land Be Bright* and **80** *The Night Watch* and ask students to compare the use of informal balance in the two images. Did the artists rely mostly on size, color, texture, or position in creating informal balance? Also have students identify the influence of political events in each **Large Print**.
NSAE 4.b

Informal Assessment
- For standardized-format test practice using this lesson's art content, see page 46–47 in *Reading and Writing Test Preparation*.

Art Journal: Critical Thinking
Have students answer the four art criticism questions—Describe, Analyze, Interpret, and Decide—in their Art Journals. Have students display their work and discuss how they used informal balance. Ask the students to discuss their selection of objects and how they chose to arrange them.

Art Across the Curriculum

Use these simple ideas to reinforce art concepts across the curriculum.

★ **Narrative Writing** Have students write a dialogue for the two women pictured in *The Tea*.

★ **Math** Have students look at *The Tea* and estimate how much smaller the teacup is than the teapot.

★ **Science** Explain to students that weathering can cause waterfalls to move or to change shape.

★ **Social Studies** Have students describes things in the United States that were originated in Japan.

★ **Technology** Using a paint or draw program, have students create a landscape that shows informal balance. Visit **SRAonline.com** to print detailed instructions for this activity.
NSAE 6.b

LESSON 3 • Informal Balance **137**

Lesson 3 Wrap-Up: Informal Balance

Extra! For the Art Specialist
Time: About 45 minutes

Focus
Study **Large Print 80** *The Night Watch* and discuss how informal balance was used. What art elements or objects are repeated? How are they arranged?

Teach
Explain to the students that they will be creating a still life using markers and washes of acrylic paint on a canvas. Have them work together to create a class arrangement of objects for a still life. Then have them complete the Alternate Activity.

Reflect
Have students use the four steps of art criticism to evaluate their work. Describe the objects used and how they were arranged in the still life. Did the students successfully use asymmetrical balance in their still-life painting? Was at least one object coming off the composition?

Alternate Activity

Materials:
- sketchbook, pencils, erasers
- objects for still life, any size canvas
- black permanent marker, acrylic paints
- brushes, containers, towels, newspaper
- glaze medium (optional)

1. Have students create several sketches of the class still life from different points of view. At least one object should be coming off the composition to create informal balance. Select the best sketch.
2. Have students use a black permanent marker to draw the still life image on the canvas. Textures can be added with the marker using stippling and hatching.
3. Demonstrate adding large amounts of water or a glaze medium to create washes of color onto the canvas. Then have students finish their still lifes, using the same technique.
4. Display completed paintings for class critique.

Research in Art Education

"There is more to learning about art than learning to do it. Most people will not actually seek to make art in their lifetime, but all of us have daily contact with visual stimuli that deliberately (in package design, fashion, or good building) or accidentally (a pattern of leaves on snow or an unexpected bright color against a faded doorway) appeal to our aesthetic sense and offer a bit of visual order in the bustle of the everyday." (Elizabeth Vallance. "Criticism as Subject Matter in Schools and in Art Museums." *Journal of Aesthetic Education* 22. 1988.)

Have students complete page 49 or 50 in their *Assessment* books.

Assessment
Use the following rubric to evaluate the artwork students made in the Creative Expression activity and to assess students' understanding of how informal or asymmetrical balance is used in two-dimensional works of art.

	Art History and Culture	Aesthetic Perception	Creative Expression	Art Criticism
3 POINTS	The student demonstrates knowledge of the lives and work of Hokusai and Cassatt.	The student accurately identifies the use of informal or asymmetrical balance in two-dimensional works of art.	The student's still life demonstrates how to use informal or asymmetrical balance.	The student thoughtfully and honestly evaluates own work using the four steps of art criticism.
2 POINTS	The student's knowledge of the lives and work of Hokusai and Cassatt is weak or incomplete.	The student shows an emerging awareness of informal or asymmetrical balance in two-dimensional works of art, but cannot consistently identify them.	The student's still life shows some awareness of how to use informal or asymmetrical balance.	The student attempts to evaluate own work but shows an incomplete understanding of evaluation criteria.
1 POINT	The student cannot demonstrate knowledge of the lives and work of Hokusai and Cassatt.	The student cannot identify how informal or asymmetrical balance is used in two-dimensional works of art.	The student's still life shows no understanding of how to use informal or asymmetrical balance.	The student makes no attempt to evaluate own work.

137A UNIT 4 • Balance and Emphasis

Lesson 4 Overview: Radial Balance

Lesson 4 introduces another type of balance called radial balance. **Radial balance** is a type of balance that occurs when the art elements come out, or radiate, from a central point. The **focal point** is the area of an artwork that is emphasized.

Objectives

Art History and Culture
To demonstrate knowledge of the soul discs of the Asante, and *Bull's Eye Quilt*

Creative Expression
To create a radial design using repeated shapes and a color scheme

Aesthetic Perception
To identify how radial balance is used in a variety of works of art

Art Criticism
To evaluate own work using the four steps of art criticism

Lesson Materials
- 4" × 4" or larger construction paper
- pencils, erasers, rulers
- 12" × 12" heavy white drawing paper
- fine-tipped black permanent marker
- color pencil, markers
- circle patterns
- compass (optional)

Alternate materials
- self-adhesive notes
- white construction paper
- crayons, precut circles

Program Resources
- *Reading and Writing Test Prep.*, pp. 48–49
- *Transparency* 22
- *Flash Card* 14
- *Artist Profiles*, pp. 68, 70
- *Animals Through History Time Line*
- *Assessment*, pp. 51–52
- *Large Prints 79 Long May Our Land Be Bright* and *80 The Night Watch*
- *Art Around the World Collection*

Concept Trace
Radial Balance
Introduced: Level 5, Unit 5, Lesson 6
Reinforced: Level 7, Chapter 3, Lesson 2

Vocabulary
Review the following vocabulary words with students before beginning the lesson.

focal point *punto focal*—the area of an artwork that is emphasized

radial balance *equilibrio radial*—a type of balance that occurs when the art elements come out, or radiate, from a central point

See page 149B for additional vocabulary and Spanish vocabulary resources.

Art Journal: Vocabulary
Have students add these words to the Vocabulary section of their Art Journals.

Lesson 4 Arts Integration

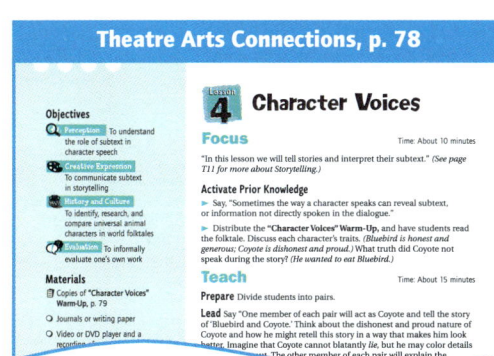

Theatre
Complete Unit 4, Lesson 4, on pages 78–79 of *Theatre Arts Connection*.

Music
Musical forms have balance. Music in the Western tradition also has forms that create balance. Rondo form occurs when one main musical idea is repeated with contrasting sections in between the main idea. The form is written ABACADA. Have students listen to *Rage over a Lost Penny* by Ludwig van Beethoven. Can students hear the repetition of the A section?

Movement & Dance
Have students make three circles: an outer circle, middle circle, and an inner circle. In each circle, have students stand with their left shoulders facing the center. Have everyone simultaneously extend their right feet, reaching out like rays from the sun. Experiment with variations on this idea.

Focus

Time: About 10 minutes

Activate Prior Knowledge

"Have you ever looked at a design in a kaleidoscope?" "¿Han visto alguna vez un diseño en un calidoscopio?"

- Discuss students' responses. Explain that radial designs, like those seen in a kaleidoscope, are often created for decorative purposes.

Using Literature ⭐ Reading

- Look at the cover illustration of *Fair Weather* by Richard Peck. Discuss how radial balance is used. The radial balance in a Ferris wheel is not only decorative but also functional.

Thematic Connection ⭐ Math

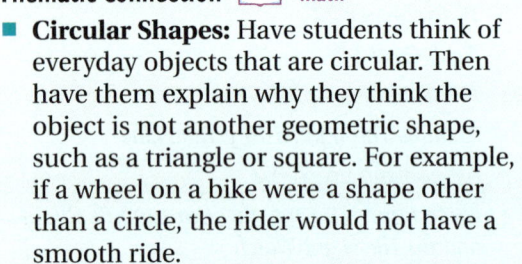

- **Circular Shapes:** Have students think of everyday objects that are circular. Then have them explain why they think the object is not another geometric shape, such as a triangle or square. For example, if a wheel on a bike were a shape other than a circle, the rider would not have a smooth ride.

Introduce the Art

Look

"Look closely at how repeated lines, shapes, and colors are arranged in the *soul discs* and *Bull's Eye Quilt*." "Observen detalladamente cómo líneas repetidas, figuras y colores son arreglados en el *soul discs* y *Bull's Eye Quilt*."

Division and Rounding ⭐ Math

- Have students look at the dimensions of the works of art in this lesson. Then have them estimate the number of discs that could fit along the length or the width of the quilt. Approximately nineteen discs would fit along the length and width of the quilt.

Art History and Culture

Possible answer: These pieces are utilitarian because they served a useful purpose at one point in their existence.

💻 Web Connection

Visit www.folkartmuseum.org for more information about the American Folk Art Museum in New York.

138 UNIT 4 • Balance and Emphasis

Lesson 4: Radial Balance

◀ Attributed to **Alverda Herb.** (American). *Bull's Eye Quilt*. c. 1900–1920.

Cotton. 84½ × 86 inches (214.63 × 218.44 cm.). American Folk Art Museum, New York, New York.

Look at the works of art on these two pages. Do you see the designs radiating from the center of each artwork? These images are examples of radial balance. *Bull's Eye Quilt* is attributed to Alverda Herb, because evidence suggests that someone in the family made the quilt. However, historians are not completely certain who it was. The akrafokonmu were made by the Asante people, who live along the Gold Coast of West Africa. These discs act as a talisman or amulet, and are worn by individuals who represent the soul of the chief. The discs are found in many places in West Africa and are usually worn around the neck, hanging from a fiber cord or a gold chain.

Art History and Culture

Would you classify these pieces of art as abstract or utilitarian?

138   Unit 4 • Lesson 4

Art History and Culture

Bull's Eye Quilt

Bull's Eye Quilt (c. 1900–1920) is attributed to Alverda Herb (al´ vâr də hûrb), whose name appears on a label sewn onto the back of the quilt. Ironically, her family said that she was not adept at sewing and would not have been able to make a quilt. Herb and other family members commonly placed labels on their textiles to show ownership, not to show that they created the pieces. *Bull's Eye Quilt* might have been sold at an estate sale for Herb's stepfather. It has not been determined whether the true maker of this quilt adapted the pattern from an earlier quilt or found it published locally. It was common to find patchwork patterns in magazines.

See pages 24–25 and 16–21 for more about art history and the subject matter.

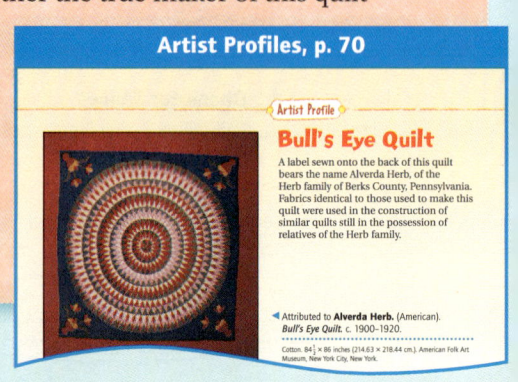

Artist Profiles, p. 70

Artist Profile

Bull's Eye Quilt

A label sewn onto the back of this quilt bears the name Alverda Herb, of the Herb family of Berks County, Pennsylvania. Fabrics identical to those used to make this quilt were used in the construction of similar quilts still in the possession of relatives of the Herb family.

◀ Attributed to **Alverda Herb.** (American). *Bull's Eye Quilt*. c. 1900–1920.

Cotton. 84½ × 86 inches (214.63 × 218.44 cm.). American Folk Art Museum, New York City, New York.

Study how radial balance is used by looking closely at the works of art.

- Describe the shapes and how they are arranged in the works of art.
- Look closely at *Akrafokonmu (Soul Discs)*. Which area attracts your eye? Why?
- Of the designs on these pages, which show the most movement? Why?
- Where do the designs begin and end in *Bull's Eye Quilt*?

Artist unknown. (Asante). *Akrafokonmu (Soul Discs)*. Twentieth century.
Gold. Largest diameter: $4\frac{1}{2}$ inches (11.43 cm.). The Museum of Fine Arts, Houston, Texas.

Aesthetic Perception

Design Awareness Think about other objects you have seen that radiate, or come out, from the center.

Unit 4 • Lesson 4

Study

- *Bull's Eye Quilt:* Diamonds and triangles repeat themselves and radiate from the center. *Soul Discs:* The circle in the center of each disc is topped by what looks like a jewel or bead. Each disc uses a different element.
- The center, because it is the largest shape on all three discs and no lines are intersecting it. The circles are the focal point, and all the other shapes and lines flow toward it.
- Student responses will vary based on personal experience. Many may say the quilt because of the rhythm of the white shape starting every ring from the center outward. Others will say the soul disc on the far left because the diagonal lines make the piece seem as if it is turning in circles.
- Student responses will vary based on how they interpret the quilt. Some may say that the quilt starts in the center and that the other fabrics were added to it in an outward pattern.
- For more examples art from Africa, see the **Art Around the World Collection.**

Art Journal: Writing

Have students explain what the word *radial* means in the Concepts section of their Art Journals. What else do they want to know about radial balance?

Aesthetic Perception

Design Awareness Have the students discuss the various types of radial designs they have noticed. Explain that radial balance is found in nature and in objects made by people. Sometimes we notice the design immediately; other times it is not as obvious.

Developing Visual Literacy Discuss the use of repeated shapes and lines in each artwork. Have students look closely at how the two pieces are arranged. Can they find the central axis? Why do they think these objects were designed this way? Ask students to explain their answers.
NSAE 4.a; 4.b

Web Connection

Visit www.mfah.org for more information about The Museum of Fine Arts, Houston.

Art History and Culture

Akrafokonmu

Akrafokonmu (twentieth century) are gold, disk-shaped chest ornaments made by the Asante people, who live along the Gold Coast of Western Africa. Known as *soul discs* or *soul washers' badges*, these discs act as a talisman or amulet, and are worn by individuals who represent the soul of the chief. These discs are found in many places and hang around the neck by a white, pineapple fiber cord or a gold chain. These discs also have been found as decoration on other surfaces such as swords, ritual containers, and stools. The design elements on many of the soul discs have been identified as stylized images of cowry shells, leaves, insects, and moon and star motifs.

See pages 24–25 and 16–21 for more about art history and the subject matter.

Artist Profiles, p. 68

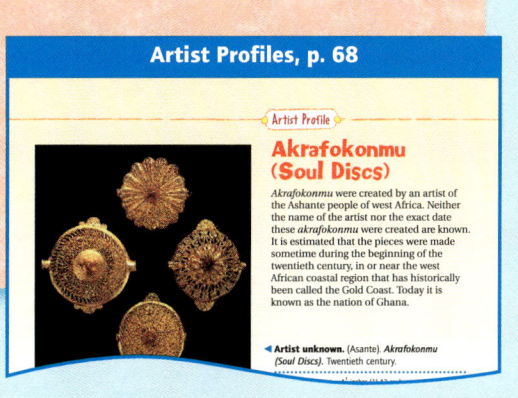

LESSON 4 • Radial Balance

Teach

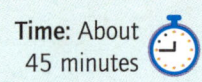

Time: About 45 minutes

"How will you create your radial design?"
"¿Cómo crearan su diseño radial?"

- Read and discuss using radial balance on page 140.

Practice

Materials: 4" × 4" or larger construction paper

Alternate Materials: self-adhesive notes

- Distribute the materials and have students follow the directions on page 140.

Creative Expression

Materials: pencils, erasers, 12" × 12" or 18" × 18" white drawing paper, ruler, fine-tipped black permanent marker, color pencil, markers, circle patterns

Alternate materials: crayons, pre-cut circles, compass

- Distribute the materials and have students follow the directions on page 141.
- Have students demonstrate their technical skills, using a variety of art media and materials to produce their radial designs.
  NSAE 1.a; 1.b
- Review the Activity Tips on page 240 for visual examples of techniques if needed.

Art Journal: Drawing

Have students draw a variety of geometric and free-form shapes in the Idea section of their Art Journals. These shapes will be used in their designs for their Creative Expression activity.

140 UNIT 4 • Balance and Emphasis

Using Radial Balance

Radial balance is a type of balance that occurs when the art elements come out, or radiate, from a central point. Radial balance is a variation of symmetry. Instead of having two matching units, it has four or more. In radial design, the central axis is the center point. Another name for this center point is the focal point. The **focal point** is the area of an artwork that is emphasized.

Radial balance occurs frequently in nature. If you look at a daisy or sunflower, you will notice that the petals radiate outward from the center. People have imitated nature by producing many objects that have radial designs. Spokes on a bicycle and hands on a clock are examples of radial balance.

A radial design created with straight lines radiating from the axis produces a calming effect. If a radial design is swirling outward from the center, it gives a feeling of excitement.

Practice

Fold a paper to create radial balance.

1. Fold a square piece of paper in half. Open the paper. Notice how the two sides are symmetrical. Close the paper.
2. Fold the paper a second time so that it becomes square again. What happens when you open it? Keep the paper open.
3. Create a third and fourth fold so that the corners of the paper touch. Your paper should be divided into eight sections, all radiating outward from the axis.

140 Unit 4 • Lesson 4

Differentiated Instruction

Reteach
Using pieces of yarn, have students demonstrate radial balance.

Special Needs
Activate student's prior knowledge of color schemes by providing visual examples for students to refer to as they complete their project.

ELL
Present the information on radial balance using a visual example such as a flower. Point to the petals and show that they move outward from the center.

◀ Harry Jones.
Age 11.

Think about what shapes the student artist began with when creating this radial design.

Creative Expression

Use shapes and a color scheme to create a radial design.

1. Lightly trace a circle on your paper with eight pie shapes.
2. Draw one shape in the center of your radial design for your focal point. Complete your design by using the shapes you made in your Art Journal. Outline your drawing using a fine-tip permanent marker.
3. Select a color scheme using three or more colors that you like. Use color pencils or markers to complete your radial design.
4. Display it for your classmates to see.

Art Criticism

Describe What shape did you use as your focal point?

Analyze What shapes and color scheme did you select for the rest of your design? Why?

Interpret What does your radial design remind you of?

Decide Do you feel you were able to successfully create a radial design using repeated shapes and a color scheme? Explain.

Unit 4 • Lesson 4   **141**

Reflect

Time: About 5 minutes

Review and Assess

"How was radial balance used?" "¿Cómo usaron el equilibrio radial?"

Think

The artist began with simple circular shapes to create his radial design.

- Use **Large Prints 79** *Long May Our Land Be Bright* and ask students to analyze how the artist created radial balance.

Informal Assessment

- Have students create portfolios of their artwork. Have students exchange their portfolios to analyze and form conclusions about the formal properties that were used. What kind of balance do they notice?
  NSAE 5.c; 6.a
- For standardized-format test practice using this lesson's art content, see page 48–49 in **Reading and Writing Test Preparation.**

Art Journal: Critical Thinking

Have students answer the four art criticism questions—Describe, Analyze, Interpret, and Decide—in their Art Journals. Have students discuss within groups how they created their radial design. Ask them to notice the similarities and differences. Have the groups share their findings with the class.

Art Across the Curriculum

Use these simple ideas to reinforce art concepts across the curriculum.

★ **Expository Writing** Have students write a paragraph explaining how the soul discs could be attached to a piece of fabric.

★ **Math** Have students measure the diameter of the circle images in the works of art.

★ **Science** Explain to students that the element symbol for gold is *Au*.

★ **Social Studies** Explain that gold can be found in 42 of the 50 United States, but it is not necessarily the kind that can be used in jewelry.

★ **Technology** Using the shape tool in a paint or draw program, have students create a design that demonstrates radial balance. Visit **SRAonline.com** to print out detailed instructions for this activity.
NSAE 6.b

LESSON 4 • Radial Balance   **141**

Lesson 4 Wrap-Up: Radial Balance

Extra! For the Art Specialist
Time: About 45 minutes

Focus
Study **Large Print 79** *Long May Our Land Be Bright* and discuss how radial balance was used. What art elements are repeated? How are these elements and forms arranged?

Teach
Explain to the students that they will be making a radial design based on shapes they find in nature. Take students outside, or bring natural examples to the classroom, and have students create several sketches. Then have them complete the Alternate Activity.

Reflect
Have students use the four steps of art criticism to evaluate their work. Describe the shapes and colors used and how they are arranged. What object in nature influenced the design? Did the students successfully create a radial design?

Alternate Activity
Materials:
- sketchbook
- pencils, erasers
- rulers
- white drawing paper
- fine-tip black permanent marker
- color pencils

1. Have students lightly draw a six- to eight-inch circle on the paper using a compass or a pattern. Students may choose to draw smaller circles within the larger one.
2. Have students draw diagonal lines to create an eight-pie design. Then have them draw two more diagonal lines to create a twelve-pie design.
3. Have students create simple shapes based on their sketches to include in their design.
4. Once the radial is complete, have students use the fine-tip black permanent marker to outline the design. Use black and white and one color to create a pattern.

Research in Art Education
Not only do students who are involved in the arts tend to have positive academic development, but "the comparative gains for arts-involved youngsters generally become more pronounced over time" ("Involvement in the Arts and Human Development: General Involvement and Intensive Involvement in Music and Theater Arts" in *Champions of Change,* pp. 2–7). The longer students pursue the arts, the greater the benefit.

Assessment
Use the following rubric to evaluate the artwork students made in the Creative Expression activity and to assess students' understanding of how radial balance is used in works of art.

	Art History and Culture	Aesthetic Perception	Creative Expression	Art Criticism
3 POINTS	The student demonstrates knowledge of *Bull's Eye Quilt* and the soul discs.	The student accurately identifies the use of radial balance in a variety of works of art.	The student's radial design demonstrates how to use radial balance.	The student thoughtfully and honestly evaluates own work using the four steps of art criticism.
2 POINTS	The student's knowledge of *Bull's Eye Quilt* and the soul discs is weak or incomplete.	The student shows an emerging awareness of radial balance in a variety of works of art, but cannot consistently identify them.	The student's radial design shows some awareness of how to use radial balance.	The student attempts to evaluate own work but shows an incomplete understanding of evaluation criteria.
1 POINT	The student cannot demonstrate knowledge of *Bull's Eye Quilt* and the soul discs.	The student cannot identify how radial balance is used in an artwork.	The student's radial design shows no understanding of how to use radial balance.	The student makes no attempt to evaluate own work.

Have students complete page 51 or 52 in their *Assessment* books.

Lesson 5 Overview: Emphasis of an Element

Lesson 5 introduces the art principle of emphasis and techniques artists use to create emphasis. **Emphasis** is the principle of design that stresses one area in an artwork over another area.

Objectives

Art History and Culture
To demostrate knowledge of the lives and work of William Sharp and Susan Rothenberg

Creative Expression
To make a collograph using contrast, isolation, or placement to create emphasis

Aesthetic Perception
To understand how artists use emphasis through contrast, isolation and placement of an art element

Art Criticism
To evaluate own work using the four steps of art criticism

Lesson Materials
- Art Journal
- pencils, erasers
- crayons, glue, brayer
- $4\frac{1}{2}" \times 6"$ tagboard
- thin white paper
- $9" \times 12"$ construction paper
- white printing ink
- sponge or washcloth
- paper towels or newspaper
- plate or tray to hold ink

Alternate Materials
- paper scraps
- tempera paint or black printing ink
- 1-inch brushes
- paper plates for ink

Program Resources
- *Reading and Writing Test Prep.*, pp. 50–51
- *Transparency 23*
- *Flash Card* 15
- *Artist Profiles*, pp. 53, 60
- *Animals Through History Time Line*
- *Assessment*, pp. 53–54
- *Large Prints 79 Long May Our Land Be Bright* and *80 The Night Watch*
- *The National Museum of Women in the Arts Collection*

Vocabulary

Review the following vocabulary words with students before beginning the lesson.

collograph colografía—a printmaking technique in which cut papers or thin boards are arranged to create an image on a stiff printing plate

printing plate placa de imprimir—a plate that holds the image that will be used to create a print

See page 149B for additional vocabulary and Spanish vocabulary resources.

Art Journal: Vocabulary
Have students add these words to the Vocabulary section of their Art Journals.

Concept Trace
Emphasis of an Element
Introduced: Level 5, Unit 6, Lesson 3
Reinforced: Level 7, Chapter 3, Lesson 3

Lesson 5 Arts Integration

Theatre
Complete Unit 4, Lesson 5, on pages 80–81 of *Theatre Arts Connection*.

Music
The most famous example of emphasis by dynamics, or "accent," is in *The Surprise Symphony No. 94* by Franz Joseph Haydn. When Haydn was frustrated that his audiences were getting sleepy during his after-dinner entertainment, he added the famous accents to wake them up. Have students listen to the symphony and identify the emphasis.

Movement & Dance
Have students walk, weaving in and around each other, to the beat of a drum or other percussive instrument. Students should emphasize a part of their bodies by having it pull them through the room. Name each body part, so students can adjust their bodies.

LESSON 5 • Emphasis of an Element **141B**

Focus

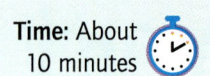

Time: About 10 minutes

Activate Prior Knowledge

"Have you ever seen a flower up close or a horse running by itself?" "¿Han visto alguna vez una flor de cerca o un caballo corriendo sólo?"

- Discuss students' answers. Explain that artists use techniques to have the viewer focus on the most important object or art element in an artwork.

Using Literature ⭐ Reading

- Read *A Mouse Called Wolf* by Dick King-Smith. Have students look at the cover illustration. Illustrator Jon Goodell used emphasis by placing the mouse toward the center of the composition and casting it in a white light.

Thematic Connection ⭐ Language Arts

- **Things That Stand Out:** Have students describe objects that have caught their attention. Students can select items they have seen in person, in a magazine, or on television.

Introduce the Art

Look

"Let's compare the two works of art to learn more about emphasis through contrast." "Comparemos las dos obras de arte para aprender sobre énfasis a través de contraste."

Environment ⭐ Science

- Have students discuss what kinds of environments are suitable for a horse and a water lily. Answers will vary. Some students will say that a horse can be in found in warm or cold environments. The water lily could survive only in a warm environment.

Art History and Culture

Possible answer: *Cabin Fever* appears to be older. Students might comment that it looks like a cave painting. Students also might say that *Complete Bloom* appears brighter and the image is sharper.

💻 Web Connection

Visit www.mamfw.org for more information about the Modern Art Museum of Fort Worth.

142 UNIT 4 • Balance and Emphasis

Lesson 5: Emphasis of an Element

▲ **Susan Rothenberg.** (American). *Cabin Fever.* 1976.
Acrylic and tempera on canvas. 67 × 84¼ inches (170.18 × 213.67 cm.). Modern Art Museum of Fort Worth, Texas.

Look at the two works of art. William Sharp created *Great Water Lily of America* using a technique called *chromolithography*. Like lithography, the image is drawn on a litho stone. However, Sharp used multiple stones, one for each color. Susan Rothenberg is best known for her abstract images of horse silhouettes. She began creating her paintings accidentally. She doodled a rough horse image onto a small sheet of paper and liked what she saw. Both works of art are examples of emphasis through contrast. For instance, in *Cabin Fever*, the shape of the horse dominates the image because it is the only shape. The color red is important, but not as important as the horse's shape.

Art History and Culture

Examine these works of art. Before looking at the dates, decide which one looks older.

142   Unit 4 • Lesson 5

Art History and Culture

Susan Rothenberg

From an early age, Susan Rothenberg (sōō´ zən rô thən berg) (1945–) was encouraged by family, teachers, and friends to pursue her interests in art. Rothenberg moved to New York in 1969 and lived among a dedicated community of young and established artists. In 1973 Susan Rothenberg's intuitive approach to painting led to spontaneously sketch the image of a horse—a subject that would preoccupy her until 1980. Rothenberg's primitive horses recall a friezelike classicism and suggest the chalky cave paintings at Lascaux. As Rothenberg developed her expressionist brushwork and the illusion of depth in her work, she fragmented the horse imagery and eventually moved away from it entirely.

See pages 24–25 and 16–21 for more about art history and the subject matter.

Artist Profiles, p. 53

Artist Profile
Susan Rothenberg
b. 1945

Susan Rothenberg (sōō´ zən rô thən berg) was born in Buffalo, New York. She attended Cornell University and took classes at the Corcoran School of Art and George Washington University in Washington, D.C. When she moved to New York City in 1969, she studied dance and eased her way into the abstract expressionist art scene of the 1970s. This background in dance and performance contributed to her appreciation of movement, and she became fascinated with depicting speed and movement on canvas in her abstract horse paintings and later figurative works.

Study both works of art and compare how the artist used emphasis through contrast.
- Describe the objects in both works of art.
- What object or area do you see first in each work of art? Why?
- Where in the painting are the main objects located?
- Which painting is active, and which one is calm?

▲ **William Sharp.** (English/American). *Great Water Lily of America.* 1854.
Chromolithograph on woven white paper. 21¼ × 27 inches (53.98 × 68.58 cm.). Amon Carter Museum, Fort Worth, Texas.

Aesthetic Perception

Design Awareness Think about a time when you have seen a line of cars on the expressway or on a busy street. Did any one car stand out more than the others? If so, why?

Unit 4 • Lesson 5 **143**

Art History and Culture

William Sharp

William Sharp (wil´ yəm shärp) (1803–1875) was a commercial printer in Boston who is credited with introducing color lithography, or chromolithography, to the United States. Before arriving in the United States, Sharp converted oil portraits to black and white lithographs. In the 1930s, he began creating chromolithographs. Chromolithography involves overprinting many colored printing stones to create a final product that had rich depth and visual variety. Sharp eventually made a book of prints created from his drawings, which were probably the finest chromolithographs in America up to that time.

See pages 24–25 and 16–21 for more about art history and the subject matter.

Artist Profiles, p. 60

Study

▶ Possible answer: *Complete Bloom:* There is a large white flower with a yellow-red center with tiny small petals pointing towards the center. There is a closed bloom of a lily that has a brown and orange cast to it behind the white flower. Three green lily pads fill up the background. *Cabin Fever:* There is a silhouette of a horse which looks to be running. A dark shadow outlines portions of the horse.

▶ *Complete Bloom:* The large white flower. It is the largest object in the picture. *Cabin Fever:* The horse, because it is the only object in the painting.

▶ *Complete Bloom:* The flower is in the middle ground. *Cabin Fever:* The horse is in the middle ground.

▶ *Complete Bloom* is calm. The lily is peacefully floating on calm water, which is created by repeated horizontal lines. *Cabin Fever* is active. The horse's head and legs appear to be moving, through the use of subtle repeated blended lines and the dark shadows around the feet.

Art Journal: Writing

Have students explain in the Concepts section of their Art Journals what the word *emphasis* means. What else do they want to know about emphasis of an element?

Aesthetic Perception

Design Awareness Discuss with students that when an object is lighter or brighter in color, different in shape, or in the center of a grouping, it is noticed more often. If you see a line of blue and green cars with a red car in the group, the red one will be noticed first. This is because of the contrasting color.

Developing Visual Literacy Compare the two works of art. How did each artist create emphasis in their work? Encourage students to share personal experiences that contribute to their understanding of the works of art.
NSAE 5.c

Web Connection

Visit **www.cartermuseum.org** for more information about the Amon Carter Museum.

LESSON 5 • Emphasis of an Element **143**

Teach

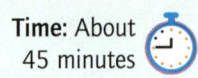

Time: About 45 minutes

"How can you create emphasis in your print?"
"¿Cómo pueden crear énfasis en su impresión?"

- Read and discuss using various techniques to create emphasis in two-dimensional art on page 144.

Practice

Materials: crayons, $4\frac{1}{2}"\times 6"$ tagboard, thin white paper

Alternate Materials: paper scraps

- Demonstrate the layering of the shapes and how an outline will be created by each individual shape's edge that directly touches the paper underneath. If one shape partially covers another, only part of the outline of the covered shape will transfer.
- Distribute the materials and have students follow the directions on page 144.

Creative Expression

Materials: Art Journal, pencils, erasers, $4\frac{1}{2}"\times 6"$ tagboard glue, $9"\times 12"$ construction paper, printing ink, brayer, sponge or washcloth, paper towels, newspaper, plate or tray to hold ink

Alternate Materials: tempera paint, black printing ink, 1" brushes, paper plates for ink

- Distribute the materials and have students follow the directions on page 145.
- Have students demonstrate their technical skills, using a variety of art materials to produce their collograph prints.
  NSAE 1.a; 1.b
- Review the Activity Tips on page 241 for visual examples of techniques if needed.

Art Journal: Planning
Have students focus on drawing images using simple shapes and contour lines. Explain that they must create emphasis of an art element. Ask students to select their best sketch and to keep their plans in their Art Journals to be used for the Creative Expression activity.

144 UNIT 4 • Balance and Emphasis

Using Emphasis of an Element

In advertisements, music, and your day-to-day communications, you see and hear certain ideas and feelings emphasized over others. In art, emphasis is used in the same way.

Emphasis is the principle of design that stresses one area in an artwork over another area. Emphasis of an art element occurs when one art element dominates the entire work, and the other elements become less important.

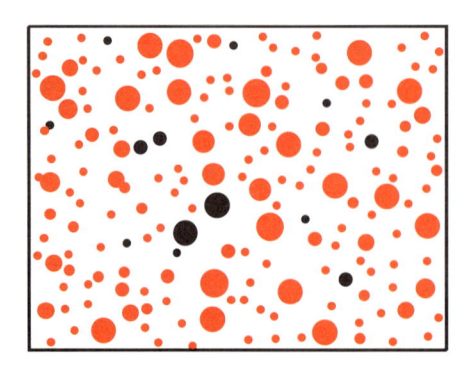

Practice

Cut three shapes and create a crayon rubbing to show emphasis.

1. Cut out your shapes from tagboard. Make two geometric and one free-form shape.
2. Place a shape on the table and place your paper on top of the shape. Rub the top of the paper with the side of a crayon. The outline of the shape below will transfer onto the paper.
3. Experiment with creating a crayon rubbing of each shape, with overlapping shapes, and with using contrasting colors. What happens when you overlap shapes?

144 Unit 4 • Lesson 5

Differentiated Instruction

Reteach
Have students look through their books to find three examples of emphasis of an element.

Special Needs
Students with low vision or gross motor skills may benefit from having both the plate and the paper stabilized by tape.

ELL
Have students create a chart of pictures from magazines that demonstrate emphasis of an element.

◀ Shawna Sullivan.
Age 11.

Think about what art element or object the student artist used to create emphasis in this artwork.

Creative Expression

Make a **collograph** print using contrast, isolation, or placement to create emphasis.

1. You will be layering each of your shapes to create a collage of your image. Look at your plant sketch in your Art Journal. Draw and cut out your large shape first. If you are creating a flower, cut out the individual petals and glue these on top of your paper. Glue the center portion last. This is called a printing plate.
2. Once you have glued down all of your shapes, make a crayon rubbing of it. This will allow you to see what your print will look like when it is finished. Make any necessary changes.
3. Set up your printing area, and create a print of your collaged image.

Art Criticism

Describe What plant form did you choose for your print?

Analyze Which art element was emphasized? Which technique did you use?

Interpret Write a poem based on your print.

Decide Do you feel you were successful in creating a collograph print using emphasis? Explain.

Unit 4 • Lesson 5   **145**

Reflect
Time: About 5 minutes

Review and Assess
"Can you explain different techniques an artist uses when creating emphasis in two-dimensional works of art?" "¿Pueden explicar técnicas diferentes que un artista usa cuando crea énfasis en obras de arte bidimensional?"

Think
The artist used color and placement to create emphasis.

- Use **Large Prints** 79 *Long May Our Land Be Bright* and 80 *The Night Watch* and have students identify how emphasis was created.

Informal Assessment
- For more examples of still lifes, see *The National Museum of Women in the Arts Collection.*
- For standardized-format test practice using this lesson's art content, see page 50–51 in *Reading and Writing Test Preparation.*

Art Journal: Critical Thinking
Have students answer the four art criticism questions—Describe, Analyze, Interpret, and Decide—in their Art Journals. Lead a class discussion on the different techniques used to create emphasis in the prints by the students. Compare how the students emphasized different art elements in their work.

Art Across the Curriculum

Use these simple ideas to reinforce art concepts across the curriculum.

★ **Descriptive Writing** Have students describe the flower in *Complete Bloom.*

★ **Math** Tell students that the average velocity for a thoroughbred horse is about 17 meters per second, or approximately 38 miles per hour.

★ **Science** Explain to students that hybrid flowers are created by crossing parents that have two different forms of the same trait.

★ **Social Studies** Have students compare *Cabin Fever* to ancient cave paintings.

★ **Technology** Using a word processing program, have students create a sign that demonstrates the emphasis of an element. Visit SRAonline.com to print detailed instructions for this activity.
NSAE 6.b

LESSON 5 • Emphasis of an Element   **145**

Lesson 5 Wrap-Up: Emphasis of an Element

Extra! For the Art Specialist
Time: About 45 minutes

Focus
Study **Large Print 80** *The Night Watch* and discuss which art element was used to create emphasis. Which object attracts your eye first? Why?

Teach
Explain to students that they will be making either a collograph or a linoleum print. Have students gather a variety of plants from various resources. Then have students create several sketches of the plants and then complete the Alternate Activity.

Reflect
Have students use the four steps of art criticism to evaluate their work. Did they effectively create emphasis in their print using one of the art elements? What problems did they encounter? How did they solve these problems?
NSAE 1.a; 1.b

Alternate Activity

Materials:
- sketchbook, pencils, erasers
- paper and linoleum cut to the same size
- brayer
- printing ink and tray
- paper at least 2" larger than the printing plate
- c-clamp or bench hook

1. Students need to choose whether to create a collograph or linoleum print. To create a linoleum print, students need to begin by transferring the completed drawing onto a piece of linoleum. Have them use a marker to color the lines and areas that will be printed.

2. Help students use a c-clamp to secure the linoleum to the table. Demonstrate moving the cutting tool in an outward motion away from the body. **Never** place the free hand in front of the direction in which the cuts are being made. Assist students with the linoleum cutting tools.

3. Have students make an edition of at least three prints, numbering them $\frac{1}{3}, \frac{2}{3}, \frac{3}{3}$.

Research in Art Education

It has been noted that "The arts can provide engaging learning environments for students who may lack interest in other classes." These classes have greatly improved "attitudes relating to self-expression, trust, self-acceptance, acceptance by others, self-awareness, and empowerment ("The Impact of an Improvisational Dramatics Program on Students Attitudes and Achievement" in *Schools, Communities, and the Arts*, p. 52).

Assessment
Use the following rubric to evaluate the artwork students make in the Creative Expression activity and to assess students' understanding of how the art elements are used to create emphasis in two-dimensional art.

Have students complete page 53 or 54 in their *Assessment* books.

	Art History and Culture	Aesthetic Perception	Creative Expression	Art Criticism
3 POINTS	The student demonstrates knowledge of the lives and work of Sharp and Rothenberg.	The student accurately identifies the use of emphasis in two-dimensional works of art.	The student's collograph print clearly demonstrates an understanding of how to use an art element to create emphasis.	The student thoughtfully and honestly evaluates own work using the four steps of art criticism.
2 POINTS	The student's knowledge of the lives and work of Sharp and Rothenberg is weak or incomplete.	The student shows an emerging awareness of how emphasis is used in two-dimensional works of art, but cannot consistently identify it.	The student's collograph print shows some awareness of how to create emphasis using an art element.	The student attempts to evaluate own work but shows an incomplete understanding of evaluation criteria.
1 POINT	The student cannot demonstrate knowledge of the lives and work of Sharp and Rothenberg.	The student cannot identify how emphasis is used.	The student's collograph print shows no understanding of how to create emphasis.	The student makes no attempt to evaluate own work.

145A UNIT 4 • Balance and Emphasis

Lesson 6 Overview: Emphasis of an Area

Lesson 6 looks at how emphasis is used in an area and how it is used as a focal point in an arrangement of three-dimensional objects.

Objectives

Art History and Culture
To demonstrate knowledge of the lives and work of George Segal and Juan Muñoz

Creative Expression
To create an individual, small-scale sculpture, then place it within a group to create emphasis of an area

Aesthetic Perception
To understand how artists emphasize an area in a grouping of three-dimensional forms

Art Criticism
To evaluate own work using the four steps of art criticism

Lesson Materials
- sketch paper, any size
- crayons, pliable wire
- scissors or wire cutters
- aluminum foil

Alternate Materials:
- pencils
- pipe cleaners
- matboard scraps

Program Resources
- *Reading and Writing Test Prep.*, pp. 52–53
- *Transparency 24*
- *Flash Card* 15
- *Artist Profiles*, pp. 42, 59
- *Animals Through History Time Line*
- *Assessment*, pp. 55–56
- *Large Prints 79* Long May Our Land Be Bright and *80* The Night Watch
- *Art Around the World Collection*

Concept Trace
Emphasis of an Area
Introduced: Level 5, Unit 6, Lesson 4
Reinforced: Level 7, Chapter 3, Lesson 3

Vocabulary

Review the following vocabulary words with students before beginning the lesson.

armature *armadura*—a framework for supporting material used in sculpting

installation *instalación*—an artwork that was created for a specific place, such as a gallery or outdoor location

See page 149B for additional vocabulary and Spanish vocabulary resources.

Art Journal: Vocabulary
Have students add these words to the Vocabulary section of their Art Journals.

Lesson 6 Arts Integration

Theatre
Complete Unit 4, Lesson 6, on pages 82–87 of *Theatre Arts Connection*.

Music
There are various musical devices for creating emphasis in music. One way is with dynamics. To create meter in music, a strong beat is combined with weak beats to create duple or triple meter, as in boom-chick boom-chick or boom-chick-chick boom-chick-chick. Have students sing or listen to "Turn the World Around" by Robert M. Freedman and Harry Belafonte. Have them clap the rhythm of the refrain while you count 1-2-3-1-2. Have students put the emphasis on beat one.

Movement & Dance
Mark off a canvas on the floor, outlining it with string or tape. Have one student enter the canvas and find a place to stand, so that attention is drawn to a certain area. Add students one at a time, until there are ten students standing on the canvas. On a signal, have the group move to different areas.

LESSON 6 • Emphasis of an Area **145B**

Focus

Time: About 10 minutes

Activate Prior Knowledge

"Have you ever seen a grouping of sculptures in an outside location?" "¿Han visto alguna vez grupos de esculturas en una ubicación en el exterior?"

- Discuss students' comments and explain that these sculptures were created based on common everyday events. Ask students if they have ever seen sculptures depicting traditional events. **NSAE 2.b**

Using Literature — Reading

- Look at the cover illustration of *Coroline* by Neil Gaiman. Notice how the illustrator created emphasis of an area.

Thematic Connection — Social Studies

- **Location:** Ask students if they have ever visited or seen a picture of a lighthouse. Have them describe the location of the lighthouse, if possible. Explain to them that location plays an important role when building an object for a specific purpose.

Introduce the Art

Look

"Let's take a closer look at the way Segal and Muñoz created emphasis of an area in their installations." "Vamos a observar detalladamente en la manera que Segal y Muñoz crearon énfasis de un área de sus instalaciones."

Classifying — Math

- Have students classify the types of figures represented in each work of art. *Answers will vary. Some possibilities are: human and nonhuman, men and women, or sitting or standing figures.*

Art History and Culture

Answers will vary. Because these sculptures are not particularly old, have students discuss whether they think people 100 years from now will understand or like the sculptures.

Web Connection

Visit www.noma.org for more information about the New Orleans Museum of Art.

146 UNIT 4 • Balance and Emphasis

Lesson 6: Emphasis of Area

▲ **George Segal.** (American). *Three People on Four Park Benches.* 1979.

Plaster and real benches. Life-size. New Orleans Museum of Art, New Orleans, Louisiana.

Look closely at the sculptures by George Segal and Juan Muñoz. Both works are examples of sculpture installations in which the environment becomes part of the artwork. Segal creates sculptures of everyday people in everyday situations. He creates the molds using surgical gauze and plaster. His models pose as he wraps the gauze in sections on their bodies. As each section dries, he cuts the gauze off. He then puts the sections together again using plaster until he has created a whole person. *Conversation Piece* by Juan Muñoz is based on a concept from the Renaissance and was influenced by Segal's work. One or more figures interact with one another to create a lifelike situation. What do you think the groups of people are talking about?

Art History and Culture

Look at the dates of these sculptures. Do you think the meaning of these works of art have changed over time?

146 Unit 4 • Lesson 6

Art History and Culture

George Segal

In 1958 George Segal (jorj sē´gəl) (1924–2000) began experimenting with plaster, burlap, and wire mesh in sculptures. He discovered the technique of using medical bandages as material for his work. He was best known for his life-size plaster sculptures of ordinary people doing ordinary things, which he created by covering friends and relatives with the plaster-soaked bandages. He placed his figures in realistic, commonplace environments that can be seen around the country. In 1983 he designed a cover for *Time* magazine. He was also the winner of a competition for the design of a Holocaust memorial.

See pages 24–25 and 16–21 for more about art history and the subject matter.

Artist Profiles, p. 59

Artist Profile

George Segal
1924–2000

Not long before George Segal (jorj sē´gəl) was born, his parents emigrated from eastern Europe to the Bronx in New York. They did not consider art to be a legitimate profession, but Segal insisted on studying art in college. After graduating in 1947, he started a chicken farm in New Jersey and taught at a high school to support his wife and two children. In 1958, he sold his chickens and used the buildings the chickens were housed in as his studio. For the next two years he created plaster figures on wood and chicken wire frames. All the art teachers in that area received surplus gauze embedded with plaster from a nearby Johnson & Johnson plant to give to Segal. He used this gauze to create his sculptures.

▲ **Juan Muñoz.** (Spanish). *Conversation Piece.* 1994–1995. Bronze. Variable dimensions, each approximately 64½ × 204 × 228 inches (163.8 × 518.2 × 579.1 cm.). Hirshhorn Museum and Sculpture Garden, Washington, D.C.

Study both sculptures to gain a better understanding of how emphasis of area is used.

▶ Which elements or objects do you see repeated in each artwork?

▶ How did George Segal create the feeling of isolation in *Three People on Four Park Benches?*

▶ How did Juan Muñoz arrange his figures?

▶ Which part of each of these works of art do you notice first?

Aesthetic Perception

Design Awareness Think about a sporting event or dance you have attended. Describe how people interacted with one another.

Unit 4 • Lesson 6   147

Art History and Culture

Juan Muñoz

Juan Muñoz (hwän moōn´ yōs) (1953–) became noticed in the mid-1980s with his gallery installations. These installations consisted of a single figure, usually a clown or a dwarf, or an architectural element that was isolated through perspective techniques. Eventually Muñoz chose settings in which his creations could interact with their surroundings. No clear interpretation of Muñoz's work is given because he meant to generate a sense of mystery.

See pages 24–25 and 16–21 for more about art history and the subject matter.

Artist Profiles, p. 42

Artist Profile
Juan Muñoz
1953–2001

Born in Madrid, Spain, Juan Muñoz (hwän moōn´ yōs) was convinced he did not want to grow up to become an artist, but when he ran away from home to London at the age of 17, he worked and studied printmaking, easing himself into a career as an artist. He traveled often in the 1970s, searching for his own style and producing little work. In the 1980s, he began to create famous installations and bronze figures and participate in major exhibitions throughout Europe.

Study

▶ *Three People on Four Park Benches:* Three seated figures, four park benches, the color white in the figures. *Conversation Piece:* Five figures, which have a green patina and have rounded bases.

▶ They are separated from one another physically and conversationally. Each appears to be isolated and separate from the other; however, the two figures sitting closest to one another seem to be comfortable in their proximity.

▶ He grouped three figures together whose heads are tilted toward one another, and one arm reaches around to touch the back of one of the figures. Two figures are placed away from the group—one to the far right, the other to the far left.

▶ *Three People on Four Park Benches:* the two people sitting closest together. *Conversation Piece:* The group of three figures.

Art Journal: Writing

Have students explain in the Concepts section of their Art Journals what it means to emphasize an area. What else do they want to know about emphasis of an area?

Aesthetic Perception

Design Awareness Discuss with students how we are intrigued with watching the interactions of small groups of people, especially when huddled close together. A grouping attracts the eye quicker than a solitary figure, which often may be overlooked.

Developing Visual Literacy Discuss the subject matter of the sculpture installations by Segal and Muñoz. Are they both based upon real situations? What did the artists do to show how people interact with one another in these works? Invite students to share personal experiences that contribute to their understanding of the sculptures.

Web Connection

Visit **www.hirshhorn.si.edu** for more information about the Hirshhorn Museum and Sculpture Garden.

LESSON 6 • Emphasis of an Area   **147**

Teach

Time: About 45 minutes

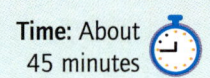

"How do you think you might be able to create a group sculpture showing emphasis of an area?" "¿Cómo piensan que podrían crear una escultura de grupo enseñando énfasis de un área?"

- Read and discuss using emphasis of an area on page 148.

Practice

Materials: any size of sketch paper, crayons

Alternate Materials: pencils

- Demonstrate creating a gesture drawing by having a student pose for 30 to 45 seconds using a crayon at an angle. Begin with the head as a solid shape, color in the neck, the body, and the thickness of the legs. Add the arms last. As you demonstrate, explain to the students that you are trying to capture the pose and position of the body, not a likeness of the person.
- Distribute the materials and have students follow the directions on page 148.

Creative Expression

Materials: gesture drawings, pliable wire, scissors or wire cutters, aluminum foil, small scraps of wood, staple gun (teacher use only)

Alternate Materials: chenille sticks, mat board scraps, acrylic paint

- Distribute the materials and have students follow the directions on page 149.
- Have students demonstrate their technical skills using a variety of art media and materials to produce their foil sculptures
  NSAE 1.a; 1.b
- Review the Activity Tips on page 241 for visual examples of techniques if needed.

Art Journal: Brainstorming

Explain to students that they will be creating a group installation for an outside location. Have students create a list of possible locations, such as the schoolyard or the library, in the Idea section of their Art Journal. The class will select a location as the first step of their Creative Expression activity.
NSAE 1.a

148 UNIT 4 • Balance and Emphasis

Using Emphasis of Area

You have learned that **emphasis** is the principle of design that stresses one area in an artwork over another area. Two types of visual emphasis can be used: emphasis of an art element and emphasis of an area. Sometimes a specific area in an artwork is emphasized. This area is called the **focal point**. There are several techniques that artists use to create emphasis.

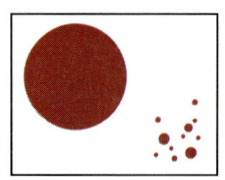

Contrast

Contrast occurs when one element stands out from the rest of the work. A bright color stands out from a dull color. A large shape stands out from small shapes. An angular shape among round shapes catches the viewer's attention. A rough texture against a smooth texture catches the viewer's eye.

Isolation

Isolation occurs when an object is placed alone and away from the other objects in an artwork. The viewer's eye is drawn to the isolated object.

Location

Location occurs when the eyes are naturally drawn toward the center of an artwork. Anything placed near the center of the work will be noticed first.

Practice

Create a focal point in a gesture drawing.

1. Create a series of gesture drawings using crayons. Look at the list you generated in the Idea section of your Art Journal. Take turns posing based on the ideas in your list.
2. Make drawings quickly with few or no details.
3. Create several of your gesture drawings, using one or two colors. At some point, create one of your gestures in a third color. Try to fit as many gestures as you can onto your paper.

148 Unit 4 • Lesson 6

Differentiated Instruction

Reteach
Have students get in groups and discuss what the focal point of the school is.

Special Needs
Encourage the participation of students with disabilities by eliciting and valuing their feedback regarding ideas for location and content of the group sculpture.

ELL
Have students think of a word that is similar to focal, such as focus. Then have them explain what *focus* means to them.

◀ Michelle Leonard's sixth-grade class.

Think about how the students created an area of emphasis in their group sculpture.

Creative Expression

Create an individual foil sculpture to be displayed together with other foil sculptures to emphasize an area.

1. Review your list of locations in your Art Journal. As a class, select one location. Look over your Practice gesture drawings and select one, or create a new one.
2. Create a wire figure based on your selected gesture. The wire figure is an **armature,** the framework for supporting the foil that will be used for your sculpture.
3. Using pieces of aluminum foil no larger than your hand, cover the wire sculpture. You can pinch out a nose or add clothing with more foil.
4. Attach your completed foil sculpture to a base, if necessary. As a class, arrange your sculptures for display.

Art Criticism

Describe Describe the location of your group sculpture.

Analyze How did you create an area of emphasis?

Interpret Does your group sculpture communicate the idea you selected? Explain.

Decide Were you successful in creating your individual sculpture? As a group, were you able to create an area of emphasis? Explain.

Unit 4 • Lesson 6 149

Reflect

Time: About 5 minutes

Review and Assess
"Describe how emphasis was used by the artists in their sculptures." "Describan cómo énfasis fue usada por los artistas en sus esculturas."

Think
The artists created an area of emphasis by placing a group of figures on the right side and a single figure on the left side.

- Use **Large Prints 79** *Long May Our Land Be Bright* and **80** *The Night Watch* and have students identify how emphasis was used.

Informal Assessment
- For more examples of art from North America, see the *Art Around the World Collection.*
- For standardized-format test practice using this lesson's art content, see pages 52–53 in *Reading and Writing Test Preparation.*

Art Journal: Critical Thinking
Have students answer the four art criticism questions—Describe, Analyze, Interpret, and Decide—in their Art Journals. Lead a class discussion on how the group sculptures were based on different themes and how each group emphasized an area.
NSAE 5.a; 5.b

Art Across the Curriculum

Use these simple ideas to reinforce art concepts across the curriculum.

★ **Poetic Writing** Have students write a poem about the figures in *Conversation Piece.*

★ **Math** Have students identify any geometric shapes in the works of art from this lesson.

★ **Science** Explain to students that bronze is made of copper and tin, or sometimes tin or another metal.

★ **Social Studies** Have students compare the sculptures of two Spanish artists, Picasso and Muñoz.

★ **Technology** Using a paint or draw program, have students draw a person and place him or her in an everyday setting. Visit **SRAonline.com** to print detailed instructions for this activity.
NSAE 6.b

LESSON 6 • Emphasis of an Area 149

Lesson 6 Wrap Up: Emphasis of an Area

Extra! For the Art Specialist
Time: About 45 minutes

Focus
Study **Large Print 80** *The Night Watch* and discuss how emphasis of an area was used. Have students discuss the use of location in the sculptural installations.

Teach
Explain to students that they will be creating models of sculptures of an imaginary public garden and amusement park. Have students begin by creating several gesture drawings of their classmates. Then have them complete the Alternate Activity.

Reflect
Have students use the four steps of art criticism to evaluate their work. Did they effectively create an area of emphasis? Describe the pose used. Where would this sculpture be installed if it were life-size?

Alternate Activity

Materials:
- gesture sketches
- wire cutters, pliers
- pliable wire, scissors
- gauze embedded with plaster
- wood scraps for sculpture platforms (optional)

1. Ask students to select one drawing to use for their sculptures. Some of the sculptures can be created with the intention of being displayed together.
2. Demonstrate and show how to form a wire figure. The wire figure will be used as the armature. Have students bend and form the armature in the desired pose.
3. Have students follow the directions on the packaging of the plaster-embedded gauze and cover the wire. The plaster sculptures should have some volume to them. After the figures have dried, display them in small groupings or areas of the park. Real items can be used with the figures for display.

Research in Art Education

It has been noted that the economic competitiveness in the United States has been enhanced by the study of the arts. It helps in the development of "creative problem-solving skills, imagination, self-discipline, and attention to detail" (U.S. Department of Education *NEWS*, February 22, 1993).

Assessment

Use the following rubric to evaluate the artwork students made in the Creative Expression activity and to assess students' understanding of how an area in a sculpture installation can be emphasized using various techniques.

Have students complete page 55 or 56 in their *Assessment* books.

	Art History and Culture	Aesthetic Perception	Creative Expression	Art Criticism
3 POINTS	The student demonstrates knowledge of the lives and works of Segal and Muñoz.	The student accurately identifies the use of emphasis in an arrangement of three-dimensional objects.	The student's group sculpture demonstrates using emphasis of an area.	The student thoughtfully and honestly evaluates own work using the four steps of art criticism.
2 POINTS	The student's knowledge of the lives and works of Segal and Muñoz is weak or incomplete.	The student shows an emerging awareness of emphasis in three-dimensional objects but cannot consistently identify it.	The student's group sculpture shows some awareness of emphasis of an area.	The student attempts to evaluate own work but shows an incomplete understanding of evaluation criteria.
1 POINT	The student cannot demonstrate knowledge of the lives and works of Segal and Muñoz.	The student cannot identify how emphasis of an area is created.	The student's group sculpture shows no understanding of how to use emphasis of an area.	The student makes no attempt to evaluate own work.

149A UNIT 4 • Balance and Emphasis

Unit 4 Vocabulary Review

approximate symmetry—a type of balance that is almost symmetrical but small differences in the artwork make it more interesting **simetría aproximada**—un tipo de equilibrio que es casi simétrico pero pequeñas diferencias en la obra de arte la hace más interesante

armature—a framework for supporting material used in sculpting **armadura**—un esqueleto de material de apoyo usado en la escultura

asymmetrical balance—another name for informal balance **equilibrio asimétrico**—otro nombre para equilibrio informal

balance—the principle of design that deals with visual weight in an artwork **equilibrio**—el principio del diseño que trata sobre el peso visual en una obra de arte

central axis—a real or imaginary dividing line which can run in two directions, vertically and horizontally **eje central**—una línea real o imaginaria que divide y puede correr en dos direcciones, vertical y horizontalmente

collage—a two-dimensional work of art made up of pieces of paper and/or fabric to create the image **collage**—una obra de arte bidimensional hecha de pedazos de papeles y/o tela para crear el imagen

collograph—a printmaking technique where cut papers or thin boards are arranged to create an image on a stiff printing plate **colografía**—una técnica de imprimir donde papeles cortados o tablas finas son arregladas para crear una imagen en una placa firme de imprimir

emphasis—the principle of design that stresses one area in an art work over another area **énfasis**—el principio del diseño que da importacia a un área de la obra de arte sobre la otra

focal point—the first part of the work to attract the attention of the viewer **punto focal**—la primera parte de la obra que atrae la atención del observador

formal balance—occurs when equal or similar elements are placed on opposite sides of a central axis **equilibrio formal**—ocurre cuando elementos iguales o parecidos son colocados en lados opuestos de un eje central

gesture drawings—quick drawings used to capture the position or pose of the body **dibujos de ademanes**—dibujos rápidos usados para capturar la posición o postura corporal

informal balance—a way of organizing parts of a design so that unlike objects have equal visual weight balance **equilibrio informal**—una manera de organizar partes de un diseño para que objetos diferentes tengan el mismo equilibrio peso visual

installation—an artwork which was created for a specific place, such as a gallery or outdoor location **instalación**—un obra de arte que fue creada para un lugar específico, como una galería o ubicación en el exterior

picture plane—the surface of a drawing or painting **plano de pintura**—la superficie de un dibujo o una pintura

printing plate—a plate that holds the image that will be used to create a print **placa de imprimir**—una placa que contiene la imagen que sera usada para crear una impresión

radial balance—a type of balance that occurs when the art elements come out, or radiate, from a central point **equilibrio radial**—un tipo de equilibrio que ocurre cuando los elementos artísticos salen o irradian, de un punto central

still life—the arrangement of common in animate objects from which artists draw or paint **naturaleza muerta**—los arreglos comunes en objetos inanimados de donde los artistas dibujan o pintan

symmetry—a type of formal balance in which two halves of a balanced artwork are identical, mirror images of each other **simetría**—un tipo de equilibrio formal en que dos mitades de una obra de arte equilibrada son idénticas, el reflejo de los imágenes de cada uno

Wrapping Up Unit 4

Balance and Emphasis

Art Criticism

Critical Thinking Art criticism is an organized system for looking at and talking about art. You can criticize art without being an expert. The purpose of art criticism is to get the viewer involved in a perception process that delays judgment until all aspects of the artwork have been studied. Push the students to expand beyond the art criticism questions.

- See pages 28–29 for more about art criticism.

Describe

- In the foreground is a yellow floor, on which a red chair sits at an angle on the left side of the composition.
- A light-colored wall with a large, rectangular window with a black shade pulled almost halfway down, two large windowpanes
- Two smaller windows on a white wall can be seen in the background through the large window.

Analyze

- Warm colors of yellow, red, and orange dominate.
- Informal or asymmetrical balance because the red chair is placed on the left side of the composition and there is not another object to the right to balance it.
- The viewer sees the red chair first because it is the only free-form shape. Another reason is the warm, red color with the bright sunlight hitting it draws our attention. Next, the viewer notices the window because it is very light and slightly above and behind the chair. The window takes up the largest area of space and is in the center of the composition.

Wrapping Up Unit 4

Balance and Emphasis

◀ **Alice Neel.** (American). *Loneliness.* 1970.
Oil on canvas. 80 × 38 inches (203.2 × 96.52 cm.).
National Gallery of Art, Washington, D.C.

150 Unit 4

Art History and Culture

Alice Neel

Alice Neel (aˊləs nēl) (1900–1984) studied at the Philadelphia School of Design for Women (currently called Moore College of Art). She was exposed to the abstract expressionists' work in which images were created to express an emotion. She moved to New York and became interested in the faces she saw around her. Portraits became her main subject matter. She often stopped people in the street and asked them to model for her. Few of her paintings sold because most people did not want to purchase portraits of people they did not know. They were also too expensive for the models to buy. When Neel died in 1984, most of her work was still in her collection.

See pages 24–25 and 16–21 for more about art history and the subject matter.

Artist Profiles, p. 43

Artist Profile
Alice Neel
1900–1984
Alice Neel (aˊləs nēl) was raised in rural Pennsylvania but abandoned her working middle-class heritage to pursue art and political activism. She began painting when it was difficult for a woman to receive critical recognition, especially if the woman ignored the prevalent style of American abstraction, which is what Neel did. Without the aid of a studio or sales, Neel developed her own style and painted numerous compositions of her friends, family, fellow artists, neighbors and famous contemporary figures. By the time she was in her 60s, Neel finally began to receive national attention, which continued throughout the rest of her career.

150 UNIT 4 • Balance and Emphasis

Art Criticism — Critical Thinking

Describe What do you see?
During this step you will collect information about the subject of the artwork.
- List all of the things you see in the foreground.
- List all of the objects you see in the middle ground.
- List all of the things you see in the background.

Analyze How is this work organized?
Think about how the artist used the elements and principles of art.
- What colors or color scheme dominates the painting?
- What type of balance was used to place the chair?
- What object do you see first? What makes it stand out? What object do you see next?

Interpret What does the artwork say?
Combine clues you collected during Describe and Analyze with your personal experiences to find out what this painting is about.
- What time of day is it?
- What type of building do you think this room is in? Why?
- Who do you think sits in the chair?
- Why do you think Alice Neel titled this work *Loneliness*?

Decide What do you think about the work?
Use all the information you have gathered to decide why this is a successful work of art.
- Is this work of art successful because it is realistic, because it is well organized, or because it conveys a message?

Interpret

- It is midday because of how bright the sun is shining.
- It could be an apartment building because the windows that can be seen out the large windows look like they are part of an apartment, and they have the same shape as the large window in the painting.
- Answers will vary. Make sure students' explanations are reasonable.
- Answers will vary. Some students may comment about there not being many items in the room or that there is only one chair.

Decide

- Students answers will vary based on individual experiences. They may use more than one aesthetic theory to explain the success of this work.

Art Journal: Writing
Have students write answers to Aesthetic Perception in their Art Journals. Have them discuss their answers in small groups.

Aesthetic Perception

Design Awareness Ask students to think about their bedroom. Then have students compare their bedroom with the room depicted in *Loneliness*.

Describe
- List and describe the items in the bedroom.

Analyze
- What area of your room is emphasized?
- How are the items arranged in front of your bedroom window, if you have one?

Interpret
- How does the balance and emphasis in your bedroom make you feel? Why?

Decide
- How do you feel about the arrangement of your bedroom?

"Artists use the art principles of balance and emphasis to help organize the art elements in two- and three-dimensional works of art."

"Los artistas usan los principios artísticos de equilibrio y énfasis para ayudar organizar los elementos artísticos en obras de arte bi y tridimensional."

T Review unit vocabulary with students using **Transparency 40.**

Art Journal: Writing
Have students answer the questions on page 152 in their Art Journals or on a separate sheet of paper. **Answers: 1. B, 2. C, 3. A, 4. C, 5. B**

T For further assessment, have students complete the unit test on **Transparency 46.**

VISIT A MUSEUM
Norton Simon Museum

▶ **Explain Norton Simon's philosophy about art.** Norton Simon stated that although a museum should be a place in which major art is constantly on view, it also should be used for teaching, seeing, and for formal and informal education. "Because for me," he said, "the respect for what art is all about comes out of looking more than reading, more than formal instruction." The Norton Simon Museum continues to hold true to its namesake's vision while organizing exhibits that demonstrate the richness and history of the collections.

"The place where I had freedom most was when I painted. I was completely and utterly myself."
　　　　　　　　　－Alice Neel

152　UNIT 4 • Balance and Emphasis

Wrapping Up Unit 4
Balance and Emphasis, continued

Show What You Know
Answer these questions on a separate sheet of paper.

❶ _____ is a type of balance that is almost symmetrical, but small differences in the artwork make it more interesting.
   A. Average symmetry
   B. Approximate symmetry
   C. Appropriate symmetry

❷ _____ is the principle of design that relates to visual weight in an artwork.
   A. Color
   B. Emphasis
   C. Balance

❸ _____ is the principle of design that stresses one area in an artwork over another area.
   A. Emphasis
   B. Line
   C. Balance

❹ _____ is a type of formal balance in which two halves of a balanced artwork are identical, mirror images of each other.
   A. Asymmetry
   B. Radial balance
   C. Symmetry

❺ The _____ is the area of an artwork that is emphasized.
   A. center
   B. focal point
   C. frame

152　Unit 4

VISIT A MUSEUM
Norton Simon Museum

The Norton Simon Museum is located in Pasadena, California. It was originally founded in 1924 as the Pasadena Art Institute and reorganized by Norton Simon in 1974. The museum consists of 38 galleries and a sculpture garden. The permanent collection contains Western and Asian art that spans a 2,000-year period. The museum owns works of art by Renaissance artists, such as Raphael and Boticelli, and impressionists, including Monet and Renoir. Pieces created by Picasso, van Gogh, and Matisse also can be found there, as well as works of art by other master artists. The public can visit the museum and view 1,000 works of art on a regular basis. The museum also has rotating special exhibits, so it can present different parts of the permanent collection.

Unit Assessment Options

Aesthetic Perception

Practice Have students select one of the concepts in the Show What You Know section on page 152, then find examples of each concept in the classroom.

Creative Expression

Student Portfolio Have students review the artwork they have created during this unit and select the pieces they wish to keep in their portfolios.

Art Criticism

Activity Have students select an artwork from this unit and study it using the four steps of art criticism. (See pages 28–29 for more information about art criticism.) Have students work in small groups and present their findings aloud or in writing.

Balance in Dance

The Pilobolus Dance Theatre works with weight and balance to create sculptural dance forms. Each dance starts with "creative play," when the dancers are directed to find new ways of moving and supporting each other's weight. During this improvisation time, there are no rules, just experimentation to find new ideas. These dancers are known for their daring body sculptures, lifts, and balances. Using their knowledge of scientific physics principles, they create inventive body designs and motion. They develop great trust in each other as they work in partnerships to find a center of gravity and balance, to use moving or kinetic energy, and to explore weight, mass, and force.

What to Do With a partner, create sculptural studies that use balance and counterbalance.

1. Work with a partner to explore the following:
   - Face each other and firmly hold wrists. Tuck your hips forward, lean with shoulders back, and bend your knees. Find the balance between you. When you are balanced, keep leaning away and slowly lower your level.
   - Now explore ways to balance, holding only right or left hands in a diagonal hold. When you have found your center of gravity, try lifting a leg.
   - Back to back, press against each other to find balance. Try lowering yourselves while maintaining balance. Experiment by pressing against shoulders or hands.
2. Perform your two best ideas for others in the class.

▲ Pilobolus Dance Theatre. "The Brass Ring" excerpt.

Art Criticism

Describe Describe the scientific principles of "opposing forces."

Analyze What choices did you make in finding pulling or pressing designs?

Interpret What feelings did you have as you tried to find the balance, and when you actually found the balance point?

Decide Did your sculptural studies have symmetry or approximate symmetry?

Unit 4   153

Art History and Culture

Pilobolus Dance Theatre

Pilobolus Dance Theatre was created at Dartmouth College in 1971. They boldly introduced a new dance style that relies on trust, collaboration, and a weight-sharing approach to partnering. Each new project begins with several days of improvisation where the dancers are called upon to find inventive movements and amazing ways to balance and counterbalance with each other. "The Brass Ring" is a work about the relationship between dance, games and athletics. It had its premier at the 2000 Olympic Games in Salt Lake City. There are nine different musical and dance sections that have a different theme and mood. They all connect like a jigsaw puzzle.

Balance and Emphasis in Dance

Objective: To create counterbalance designs with a partner

Materials: "The Brass Ring," performed by Pilobolus Dance Theatre. Running time: 3:14.

Focus
Time: About 5 minutes

- Discuss the information on page 153.

Art History and Culture
- Have students discuss the difference between balance in visual art and balance and counterbalance in dance.

Teach
Time: About 20 minutes

Aesthetic Perception
- Have students look around the room and notice how objects are balanced. Do they notice anything that looks like it is going to fall?

Creative Expression
- Introduce the scientific principles of opposing forces and how they can be demonstrated in dance. The energy and weight are either directed toward or away from each other. Direct students to find partner designs that pull away from and press in to each other.

- **Informal Assessment** When students perform their counterbalance designs, comment positively on their efforts.

Reflect
Time: About 10 minutes

Art Criticism
- Have students answer the four art criticism questions on page 153 aloud or in writing.

- Were the students able to successfully show two different counterbalance partner designs?

UNIT 4 • Balance and Emphasis   153

Unit 5 Planning Guide

	Lesson Title	Suggested Pacing	Creative Expression Activity
Lesson 1	Facial Proportions	1 hour	Create a self-portrait.
Lesson 2	Figure Proportion	1 hour	Make a series of line drawings.
Lesson 3	Facial Distortion	1 hour	Make a face jug from clay.
Lesson 4	Figure Distortion	1 hour	Use a computer to distort a photograph.
Lesson 5	Realistic Scale	1 hour	Design a chair.
Lesson 6	Unrealistic Scale	1 hour	Create a surrealistic collage.
ARTSOURCE	Proportion and Distortion in Theatre	35 minutes	Create a character and a walk.

154A UNIT 5 • Proportion, Distortion, and Scale

Materials	Program Resources	Fine Art Resources	Literature Resources
pencils, erasers, Art Journal, white or black paper, mirrors, yellow or white chalk, scrap paper, oil pastels, paper towels, newspaper	*Assessment*, pp. 57–58 *Reading and Writing Test Preparation*, pp. 54–55 *Home and After-School Connections* *Flash Card* 18	*Transparency 25* *Artist Profiles*, pp. 8, 18 *Large Prints 81* and *82* *The National Museum of Women in the Arts Collection*	*A Face First* by Priscilla Cummings
pencils, fine-point markers, sketch paper or sketchbook, white paper	*Assessment*, pp. 59–60 *Reading and Writing Test Preparation*, pp. 56–57 *Flash Card* 18	*Transparency 26* *Artist Profiles*, pp. 69, 75 *Large Prints 81* and *82* *Art Around the World Collection*	*Run Away Home* by Patricia C. McKissack
Art Journals, pencils, erasers, clay, burlap, pencils or nails to draw into clay, cloth to work on, wire cutter for clay, kiln, glaze, clay tools	*Assessment*, pp. 61–62 *Reading and Writing Test Preparation*, pp. 58–59	*Transparency 27* *Artist Profiles*, pp. 41, 77 *Large Prints 81* and *82* *The National Museum of Women in the Arts Collection*	*Tales from the Brothers Grimm and the Sister's Weird* by Vivian Vande Velde
Art Journals, digital camera, computer monitor, draw or paint software, printer, paper	*Assessment*, pp. 63–64 *Reading and Writing Test Preparation*, pp. 60–61	*Transparency 28* *Artist Profiles*, pp. 10, 27 *Large Prints 81* and *82* *Art Around the World Collection*	*Treasure of Green Knowe* by L. M. Boston
Art Journals, pencils, erasers, rulers, white paper, color pencils	*Assessment*, pp. 65–66 *Reading and Writing Test Preparation*, pp. 62–63 *Flash Card* 19	*Transparency 29* *Artist Profiles*, pp. 55, 56 *Large Prints 81* and *82* *Art Around the World Collection*	*Lily's Crossing* by Patricia Reilly Giff
Art Journals, tagboard, magazines, scissors, glue, oil pastels, fine-line markers	*Assessment*, pp. 67–68 *Reading and Writing Test Preparation*, pp. 64–65 *Flash Card* 19	*Transparency 30* *Artist Profiles*, pp. 19, 48 *Large Prints 81* and *82* *Art Around the World Collection*	*Where the Sidewalk Ends* by Shel Silverstein
The Mask Messenger			

UNIT 5 • Proportion, Distortion, and Scale **154B**

Unit Overview

5 Proportion, Distortion, and Scale

Lesson 1: Facial proportions are the relationship of one feature of a face to other features.

Lesson 2: Proportion is used to create the human figure accurately. A **ratio** is a comparison of size between two things.

Lesson 3: Distortion is a deviation from normal or expected proportions.

Lesson 4: One way to create distortion is through the **exaggeration** of a feature or a figure.

Lesson 5: Realistic scale is size as measured against a standard reference.

Lesson 6: Unrealistic scale is used to make size relationships that do not make sense.

Introduce Unit Concepts

"Artists use the art principles of proportion, distortion, and scale to draw human faces and bodies and to create meaning in works of art." "Los artistas usan los principios artísticos de proporción, distorsión y escala para dibujar caras y cuerpos humanos y para crear sentido."

Proportion and Distortion
- Have students look up the definitions of *portion* and *proportion* in the dictionary.
- What does it mean to distort something? Have students come up with as many phrases as possible using the word *distort*.

Scale
- What are scales used for traditionally? Discuss the types of scales that students may have used or seen.

Cross-Curricular Projects
- See the *Language Arts and Reading, Mathematics, Science,* and *Social Studies Art Connections* books for activities that further develop proportion, distortion, and scale concepts.

154 UNIT 5 • Proportion, Distortion, and Scale

Unit 5

Proportion, Distortion, and Scale

Artists use proportion, distortion, and scale in both sculptural forms and pictures.

Mexican artist Frida Kahlo is best known for her series of self-portraits depicting her life. She used color and objects symbolically to communicate her feelings and experiences. She also used the ongoing theme of pain in her paintings as a result of the hardships she endured during her short life.

▲ **Frida Kahlo.** (Mexican). *Frida y Diego Rivera.* 1931.
Oil on canvas. $39\frac{3}{8} \times 31$ inches (100.01 × 78.74 cm.). San Francisco Museum of Modern Art, San Francisco, California.

154   Unit 5

Fine Art Prints

Display **Large Prints 81** *Self-Portrait* and **82** *Ruckus Rodeo.* Refer to the prints throughout this unit as students learn about proportion, distortion, and scale.

Large Print 81

Large Print 82

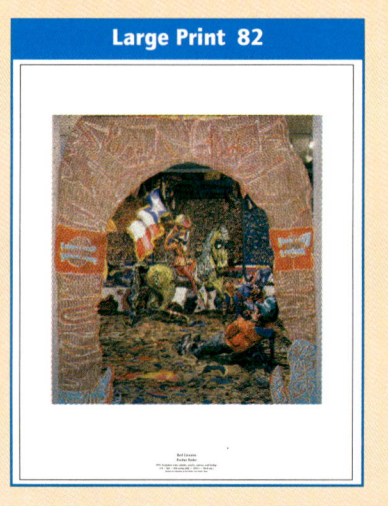

Artists use **proportion** to portray human size in two- and three-dimensional works of art.
- What objects do you see?
- Use your fingers to measure the size of the woman's head. About how many heads tall is she? Measure the man in the same way.

Distortion is used by artists to express feelings and ideas in works of art.
- What feeling was Kahlo trying to communicate in her wedding portrait?
- Which objects, if any, are larger or smaller than normal?

Scale is used by artists to show the size of one object in relation to another object.
- How big are the people in the painting? What gives you a clue about their size?

In This Unit you will learn how artists use proportion. Using a variety of media, you will create personal artwork based on proportion, distortion, and exaggeration. You also will learn about scale as an art principle and how it relates to size. Here are the topics you will study:
- Proportion
- Ratio
- Distortion
- Exaggeration
- Scale
- Surrealism

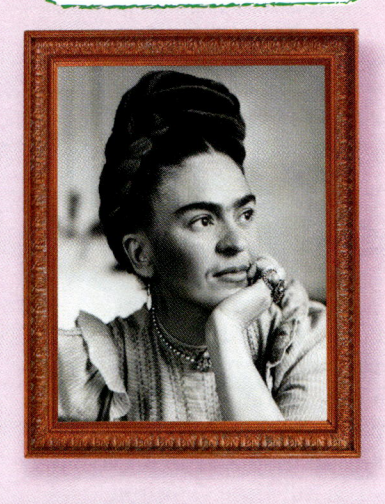

Master Artist Profile

Frida Kahlo
(1907–1954)

Frida Kahlo was born in Mexico City. As a child she had polio, which caused one leg to grow smaller than the other. During her teens, Kahlo was in a bus accident, which left her severely injured. She endured thirty-five surgical operations and a life of pain. It was while in the hospital that Kahlo taught herself to paint, out of boredom. Later, she became reacquainted with and married muralist Diego Rivera, whom she had met when he was painting a mural in her high school. Many of her paintings are based on her marriage, her pain, and the history of the Mexican people.

Unit 5   **155**

Art History and Culture

Frida Kahlo

Frida Kahlo (frēˊ da käˊ lō)(1907–1954) was born in Mexico City, Mexico. As a child she had polio, which caused one leg to be smaller than the other. She had hoped to study medicine, but a serious accident as a teenager fractured her spine and crushed her pelvis. While convalescing, Kahlo taught herself to paint. She met muralist Diego Rivera, whom she later married. Her life was full of pain and tragedy, and her marriage to Rivera was stormy. She used her life as her subject matter for her art.

See pages 24–25 and 16–21 for more about art history and subject matter.

Artist Profiles, p. 33

Examine the Artwork

"Let's study the wedding portrait by Frida Kahlo." "Vamos a estudiar el retrato de boda por Frida Kahlo."

- Have students study Frida Kahlo's wedding portrait and ask them to describe how the principles of proportion and scale were used.

- Have students answer the questions about proportion, distortion, and scale on page 155.

  ▸ A man, Diego Rivera, wearing a dark suit, blue shirt, brown belt, and shoes is holding a paint palette and brushes. A woman, Frida Kahlo, is in a long, full dress and a large red wrap. She wears two necklaces and a ribbon braided into her hair. A bird holding a banner with written words flies above the couple.

  ▸ Diego Rivera is $7\frac{1}{2}$ heads tall; Frida Kahlo is $6\frac{1}{2}$ heads tall.

  ▸ Student responses will vary. Neither of them is smiling, and Kahlo is a little behind Rivera. She is also much smaller, but her clothing makes her look bigger than she is. Perhaps she was communicating the feeling of being less important than her husband, who was a very dominating person.

  ▸ Rivera's hands are a little smaller than normal, as are Kahlo's feet.

  ▸ The man looks a little shorter than average, and the woman looks small. The palette and brushes are large in the man's small hands, and the woman's feet look very small, while her clothing looks large.

Unit Pretest

T Display **Transparency 47** as a pretest. Have students write their answers on a separate piece of paper. Answers: 1. A, 2. C, 3. A, 4. B, 5. C

Home Connection

- See **Home and After-School Connections** for family newsletters and activities for this unit.

UNIT 5 • Proportion, Distortion, and Scale   **155**

Unit 5 Arts Integration

ILLUSTRATOR PROFILE
Chris Van Allsburg
(1949–)

Chris Van Allsburg was born in Grand Rapids, Michigan. As long as he can remember, Van Allsburg has always loved to draw, but he began his art career as a sculptor. Many of his sculptures tell stories and show the funny and dark qualities that appear in his picture books. Even when he was a full-time sculptor, Van Allsburg still had time to draw at home during the evenings. David Macaulay, another author and illustrator, saw Van Allsburg's drawings and encouraged him to send them to book companies. With this encouragement and that of his wife, Van Allsburg was able to begin his writing and illustrating career.

Van Allsburg has said that his love for drawing developed into a love for telling stories through pictures. When he begins a story, he poses questions to himself that he calls his "what if" or "what then" approach to story writing. Once he poses questions, he imagines the pictures and the story. The next step for him is putting the story and pictures on paper. Van Allsburg has won Caldecott Medals for *Jumanji* and *The Polar Express*. Generally his books are thought of as children's books, but he actually makes them for people of all ages.

Throughout Unit 5, share Van Allsburg's illustrations with the class, and discuss the use of proportion, distortion, and scale in his books. Which faces and figures are in proportion? Are there any distorted faces or figures? Which illustrations have examples of realistic and unrealistic scale?

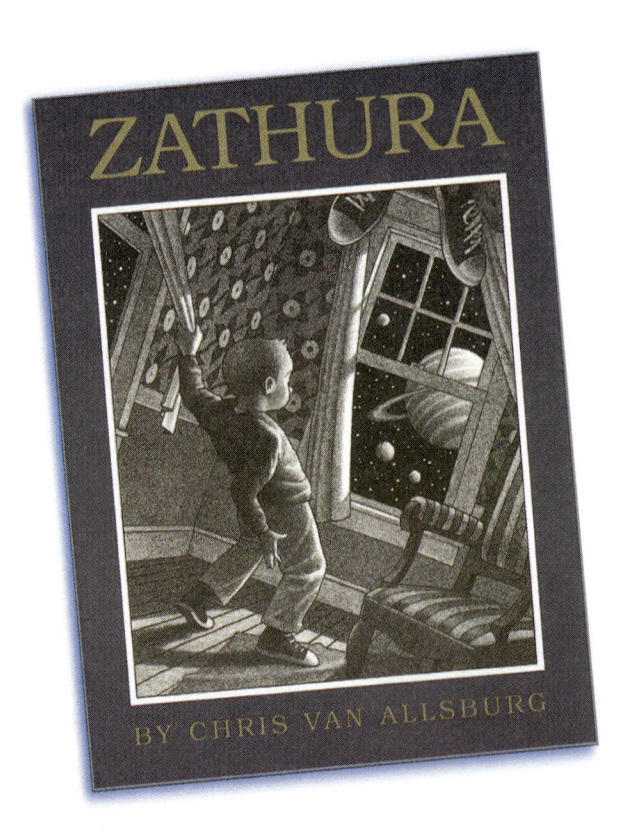

Music
Although proportion is not a musical term, it is always in the mind of a composer with regard to balancing various aspects of a composition. Distortion is sometimes used in music for dramatic effect; in *Tubby the Tuba*, the tuba's sound is distorted when Tubby accidentally "sits" on the tuba.

Literature
Show the video *The Grey Lady and the Strawberry Snatcher* to introduce the concepts of proportion, distortion, and scale. Pause the video and have students identify images that look exaggerated or realistic.

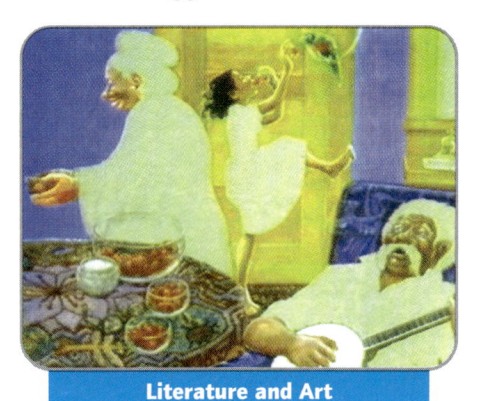

Literature and Art

Performing Arts
Show *The Mask Messenger*. Have students identify proportion and distortion.

Artsource®

155A UNIT 5 • Proportion, Distortion, and Scale

SHADED BOTTLES

Written by: Amy Shapley [Amy is an art educator from Notre Dame de Sion, in Kansas City, MO]

Grade: K-6

Age: 5-12

Activity Summary:

Students will learn how to draw (paint) bottles on their papers which appear to be three dimensional.

Objectives:

- Students will learn about shading and value.
- Students will learn basic techniques of watercolor painting.

What You Need:

- assortment of colored (or clear) bottles in a variety of shapes
- pencils
- brushes
- heavy white construction paper or inexpensive watercolor paper
- scissors
- glue stick
- pan watercolors
- back ground paper for display
- a light source (small desk lamp will do)
- Optional: chalk pastel

What You Do:

1. Arrange bottles on a desk or table so they can be seen clearly by all students. (You might need to set up several "stations" around the classroom).
2. After students have looked at the bottles with no light source, add a light source (small desk lamp) coming from the side and discuss with students how highlights and shadows are made and how they affect the way the bottles look.
3. Demonstrate the way different amounts of water can be used with watercolor to show different values.
4. Students then draw the outlines of 3 to 6 bottles on the white paper.
5. Using light wash, encourage students to paint one bottle with one color of water paint.
6. In the center section of the bottle, they should paint a darker value.
7. On the shadowed side, they should paint the darkest value.
8. On the light source side, they should use less paint.
9. Students should be encouraged to use a wet brush to blend the three values together.
10. Optional: Students can use chalk pastels to add additional details to the artwork (as shown in examples).
11. Optional: Once they have finished, cut out each of their bottle paintings and glue them onto the background paper for display.

Recommended Books:

Drawing With Children
by Mona Brookes
Founded on the belief that any child can learn to draw realistic pictures using her "alphabet of shapes" while in a noncompetitive environment, Mona Brookes' easy-to-follow, lesson-by-lesson approach to drawing has yielded astounding results with children of all ages. This is *THE BEST* learning to draw book we've ever seen. (for ages 3-4 and up)

▶ More Activities Like This

© KinderArt ®

Lesson 1 Overview: Facial Proportions

Lesson 1 introduces the art principle of proportion. **Proportion** is the principle of art that is concerned with the size relationship of one part to another. **Facial proportions** are the relationship of one feature of a face to other features.

Objectives

Art History and Culture
To demonstrate knowledge of the lives and works of Isabel Bishop and John Singleton Copley

Creative Expression
To create a self-portrait using facial proportions

Aesthetic Perception
To identify how facial proportions are used in two-dimensional portraits

Art Criticism
To evaluate own work using the four steps of art criticism

Lesson Materials
- pencils, erasers
- Art Journal, mirror
- scrap paper
- 12" × 18" heavy white or black drawing paper
- white or yellow chalk
- oil pastels, paper towels
- newspaper

Alternate Materials:
- copier paper
- 9" × 12" white paper
- crayons, color pencils

Program Resources
- *Reading and Writing Test Prep.*, pp. 54–55
- *Transparency 25*
- *Flash Cards* 18
- *Artist Profiles*, pp. 8, 18
- *Animals Through History Time Line*
- *Assessment*, pp. 57–58
- *Large Prints 81 Self-Portrait* and *82 Ruckus Rodeo*
- *The National Museum of Women in the Arts Collection*

Concept Trace
Facial Proportions
Introduced: Level 5, Unit 4, Lesson 3
Reinforced: Level 7, Chapter 3, Lesson 4

Vocabulary

Review the following vocabulary words with students before beginning the lesson.

portrait *retrato*—a two- or three-dimensional artwork created in the image of a person or animal

self-portrait *autorretrato*—a two or three-dimensional artwork that an artist makes of him- or herself

See page 179B for additional vocabulary and Spanish vocabulary resources.

Art Journal: Vocabulary
Have students add these words to the Vocabulary section of their Art Journals.

Lesson 1 Arts Integration

Theatre
Complete Unit 5, Lesson 1, on pages 90–91 of *Theatre Arts Connections*.

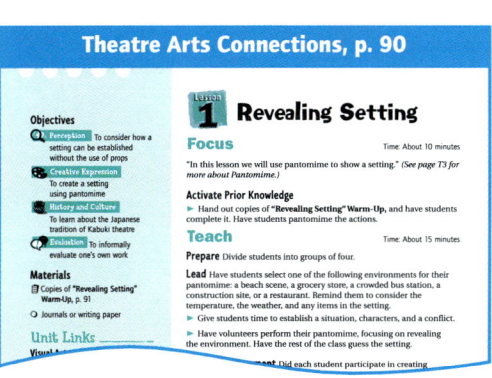

Music
In art, faces have symmetry. In music, songs have symmetry. In ABA form, for example, the outer two sections are the same with a contrasting section in the middle. Sing or listen to *Cumbia del Sol*. The form is refrain, verse, refrain. Is this the form of *Shoo Fly?*

Movement & Dance
Have students explore a variety of facial expressions. Have them warm up their faces, using the following: chewing movements, open yawns, stretching and contracting the face. Then have students explore different facial expressions, such as sad, happy, relaxed, and anxious. Discuss the difference between each feeling.

LESSON 1 • Facial Proportions 155B

Focus

Time: About 10 minutes

Activate Prior Knowledge

"Have you seen a drawn or painted portrait before? Do you know how one is started?"

"¿Han visto antes un retrato pintado o dibujado? ¿Saben como se empiezan?"

- As a class, discuss student responses. Discuss the differences between a drawn or painted portrait and a photograph of a person.

Using Literature ⭐ Reading

- Have students look at the cover illustration of *A Face First* by Priscilla Cummings. Discuss how facial proportions were used to draw the image of the girl on the cover.

Thematic Connection ⭐ Social Studies

- **Friendship:** Have students discuss what friendship means to them. Explain that not only humans can be friends. Many humans consider animals to be their friends, especially animals that assist disabled people.

Introduce the Art

Look

"Look closely at how facial proportions are used in these two paintings." "Miren detalladamente cómo se usan las proporciones faciales en estas dos pinturas."

Looking at Details ⭐ Reading

Have students look at the details in both paintings. What objects are not the focus of each painting? *Bishop: a cup, a saucer, and a piece of paper; Copley: a leash for the squirrel, a cup of water, and pieces of food*

Art History and Culture

Most students will say that the clothes are appropriate but may comment that the people look dressed up. Explain that hats for women were fashionable during the 1930s and that children dressed more formally during the 1700s.
NSAE 5.b

💻 Web Connection

Visit www.metmuseum.org for more information about the Metropolitan Museum of Art.

156 UNIT 5 • Proportion, Distortion, and Scale

Lesson 1: Facial Proportions

▲ **Isabel Bishop.** (American). *Two Girls.* 1935.
Oil and tempera on masonite.
20 × 24 inches (50.8 × 60.96 cm.).
The Metropolitan Museum of Art, New York, New York.

Look at the paintings by Isabel Bishop and John Singleton Copley. Bishop traveled daily from her home in Riverdale, New York, to her studio in Union Square, Manhattan. During her long daily commute, she sketched. Her subject matter was the working girls she saw as she rode the train. The blonde woman in *Two Girls* is a waitress from the cafe where Bishop ate breakfast. The woman whose face we see was the waitress's friend. Copley was a self-taught artist and was the first American artist to be recognized for his work both in the United States and in Europe. *Henry Pelham* is a painting of Copley's half-brother. This painting was for an exhibition in London to see how the leading artists of England would rate Copley's work. *Henry Pelham* is one of Copley's earliest paintings and is considered one of his finest works.

Art History and Culture

Study the clothes the people are wearing. Do you think they fit the period in which the paintings were created?

156 Unit 5 • Lesson 1

Art History and Culture

Isabel Bishop

At 15 years of age, Isabel Bishop (iˊ za bel biˊ shəp) (1902–1988) moved to New York City and attended art school. One school she attended was the Art Students League. While there, she took a cubism class from Max Weber, who intimidated her and was critical of her work. Bishop was not able to handle the criticism and went to study with Kenneth Hayes Miller. Miller taught her what was required to be a serious artist: total dedication to work. Bishop rented her first studio in the middle of Union Square in New York. She would frequently stare out her window and watch the people of Union Square. *Two Girls* was painted at her Union Square studio.

See pages 24–25 and 16–21 for more about art history and subject matter.

Artist Profiles, p. 8

Artist Profile
Isabel Bishop
1902–1988

Isabel Bishop (iˊ a bel bishˊ ap) was born in Cincinnati, Ohio. A year later, her family moved to a run-down neighborhood in Detroit, Michigan, where her father was employed as the principal of a nearby high school. Her parents didn't think the neighborhood children made good playmates, so Bishop spent much of her time alone. She graduated from high school at age 15 and then studied art. She moved to New York City, where she continued to study art and began exhibiting her work. She loved to paint the people in Union Square.

Bishop married in 1934, moved to the suburbs, and had a son. She commuted

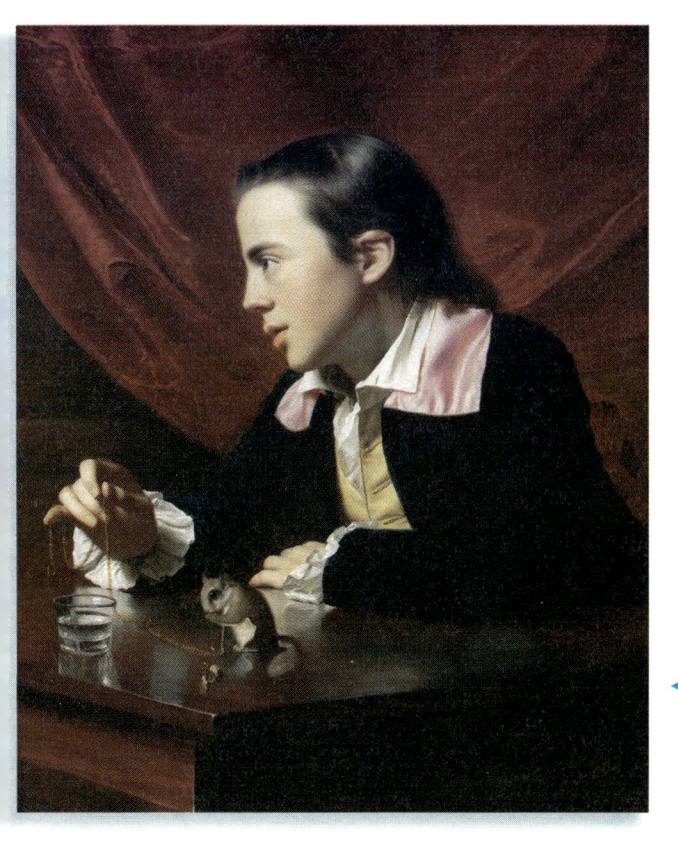

John Singleton Copley. (American). *Henry Pelham (Boy with a Squirrel).* 1765. Oil on canvas. 30¼ × 25 inches (76.84 × 63.5 cm.). Museum of Fine Arts, Boston, Massachusetts.

Study the two paintings to better understand facial proportions.
- Describe the positions of the faces in the two paintings.
- What are the differences in the way the eyes are portrayed? How do the mouths look different?
- Where are the ears in relation to the eyes and nose?
- Describe where the hairline is in relation to the top of the head in Copley's painting.

Aesthetic Perception

Design Awareness Look at the faces around you. Notice how everyone's features are arranged similarly.

Unit 5 • Lesson 1   **157**

Study

- Bishop: The viewer sees the profile of the woman with blond hair in the foreground. The other woman's face is a frontal view.
- Bishop: The woman who is facing the viewer has eyes that are fully shaped and her face is in full view. Her eyes are looking toward the other woman. The woman in profile has her eyes partially closed, and the viewers can see only part of her mouth. Copley: The viewer can see one of Henry Pelham's eyes; he is looking straight ahead with his eye open. His mouth is a little more than halfway visible.
- Bishop: Frontal view; the top of the ear lines up with the top of the eye, and the bottom of the ear lines up with the bottom of the nose. Profile: The top of the ear lines up with the top of the brow, and the bottom of the ear lines up with the bottom of the nose. Copley: The top of the ear lines up with the top of the brow, and the bottom of the ear lines up with the bottom of the nose.
- The hairline begins one quarter of the way down from the top of the head. The side of the hairline is halfway between the face and the back of the head and is in front of the ear.
- For more examples of portraits, see *The National Museum of Women in the Arts Collection.*

Art Journal: Writing
Have students explain what *proportion* means to them in the Concepts section of their Art Journals. What else do they want to know about facial proportions?

Aesthetic Perception

Design Awareness Discuss how all of the students have similar head shapes, which are basically oval.

Developing Visual Literacy Have students look closely at the details in the two paintings. Do they think the details are necessary? Why are details important? How do they impact the painting?

Web Connection
Visit **www.mfa.org** for more information about the Museum of Fine Arts, Boston.

LESSON 1 • Facial Proportions   **157**

Art History and Culture

John Singleton Copley

John Singleton Copley (jän sing´ gəl tən kä´ plē) (1738–1815) is considered one of the finest painters of colonial America. In about 1755 Copley met English artist Joseph Blackburn, whose use of rococo lightness and coloring Copley quickly adopted. He also made use of the rococo device called *portrait d'apparat,* or portrayal of the subject with objects associated with daily life. His style was straightforward and realistic, creating portraits of great strength. Copley wanted to see how his art would be received overseas, so he sent *Henry Pelham, Boy with Squirrel* to England. His work was praised, and he decided to move to England in 1774.

See pages 24–25 and 16–21 for more about art history and subject matter.

Artist Profiles, p. 18

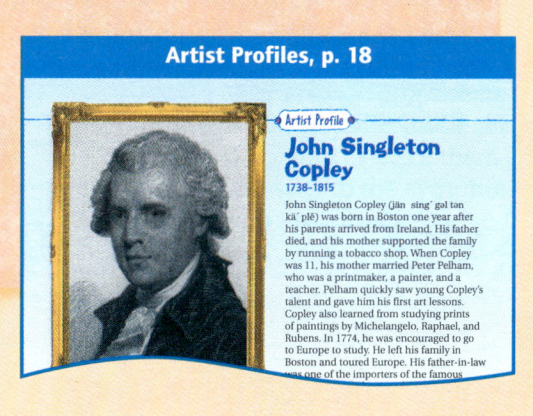

Teach

Time: About 45 minutes

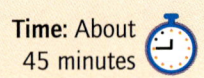

"How will you use facial proportions?"
"¿Cómo usarían las proporciones faciales?"

- Read and discuss using facial proportions on page 158.

Practice

Materials: fine-line permanent black marker, 9" × 12" sketch paper

Alternate Materials: crayon

- Distribute the materials and have students follow the directions on page 158.

Creative Expression

Materials: pencils, erasers, Art Journal, 12" × 18" heavy white or black drawing paper, mirrors, yellow or white chalk, scrap paper, oil pastels, paper towels, newspaper

Alternate Materials: color pencils, 9" × 12" white paper

- Distribute the materials and have students follow the directions on page 159.
- Have students demonstrate their technical skills, using a variety of art media and materials to produce their self-portraits. NSAE 1.a; 1.b
- Review the Activity Tips on page 242 for visual examples of techniques if needed.

Art Journal: Sketching

Discuss the difference between a portrait and a self-portrait. Ask students to look at themselves in a mirror. What makes them different from the other students in the class? Ask students to create two or three quick sketches of their faces in their Art Journals. Their sketches will be used for their self-portraits in the Creative Expression activity.

158 UNIT 5 • Proportion, Distortion, and Scale

Using Facial Proportions

The principle of art concerned with the size relationship of one part to another is called **proportion.** In realistic portraits, artists use correct proportions. They use facial proportions to help place features correctly on the human face. **Facial proportions** are the relationship of one feature of a face to other features.

Frontal proportions A front view of the head can be divided by drawing three horizontal lines across a vertical center line called the **central axis.** In the example, notice how the eyes are drawn on the center line, the lips just below the bottom line, and the ears between the center and lower horizontal lines. The nose is above the bottom line on the central axis. The hairline is near the top line.

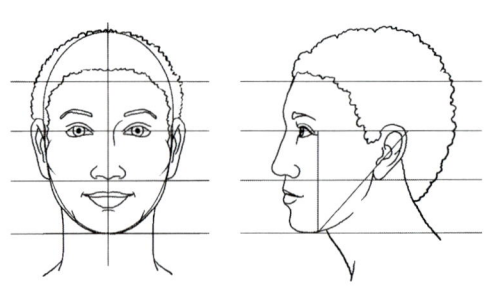

Profile Proportions When you view a head in profile, or from a side view, all the horizontal proportion lines remain the same as in the front view. However, the shape of the head and the shapes of the features change. In the example, notice that the shape of the head in the profile is different from that of the front view. Notice the spaces between the eye, the ear, and the chin.

Practice

Using a marker, make a blind contour drawing.

1. Select a partner, and take turns drawing a blind contour.
2. Look closely at your partner. Place the marker tip on the paper and slowly move the pen as your eyes follow the contours of your partner's face.
3. Try not to pick up the pen or look down at your paper when you draw your partner's profile. See if you can draw your partner's profile in proportion.

158 Unit 5 • Lesson 1

Differentiated Instruction

Reteach
Have each student find an example of a face in a magazine. Ask them to draw a line down the center, called the central axis, and the three guidelines showing the eyes, the bottom of the nose, and the hairline.

Special Needs
Students will need to review the properties of color and color schemes in order to successfully achieve the objectives of this activity. Provide color wheels and examples of color schemes and portraits.

ELL
When explaining facial proportions to students, point to where the central axis and the three guidelines would be on your face. Then have students demonstrate on their own face.

◀ Jonathan Lizcano.
Age 12.

Think about how the student artist used facial proportions.

Creative Expression

Use oil pastels to create a self-portrait using facial proportions.

1. Choose one of the sketches from your Art Journal. Begin by using chalk to draw in your facial proportions. Add your features, hair, and clothing to fill the page.
2. Select a color scheme that you think best reflects your personality.
3. Practice blending colors on a scrap piece of paper. Do this by overlapping colors and working them with your oil pastels. Try using a paper towel to blend colors.
4. Use oil pastels to complete your self-portrait.

Art Criticism

Describe List the steps you took in creating your self-portrait.

Analyze Describe how you used a central axis and guide lines to create facial proportions. What color scheme did you use?

Interpret How does your color scheme affect the mood of your self-portrait?

Decide Were you able to use facial proportions successfully in your portrait? Explain.

Unit 5 • Lesson 1   **159**

Art Across the Curriculum

Use these simple ideas to reinforce art concepts across the curriculum.

★ **Narrative Writing** Have students write a paragraph about what Henry Pelham is thinking.

★ **Math** Explain to students that a proportion is a statement that two ratios are equal.

★ **Science** Discuss with students whether twins have identical facial proportions.

★ **Social Studies** Have students explain what they know about Colonial America.

★ **Technology** Have students create a collage using a word-processing program by finding examples of clip art that show facial proportions. Visit **SRAonline.com** to print detailed instructions for this activity.
NSAE 6.b

Reflect

Time: About 5 minutes

Review and Assess

"How were facial proportions used in these self-portraits?" "¿Cómo fueron usadas las proporciones faciales en estos autorretratos?"

Think

The artist used correct facial proportions. The eyes are spaced evenly with the nose in between them. Students may note that the nose seems distorted, but remind them that this is how the artist sees himself.

- Use **Large Prints 81** *Self-Portrait* and **82** *Ruckus Rodeo* and ask students to compare how the two images use facial proportions. How are they similar? How are they different?

Informal Assessment

- Have students exchange portfolios with classmates, so they can form conclusions about historical and cultural contexts.
NSAE 4.b; 4.c
- For standardized-format test practice using this lesson's art content, see pages 54–55 in *Reading and Writing Test Preparation.*

Art Journal: Critical Thinking

Have students answer the four art criticism questions—Describe, Analyze, Interpret, and Decide—in their Art Journals. Have students discuss within groups how they used facial proportions. Ask them to notice the similarities and differences in their self-portraits. Have the groups share their findings with the class.

LESSON 1 • Facial Proportions **159**

Lesson 1 Wrap-Up: Facial Proportions

Extra! For the Art Specialist
Time: About 45 minutes

Focus
Study *Large Print 81 Self-Portrait* and discuss how facial proportions were used. What techniques do students think the artists used for organizing the features on the faces?

Teach
Explain to students that they will be selecting an unusual point of view to create a portrait, using facial proportions. Give students the option of doing a self-portrait or a portrait. They may use both photographs and/or real models. As an alternative, students also can draw self-portraits or portraits on the computer.

Reflect
Have students use the four steps of art criticism to evaluate their work. Have them describe the steps they used for creating a portrait. Did students successfully draw a portrait or self-portrait, using facial proportions?

Alternate Activity
Materials:
- sketchbook, pencils
- erasers, mirrors
- 12" × 18" black or color drawing paper
- conte crayons
- student-supplied photographs (optional)
- color pencils (optional)

1. Have students begin by creating several sketches in their sketchbooks.
2. Ask students to use conte crayon on either a black or colored piece of drawing paper. Have them begin by using light-colored conte crayons to color their composition. They can use the darker colors to add value and highlights.
3. Students can keep these as neutral-color drawings, or color pencils can be used to add color.

Research in Art Education
Opportunities for students to become involved with the arts are "inequitably distributed in our society" ("Involvement in the Arts and Human Development: General Involvement and Intensive Involvement in Music and Theater Arts" in *Champions of Change*, p. 17). Because of the research showing that learning and the arts are linked, it is important to create arts-involvement opportunities for students of every economic background.

Assessment
Use the following rubric to evaluate the artwork students make in the Creative Expression activity and to assess students' understanding of how facial proportions are used in creating portraits.

	Art History and Culture	Aesthetic Perception	Creative Expression	Art Criticism
3 POINTS	The student demonstrates knowledge of the lives and work of Bishop and Copley.	The student accurately identifies the use of facial proportions in portraits.	The student's self-portrait demonstrates use of facial proportions.	The student thoughtfully and honestly evaluates own work using the four steps of art criticism.
2 POINTS	The student's knowledge of the lives and work of Bishop and Copley is weak or incomplete.	The student shows an emerging awareness of facial proportions in portraits, but cannot consistently identify them.	The student's self-portrait shows some awareness of how to use facial proportions.	The student attempts to evaluate own work but shows an incomplete understanding of evaluation criteria.
1 POINT	The student cannot demonstrate knowledge of the lives or work of Bishop and Copley.	The student cannot identify how facial proportions are used in portraits.	The student's self-portrait shows no understanding of how to use facial proportions.	The student makes no attempt to evaluate own work.

Have students complete page 57 or 58 in their *Assessment* books.

UNIT 5 • Proportion, Distortion, and Scale

Lesson 2 Overview: Figure Proportions

Lesson 2 extends the concept of the art principle of proportion and explains how figure proportion is based on a ratio. A **ratio** is a comparison of size between two things. **Figure proportion** is based on the average size of the human figure, which is $7\frac{1}{2}$ heads tall.

Objectives

Art History and Culture
To demonstrate knowledge of *Armor of George Clifford* and *Dancing Lady*

Creative Expression
To create a series of line drawings using body proportions

Aesthetic Perception
To better understand how figure proportions are used to convey realistic human forms in a variety of works of art

Art Criticism
To evaluate own work using the four steps of art criticism

Lesson Materials
- magazines
- pencils
- fine-tip markers
- sketch paper or sketchbook
- 9" × 12" or 12" × 18" white drawing paper

Alternate Materials:
- crayons
- construction paper

Program Resources
- *Reading and Writing Test Prep.,* pp. 56–57
- *Transparency 26*
- *Flash Cards* 18
- *Artist Profiles,* pp. 69, 75
- *Animals Through History Time Line*
- *Assessment,* pp. 59–60
- *Large Prints 81 Self-Portrait* and *82 Ruckus Rodeo*
- *Art Around the World Collection*

Concept Trace
Figure proportion
Introduced: Level 5, Unit 4, Lesson 1
Reinforced: Level 7, Chapter 3, Lesson 3

Vocabulary

Review the following vocabulary word with students before beginning the lesson.

figure proportion *proporción de figura*—the size relationship of one part of the body to another

See page 179B for additional vocabulary and Spanish vocabulary resources.

Art Journal: Writing
Have students add this word to the Vocabulary section of their Art Journals.

Lesson 2 Arts Integration

Theatre
Complete Unit 5, Lesson 2, on pages 92–93 of *Theatre Arts Connections.*

Music
In a large form of music that has movements, acts, or stand-alone compositions (such as a suite), the composer takes care to make each part fit with the whole. Listen to "Nessun Dorma" from the opera *Turandot* by Giacomo Puccini. The form of opera is so large that all action can stop for the singing of an aria.

Movement & Dance
Divide students into groups of four. Each person should take a turn being the model. The model should create an interesting pose and hold it. The members of the group, while keeping their eyes on the model at all times, should trace the outline of the model. Students should start looking at the head or at the feet and walk clockwise around the model.

LESSON 2 • Figure Proportions 159B

Focus

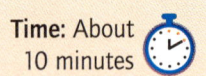

Time: About 10 minutes

Activate Prior Knowledge

"Have you ever seen a realistic sculpture of a person before?" "¿Han visto alguna vez una escultura realista de una persona?"

- Discuss responses with students. The Greeks created sculptures that were based on ideal beauty and proportions. Today artists measure to get exact proportions, and some even create a mold of a person to make the sculpture more realistic.

Using Literature ⭐ Reading

- Look at the cover illustration of *Run Away Home* by Patricia C. McKissack. Discuss how figure proportions were used for the two children on the cover illustration.

Thematic Connection ⭐ Social Studies

- **Journeys and Quests:** Have students name some journeys or quests that knights undertook in the Middle Ages. Also have them do the same for people who lived in ancient Greece.

Introduce the Art

Look

"Look closely at how the works of art are based on body proportions." "Miren detalladamente cómo obras de arte están basada en proporciones del cuerpo."

Logical Reasoning ⭐ Math

- Ask students if they have seen armor for anyone or anything other than a man. Can they think of a reason why someone or something else might need armor? Armor was made not only for men but also for boys and horses. Boys wore it mostly for ceremonial purposes.

Art History and Culture

Explain to students that some works of art are damaged because they are very old. *Dancing Lady* is more than 2,000 years old and, despite a few blemishes, is in excellent condition.

💻 Web Connection

Visit www.metmuseum.org for more information about the Metropolitan Museum of Art.

160 UNIT 5 • Proportion, Distortion, and Scale

Lesson 2: Figure Proportions

Look at the works of art on these pages. *Armor of George Clifford, Third Earl of Cumberland,* was made for a man who stands five feet nine and a half inches tall. By today's standard this would be considered smaller than average. The marble sculpture *Dancing Lady* was carved around 50 B.C. During this time in ancient Greece it was believed that the human body was the true expression of order. Statues, like *Dancing Lady*, were not realistic portraits, but rather the perfect, or ideal, form. This is why many Greek sculptures from this time period, the Golden Age, look so much alike.

◀ **Royal Workshops.** (England). *Armor of George Clifford, Third Earl of Cumberland.* c. 1580–1585.
Steel, etched, blued, and gilded. $69\frac{1}{2}$ inches tall (176.53 cm.). The Metropolitan Museum of Art, New York, New York.

Art History and Culture

Look at the condition of these works of art. Why do you think they belong in a museum?

160 Unit 5 • Lesson 2

Art History and Culture

Armor of George Clifford, Third Earl of Cumberland

George Clifford was appointed Queen's Champion in 1590 and was made a Knight of the Garter two years later. He is best remembered for his capture of the Spanish fort in San Juan, Puerto Rico. A favorite of Queen Elizabeth I, he chose for the decoration of this armor the Tudor rose, the French fleur-de-lis (a part of the English arms at that time), and the cipher of Elizabeth, two *E*s back to back. The Cumberland armor is the best preserved, most extensive armor garniture from the Royal Workshops at Greenwich.

See pages 24–25 and 16–21 for more about art history and subject matter.

Artist Profiles, p. 69

Study the armor and the statue to learn about figure proportions.

- Use your fingers to measure the length of the head on both works of art. How many heads tall is each piece?
- Look at both works of art and describe the similarities.
- How tall do you think the statue *Dancing Lady* is? Now look at the size of the image listed in the caption. Explain why you guessed the size that you did.
- What did the artist do to make *Dancing Lady* look realistic in size?

◀ **Artist unknown.** (Greece). *Dancing Lady.* c. 50 B.C.
Marble. $33\frac{5}{8}$ inches tall including base (85.4 cm.). The Cleveland Museum of Art, Cleveland, Ohio.

Aesthetic Perception

Design Awareness Think about shopping for clothes. How are the clothes usually arranged? Think about the range of sizes and lengths.

Unit 5 • Lesson 2   **161**

Art History and Culture

Dancing Lady

In ancient Greece, artists were also philosophers and mathematicians. Proportion was central to the design, and artists devised the classical, or perfectly proportioned, human figure. Statues did not represent real people. If the model who posed for *Dancing Lady* stood next to the artist's artwork, she would not resemble it. Euclid, a Greek mathematician, discovered what he thought was the perfect ratio. This ratio was called the Golden Mean, which was a line that divided two parts so that the smaller line has the same proportion to the larger line as the larger line has to the whole line. This ratio is written 1:1.6.

See pages 24–25 and 16–21 for more about art history and subject matter.

Artist Profiles, p. 75

> *Artist Profile*
> **Dancing Lady**
> This dancing lady sculpture was created by an unknown Greek sculptor sometime during the 1st century, B.C. The time period between the years 320 B.C. and 30 B.C. is known as the *Hellenistic* period of Greek history. The artist who created this sculpture must have subscribed to the classical style of sculpture practiced by artists of the fourth century B.C. This style was characterized by attention to detail and proportions considered to be the ideal of the human figure. Sculptors of the Hellenistic period often portrayed everyday subjects rather than the more mythological and heroic figures sculpted by artists of previous periods.
>
> **Artist unknown.** (Greece).

Study

- Both the armor and marble sculpture are approximately $7\frac{1}{2}$ heads tall.
- They are similar in the way they are arranged. Both figures are standing, the heads look the right size for the bodies, and the arms and legs look like the correct size for the bodies and heads. Both are standing in natural poses.
- Answers will vary; however, some students will say that it is life-size. Have students look at the actual size, and discuss why many of them may have thought it was a different size.
- All body parts are in proportion for the head. The head and body ratio is 1: $7\frac{1}{2}$, or 1 head length to a body length of $7\frac{1}{2}$ heads tall. This is the proportion of an average person.
- For more examples of art from Europe, see the *Art Around the World Collection.*

Art Journal: Writing

Have students explain what the word *figure* means to them in the Concepts section of their Art Journals. What else do they want to know about figure proportion?

Aesthetic Perception

Design Awareness Discuss with students that most clothing is made for people of an average height. However, explain that some clothing is made for small and taller people.

Developing Visual Literacy Discuss the use of figure proportion in each artwork. Have students notice how the head on the armor looks like the right size for the body. The body is $7\frac{1}{2}$ times the size of the head. Have students notice how the Greek sculpture *Dancing Lady* looks life-sized. This is because the figure has been carved in perfect proportion.

Web Connection

Visit **www.clemusart.com** for more information about the Cleveland Museum of Art.

LESSON 2 • Figure Proportions   **161**

Teach

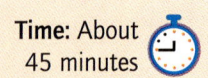

Time: About 45 minutes

"How can you use figure proportions in a drawing?" "¿Cómo pueden usar proporciones de figura en un dibujo?"

- Read and discuss using figure proportions on page 162.
- Have students analyze and form generalizations about the interdependence of art principles, such as proportion and balance, using art vocabulary appropriately. NSAE 2.b

Practice

Materials: magazines

- Distribute the materials and have students follow the directions on page 162.

Creative Expression

Materials: pencils, fine-tip markers, sketch paper or sketchbook, 9" × 12" or 12" × 18" white drawing paper

Alternate Materials: crayons, construction paper

- Distribute the materials and have students follow the directions on page 163. NSAE 3.a; 3.b
- Have students express a variety of ideas based on direct observations.
- Review the Activity Tips on page 242 for visual examples of techniques if needed.

Art Journal: Writing

Ask students to work with a partner to list questions and observations based on figure proportion in their Art Journals. Have them each give a personal definition of *figure proportion*. Ask them what questions they may have or comments they may want to share about proportion. Student notes will be used in their discussion as part of their Practice activity.

Using Figure Proportions

Look around and you will notice that people come in all different shapes and sizes. Still, most people's bodies have similar proportions.

You learned in the previous lesson that **proportion** is the principle of art concerned with the size relationship of one part to another. For example, someone who is six feet tall may have the same proportions as someone who is five feet tall. This means that the taller person's limbs have the same ratio as the shorter person's limbs. A **ratio** is a comparison of size between two things. Artists often use the head as the ratio of *one* to the length of an adult body, which is about seven and a half head lengths. Therefore, the ratio is written as 1:7.5, which means the ratio is 1 (the head) to 7.5 (heads per body length).

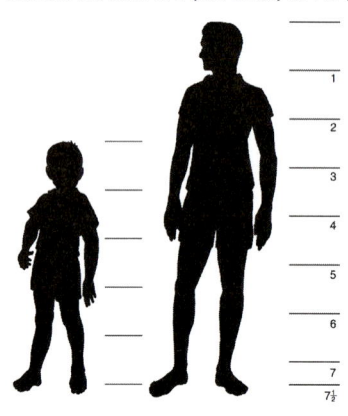

Practice

Compare body proportions.

1. Look through a magazine and cut out a picture of an adult and a child. Make sure that the picture you find is a complete image of the adult and child standing or walking.
2. Measure the head of each person. Use that measurement to see how many head lengths the body is.
3. Compare the ratio of the adult with the ratio of the child. As a class, discuss your findings. Use questions and observations from your Art Journal as part of the discussion if possible.

162 Unit 5 • Lesson 2

Differentiated Instruction

Reteach
Have students look through their textbooks and/or *Large Prints* for examples of figure proportion. Have them measure how many heads tall the examples are.

Special Needs
To ensure student success in the lesson activity, have visual prompts available, such as figures with proportion guidelines.

ELL
When explaining the concept of ratio to students, provide different visual examples, such as three large erasers to one pencil or two tennis balls to one aluminum can.

162 UNIT 5 • Proportion, Distortion, and Scale

◀ Kimberly Capel. Age 13.

Think about how the student artist used body proportions in this line drawing.

Creative Expression

Create a series of line drawings using body proportions.

1. Take turns with your partner posing for one another and making several sketches. Use the sighting technique. Think about body proportions as you create your sketches.
2. Select the sketch you like best and transfer it to drawing paper. Add a prop to your drawing that looks like it belongs, such as a tennis racket. Use a combination of simple thick and thin lines, and draw your image large so that your figure fills the page. Include a background in your drawing.
3. Use a marker to outline your drawing and to add textures. Use hatching, cross-hatching, or stippling techniques to create value.

Art Criticism

Describe Describe the pose you chose. What props did you add?

Analyze How did you use the sighting technique? What techniques did you use to add value?

Interpret What type of mood does your selected pose communicate?

Decide Were you able to use body proportions successfully in your drawing? Explain.

Unit 5 • Lesson 2 **163**

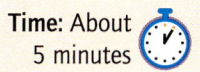

Reflect
Time: About 5 minutes

Review and Assess
"How was figure proportion used in your final drawing?" "¿Cómo fueron usadas las proporciones de figura en su dibujo final?"

Think
The artist used correct body proportions for a child. The ratio the artist used was 1:5.

- Use **Large Prints 81** *Self-Portrait* and **82** *Ruckus Rodeo* and ask students to compare how figure proportions were used in the two images. Explain the differences and similarities.

Informal Assessment

- Have students compare the career and avocational opportunities for portrait artists. Invite a local painter or photographer to the class, if possible.
- For standardized-format test practice using this lesson's art content, see pages 56–57 in *Reading and Writing Test Preparation.*

Art Journal: Critical Thinking
Have students answer the four art criticism questions—Describe, Analyze, Interpret, and Decide—in their Art Journals. Have students discuss as a class how they used figure proportions in their drawings. Had they used sighting techniques before? What type of measurement, if any, have they based their drawings on before?

Art Across the Curriculum

Use these simple ideas to reinforce art concepts across the curriculum.

★ **Persuasive Writing** Have students write a letter to a queen stating why he or she should be allowed to participate in a tournament.

★ **Math** Explain to students that a ratio is a comparison of two numbers.

★ **Science** Explain to students that marble is a material that was used in classical architecture and is still used today.

★ **Social Studies** Explain to students that democracy as a form of government was developed in ancient Greece.

★ **Technology** Using a paint or draw program, have students create a drawing of a person using figure proportion. Visit **SRAonline.com** to print detailed instructions for this activity.
NSAE 6.b

LESSON 2 • Figure Proportions **163**

Lesson 2 Wrap-Up: Figure Proportions

Extra! For the Art Specialist
Time: About 45 minutes

Focus
Study **Large Print 82** *Ruckus Rodeo* and discuss how figure proportion was used. How are the body parts arranged? Which technique do students think was used—sighting or measurement—to get the figure proportions?

Teach
Tell students they will be using the sighting technique for measuring the figure proportions of people in a busy area, such as the playground, hallways, or commons area. Explain that they will be creating a series of quick studies of the people, concentrating on the poses and figure proportions.

Reflect
Have students use the four steps of art criticism to evaluate their work. Have them describe the pose of their person and how their composition was arranged. Did students successfully create a figure drawing showing figure proportion?

Alternate Activity

Materials:
- sketchbooks
- pencils, drawing paper
- light-colored chalk, charcoal
- kneaded erasers
- towels, newspaper

1. After several sketches have been completed ask students to select their best one. Have them use this sketch as a basis for their final drawing.
2. Have students lightly sketch the basic shapes of their selected sketch onto their drawing paper with light-colored chalk. Tell students to make sure they keep the figure in the correct proportions. Have them use the charcoal to darken the important lines and to add some details. Shading techniques, such as hatching and cross-hatching, can be added.

Research in Art Education

"Children respond to art in a holistic manner; their reactions are immediate, subjective, and rarely go beyond the 'like/don't like' stage . . . It takes a sensitive teacher to help educate the vision of the child so that appreciation may occur." (Hurwitz, Al, and Stanley Madeja. *The Joyous Vision*. New Jersey: Prentice Hall, 1997.)

Assessment
Use the following rubric to evaluate the artwork students make in the Creative Expression activity and to assess students' understanding of how figure proportion is used in various works of art.

Have students complete page 59 or 60 in their *Assessment* books.

	Art History and Culture	Aesthetic Perception	Creative Expression	Art Criticism
3 POINTS	The student demonstrates knowledge of *Armor of George Clifford* and *Dancing Lady*.	The student accurately identifies the use of figure proportions in various works of art.	The student's figure drawing demonstrates how to use figure proportions.	The student thoughtfully and honestly evaluates own work using the four steps of art criticism.
2 POINTS	The student's knowledge of *Armor of George Clifford* and *Dancing Lady* is weak or incomplete.	The student shows an emerging awareness of figure proportions in various works of art, but cannot consistently identify them.	The student's figure drawing shows some awareness of how to use figure proportions.	The student attempts to evaluate own work but shows an incomplete understanding of evaluation criteria.
1 POINT	The student cannot demonstrate knowledge of *Armor of George Clifford* and *Dancing Lady*.	The student cannot identify how figure proportions are used in any works of art.	The student's figure drawing shows no understanding of how to use figure proportions.	The student makes no attempt to evaluate own work.

UNIT 5 • Proportion, Distortion, and Scale

Lesson 3 Overview: Facial Distortion

Lesson 3 introduces another type of proportion, known as distortion. **Distortion** is a deviation from normal or expected proportions.

Objectives

Art History and Culture
To demonstrate knowledge of Edvard Munch and face jugs

Creative Expression
To create a face jug using a distorted feature

Aesthetic Perception
To identify how face distortion is used in both two- and three-dimensional works of art

Art Criticism
To evaluate own work using the four steps of art criticism

Lesson Materials
- Art Journals
- pencils, erasers
- clay, glaze, kiln
- wire cutter (for clay)
- burlap or cloth to work on
- clay tools

Alternate Materials:
- self-hardening clay
- wallpaper scraps to work on
- white clay for eyes

Program Resources
- *Reading and Writing Test Prep.*, pp. 58–59
- *Transparency 27*
- *Artist Profiles*, pp. 41, 77
- *Animals Through History Time Line*
- *Assessment*, pp. 61–62
- *Large Prints 81 Self-Portrait* and *82 Ruckus Rodeo*
- *The National Museum of Women in the Arts Collection*

Concept Trace
Facial Distortion
Introduced: Level 5, Unit 4, Lesson 5
Reinforced: Level 7, Chapter 12, Lesson 1

Vocabulary

Review the following vocabulary words with students before beginning the lesson.

score muesca—the repeated scratching of a clay surface at the area where another scored piece will be attached

slip barbotina—a mixture of clay and water that is creamy to the touch and is used to attach two scored pieces of clay together

See page 179B for additional vocabulary and Spanish vocabulary resources.

Art Journal: Vocabulary
Have students add these words to the Vocabulary section of their Art Journals.

Lesson 3 Arts Integration

Theatre
Complete Unit 5, Lesson 3, on pages 94–95 of *Theatre Arts Connections*.

Music
Sing or listen to *Mongolian Night Song*. One melodic pattern is used repeatedly. The speed of the melody changes, however. This is called diminution when the melody speeds up and augmentation when it slows down.

Movement & Dance
Have students create three distorted facial expressions. Have them incorporate hand gestures as well. Have students share the three expressions with a partner and then have them try to copy each other. This allows each person to see their expressions performed on a different face.

LESSON 3 • Facial Distortion **163B**

Focus

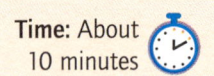

Time: About 10 minutes

Activate Prior Knowledge

"Have you seen a mime or clown act out a scene?" "¿Han visto un mimo o payaso actuando una escena?"

- Discuss student responses. Explain that exaggerated facial expressions and body language can be used to convey a message without words. Controlled movements are often used by mimes and clowns to convey emotions and to communicate scenarios. Silent movies used exaggerated expressions to convey messages.

Using Literature ⭐ Reading

- Have students look at the cover illustration of *Tales from the Brothers Grimm and the Sister's Weird* by Vivian Vande Velde. Discuss how face distortion is used in the masks on the cover illustration.

Thematic Connection ⭐ Science

- **Being Afraid:** Have students discuss times when they were afraid of something. Then ask them if they were able to overcome that fear and how they were able to do it.

Introduce the Art

Look

Look closely at how facial distortions are used in these works of art." "Miren detalladamente cómo en estas obras de arte se usan las distorsiones faciales."

Artist's Purpose ⭐ Reading

- Ask students what they think the artists' intentions were for *The Scream* and *Face Jugs*. Answers will vary, but some students may say that their purposes are to scare the viewer or to make them laugh.

Art History and Culture

The following works of art look similar because the subjects' faces are distorted: *Last Conversation Piece* by Juan Muñoz, *Portrait of Dora Maar* by Pablo Picasso, and *Portrait of Emy* by Karl Schmidt-Rotluff.

💻 Web Connection

Visit museumsnett.no/munchmuseet for more information about Edvard Munch.

164 UNIT 5 • Proportion, Distortion, and Scale

Lesson 3: Facial Distortion

▲ **Edvard Munch.** (Norwegian). *The Scream.* 1893.
Tempera and casein on cardboard. 36 × 29 inches (91.44 × 73.66 cm.). Munch-Museet, Oslo, Norway.

Look closely at the artwork on these two pages. When it was first exhibited, *The Scream*, by Edvard Munch, shocked viewers because it communicates the emotion of fear. During this time period, paintings usually conveyed happy emotions and were painted with bright colors. *Face Jugs*, from Georgia and South Carolina, are examples of Southern folk pottery. They were first made in the 1800s by the African American potters of the Edgefield District of South Carolina. No one really knows their purpose. The techniques of these early potters filtered into Georgia and eventually throughout the United States.

Art History and Culture

Examine these works of art. Do they remind you of any other pieces you have studied?

164 Unit 5 • Lesson 3

Art History and Culture

Edvard Munch

Edvard Munch (ed´ värd mungk) (1863–1944) was influenced by the nabis and the post-impressionists, particularly Gauguin, van Gogh, and Toulouse-Lautrec. At the same time, Munch created his own symbolism based on his own traumatic experiences. During the 1890s, he made a series of paintings called *The Frieze of Life*. He referred to this work as "a poem of life, love, and death." *The Scream* is from this series and expresses conflict and tension. Because Munch emphasized mental anguish and the distortion of colors and form, he, along with van Gogh, is considered to be a great influence on German expressionism.

See pages 24–25 and 16–21 for more about art history and subject matter.

Artist Profiles, p. 41

Artist unknown. (United States). *Face Jugs.* c. Twentieth century.
Private collection.

Study the faces portrayed on these two pages to learn more about facial distortion.

- What normal human features have been changed in *The Scream?* How have they been altered?
- What features look larger than normal in *Face Jugs?* Are any of the features smaller than normal? Explain.
- What emotions do you think Munch was communicating in his painting?
- What purpose do you think the face jugs served?

Aesthetic Perception

Design Awareness Think about the facial expressions you have seen people make. What feelings do they communicate?

Unit 5 • Lesson 3 **165**

Art History and Culture

Face Jugs

Historians are not sure of the purpose of face jugs. Some believe they were influenced by the carved wooden figures of Central Africa, while others believe they were influenced by the figural jugs of England. In the United States, the most famous face jugs were made by the African American potters of the Edgefield District of South Carolina during the 1800s, although several potters were making similar jugs in the North at the same time. Several construction methods and types of clay were used to create these forms. A high level of skill was needed to combine wheel throwing and hand building with porcelain and stoneware clay.

See pages 24–25 and 16–21 for more about art history and subject matter.

Artist Profiles, p. 77

Artist Profile
Face Jugs
These face jugs were made by an unknown artist or artists sometime during the twentieth century. Face jug pottery is a traditional art form from the American South and the Appalachian Mountains. Because face jugs have been made in thousands of American communities for nearly two hundred years, it is often difficult to find information about the individual creator of a particular piece.

Artist unknown. (United States). *Face Jugs.* c. Twentieth century.
Earthenware. Private collection.

Study

- The head, mouth, and body of the single figure and the bodies of the two figures in the background. The shape of the head, the jaw, and the mouth look stretched out. The body is curved and thin. The figures in the background look tall and elongated.

- The noses on the small and far-right faces, the lips on the center jug, and the ears on the left jug are large. The eyes and teeth on the far-right and small jugs are large. On the center jug, the ears are smaller than normal.

- Student responses will vary; however, many will respond with fear and sadness.

- Student responses will vary. Historians are not sure of the purpose of the face jugs.

■ For more examples of abstract and nonobjective art, see *The National Museum of Women in the Arts Collection.*

Art Journal: Writing
Encourage students to write their explanations of distortion in the Concepts section of their Art Journals. What else do they want to know about facial distortion?

Aesthetic Perception

Design Awareness Discuss with students how a frown communicates sadness, and a smile communicates happiness. Explain that artists often distort features to better communicate feelings or emotions. Facial distortion not only communicates feelings or emotions but also makes a composition more interesting.

Developing Visual Literacy Discuss the faces in each of the works of art. Discuss how the artists distorted the features to communicate messages or emotions. Which features are distorted? Do students associate distorted facial features with any traditional life events? Ask students to share personal experiences that contribute to their interpretations.

Web Connection
Visit www.amesgallery.com/FolkArtPages/FaceJugs.html for more examples of face jugs.

LESSON 3 • FACIAL DISTORTION **165**

Teach

Time: About 45 minutes

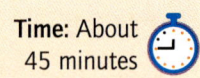

"What feature will you distort when making your face jug?" "¿Qué rasgo van a distorsionar cuando están haciendo un jarro de cara?"

- Read and discuss using facial distortion on page 166.

Practice

Materials: pieces of paper with names of emotions and expressions written on them, envelopes

Alternate Materials: *Art Connections* textbook

- On pieces of paper, write names of emotions or expressions. Place these in an envelope.
- Distribute the materials and have students follow the directions on page 166.

Creative Expression

Materials: Art Journals, pencils, erasers, clay, burlap, pencils or nails to draw into clay, cloth to work on, wire cutter for clay, kiln, glaze, clay tools

Alternate Materials: self-hardening clay, wallpaper scraps to work on, white clay for eyes

- Distribute the materials and have students follow the directions on page 167.
- Have students demonstrate their technical skills, using a variety of art media and materials to produce their face jugs. NSAE 1.a; 1.b
- Review the Activity Tips on page 243 for visual examples of techniques if needed.

Art Journal: Sketching

Have students create two sketches for their face jugs and distort at least one of the features. Ask the students to think about an expression or emotion they may want to portray. Have them work out their ideas in their Art Journals.

166 UNIT 5 • Proportion, Distortion, and Scale

Using Facial Distortion

Distortion is based on the art principle of proportion. **Distortion** is a deviation from normal or expected proportions. Artists use distortion to express personal feelings and to communicate emotions. Distortion is a powerful means of expression and can convey feelings or meanings that normal proportions cannot.

Think about other places where you have seen distortion. Cartoonists often use facial distortion in their art to emphasize character traits. If you have ever seen caricatures of famous people you have probably noticed that one feature is often exaggerated or distorted. Distortion is also commonly used in masks. Many cultures distort the features on masks used for religious or celebratory purposes.

Practice

Work in groups to act out an emotion using facial expressions.

1. Work in small groups. Your teacher will select the name of an emotion or expression from an envelope for your group to perform.
2. Look at the name of the emotion or expression. As a group, practice exaggerating the facial expression assigned.
3. Take turns with the other groups in your class performing the emotions or expressions. Can you correctly identify the emotions expressed?

166   Unit 5 • Lesson 3

Differentiated Instruction

Reteach
Have students look through the **Large Prints** for examples of facial distortion. Have them list the works of art that have facial distortion and the features that are distorted.

Special Needs
Use this activity as an opportunity to nurture emotional intelligence. Have students think about a positive character trait they have or one that they would like to develop. Then ask them to emphasize or distort the area of the face that represents that trait.

ELL
When explaining facial distortion to students, show them several pictures of the same face with a different feature distorted each time. Have them explain what is different about the pictures.

◀ Mrs. Cox's sixth-grade class.

Think about which features the student artists distorted in their face pots.

Creative Expression

Create a clay face jug, using a distorted feature.

1. Create various sketches of a face jug and select one. Look at your selected sketch, and then make a clay sphere. Gently pat your form, turning it in your hands to make it even all around. Flatten the bottom to sit upright.
2. Pinch out a spout at the top of your form, but do not make a hole. Lightly draw the facial features.
3. Form and attach the features using the scoring method. Make the eyes from small balls of clay, and make the lids from small coils of clay.
4. Use a pencil to pierce a hole in the spout as you support it with your fingers. Add color with glaze.

Art Criticism

Describe Describe the expression on your face jug.

Analyze What forms did you use? How did you distort a feature?

Interpret What emotion or mood does your face jug communicate?

Decide Were you successful in creating a face jug using distortion? Explain.

Reflect

Time: About 5 minutes

Review and Assess

"How was facial distortion used?" "¿Cómo usaron la distorsión facial?"

Think

The artists distorted the eyes, the noses, and the mouths of their face jugs.

- Use **Large Prints 81** *Self-Portrait* and **82** *Ruckus Rodeo* and ask students to compare the use of facial distortion in the two images. What areas were distorted? Why do students think the artist chose to distort this area?

Informal Assessment

- For standardized-format test practice using this lesson's art content, see pages 58–59 in *Reading and Writing Test Preparation.*

Art Journal: Critical Thinking

Have students answer the four art criticism questions—Describe, Analyze, Interpret, and Decide—in their Art Journals. Have students create a display of their work and analyze how their classmates used facial distortion. Can students form any conclusions about historical or cultural contexts? Then ask students to discuss the features they chose to distort and why.
NSAE 4.b

Art Across the Curriculum

Use these simple ideas to reinforce art concepts across the curriculum.

★ **Descriptive Writing** Have students write a descriptive paragraph about the background of *The Scream*.

★ **Math** Have students estimate the size difference between the largest and smallest face jugs.

★ **Science** Explain to students that researchers believe we dream every night, even though we do not always remember our dreams.

★ **Social Studies** Have students discuss folk art they have seen in the United States. NSAE 4.b; 4.c

★ **Technology** Using a paint or draw program, have students create a drawing similar to *The Scream*. Visit **SRAonline.com** to print detailed instructions for this activity.
NSAE 6.b

Lesson 3 Wrap-Up: Facial Distortion

Extra! For the Art Specialist
Time: About 45 minutes

Focus
Study **Large Print 82** *Ruckus Rodeo* and discuss how facial distortion was used in the artwork. What area was distorted? How was it distorted?

Teach
Explain to students that they will create self-portraits in clay. They will distort the faces to express emotions. Have them create several sketches to work from. Then have them complete the Alternate Activity.

Reflect
Have students use the four steps of art criticism to evaluate their work. Have them describe the emotion that was portrayed in the self-portrait. Did students successfully use facial distortion in their self-portraits? Which features were distorted?
NSAE 1.a; 1.b

Alternate Activity

Materials:
- Art Journals
- pencils, erasers
- clay, kiln
- burlap
- pencils or nails to draw into clay
- cloth to work on
- wire cutter for clay

1. Have students begin by forming the clay into an oval. They also should shape the shoulders, neck, and head.
2. Have students pinch out the nose and use a pencil to draw where they want the mouth and eyes.
3. Explain to students that hair can be added as individual coils, braids, or repeated lines drawn on the head.
4. Have students use a clay tool to scrape out the excess clay in the base so that the walls are no thinner than the thickness of a finger. Then have them use a pencil to carefully poke a hole from the bottom into the head.
5. Fire the completed face jugs for students.

Research in Art Education

"Only through a multifaceted education program that develops divergent as well as convergent thinking—that encourages intuitive as well as rational thought processes—can today's young learner begin to be prepared to cope with the rapidly changing aspects of a technology-oriented world." (Herberholz, Barbara, and Lee Hanson. *Early Childhood Art*. New York: McGraw-Hill, 1994.)

Assessment
Use the following rubric to evaluate the artwork students make in the Creative Expression activity and to assess students' understanding of how facial distortion is used in two- and three-dimensional works of art.

Have students complete page 61 or 62 in their *Assessment* books.

	Art History and Culture	Aesthetic Perception	Creative Expression	Art Criticism
3 POINTS	The student demonstrates knowledge of Edvard Munch and face jugs.	The student accurately identifies the use of facial distortion in two- and three-dimensional works of art.	The student's face jug demonstrates how to use facial distortion.	The student thoughtfully and honestly evaluates own work using the four steps of art criticism.
2 POINTS	The student's knowledge of Edvard Munch and face jugs is weak or incomplete.	The student shows an emerging awareness of facial distortion in two- and three-dimensional works of art but cannot consistently identify them.	The student's face jug shows some awareness of how to use facial distortion.	The student attempts to evaluate own work but shows an incomplete understanding of evaluation criteria.
1 POINT	The student cannot demonstrate knowledge of Edvard Munch and face jugs.	The student cannot identify how facial distortion is used in two- or three-dimensional works of art.	The student's face jug shows no understanding of how to use facial distortion.	The student makes no attempt to evaluate own work.

167A UNIT 5 • Proportion, Distortion, and Scale

Lesson 4 Overview: Figure Distortion

Lesson 4 takes a closer look at proportion and how figure distortion is created through various techniques such as exaggeration. **Exaggeration** is an increase or enlargement beyond what is expected or normal.

Objectives

Art History and Culture
To demonstrate knowledge of the lives and work of Alberto Giacometti and Fernando Botero

Creative Expression
To create figure distortion by manipulating a digital photograph in a draw or paint program

Aesthetic Perception
To identify how figure distortion is used in two- and three-dimensional works of art

Art Criticism
To evaluate own work using the four steps of art criticism

Lesson Materials
- comic strips
- Art Journals
- pencils, erasers
- digital camera
- computer
- draw or paint software
- printer, paper
- scanner (optional)

Alternate materials:
- *Art Connections* textbook
- photographs from home
- word-processing program

Program Resources
- *Reading and Writing Test Prep.*, pp. 60–61
- *Transparency 28*
- *Artist Profiles*, pp. 10, 27
- *Animals Through History Time Line*
- *Assessment*, pp. 63–64
- *Large Prints 81 Self-Portrait* and *82 Ruckus Rodeo*
- *Art Around the World Collection*

Concept Trace
Figure Distortion
Introduced: Level 5, Unit 4, Lesson 4
Reinforced: Level 7, Chapter 4, Lesson 6

Vocabulary

Review the following vocabulary words with students before beginning the lesson.

distortion distorsión—a deviation from normal or expected proportions

elongate alargar—to stretch out or make long

See page 179B for additional vocabulary and Spanish Vocabulary resources.

Art Journal: Vocabulary
Have students add these words to the Vocabulary section of their Art Journals.

Lesson 4 Arts Integration

Theatre
Complete Unit 5, Lesson 4, on pages 96–97 of *Theatre Arts Connections*.

Music
The sound of an instrument may be distorted through change of tone production. Contemporary composers often find new ways to produce sound on traditional instruments. The musical style of another culture may sound different and "distorted" when first heard. Listen to a recording of Chinese opera or Balkan folk songs to hear styles different from our Western ideas of vocal production.

Movement & Dance
Have students form a large circle. While they hold hands, have students explore ways that the circle can be distorted. Have some students stretch high and some bend low, or have half of the circle move with one type of energy and the other half move with another type.

LESSON 4 • Figure Distortion **167B**

Focus

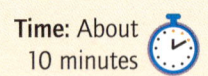

Time: About 10 minutes

Activate Prior Knowledge

"Have you ever seen a toy that was distorted?" "¿Han visto alguna vez un juguete distorsionado?"

- As a class, discuss the student responses. Explain that many toy manufacturers have used figure distortion in many products. These toys have been designed for children to use their imagination in play, as well as to promote or sell the product.

Using Literature ⭐ Reading

- Look at the cover illustration of *Treasure of Green Knowe* by L. M. Boston. Discuss how figure distortion is used on the cover illustration. The arms on the boy are disproportional for his body. They are stretched out a little longer than would be natural.

Thematic Connection ⭐ Science

- **Human Body:** Ask students how they would feel if everyone looked exactly the same. How do they think that would affect the work of artists?

Introduce the Art

Look

"Look closely at how the figures are distorted in the two works of art on these pages."
"Miren detalladamente cómo las figuras están distorsionadas en las dos obras de arte en estas páginas."

Health ⭐ Science

- Have students look at the works of the art in this lesson and describe any activities in them that could be considered a form of exercise. In *City Square*, the figures appear to be walking. In *Dancing in Colombia*, the couple is dancing.

Art History and Culture

Both of these pieces will remind students of cartoons because of the distorted characters created by each artist. Cartoon illustrators often distort their characters to make a point or to create a mood.

🖥 Web Connection

Visit www.moma.org for more information about the Museum of Modern Art.

168 UNIT 5 • Proportion, Distortion, and Scale

Lesson 4: Figure Distortion

Look at the works of art on these pages. Notice the extreme proportions these artists used. Alberto Giacometti originally made his figures from wire covered in plaster. He was part of a group of artists known as surrealists, who were inspired by dreams and fantasy. *Dancing in Colombia* is typical of Colombian-born artist Fernando Botero. His figures have plump proportions, which he calls "plasticity." Not only his figures are rounded, but so are all of the other objects in his paintings. Each of these works of art is an example of figure distortion.

▲ **Alberto Giacometti.** (Swiss). *City Square.* 1948.
Bronze. 8½ × 25¾ × 17¼ inches (21.59 × 65.41 × 43.82 cm.). Museum of Modern Art, New York, New York.

Art History and Culture

As a child, Giacometti wanted to be an illustrator. Botero had a job as an illustrator. In what ways do these works of art remind you of cartoons?

168   Unit 5 • Lesson 4

Art History and Culture

Alberto Giacometti

Alberto Giacometti (äl ber´ tō jä kə me´ tē) (1901–1966) was always interested in art. As a child, he wanted to illustrate stories. In Geneva between 1935 and 1940, Giacometti began to make sculptures of heads and standing figures from memory, but they became smaller and smaller. When he returned to Paris after World War II, he was able to make sculptures of more normal dimensions, but they were tall and thin. After World War II, his reputation as a sculptor grew. In 1956 he decided to produce paintings but each portrait required many sittings because Giacometti was unable to capture precisely what he wanted.

See pages 24–25 and 16–21 for more about art history and subject matter.

Artist Profiles, p. 27

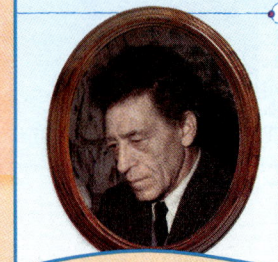

▲ **Fernando Botero.**
(Colombian). *Dancing in Colombia.* 1980.
Oil on canvas. 74 × 91 inches (187.96 × 231.14 cm.). The Metropolitan Museum of Art, New York, New York.

Study the two works of art to learn how figure distortion is used.
▶ Which figures are elongated, or stretched?
▶ How did Botero distort the people in *Dancing in Colombia*?
▶ Describe the negative space around and between the figures in *City Square*. How does this affect the feeling of the work?
▶ Describe the images and emotions that come to mind when you view each work of art.

Aesthetic Perception

Design Awareness Think of a time when you were part of a crowd but did not know anyone or just did not want to be there. What did you seem to notice the most?

Unit 5 • Lesson 4   **169**

Study
▶ The figures in Alberto Giacometti's *City Square*.
▶ Fernando Botero rounded all of the people in *Dancing in Colombia*. The figures look as if they are blown up or inflated. The size of the features is small in comparison to the face size.
▶ The figures are very close together, overlapped, and crowded on a stagelike setting. There is no negative space between the figures, only around them. This arrangement gives the feeling that the figures are comfortable being together, but there also is a crowded feeling.
▶ Student responses will vary; however, most will respond as follows: *City Square*: The figures are spaced away from one another and do not seem to recognize or acknowledge each other. *Dancing in Colombia*: Seven large figures are in the middle ground, and two smaller dancing figures are in the foreground. They seem not to notice one another.

■ For more examples of art from South America, see the **Art Around the World Collection**.

Art Journal: Writing
Encourage students to write about other paintings and sculptures with distorted figures that they have seen in the Concepts section of their Art Journals. What else do they want to know about figure distortion?

Art History and Culture

Fernando Botero

In 1948, Fernando Botero (fer nän′ dō bō tār′ ō) (1932–) started work as an illustrator. In his own work, he introduced inflated forms, exaggerated human figures, and natural features, celebrating the life within them while mocking their role in the world. He combined the regional with the universal, constantly referring to his native Colombia. He also created elaborate parodies of works of art from the past. In Botero's words, "When I deform things, I enter a subconscious world rich in folk images. For me rotundity in art is linked to pleasure. Basically it's a matter of rationalizing natural impulses."

See pages 24–25 and 16–21 for more about art history and subject matter.

Artist Profiles, p. 10

Artist Profile
Fernando Botero
b. 1932

As a young man, this Colombian spent two years learning to be a matador. Fernando Botero (fer nän′ dō bōtä′ rō) changed his career plans and studied art in Colombia, Spain, France, and Italy. During this time, Botero had several exhibitions, but received little praise for his work—and fewer sales. After he began painting in a rounded style in 1956, his pictures sold well. By 1958, he was Colombia's most famous young artist. In 1960, he opened a studio in New York City. In 1973, he moved to Paris and began sculpting. He has married twice and has four children.

Aesthetic Perception

Design Awareness Have students discuss the various groupings of people they may have observed. A crowd of people at a concert is different from a group of close family members or friends.

Developing Visual Literacy Talk about the use of distorted figures, and have students notice the differences in negative space in each artwork.

Web Connection
Visit **www.metmuseum.org** for more information about the Metropolitan Museum of Art.

LESSON 4 • Figure Distortion **169**

Teach

Time: About 45 minutes

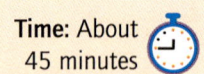

"How will you use figure distortion in your art?" "¿Cómo usarian la distorsión de una figura en su arte?"

- Read and discuss using figure distortion on page 170.

Practice

Materials: comic strips

Alternate Materials: *Art Connections* textbook

- Distribute the materials and have students follow the directions on page 170.

Creative Expression

Materials: Art Journals, digital camera, computer monitor, draw or paint software, printer, paper, scanner (optional)

Alternate Materials: photographs from home, word-processing program, pencils

- Distribute the materials and have students follow the directions on page 171.
- Have students conduct in-progress analyses and critiques of their computer images.
  NSAE 2.b; 2.c
- Have students demonstrate their technical skills, using a variety of art media and materials to distort their photographs and make prints of them.
  NSAE 1.a; 1.b
- Review the Activity Tips on page 243 for visual examples of techniques if needed.

Art Journal: Brainstorming

Ask students to list ideas they have for creating a distorted figure. Have them write their list, along with any questions they may have, in their Art Journals. Their list and questions will be used in their Creative Expression activity as well as the class art criticism of the completed project.

170 UNIT 5 • Proportion, Distortion, and Scale

Using Figure Distortion

In the last lesson you learned that artists use distortion to express feelings and emotions. Artwork created with distorted figures often produces intense feelings in the viewer. Sometimes the distortions create feelings of love and happiness; other times they create feelings of fear or loneliness.

Artists communicate these moods or feelings so their works can be better understood by viewers. An artist can elongate or lengthen a form, as Giacometti did in *City Square*. Other artists, like Botero, inflate or enlarge a figure to create a result that is monumental, large, or imposing. The figures in *Dancing in Colombia* were created with exaggerated proportions. Exaggeration is a form of distortion. **Exaggeration** is an increase or enlargement of an object beyond what is expected or normal. When artists exaggerate things, they might make them extra long or extra wide. Artists can also bend, warp, twist, and deform parts, or all, of the human body to create figure distortions.

Practice

Look through comic strips for examples of figure distortion.

1. Work in groups of three or four. Look through comic strips and collect images of distorted figures.
2. Create a grid on the board as a class. Use these categories: Elongated/Stretched, Exaggerated/Enlarged, Twisted/Bent.
3. Share collected images of comic strips with the class. Categorize and record each of the comic-strip images on the grid. Which type of distortion was used most often? Which was used least often?

170   Unit 5 • Lesson 4

Differentiated Instruction

Reteach
Have students find examples of figure distortion in magazines. Ask them to describe how the figures are distorted.

Special Needs
Students develop confidence as they master different art media, including the computer. Allow students with disabilities the opportunity to experiment, to develop competence in this medium, and to share their knowledge with other classmates.

ELL
Have students draw a funny picture of themselves. Ask them why they think the drawing is funny and identify whether they used exaggeration or another type of distortion.

◀ Brianna Ruch.
Age 12.

Think about how the student artist distorted this figure.

Creative Expression

Use the computer to distort a photograph.

1. Use a digital camera, and take several photographs of a family member or friend. Choose one or two of your photographs.
2. Begin by loading the image into the computer. If you have regular photographs, scan them into the computer.
3. Use a draw or paint program to create a copy of the image, and then save it. Use a variety of tools on the menu to create a distortion of the image.
4. Add textures to the background or alter the colors. Title and save your work.

Art Criticism

Describe What tools did you use to distort your image?

Analyze Describe the textures and/or color schemes you used to alter your image. What type of distortion did you use?

Interpret How did distortion affect the mood of your work? Explain.

Decide Were you successful in creating figure distortion in your artwork? Explain.

Unit 5 • Lesson 4   **171**

Reflect

Time: About 5 minutes

Review and Assess

"How was figure distortion used in this artwork?" "¿Cómo se usó la distorsión de figura en esta obra de arte?"

Think

The artist created a spiral, swirling effect in the middle of the photograph.

- Use **Large Prints 81** *Self-Portrait* and **82** *Ruckus Rodeo* and ask students to compare how the artists used figure distortion in their works of art. How are they different? How are they similar? What techniques were used to distort the figures in each work?

Informal Assessment

- For standardized-format test practice using this lesson's art content, see pages 60–61 in *Reading and Writing Test Preparation*.

Art Journal: Critical Thinking

Have students answer the four art criticism questions—Describe, Analyze, Interpret, and Decide—in their Art Journals. Have students discuss within groups how they created their figure distortions. Ask them to notice the similarities and differences including formal properties and historical and cultural contexts. Have the groups share their discussion with the class.
NSAE 5.a; 5.c

Art Across the Curriculum

Use these simple ideas to reinforce art concepts across the curriculum.

★ **Expository Writing** Have students write a paragraph explaining why the instruments in *Dancing in Colombia* do not have strings.

★ **Math** Explain to students that a squared number is a number multiplied by itself.

★ **Science** Discuss with students that genes determine how tall or short a person will be.

★ **Social Studies** Explain to students that many large cities were developed on a grid system.

★ **Technology** Using a word-processing program, have students insert a piece of clip art that contains people and distort the figures. Visit **SRAonline.com** to print detailed instructions for this activity.
NSAE 6.b

LESSON 4 • Figure Distortion **171**

Lesson 4 Wrap-Up: Figure Distortion

Extra! For the Art Specialist

Time: About 45 minutes

Focus
Have students study **Large Print 82** *Ruckus Rodeo* and discuss how figure distortion was used. What technique was used to distort the figures in this artwork?

Teach
Discuss with the students figure distortion and the various techniques used: exaggeration, elongation, twisting, and bending. Have students either find a full-body image in a magazine or bring a photograph to class from home.

Reflect
Have students use the four steps of art criticism to evaluate their work. Have them describe the technique used to distort the figure. What image was used? Did students successfully create a drawing, using figure distortion?

Alternate Activity

Materials:
- sketchbooks
- pencils, erasers
- 12" × 18" drawing paper (any color)
- colored chalk or charcoal
- kneaded eraser

1. Ask students to create two or three sketches in their sketchbooks from their photographs. Have them create the images using one distortion technique. Ask students to select their best sketches.
2. Have students use a light-colored chalk to draw their figures on drawing paper.
3. Have students complete the drawings with either color chalk or charcoal.

Research in Art Education

" . . . the kind of deliberately designed tasks students are offered in school help define the kind of thinking they will learn to do. The kind of thinking students learn to do will influence what they come to know and the kind of cognitive skills they acquire." (Eisner, Elliot W. *The Arts and the Creation of Mind*. New Haven: Yale Univ. Press, 2002.)

Assessment
Use the following rubric to evaluate the artwork students make in the Creative Expression activity and to assess students' understanding of how figure distortion is used in two- and three-dimensional works of art.

Have students complete page 63 or 64 in their *Assessment* books.

	Art History and Culture	Aesthetic Perception	Creative Expression	Art Criticism
3 POINTS	The student demonstrates knowledge of the lives and work of Giacometti and Botero.	The student accurately identifies the use of figure distortion in a variety of works of art.	The student's artwork demonstrates how to use figure distortion.	The student thoughtfully and honestly evaluates own work using the four steps of art criticism.
2 POINTS	The student's knowledge of the lives and work of Giacometti and Botero is weak or incomplete.	The student shows an emerging awareness of figure distortion in a variety of works of art but cannot consistently identify it.	The student's artwork shows some awareness of how to use figure distortion.	The student attempts to evaluate own work but shows an incomplete understanding of evaluation criteria.
1 POINT	The student cannot demonstrate knowledge of the lives and work of Giacometti or Botero.	The student cannot identify how figure distortion is used in an artwork.	The student's artwork shows no understanding of how to use figure distortion.	The student makes no attempt to evaluate own work.

171A UNIT 5 • Proportion, Distortion, and Scale

Lesson 5 Overview: Realistic Scale

Lesson 5 introduces scale and compares it to proportion; the focus is on realistic scale as used in everyday objects. **Scale** is size as measured against a standard reference. **Realistic scale** is when everything fits together and makes sense in size relation.

Objectives

Art History and Culture
To demonstrate knowledge of the lives and work of Moshe Safdie and Julia Russell

Creative Expression
To design a chair using realistic scale

Aesthetic Perception
To identify and better understand how realistic scale is used in two- and three-dimensional works of art

Art Criticism
To evaluate own work using the four steps of art criticism

Lesson Materials
- magazines
- Art Journals
- pencils, erasers
- scissors
- rulers, glue
- 9" × 12" white drawing paper
- colored pencils

Alternate Materials:
- photographs from home
- crayons

Program Resources
- *Reading and Writing Test Prep.,* pp. 62–63
- *Transparency* 29
- *Flash Cards* 19
- *Artist Profiles,* pp. 55–56
- *Animals Through History Time Line*
- *Assessment,* pp. 65–66
- *Large Prints 81 Self-Portrait* and *82 Ruckus Rodeo*
- *Art Around the World Collection*

Concept Trace
Scale
Introduced: Level 5, Unit 4, Lessons 2, 6
Reinforced: Level 7, Chapter 14, Lesson 1

Vocabulary

Review the following vocabulary words with students before beginning the lesson.

proportion proporción—refers to the relationship of one part to another part

scale escala—size as measured against a standard reference

See page 179B for additional vocabulary and Spanish Vocabulary resources.

Art Journal: Vocabulary
Have students add these words to the Vocabulary section of their Art Journals.

Lesson 5 Arts Integration

Theatre
Complete Unit 5, Lesson 5, on pages 98–99 of *Theatre Arts Connections.*

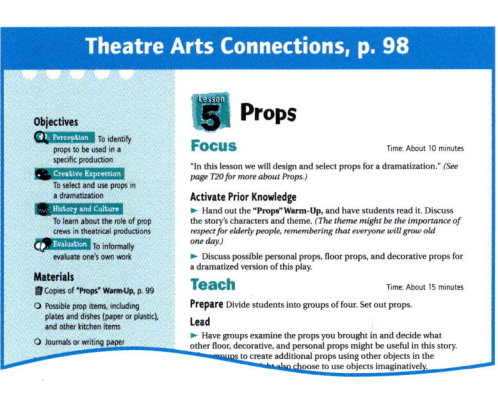

Music
Musical compositions can be composed on any scale, from chamber music to symphonic form. Chamber music is written for a small group of musicians to perform in a "chamber" instead of a large concert hall. Listen to Quintet 114 "The Trout" by Franz Schubert. Is one instrument of greater importance in this composition?

Movement & Dance
Have students go outside and choose three objects, such as a doorway, a tree, and a building. Have one student stand next to each of the objects. Then have the class look at the student in relation to the object, viewing them from close up and then far away.

LESSON 5 • Realistic Scale **171B**

Focus

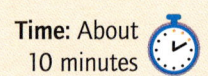

Time: About 10 minutes

Activate Prior Knowledge

"Have you ever been inside a playhouse?" "¿Han estado adentro de una casita de juguete?"

- As a class, discuss student responses. Explain that a lot of designers create furniture, housing, and functional items to scale based on average human dimensions. Architects and designers create objects based on realistic scale.

Using Literature ⭐ Reading

- Have students look at the cover illustration of *Lily's Crossing* by Patricia Reilly Giff. Discuss how the image of the girl on the cover and the scene behind her are in realistic scale.

Thematic Connection ⭐ Science

- **Homes:** Have students describe different types of homes. Do they or someone else they know own any interesting pieces of furniture?

Introduce the Art

Look

"Look closely at how realistic scale is used in the two works of art on these pages." "Miren detalladamente cómo es usada la escala realista en la dos obras de arte en estas páginas?"

Similarity ⭐ Math

- Have students identify similar shapes and forms within each work of art. In *Habitat*, there are squares and rectangles that are similarly shaped and tree forms that look similar. In *Leonardo da Vinci Chair*, there are similar butterfly forms and oval shapes for the eyes.

Art History and Culture

The apartment building might remind students of pueblos in Mexican societies. Even though the chair looks contemporary, it might remind them of Italy during the Renaissance.

💻 Web Connection

Visit cac.mcgill.ca/safdie/habitat/ for more information about *Habitat*.

172 UNIT 5 • Proportion, Distortion, and Scale

Lesson 5: Realistic Scale

▲ **Mosche Safdie.** (Israeli). *Habitat.* 1967.
Concrete. Montreal, Canada.

Look closely at the two works of art on these pages. Notice how both artists created artwork using realistic scale. Mosche Safdie designed *Habitat* for the Expo in Montreal in 1967. Each of the single cubes is a precast concrete unit. The units were mass-produced, then transported to the site and assembled. The units vary in size and have different interiors. Julia Russell painted *Leonardo da Vinci's Chair* for a fundraiser for the arts. The work was so successful that she began to create compositions based on her favorite artists for other chairs. Russell studies an artist's style and artwork, creates a detailed composition, and then transfers it onto a specially prepared chair. After she draws the details, she uses acrylic paint to complete the work.

Art History and Culture

Examine these pieces of art. Do they remind you of other cultures?

172 Unit 5 • Lesson 5

Art History and Culture

Moshe Safdie

Moshe Safdie (mō shā´ saf´ dē) (1938–) was born in Haifa, Israel, and received his architecture degree from McGill University in Montreal. He started his first practice in Montreal and then moved to the United States, where he established a practice and taught at Harvard. Influenced by his graduate thesis, Safdie created *Habitat* for the Expo in Montreal. Each apartment is ready-made and can be stacked in a variety of ways. This contemporary structure resembles the towns of Mesopotamia or pueblos found in the Southwestern United States.

See pages 24–25 and 16–21 for more about art history and subject matter.

Artist Profiles, p. 56

Artist Profile
Moshe Safdie
b. 1938

Moshe Safdie (mō shā´ saf´ dē) was born in Haifa, Israel, and received his architecture degree from McGill University in Montreal, Canada, in 1961. He has been commissioned by cities around the world to create designs for public buildings and civic organizations. The Salt Lake City Public Library and the Peabody Essex Museum, both designed by Safdie, opened to positive acclaim in 2003. Safdie also designed the United States Institute of Peace Headquarters in Washington, D.C. and the National Campus for the Archaeology of Israel in Jerusalem.

Study the two works of art to learn how artists use realistic scale.

- How tall do you think you would be in relation to Russell's chair? On what are you basing your guess?
- How large do you think Safdie's buildings are? What objects in the photograph give you a clue about their size?
- What do you think Safdie used as the basis for the building's dimensions? Why?
- Would you want to live in *Habitat*? Explain your answer.
- If you owned Julia Russell's chair, what room would you place it in and how would you use it?

◀ **Julia Russell.** (American). *Leonardo da Vinci Chair.* Twentieth century.
Private Collection.

Aesthetic Perception

Design Awareness Think of a time when you sat in a chair that was too small or too big. Share with the class how it felt to sit in that chair.

Unit 5 • Lesson 5   **173**

Art History and Culture

Julia Russell

Julia Russell (jōōl´ yə rə´ səl) (1949–) creates her painted chairs using layered acrylic washes on gessoed canvas seats. Russell studies the works of the selected artist and carefully plans how to arrange images and elements on the surface of the chair to create a unified composition. She draws in the details before adding paint. These homage paintings combine both function and beauty that pay stylistic tribute to the artist portrayed. To complete her chairs, Russell applies several coats of acrylic medium as a sealant for protection.

See pages 24–25 and 16–21 for more about art history and subject matter.

Artist Profiles, p. 55

Study

- Student responses will vary based on personal experiences. However, many students will say that they believe the chair would be as tall as they are.
- Safdie's buildings look as if they are about six stories high, similar to an apartment building. The alternating boxes and low windows make it difficult to tell the actual height of each apartment. The trees and the street area help in establishing the scale of this building.
- Safdie used the human form as the basis for the building's dimensions because the building will be used by people to live in.
- Each student will answer this question differently based on their personal experiences.
- Each student will answer this question differently based on their personal experiences.
- For more examples of art from North America, see the *Art Around the World Collection*.

Art Journal: Writing

Encourage students to write about what the word *scale* means to them in the Concepts section of their Art Journals. What else do they want to know about realistic scale?

Aesthetic Perception

Design Awareness When designers create furniture for people to use, they think about several things: the size of the person who will use it; its functionality; and the look that is desired. Discuss the sizes and functions of chairs.

Developing Visual Literacy Talk about how both designers and architects have to work with realistic scale to make products that are functional. Have students ever been in a modern building where the exterior looked out of scale, but once they entered, everything seemed to be a normal size?

Web Connection

Visit www.dundee.ac.uk/museum/Design.html for more information about chair design. **Note:** This Web site is for teacher use only.

LESSON 5 • Realistic Scale   **173**

Teach

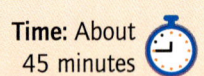

Time: About 45 minutes

"How is realistic scale used in two- and three-dimensional art? How can you use it?"
"¿Cómo se usó la escala realista en arte bi y tridimensional? ¿Cómo se puede usar?"

- Read and discuss using realistic scale on page 174.

Practice

Materials: magazines, Art Journals, pencils, erasers, scissors, rulers

- As an alternative, students can measure each other and their chairs and compare the size differences.
- Distribute the materials and have students follow the directions on page 174.

Creative Expression

Materials: Art Journals, pencils, erasers, rulers, 9" × 12" white drawing paper, color pencils

Alternate Materials: crayons

- Distribute the materials and have students follow the directions on page 175.
- Have students express a variety of ideas in their chair designs based on personal experience.
- Review the Activity Tips on page 244 for visual examples of techniques if needed.

Art Journal: Planning

Have students each generate a list of rooms and places where chairs are used. Then have them collect images and ideas for their chair designs from nature and human-made objects. Have students place their lists, along with their collected images, in their Art Journals. These will be used in the Creative Expression activity.

Using Realistic Scale

Scale, like proportion, is about size relationships. **Scale** refers to size as measured against a standard reference. An average-sized person is a good scale reference. If you saw a professional basketball player standing with other basketball players, he would not look tall. However, if that same person were in a crowd of fans, he would look very tall. With scale, you can compare the size of various objects in relation to objects you know are always a consistent size.

One type of scale is the actual size of an artwork. This is realistic scale. Realistic scale is used in a work of art in which everything fits together and makes sense in relation to size. Often this size relation is based on averages or standards. Objects that people use for daily living are made to scale based on average human proportions. Chairs, tables, buildings, clothing, and dinnerware are just a few examples of objects that are based on realistic scale.

Practice

Look through a magazine to find examples of realistic scale.

1. Collect images of three different people. Cut out the images so that you have removed most of the excess paper from around the people.
2. On a separate sheet of paper, glue the pictures of the three people so that there is a space next to each one.
3. Use a ruler to find the height and width of each person. Write your measurements next to each of your cut-out people. Save your work for the Creative Expression activity.

Differentiated Instruction

Reteach
Have students look for examples of realistic scale around the classroom. Ask them to explain why it is important that these items be in realistic scale.

Special Needs
Cultivate disability awareness in students by including persons with physical disabilities among those for whom furniture is designed. Introduce students to universal design, a process where spaces and places are created to accommodate the largest possible number of people.

ELL
Explain to students the different meanings of *scale*. Have them create sentences using the various meanings.

◀ **Lauren Shaw.**
Age 12.

Think about whether a child or an adult would use this chair.

Creative Expression

How does a designer decide on the size of a piece of furniture? Use images from a magazine to design a chair, using realistic scale.

1. Look at the list of rooms and images in your Art Journal. Select one of the people from the Practice activity as your client.
2. Begin planning a chair for your client. Think about where it will be used and the image you will use for your design. Create several sketches until you make one you like.
3. Use a pencil and a ruler to draw your chair to scale.
4. Use color pencils to add details and to complete your design.

Art Criticism

Describe Who is your chair for? What object did you use as the basis for your design?

Analyze Describe your color scheme. Explain how you used realistic scale.

Interpret Why do you think your client would like your chair?

Decide Were you able to design a chair successfully for a specific person, using realistic scale? Explain.

Unit 5 • Lesson 5   175

Reflect
Time: About 5 minutes

Review and Assess
"How was realistic scale used in this artwork?" "¿Cómo se usó la escala realista en esta obra de arte?"

Think
Both a child and an adult could use the chair created by the student artist, but it was designed for a child and an adult would look awkward sitting in it.

- Use **Large Prints 81** *Self-Portrait* and **82** *Ruckus Rodeo* and ask students to compare how the artists each used realistic scale in their works of art. How are they different? How are they similar? What were the proportions based on for each work? Can students tell whether realistic scale was used?

Informal Assessment
- For standardized-format test practice using this lesson's art content, see pages 62–63 in ***Reading and Writing Test Preparation.***

Art Journal: Critical Thinking
Have students answer the four art criticism questions—Describe, Analyze, Interpret, and Decide—in their Art Journals. Have students discuss within groups how they measured to create realistic scale for their chair designs. Ask individual students to share where the chair will be used, who it was designed for, and what object inspired the design. Have groups share interesting findings with the class.

Art Across the Curriculum

Use these simple ideas to reinforce art concepts across the curriculum.

★ **Persuasive Writing** Have students write a paragraph persuading someone to buy a chair.

★ **Math** Have students estimate what size *Leonardo da Vinci Chair* would have to be for a child.

★ **Science** Have students discuss whether they think it is harder to smile than to frown.

★ **Social Studies** Have students discuss the inventions of Leonardo da Vinci.

★ **Technology** Using a paint or draw program, have students create an apartment building using a geometric shape. Visit **SRAonline.com** to print detailed instructions for this activity.
NSAE 6.b

LESSON 5 • Realistic Scale   **175**

Lesson 5 Wrap-Up: Realistic Scale

Extra! For the Art Specialist
Time: About 45 minutes

Focus
Have students study **Large Print 81** *Self-Portrait* and discuss how realistic scale was used. What in this artwork tells them that realistic scale was used?

Teach
Explain to students that they will make an acrylic painting that pays homage to a selected artist. They will research an artist and study the period and style of the artist, major influences on the artist's work, and famous pieces the artist created. Have students each bring in a used object, such as a drink can, an old vase, or a wooden chair. Explain that they will be using realistic scale in their design.

Reflect
Have students use the four steps of art criticism to evaluate their work. Describe the techniques they used to create realistic scale. What artist and image was used?

Alternate Activity

Materials:
- sketchbooks
- three-dimensional objects
- paint for primer
- pencils, erasers
- towels, water containers
- newspaper
- acrylic paint
- various-sized brushes

1. Have students use two coats of primer as a base coat for their selected objects. Make sure they let the paint dry completely between coats.
2. Have students carefully transfer their designs onto their objects, developing the images or combination of images around each surface of the objects.
3. Once the base coat is dry, have students begin painting their objects by first outlining the shapes with small brushes and filling them with larger brushes.

Research in Art Education
One case study showed that students who were "learning disabled and who were 'reluctant' readers" were better able to engage in reading when the creation and analysis of visual art was incorporated into their discussions of stories. This suggests that combining visual art with reading may help certain readers ("Reading *Is* Seeing: Using Visual Response to Improve the Literary Reading of Reluctant Readers" in *Critical Links,* p. 144).

Assessment
Use the following rubric to evaluate the artwork students make in the Creative Expression activity and to assess students' understanding of how realistic scale is used in three-dimensional works of art.

	Art History and Culture	Aesthetic Perception	Creative Expression	Art Criticism
3 POINTS	The student demonstrates knowledge of the lives and work of Safdie and Russell.	The student accurately identifies the use of realistic scale in three-dimensional works of art.	The student's chair design demonstrates how to use realistic scale.	The student thoughtfully and honestly evaluates own work using the four steps of art criticism.
2 POINTS	The student's knowledge of the lives and work of Safdie and Russell is weak or incomplete.	The student shows an emerging awareness of realistic scale in three-dimensional works of art but cannot consistently identify it.	The student's chair design shows some awareness of how to use realistic scale.	The student attempts to evaluate own work but shows an incomplete understanding of evaluation criteria.
1 POINT	The student cannot demonstrate knowledge of the lives and work of Safdie or Russell.	The student cannot identify how realistic scale is used in an artwork.	The student's chair design shows no understanding of how to use realistic scale.	The student makes no attempt to evaluate own work.

Have students complete page 65 or 66 in their *Assessment* books.

175A UNIT 5 • Proportion, Distortion, and Scale

Lesson 6 Overview: Unrealistic Scale

Lesson 6 takes a closer look at scale and how unrealistic scale is used. **Unrealistic scale** is used when an artist makes size relationships that do not make sense.

Objectives

Art History and Culture
To demonstrate knowledge of the lives and work of Pablo Picasso and Salvador Dalí

Creative Expression
To create a surrealistic landscape collage showing unrealistic scale

Aesthetic Perception
To identify and better understand how unrealistic scale is used in both two- and three-dimensional works of art

Art Criticism
To evaluate own work using the four steps of art criticism

Lesson Materials
- Art Journals
- pencils, erasers
- *Art Connections* textbooks
- *Large Prints*, magazines
- masking tape
- ruler or yardsticks
- 9" × 12" or 12" × 18" tagboard
- scissors, glue
- oil pastels
- fine-line markers

Alternate Materials
- construction paper
- crayons

Program Resources
- *Reading and Writing Test Prep.*, pp. 64–65
- *Transparency* 30
- *Flash Card* 19
- *Artist Profiles*, pp. 19, 48
- *Animals Through History Time Line*
- *Assessment*, pp. 67–68
- *Large Prints 81 Self-Portrait* and *82 Ruckus Rodeo*
- *Art Around the World Collection*

Concept Trace
Unrealistic Scale
Introduced: Level 5, Unit 4, Lesson 2
Reinforced: Level 7, Chapter 5, Lesson 4

Vocabulary

Review the following vocabulary word with students before beginning the lesson.

surrealism surrealismo—an art movement that emphasized art in which dreams, fantasy, and the subconscious served as inspiration for artists

See page 179B for additional vocabulary and Spanish Vocabulary resources.

Art Journal: Vocabulary
Have students add this word to the Vocabulary section of their Art Journals.

Lesson 6 Arts Integration

Theatre
Complete Unit 5, Lesson 6, on pages 100–101 of *Theatre Arts Connections*.

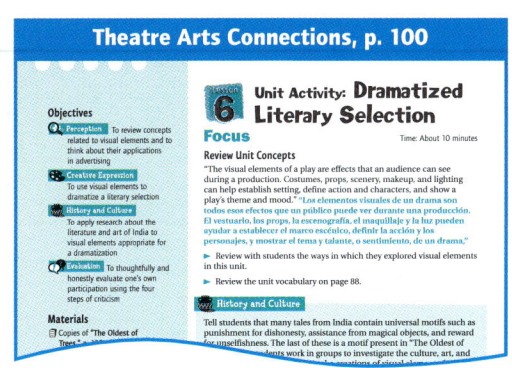

Music
Like surrealist art, contemporary music can have sounds, melodies, and rhythms placed in surprising places. Listen to *The Firebird* by Igor Stravinsky. Stravinsky was known for breaking rules of form and melody. He used forceful, exotic rhythms and juxtaposed short fragments of melody upon one another.

Movement & Dance
Have students imagine that they have to create a dance piece based on the story, *Alice in Wonderland*. In parts of the story, Alice grows larger or smaller. In the live performance, how would they solve this problem? What would Alice do in her movements to suggest her change in size? What could be done with sets or costumes?

LESSON 6 • Unrealistic Scale 175B

Focus

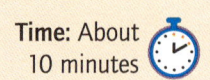

Time: About 10 minutes

Activate Prior Knowledge

"Have you ever seen an object that caught your attention because it was larger or smaller than normal?" "¿Han visto algún objeto que tomó su atención porque era más grande o pequeño que lo normal?"

- Discuss students' responses. Explain that some artists will get ideas from dreams, a story, or just by looking at an object and imagining it in unrealistic scale.

Using Literature ⭐ Reading

- Read the poem "One Inch Tall" in the book *Where the Sidewalk Ends* by Shel Silverstein. Discuss how the poem lends itself to imagining unrealistic scale.

Thematic Connection ⭐ Social Studies

- **Taking a Stand:** Have students describe times they stood up for someone or something they believed in, even though other people did not agree with them. Explain to students that many artists believe it is important to be true to their art and not give in to popular opinion.

Introduce the Art

Look

Why do these images not look real? "¿Por qué estos imágenes no lucen real?"

Asking Questions ⭐ Science

- Have students create a list of questions that they have about these works of art. **Possible questions:** Is *Chicago Picasso* an animal? Is that a beach in *Persistence of Memory*? Why are the clocks melting?

🏺 Art History and Culture

In *Persistence of Memory*, the cliffs and water in the background could possibly be the coast of Spain where Dalí's family had a summer home. Other works by Dalí and Picasso depict images of Spain, but not necessarily the ones in this lesson.

💻 Web Connection

Visit www.salvadordalimuseum.org/ for more information about Salvador Dalí. **Note:** This Web site is for teacher use only.

176 UNIT 5 • Proportion, Distortion, and Scale

Lesson 6: Unrealistic Scale

▲ **Salvador Dalí.** (Spanish). *Persistence of Memory.* 1931.

Oil on canvas. 9½ × 13 inches (24.13 × 33.02 cm.). The Museum of Modern Art, New York, New York.

Look at the works of art on these pages to learn more about scale. Pablo Picasso was asked by Chicago architect William Hartmann to produce a monumental sculpture to be placed in front of the Civic Center. Picasso, who never visited Chicago or the United States, gave his work as a gift to the people of Chicago. His sculpture came to be called the *Chicago Picasso*. Salvador Dalí painted the dreamlike images of *Persistence of Memory* during the peak of surrealism. Surrealism emphasized art in which dreams, fantasy, and the subconscious served as inspiration for artists. Dalí's images were painted in a precise, realistic manner and include commonplace objects. He distorted the objects so they do not look real. Notice how he placed unrelated objects together. The landscape contains strange objects that do not seem to belong there and appear to be made of unexpected materials.

🏺 Art History and Culture

Both Dalí and Picasso were born in Spain. Do either of their works of art remind you of Spain or of something Spanish?

176 Unit 5 • Lesson 6

🏺 Art History and Culture

Salvador Dalí

Early recognition of Salvador Dalí's (sal´ və dor dä´ lē) (1904–1989) talent came with his first one-man show in Barcelona in 1925. Dalí joined the surrealists and soon became a leader of the surrealist movement. His painting *Persistence of Memory* is still one of the best-known surrealist works. As an artist, Dalí was not limited to a particular style or medium. The body of his work from early impressionist paintings through his transitional surrealist works, and into his classical period, reveals an evolving artist. Dalí worked in all media, including oils, watercolors, drawings, graphics, sculptures, and jewelry.

See pages 24–25 and 16–21 for more about art history and subject matter.

Artist Profiles, p. 19

Artist Profile
Salvador Dalí
1904–1989

Salvador Dalí (sal´ və dor dä´ lē´) was born in Spain and grew up in a prosperous family. During his childhood he spent summers in a small coastal village in Spain, where his parents built his first studio, and many of his paintings portray his love of that area. Dalí earned fame and recognition early in his career with exhibitions in both Europe and the United States, and he continued to receive attention throughout his career, which spanned many styles and artistic experiments. Dalí was a surrealist, and he considered his paintings to be "dream photographs." He explored many different techniques and materials which influenced the surrealist movement everywhere. He moved to America and then Spain, where he...

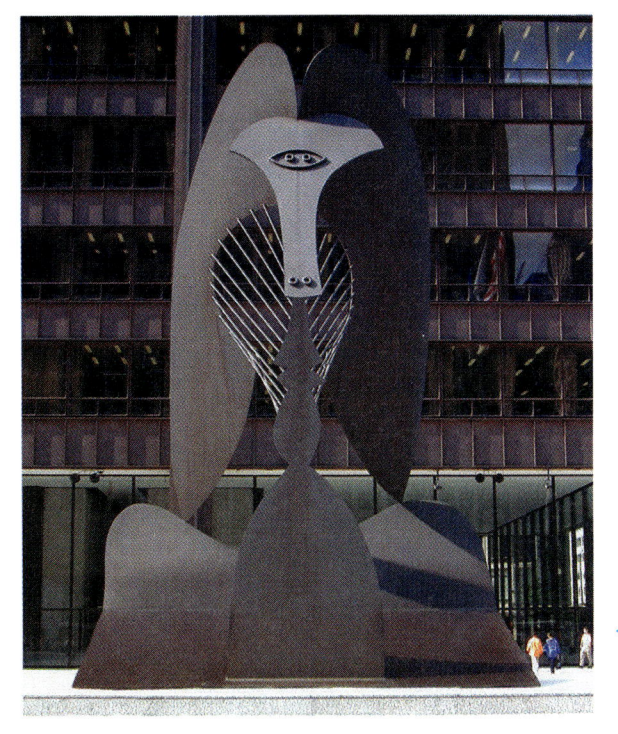

◀ **Pablo Picasso.** (Spanish).
Chicago Picasso. 1967.
Steel. 50 feet tall (15.24 meters).
Civic Center Plaza, Chicago, Illinois.

Study the two works of art to learn how unrealistic scale is used.
▶ Describe the unusual objects in *Persistence of Memory*.
▶ What is unusual about the size of the objects in *Persistence of Memory*?
▶ Would the *Chicago Picasso* have the same effect if it were a tabletop sculpture? Why?
▶ How do you think it would feel to walk under the *Chicago Picasso*?
▶ What would it be like to walk into Dalí's painting? What sounds might you hear? What do you think the clocks would feel like if you could touch them?

Aesthetic Perception

Design Awareness Imagine that you are only six inches tall. How would the objects around you look?

Unit 5 • Lesson 6   **177**

Study

▶ A portion of a face is on the ground. It looks like a tongue is coming out of the nose. A clock lies limply over the edge of the face. On the left side of the painting is a tree on an angled edge of land with a melted clock on the edge. A pocket watch is covered with ants. A portion of a small tree stands with another melted clock hanging on to its single limb.

▶ The clocks are larger than the tree and in proportion to the size of the face.

▶ Student answers will vary; however, some will say no. The effect it has on the viewer is a result of its large size.

▶ Each student will answer this question differently based on their personal experiences.

▶ Each student will answer this question differently based on their personal experiences.

■ For more examples of art from Europe, see the **Art Around the World Collection.**

Art Journal: Writing
Encourage students to write what the word *unrealistic* means to them in the Concepts section of their Art Journals. What else do they want to know about unrealistic scale?

Aesthetic Perception

Design Awareness Discuss how many movies, comics, stories, and works of art have developed from the concept of being smaller or larger than normal. Ask the students if they can give examples of how unrealistic scale has been used.

Developing Visual Literacy Talk about the use of realistic objects that have been altered in size relative to other objects or the surrounding area. Explain that when items are created using unrealistic scale, they produce a dreamlike quality. Ask students if they have ever seen a sculpture that was designed using unrealistic scale.

Web Connection
Visit **www.tamu.edu/mocl/picasso/** for more information about Pablo Picasso.

LESSON 6 • Unrealistic Scale   **177**

Art History and Culture

Pablo Picasso
About four years before the unveiling of *Chicago Picasso*, Chicago architect William Hartmann approached Pablo Picasso (pä´ blō pi kä´ sō) (1881–1973) with an invitation to produce a model for a monumental sculpture that would be erected in the Civic Center. Created from Picasso's 42-inch steel model, the completed *Chicago Picasso* is 50 feet high and weighs 162 tons. The sculpture is made from the same type of steel as the exterior of the Civic Center building, and it will gradually develop a similar patina. Picasso refused a fee for his work but preferred to give the design and the model as a "gift to the people of Chicago." *Chicago Picasso* was unveiled in the Civic Center Plaza on August 15, 1967.

See pages 24–25 and 16–21 for more about art history and subject matter.

Artist Profiles, p. 48

Artist Profile
Pablo Picasso
1881–1973
Pablo Picasso (pä´ blō pi kä´ sō) was born in Málaga, Spain. He did poorly in school but his father, an art teacher, taught him to draw and paint. Picasso learned quickly. When he was only 14 he had a painting accepted for an exhibition. Picasso moved to Paris, France when he was 18. At the time he was very poor. Thieves stole what little he had, yet they left his now valuable drawings. In time the outgoing Picasso made many friends. Among them were the American writers Ernest Hemingway and Gertrude Stein and the Russian composer Igor Stravinsky. Picasso painted at night and slept late most mornings. He worked hard his entire life. He completed 200 paintings

Teach

Time: About 45 minutes

"How will you use unrealistic scale in your landscape?" "¿Cómo usarían una escala irreal en su paisaje?"

- Read and discuss using unrealistic scale on page 178.

Practice

Materials: *Art Connections* textbooks, *Large Prints*, rulers or yardsticks, masking tape

- Distribute the materials and have students follow the directions on page 178.

Creative Expression

Materials: Art Journals, 9" × 12" or 12" × 18" tagboard, magazines, scissors, glue, oil pastels, fine-line markers

Alternate materials: construction paper, crayons

- Distribute the materials and have students follow the directions on page 179.
- Review the Activity Tips on page 244 for visual examples of techniques if needed.

Art Journal: Researching

Ask students to look through magazines and collect images of human-made objects that might be interesting to use in a surrealism design. Have them place their collected images, along with any notes they may have taken, in the Research section of their Art Journals. These items will be used in the Creative Expression activity.

Using Unrealistic Scale

One type of scale is the actual size of an object or artwork in relation to human scale. When a person stands next to an artwork you can see the difference in scale. A second type of scale is the size relationship of the objects or elements within a design. Sometimes the objects or elements relate to one another based on realistic scale, for example, the size of the furniture in relation to the people in an artwork. At other times, the objects or elements relate to one another based on unrealistic scale.

Unrealistic scale is used when an artist makes size relationships that do not make sense. For example, making a small object, such as a button, larger than the hand holding it creates unrealistic scale. Artists use unrealistic scale in both two- and three-dimensional artwork. Variation in scale within an artwork can change the work's total impact. When unrealistic scale is used, it creates dreamlike or fantasy qualities in the work. The effect often captures the viewer's attention because it is so different from what is normally seen.

Practice

Look for examples of unrealistic scale.

1. Work in groups of three or four. Look through your textbook and the *Large Prints* for examples of unrealistic scale. Unrealistic scale can be either smaller or larger than normal.
2. Read the measurements in the credit lines. Select the dimensions of one of the works of art and measure that area on a table, a wall, or the floor. Use tape to show the dimensions.
3. Share your measurements with the class.

178 Unit 5 • Lesson 6

Differentiated Instruction

Reteach
Have students think about times when they were younger and encountered unrealistic scale from their point of view.

Special Needs
As an extension to this activity, students could create a shadowbox that uses unrealistic scale in the juxtaposition of objects.

ELL
Have students look at the works of art in this lesson and explain what does not make sense to them. Help them identify any of their answers that relate to unrealistic scale.

---

178 UNIT 5 • Proportion, Distortion, and Scale

◄ Eric Flynn.
Age 11.

Think about how the student artist used unrealistic scale in this collage.

Creative Expression

Create a surrealistic collage, showing unrealistic scale.
1. Begin by sketching several designs. Select your best one. Look at the collected cutouts in your Art Journal and place them on the table. Select three of the images to use in your collage.
2. Look through magazines to find at least four examples of natural elements, such as trees and rocks. Cut these out.
3. Lightly transfer your sketch onto paper. Combine your collected images to create a surreal collage.
4. Use oil pastels to add color and complete your work.

Art Criticism

Describe What images did you use?
Analyze Describe how you used unrealistic scale.
Interpret How does your use of unrealistic scale affect the mood of your work? Explain.
Decide Were you successful in creating a collage, using unrealistic scale? Explain.

Unit 5 • Lesson 6   179

Art Across the Curriculum

Use these simple ideas to reinforce art concepts across the curriculum.

★ **Poetry Writing** Have students write a poem about time.

★ **Math** Explain to students that time can be divided into smaller increments than seconds.

★ **Science** Explain to students that inside an electric clock there is a motor that turns gears.

★ **Social Studies** Have students discuss what they know about Spain.

★ **Technology** Using a word-processing program, have students create a surrealistic scene with clip art. Visit **SRAonline.com** to print detailed instructions for this activity.
NSAE 6.b

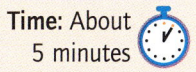

Reflect
Time: About 5 minutes

Review and Assess
"What impact does the artists' use of scale have on the artwork?" "¿Qué impacto tiene el uso de escala por un artista en la obra de arte?"

Think
The artist created unrealistic scale by placing a close-up photograph of a woman in the background and full-body images of children in the foreground, who look like they are climbing on the woman's face.

■ Use **Large Prints 81** *Self-Portrait* and **82** *Ruckus Rodeo* and ask students to compare how the artists used unrealistic scale in their works of art. How are they different? How are they similar? What objects are not in realistic scale in each work?

Informal Assessment

■ Have students evaluate their portfolios. Have them exchange portfolios with classmates, so they can form conclusions about properties. NSAE 6.a

■ For standardized-format test practice using this lesson's art content, see pages 64–65 in *Reading and Writing Test Preparation.*

Art Journal: Critical Thinking
Have students answer the four art criticism question—Describe, Analyze, Interpret, and Decide—in their Art Journals. Have students discuss within groups how they created their collaged surreal landscapes. What areas have unrealistic scale? How does this affect the works? Ask students to discuss the similarities and differences of their works of art and share them with the class.

LESSON 6 • Unrealistic Scale   179

Lesson 6 Wrap-Up: Unrealistic Scale

Extra! For the Art Specialist
Time: About 45 minutes

Focus
Have students study *Large Print 82 Ruckus Rodeo* and discuss how unrealistic scale was used. What objects are not in realistic scale in this artwork?

Teach
Explain to students that they will create surrealist drawings, using oil pastels. Discuss the surrealists with students and how they created dreamlike images. Explain that one way this was achieved was by combining unrelated objects or using unrealistic scale in works of art that were realistically rendered. Then have students complete the Alternate Activity.

Reflect
Have students use the four steps of art criticism to evaluate their work. Have them describe the images used to create their surrealist drawing. Where was unrealistic scale used?

Alternate Activity

Materials:
- sketchbooks, magazines
- pencils, erasers
- bag for cut images
- 12" × 18" drawing paper (any color)
- oil pastels

1. Ask each student to find in a magazine three to five images that they think would work well for a surrealist drawing. Explain that they should be commonplace objects.
2. Place the cut images in a bag and ask students to draw three images from the bag.
3. Ask students to use the three images to create several compositions in their sketchbooks. Make sure they use unrealistic scale by making some objects larger and others smaller than normal.
4. Have students select their best images and transfer and complete it on drawing paper, using oil pastels.

Research in Art Education

The subjects upon which schools typically focus give only students with "logical-mathematical and linguistic intelligences" an opportunity to excel. One benefit of arts curricula is that they offer "many approaches to subject matter; therefore, they provide better learning opportunities for low-achieving and 'problem' students" ("The Fourth R: The Arts and Learning" in *Schools, Communities, and the Arts: A Research Compendium*).

Assessment

Use the following rubric to evaluate the artwork students make in the Creative Expression activity and to assess students' understanding of how unrealistic scale is used in two- and three-dimensional works of art.

	Art History and Culture	Aesthetic Perception	Creative Expression	Art Criticism
3 POINTS	The student demonstrates knowledge of the lives and work of Picasso and Dalí.	The student accurately identifies the use of unrealistic scale in a variety of works of art.	The student's surreal landscape collage demonstrates how to use unrealistic scale.	The student thoughtfully and honestly evaluates own work using the four steps of art criticism.
2 POINTS	The student's knowledge of the lives and work of Picasso and Dalí is weak or incomplete.	The student shows an emerging awareness of unrealistic scale in a variety of works of art but cannot consistently identify it.	The student's surreal landscape collage shows some awareness of how to use unrealistic scale.	The student attempts to evaluate own work but shows an incomplete understanding of evaluation criteria.
1 POINT	The student cannot demonstrate knowledge of the lives and work of Picasso or Dalí.	The student cannot identify how unrealistic scale is used in an artwork.	The student's surreal landscape collage shows no understanding of how to use unrealistic scale.	The student makes no attempt to evaluate own work.

Have students complete page 67 or 68 in their *Assessment* books.

Unit 5 Vocabulary Review

body proportion—the size relationship of one part of the body to another **proporción corporal**—la relación de tamaño de una parte del cuerpo a la otra.

central axis—a real or imaginary line that is down the center of an object **eje central**—una línea imaginaria o real que está en el centro de un objeto.

distortion—a deviation from normal or expected proportions **distorsión**—una desviación de proporciones normales o esperadas

elongate—to stretch out or to make long **alargar**—extender o hacer más largo

exaggeration—an increase or enlargement beyond what is expected or normal **exageración**—un aumento más de lo esperado o normal

facial proportions—the relationship of one feature of a face to other features **proporciones faciales**—la relación de un rasgo de la cara a otros rasgos

portrait—a two- or three-dimensional artwork created in the image of a person or animal **retrato**—obra de arte bi o tridimensional creada en la imagen de una persona o animal

profile—a side view of a person or animal **perfil**—una vista lateral de una persona o animal

proportion—the principle of art that is concerned with the size relationship of one part to another **proporción**—el principio artístico que se interesa con la relación de tamaño de una parte a la otra

self-portrait—a two- or three-dimensional artwork that an artist makes of him- or herself **autorretrato**—una obra de arte bi o tridimensional que un artista hace de sí mismo

realistic scale—is used in a work of art in which everything fits together and makes sense in size relation **escala realista**—es usado en una obra de arte en que todo se adapta junto y tiene sentido en relación a tamaño

scale—size as measured against a standard reference **escala**—tamaño comparado contra una referencia normal

score—the repeated scratching of a clay surface at the area that another scored piece will be attached **muesca**—rascar repetidamente a una superficie de arcilla en el área que otra pieza rayada será atada

slip—a mixture of clay and water that is creamy to the touch and is used to attach two scored pieces of clay together **barbotina**—una mezcla de arcilla y agua que es cremosa al toque y se usa para atar juntas dos piezas de arcilla con muescas

surrealism—an art movement that emphasized art in which dreams, fantasy, and the subconscious served as inspiration for artists **surrealismo**—un movimiento artístico que da énfasis al arte en que sueños, fantasía y la subconciencia sirve como inspiracion para los artistas

unrealistic scale—relationships that do not make sense **escala irreal**—relaciones que no tienen sentido

Vocabulary Practice

T Display *Transparency 41* to review unit vocabulary words.

Dictionary Entries ⭐ Vocabulary
Have students look up the definition of *scale* in a dictionary. Is the dictionary definition similar to the definition in their textbooks? Have students explain their answers.

Demonstrate Meanings ⭐ Vocabulary
Display *Large Print 82 Ruckus Rodeo*. Have volunteers select a vocabulary word such as *proportion* and explain how it is shown in the artwork.

Antonyms and Synonyms ⭐ Vocabulary
Have students create a list of antonyms and synonyms for the word *distortion*. Have students refer to a thesaurus, if necessary. Repeat the process for other unit vocabulary words.

Wrapping Up Unit 5
Proportion, Distortion, and Scale

Art Criticism

Critical Thinking Art criticism is an organized system for looking at and talking about art. You can criticize art without being an expert. The purpose of art criticism is to get the viewer involved in a perception process that delays judgment until all aspects of the artwork have been studied. Push the students to expand beyond the art criticism questions.

- See pages 28–29 for more about art criticism.

Describe

- Ginevra's skin is pale and smooth. Her eyelids are half closed. Her eyes are staring straight ahead. She is not smiling, and her lips are straight. Her brown hair frames her face in ringlets. She is most likely wearing a brown dress. A gold embroidered ribbon decorates the top edge of the dress, and a black sash hangs around her neck.
- Directly behind her head is a juniper bush. On the right side of the painting we see a landscape with two church spires and a body of water in the distance.

Analyze

- The proportions are accurate. Students may feel that something is wrong because Ginevra's forehead is so high. In that period noble ladies plucked their hair to create a higher forehead because it was thought to be a sign of intelligence.
- The eyes are placed halfway between the top of the head and the chin on a central horizontal axis. The bottom edge of the nose is halfway between the chin and the eyes. The center line of the lips is closer to the nose than the chin.
- The juniper bush needles are the correct size in relationship to her head, which is in realistic scale. The landscape is small in scale in relation to her head. The church spires are smaller than her nose.

Wrapping Up Unit 5
Proportion, Distortion, and Scale

▲ **Leonardo da Vinci.** (Italian). *Ginevra de' Benci.* c. 1474.
Oil on canvas. $16\frac{1}{2} \times 14\frac{9}{16}$ inches (42.7 × 36.98 cm.). National Gallery of Art, Washington, D.C.

Art History and Culture

Leonardo da Vinci

Leonardo da Vinci (lē ə när´ dō də vin´ chē) (1452–1519) is considered one of the greatest artists and scientists of all times. He was proficient in just about everything intellectual and cultural. Da Vinci was constantly experimenting with new media and although he had many ideas, he did not complete many of his works. He is still considered a genius even by today's standards. The *Ginevra de' Benci* is the only certified da Vinci work in the United States. It is the first psychological portrait ever painted, and *Mona Lisa* was the second.

See pages 24–25 and 16–21 for more information about art history and subject matter.

Artist Profiles, p. 20

Art Criticism — Critical Thinking

Describe What do you see?
During this step you will collect information about the subject of the work.
- Describe the woman, including her clothing, her hair, and the features of her face.
- What do you see behind Ginevra?

Analyze How is this work organized?
Think about how the artist used the elements and principles of art.
- Did Leonardo da Vinci use realistic proportions or distortion?
- Measure the face and describe how da Vinci used facial proportions.
- Describe the scale of the background in relation to Ginevra.

Interpret What does the artwork say?
Combine clues you collected during your description and analysis with your personal experiences to find out what this painting is about.
- What is unusual about Ginevra's eyes and mouth?
- What feelings does her face express?
- How does da Vinci's use of proportion affect the expressive quality of the painting?
- If Leonardo da Vinci were alive today, whose portrait do you think he would choose to paint? Why?

Decide What do you think about the work?
Use all the information you have gathered to decide why this is a successful work of art.
- Is this work successful because it is realistic, because it is well organized, or because it conveys a message?

Unit 5 **181**

Interpret

- Her eyes have no shadows. The dark brown color of her irises is the darkest area on her face. Her mouth is closed and looks relaxed, almost pouty, with a slight downward turn of the lower lip.
- Answers may vary. Some will say she looks sad, some that she looks serious, others that she looks stern, and some that she looks thoughtful. This is the first psychological portrait ever painted.
- The use of realistic proportion gives the painting a formal or serious quality. It shows that the artist cared about the person.
- Student answers will vary. No one answer is correct, but make sure that students' explanations are reasonable.

Decide

- Students' answers will vary based on individual experiences. They may use more than one aesthetic theory to explain the success of this work.

Art Journal: Writing
Have students write answers to Aesthetic Perception in their Art Journals. Have them discuss their answers in small groups.

Aesthetic Perception

Seeing Like an Artist Ask students to think about some photographs that have been taken of them. Then have students compare these photographs to *Ginevra de' Benci*.

Describe
- Describe one photo you like and one you do not like.

Analyze
- Is everything in proportion in the photograph you like?
- Is anything distorted in the photograph you do not like?

Interpret
- What feelings are created by the proportion or distortion in the photographs? Why?

Decide
- If you could retake the photographs, what would you change?

UNIT 5 • Proportion, Distortion, and Scale **181**

"Artists use proportion, distortion, and scale in two- and three-dimensional works of art."
"Los artistas usan proporción, distorsión y escala en obras de arte bi y tridimensional."

T Review unit vocabulary with students, using **Transparency 41**.

Art Journal: Writing
Have students answer the questions on page 182 in their Art Journals or on a separate sheet of paper. **Answers: 1. A, 2. B, 3. A, 4. C, 5. B**

T For further assessment, have students complete the unit test on **Transparency 47**.

CAREERS IN ART
Graphic Design

▶ Ask students if they know anyone who is a graphic designer. Have them explain the type of work the person performs, if possible.

▶ Have students create a list of font names, such as *Impact*, *Comic Sans*, and *Times New Roman*. Ask them what feelings or moods they associate with these fonts. Remind students that every font they encounter took a graphic designer a considerable amount of time to create.

"Learn diligence before speedy execution."
        —Leonardo da Vinci

182 UNIT 5 • Proportion, Distortion, and Scale

Wrapping Up Unit 5
Proportion, Distortion, and Scale, continued

Show What You Know
Answer these questions on a separate sheet of paper.

1. A _____ is a comparison of size between two things.
   A. ratio
   B. scale
   C. scheme

2. _____ is an increase or enlargement beyond what is expected or normal.
   A. Proportion
   B. Exaggeration
   C. Elaboration

3. The principle of art concerned with the size relationship of one part to another is called _____.
   A. proportion
   B. distortion
   C. scale

4. _____ refers to size as measured against a standard reference.
   A. The central axis
   B. Ratio
   C. Scale

5. _____ is a deviation from normal or expected proportions.
   A. Realistic scale
   B. Distortion
   C. Variation

182 Unit 5

Unit Assessment Options

Aesthetic Perception
Practice Have students select one of the concepts in the Show What You Know section on page 182, then find examples of each concept in the classroom.

Creative Expression
Student Portfolio Have students review the artwork they have created during this unit and select the pieces they wish to keep in their portfolios.

Art Criticism
Activity Have students select an artwork from this unit and study it, using the four steps of art criticism. (See pages 28–29 for more information about art criticism.) Have students work in small groups and present their findings aloud or in writing.

CAREERS IN ART
Graphic Design

Graphic designers create a pleasing layout with text and graphics. They use a variety of print, electronic, and film media.

Book designers are responsible for designing the outsides and insides of books. A book designer wants the outside of a book to be as unique as it possibly can be, and the focus is usually on color. On the inside, the book is designed to be well organized and easy for the reader to follow.

Font designers usually study and practice for about seven years before they are established. Their skill is acquired through study of the visual forms and practice in making them. Most font designers work individually. Designing a font can take several months to several years. A *font* is a complete set of letters, numbers, and symbols, all of the same style.

Packaging designers have the job of making the outside of a product grab the buyer's attention. They do this by combining colors, graphics, unique shapes, and any other eye-catching designs they think will help sell the product.

▲ Book designer

Proportion and Distortion in Theatre

By wearing different masks, Robert Faust can make himself into many characters. He surprises everyone with his odd postures and the strange features of his masks. He alters the proportion of his human form by making some masks huge and some very small. He also exaggerates the shapes of noses, eyes, and mouths.

What to Do Create a character by exaggerating the way they walk.

A character can be defined by exaggerating the way they walk. You can change the size of the steps, give the walk a rhythm, and alter the speed. Posture also affects the way one walks Also, the emotion of the character is important.

1. Try walking in various exaggerated ways. Take very large steps, then tiny ones. Walk slowly, then quickly. Walk in a stiff, then loose, way. Walk as if you were curious about everything, then disinterested.
2. Think of a character you would like to show. Explore how this character might walk. Exaggerate the movement so that it clearly shows the posture, attitude, emotion, and size of the character.
3. Share your character and walk with a partner or small group. Discuss the traits of each character.

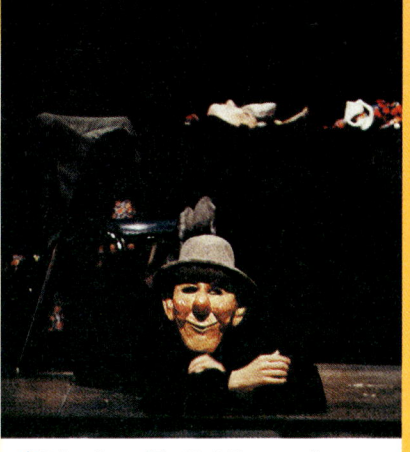

▲ Robert Faust. "The Mask Messenger."

Art Criticism

Describe Describe the character you created.

Analyze How did you exaggerate the walk to clearly show the traits of your character?

Interpret How did it feel to walk as your character?

Decide Were you successful in creating a character and a walk that communicated his/her traits?

Art History and Culture

Masks

In many cultures throughout the world, masks are worn at festivals, celebrations, and rituals. The use of masks evolved from religious practices in ancient Greece. The first masks were used to imitate a god and were simple. As ceremonies became more theatrical, the masks became more elaborate. The traditional masks depicting tragedy and comedy are derived from Greek theatrical traditions. Robert Faust draws on these ancient traditions in creating contemporary masks.

Proportion and Distortion in Dance

Objective: To create a character and a walk that shows the traits of a character

Materials: *The Mask Messenger* performed by Robert Faust. Running time: 4:40

Focus
Time: About 5 minutes

- Discuss the information on page 183.

Art History and Culture

- Have students think of historical figures who had unique physical traits.

Teach
Time: About 20 minutes

Aesthetic Perception

- Have students walk around the classroom and study how other students walk.

Creative Expression

- Have students vary their walks, such as length of strides, tempo, rhythm, energy, weight, attitude, and emotion.

- **Informal Assessment** When students demonstrate their walks, comment positively on how the walks match the characters they created.

Reflect
Time: About 10 minutes

Art Criticism

- Have students answer the four art criticism questions on page 183 aloud or in writing.

- Were students able to successfully create a character and a walk?

Unit 6 Planning Guide

	Lesson Title	Suggested Pacing	Creative Expression Activity
Lesson 1	Variety Through Line, Shape, and Color	1 hour	Make a collage.
Lesson 2	Variety Through Contrast	1 hour	Hand color a photograph.
Lesson 3	Harmony in Two-Dimensional Art	1 hour	Design a harmonious embroidery.
Lesson 4	Harmony in Three-Dimensional Art	1 hour	Create a group assemblage.
Lesson 5	Unity in Weaving	1 hour	Make a cardboard-loom weaving.
Lesson 6	Unity in Three-Dimensional Art	1 hour	Create a human-like sculpture.
ARTSOURCE	Variety, Harmony, and Unity in Animation	35 minutes	Create a storyboard.

184A UNIT 6 • Variety, Harmony, and Unity

Materials	Program Resources	Fine Art Resources	Literature Resources
Art Journals, pencils, erasers, 9" × 12" or larger construction paper, $4\frac{1}{2}$" × 6" construction paper, scissors, glue, fine-tip black markers, newspaper	*Assessment,* pp. 69-70 *Reading and Writing Test Preparation,* pp. 66-67 *Home and After-School Connections* *Flash Card* 18	*Transparency 31* *Artist Profiles,* pp. 7, 13 *Large Prints 83* and *84* *Art Around the World Collection*	*The Circuit* by Francisco Jimenez
Art Journals, pencils, erasers, 35-mm camera, black-and-white film, color pencils, water-based color markers, watercolor paints, small paintbrushes, cotton swabs, water containers, newspaper	*Assessment,* pp. 71-72 *Reading and Writing Test Preparation,* pp. 68-69 *Flash Card* 16, 18	*Transparency 32* *Artist Profiles,* pp. 11, 50 *Large Prints 83* and *84* *The National Museum of Women in the Arts Collection*	*Troubling a Star* by Madeleine L'Engle
Art Journals, pencils, burlap, light-colored chalk, yarn in various colors, scissors, tapestry needles	*Assessment,* pp. 73-74 *Reading and Writing Test Preparation,* pp. 70-71 *Flash Card* 17-18	*Transparency 33* *Artist Profile,* pp. 28, 82 *Large Prints 83* and *84* *Art Around the World Collection*	*A Bone from a Dry Sea* by Peter Dickinson
flat open boxes of a consistent size, a variety of collected cardboard and plastic recycled items, craft glue, acrylic paint	*Assessment,* pp. 75-76 *Reading and Writing Test Preparation,* pp. 72-73	*Transparency 34* *Artist Profiles,* pp. 23, 44 *Large Prints 83* and *84* *The National Museum of Women in the Arts Collection*	*Body Parts in Rebellion* by Regan Dunnick
Art Journals, pencils, yarn of various colors, ruler, cardboard box, heavy string, tapestry needle, scissors	*Assessment,* pp. 77-78 *Reading and Writing Test Preparation,* pp. 74-75	*Transparency 35* *Artist Profiles,* pp. 34, 72 *Large Prints 83* and *84* *The National Museum of Women in the Arts Collection*	*The Monkey Thief* by Aileen Kilgore Henderson
wire, heavy string, tacky craft glue, pliers, scissors, screw drivers, wire clippers, packaging, electrical or duct tape, student/teacher collected machine/technology parts	*Assessment,* pp. 79-80 *Reading and Writing Test Preparation,* pp. 76-77	*Transparency 36* *Artist Profiles,* pp. 37, 46 *Large Prints 83* and *84* *Art Around the World Collection*	*A Wrinkle in Time* by Madeleine L'Engle
Every Picture Tells a Story and *Full Fathoms Five, Turbo Power, Spirit of the Landscape,* paper, pencils, markers			

UNIT 6 • Variety, Harmony, and Unity **184B**

Unit Overview

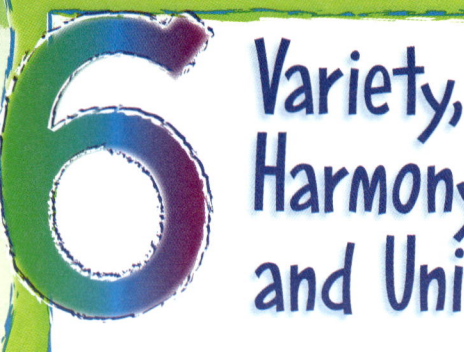

6 Variety, Harmony, and Unity

Lesson 1: Variety is the principle of art that relates to differences or contrasts.

Lesson 2: Variety can be created through contrast of value.

Lesson 3: Harmony is the principle of art that creates unity by stressing similarities of separate but related parts.

Lesson 4: The art principle of **harmony** can be used in three-dimensional sculptures.

Lesson 5: Unity is the oneness that is achieved by properly using the elements and principles of art.

Lesson 6: The art principle of **unity** in three-dimensional forms is explored.

Introduce Unit Concepts

"Artists use the art principles of variety, harmony, and unity to help organize the art elements in works of art." "Los artistas usan los principios artísticos de variedad, armonía y unidad para organizar los elementos artísticos en obras de arte bi y tridimensionales."

Variety and Harmony
- Have students look around the room to find examples of what *variety* means to them.
- Have students think about harmony as it relates to music. Harmony refers to different pitches played or sung together to create a melodic sound.

Unity
- Have students explain what a *unit* is. Have students come up with phrases in which the word *unity* is used.

Cross-Curricular Projects
- See the *Language Arts and Reading, Mathematics, Science,* and *Social Studies Art Connections* books for activities that further develop the concepts of variety, harmony, and unity.

184 UNIT 6 • Variety, Harmony, and Unity

Unit 6

Variety, Harmony, and Unity

Variety, harmony, and unity are used by artists to arrange the art elements in both two- and three-dimensional art.

Paul Gauguin is best known in the art world as a rebel. He used color and shape to create unconventional works of far-off lands and primitive life. He traveled often and settled on the tropical island of Tahiti, where he produced his most famous works. Notice how Gauguin used color to express emotion in *The Brooding Woman*.

▲ **Paul Gauguin.** (French).
The Brooding Woman (Te Faaturuma). 1891.
Oil on canvas. 35 15/16 × 27 1/16 inches (91.2 × 68.7 cm.).
Worcester Art Museum, Worcester, Massachusetts.

Fine Art Prints

Display **Large Prints 83** *The Brueghel Series (A Vanitas for Style)* and **84** *Milagros Memories*. Refer to the prints throughout this unit as students learn about variety, harmony, and unity.

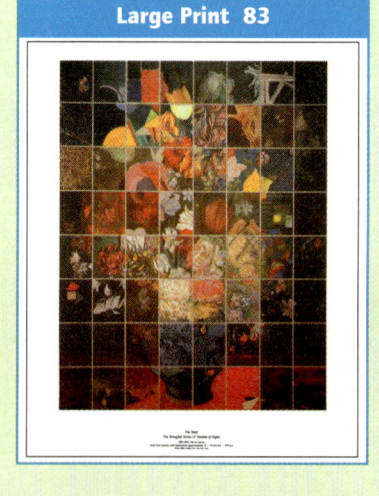

Large Print 83

Large Print 84

Artists use **variety** to show differences or contrasts in a work of art.
- What different objects do you see?
- Describe the contrasting colors, lines, and shapes.

Artists can stress the similarities of separate but related parts in an artwork by using **harmony**.
- How did Gauguin relate the outside scene to the interior?
- What element of this painting gives it a feeling of oneness or wholeness?

Unity is the feeling of oneness that artists create in their works of art.
- What about this work makes all the pieces look like they belong?

In This Unit you will learn how artists use variety and harmony. You will create works of art using a variety of media. You will create a weaving using two-dimensional decorations and a sculpture using a three-dimensional form. You will also learn how artists use unity to bring together art elements and objects.

Here are the topics you will study:
▶ Variety
▶ Harmony
▶ Weaving
▶ Unity

Master Artist Profile

Paul Gauguin
(1848–1903)

Paul Gauguin began painting as a hobby. In 1883 he quit his job as a stockbroker and decided to paint full-time. Gauguin used color and shape in new and exciting ways. *The Brooding Woman* shows a scene from the South Seas, where Gauguin spent the later part of his life. *The Brooding Woman* was painted during the first of Gauguin's two visits to Tahiti. It shows Gauguin's use of bright colors and simple forms. He considered this painting to be among his best. French impressionist artist Edgar Degas owned this painting and several other works by Gauguin.

Unit 6   **185**

Art History and Culture

Paul Gauguin

Paul Gauguin (pôl gō gan´) (1848–1903) was one of the leading French painters of the postimpressionist period. After spending a brief period with Vincent van Gogh, Gauguin increasingly abandoned imitative art for expressiveness through color. He used colors and shapes in new and exciting ways. The painting *The Brooding Woman* shows a scene from the South Seas and was painted during the first of Gauguin's two visits to Tahiti. The quiet, thinking girl shows the sense of mystery that the Tahitian people evoked in the artist.

See pages 24–25 and 16–21 for more about art history and subject matter.

Artist Profiles, p. 26

Artist Profile
Paul Gauguin
1848–1903

As one of France's leading postimpressionist painters, the artistic career of Paul Gauguin (pôl gō gan´) did not begin until he was a 25-year-old stockbroker. He decided to become a painter when he saw the first impressionist exhibit in Paris, France, in 1874, and throughout the next 30 years he developed his own style independent from impressionism and full of influences and experiences from his life. He was not content or fulfilled in Europe, however, and in 1891 he left his family and job to move to Tahiti and various other destinations in the South Pacific. With the exception of a two-year absence, Gauguin remained in Tahiti for the rest of his life, painting until his death in 1903.

Examine the Artwork

"Let's examine this painting by Paul Gauguin."
"Vamos a examinar esta pintura de Paul Gauguin."

- Have students study Paul Gauguin's painting *The Brooding Woman*. Ask them to describe how the principles of variety, harmony, and unity are used.

- Have students answer the questions about variety, harmony, and unity on page 185.
  ▶ There is a hat with a red piece of fabric on it, two apples, a dark container, a woman sitting cross-legged on the floor wearing a white dress, an orange floor, a blue wall and porch, and tree, plant, and animal forms.
  ▶ The yellow hat contrasts with the red piece of fabric. The brown, neutral tones of the woman contrast with the white dress. The curved free-form lines of the woman and the animals contrast with the straight vertical and horizontal forms of the room and wall. The free-form shapes contrast with the geometric shapes.
  ▶ Gauguin did this by placing fruit on the floor in front of the woman. By leaving the doorway open, he also connected the interior of the room with the exterior.
  ▶ The use of curved, free-form shapes: the hat, fruit, bowl; curves in the face, legs, arms, and clothing; the shapes in the wall; the animal and plant forms.
  ▶ Student responses will vary. Some will say it is the repeated shapes, others that it is the use of color or that it is the place and climate.

Unit Pretest

Display **Transparency 48** as a pretest. Have students write their answers on a separate piece of paper.
Answers: 1. A, 2. C, 3. B, 4. A, 5. C

Home Connection

- See *Home and After-School Connections* for family newsletters and activities for this unit.

UNIT 6 • Variety, Harmony, and Unity   **185**

Unit 6 Arts Integration

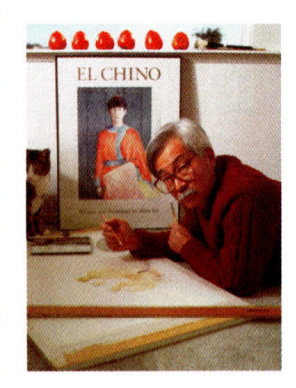

ILLUSTRATOR PROFILE
Allen Say
(1937–)

Allen Say was born in Yokohama, Japan. The breakup of his parents' marriage eventually caused Say to be sent to a grandmother with whom he did not get along and who agreed to let him live on his own at the age of 12. However, Say describes the four years he lived alone in his small apartment as the happiest time of his life. It was during this period that Say worked as an apprentice to his favorite cartoonist, Noro Shinpei.

When Say was 16, he moved with his father to the United States. He experienced discrimination at the military school that he attended, and he was eventually expelled. After roaming for several years, Say enrolled as an architectural student at the University of California at Berkeley. Then, in 1962, he was drafted into the army, where an officer noticed Say's photographic work. His photos were first published in the newspaper *Stars and Stripes*.

In California, Say pursued photography as a career. His practice of sketching ideas for his photographs caught the attention of other artists and designers, who encouraged Say to become a freelance illustrator. Beginning in 1972, Say alternated between writing and illustrating books and photography. In 1984 Say decided to give up illustrating, but agreed to do one more book. That book was *The Boy of the Three-Year Nap,* which earned a Caldecott Honor Award and convinced Say that he had found his calling. *Grandfather's Journey,* which Say wrote and illustrated, won the Caldecott Medal in 1994.

Throughout Unit 6, share Say's illustrations with the class and discuss the use of harmony, variety, and unity in his works of art. How does Say create unified illustrations?

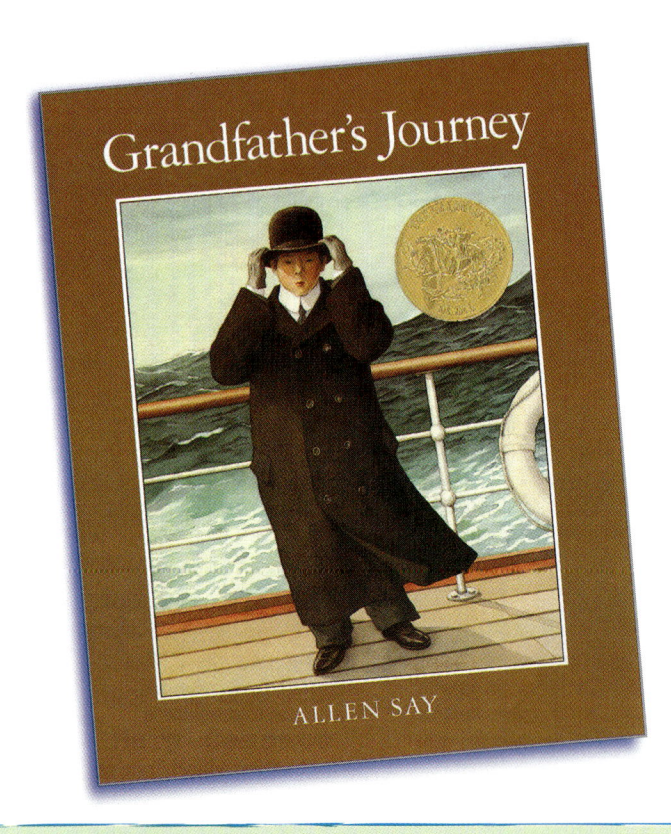

Music

Harmony in music refers to different pitches played or sung at the same time, producing chords. Have students play combinations of three pitches with one pitch in between them and observe the effect. Unity and variety are much of what gives each composition identity and character. Have students sing a song or listen to a recording and hear what seems to create unity and variety.

Literature

Show the video or DVD *The Hundred Penny Box* to introduce the concepts of variety, harmony, and unity. Pause the video and have students describe the variety, harmony, or unity of various scenes.

Literature and Art

Performing Arts

Show *Every Picture Tells a Story*. Have students look for harmony, variety, and unity.

Artsource®

185A UNIT 6 • Variety, Harmony, and Unity

Lesson 1 Overview: Variety through Line, Shape, and Color

Lesson 1 introduces the art principle of **variety**, which is concerned with differences or contrasts. It can be created through the use of the art elements of line, shape, and color.

Objectives

Art History and Culture
To demonstrate knowledge of the lives and work of Nathaniel Bustion and Lee Bennion

Creative Expression
To use variety to create a paper collage using a human or animal form

Aesthetic Perception
To identify and understand how variety through line, shape, and color is used in two-dimensional art

Art Criticism
To evaluate own work using the four steps of art criticism

Lesson Materials
- Art Journals
- sketch paper
- scissors
- 9" × 12" or larger paper (any color)
- $4\frac{1}{2}$" × 6" paper in a variety of colors
- glue
- fine-tip black markers
- newspaper

Alternate Materials:
- construction paper
- crayons
- markers

Program Resources
- *Reading and Writing Test Prep.,* pp. 66–67
- *Transparency 31*
- *Flash Card 18*
- *Artist Profiles,* pp. 7, 13
- *Animals Through History Time Line*
- *Assessment,* pp. 69–70
- *Large Prints 83 The Brueghel Series (A Vanitas for Style)* and *84 Milagros Memories*
- *Art Around the World Collection*

Concept Trace
Variety
Introduced: Level 5, Unit 6, Lesson 2
Reinforced: Level 7, Chapter 3, Lesson 3

Vocabulary

Review the following vocabulary words with students before beginning the lesson.

contrast *contraste*—a technique for creating a focal point or area of interest in a work of art, using differences in elements

variety *variedad*—the principle of art concerned with differences or contrasts

See page 209B for additional vocabulary and Spanish vocabulary resources.

Art Journal: Vocabulary
Have students add these words to the Vocabulary section of their Art Journals.

Lesson 1 Arts Integration

Theatre
Complete Unit 6, Lesson 1, on pages 108–109 of *Theatre Arts Connections.*

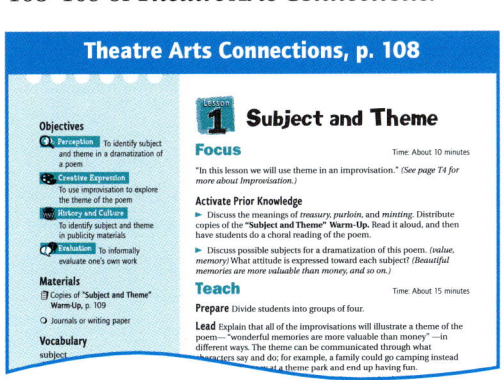

Music
Listen to the melody change color as it moves around the band in "East St. Louis Toddle-o" by Duke Ellington. Duke worked with superb artists who could improvise on a melody to the point that a listener might not know it is still there.

Movement & Dance
Have students explore variety through line, shape, and color by looking at the principle elements of dance: space, time and force/energy. Working with four counts, have students create a simple gesture that they can move through space using strong energy or force. Have them repeat the gesture standing in place and using soft energy for eight counts.

LESSON 1 • Variety through Line, Shape, and Color **185B**

Focus

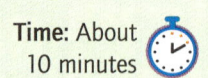

Time: About 10 minutes

Activate Prior Knowledge

"Have you ever seen a quilt with various fabric swatches?" "¿Alguna vez han visto una colcha con varias muestras de telas?"

- As a class, discuss students' responses. Explain that many designers use lines, shapes, and colors to create patterns and designs that are interesting to view. Variety is so intriguing that the viewer often looks at a work with variety for a long period of time.

Using Literature ⭐ Reading

- Have students study the cover illustration of *The Circuit* by Francisco Jimenez. Discuss how variety of line, shape, and color is used to create interest in the illustration.

Thematic Connection ⭐ Social Studies

- **Journeys:** Have students discuss what types of journeys they might experience as they grow older. What journeys have they already completed in their lives?

Introduce the Art

Look

"Look closely at how variety is used in the two works of art on these pages." "Miren detalladamente en la manera que se usó la variedad en las dos obras de arte de estas páginas."

Looking at Details ⭐ Reading

- Have students look at both works of art and list the details in each. Does one artwork have more details than the other?

🏺 Art History and Culture

Possible answers: Some artists who use color as a dominant element are Miriam Schapiro, Stanton MacDonald-Wright, and Karl Schmidt-Rottluff.

💻 Web Connection

Visit www.nathanielbustion.com for more information about Nathaniel Bustion.

186 UNIT 6 • Variety, Harmony, and Unity

Lesson 1: Variety through Line, Shape, and Color

Look at the works of art on these pages. Notice that both works of art include a variety of lines, shapes, and colors. Lee Bennion painted an image of Adah, the youngest of her three daughters, standing in the window in her pajamas. The colors and lines add interest to the painting. Bustion's serigraph expresses the joy and excitement of a festival. Bustion used a variety of shapes and patterns, which makes his work interesting to view. See how many hidden masks you can find in this composition.

◀ **Nathaniel Bustion.** (American). *Bo Bo Festival Series 3.* Twentieth century.
Serigraph. $18\frac{1}{2} \times 12$ inches (47×30.5 cm.). Collection of the artist.

🏺 Art History and Culture

Color is a dominant element in the artwork of both Bustion and Bennion. What other artists use color as a dominant element?

186 Unit 6 • Lesson 1

🏺 Art History and Culture

Nathaniel Bustion

Nathaniel Bustion (nə than´ yəl bū tən) (1942–) received his formal art education in the United States and Europe. In 1968 and in conjunction with the Belgium Antwerp Academy, Bustion created a series of travel-research projects designed to develop concepts for ceramics and ceramic sculptures. He has lectured or taught at colleges and universities in the United States and Nigeria, and has also worked as an instructor in many community art programs. Bustion has traveled all over the world, and his paintings, prints, and sculptures reflect these travels.

See pages 24–25 and 16–21 for more about art history and subject matter.

Artist Profiles, p. 13

Artist Profile
Nathaniel Bustion
b. 1942

Nathaniel Bustion (nə than´ yəl bū tən) was born in Gadsden, Alabama, in 1942. He graduated from the Otis Art Institute where he received a master of fine arts degree. He also studied at the Belgium Antwerp Academy and attended several workshops at Ife University in Nigeria. Bustion's paintings, prints, and sculptures reflect his worldwide travels.

Study the two paintings closely to learn about variety.

- Describe the shapes, colors, and patterns in Bustion's serigraph.
- Describe the shapes, colors, and patterns in *Snow Queen, Portrait of Adah*.
- Compare the shapes in the two works of art.
- In what ways did both artists use contrast?

▲ **Lee Bennion.** (American). *Snow Queen, Portrait of Adah.* 1992. Oil on canvas. 48 × 36 inches (121.9 × 91.4 cm.). Springville Museum of Art, Springville, Utah.

Aesthetic Perception

Design Awareness Think of a window display you have seen at a store. What did you notice about the items on display?

Unit 6 • Lesson 1 **187**

Art History and Culture

Lee Bennion

Lee Bennion (lē ben´ yən) (1956–) has three daughters and is active in the family-oriented life of Spring City. Bennion's commitment to family is reflected in the subject matter of many of her paintings. Her distinctive style, with its pensive, elongated figures, is not so much portraiture as it is her own special harmony among a subject, emotional atmosphere, and viewer. Her paintings are at once intensely personal and broadly universal. Bennion believes that the only real change in her work over the years has been her increased ability to get the paint to do what she wants it to.

See pages 24–25 and 16–21 for more about art history and subject matter.

Artist Profiles, p. 7

Study

- Almost all of the large shapes in this work are free-form shapes. Bustion created patterns, using triangles, circles, and dots. He used all six spectral colors as well as dark red, dull orange, black, white, and gray.
- Geometric shapes: windows, snowflakes, and the painted frame around the image. Free-form shapes: Adah and her clothing. Color: red stripes, red socks, warm skin tones against cool green, and neutral colors in the background. Patterns: stripes on the dress, radial patterns in the snowflakes, and patterns in the window and outer frames.
- In Bustion's work, free-form shapes dominate. Bennion contrasted free-form and geometric shapes.
- Both show contrasts of shape and size and warm and cool colors. Bennion used some contrast of patterns. In Bustion's work, there is a strong contrast of patterns.

■ For more examples of art from North America, see the *Art Around the World Collection.*

Art Journal: Writing

Have students explain what *variety* means to them in the Concepts section of their Art Journals. What else do they want to know about variety?

Aesthetic Perception

Design Awareness Discuss with students how a window display is carefully arranged with a variety of objects. By using variety, the designer is able to create an attractive display.

Developing Visual Literacy Talk about the use of variety and how artists use various lines, shapes, and colors in their works of art to make them more interesting. Ask students to look at how both artists created variety in their works.

Web Connection

Visit www.shs.nebo.edu/Museum/Museum.html for more information about the Springville Museum of Art.

LESSON 1 • Variety through Line, Shape, and Color **187**

Teach

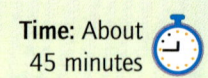

Time: About 45 minutes

"How is variety used in two-dimensional art? How can you use it in your work?" "¿Cómo se usa la variedad en el arte bidimensional? ¿Cómo pueden usarla en su obra?"

- Read and discuss using variety through line, shape, and color on page 188.

Practice

Materials: paper in a variety of colors, scissors

- Distribute the materials and have students follow the directions on page 188.
- Make sure that students leave some of the paper above and below the cut shape.

Creative Expression

Materials: Art Journals, pencils, erasers, 9" × 12" or larger construction paper $4\frac{1}{2}$" × 6" construction paper, scissors, glue, fine-tip black markers, newspaper

Alternate Materials: white paper, markers, crayons

- Distribute the materials and have students follow the directions on page 189.
- Review the Activity Tips on page 245 for visual examples of techniques if needed.

Art Journal: Ideas/Sketches

Have students generate three lists of ideas to use for their collages: one of animals, another of people, and a third of environments. Have students select their main subject from either the animal or people list and a second topic from the environment list. In their Art Journals have students work out their ideas for their collages based on their list selections. These will be used for the Creative Expression activity.

188 UNIT 6 • Variety, Harmony, and Unity

Using Variety Through Line, Shape, and Color

Think about walking through a shopping center. The displays, signs, and the ways the items are displayed are all varied. If every store looked the same or sold the same product, the stores' owners would have a hard time staying in business. People like to have choices and are attracted to differences. Owners and managers put a great deal of time and effort into creating variety in their stores.

Artists use variety as well. **Variety** is the principle of art that relates to differences or contrasts. A work of art that is all the same is dull and will not hold the viewer's attention for long. Think about a painting that has only one color. Unless there is another art element in it, the painting will not be interesting to look at. Variety is achieved by adding something different to a design to provide a break in the repetition.

Lines, shapes, and colors are three of the art elements that are used to create variety in a work of art.

Practice

Create a pattern out of a piece of paper.

1. Fold a sheet of paper in half and draw a triangle on the fold, leaving room above and below it. Cut out the shape and open the sheet of paper. What shape do you see?
2. Fold the paper in half again and cut out another shape. What happens to the shape when you open the paper? Fold and cut out your last shape. Notice the variety of the pattern.

188 Unit 6 • Lesson 1

Differentiated Instruction

Reteach
Have students look through their textbooks and the *Large Prints* for examples of variety using line, shape, and color.

Special Needs
Consider teaching different paper cutting techniques to extend students' knowledge during this project.

ELL
When explaining variety to students, use visuals such as a group of different types of fruit and a group of oranges.

◀ Ashley Guzini.
Age 11.

Think about how the student artist used variety in this collage.

Creative Expression

Choose either an animal or a person to represent in a paper collage. Use a variety of lines, shapes, and colors in your composition.

1. Select your best sketch from your Art Journal. Then select a colored sheet of paper for your background.
2. Begin by cutting out the shape of the person or animal from paper whose color contrasts with your background color.
3. Use a variety of colors and shapes to cut out objects for your environment. Overlap your shapes to make them more interesting.
4. Glue your arrangement in place. Use a felt-tip marker to make a variety of repeated lines to complete your collage.

Art Criticism

Describe What subject matter and environment did you use for your collage?

Analyze Describe the lines, shapes, and colors you used to create variety.

Interpret How does your use of variety affect the mood of your work? Explain.

Decide Do you think you were successful in arranging lines, shapes, and colors to create variety in your collage? Explain.

Unit 6 • Lesson 1   **189**

Art Across the Curriculum

Use these simple ideas to reinforce art concepts across the curriculum.

★ **Descriptive Writing** Have each student write a paragraph about how Adah is dressed.

★ **Math** Have students examine the snowflakes in *Snow Queen* to see if they are symmetrical.

★ **Science** Explain to students that no two complex snowflakes are exactly alike.

★ **Social Studies** Explain to students that African masks are made of various materials, including leather, metal, fabric, and various types of wood.

★ **Technology** Have students use a paint or draw program to create a collage of masks. Visit **SRAonline.com** to print detailed instructions for this activity.
NSAE 6.b

Reflect

Time: About 5 minutes

Review and Assess

"What art elements were used to create variety in these works of art?" "¿Qué elementos artísticos se usaron para crear variedad en estas obras de arte?"

Think

The artist used a variety of geometric and free-form shapes in the collage. The free-form shapes have curved lines and the geometric shapes have straight or diagonal lines.

■ Use **Large Prints 83** *The Brueghel Series (A Vanitas for Style)* and **84** *Milagros Memories* and ask students to compare how the artists used variety in their works of art. What art elements did they use? Does any one element dominate either of the compositions?

Informal Assessment

■ For standardized-format test practice using this lesson's art content, see page 66–67 in *Reading and Writing Test Preparation.*

Art Journal: Critical Thinking

Have students answer the four art criticism questions—Describe, Analyze, Interpret, and Decide—in their Art Journals. Have students discuss within table groups how they created variety in their completed collages. What subject matter was selected for the collage, an animal or a person? What type of environment was chosen? Ask students to discuss which element dominated their work. As a class discuss the differences and similarities among the students' works of art.

LESSON 1 • Variety through Line, Shape, and Color **189**

Lesson 1 Wrap-Up

Variety Through Line, Shape, and Color

Extra! For the Art Specialist

Time: About 45 minutes

Focus
Have students study **Large Print 83** *The Brueghel Series (A Vanitas for Style)* and discuss how line, shape, and color were used to create variety. How was variety used in this work?

Teach
Explain to students that they will create a collage, using felt and fabric. Ask students to brainstorm a list of possible subject matter for their collages. Then explain that they need to create variety in their works through the use of line, shape, and color. Have students sketch their ideas in their sketchbooks.

Reflect
Have students use the four steps of art criticism to evaluate their work. Have them describe the subject matter. What types of lines, shapes, and colors were used?

Alternate Activity

Materials:
- sketchbooks
- pencils and erasers
- newspaper
- felt and fabric scraps
- glue
- scissors
- ribbon, buttons, and beads
- thread and needles

1. Have students begin by selecting a solid background color. Have them use the fabric to cut out the shapes and figures needed for their designs.
2. Students should arrange the shapes and glue them into place once the layout is satisfactory.
3. Students can embellish their designs using ribbon, buttons, beads, and thread. A fine-tip permanent marker can be used to add details.

Research in Art Education

Research has shown that artistically talented at-risk students make greater gains in reading scores on standardized tests when the arts are integrated into the curriculum ("Using Art Processes to Enhance Academic Self-Regulation," in *Critical Links*, p. 64). The amount of training in arts-integration their teachers had received was a predictor of how great these gains were.

Assessment

Use the following rubric to evaluate the artwork students made in the Creative Expression activity and to assess students' understanding of how variety through line, shape, and color is used in two-dimensional works of art.

	Art History and Culture	Aesthetic Perception	Creative Expression	Art Criticism
3 POINTS	The student demonstrates knowledge of the lives and work of Bustion and Bennion.	The student accurately identifies the use of variety through line, shape, and color in two-dimensional works of art.	The student's collage demonstrates how to create variety through line, shape, and color.	The student thoughtfully and honestly evaluates own work using the four steps of art criticism.
2 POINTS	The student's knowledge of the lives and work of Bustion and Bennion is weak or incomplete.	The student shows an emerging awareness of the use of variety through line, shape, and color but cannot consistently identify it.	The student's collage shows some awareness of how to create variety through line, shape, and color.	The student attempts to evaluate own work but shows an incomplete understanding of evaluation criteria.
1 POINT	The student cannot demonstrate knowledge of the life and work of Bustion or Bennion.	The student cannot identify how variety through line, shape, and color is used in an artwork.	The student's collage shows no understanding of how to create variety through line, shape, and color.	The student makes no attempt to evaluate own work.

Have students complete page 69 or 70 in their *Assessment* books.

Assessment, p. 69

Variety Through Line, Shape, and Color

A. Short Answer — Complete the sentence. Variety is the principle of art that _____

B. Drawing — Draw a picture of your school. Use variety in your picture.

C. Writing — Study Lee Bennion's *Snow Queen, Portrait of Adah*, and write a paragraph describing the variety in this artwork.

189A UNIT 6 • Variety, Harmony, and Unity

Lesson 2 Overview: Variety through Contrast

Lesson 2 introduces variety through contrast of value. **Variety** is the principle of art that is concerned with differences or contrasts. **Value** is the lightness or darkness of a color.

Objectives

Art History and Culture
To demonstrate knowledge of the lives and work of Rosalind Ragans and Paul Brach

Creative Expression
To add color to a black-and-white photograph to create variety

Aesthetic Perception
To identify and better understand how artists create variety using contrast of value in two-dimensional works of art

Art Criticism
To evaluate own work using the four steps of art criticism

Vocabulary

Review the following vocabulary words with students before beginning the lesson.

contrast *contraste*—a technique for creating a focal point or area of interest in a work of art, using differences in elements

value *valor*—the lightness or darkness of a color

See page 209B for additional vocabulary and Spanish vocabulary resources.

Art Journal: Vocabulary
Have students add these words to the Vocabulary section of their Art Journals.

Lesson Materials
- Art Journals
- newspapers
- scissors, glue
- crayons
- 9" × 12" paper (any color)
- 35-mm camera, black-and-white film
- color pencils
- water-based color markers
- watercolor paints
- small paintbrushes
- cotton swabs
- water containers

Alternate Materials:
- disposable camera (black-and-white)
- digital camera
- black-and-white copier images of photographs
- crayons

Program Resources
- *Reading and Writing Test Prep.*, pp. 68–69
- *Transparency 32*
- *Flash Cards 16, 18*
- *Artist Profiles*, pp. 11, 50
- *Animals Through History Time Line*
- *Assessment*, pp. 71–72
- *Large Prints 83 The Brueghel Series (A Vanitas for Style)* and *84 Milagros Memories*
- *Art Around the World Collection*

Concept Trace
Variety
Introduced: Level 5, Unit 6, Lesson 2
Reinforced: Level 7, Chapter 3, Lesson 3

Lesson 2 Arts Integration

Theatre
Complete Unit 6, Lesson 2, on pages 110–111 of *Theatre Arts Connections*.

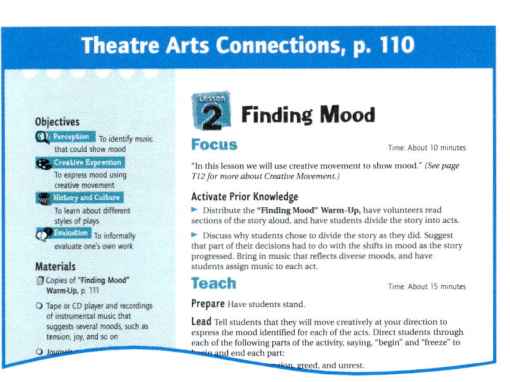

Music
Listen to "Variations on the Theme Pop! Goes the Weasel" by Lucien Caillet. How does the composer take this children's song and change the tune, the meter, the orchestration, the tempo, and the harmonization? Can students always recognize the theme?

Movement & Dance
Have students build a simple combination, using contrasting elements such as actions and time. For example; run for four counts, turn for two counts, fall and rise in four counts, and freeze in a shape for one count.

LESSON 2 • Variety through Contrast 189B

Focus

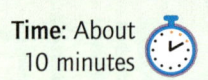

Time: About 10 minutes

Activate Prior Knowledge

"Have you ever noticed an artwork that had light areas next to dark areas, similar to these paintings?" "¿Alguna vez han notado una obra de arte que tenía áreas claras al lado de áreas oscuras, parecido a lo que ven en estas pinturas?"

- As a class discuss students' responses. Explain that artists often create contrast of value to make works of art more interesting. Contrast is also used in advertising, clothing, and photography.

Using Literature ⭐ Reading

- Have students look at the cover of *Troubling a Star* by Madeleine L'Engle. Discuss how the image on the cover uses contrast through value. How does the light reflecting on the water lead the viewer's eyes through the illustration? How does the use of variety create a feeling of mystery in the illustration?

Thematic Connection ⭐ Language Arts

- **Communication:** Have students discuss how a piece of art can communicate the way someone feels about a subject. What were the artists in this lesson trying to communicate through their artwork?

Introduce the Art

Look

"Let's study how these two artists used variety through contrast." "Vamos a estudiar cómo estos dos artistas usaron la variedad a través del contraste."

Diversity ⭐ Social Studies

- Have students look at the works of art in this lesson and discuss diversity in terms of things people like do in their spare time, such as dancing or horseback riding.

Art History and Culture

Possible Answers: Some students may say that Susan Rothenberg's *Cabin Fever* is similar to Brach's painting. They may also connect the dancing in Ragans's painting to the dancers in the works by Schapiro and Botero.

💻 Web Connection

Visit www.serve.com/aberges/batikpag.htm for more information about batik. Note: This Web site is for teacher use only.

190 UNIT 6 • Variety, Harmony, and Unity

Lesson 2: Variety Through Contrast

▲ **Rosalind Ragans.** (American). *Pas de Deux.* 2003.
Batik on cotton. 36 × 24 inches (91.4 × 61 cm.). Private collection.

Look at the two works of art on these pages. Both of these works include variety through contrasts of value. As a child, Rosalind Ragans suffered from polio and was paralyzed on her right side. She regained nearly all the movement in her body with the help of therapy. In *Pas de Deux,* Ragans was able to express her mind's ability to dance, even though her body could not. In *Chuska,* there are images of five horses running in front of a mountain range. It is hard for the viewer to take his or her eyes away from the dark horses because of the contrast in value with the light area around the horses.

Art History and Culture

What other American artists have you studied whose works of art have subject matter similar to these works of art?

190 Unit 6 • Lesson 2

Art History and Culture

Rosalind Ragans

Rosalind Ragans (ro´ zə lind rā´ gənz) (1933–) received a B.F.A. at Hunter College, The City University of New York, New York, and earned a M.Ed. in elementary education at Georgia Southern College and a Ph.D. in art education at the University of Georgia. She is one of the authors of several art textbooks for elementary, middle-school, and high-school students. Ragans has taught art in grades K–12 and has earned several honors, including National Art Educator of the Year for 1992. She is currently Associate Professor of Art Education Emerita at Georgia Southern University.

See pages 24–25 and 16–21 for more about art history and subject matter.

Artist Profiles, p. 50

Artist Profile
Rosalind Ragans
b. 1933

Rosalind Ragans (ro´ zə lind rā´ gənz) was born and grew up in New York City. When she was 11, polio paralyzed the right side of her body. Fortunately two years of therapy helped her regain nearly all the movement she had lost. Ragans had planned to be a stage designer but discovered that she loved teaching art. She began teaching in New Jersey in 1956. She earned a doctoral degree in education. While teaching art in Georgia in 1975, she began developing *ArtTalk.* This art education program presents art as a language, or way of communicating. Published in 1987, it has been well received by art teachers across the nation. Since then Ragans has created *Art Connections,* which you are using now. She still finds time to

▲ **Paul Brach.** (American). *Chuska.* 1982.
Oil and gold leaf on canvas. 50 × 60 inches (127 × 152.4 cm.). Private collection.

Study how contrast is used to create variety in these two-dimensional works of art.
- Where are the dark values in each work of art?
- Where are the lightest values in each work?
- What is mysterious about both artists' use of value?
- What type of music do you think the figures in *Pas de Deux* are dancing to? What sounds would you hear if you were standing in Brach's painting?

Aesthetic Perception

Seeing Like an Artist Think about a sunset and how the sky changes as night approaches. What kind of contrast do you notice?

Unit 6 • Lesson 2   **191**

Art History and Culture

Paul Brach

Paul Brach (pôl brak) (1924–) earned a B.F.A. and an M.F.A. from the University of Iowa. He has had more than two dozen one-man shows. His work is in many public collections, including those at the Museum of Modern Art in New York, the Whitney Museum of American Art in New York, the Los Angeles County Museum of Art, and the New York Public Library. Brach is married to artist Miriam Shapiro. In the early 1980s, he was interested in combining the patterns of Navajo blankets with the landscapes in which the weavers live. *Chuska* is the name of a mountain range in the northeastern corner of the Navajo reservation in Arizona.

See pages 24–25 and 16–21 for more about art history and subject matter.

Artist Profiles, p. 11

Study

▶ Ragans: the shape in the upper-left corner and the free-form shape that starts in the upper-right corner and swirls through the work to the bottom. This dark shape surrounds the two figures. Brach: the stripes on the painted frame, around the crosses, and around the gold-leaf outline; inside the painting on the mountain edges and dark-red horses against the light-red ground.

▶ Ragans: the white lines and the blue negative space around the shapes. Brach: the gold-leaf outline around the central red shape and the white stripe in the painted frame.

▶ Ragans: the two figures emerging from the area of dark value. Brach: The dark-red horses are emerging from the lighter-red ground, and the dark mountain is emerging from the lighter-red ground. The value of the sky is the same as the value of the ground, which adds to the feeling of mystery.

▶ Student answers will vary based on personal experiences.

■ For more examples of landscapes, see *The National Museum of Women in the Arts Collection.*

Art Journal: Writing

Have students explain what *contrast* means to them in the Concepts section of their Art Journals. What else do they want to know about variety through contrast?

Aesthetic Perception

Design Awareness Ask students what attracts our attention when we see a sunset. Have students share their experiences with sunsets and discuss how the contrast of value in the sky affects the viewer.

Developing Visual Literacy Have students look at both works of art in this lesson. What real experiences do students think might have affected the way the artists responded to their subject matter?

Web Connection

Visit www.goldleafstudios.com/framemaking/traditonal_steps_gild.htm for more information about gold leaf. Note: This Web site is for teacher use only.

LESSON 2 • Variety through Contrast   **191**

Teach

Time: About 45 minutes

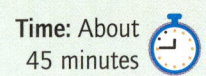

"How can you use variety through contrast in your work?" "¿Cómo pueden usar la variedad a través del contraste en su obra?"

- Read and discuss using variety through contrast of value on page 192.

Practice

Materials: newspapers, scissors, crayons, glue, 9" × 12" paper (any color)

Alternate Materials: color pencils

- Distribute the materials and have students follow the directions on page 192.

Creative Expression

Materials: Art Journals, pencils, erasers, 35-mm camera, black-and-white film, color pencils, water-based color, markers, watercolor paints, small brushes, cotton swabs, water containers, newspaper

Alternate Materials: disposable camera with black-and-white film, digital camera, black-and-white copier images of photographs, crayons, printer

- Distribute the materials and have students follow the directions on page 193.
- Review the Activity Tips on page 245 for visual examples of techniques if needed.

Art Journal: Brainstorming

As a class, brainstorm a list of themes to use for the photography lesson. What would be a good subject to use for the photographs? What are some things that are important to know about composition when taking a picture? What effect do different colors and textures have on black-and-white images? Write these questions on the board and have students answer them, as a class in their Art Journals. Students can refer back to their notes for the Creative Expression activity.

192 UNIT 6 • Variety, Harmony, and Unity

Using Variety Through Contrast

Have you ever noticed that when a film is playing in a darkened theater, it is hard to turn your head away from the screen? This is because several things are happening. A story is unfolding, and the light from the screen contrasts with the darkened theater. The contrast of light against dark adds variety to the environment. **Variety** is the principle of art that relates to differences or contrasts.

An artist often uses contrast to keep the viewer's attention on a certain part of an artwork. This is done in a manner similar to that of a lighted movie screen in a darkened theater. Sometimes the contrast in value is subtle, as in Brach's *Chuska,* which is made up of values of red. Other times the contrast of value is very noticeable. *Pas de Deux* by Rosalind Ragans is an example of an artist's use of high contrast. Ragans placed a light value of a color against a dark value of another color.

Practice

Create variety through color contrast in a black-and-white image.

1. Cut out two black-and-white images from a newspaper showing a range of values. Glue the images next to each other on a background sheet of paper. Use a dot of glue in each corner of the images to keep them from tearing.
2. Add a single color to only one of your images. Color in two areas you want to emphasize.

192 Unit 6 • Lesson 2

Differentiated Instruction

Reteach
Have students review the lesson on value in Unit 2 of their textbooks and explain the use of value in each work of art.

Special Needs
Develop students' emotional intelligence in this project by discussing the subject matter of Ragans's art. Ask students to think of how to overcome the limitations that they face. Allow them to explore these ideas further in the subject matter of their photographs.

ELL
Have students look for examples of variety through contrast of value in magazines.

◀ Jacqueline Mayo.
Age 12.

Think about how the student artist created variety in this photograph.

Creative Expression

What theme will you use for your hand-colored photograph? Hand-color a photograph to create variety.

1. Decide on a theme and take several black-and-white photographs.
2. Look at your developed images carefully. Choose one or two photographs that show a range of gray values. Put these aside to hand-color.
3. Select a third image for practice. See Technique Tip, Hand-Coloring a Photograph. Experiment with the various techniques.
4. Add variety to your two selected images by adding color to one or three areas in each photograph. Use one hand-coloring technique you like for each image.

Art Criticism

Describe What images did you choose? Why?

Analyze Describe the techniques you used to add variety to each photograph.

Interpret How does the hand-coloring affect the mood of each photograph?

Decide Do you think you were successful in creating variety in your photographs? Explain.

Unit 6 • Lesson 2   **193**

Reflect

Time: About 5 minutes

Review and Assess

"How was variety of contrast used in these works of art?" "¿Cómo se usó la variedad de contraste en estas obras de arte?"

Think

The artist created variety by hand coloring the black-and-white photography, so the viewer will notice each section of the photograph.

- Use **Large Prints 83** *The Brueghel Series (A Vanitas for Style)* and **84** *Milagros Memories* and ask students to compare the differences and similarities between the two works. How was variety through contrast of value achieved? What effect does this have on each work? Do students think the works would be as effective if only solid areas of color had been used?

Informal Assessment

- For standardized-format test practice using this lesson's art content, see page 68–69 in *Reading and Writing Test Preparation.*

Art Journal: Critical Thinking

Have students answer the four art criticism questions—Describe, Analyze, Interpret, and Decide—in their Art Journals. Create a class gallery, using the completed photographs. Ask students to study how their classmates used variety through contrast of value in their work. As a class, discuss the similarities and differences and what effect the different hand-coloring techniques have on the works of art.

Art Across the Curriculum

Use these simple ideas to reinforce art concepts across the curriculum.

★ **Poetry Writing** Have each student write a poem about dancing.

★ **Math** Explain to students that the horses in *Chuska* are running parallel to the mountains.

★ **Science** Explain to students that cacti are one type of vegetation that grows in the desert.

★ **Social Studies** Have students look at a map and identify the mountainous regions in the United States.

★ **Technology** Using a paint or draw program, have students create a nonobjective image that shows variety through contrast. Visit **SRAonline.com** to print detailed instructions for this activity.
NSAE 6.b

LESSON 2 • Variety through Contrast   **193**

Lesson 2 Wrap-Up

Variety Through Contrast

Extra! For the Art Specialist

Time: About 45 minutes

Focus
Have students study **Large Print 83** *The Brueghel Series (A Vanitas for Style)* and discuss how variety through contrast of value was used. Where are the value changes in this work?

Teach
Explain to students that they will be hand-coloring a black-and-white photograph. The easiest photographs to color are those with many overall gray values. Have students start by taping the photograph onto a work surface and placing a piece of tissue on it to protect it while working. Students can make their own pinhole camera and develop their film for the project, if time permits.

Reflect
Have students use the four steps of art criticism to evaluate their work. Have them describe the techniques used to create variety through contrast of value. What images did they use?

Alternate Activity

Materials:
- black-and-white photographs
- water-based markers
- oil pastels
- watercolors
- color chalk, crayons
- cotton swabs
- cotton balls
- half-turpentine and half-vegetable oil solution (mixed by teacher)
- towels, water containers
- newspaper, small brushes

1. Have students experiment on one photograph first with various materials.
2. Have students dip the end of a cotton swab in a solution of half turpentine and half vegetable oil. They should use this to rub the colors so the strokes blend into each other.
3. Have students apply watercolors with either a small brush or a cotton ball. Each layer needs to dry before students start on the next.
4. Students can add fine details with color pencils on top of the watercolor areas.

Research in Art Education

"The elementary classroom offers an environment that can foster creativity, independence, self-awareness, self-expression, and an understanding of the visual world. Education through art can provide opportunities for exploring one's creativity, for communicating ideas, and enabling students to express themselves through the use of materials, processes, and tools." (Andra Nyman, "Cultural Content, Identity, and Program Development: Approaches to Art Education for Elementary Educators," in *Contemporary Issues in Art Education*, edited by Y. Gaudelius and P. Speirs, 61–69. New Jersey: Prentice Hall, 2002.)

Assessment
Use the following rubric to evaluate the artwork students made in the Creative Expression activity and to assess students' understanding of how variety through contrast of value is used in two-dimensional works of art.

Have students complete page 71 or 72 in their *Assessment* books.

	Art History and Culture	Aesthetic Perception	Creative Expression	Art Criticism
3 POINTS	The student demonstrates knowledge of the lives and work of Ragans and Brach.	The student accurately identifies the use of variety through contrast of value in two-dimensional works of art.	The student's hand-colored photograph demonstrates variety through contrast of value.	The student thoughtfully and honestly evaluates own work using the four steps of art criticism.
2 POINTS	The student's knowledge of the lives and work of Ragans and Brach is weak or incomplete.	The student shows an emerging awareness of variety through contrast of value in two-dimensional works of art but cannot consistently identify it.	The student's hand-colored photograph shows some awareness of variety through contrast of value.	The student attempts to evaluate own work but shows an incomplete understanding of evaluation criteria.
1 POINT	The student cannot demonstrate knowledge of the life and work of Ragans or Brach.	The student cannot identify how variety through contrast of value is used in an artwork.	The student's hand-colored photograph shows no understanding of variety through contrast of value.	The student makes no attempt to evaluate own work.

Assessment, p. 71

193A UNIT 6 • Variety, Harmony, and Unity

Lesson 3 Overview: Harmony in Two-Dimensional Art

Lesson 3 introduces the art principle of harmony as used in two-dimensional decorations. **Harmony** is the principle of art that creates unity by stressing similarities of separate but related parts. A **two-dimensional decoration** is a flat decoration on the surface of a work of art.

Objectives

Art History and Culture
To demonstrate knowledge of Grandma Moses and Guatemalan culture

Creative Expression
To design and create a harmonious embroidery piece based on a life event

Aesthetic Perception
To understand how harmony is used in two-dimensional decorations

Art Criticism
To evaluate own work using the four steps of art criticism

Lesson Materials
- Art Journals
- pencils and erasers
- burlap
- light-colored chalk
- yarn in various colors
- scissors
- tapestry needles

Alternate Materials:
- paper
- markers

Program Resources
- *Reading and Writing Test Prep.,* pp. 70–71
- *Transparency 33*
- *Flash Cards 17–18*
- *Artist Profiles,* pp. 28, 82
- *Animals Through History Time Line*
- *Assessment,* pp. 73–74
- *Large Prints 83 The Brueghel Series (A Vanitas for Style)* and *84 Milagros Memories*
- *Art Around the World Collection*

Concept Trace
Harmony
Introduced: Level 5, Unit 6, Lesson 1
Reinforced: Level 7, Chapter 3, Lesson 3

Vocabulary

Review the following vocabulary words with students before beginning the lesson.

harmony *armonía*—the principle of art that creates unity by stressing similarities of separate but related parts

two-dimensional decoration *decoración bidimensional*—a flat decoration on the surface of a work of art

See page 209B for additional vocabulary and Spanish vocabulary resources.

Art Journal: Vocabulary
Have students add these words to the Vocabulary section of their Art Journals.

Lesson 3 Arts Integration

Theatre
Complete Unit 6, Lesson 3, on pages 112–113 of *Theatre Arts Connections.*

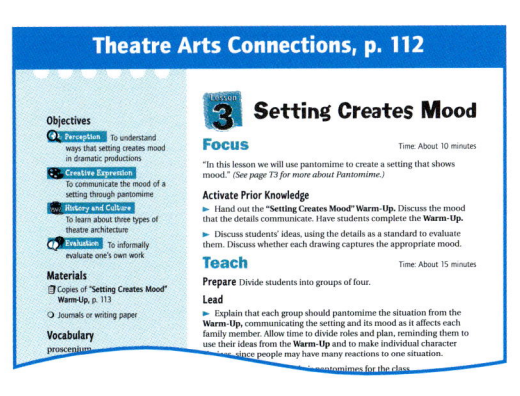

Music
The life work of Johann Sebastian Bach set down the harmonies that Western music is built upon. Listen to the last movement of "Brandenburg Concerto No. 5." He wrote six of these concertos, named after the Margrave of Brandenburg who commissioned them.

Movement & Dance
Have students explore two-dimensional harmony by looking at Egyptian art. As a class, choose one posture with which everyone will work. Standing in a line, have students create an "Egyptian wall of art." Each person must take on the same basic posture, but it can be at a low, middle, or high level. Using eight counts, everyone must slowly change their level and freeze.

LESSON 3 • Harmony in Two-Dimensional Art **193B**

Focus

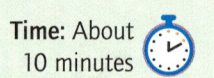

Time: About 10 minutes

Activate Prior Knowledge

"When creating a personal piece of art, what do you do to make each separate part look as if it belongs with the other parts?" "Cuando crean una obra de arte personal, ¿qué hacen para que cada parte separada parezca que concuerda con las otras partes?"

- As a class, discuss students' responses. Explain that artists often use harmony to bring together unrelated parts.

Using Literature — Reading

- Have students look at the cover illustration of *A Bone from a Dry Sea* by Peter Dickinson. Discuss how the image on the cover uses harmony through color. How does the use of warm colors bring together the image of the girl, the background, and the animal face?

Thematic Connection — Social Studies

- **Neighborhoods/Communities:** Have students describe their neighborhoods or communities. Is there a particular style of clothing people tend to wear?

Introduce the Art

Look

"Look closely at both *Mt. Nebo on the Hill* and *Woman's Headcloth*." "Miren detalladamente las obras *Mt. Nebo on the Hill* y *Woman's Headcloth*."

Drawing Conclusions — Science

- Have students examine the artwork in this lesson. Have them draw conclusions about each artist based only on the works of art. Then have students compare their conclusions with real facts.

Art History and Culture

Explain to students that recorded history and works of art depict people of various ancient civilizations wearing embroidered clothing dating back more than 3,000 years. Archaeological digs in Ur in 1944 revealed a pure gold-thread embroidered and woven shroud in the tomb of Empress Honorius dating to 400 A.D.

Web Connection

Visit www.artnet.com/etienne.html for more information about the Galerie St. Etienne.

194 UNIT 6 • Variety, Harmony, and Unity

Lesson 3: Harmony in Two-Dimensional Art

▲ **Grandma Moses.** (American). *Mt. Nebo on the Hill.* 1940 or earlier. Embroidery yarn on fabric. 10 × 14 inches (25.4 × 35.6 cm.). Galerie St. Etienne, New York, New York.

Look at the two works of art on these pages. Anna Mary Robertson, known as Grandma Moses, is most famous for painted landscapes based on her childhood experiences. Before she began painting, she created original needlepoint pieces depicting scenes of her home and community. When she was well into her seventies and her eyesight began to fail, she turned to painting. Moses was the originator of the style known as memory painting. *Woman's Headcloth* is handwoven. Some women in hot climates fold cloths like these on top of their heads and use them as sunshades. These textiles can also be used as carrying cloths for babies and various items. The figures on the headcloths vary in size and shape, which makes them unique pieces of art.

Art History and Culture

Embroidery and other fiber and needlework arts most likely originated in Asia and the Middle East.

194 Unit 6 • Lesson 3

Art History and Culture

Grandma Moses

Grandma Moses' real name was Anna Mary Robertson Moses (an´ a mâr´ ē ro´ bərt sən mō´ z´əz) (1860–1961). She lived in the New York countryside and began painting in her seventies, when her daily activities on the farm no longer took up her time. Moses' work was first noticed by a New York City art collector who saw her paintings in the window of a local drugstore. Moses' paintings of rural American landscapes were well received during a time when the world was starting to focus on technology. By the time of her death, Moses had created more than 1,500 works of art.

See pages 24–25 and 16–21 for more about art history and subject matter.

Artist Profiles, p. 28

Artist Profile

Grandma Moses
1860–1961

Anna Mary Robertson Moses (an´ a mâr´ ē ro´ bərt sən mō´ zəz) was always interested in art but was too busy raising children and doing farm work to devote much time to her creative talents. It was not until she was in her late 70s that she took up painting. In 1938 her work was discovered when an art collector saw one of her paintings hanging in a drugstore window. Within two years her work was being exhibited at the Museum of Modern Art and the Galerie St. Etienne, both in New York City. In the last 20 years of her life, her paintings appeared in museums and galleries throughout the United States and Europe. She continued to paint until the year she died at age 101.

◀ **Artist unknown.** (Guatemala). *Woman's Headcloth.* c. 1935–1945.
Cotton, silk, and wool.
50 × 44 inches (127 × 111.8 cm).
Dallas Museum of Art, Dallas, Texas.

Study how harmony is used in both works of art.
▸ Describe any repeated lines, shapes, colors, and textures you see in each work of art.
▸ Describe any one area in either artwork that seems to stand out.
▸ Which art element in *Mt. Nebo on the Hill* ties the work together?
▸ Which work of art do you think was more difficult to create? Explain.

Aesthetic Perception

Design Awareness Look at the clothing you have on. What about it makes it look like the separate pieces go together?

Unit 6 • Lesson 3 **195**

Study

▸ Possible answers: *Mt. Nebo on the Hill:* There are repeated vertical lines in the buildings and trees. There are diagonal lines in the branches of the trees, leaves, and roof. Free-form shapes include the trees, clouds, and sky. There are both cool and warm colors. The yarn has a soft, matte, bumpy texture. *Woman's Headcloth:* There are horizontal, vertical, and diagonal lines in various objects. There is an abundance of triangular shapes used to create the figures. The people and animals are free-form shapes. There are mostly warm colors in the embroidery and orange in the flower. The thread has a soft, matte, bumpy texture.

▸ *Mt. Nebo on the Hill:* the white buildings and structure in the middle ground. *Woman's Headcloth:* the two yellow animals

▸ Student responses may vary, but many will say the use of cool and neutral colors.

▸ Student answers will vary based on personal experiences.

■ For more examples of art from Latin America, see the **Art Around the World Collection.**

Art Journal: Writing

Have students explain what *harmony* means to them in the Concepts section of their Art Journals. What else do they want to know about harmony in two-dimensional art?

Art History and Culture

Woman's Headcloth

This woman's headcloth is an example of a weaving style from Guatemala. The figures on these types of textiles have their own quirks. For example, all the feet in the design look the same no matter whether they belong to an animal or person, the female figures have triangular skirts, and the deer have diamond spots. There is no regular pattern to how the motifs are positioned on these headcloths, but the overall designs focus on negative space and asymmetrical balance.

See pages 24–25 and 16–21 for more about art history and subject matter.

Artist Profiles, p. 82

Artist Profile
Woman's Headcloth
This headcloth was made by an unidentified Mayan artist from Chichicastenango, located in the highlands of Guatemala. Art historians estimate that the piece was made between 1935 and 1945. The Mayan people, founders of a vast, powerful, and ancient kingdom, have historically lived throughout an enormous geographic area of what is today Mexico and Central America.

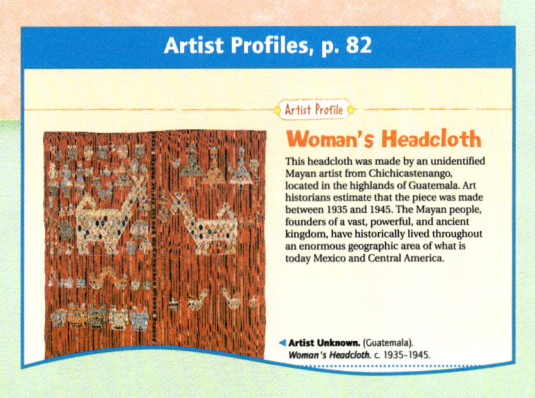

◀ **Artist Unknown.** (Guatemala).
Woman's Headcloth. 1935–1945.

Aesthetic Perception

Design Awareness Talk about the types of lines, colors, and shapes in the various articles of clothing worn by students. Explain that harmony makes the separate pieces of a suit or costume seem to go together.

Developing Visual Literacy Discuss the use of lines, shapes, colors, and textures in each artwork. How did the artists use these elements to communicate their ideas? Ask students to share personal experiences that contribute to their interpretations.

Web Connection

Visit **www.guatemaltecos.com/default.aspx** for more information about Guatemala. Note: This Web site is for teacher use only.

LESSON 3 • Harmony in Two-Dimensional Art **195**

Teach

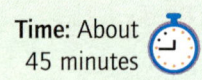

Time: About 45 minutes

"Can you use harmony in an artwork that tells a personal story?" "¿Pueden usar armonía en una obra de arte que cuenta una historia personal?"

- Read and discuss using harmony on page 196.

Practice

Materials: 6" × 6" burlap, light-colored chalk, yarn, scissors, tapestry needles

Alternate Materials: markers and construction paper to draw simulated stitches

- Distribute the materials and have students follow the directions on page 196.

Creative Expression

Materials: Art Journals, pencils, 6" × 9" or larger burlap, light-colored chalk, yarn in various colors, scissors, tapestry needles

Alternate Materials: muslin or cotton fabric, embroidery floss

- Distribute the materials and have students follow the directions on page 197.
- Have students demonstrate their technical skills, using a variety of art media and materials to produce their embroidery design. NSAE 1.a; 1.b
- Review the Activity Tips on page 246 for visual examples of techniques if needed.

Art Journal: Brainstorming

Have each student think of a personal event, such as moving, discovering a special place, or meeting a best friend, and write a brief story of the event and create several sketches. The drawings do not have to be realistic; they can be symbols to represent the event. Ask students to keep their sketches and stories in their Art Journals. Have students look over their sketches and select their best one for the Creative Expression activity.

196 UNIT 6 • Variety, Harmony, and Unity

Using Harmony in Two-Dimensional Art

You have probably heard the term *harmony* used in connection with music. When voices harmonize, they blend together to create a unified sound. Artists use this same concept, but instead of combining sounds, they combine the art elements. **Harmony** is the principle of art that creates unity by stressing similarities of separate but related parts. Artists create harmony in two-dimensional works of art by repeating shapes, colors, and textures. Harmony can also occur when the spaces between different shapes, colors, and/or textures are even.

Look at Grandma Moses's embroidery again. Even though there is a variety of shapes, lines, and yarn textures, the use of cool colors and neutral colors unifies the separate parts. The purples in the hillside and sky, the greens in the grass and plants, and the grays, browns, black, and white in the buildings and trees create harmony.

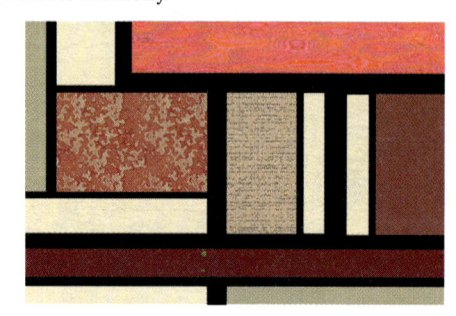

Practice

Practice using various embroidery techniques.

1. Look at the Techniques Tips for embroidery.
2. With a permanent marker draw one line of any type on your burlap. Draw any type of shape no larger than a quarter.
3. Use the running, back, or outline stitch on the line you made. Practice the satin stitch on the shape you made. If you have time, you may want to try another embroidery technique.

196   Unit 6 • Lesson 3

Differentiated Instruction

Reteach
Ask students to look through their textbooks for examples of works of art that best illustrate harmony. Have students list the art elements that are used to create harmony in the works they find.

Special Needs
Provide students with alternate means of expression for this project. Some students may prefer to create symbols about important events in their life rather than drawing a scene.

ELL
Have students listen to choral music to help them comprehend the concept of harmony.

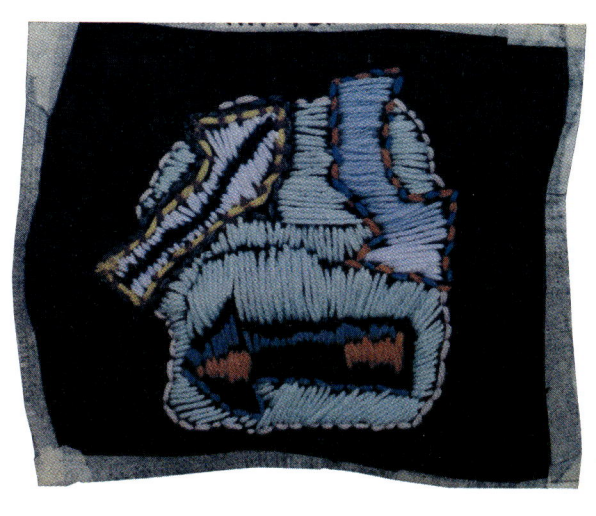

◀ Tiffany Zim.
Age 11.

Think about which art element the student artist used in this artwork to create harmony.

Creative Expression

Think about an important event in your life. Create a harmonious embroidery based on this event.

1. Look over your planned sketch in your Art Journal or create a new one. Use a light piece of chalk to transfer your design to the burlap. Make your image large, and keep your design simple.
2. Use masking tape to tape around the edges of the burlap before you begin stitching. This will keep it from unraveling.
3. Look at your practice embroidery piece and the Technique Tips on page 214. Outline your image first using either a running, back, or outline stitch. Use a contrasting color of yarn and a satin stitch to complete your work. Make sure you have used at least one art element in your embroidery to create harmony.

Art Criticism

Describe Describe the image you used in your embroidery. What embroidery techniques did you use?

Analyze List the lines, shapes, colors, and textures you used in your embroidery. Which element did you use to create harmony? Explain.

Interpret Give your completed work a descriptive title.

Decide Do you feel your embroidery piece is a success? Explain.

Unit 6 • Lesson 3   **197**

Reflect
Time: About 5 minutes

Review and Assess
"Explain how you created harmony in your embroidery piece. Which art element ties your work together?" "Expliquen cómo crearon armonía en su bordado. ¿Qué elemento artístico unifica su obra?"

Think
The artist used cool colors to create harmony in the design.

- Use **Large Prints 83** *The Brueghel Series (A Vanitas for Style)* and **84** *Milagros Memories* to have students identify how harmony was used. Which art element was used to create harmony in each work of art?

- Have students exchange portfolios with a classmate. Have them analyze their peer's portfolio to form conclusions about historical and cultural contexts and formal properties.
NSAE 4.b

Informal Assessment
- For standardized-format test practice using this lesson's art content, see pages 70–71 in *Reading and Writing Test Preparation*.

Art Journal: Critical Thinking
Have students answer the four art criticism questions—Describe, Analyze, Interpret, and Decide—in their Art Journals. Within their table groups, have students discuss the different types of embroidery techniques they used in their work. Have them compare how some people used line, while others used color or shape to create harmony in their work.

Art Across the Curriculum

Use these simple ideas to reinforce art concepts across the curriculum.

★ **Expository Writing** Have students write instructions to help someone create an embroidery piece.

★ **Math** Have students locate horizontal, vertical, and diagonal lines in each embroidery.

★ **Science** Explain to students that technology has made it faster to create embroidered pieces.

★ **Social Studies** Have students explain what they know about Guatemala.

★ **Technology** Have students create a harmonious landscape, using a paint or draw program. Visit **SRAonline.com** to print detailed instructions for this activity.
NSAE 6.b

LESSON 3 • Harmony in Two-Dimensional Art **197**

Lesson 3 Wrap-Up: Harmony in Two-Dimensional Art

Extra! For the Art Specialist
Time: About 45 minutes

Focus
Have students study **Large Print 84** *Milagros Memories* and discuss how the artist used harmony. How does the use of harmony affect the mood of the artwork? Is it calm or active? Have student explain their responses.

Teach
Have students collect images of cities. Some resources are personal photographs, images from magazines, postcards, and the Internet.

Reflect
Have students use the four steps of art criticism to evaluate their work. Did they effectively use a variety of lines and shapes in their cityscapes? Which colors were used to create harmony?

Alternate Activity

Materials:
- collected city images
- sketchbooks
- pencils, erasers
- rulers
- white drawing paper
- black fine-tip marker
- watercolors, paintbrushes

1. From a selected image, ask students to create several sketches. Explain that the drawing does not have to be exactly like the image they select. Explain that they should include in their sketches a variety of lines and shapes to make their compositions interesting.

2. Ask students to select their best sketches and transfer them onto drawing paper. Have them draw the basic shapes first, then the details. They should use markers to outline the drawings.

3. Have students use color to create harmony in their cityscapes. Have them use washes of watercolor.

Research in Art Education

Research has shown that assessing knowledge through a combination of drawing and writing can lead to higher scores for content knowledge. This applies to native English speakers and limited English speakers alike. This suggests "that drawing may be one way to reveal what students know but cannot put into words" ("The Arts, Language, and Knowing: An Experimental Study of the Potential of the Visual Arts for Assessing Academic Learning by Language Minority Students," in *Critical Links*, p. 141).

Assessment
Use the following rubric to evaluate the artwork students make in the Creative Expression activity and to assess students' understanding of how harmony is used in two-dimensional decorations.

Have students complete page 73 or 74 in their *Assessment* books.

	Art History and Culture	Aesthetic Perception	Creative Expression	Art Criticism
3 POINTS	The student demonstrates knowledge of Grandma Moses and Guatemalan culture.	The student accurately identifies the use of harmony in two-dimensional decorations.	The student's embroidery piece demonstrates harmony in two-dimensional decoration.	The student thoughtfully and honestly evaluates own work using the four steps of art criticism.
2 POINTS	The student's knowledge of Grandma Moses and Guatemalan culture is weak or incomplete.	The student shows an emerging awareness of harmony in two-dimensional decorations but cannot consistently identify it.	The student's embroidery piece shows some awareness of harmony in two-dimensional decoration.	The student attempts to evaluate own work but shows an incomplete understanding of evaluation criteria.
1 POINT	The student cannot demonstrate knowledge of Grandma Moses or Guatemalan culture.	The student cannot identify how harmony is used in an artwork.	The student's embroidery piece shows no understanding of harmony in two-dimensional decoration.	The student makes no attempt to evaluate own work.

Lesson 4 Overview

Harmony in Three-Dimensional Art

Lesson 4 introduces how the art principle of harmony is used in three-dimensional sculptures. **Harmony** is the principle of art that creates unity by stressing similarities of separate but related parts. An **assemblage** is a variety of objects that are arranged to create one complete piece.

Objectives

Art History and Culture
To demonstrate knowledge of the lives and work of Louise Nevelson and Randy Ellett

Creative Expression
To collect a variety of discarded objects and make a harmonious group assemblage

Aesthetic Perception
To understand how harmony is used in three-dimensional sculptures

Art Criticism
To evaluate own work using the four steps of art criticism

Lesson Materials
- Art Journals
- wide, open boxes of a consistent size
- a variety of collected cardboard and plastic recycled items
- tacky craft glue
- acrylic paint

Alternate Materials:
- cardboard boxes
- construction paper
- white school glue

Program Resources
- *Reading and Writing Test Prep.*, pp. 72-73
- *Transparency 34*
- *Artist Profiles*, pp. 23, 44
- *Animals Through History Time Line*
- *Assessment*, pp. 75-76
- *Large Prints 83 The Brueghel Series (A Vanitas for Style)* and *84 Milagros Memories*
- *Art Around the World Collection*

Concept Trace
Harmony
Introduced: Level 5, Unit 6, Lesson 1
Reinforced: Level 7, Chapter 3, Lesson 3

Vocabulary

Review the following vocabulary words with students before beginning the lesson.

assemblage *montaje*—when a variety of objects are assembled to create one complete piece.

harmony *armonía*—the principle of art which creates unity by stressing similarities of separate but related parts

See page 209B for additional vocabulary and Spanish vocabulary resources.

Art Journal: Vocabulary
Have students add these words to the Vocabulary section of their Art Journals.

Lesson 4 Arts Integration

Theatre
Complete Unit 6, Lesson 4, on pages 114–115 of *Theatre Arts Connections.*

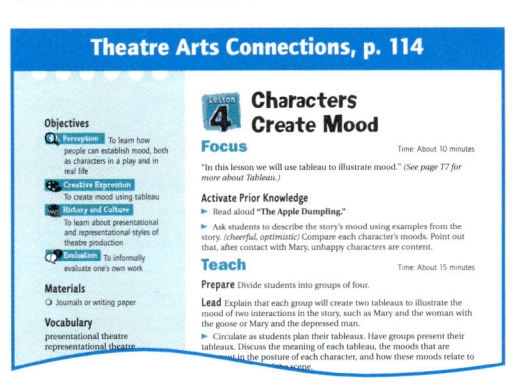

Music
During the twentieth century, composers broke from traditional ideas of harmony. Listen to "Infernal Dance of King Kaschei" from *Firebird Suite*. Stravinsky wrote this in 1910, three years before "The Rite of Spring," which caused a riot at its premier.

Movement & Dance
A sense of harmony can be felt when movement comes from breath. Breath is continuous. When we are relaxed, our breathing is even and slow, deep and flowing. Have students sit in groups of three and practice breathing in and out deeply together. Have each group find a movement they can do together as they inhale and a different movement they can do in unison as they exhale.

LESSON 4 • Harmony in Three-Dimensional Art **197B**

Focus

Time: About 10 minutes

Activate Prior Knowledge

"Have you ever created or seen a sculpture that was composed of different materials?"

"¿Alguna vez han creado o visto una escultura compuesta de diferentes materiales?"

- As a class discuss students' responses. Explain that sometimes artists use materials that are not normally thought of as art materials. Artists use harmony to bring together these unusual materials in a unified piece.

Using Literature ⭐ Reading

- Have students look at the cover of *Body Parts in Rebellion* by Regan Dunnick and notice how the various body parts seem to float around the head, which is centrally placed. Discuss how the image uses harmony through color and subject matter.

Thematic Connection ⭐ Social Studies

- **Cooperation:** Have students discuss how working together in a group can create harmony. How do people feel if there is harmony in a group?

Introduce the Art

Look

"Look closely at both sculptures to compare how Nevelson and Ellett use harmony in their works." "Miren detalladamente ambas esculturas para comparar cómo Nevelson y Ellett usaron la armonía en sus obras."

Probability ⭐ Math

- Have students examine the works of art in this lesson and determine what other shapes each sculpture could have taken, such as a square.

Art History and Culture

Possible answers: David Smith and George Hart use geometric elements in their sculptures.

Web Connection

Visit www.albrightknox.org for more information about the Albright Knox Museum.

198 UNIT 6 • Variety, Harmony, and Unity

Lesson 4: Harmony in Three-Dimensional Art

Look at the works of art on these pages. Many of the wood forms Louise Nevelson used in *White Vertical Water* are similar to those she grew up with in her father's lumber yard. She gathered the discarded wood pieces for her sculptures from renovations of Victorian homes. She then arranged the various pieces in boxes. As she was stacking boxes in her studio to make more room, she noticed a sculptural form. Like Nevelson, Randy Ellett was influenced by his surroundings. Working as a forklift driver, he would move objects around a warehouse on wooden pallets. The writing and images on the pallets intrigued him and were the inspiration for *National Parts*. Notice how the various images are arranged. Each individual shape represents one pallet.

◀ **Louise Nevelson.** (Russian/American). *White Vertical Water*. 1972.
Painted wood. 26 sections. 216 × 108 inches overall (548.6 × 274.3 cm.). Solomon R. Guggenheim Museum, New York, New York.

Art History and Culture

Both Nevelson and Ellet used geometric elements in their sculptures. Can you name another artist who did the same?

198 Unit 6 • Lesson 4

Art History and Culture

Louise Nevelson

Louise Nevelson (lōō ēz´ ne´ vəl sən) (1900–1988) was born Louise Berliawsky in Kiev, Russia. By 1905, her family had emigrated to the United States and settled in Rockland, Maine. She was one of the most important sculptors of the twentieth century. Her sculptures are wood assemblages usually painted in black, white, or gold. They range in size from the small and personal to the large and monumental. They consist of intricate forms that are often grouped within boxlike frames, inviting viewers to observe a new type of world.

See pages 24–25 and 16–21 for more about art history and subject matter.

Artist Profiles, p. 44

Artist Profile
Louise Nevelson
1900–1988

Louise Nevelson (lōō ēz´ ne´ vəl sən), one of the most important and successful American sculptors of the twentieth century, was born in Kiev, Russia. Her family resettled in Rockland, Maine, when she was five years old. As a child she began assembling wood scraps from her father's contracting business. Her education was rich and varied, including music, theatre, dance, and visual art. She studied in New York, New York and Paris, France. At first she made both paintings and sculptures, but eventually concentrated on sculpture, which she exhibited irregularly from the 1930s onward. It was not until the late 1950s that she began to receive critical acclaim. Before her death, she had received more...

Study how Nevelson and Ellett used harmony in their works of art.

- Describe the types of lines and shapes used in each artwork.
- Is there any one element in each artwork that seems to stand out?
- How do you think these works were assembled?
- Why do you think Nevelson named her work *White Vertical Water*? Why do you think Ellett named his work *National Parts*?

◀ **Randy Ellett.** (American). *National Parts.* 1996.
Wooden pallets. $73\frac{5}{8} \times 15\frac{1}{2} \times 2\frac{3}{8}$ inches ($187 \times 39.4 \times 5.4$ cm). Collection of the artist.

Aesthetic Perception

Design Awareness Think about how the various parts of playground equipment are put together.

Unit 6 • Lesson 4   **199**

Study

- Nevelson: Lines: Vertical, diagonal, and horizontal; straight and curved. The shapes are both free-form and geometric. Ellett: Lines: straight, both vertical and horizontal. The shapes are geometric.

- Nevelson: color (white) and the rectangular boxes that hold the wooden forms. Ellett: color (natural wood) and repeated rectangular shapes

- Student responses will vary, but many will say Nevelson's work was assembled using wood scraps nailed or glued into separate boxes, then stacked and nailed or glued together. *National Parts* was measured and cut to size and nailed or glued inside a rectangular box.

- Student responses will vary based on personal experiences. Some may respond that Nevelson chose this name because of the color used, or because it looks like water. Some may respond that Ellett named his work *National Parts* because of the words *National Parts* in the sculpture.

- For more examples of abstract and nonobjective art, see *The National Museum of Women in the Arts Collection.*

Art Journal: Writing

Have students explain what *assemblage* means to them in the Concepts section of their Art Journals. What else do they want to know about harmony in three-dimensional art?

Art History and Culture

Randy Ellett

Randy Ellett (rân´ dē l´ let) (1959–) was born in Gainesville, Georgia. He earned a degree in printmaking from the University of Georgia and admires the work of Albrect Dürer, Rembrandt, and M.C. Escher. Ellett considers himself a printmaker and focuses on the etching process. He also carves and works with wood. *National Parts* was directly influenced by his working as a fork-lift driver in a warehouse. Ellett's environment often has a direct influence on his work. The images that make up *National Parts* are taken from the pallets Ellet used as a fork-lift driver.

See pages 24–25 and 16–21 for more about art history and subject matter.

Artist Profiles, p. 23

Artist Profile
Randy Ellett
b. 1959

Randy Ellett (rân´ dē el´ let) was born in Gainesville, Georgia, and grew up in a family that encouraged him to make art. His father was a dentist who used the intricately detailed work of his profession to create cast jewelry. Ellett's mother continues to paint and draw today. Having artistic parents meant that art materials were always accessible in his childhood home. Ellett also took drawing classes when he was young, and had one of his drawings published right after graduating from high school. This early success further encouraged Ellett's artistic path as he went on to receive a degree in printmaking from the University of Georgia and establish a career in printmaking and woodworking.

Aesthetic Perception

Design Awareness Industrial engineers and architects create playscapes from a variety of materials. The designers usually harmonize the various pieces through color and shape.

Developing Visual Literacy Explain that artists are often inspired by the environment in which they live and work. Have students ever seen an object in their environment that inspired them to create an artwork, story, poem, or piece of music?

Web Connection

Visit www.sculpturesite.com for more information about contemporary sculpture. Note: This Web site is for teacher use only.

LESSON 4 • Harmony in Three-Dimensional Art   **199**

Teach

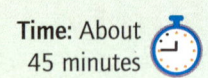

Time: About 45 minutes

"How can you harmonize a variety of objects in a group sculpture?" "¿Cómo pueden armonizar una variedad de objetos en una escultura de grupo?"

- Read and discuss harmony on page 200.

Practice

Materials: objects from around the room that share a common element, for example, various-sized books, objects that are all blue, or objects that are made of the same material

Alternate Materials: magazine images that share an element

- Distribute the materials and have students follow the directions on page 200.

Creative Expression

Materials: flat, open boxes of a consistent size, a variety of collected cardboard and plastic recycled items, (toilet- and paper-towel rolls, plastic bottles, milk-container tops, egg cartons), craft glue, acrylic paint

Alternate Materials: paper boxes, white school glue

- Distribute the materials and have students follow the directions on page 201.
- Review the Activity Tips on page 246 for visual examples of techniques if needed.

Art Journal: Brainstorming

Have students research the term *assemblage* and find examples to include in their Art Journals. As a class, brainstorm a list of recyclable objects that could be used in the individual assemblages. Explain that the individual works will be arranged to create one or two group sculptures. Have students write the list in their Art Journals to be used for the Creative Expression activity.

200 UNIT 6 • Variety, Harmony, and Unity

Using Harmony in Three-Dimensional Assemblages

Harmony is the principle of art that creates unity by stressing similarities of separate but related parts. Artists create harmony in three-dimensional works of art by repeating shapes, colors, or similar materials. When an artist works with an **assemblage**, a variety of objects put together to create one complete piece, he or she uses harmony.

Notice how Louise Nevelson used a variety of wooden objects in *White Vertical Water*. Even though there is a variety of shapes and forms, the use of white and the rectangular boxes unify the separate pieces. The repetition of rectangular shapes harmonizes the various words and images in *National Parts*.

Practice

Work as a class or table group to harmonize a variety of objects.

1. Look around your classroom. What colors, shapes, textures, and materials do you see?
2. Decide which art element you will use. Gather several objects from around the room that are made up of this element. For example, you might choose all wood objects or objects that are geometric shapes.
3. Arrange the collected objects. What do you notice?

200 Unit 6 • Lesson 4

Differentiated Instruction

Reteach
Ask students to look at the architecture in their neighborhoods for examples of harmony.

Special Needs
Encourage students to develop their composition skills by asking them to try several arrangements of their objects in order to find the one that their eyes like best.

ELL
Have students group together different objects in the classroom to create harmony.

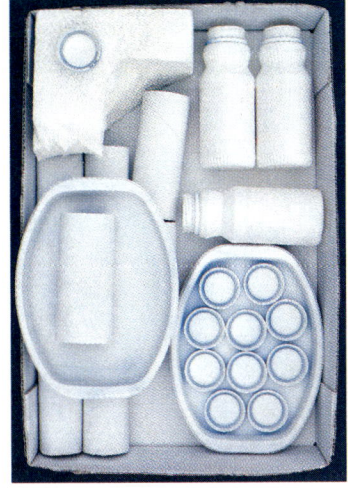

◀ Bobby Braswell.
Age 11.

Think about how the student artist used harmony to bring together the various objects in this work of art.

Creative Expression

Collect a variety of discarded objects and make a harmonious group assemblage.

1. Look over the list of recycled objects in your Art Journal and try to collect several of the objects.
2. Begin by arranging the objects in the box. None of the objects should stick out beyond one inch from the box's edge. Think about repeating similar shapes in one area of the box and using different shapes in another area.
3. Once you have arranged your objects, glue them in place. Use one harmonious color to paint all of the assemblages of your group members. Arrange the individual works to create one or two harmonious sculptures.

Art Criticism

Describe List the objects you used in your assemblage.

Analyze List the lines, shapes, colors, and textures used in the group sculpture. Which element was used to create harmony?

Interpret Imagine that you are an art critic and write a review of the sculpture for a newspaper.

Decide Do you feel your assemblage is a success? Is the group sculpture a success? Explain.

Unit 6 • Lesson 4 **201**

Reflect
Time: About 5 minutes

Review and Assess
"Explain how you created harmony in your assemblage. Which art element ties your work together? "Expliquen cómo crearon armonía en su montaje. ¿Qué elementos artísticos unifican su obra?"

Think
The artist painted the box and the items inside of it white, which creates harmony.

- Use **Large Prints 83** *The Brueghel Series (A Vanitas for Style)* and **84** *Milagros Memories* to have students identify how harmony was used. Have them describe the lines, shapes, colors and objects in each work. Which art element was used to create harmony in each work of art?

Informal Assessment
- For standardized-format test practice using this lesson's art content, see pages 72–73 in *Reading and Writing Test Preparation.*

Art Journal: Critical Thinking
Have students answer the four art criticism questions—Describe, Analyze, Interpret, and Decide—in their Art Journals. As a class, discuss the use of harmony in the completed sculptures. What types of lines, shapes, and objects were used? How did color harmonize the separate pieces? Would the effect have been the same if each individual box were a different color?

Art Across the Curriculum

Use these simple ideas to reinforce art concepts across the curriculum.

★ **Persuasive Writing** Have each student write a paragraph persuading a museum director to include *National Parts* in his or her modern sculpture collection.

★ **Math** Have students imagine that each artwork is a solid and calculate its volume.

★ **Science** Explain to students that large wooden sculptures may appear heavier than they actually are, depending on the density of the wood.

★ **Social Studies** Have students discuss how a person's job can influence the type of art he or she creates.

★ **Technology** Using a paint or draw program, have students create a design for an abstract sculpture that shows harmony. Visit SRAonline.com to print detailed instructions for this activity.
NSAE 6.b

LESSON 4 • Harmony in Three-Dimensional Art **201**

Lesson 4 Wrap-Up: Harmony in Three-Dimensional Art

Extra! For the Art Specialist

Time: About 45 minutes

Focus
Have students study **Large Print 83** *The Brueghel Series (A Vanitas for Style)* and discuss how harmony was used in this work. Which art element ties it all together?

Teach
Explain to students that they will be making a soft-covered book. Using various types of papers, students will design unique books to use as journals or sketchbooks. Begin by having students decide on the shape of their books. The shape must have one straight edge. Then have students complete the Alternate Activity.

Reflect
Have students use the four steps of art criticism to evaluate their work. Did they effectively use harmony to bring together the various-colored paper in their books? How were the covers decorated? What will the books be used for?

Alternate Activity

Materials:
- pencils, erasers
- rulers, scissors
- white drawing paper
- various types of paper
- embroidery floss
- tapestry needles
- large clips

1. Students should select thick paper for the front and back covers. Then have them trace the shape of the book onto the number of pages they plan to have.

2. Have students stack the sheets of paper and use a ruler to mark every half or whole inch on the straight edge. Then have them poke holes through the marks on the first sheet of paper.

3. Students should place the first sheet of paper back on the stack, trace the holes that were punched out, and make holes in the remaining sheets, one at a time.

4. Have students use a clip to hold the pages together while they sew the pages together.

5. Students can decorate the cover, using any media of choice.

Research in Art Education

"At a time when the development of thinking skills is particularly important . . . the presence of a program that fosters flexibility, promotes a tolerance for ambiguity, encourages risk taking and depends upon the exercise of judgment outside the sphere of rules is an especially valuable resource." (Eisner, Elliot W. *The Arts and the Creation of Mind.* New Haven: Yale Univ. Press, 2002.)

Have students complete page 75 or 76 in their *Assessment* books.

Assessment

Use the following rubric to evaluate the artwork students make in the Creative Expression activity and to assess students' understanding of how harmony is used in sculpture.

	Art History and Culture	Aesthetic Perception	Creative Expression	Art Criticism
3 POINTS	The student demonstrates knowledge of the lives and work of Nevelson and Ellett.	The student accurately identifies the use of harmony in sculpture.	The student's assemblage demonstrates harmony in sculpture.	The student thoughtfully and honestly evaluates own work using the four steps of art criticism.
2 POINTS	The student's knowledge of the lives and work of Nevelson and Ellett is weak or incomplete.	The student shows an emerging awareness of harmony in sculpture but cannot consistently identify it.	The student's assemblage shows some awareness of harmony.	The student attempts to evaluate own work but shows an incomplete understanding of evaluation criteria.
1 POINT	The student cannot demonstrate knowledge of the life and work of Nevelson or Ellett.	The student cannot identify how harmony is used in an artwork.	The student's assemblage shows no understanding of harmony.	The student makes no attempt to evaluate own work.

Lesson 5 Overview: Unity in Weaving

Lesson 5 introduces the art principle of unity and explains how variety and harmony are used together to create a harmonious weaving. **Unity** is the sense of oneness that is achieved by properly using the elements and principles of art. Unity is created when the art principles of variety and harmony work together.

Objectives

Art History and Culture
To demonstrate knowledge of Louisa Keyser and Indonesian culture

Creative Expression
To design a weaving using variety and harmony to create unity

Aesthetic Perception
To identify and understand how unity is used in two types of weaving

Art Criticism
To evaluate own work using the four steps of art criticism

Lesson Materials
- ruled paper
- Art Journals
- pencils, rulers
- yarn of various colors
- cardboard boxes
- heavy string
- tapestry needles
- scissors

Alternate Materials:
- construction-paper weaving
- fabric scraps
- masking tape

Program Resources
- *Reading and Writing Test Prep.,* pp. 74–75
- *Transparency 35*
- *Artist Profiles,* pp. 34, 72
- *Animals Through History Time Line*
- *Assessment,* pp. 77–78
- *Large Prints 83 The Brueghel Series (A Vanitas for Style)* and *84 Milagros Memories*
- *Art Around the World Collection*

Concept Trace
Unity
Introduced: Level 5, Unit 6, Lesson 5
Reinforced: Level 7, Chapter 3, Lesson 7

Vocabulary

Review the following vocabulary word with students before beginning the lesson.

unity *unidad*—the feeling of wholeness or oneness that is achieved by properly using the elements and principles of art

See page 209B for additional vocabulary and Spanish vocabulary resources.

Art Journal: Vocabulary
Have students add this word to the Vocabulary section of their Art Journals.

Lesson 5 Arts Integration

Theatre
Complete Unit 6, Lesson 5, on pages 116–117 of *Theatre Arts Connections*.

Music
Listen to "Tuileries" from *Pictures at an Exhibition*. The instrumental sounds stay high and light throughout the piece. There is a contrasting middle section where the melody smoothes out. Ask students why the total piece has a feeling of unity even with the contrasting rhythms and phrasing of the section in the middle.

Movement & Dance
Make a large circle and number students 1 or 2. Have all the 1s turn to face the 2s. Each person should be facing someone. The 1s will go clockwise in the circle, and the 2s will go counterclockwise. Have students hold the right hand of the person they are facing and start to walk in opposite directions until they take the left hand of the next person they meet. Students should continue moving until they get back to their original place.

Focus

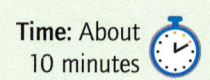

Time: About 10 minutes

Activate Prior Knowledge

"Have you ever seen a weaving before?"
"¿Alguna vez han visto un tejido?"

- As a class, discuss students' responses. Explain that many contemporary weavers use the traditional methods that were developed by the Navajo people. Although there are a variety of looms available today, they are all based on the simple weaving loom of the Navajo people. Have students discuss their experiences with weaving.

Using Literature ⭐ Reading

- Have students look at the cover of *The Monkey Thief,* by Aileen Kilgore Henderson. Discuss how the image uses a variety of shapes in the plant forms and how they contrast in color with the monkeys and the person. Even though there are a variety of shapes and objects, the color green unifies the illustration.

Thematic Connection ⭐ Social Studies

- **Jobs:** Have students discuss the skills needed to become a weaver. What other kinds of jobs do they associate with artists?

Introduce the Art

Look

"Let's compare how unity is used in *Basket* and *Ceremonial Hanging*." "Vamos a comparar cómo se usó la unidad en la obra *Basket* y *Ceremonial Hanging*."

Geography ⭐ Social Studies

- Ask students what other countries or societies they associate with creating baskets and/or wall hangings. Have students locate the corresponding areas on a map and discuss why these places are known for making these items.

Art History and Culture

Possible answer: Both the basket and the wall hanging have a similar color scheme.

💻 Web Connection

Visit www.philbrook.org for more information about the Philbrook Art Center.

202 UNIT 6 • Variety, Harmony, and Unity

Lesson 5: Unity in Weaving

▲ **Louisa Keyser (Dat So La Lee).** (Washoe/North American). *Basket.* c. 1917–1918.
Redbud and braken fern. 12 × 16¼ inches (30.5 × 41.3 cm.). Philbrook Museum of Art, Tulsa, Oklahoma.

Look at the two woven works of art on these pages. *Basket* was created through weaving. Louisa Keyser was a member of the Washoe tribe of the American Northwest. The method of weaving used is called *coiling* because the basket was woven in one continuous coil. Washoe baskets are watertight and were used to carry various items. *Basket* is based on a *degikup (deh gee' kup)*, a small, round basket used for ceremonies. In Indonesia, a ceremonial hanging is called a *palepai (pah lee' peye)*. A *palepai* can be hung during ceremonies for important life events, and only by titled members of the nobility. *Ceremonial Hanging* includes images of animals carrying riders, trees, and a ship.

Art History and Culture

Do you notice any similarities between the Washoe basket and the Indonesian ceremonial hanging? Explain.

202 Unit 6 • Lesson 5

Art History and Culture

Louisa Keyser

Louisa Keyser (lü ē sǝ kī zǝr) (c. 1850–1925) was also known as Dat So La Lee. Her Washoe Indian tribe gave her this name, which means "The Queen of Washoe Indian Basketmakers." Keyser single-handedly changed the art of Washoe basket weaving. She changed and refined the stitching technique to create a new shape of basket called a *degikup*. A *degikup* is a larger basket that curves in toward the top. Keyser also expanded the design to cover most of the basket surface. Then she introduced a dye called redbud. This was used along with a black dye for decoration.

Keyser was also influential in establishing the direction for the new curio style and the three-coil method.

See pages 24–25 and 16–21 for more about art history and subject matter.

Artist Profiles, p. 34

Artist Profile
Louisa Keyser (Dat So La Lee)
1850-1925

Louisa Keyser (lü ē' sǝ kī' zǝr) was a Washoe Indian born in Nevada. Her handwoven baskets were quite valuable during her lifetime and are now exhibited in museums and collections throughout the country. Keyser's baskets are even more impressive because she was nearly blind. The extreme precision with which she created her artwork is especially inspiring; she could barely see her own artwork and yet it was perfectly made. With her innovative new styles and techniques Keyser changed the nature of traditional Washoe basket making.

Study the works of art to see how unity is used in weaving.
- Which art elements create variety in each weaving?
- Which art elements create harmony in each weaving?
- How are all the images brought together to make *Ceremonial Hanging* work?
- How did Keyser balance all the different parts in *Basket*?

▲ **Artist unknown.** (Indonesia). *Ceremonial Hanging.* c. 1900.
Cotton and metal wrapped yarns. 24¼ × 95¾ inches (61.6 × 243.2 cm.). Dallas Museum of Art, Dallas, Texas.

Aesthetic Perception

Design Awareness Think about a patterned blanket you have seen before. What about this blanket gave it the feeling of oneness?

Unit 6 • Lesson 5   203

Art History and Culture

Ceremonial Hanging

Ceremonial Hanging is from Indonesia. The islands of this region were the crossroads of ancient trading routes and brought foreign travelers into the area. *Ceremonial Hanging* contains symbolic and representational images in Lampung society. They include a large ship with multiple prows, trees, and animals with riders. The ship may be a symbol of spiritual transition in the face of crisis or other difficulty in life. The trees may represent the Tree of Life. Ceremonial cloths like this one were used by the aristocracy during celebrations and rituals of importance, such as weddings, funerals, and naming ceremonies for infants.

See pages 24–25 and 16–21 for more about art history and subject matter.

Artist Profiles, p. 72

Study

- *Basket:* There is a contrast between the shape of the basket and the shapes of the design. *Ceremonial Hanging:* There is a contrast between the black images and the beige background stripes and the red diamond shapes.
- *Basket:* the shape of the basket, repeated coils, and gradual change in size of the pattern. *Ceremonial Hanging:* Harmony is created in the symmetrical arrangement of the design and the repeated patterns and shapes.
- The wall hanging was woven on a loom, giving it a uniform shape and symmetry.
- Keyser balanced all the parts by forming the materials into the uniform shape of a basket.
- For more examples of utilitarian art, see *The National Museum of Women in the Arts Collection.*

Art Journal: Writing
Have students explain what *unity* means to them in the Concepts section of their Art Journals. What else do they want to know about weaving?

Aesthetic Perception

Design Awareness A variety of colors, lines, and shapes is brought together using the principle of art called unity. Unity is what makes sense of all the different parts. Explain that each of the separate and varied parts contribute to the whole. No single part is more important than the others, but the pieces work as a whole.

Developing Visual Literacy Discuss with student how unity is used in both works. Point out to students that the wall hanging works as a whole because of the repetition of the shapes and colors. *Basket* is unified through the adjustment of the parts. Ask students to contribute personal experiences by asking questions. Do they know someone who weaves, or have they made weavings before?

Web Connection
Visit www.dm-art.org for more information about Dallas Museum of Art.

LESSON 5 • Unity in Weaving   203

Teach

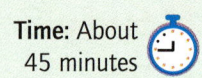

Time: About 45 minutes

"How is unity used in weaving? How can you use it in your weaving?" "¿Cómo se usa la unidad en el tejido? ¿Cómo pueden usarla en su tejido?"

- Read and discuss unity in weaving on page 204.

Practice

Materials: ruled paper, pencils

- Distribute the materials and have students follow the directions on page 204.

Creative Expression

Materials: Art Journals, pencils, yarn of various colors, rulers, cardboard boxes heavy string, tapestry needles, scissors

Alternate Materials: construction-paper weaving, fabric scraps woven after being cut into thin strips, masking tape

- Distribute the materials and have students follow the directions on page 205.
- Review the Activity Tips on page 247 for visual examples of techniques if needed.

Art Journal: Brainstorming

A weaving with a lot of detail can become very difficult and time consuming. Have students look at the Weaving Technique Tips. In their Art Journals, have students create two weaving designs, using simple lines. Have them use color pencils or crayons to help in planning the color. Students can select one design to work from in the Creative Expression activity.

204 UNIT 6 • Variety, Harmony, and Unity

Using Unity in Weaving

Unity is oneness. For example, the separate states are brought together or unified as one United States. In art, **unity** is the feeling of wholeness or oneness that is achieved by properly using the elements and principles of art. Unity is created when the art principles of variety and harmony work together.

In a weaving, the separate parts relate to one another to make the whole weaving. Various lines, shapes, and colors are woven together. One way in which variety and harmony work together to create unity or oneness in a weaving is the very technique of weaving. Most weaving is done on a loom. The shape and consistent technique of weaving on a loom unify the whole. Notice the image of the weaving loom and tools below. These are what a weaver needs to created a completely unified weaving.

Practice

Discuss how unity occurs in architecture.

1. In a small group, create a list of all of the elements or parts needed to construct a house.
2. Answer these questions: Why do you need each part? How do each of these separate parts fit together?
3. Share your answers with the class. Discuss how variety and harmony are used together to create unity in architecture.

204   Unit 6 • Lesson 5

Differentiated Instruction

Reteach
Have students look for examples of woven fabric in the room. Explain that even though clothing does not always look woven, it actually is.

Special Needs
Assess students' knowledge of unity by asking them to choose a picture from a magazine that is not unified. Have them redraw the picture so that it is unified and describe the art elements they repeated.

ELL
When explaining unity in weaving, show students the yarn before and after it is woven together.

◀ Bethany Ullrich.
Age 11.

Think about how the student artist used unity in this weaving.

Creative Expression

How can you use unity in your cardboard-loom weaving?

1. Prepare your loom following the Technique Tips. Look at your loom design in your Art Journal. Select a yarn and attach it to the first warp string.
2. Begin by using the tabby (basket) weave for the first few rows. Your teacher will demonstrate other weaving techniques you can use.
3. Look at your sketch and try to follow your plan. Make any adjustments to your design.
4. When finished, take your weaving off the loom. Turn it over, and cut the warp strings across the center. Cut two strings at a time. Gently lift the top two strings and knot them together. The knot should be close to the weaving. Repeat this process until all the strings are cut and tied.

Art Criticism

Describe What weaving techniques did you use? List the colors you used in your weaving.

Analyze Describe how variety and harmony were used to create unity in your weaving.

Interpret If you could enlarge your weaving, what size would you make it? What would it be used for?

Decide Were you successful in using unity in your weaving? Explain.

Unit 6 • Lesson 5   **205**

Reflect

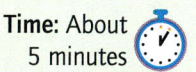

Time: About 5 minutes

Review and Assess
"How were variety and harmony used to create unity in these works of art?" "¿Cómo se usaron la variedad y la armonía para crear unidad en estas obras de arte?"

Think
The artist used yarn, one type of media, to create unity in the weaving.

- Use **Large Prints 83** *The Brueghel Series (A Vanitas for Style)* and **84** *Milagros Memories* and ask students to compare how the artists each used unity in their works of art. Which elements create variety in each artwork? Which elements create harmony? How were the separate elements unified?

Informal Assessment

- For standardized-format test practice using this lesson's art content, see pages 74–75 in *Reading and Writing Test Preparation*.

Art Journal: Critical Thinking
Have students answer the four art criticism questions—Describe, Analyze, Interpret, and Decide—in their Art Journals. Have students discuss within table groups how they created unity in their weavings. What colors did they use? What weaving techniques were used? What difficulties did they have, and how did they solve them? How closely did they follow their weaving plans? Have the groups share some of their discoveries with the class.

Art Across the Curriculum

Use these simple ideas to reinforce art concepts across the curriculum.

★ **Personal Writing** Have students imagine that they received one of the works of art in this lesson as a gift and write a thank-you note.

★ **Math** Have students convert the measurements of each artwork into millimeters.

★ **Science** Have students create a list of different types of fibers.

★ **Social Studies** Have students locate Indonesia on a world map.

★ **Technology** Have students make a weaving design, using a paint or draw program. Visit **SRAonline.com** to print detailed instructions for this activity.
NSAE 6.b

LESSON 5 • Unity in Weaving   **205**

Lesson 5 Wrap-Up: Unity in Weaving

Extra! For the Art Specialist

Time: About 45 minutes

Focus
Have students study **Large Print 84** *Milagros Memories* and discuss how variety and harmony were unified in the artwork. Which elements were used to create unity?

Teach
Explain to students that they will make coil baskets, using a technique similar to the one used by Louisa Keyser. Explain that they will be selecting two colors of yarn to complete their baskets. Have students practice the coil basket method. Then have them complete the Alternate Activity.

Reflect
Have students use the four steps of art criticism to evaluate their work. What colors did they use? Did students successfully use unity in their woven baskets?

Alternate Activity

Materials:
- sketchbooks
- pencils, erasers
- yarn, tape
- heavy cord
- tapestry needles
- scissors

1. Have students create a sketch of a basket using two colors.
2. Using the sketch as a guide, have students use about three feet of cording. The cording will be the warp.
3. Demonstrate holding the position of the warp cord as the stitches are sewn to connect one coil to the next. Show how the warp coils can either be stacked vertically or moved up at a slant.
4. Have students finish their baskets using the taper method.

Research in Art Education

"When we teach a child to sing or play an instrument, we teach her to listen. When we teach a child to draw, we teach her to see. When we teach a child to dance, we teach him about body and about space. When we teach a child design, we teach the geometry of the world. When we teach children about the folk and traditional arts and great masterpieces, we teach them to celebrate their roots and find their place in history" (Town Hall Meeting with Jane Alexander, November 23, 1994). Continue to remind students about the cultures of the artists they are learning about so they have an understanding of various cultures around the world.

Assessment
Use the following rubric to evaluate the artwork students make in the Creative Expression activity and to assess students' understanding of how unity is used in weaving.

	Art History and Culture	Aesthetic Perception	Creative Expression	Art Criticism
3 POINTS	The student demonstrates knowledge of Keyser and Indonesian culture.	The student accurately identifies the use of unity in a weaving.	The student's weaving demonstrates unity.	The student thoughtfully and honestly evaluates own work using the four steps of art criticism.
2 POINTS	The student's knowledge of Keyser and Indonesian culture is weak or incomplete.	The student shows an emerging awareness of unity in a weaving but cannot consistently identify it.	The student's weaving shows some awareness of unity.	The student attempts to evaluate own work but shows an incomplete understanding of evaluation criteria.
1 POINT	The student cannot demonstrate knowledge of Keyser or Indonesian culture.	The student cannot identify how unity is used in a weaving.	The student's weaving shows no understanding of unity.	The student makes no attempt to evaluate own work.

Have students complete page 77 or 78 in their *Assessment* books.

Assessment, p. 77

205A UNIT 6 • Variety, Harmony, and Unity

Lesson 6 Overview: Unity in Three-Dimensional Art

Lesson 6 introduces the art principle of unity in three-dimensional forms. Unity is created when the art principles of variety and harmony work together. A **three-dimensional form** is anything that can be measured by height, width, and depth.

Objectives

Art History and Culture
To demonstrate knowledge of the lives and work of Nam June Paik and Christina Lemon

Creative Expression
To create a humanlike form using discarded machine and technology parts

Aesthetic Perception
To identify and understand how unity is used in three-dimensional forms

Art Criticism
To evaluate own work using the four steps of art criticism

Lesson Materials
- Art Journals
- pencils
- wire, pliers
- heavy string
- tacky craft glue
- scissors
- screwdrivers
- wire clippers
- packaging, electrical, or duct tape
- student/teacher collected machine/technology parts

Alternate Materials:
- hot-glue gun and glue sticks (teacher use only)
- cardboard products (paper-towel rolls or egg cartons)
- leaves, sticks, and pinecones

Program Resources
- *Reading and Writing Test Prep.*, pp. 76–77
- *Transparency 36*
- *Artist Profiles*, pp. 37, 46
- *Animals Through History Time Line*
- *Assessment*, pp. 79–80
- *Large Prints 83 The Brueghel Series (A Vanitas for Style)* and **84** *Milagros Memories*
- *Art Around the World Collection*

Concept Trace
Unity
Introduced: Level 5, Unit 6, Lesson 6
Reinforced: Level 7, Chapter 3, Lesson 7

Vocabulary
Review the following vocabulary word with students before beginning the lesson.

unity *unidad*—the feeling of wholeness or oneness that is achieved by properly using the elements and principles of art

See page 209B for additional vocabulary and Spanish vocabulary resources.

Art Journal: Vocabulary
Have students add this word to the Vocabulary section of their Art Journals.

Lesson 6 Arts Integration

Theatre
Complete Unit 6, Lesson 6, on pages 118–123 of *Theatre Arts Connections.*

Music
Listen to "Canon in D Major" by Pachebel. The three high melodies start at different times, creating a "canon." (Singing a round has the effect of a canon, except in a canon every part finishes at the same time.) The bass line has a very simple job to create unity. Ask students what happens to the bass line. Students should reply it creates unity.

Movement & Dance
A sense of unity can be created by working with a common theme. For example, use various harvesting movements: pull, rake, push, pick, and gather. In groups of five, assign students one of the actions. Have them spread out and explore the action for eight counts. Each student will show a different idea, but a strong sense of unity exists because they have the same theme.

LESSON 6 • Unity in Three-Dimensional Art **205B**

Focus

Time: About 10 minutes

Activate Prior Knowledge

"Do you own an electronic toy, or have you seen one before?" "¿Tienen un juguete electrónico o han visto uno anteriormente?"

- Discuss students' responses. Explain that people today are very accustomed to machines and technology. We are said to be living in the "technological age." Ask students what this means and how they use machines and technology every day.

Using Literature ⭐ Reading

- Have students look at the cover of *A Wrinkle in Time* by Madeleine L'Engle. Discuss how the various objects are unified by the harmonious use of blue. Also the common characteristics of the objects and the things related to a bird unify the illustration.

Thematic Connection ⭐ Language Arts

- **A Question of Value:** Have students discuss who decides if someone's creation is art. Do they think the pieces of fine art in this lesson should be called art?

Introduce the Art

Look

"Let's compare how unity is used in three-dimensional forms by looking at the work of Nam June Paik and Christina Lemon."

"Vamos a comparar cómo la unidad se usa en formas tridimensionales mirando a la obra de Nam June Paik y Christina Lemon."

Create a Model ⭐ Science

- Have each student invent a new piece of machinery. Ask them to combine two or three objects and create a drawing of a new machine that would benefit our lives. Ask students to write a description of the invention, naming it and explaining its function.

Art History and Culture

Explain to students that Paik was influenced by the Native American thunderbird, and Lemon was inspired by African masks.

💻 Web Connection

Visit www.ackland.org for more information about the Ackland Art Museum.

206 UNIT 6 • Variety, Harmony, and Unity

Lesson 6: Unity in Three-Dimensional Art

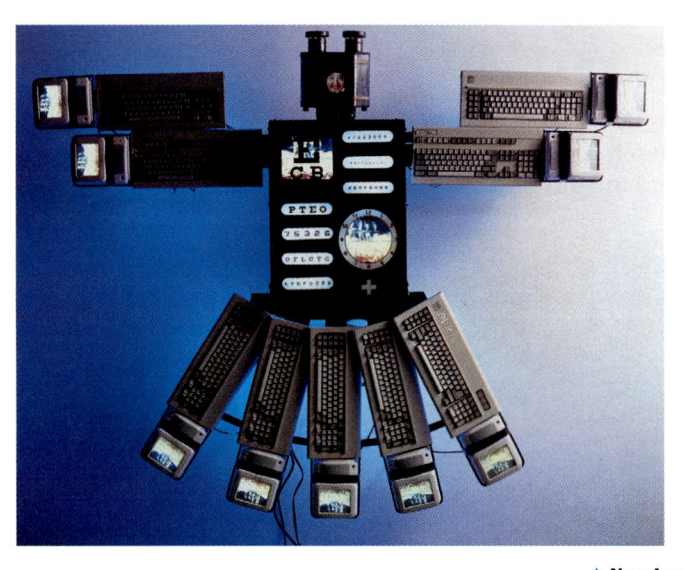

▲ **Nam June Paik.** (Korean/American). *Eagle Eye.* 1996.

Antique slide projector and eye chart, transparency of the artist, aluminum, nine computer keyboards, neon, nine Sony 5-inch televisions model FDT-5BX5, two KEC 9-inch televisions model 9BND, and DVD. $66\frac{11}{16} \times 86\frac{3}{8} \times 24\frac{1}{2}$ inches (169.4 × 219.4 × 62.2 cm.). Ackland Art Museum, Chapel Hill, North Carolina.

Look at the forms of the sculptures on these pages. Nam June Paik is considered the first artist to explore the area of video art. Paik created *Eagle Eye* based on the Native American thunderbird. He combined old technology—a slide projector and an eye chart—with the newer technology of computers, television, and DVDs. A portrait of Paik is in the work; he is the eagle, blending old technology with new. Christina Lemon is a professor of jewelry and design at Georgia Southern University. She works primarily with silver and gold, although she uses a variety of materials with her students. By using simple shapes and contrasting colors in *Mask Brooch*, Lemon was able to suggest the feeling of a mask without making a symmetrical face. Both artists use unity in their three-dimensional forms.

Art History and Culture

When creating works of art, both Nam June Paik and Christina Lemon look to other cultures for inspiration.

206 Unit 6 • Lesson 6

Art History and Culture

Nam June Paik

In 1950, Nam June Paik (1932–), and his family left their native Korea during that country's civil war. After studying aesthetics, art, music, and philosophy in Hong Kong and Japan, Paik moved to Germany. There he trained in music theory, history, and composition, piano, and electronic music. Paik began making "altered TVs," in which he manipulated television signals with magnets and used video feedback, synthesizers, and other technology to produce kaleidoscopic shapes and luminous colors. Paik, long considered the pioneer of video art, uses the medium to express the complexities of contemporary culture.

See pages 24–25 and 16–21 for more about art history and subject matter.

Artist Profiles, p. 46

Artist Profile

Nam June Paik
b. 1932

Nam June Paik (näm jōōn päk) is considered a pioneer of video art. As a child growing up in Korea, Paik was fascinated by electronics, especially the radio. When television was introduced in the early 1950s, he became interested in technology and cultural iconography. With the encouragement of his friends, Karlheinz Stockhausen and John Cage, Paik became involved in electronic art and combined ideas of composition and performance. Regarded as a father of video art, he continues to influence and teach younger generations of artists and to provide cutting-edge technology for the art world.

Study the works of art to see how unity is used in three-dimensional art.
- Which elements or objects create variety in each artwork?
- Which elements or objects create harmony in each work?
- How did Nam June Paik bring all the pieces together to make *Eagle Eye* work?
- How did Lemon balance all the different parts in *Mask Brooch*?

◀ **Christina Lemon.** (American). *Mask Brooch.* 2003.
Sterling silver and 18-karat gold laminate. 2½ × 1 inch (6.4 × 2.5 cm.). Collection of the artist.

Aesthetic Perception

Design Awareness Think about a computer system, a music system, or a media center. Describe the different parts that are needed to complete the system.

Unit 6 • Lesson 6   **207**

Study

- Paik: The different technology parts create variety. Lemon: The different metals create variety.
- Paik: The keyboards create harmony. Lemon: The shapes create harmony.
- Paik brought together all the pieces by having them represent different parts of a thunderbird. The different parts come together to make a whole.
- Lemon created balance by having an almost central axis in the brooch. The different objects are arranged around this central point, and they look balanced.
- For more examples of art from North America, see the ***Art Around the World Collection.***

Art Journal: Writing
Have students explain what *modern* means to them in the Concepts section of their Art Journals. What else do they want to know about modern art?

Aesthetic Perception

Design Awareness Have students share their experiences with computer, music, and multimedia systems. Explain that even though there are many components, or parts, to these systems, they depend on one another to work well. Unity in three-dimensional form is very similar. All of the different parts usually do not work as well alone as they do together.

Developing Visual Literacy Discuss with students how unity is used in both works. Point out that Paik's work is made of parts of machines, which are not normally considered works of art. Paik uses repetition of objects, keyboards, and televisions, to create a unified piece. Have students note how Lemon used two different metals together.

Web Connection
Visit www.gasou.edu/~clemon for more information about Christina Lemon.

LESSON 6 • Unity in Three-Dimensional Art   **207**

Art History and Culture

Christina Lemon

Christina Lemon (kris tē´ nə le´ mən) (1967–) received her B.F.A. from Radford University and her M.F.A. from East Carolina University in jewelry design and metalsmithing. Her work features one-of-a-kind jewelry designs in sterling and gold, and her work is inspired by her interest in collecting African masks and ethnic jewelry. *Mask Brooch* is fabricated from sterling sheet and 18K bimetal, a unique metal made from bonding sterling silver and gold to create a two-color material. The metal is formed over wooden stakes using plastic mallets, and soldered using a silver soldering technique to permanently join the metals. Texture is an important element in Lemon's art.

See pages 24–25 and 16–21 for more about art history and subject matter.

Artist Profiles, p. 37

Teach

Time: About 45 minutes

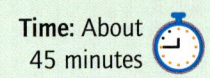

"How can you use unity in your sculptural form?" "¿Cómo pueden usar unidad en su forma escultural?"

- Read and discuss unity in three-dimensional forms on page 208.
- Have students use appropriate vocabulary to analyze and form generalizations about the interdependence of art elements, such as form, space, and color.
  NSAE 2.b

Practice

Materials: objects from around the room, in book bags and/or pockets

- Distribute the materials and have students follow the directions on page 208.

Creative Expression

Materials: wire, heavy string, tacky craft glue, pliers, scissors, screwdrivers, wire clippers, packaging, electrical or duct tape, student- or teacher-collected machine and technology parts

Alternate Materials: hot-glue gun and glue sticks, cardboard products (paper-towel rolls or egg cartons), leaves, sticks, pinecones

- Distribute the materials and have students follow the directions on page 209.
- Review the Activity Tips on page 247 for visual examples of techniques if needed.

Art Journal: Ideas

In their Art Journals have students each create a list of machine parts and objects, such as things that can be found in a hardware store. Have students use this list as things to be collected prior to doing the Creative Expression activity.

208 UNIT 6 • Variety, Harmony, and Unity

Using Unity in Three-Dimensional Forms

In art, **unity** is the feeling of wholeness or oneness that is achieved by properly using the elements and principles of art. Unity is oneness. It brings order to a work of art. It helps the viewer concentrate on the image as a whole. When an artwork does not have unity, it is very difficult to concentrate on because each part demands the viewer's separate attention. It is like trying to read a story when a lawn mower is running and a dog is barking. To create unity, an artist adjusts the parts so that they work together. This is done by using the art principles of variety and harmony together. When an artist uses unity, he or she harmonizes the variety, or different elements or objects, by making them relate to one another.

By combining like objects, or things that relate, and organizing them in an understandable manner, an artist creates unity. Look at the sets of objects below. Even though these are not art objects their arrangement and dependency on each other make them unified sets.

Practice

Try creating a face or human form from a variety of objects.

1. Pull an assortment of objects from your desk, book-bag, or pockets. Look around the room for small objects as well.
2. Once you have collected several objects, as a group, arrange them to make a human figure or face.
3. Share your sculpture with the class and discuss how unity occurs in each form. How is variety used? How is harmony used?

208 Unit 6 • Lesson 6

Differentiated Instruction

Reteach
Have students look around the room for things that are made of different parts but go together, for example, a computer system and printer or a table and chairs.

Special Needs
Model group norms of support and collaboration by encouraging students to verbally recognize the way that their classmates have created unity in their works of art.

ELL
When discussing unity, draw unified images on the board, and show how the different parts make up the whole.

◀ Alan McCormack.
Age 12.

Think about how the student artist used unity in this sculpture.

Creative Expression

How can you use unity to create a human or animal form using discarded machine or technology parts?

1. Begin by collecting a variety of machine and/or technology parts. Look at your list in your Art Journal for ideas. Place any extra objects you have in an area to share with your classmates.
2. Place your collected objects on your table and try to create a human or animal form. Arrange your items until you find an arrangement you like.
3. Create a class display with your completed sculpture and those of your classmates.

Art Criticism

Describe List the objects you used in your sculpture. Describe the form you made. Is it an animal or a person?

Analyze Describe how you used variety and harmony to create unity in your sculpture.

Interpret Give your sculpture a title. Create a fantasy story based on your sculpture.

Decide Were you successful in using unity in your sculpture? Explain.

Unit 6 • Lesson 6   **209**

Art Across the Curriculum

Use these simple ideas to reinforce art concepts across the curriculum.

★ **Narrative Writing** Have students each write a short story about how one of the artists got the idea for his or her artwork.

★ **Math** Have students make a pie graph that shows the gender makeup of the class.

★ **Science** Have students discuss the different parts of a computer system.

★ **Social Studies** Have students discuss how the Internet has made worldwide communication easier.

★ **Technology** Have students use a paint or draw program to design a piece of jewelry. Visit **SRAonline.com** to print detailed instructions for this activity.
NSAE 6.b

Reflect
Time: About 5 minutes

Review and Assess
"How were variety and harmony used to create unity in these three-dimensional forms?" "¿Cómo se usaron la variedad y la armonía para crear unidad en estas formas tridimensionales?"

Think
The artist created unity by using various found objects and technology parts to assemble a humanlike form.

■ Use *Large Prints 83 The Brueghel Series (A Vanitas for Style)* and *84 Milagros Memories* and ask students to compare how the artists each used unity in their works of art. Which elements create variety in each artwork? Which elements create harmony? How were the separate elements unified? What objects were used? Are they all objects students would normally associate with one another, or are they unrelated?

Informal Assessment

■ For standardized-format test practice using this lesson's art content, see pages 76–77 in *Reading and Writing Test Preparation.*

Art Journal: Critical Thinking

Have students answer the four art criticism questions—Describe, Analyze, Interpret, and Decide—in their Art Journals. Have students describe their sculptures. What objects did they use? Which methods were used for assembling them? What difficulties did students have, and how did they solve them? What function, if any, do their forms have?

LESSON 6 • Unity in Three-Dimensional Art   **209**

Lesson 6 Wrap-Up: Unity in Three-Dimensional Art

Extra! For the Art Specialist

Time: About 45 minutes

Focus
Have students study **Large Print 83** *The Brueghel Series (A Vanitas for Style)* and discuss how variety and harmony were used to unify the various parts of the artwork.

Teach
Explain to students that they will make pieces of jewelry using unusual objects. Have them look again at Christina Lemon's *Mask Brooch*. Point out that she limited her materials to two types of metal. Explain that each student will select two or three different types of objects to combine to create a necklace or pendent. Students can use more that one piece of each type of object. For example, a student might want to use six washers and one bolt. Then have students complete the Alternate Activity.

Reflect
Have students use the four steps of art criticism to evaluate their work. What type of jewelry did they make? How was unity used in the finished pieces?

Alternate Activity

Materials:
- sketchbooks
- pencils, erasers
- scissors tape
- a variety of glue
- hot-glue gun, glue sticks
- wire
- embroidery floss
- thin cording for necklaces
- various found objects

1. Have students begin by brainstorming a list of possible small objects that they can collect. Encourage them to think of things that would not normally be used. Then have students collect several of the items prior to the activity. A good place to find items is at a hardware store.

2. Once the objects are collected, have students create sketches of what they want their jewelry pieces to look like.

3. Have students assemble their jewelry, using their sketches as a guide.

Research in Art Education

"All the evidence points to a relationship between the arts and the other academic disciplines that is clear and compelling, indicating to both fields that one cannot really flourish without the influence of the other" (Letter from Jerrold Ross to Milton Goldberg, May 22, 1992).

Assessment
Use the following rubric to evaluate the artwork students make in the Creative Expression activity and to assess students' understanding of how unity is used in three-dimensional forms.

	Art History and Culture	Aesthetic Perception	Creative Expression	Art Criticism
3 POINTS	The student demonstrates knowledge of the lives and work of Paik and Lemon.	The student accurately identifies the use of unity in three-dimensional art.	The student's sculpture demonstrates unity.	The student thoughtfully and honestly evaluates own work using the four steps of art criticism.
2 POINTS	The student's knowledge of the lives and work of Paik and Lemon is weak or incomplete.	The student shows an emerging awareness of unity in three-dimensional art but cannot consistently identify it.	The student's sculpture shows some awareness of unity.	The student attempts to evaluate own work but shows an incomplete understanding of evaluation criteria.
1 POINT	The student cannot demonstrate knowledge of the life and work of Paik or Lemon.	The student cannot identify how unity is used in three-dimensional art.	The student's sculpture shows no understanding of unity.	The student makes no attempt to evaluate own work.

Have students complete page 79 or 80 in their *Assessment* books.

Unit 6 Vocabulary Review

assemblage—a variety of objects that are arranged to create one complete piece **montaje**—una técnica en que un artista recoge materiales que encuentra y los agrupa en una obra de arte tridimensional

contrast—a technique for creating a focal point or area of interest in a work of art using differences in elements **contraste**—una técnica para crear un punto local o área de interés en una obra de arte usando diferencias en los elementos

harmony—the principle of art that creates unity by stressing similarities of separate but related parts **armonía**—el principio artístico que crea unidad con énfasis en las semejanzas de partes separadas pero relacionadas

two-dimensional decoration—a flat decoration on the surface of a work of art **decoración bidimensional**—decoración plana producida en la superficie de una obra de arte

unity—the feeling of wholeness or oneness that is achieved by properly using the elements and principles of art **unidad**—el sentimiento de integridad o unicidad que se obtiene usando propiamente los elementos y principios artísticos

value—the lightness or darkness of a color **valor**—la brillantez u oscuridad de un color

variety—the principle of art that is concerned with differences or contrasts **variedad**—el principio artístico que trata sobre las diferencias o contrastes

Vocabulary Practice

T Display *Transparency 42* to review unit vocabulary words.

Reference ⭐ Vocabulary
Have students look up *variety* in a dictionary of quotations. Do any of the quotations refer to art? Have students explain their responses.

Connotation ⭐ Vocabulary
Have a volunteer select a vocabulary word, such as *harmony,* and explain whether it has a positive or negative connotation. Repeat for other unit vocabulary words.

Related Words ⭐ Vocabulary
Have students create a list of words related to the word *unity*. Have students refer to a dictionary, if necessary. Repeat the process for other unit vocabulary words.

Wrapping Up Unit 6

Variety, Harmony, and Unity

Art Criticism

Critical Thinking Art criticism is an organized system for looking at and talking about art. You can criticize art without being an expert. The purpose of art criticism is to get the viewer involved in a perception process that delays judgment until all aspects of the artwork have been studied. Push the students to expand beyond the art criticism questions.

- See pages 28–29 for more about art criticism.

Describe

- The young man with dark hair is wearing blue jeans, high-top athletic shoes, and a brown jacket with a pointed collar. He is sitting up straight in a chair, and his head looking forward. The woman has white hair pulled back in a bun. She is wearing a long, black dress with a tan lace collar and cuffs. She is sitting in a chair with just her toes touching the ground.
- The people are inside in a room. The floor is covered with a purple rug. There are two wooden, ladder-back chairs with a round table between them.

Analyze

- He uses sets of complementary colors throughout the composition.
- Andrews contrasts the calm vertical and horizontal lines with diagonal and curved lines.
- There is harmony through repetition of rounded shapes and repeated rectangular shapes.
- Student answers will vary. The following are some possible answers: Unity through a unified subject matter; unity through the balance of contrasting complementary colors or all the colors are tints except the blue of the boy's jeans.

210 UNIT 6 • Variety, Harmony, and Unity

Wrapping Up Unit 6
Variety, Harmony, and Unity

▲ **Benny Andrews.** (American). *Grandmother's Dinner.* 1992.
Oil on canvas. 72 × 52 inches (182.88 × 132.08 cm.).
Ogden Museum of Southern Art, New Orleans, Louisiana.

210 Unit 6

Art History and Culture

Benny Andrews

Benny Andrews (ben´ ē an´ drōōz) (1930–) was born in Plainview, Georgia, and was one of ten children. His parents were sharecroppers during the Great Depression. His mother supplied Andrews and his siblings with paper, pencils, and crayons. He and his brother would use nails and sticks to draw images in the dirt. He eventually went to the Art Institute of Chicago in 1957. His collages began when he was creating a painting of the janitors at the Art Institute. He incorporated a piece of paper towel into his composition, liked it, and has been creating collages along with his drawings and paintings ever since.

See pages 24–25 and 16–21 for more about art history and the subject matter.

Artist Profiles, p. 3

Artist Profile
Benny Andrews
b. 1930

Benny Andrews (ben´ ē an´ drŭz) was born in rural Georgia during the Great Depression. His parents were farmers. They raised ten children. Andrews grew up watching his father George paint pictures on every available surface. Benny himself scratched pictures in the dirt with sticks. After high school, he served in the United States Air Force. At the time, Georgia did not permit African American students to attend its art schools. A federal law forced the state to pay part of Andrews's tuition to an out-of-state school. Andrews was able to earn a degree at the Art Institute of Chicago. But even there, the work of African American students was not included in student shows. After a long struggle, Andrews finally

Art Criticism — Critical Thinking

Describe What do you see?
During this step you will collect information about the subject of the work.
- Describe the people, including their clothing and their postures.
- Describe the environment and the objects in it.

Analyze How is this work organized?
Think about how the artist used the elements and principles of art.
- How did the artist use contrast of colors to create variety?
- How did he use contrast of lines to create variety?
- How did he use shapes to create harmony?
- How did he make this work a unified composition?

Interpret What does the artwork say?
Combine clues you collected during description and analysis with your personal experiences to find out what this painting is about.
- What do you think is the story behind this painting?
- What is the location of this room?
- Why do you think there is a high-intensity blue on the boy's jeans when all the other colors are tints?

Decide What do you think about the work?
Use all the information you have gathered to decide why this is a successful work of art.
- Is this successful because it is realistic, because it is well organized, and/or because it conveys a message?

Unit 6 **211**

Interpret

- Answers will vary. Some students may recall Sunday dinners with their grandmothers, or visiting a nursing home. Some may recognize the importance of the role of the family matriarch in African American culture.
- Answers will vary. Some students may say this is a city apartment; others may place the room in a country home. Some students may say it is a dining room.
- Answers will vary. Some students may say that this is to bring attention to the boy's legs, which look like they are ready to move.

Decide

- Students' answers will vary based on individual experiences. They may use more than one aesthetic theory to explain the success of this work.

Art Journal: Writing
Have students write answers to Aesthetic Perception in their Art Journals. Have them discuss their answers in small groups.

Aesthetic Perception

Seeing Like an Artist Have students think about the places in which they have eaten dinner. Then have them compare the scene in one of these places to *Grandmother's Dinner*.

Describe
- Describe the people and things in the room.

Analyze
- What kind of variety was in the room?
- Did the room seem unified?

Interpret
- What feelings do you have when you think of the dinner? Why?

Decide
- If you could have the dinner again, what would you change?

UNIT 6 • Variety, Harmony, and Unity **211**

"Artists use the art principles of variety, harmony, and unity to help organize the art elements in works of art."

"Los artistas usan los principios artísticos de variedad, armonía y unidad para organizar los elementos artísticos en obras de arte bi y tridimensionales."

T Review the unit vocabulary with students, using **Transparency 42.**

Art Journal: Writing
Have students answer the questions on page 182 in their Art Journals or on a separate sheet of paper. Answers: 1. C, 2. A, 3. A, 4. B, 5. B

T For further assessment, have students complete the unit test on **Transparency 48.**

VISIT A MUSEUM
Dallas Museum of Art

▶ Explain to students that the museum facility first opened in 1909 under the name Free Public Art Gallery of Dallas. In 1932 the museum was renamed the Dallas Museum of Fine Arts.

▶ Two objectives of the Dallas Museum of Art are education through exposure to art of the highest quality and the support of young regional artists. In order to accomplish these objectives, the museum offers a full and varied exhibition schedule. What do students think of these objectives?

"My work has always had the problem of where to place it. I will always be an outsider, and I like that."

—Benny Andrews

212 UNIT 6 • Variety, Harmony, and Unity

Wrapping Up Unit 6
Variety, Harmony, and Unity, continued

Show What You Know
Answer these questions on a separate sheet of paper.

1. An _____ is a variety of objects put together to create one complete piece.
   A. abstract
   B. application
   C. assemblage

2. _____ is the principle of art that relates to differences or contrasts.
   A. Variety
   B. Unity
   C. Harmony

3. _____ is the feeling of wholeness or oneness that is achieved by properly using the elements and principles of art.
   A. Unity
   B. Harmony
   C. Variety

4. _____ is the principle of art that creates unity by stressing similarities of separate but related parts.
   A. Variety
   B. Harmony
   C. Unity

5. When an artist creates unity, he or she harmonizes _____, or the different elements or objects, by making them relate to one another.
   A. symmetry
   B. variety
   C. emphasis

212   Unit 6

Unit Assessment Options

Aesthetic Perception
Practice Have students select one of the concepts in the Show What You Know section on page 212, then find examples of the concept in the classroom.

Creative Expression
Student Portfolio Have students review all the artwork they have created during this unit and select the pieces they wish to keep in their portfolios.

Art Criticism
Activity Have students select an artwork from this unit and study it using the four steps of art criticism. (See pages 28–29 for more information about art criticism.) Have students work in small groups and present their findings aloud or in writing.

VISIT A MUSEUM
Dallas Museum of Art

The Dallas Museum of Art began as the Dallas Art Association. It was founded in 1903, and its name was changed to the Dallas Museum of Art in 1984. The museum's permanent collection includes Asian, African, Indonesian, and contemporary art, as well as photography, pre-Columbian, impressionist and post-impressionist European art. The sculpture collection is displayed both indoors and outdoors. The museum also has a model of a French country house that contains works by Renoir, van Gogh, Gauguin, Cézanne, and Degas.

Variety, Harmony, and Unity in Animation

John Ramirez is an animator and storyboard artist for feature animated films. His video "Every Picture Tells a Story" shows how he works with a creative team to make an animated film. He studies photographs of real people and scenes to know how to draw them in his storyboards.

What to Do Create a short story that is expressed in a four-frame comic strip.

Comic strips are a simple form of storyboarding. They have four frames in which to tell a joke or simple story. The style of art and the characters' postures and expressions are also integral to the success of the idea. They show the movement, pattern, and sequence of an idea from the beginning to the end.

1. Think of a simple idea or joke. Your idea should have specific characters and a beginning, middle, or end.
2. Sketch out four scenes to show the action in the story. You can also add simple dialogue or captions.
3. Use contrast to keep the viewer's attention on a specific part of your drawing. Give your characters a name, add dialogue, and title your strip.
4. Share your strip with your friends. Ask them if they understand the story.

▲ John Ramirez. "Every Picture Tells a Story."

Art Criticism

Describe Describe the scenes you chose to convey your idea or story.

Analyze How did you choose the four scenes that would best tell your story?

Interpret How did you use contrast to emphasize the point of your joke or story?

Decide Did you use some elements (line, shape, color, etc.) to create variety, and some elements to create unity?

Art History and Culture

Animation

John Ramirez has been an animator and storyboard artist for both Walt Disney and Warner Brothers Feature Animation. As a storyboard artist, he pitches the story line and describes the characters to the other members of the creative team. *Every Picture Tells a Story* shows the process of taking an idea, developing it into a story sequence with a creative team, and storyboarding it. The art of animation is about collaboration. Creative teams work in much the same way as an orchestra. Just as each musician in an orchestra is an expert on a specific instrument, each person on the animation team is highly talented in a specific field. The film director serves in a similar capacity as a conductor, coordinating the efforts of each player to work together.

Variety, Harmony, and Unity in Animation

Objective: To create a story that is portrayed in a four-frame storyboard

Materials: *Every Picture Tells a Story*, and *Full Fathoms Five, Turbo Power, Spirit of the Landscape*. (Running time: 10:07); paper, pencils, or markers

Focus
Time: About 5 minutes

- Discuss the information on page 213.

Art History and Culture
- Have students brainstorm ideas for a short story or joke that can be illustrated in four scenes of a storyboard or in a comic strip.

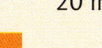

Teach
Time: About 20 minutes

Aesthetic Perception
- Explain storyboards and their function.

Creative Expression
- Direct students to think of a short original story or joke.
- Ask them to think of four scenes that could portray the idea and to sketch the scenes before drawing them. Students should have a clear idea, characters, and sequence.
- **Informal Assessment:** Have students share their storyboards and give positive feedback.

Reflect
Time: About 10 minutes

Art Criticism
- Have students answer the four art criticism questions on page 213 aloud or in writing.
- Did students effectively create four-frame storyboards?

Technique Tips
Embroidery

Running stitch
The running stitch is the simplest and most basic of all stitches. Pass the needle in and out of the fabric, making the surface stitches equal in length. The stitches on the underside should also be of equal length, but half the size or shorter than the upper stitches.

Back stitch
Bring the thread up through on the stitch line and then take a small stitch backward through the fabric. Bring the needle through again a little in front of the first stitch, then take another stitch, inserting the needle at the point where it first came through.

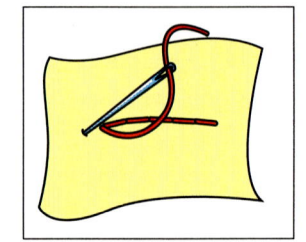

Couching
Working from left to right, position the thread or threads on the fabric. Use your thumb to hold it in place. Bring out the working couching thread from underneath the fabric, just below the laid thread. Secure the laid thread at regular intervals with a couching stitch. Finish at the end of the line by taking both the couching thread and the laid thread to the back of the fabric.

Outline stitch
The outline stitch creates a neat twisted line. Work from left to right along the line of the design, taking small regular stitches with a forward and backward motion. The thread is kept to the left of the needle after picking up a small piece of material.

Technique Tips

Drawing

Pencil

With a pencil, you can add form to your objects with shading. With the side of your pencil lead, press and shade over areas more than once for darker values. You can also use lines or dots for shading. When lines or dots are drawn close together, darker values are created. When dots or lines are drawn farther apart, lighter values are created.

Blending

Cross-hatching

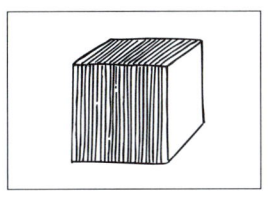

Hatching

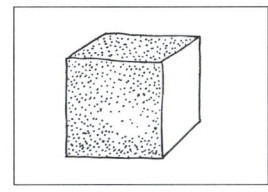

Stippling

Drawing

It is important to allow the students to experiment with the drawing media. Use gentle guidance to show them how to properly hold the drawing media. Prior to use, demonstrate the techniques as they are illustrated here. Proper handling and use will increase success and establish good habits for the future. It will also make the media last longer.

Pencil

Blending is a technique of shading in which the student holds the pencil on its side between the thumb and other fingers and shades with the side of the lead.

- Primary grade pencils with a medium-soft lead are ideal for all shading techniques.
- To create darker values, students should use the side of the pencil lead, press harder, and shade over areas more than once.
- To create lighter values, students should press lightly and shade over the area less.
- Gradations from dark to light can be created by smearing a shaded area into an area not yet shaded with a paper stump made of a tightly rolled paper towel.

Hatching is a pattern of parallel lines. How closely together the lines are drawn determines the value of that part of the drawing.

In **Crosshatching,** the parallel lines overlap each other. Like with hatching, the distance of the lines from each other determines the value.

Stippling is a series of dots that create value and value change. Careful control of the placement of all shading is important, especially stipple dots. Be sure that students are carefully drawing these dots rather than simply dotting their paper with them.

Color Pencils

- When blending colors with color pencils, it is important to color the lighter color before the darker one. A color can be darkened easily, but it is almost impossible to lighten a color.

- To create shadows, blend complementary colors. This will create browns and darker colors.

Technique Tips

Color Pencil

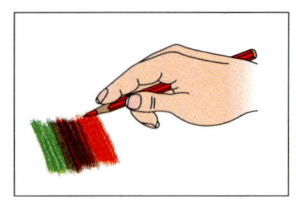

You can blend colors with color pencils. Color with the lighter color first. Gently color over it with the darker color until you have the effect you want.

With color pencils, you can use the four shading techniques.

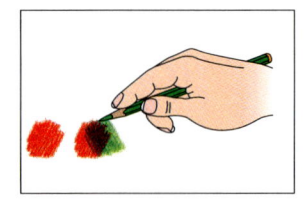

Shadows can be created by blending complementary colors.

Technique Tips

Fine-Point Felt-Tip Pen

Fine-point felt-tip pens can be used to make either sketches or finished drawings. They are ideal for contour drawings.

Use the point of a fine-point felt-tip pen to make details. Fine-point felt-tip pens can be used for hatching, cross-hatching, and stippling.

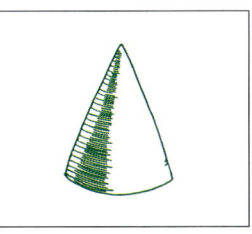

Hatching 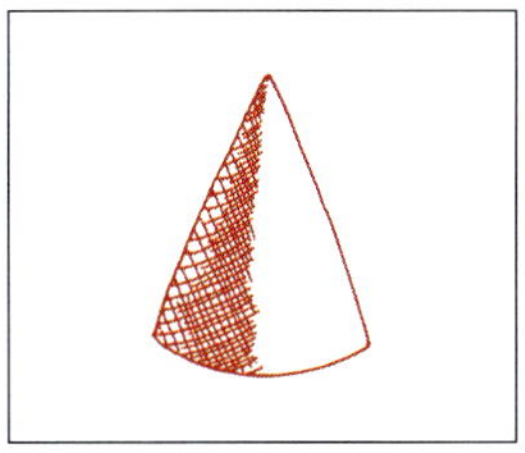   Cross-hatching 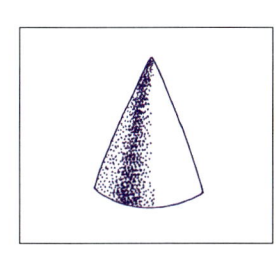   Stippling

Always replace the cap so the fine-point felt-tip pen does not dry out.

Fine-Point Felt-Tip Pen

Felt-tip pens are a practical substitute for pen and ink. Their narrow points make them ideal for drawing details and contour line drawings.

- They can be used to draw over lightly sketched pencil drawings.
- They can be used to draw a picture which can then be painted with watercolors. (The ink is water-soluble and may run when touched by wet paint.)
- Students should avoid pressing too hard when drawing so as not to damage the tip; this is especially true when stippling.
- After use, the cap should always be replaced.

Marker

- To avoid damage, students should not press hard on the marker tip. Tell them to handle the marker gently for better control.
- For thin lines and dots, a conical-tipped marker can be used.
- The side of the tip can be used to make wider lines and color in areas.
- Remind students to replace the cap to prevent drying.

218 Technique Tips

Technique Tips

Marker

Markers can be used to make sketches or finished drawings. Use the point of the marker to make thin lines and small dots.

Use the side of the tip for coloring in areas and for making thick lines.

Always replace the cap so the marker does not dry out.

Technique Tips

Color Chalk

Color chalks can be used to make colorful, soft designs.

You can use the tip of the colored chalk to create lines and shapes. You can use the side of the chalk to fill spaces. As with pencil, you can also use them for blending to create shadows.

Colored chalk is soft and can break easily. Broken pieces are still usable. Colors can be mixed or blended by smearing them together with your finger or a tissue.

Oil Pastels

Oil pastels are colors that are mixed with oil and pressed into sticks. When you press down hard with them, your pictures will look painted.

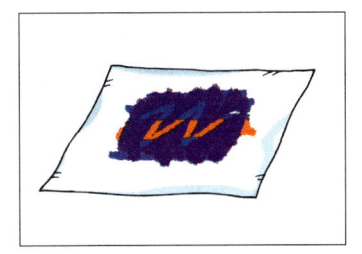

Oil pastels are soft with strong colors. You can use oil pastels to color over other media, such as tempera or crayon. Then you can scratch through this covering to create a design.

Color Chalk

- Color chalks are used to make colorful, soft designs. The use of dustless chalk is recommended for elementary classrooms. The tip of the chalk is used much like an oil pastel to make lines. To fill a space or shape with solid color, use gentle force and color over an area more than once.
- Colors can be mixed or blended by smearing them together with a paper towel wrapped around a finger.
- Like oil pastels, color chalks break easily. Reassure the students that these pieces can still be used like new ones.
- Color chalks become dirty from use. Instruct students to mark on a paper towel until the colors are clean.

Oil Pastels

- Oil pastels are pigments that are mixed with oil and compressed into sticks. They are used like crayons. By pressing with gentle force and coloring over an area several times, students can create the effect of paint.
- Students can create lines by drawing with the tip. Large spaces can be colored with the tip or the side.
- Textures can be created by making marks such as dots and lines. Textures can also be made by layering colors and scratching through with a paper clip straightened out at one end.
- Colors can be mixed or blended by smearing them with a paper towel wrapped around a finger.
- Oil pastels break easily. Reassure the students that these pieces can still be used like new ones.
- If the oil pastels become dirty from use, instruct the students to mark on a paper towel until the colors are clean again.

Painting

Tempera

- For best results, it is recommended that quality liquid tempera paint is used.

- To remove excess water from the brush, gently wipe the end of the brush on the inside edge of the container. This will allow the water to run back into the container. Discourage students from tapping their brushes on the rim of the container. This will prevent paint splatters.

- When mixing paints on a palette, always mix the darker color into the lighter color a little at a time until the desired color is reached. This reduces wasted paint. Paper plates work well as palettes and reduce cleanup.

- Use a thin brush for details.
- Use a wide brush for large spaces.

220 Technique Tips

Technique Tips

Painting

Tempera

1. Fill water containers halfway. Dip your brush in the water. Wipe your brush on the inside edge of the container. Then blot it on a paper towel to get rid of extra water. Stir the paints. Add a little water if a color is too thick or dry. Remember to clean your brush before using a new color.

2. Always mix colors on the palette. Put some of each color that you want to mix on the palette. Then add the darker color a little at a time to the lighter color. Change your water when it gets too cloudy.

3. To create lighter values, add white. To darken a value, add a tiny amount of black. If you have painted something too thickly, add water and blot it with a clean paper towel.

4. Use a thin pointed brush to paint thin lines and details. For thick lines or large areas, press firmly on the tip or use a wide brush.

5. Wash your brush when you are finished. Reshape the bristles. Store brushes with bristles up.

220 Technique Tips

Technique Tips

Watercolor

1. Fill water containers halfway. Dip your brush in the water. Wipe your brush on the inside edge of the container. Then blot it on a paper towel to get rid of extra water. With your brush, add a drop of water to each watercolor cake and stir. Remember to clean your brush whenever you change colors.

2. Always mix colors on a palette. Put some of each color that you want to mix on the palette. Then add the darker color a little at a time to the lighter color. Change your water when it gets too dark.

3. To create lighter values, add more water. To darken a value, add a tiny amount of black. If you have painted something too quickly, add water to the paint on the paper and blot it with a clean paper towel.

4. Use a thin pointed brush to paint thin lines and details. For thick lines or large areas, press firmly on the tip or use a wide brush.

5. For a softer look, tape your paper to the table with masking tape. Use a wide brush to add water to the paper, working in rows from top to bottom. This is a wash. Let the water soak in a little. Painting on wet paper will create a soft or fuzzy look. For sharper forms or edges, paint on dry paper, using only a little water on your brush.

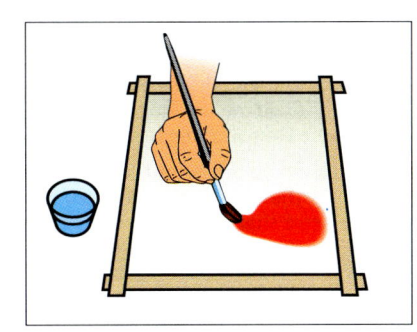

6. Wash your brushes when you are finished. Reshape the bristles. Store brushes with the bristles up.

Watercolor

- School watercolors come in semimoist cakes. Moisten each cake that is going to be used by dripping a little water from the brush onto the cake and gently stirring the water on the surface of the paint.
- Create thick lines by gently pressing down on the brush.
- Create thin lines by lightly touching the surface of the paper with the tip of the brush.
- To create textures such as stipple (dots) or lines, demonstrate these techniques:
  1. Wet a round, soft-bristled watercolor brush.
  2. Carefully squeeze excess water from the bristles.
  3. Gently divide the bristles into spikes.
  4. Carefully touch the moistened paint cake with the bristle tips so that some paint is absorbed by the bristles.
  5. Lightly touch the paper with the separated bristles. Gentle taps create irregular dots. Gentle, upward strokes create irregular lines.
  6. When finished, rinse, clean, and reshape the brush.
- To create lighter values, the hue should be thinned with water using these steps:
  1. Use a watery brush.
  2. Thin the hue on the palette with water.
  3. Brush water over an already painted area.
  4. Blot wet, painted area with a paper towel.
- To create darker values, add drops of black to the hue on the palette, *one at a time*, until the desired value is achieved.

Wash

Painting or sponging water onto the paper prior to painting will create soft lines, soft-edged shapes, and softer colors. The water should be allowed to soak into the paper before painting.

- To create sharp, clear lines and shapes, students should paint on dry paper with a damp brush.
- To create a fuzzy look, students should paint on dry paper with a dry brush and very little paint.

Technique Tips

Acrylic Paint

1. Because acrylics dry so fast, squeeze out only a little paint. If you are using a plastic palette, regularly use a spray bottle to spray a fine mist over the paint to keep it moist.

2. Keep a piece of paper towel or cloth next to your water jar, and wipe your brushes on it after you rinse them. When you are not working with your brush, keep it in the water jar.

3. If applied thickly or if mixed with a little white, all acrylic colors can be opaque. If they are diluted, they can be used like watercolors or for airbrushing.

4. Unlike a watercolor wash, when an acrylic wash dries, it is permanent and is insoluble. It can be over-painted without disturbing the existing wash.

5. Because acrylics dry rapidly, you need to work fast to blend colors. If you are working on paper, dampening the paper will increase your working time.

6. Masking tape can be put onto and removed from dried acrylic paint without damaging an existing layer. This makes it easy to produce a sharp edge. Be sure the edges of the tape are firmly pressed down. Do not paint too thickly on the edges, or you will not get a clean line when you lift the tape.

7. When you are finished painting, clean your brushes. Be sure to clean inside the bristles so no paint remains.

Technique Tips

Collograph Print

1. Place your printing plate on a prepared surface. Squeeze some ink onto a tray and smooth it out in a small section to cover your brayer with ink.

2. Use the brayer to cover the plate with ink. Roll the ink in two directions: up and down and side to side.

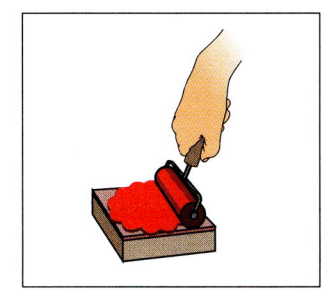

3. Move the plate to a clean area of the table. Place paper on topof the plate and gently rub the top of the paper with your fingers.

4. Carefully hold the corners of one edge of the paper and lift it off the print. Place the finished print in a safe place to dry.

Technique Tips

Handcoloring a Photograph

If you like, you can make a black and white photograph more interesting by adding color.

1. You can use water-based markers to add color to a photograph.
2. Color pencils create soft colors. Creating layers of color pencil gives a deeper hue.

3. Use a cotton swab to blend in your color pencils and an eraser to remove unwanted marks.
4. Experiment with crayons, oil pastels, and pastel chalks.

Technique Tips

Mobile

There are many ways to put together a mobile, but the assembly is always the same. Start connecting the pieces from the bottom.

1. Find or create the shapes you want to use. Lay them on a large sheet of paper. Draw lines connecting the bottom, or end, pieces.

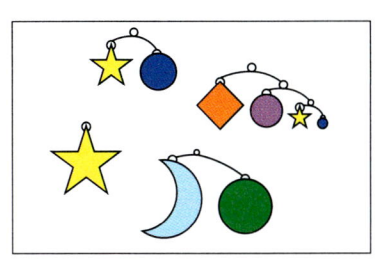

2. Wire the pieces together, starting with the small end pieces. Then connect the middle-size systems together.

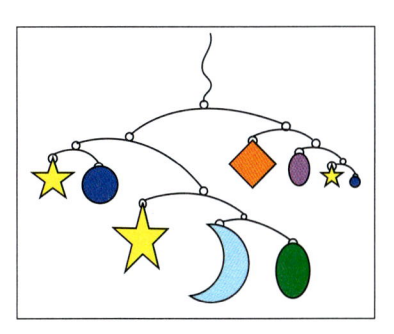

3. Connect the top bar last. Connect the middle systems to the top bar, then balance and hang the mobile.

Collage

Scissors

- It is important to teach students safety when they use scissors. They should always cut away from their bodies. Of course they should never point their scissors at others, spin them on the table, or walk around the room with them.

- There are scissors specially made to spring open for students who are physically challenged, or who are not yet developmentally ready to use standard school scissors. Many scissors on the market today can be used with the right or left hand. If these are not available, keep a supply of "lefty" scissors for students who need them.

- To cut thick yarn or fabric, encourage students to work in pairs. While one cuts, the other can stretch the yarn or fabric. This makes cutting easier and encourages cooperation.

Arranging a Design

A collage is a work of art in which bits and pieces of paper, fabric, and other materials are glued onto a surface to create a **composition.**

- Provide a variety of textured and colored papers, yarns, fabrics, and found objects for students to use. Hard-to-cut materials should be precut for students.

- When using paper, students may choose to tear and/or cut their shapes.

- Encourage students to arrange the design first. They should pay as much attention to the negative spaces as the positive ones.

- Glue only after the final colors, shapes, and textures have been chosen and arranged. White glue will attach most porous items to the background surface.

Technique Tips

Collage

In a collage, objects or pieces of paper, fabric, or other materials are pasted onto a surface to create a work of art. When planning your collage, consider such things as:

- Size of shapes and spaces
- Placement of shapes and spaces
- Color schemes
- Textures

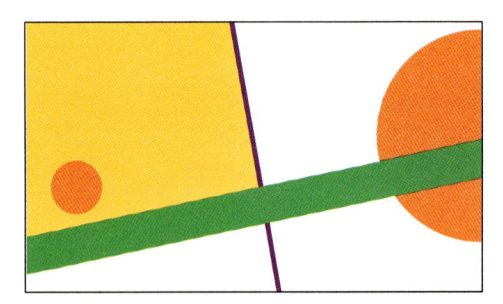

Remember that the empty (negative) spaces are also part of your design. Plan a collage as you would plan a painting or a drawing. After deciding what shapes and objects you want to use, arrange them on the paper. When you have made an arrangement you like, glue your shapes and objects to the paper.

Technique Tips
Weaving

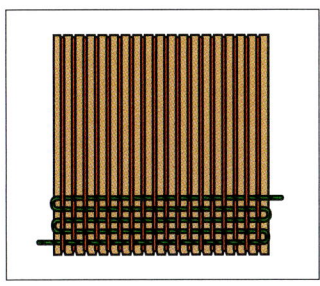

1. Measure and cut notches one-quarter inch apart and one-half inch deep on opposite sides of the cardboard.
2. Tape the warp thread to the back and string from top to bottom. Continue to wrap the thread through each notch until you reach the end. Tape the end of the thread to the cardboard.
3. Start to weave horizontally at the bottom of the loom in an over-one-under-one motion.
4. Do not pull the weft threads too tight.

Sculpting

Working with Clay

- Always protect the work area with a cloth or newspaper. Clay dust is messy. Always wash the tables after working with clay.

- To help prevent earth clay from drying and cracking, students should not overhandle the clay. Keep damp paper towels nearby for students to keep their hands moist.

- The following steps are for modeling a person or animal from clay:

    1. Roll the piece of clay into an oval-shaped form. Describe this to the students as a "potato" shape.
    2. Pinch a head shape on one end.
    3. Pinch and pull out arms and legs.
    4. Leave some, but not too much, clay for the body.
    5. Squeeze the head, arms, legs, and body into the desired shapes.

- Clay is often sold in 25 pound bags. The bags are usually strong enough to keep the clay damp, but be sure to close the bag tightly with a twist tie or some other device to keep it sealed. It is a good idea to place the bag inside a second bag, like a heavy-duty garbage bag, for long-term storage.

Joining Clay

- Clay is joined by using **slip,** a creamy mixture of clay and water. Slip can be made by putting a few dry pieces of clay in a container and covering them with water. When the clay dissolves, stir to achieve a creamy consistency.

- Joining clay also requires a scoring tool such as a straightened paper clip. The steps below are called the four *S*s—score, slip, smooth, and squeeze.

    1. **Score** the two pieces to be joined.
    2. Apply **slip** to one of the surfaces.
    3. **Smooth** the seam.
    4. **Squeeze** the two surfaces together.

Carving Clay

There are a variety of tools manufactured for carving clay. Some classroom items that will work just as well are plastic eating utensils, craft sticks, and paper clips. The straightened end of a paper clip can be used to draw in the clay. The rounded end can be used as a gouge to carve clay away.

Technique Tips

Sculpting

Clay

Pinch and pull clay into the desired shape.

Joining Two Pieces of Clay

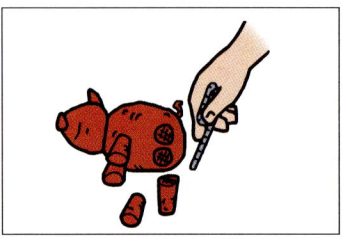

Score, or scratch, both pieces so they will stick together.

Attach the pieces with some *slip,* which is watery clay.

Squeeze the two pieces together. *Smooth* the edges.

Technique Tips

Clay Slab Construction

To roll a slab of clay, press a ball of clay into a flat shape on a cloth-covered board. Place one $\frac{1}{4}$-inch slat on each side of the clay. Use a roller to press the slab into an even thickness. With a straightened paper clip, trim the slab into the desired shape.

Wrap unfinished sculptures in plastic to keep them moist until finished.

When you are constructing a form such as a container or house with slabs of clay, it may be necessary to stuff the form with wads of newspaper to support the walls. The newspaper will burn out in the kiln.

Activity Tips

Unit 1 · Lesson 1 — Line and Qualities of Line

Creative Expression

1. Look over the directions you wrote in your Art Journal on how to make a contour drawing. Make a practice drawing of your object, or objects, following your directions.
2. Using a marker, make a second drawing of the same object.
3. Make some lines thick and some lines thin. You may pick up your marker and look at your paper to make the thick and thin lines. Always concentrate on the contours of your object.
4. Look at your first contour drawing and compare it to your second one.

Unit 1 · Lesson 2 — Geometric and Free-Form Shapes

Creative Expression

1. Collect your pattern pieces from the Practice activity. Select a background square in the color that best depicts the time or place of your scene. Select various colors of felt for each of your pattern pieces.
2. Use a piece of chalk or a pencil to outline the paper shapes onto the felt pieces. Cut out the felt shapes and arrange them on the background square. Secure your shapes with either straight pins or a dot of craft glue.
3. Thread your needle and stitch the cut shapes into place on the background. Look at the embroidery Technique Tips on page 214 to get ideas for different stitches to use.

Activity Tips

Unit 1 · Lesson 3

Geometric Forms

Creative Expression

1. Look at the sketches in your Art Journal and collect the wooden forms you will need.
2. Use either wood glue or craft glue to put your sculpture together. You may need to use a hot-glue gun and sticks for those pieces that will not hold together. Ask your teacher for assistance with this.
3. As you glue your pieces together, see if your sculpture will stand on its own. You may need to make adjustments to your sculpture as you work.
4. Apply acrylic paint to your sculpture once the glue has dried completely. You may want to test colors on a scrap piece of paper before using it on the wood.

Unit 1 · Lesson 4

Free-Form Form

Creative Expression

1. Look at the sketches you drew in your Art Journal and select one. On sketch paper, make simple contour line drawings of the main forms for your model.
2. Cut a piece of thin wire so that it is about three inches longer than the contour of your drawing. Start at the bottom of the drawing and trace around the object using the wire. Leave about $1\frac{1}{2}$ inches of extra wire at the beginning. As you bend your wire around the line, tape it in place. When you reach the bottom where you started, twist the two ends together so that you form a stake, or stick.
3. Cover your wire shapes with tissue paper.
4. Color your base with acrylic paints. Construct your model by pushing the wire stakes or sticks into the base.

Geometric Forms

- Wood scraps can be found at home improvement and lumber stores. Be sure to ask at least a few days ahead of time and they will save them for you.
- Spray paint can be used but only outdoors and by the teacher.
- A hot-glue gun should be used by the teacher only.

Free-Form Form

- Tempera paint can be used to paint a cardboard base, but not any type of foam base.
- Wire can be found at art supply or craft stores. A call to a cable company or local phone company may result in free wire. Usually two to three feet sections are cut during installations and these multicolored wires are safe and can easily be used for this project.
- Demonstrate gluing tissue paper to the wire. Dot one side of the wire with glue and place it on the tissue paper. Let this dry for about one minute so that it is tacky and carefully cut around the edge, leaving about a half of an inch. Gently fold the edge over so that it is glued in place on the back of your shape. You may need to add a little more glue.
- Demonstrate gluing one piece of wire between two pieces of tissue paper. When it is dry, leaf and grass shapes can be cut out so that the wire is in the center. The grass and leaf shapes can be curled on a pencil or a finger, and so can chenille sticks.

Space and Perspective

- Demonstrate holding a ruler. Spread the hand open so that the thumb and index finger are holding the ruler at the same time. This will keep the ruler straight when drawing a line.

Positive and Negative Space

- Have students begin to collect various objects to incorporate into their sculptures prior to starting this lesson. Buttons, aluminum-can tabs, small silk flowers, fabric scraps, wire, and beads are a few items they may want to collect.

Activity Tips

Unit 1 · Lesson 5   Space and Perspective

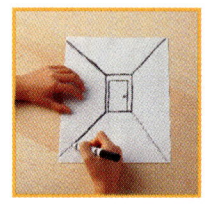

Creative Expression

1. Using a pencil, draw a horizontal or vertical rectangle in the center of your paper, no larger than three inches. This will be the end of the hall. Draw very lightly.
2. Mark a point near the center of your box—the vanishing point. Draw four lines with a ruler coming out from that point toward each corner of your paper. These lines will create the walls of your hallway. Add guide lines for the top and bottom of doors or objects on the walls or in the hall.
3. Outline your drawing with a marker. Erase any unnecessary guide lines. Use watercolor or color pencils to complete your drawing.

Unit 1 · Lesson 6   Positive and Negative Space

Creative Expression

1. Look over your selected sketch in your Art Journal. Begin cutting the geometric and free-form shapes for your sculpture. Cut slots and tabs in the shapes to construct your assemblage. Add your features separately, such as eyes, ears, nose, and mouth. Try to create a distinct personality with the facial features.
2. Arrange your shapes on your base as you work. Be sure to include negative space within your sculpture. Glue your sculpture to the base.
3. Use acrylic paints and a marker to add color and details. Glue your collected items to your sculpture to embellish it. Give your completed sculpture a descriptive title.

Activity Tips

Unit 2 · Lesson 1 — Hue

Creative Expression

1. Make a pattern of your selected shape or object and trace it twelve times on white paper. Outline your shapes using a permanent marker.
2. Mix only primary colors to make secondary and intermediate colors. Paint your first three shapes the primary colors. Paint the next three shapes the secondary colors. Paint the last shapes the intermediate colors.
3. Once your shapes are dry, cut them out. Arrange them to show the correct color relationships. Your color wheel does not have to be perfectly round, nor does it have to be a wheel. Glue your shapes onto a black or white background once you have your idea.

Unit 2 · Lesson 2 — Value

Creative Expression

1. Look over your planned sketch in your Art Journal. Lightly transfer your sketch onto your paper, filling the whole page.
2. Select any one color from the color wheel. From your paint palette, mix tints and shades and try them out on a scrap sheet of paper.
3. Paint your landscapes. Using tints and shades of your selected color, make gradual changes in the value in some areas of your painting. Show a wide range of values from almost-white highlights to dark shadows.

Hue

- Demonstrate mixing a primary and secondary color together to blend an intermediate color. It is very difficult to get a true green by mixing the primary colors in tempera paint. Once the students have shown that they can mix a green, you may choose to allow them to use a pre-mixed green for their color wheel and for mixing intermediate colors.

Value

- Demonstrate gradually blending values in a portion of a landscape. Show students how white can be added to an area in their painting to highlight that area or to blend in with the still damp paint to lighten a color.
- Pre-mixed green tempera paint can be used to mix intermediate colors because it is very hard to get a true green when mixing yellow and blue tempera.

Intensity

- If practical, have students gather around a table to demonstrate blending oil pastels.

Color Schemes

- Encourage students to mix using the primary colors when possible. Pre-mixed green tempera paint can be used to mix intermediate colors because it is very hard to get a true green when mixing yellow and blue tempera.

Activity Tips

Unit 2 · Lesson 3 — Intensity

Creative Expression

1. Choose your best sketch from your art Journal. Transfer it onto your paper, touching three edges to fill your page.
2. Select any one complementary color set. On a scrap sheet of paper, practice blending colors and creating textures.
3. Color in your portrait with oil pastels. Overlap and blend colors in some areas of your work; use bright colors in other areas. Show both high- and low-intensity colors. Keep your background simple so that it does not distract from the portrait.

Unit 2 · Lesson 4 — Color Schemes

Creative Expression

1. Divide your paper into four equal sections. Fold the paper in half, open it, and fold it in half in the opposite direction.
2. Using your sketch, make a simple line drawing on a small piece of paper. Transfer your line drawing onto each of the rectangles on your drawing paper.
3. Look at the color schemes in this unit, and select any four. Paint each of your four small landscapes using a different color scheme.
4. Use the primary and secondary colors to mix your intermediate colors. Using a small brush, paint the shapes by outlining them with a color. Then use a medium-sized brush to fill them in.

234 Activity Tips

Activity Tips

Unit 2 · Lesson 5 — Visual Texture

Creative Expression

1. Look over your sketch and draw your image using a computer program. Use any tools or options available on your software to resize and manipulate the image. When your image is completed to your satisfaction, save it as "Original Image."
2. Copy your image and save it as "Drawing 1." Use the fill bucket and other tools to add and create textures.
3. Copy several images and explore a variety of textures from each one. Label and save each drawing as you complete it.
4. Select your three best images to print.

Unit 2 · Lesson 6 — Tactile Texture

Creative Expression

1. Look over your ideas in your Art Journal. Bring in an old hat to decorate, or make a headpiece from decorated paper. Place collected textured items in a central location to be shared. Keep your personal objects in a separate envelope or bag.
2. Begin by decorating your hat with various real textures, such as beads, ribbon, lace, and fabric. Overlap some of the material, and use thread, yarn, and glue to attach it to your hat base.
3. Next think about how your personal objects will be arranged to convey the theme of your chosen event or memory. Use thread, yarn, and glue to attach your items to your hat.

Visual Texture

- As an alternative to using the computer, students can create a drawing which they fill with crayon rubbings. Have the students refer to their practice rubbing for ideas on available textures.

Tactile Texture

- Send a letter home with students to begin collecting small objects for their hats, such as buttons, small mementos, fabric scraps, wire, and beads.
- Teacher may need a hot-glue gun and glue sticks to attach some objects.

Motif and Pattern

- Demonstrate outlining a shape with a color then coloring it in using marks in the same direction.

Two-Dimensional Pattern

- Explain to students that non-objective art is art that does not contain a subject matter. Look at the student artwork as an example.

Activity Tips

Unit 3 · Lesson 1 — Motif and Pattern

Creative Expression

1. Begin by lightly drawing two or more figures dressed in costume. Refer to your sketches and the student's art above.
2. Look at the motifs you created in the Practice activity. Select one of these to begin a pattern in part of one of the costumes or create a new one. Use a ruler to help you draw straight lines.
3. Continue creating patterns based on your motifs. You may use the same motif again, but change the color.
4. Once your drawing is complete, outline it using a fine-line black marker. Use either color pencils or markers to finish your work.

Unit 3 · Lesson 2 — Two-Dimensional Pattern

Creative Expression

1. Begin by lightly drawing one large shape off center on your paper. Divide the rest of your paper using straight and curved lines. Have your lines go through your shape. You will have created a variety of shapes.
2. Look at the patterns you created in the Practice activity. Select one of these to begin a pattern in one of the shapes in your design or create a new one. Use a ruler to help you draw straight lines.
3. Continue creating patterns in each shape. Use random, regular, and alternating patterns.
4. Use either color pencils or markers to finish your patterns and complete your work.

Activity Tips

Unit 3 · Lesson 3 — Three-Dimensional Pattern

Creative Expression

1. Begin by forming your clay animal.
2. Once you have your basic animal form, add ears. You can either pinch out or attach the ear forms.
3. Think about other details that are important for your particular animal, like eyes and feet. When you have finished forming your animal, use a toothpick or pencil to add details.
4. Paint your animal using one or two base colors. Once the base color has dried, add patterns using a thin brush or paint pen. Dots and lines can be layered on top of one another.

Unit 3 · Lesson 4 — Rhythm

Creative Expression

1. Select a shape and a line. Repeat parallel lines and shapes to create visual rhythm. Place them so that your entire paper is covered. Make your design nonobjective; there should be no recognizable objects in your composition.
2. Once your design is drawn to your satisfaction, use a felt-tip marker to trace over your lines.
3. Look at the color schemes in Unit 2. Select one color scheme to use in your nonobjective design. Use color pencils to add color to complete your design.

Three-Dimensional Pattern

- Many pottery and craft shops will fire projects for you at a cost. If you do not have a kiln, contact these places and see what type of clay they can fire and the costs. Sometimes high schools have a kiln and will fire a class load.

Rhythm

- Encourage students to overlap and blend colors. Demonstrate drawing sets of parallel lines to create a basket effect.

Visual Movement

- Remind students that they may need to use a larger sized brush depending on the size of the objects or shapes.

Kinetic Movement

- If you choose to use coat hangers, send a letter home with students a week prior to starting this lesson.
- Demonstrate using the hole punch to make a hole in the mat board $\frac{1}{4}"$ in from the edge. Show students how to close the "S" hook once the cut shape is attached to the wire arm of the mobile.

Activity Tips

Unit 3 · Lesson 5 — Visual Movement

Creative Expression

1. Look over your sketches and select several of your images to transfer onto your drawing paper. Choose at least one animal to include in your composition and lightly draw it in first. As you draw, fill in any open spaces with overlapping plant shapes.
2. Practice mixing a variety of greens and testing them on a scrap piece of paper. Do this with any color you mix before applying it to your painting.
3. Begin painting the objects in your drawing. First outline your shape with a small paintbrush, then fill it in.
4. Create an area of interest by using a lighter color or a different shape.

Unit 3 · Lesson 6 — Kinetic Movement

Creative Expression

1. Look over your list in the Ideas section of your Art Journal. Select one subject and begin by sketching simple shapes or objects.
2. Select five or seven of your images to transfer onto your pieces of mat board. Punch a hole in the top of each shape. Use sandpaper to smooth out the cut edges of your board by sanding in one direction.
3. Use acrylic paints to paint your shapes.
4. Lay out your shapes on a large piece of newspaper. Draw the wire lines showing how the pieces will connect. Begin at the bottom and work your way up.
5. Follow the Mobile Technique Tip and connect your mobile. Attach the top bar last.

Activity Tips

Unit 4 · Lesson 1 — Formal Balance and Symmetry

Creative Expression

1. Use one of the ideas in your Art Journal to create two sketches. Use basic shapes and architectural elements. Look at the architectural details that you collected in your Art Journal for ideas.
2. Look over your two sketches and decide which one you like best. Lightly transfer your sketch onto drawing paper. Use a ruler to help you draw straight lines.
3. Add architectural textures such as wood or stone to make your design more interesting. Decide where your building will be located and add a background.
4. After your drawing is complete, outline it using a fine-tipped black marker. Use watercolor paints to complete your design.

Unit 4 · Lesson 2 — Approximate Symmetry

Creative Expression

1. Look at your collected images in your art Journal. Choose one or two images.
2. Use a computer draw or paint program and the mouse to draw your interpretation of the selected images. Do not include anything from the images' background.
3. Create a copy of your images and save them. Use a variety of tools on the menu to create a design using approximate symmetry.
4. After your drawing is complete, select either a warm or cool color for your background. Create interest by using a contrasting color to complete your design. Title and save your work.

Activity Tips **239**

Informal Balance

- Demonstrate drawing with the glue in a steady stream. Show students how they can use a pencil point or toothpicks to connect the glue that separates into dots. Scratch through the glue lines where the breaks are in the lines with a toothpick or pencil, as if drawing.

Radial Balance

- Large, plastic coffee-can lids are good for tracing circle patterns.

Activity Tips

Unit 4 · Lesson 3 — Informal Balance

Creative Expression

1. Arrange a variety of objects to create a still life. Include tall and short objects and items with various patterns and colors.
2. Create two quick sketches from different viewpoints using asymmetrical balance. Select the one you like best.
3. Use white chalk to transfer your sketch onto black paper. Use white glue to outline your drawing. Let it dry.
4. Use color chalk to add color to your still-life drawing.
5. Give your completed work a title.

Unit 4 · Lesson 4 — Radial Balance

Creative Expression

1. Lightly trace a circle on your paper with eight pie shapes.
2. Draw one shape in the center of your radial design for your focal point. Complete your design by using the shapes you made in your Art Journal. Outline your drawing using a fine-tip permanent marker.
3. Select a color scheme using three or more colors that you like. Use color pencils or markers to complete your radial design.
4. Display it for your classmates to see.

Activity Tips

Unit 4 · Lesson 5 — Emphasis of an Element

Creative Expression

1. You will be layering each of your shapes to create a collage of your image. Look at your plant sketch in your Art Journal. Draw and cut out your large shape first. If you are creating a flower, cut out the individual petals and glue these on top of your paper. Glue the center portion last. This is called a printing plate.
2. Once you have glued down all of your shapes, make a crayon rubbing of it. This will allow you to see what your print will look like when it is finished. Make any necessary changes.
3. Set up your printing area and create a print of your collaged image.

Unit 4 · Lesson 6 — Emphasis of Area

Creative Expression

1. Review your list of locations in your art Journal. As a class, select one location. Look over your Practice gesture drawings and select one or create a new one.
2. Create a wire figure based on your selected gesture. The wire figure is an armature, the framework for supporting the foil that will be used for your sculpture.
3. Using pieces of aluminum foil no larger that your hand, cover the wire sculpture. You can pinch out a nose or add clothing with more foil.
4. Attach your completed foil sculpture to a base, if necessary. As a class, arrange your sculptures for display.

Emphasis of an Element

- Collect a variety of plant examples, such as plastic or silk flowers, real plants or flowers, digital images or magazine photos prior to the create activity.
- Demonstrate cutting and layering shapes to create the flower or plant image. Show students how each part has to be cut and glued, sometimes on top of another shape, other times partially overlapping another shape. Demonstrate how to check the quality of the image. Do this by creating a crayon rubbing of the printing plate as it is being glued together.

Facial Proportions

- Show students that by wrapping a piece of paper towel around their index finger they can blend oil pastels together. This technique can be used to make a gradual value change.

Activity Tips

Unit 5 · Lesson 1 — Facial Proportions

Creative Expression

1. Choose one of the sketches from your Art Journal. Begin by using chalk to draw in your facial proportions. Add your features, hair, and clothing to fill the page.
2. Select a color scheme that you think best reflects your personality.
3. Practice blending colors on a scrap piece of paper. Do this by overlapping colors and working them with your oil pastels. Try using a paper towel to blend colors.
4. Use oil pastels to complete your self-portrait.

Unit 5 · Lesson 2 — Figure Proportions

Creative Expression

1. Take turns with your partner posing for one another and making several sketches. Use the sighting technique. Think about body proportions as you create your sketches.
2. Select the sketch you like best and transfer it to drawing paper. Add a prop to your drawing that looks like it belongs, such as a tennis racket. Use a combination of simple thick and thin lines, and draw your image large so that your figure fills the page. Include a background in your drawing.
3. Use a marker to outline your drawing and to add textures. Use hatching, cross-hatching, or stippling techniques to create value.

Activity Tips

Unit 5 · Lesson 3 — Facial Distortion

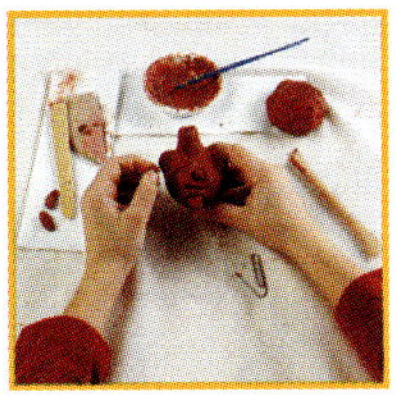

Creative Expression

1. Create various sketches of a face jug and select one. Look at your selected sketch, and then make a clay sphere. Gently pat your form, turning it in your hands to make it even all around. Flatten the bottom to sit upright.
2. Pinch out a spout at the top of your form, but do not make a hole. Lightly draw the facial features.
3. Form and attach the features using the scoring method. Make the eyes from small balls of clay, and make the lids from small coils of clay.
4. Use a pencil to pierce a hole in the spout as you support it with your fingers. Add color with glaze.

Unit 5 · Lesson 4 — Figure Distortion

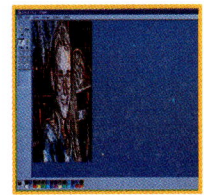

Creative Expression

1. Use a digital camera, and take several photographs of a family member or friend. Choose one or two of your photographs.
2. Begin by loading the image into the computer. If you have regular photographs, scan them into the computer.
3. Use a draw or paint program to create a copy of the image, and then save it. Use a variety of tools on the menu to create a distortion of the image.
4. Add textures to the background or alter the colors. Title and save your work.

Facial Distortion

- Demonstrate drawing lightly with the glue on the clay sphere prior to placing the features. Show students how a pencil or nail can be used to scratch or score the areas where a feature will be added. Score both the small piece of clay and the surface of the jug, apply some slip, attach so the scored areas touch, and smooth the seam.

Figure Distortion

- If computers are not available, students can draw a portrait or a character using figure distortion.

Activity Tips

Unit 5 · Lesson 5 — Realistic Scale

Creative Expression

1. Look at the list of rooms and images in your Art Journal. Select one of the people from the Practice activity as your client.
2. Begin planning a chair for your client. Think about where it will be used and the image you will use for your design. Create several sketches until you make one you like.
3. Use a pencil and a ruler to draw your chair to scale.
4. Use color pencils to add details and to complete your design.

Unit 5 · Lesson 6 — Unrealistic Scale

Creative Expression

1. Begin by sketching several designs. Select your best one. Look at the collected cutouts in your Art Journal and place them on the table. Select three of the images to use in your collage.
2. Look through magazines to find at least four examples of natural elements, such as trees and rocks. Cut these out.
3. Lightly transfer your sketch onto paper. Combine your collected images to create a surreal collage.
4. Use oil pastels to add color and complete your work.

Activity Tips

Unit 6 · Lesson 1: Variety through Line, Shape, and Color

Creative Expression

1. Select your best sketch from your Art Journal or create a new one. Then select a colored sheet of paper for your background.
2. Begin by cutting out the shape of the person or animal from paper whose color contrasts with your background color.
3. Use a variety of colors and shapes to cut out objects for your environment. Overlap your shapes to make them more interesting.
4. Glue your arrangement in place. Use a felt-tip marker to make a variety of repeated lines to complete your collage.

Unit 6 · Lesson 2: Variety Through Contrast

Creative Expression

1. Decide on a theme and take several black-and-white photographs.
2. Look at your developed images carefully. Choose one or two photographs that show a range of gray values. Put these aside to hand-color.
3. Select a third image for practice. Review the Hand-Coloring a Photograph Technique Tips. Experiment with the various techniques.
4. Add variety to your two selected images by adding color to one area in each photograph. Use one hand-coloring technique you like for each image.

Variety Through Contrast

- Try to have matte copies made. The matte texture takes the color better than the glossy finish. However, you can use a glossy print if it is the only option.
- Give students these three pointers for taking a good picture: get close to the subject; keep the background interesting but not busy; and take several photographs of the subject.

Harmony in Three-Dimensional Art

- Flat boxes can be collected from the person who stocks the vending machines at your school.
- A hot-glue gun and glue sticks can be used by the teacher to secure some objects that may be heavy.
- Paper boxes can be made from 9″ × 12″ construction paper. Cut diagonally $2\frac{1}{2}″$ into all four corners, fold the sides between the cuts, overlap the ends, and staple to create a box.

246 Activity Tips

Activity Tips

Unit 6 · Lesson 3 Harmony in Two-Dimensional Art

Creative Expression

1. Look over your planned sketch in your Art Journal or create a new one. Use a light piece of chalk to transfer your design to the burlap. Make your image large, and keep your design simple.
2. Use masking tape to tape around the edges of the burlap before you begin stitching. This will keep it from unraveling.
3. Look at your practice embroidery piece and the Technique Tips on page 214. Outline your image first using either a running, back, or outline stitch. Use a contrasting color of yarn and a satin stitch to complete your work. Make sure you have used at least one art element in your embroidery to create harmony.

Unit 6 · Lesson 4 Harmony in Three-Dimensional Art

Creative Expression

1. Look over the list of recycled objects in your Art Journal and try to collect several of the objects.
2. Begin by arranging the objects in the box. None of the objects should stick out beyond one inch from the box's edge. Think about repeating similar shapes in one area of the box and using different shapes in another area.
3. Once you have arranged your objects, glue them in place. Use one harmonious color to paint all of the assemblages of your group members. Arrange the individual works to create one or two harmonious sculptures.

246 Activity Tips

Activity Tips

Unit 6 · Lesson 5 — **Unity in Weaving**

Creative Expression

1. Prepare your loom following the Weaving Technique Tips. Look at your loom design in your Art Journal. Select your yarn and attach it to your first warp string.
2. Begin by using the tabby (basket) weave for the first few rows to get used to the rhythm of weaving.
3. Look at your sketch and try to follow your plan. You may find as you work that you need to make adjustments to your design.
4. When you are finished, take your weaving off the loom.

Unit 6 · Lesson 6 — **Unity in Three-Dimensional Art**

Creative Expression

1. Begin by collecting a variety of machine and/or technology parts. Look at your list in your Art Journal for ideas. Place any extra objects you have in an area to share with your classmates.
2. Place your collected objects on your table and try to create a human or animal form. Arrange your items until you find an arrangement you like.
3. Create a class display with your completed sculpture and those of your classmates.

Unity in Weaving

- Another alternative to cardboard boxes are the back of paper pads. Tear the back off and clean off the top so there is no leftover glue.
- Demonstrate the following weaving techniques:

  Tabby: This is the basic weave and is also called a basket weave. The pattern is over-under-over-under.

  Supplementary: Begin with two different colors of yarn. Tie one piece to the first warp string the second to the last warp string. Weave the first row using one color using the tabby weave. Weave the second row with your second color. Go back to the first color and alternate weaving each row with the two colors.

  Interlocking: Two yarn colors are woven from opposite directions and share the one central sting were they meet.

  Dovetail: Have two pieces of yarn loop together where they meet.

  Slits: Use the tabby weave from opposite sides but do not share or loop the yarns where they meet.

Unity in Three-Dimensional Art

- Demonstrate using tools to take machines or objects apart, or have that as a homework assignment prior to the lesson.
- A hot-glue gun should be used by the teacher only.

Visual Index

Artist Unknown
Dancing Lady
c. 50 B.C. (page 161)

Leonardo da Vinci
Ginevra de' Benci
c. 1474. (page 180)

Royal Workshops
Armor of George Clifford, Third Earl of Cumberland
1580–1585. (page 160)

Rembrandt van Rijn
Portrait of Rembrandt
1650. (page 124)

Thornton, Latrobe, Bulfinch, and Walter
United States Capitol
18th–19th centuries. (page 126)

Giovanni Paolo Pannini
The Picture Gallery of Cardinal Silvio Valenti Gonzaga
1749. (page 52)

John Singleton Copley
Henry Pelham (Boy with a Squirrel)
1765. (page 157)

Jean-Baptiste Simeon Chardin
Still Life with the Attributes of the Arts
1766. (page 83)

Artist Unknown
Ceremonial Skirt
19th century. (page 37)

248 Visual Index

Katsushika Hokusai
Li Bai (Imagery of the Poets)
1834. (page 134)

William Sharp
Great Water Lily of America
1854. (page 143)

Mary Cassatt
The Tea
1879. (page 135)

Paul Cézanne
Bottom of the Ravine
1879. (page 113)

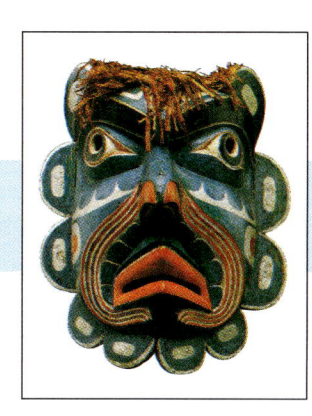

Artist Unknown
Face Mask of K̲umugwe'
c. 1880. (page 96)

Artist Unknown
Quilt
c. 1885. (page 40)

Alexandre-Gustave Eiffel
Eiffel Tower
1887–1889. (page 127)

James Ensor
Fireworks
1887. (page 78)

Vincent van Gogh
Café Terrace at Night
1888. (page 53)

Vincent van Gogh
Portrait of Joseph Roulin
1888. (page 70)

John Henry Twachtman
Snow Scene
1882. (page 71)

Mary Cassatt
Mother and Child
c. 1890. (page 90)

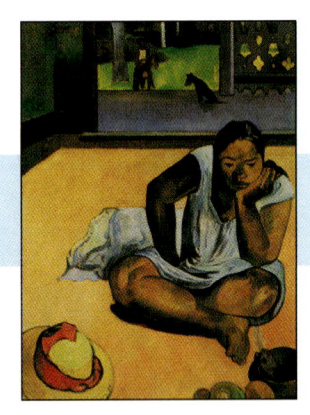

Paul Gauguin
*The Brooding Woman
(Te Faaturuma)*
1891. (page 184)

Edvard Munch
The Scream
1893. (page 164)

Harriet Powers
Pictorial Quilt
1895–1898. (page 41)

Auguste Renoir
*Young Spanish Woman
with a Guitar*
1898. (page 64)

Artist Unknown
Akrafokonmu (Soul Discs)
20th century. (page 139)

Artist Unknown
Coming of Age Hat
20th century. (page 87)

250   Visual Index

Artist Unknown
Egungun from Ogbomoso
20th century. (page 97)

Artist Unknown
Face Jugs
20th century. (page 165)

Artist Unknown
Carved Animals
20th century. (page 105)

Paul A. Baliker
Fish Story
20th century. (page 48)

Nathaniel Bustion
Bo Bo Festival Series #3
20th century. (page 186)

Susan Le Van
Two Birds in Hand
20th century. (page 82)

Julia Russell
Leonardo da Vinci Chair
20th century. (page 173)

John Warren
Dark Snapper
20th century. (page 49)

Alverda Herb (attributed to)
Bull's Eye Quilt
1900–1920. (page 138)

Visual Index **251**

Artist Unknown
Ceremonial Hanging
c. 1900. (page 203)

Gustav Klimt
Die Erfüllung (Fulfillment)
1905–1909. (page 34)

Ferdinand Hodler
James Vibert, Sculptor
1907. (page 131)

Georges Braque
Fishing Boats
1909 and 1911.
(page 79)

Henri Rousseau
Exotic Landscape
1910. (page 112)

George Bellows
Cliff Dwellers
1913. (page 60)

André Derain
Portrait of a Young Girl in Black
1914. (page 74)

Marsden Hartley
Indian Fantasy
1914. (page 100)

252 Visual Index

Franz Marc
Animals in a Landscape
1914. (page 108)

Stanton MacDonald Wright
Conception Synchromy
1914. (page 67)

Max Weber
Chinese Restaurant
1915. (page 94)

**Louisa Keyser
(Dat So La Lee)**
Basket
c. 1917–1918.
(page 202)

Karl Schmidt-Rottluff
Portrait of Emy
1919. (page 75)

Pablo Picasso
*Proposal for a Monument
to Apollinaire*
1928. (page 57)

Artist Unknown
King's Crown
c. 1930. (page 86)

Salvador Dalí
Persistence of Memory
1931. (page 176)

Visual Index   **253**

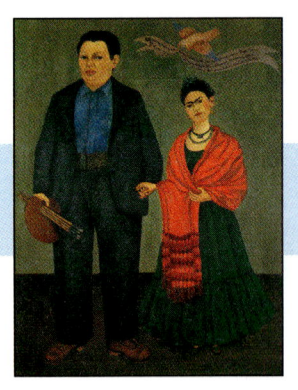

Frida Kahlo
Frida y Diego Rivera
1931. (page 154)

Georgia O'Keeffe
Cow's Skull: Red White and Blue
1931. (page 130)

Henri Matisse
Plate 24 from Poésies by Stéphane Mallarmé
1932. (page 36)

Artist Unknown
Woman's Headcloth
c. 1935–1945. (page 195)

Isabel Bishop
Two Girls
1935. (page 156)

Pablo Picasso
Portrait of Dora Maar
1938. (page 109)

Alexander Calder
Lobster Trap and Fish Tail
1939. (page 116)

Grandma Moses
Mt. Nebo on the Hill
c. 1940. (page 194)

254 Visual Index

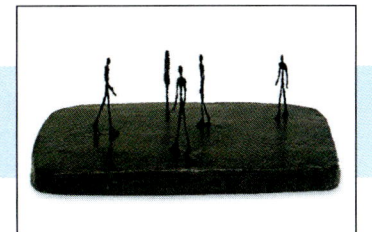

Alberto Giacometti
City Square
1948. (page 168)

Minnie Evans
King
1962. (page 101)

David Smith
Cubi XVII
1963. (page 44)

Pablo Picasso
Chicago Picasso
1967. (page 177)

Moshe Safdie
Habitat
1967. (page 172)

Alice Neel
Loneliness
1970. (page 150)

Loiuse Nevelson
White Vertical Water
1972. (page 198)

Susan Rothenberg
Cabin Fever
1976. (page 142)

Teodora Blanco
Ceramic Figures
1978. (page 104)

George Segal
Three People on Four Park Benches
1979. (page 147)

Fernando Botero
Dancing in Colombia
1980. (page 169)

Wayne Thiebaud
Down Eighteenth Street
1980. (page 120)

Paul Brach
Chuska
1982. (page 191)

Miriam Schapiro
Anna and David
1987. (page 66)

Benny Andrews
Grandmother's Dinner
1992. (page 210)

Lee Bennion
Snow Queen, Portrait of Adah
1992. (page 187)

Juan Muñoz
Last Conversation Piece
1994–1995. (page 146)

David Bates
Seated Man #4
1995. (page 56)

Nam June Paik
Eagle Eye
1996. (page 206)

Randy Ellett
National Parts
1996. (page 199)

George Hart
Roads Untaken
1998. (page 45)

Timothy Rose
Double Pan Swoosh
2001. (page 117)

Christina Lemon
Mask Brooch
2003. (page 207)

Roz Ragans
Pas de Deux
2003. (page 190)

Visual Index **257**

Glossary

Pronunciation Key: **a**t; l**ā**te; c**â**re; f**ä**ther; s**e**t; m**ē**; **i**t; k**ī**te; **o**x r**ō**se; **ô** in b**o**ught; c**oi**n; b**oo**k; t**oo**; f**o**rm; **ou**t; **u**p; **ū**se; t**û**rn; **ə** sound in **a**bout, chick**e**n, penc**i**l, cann**o**n, circ**u**s, **ch**air; **hw** in **wh**ich; ri**ng**; **sh**op; **th**in; **th**ere; **zh** in trea**s**ure.

A

alternating pattern (ôl′ tər nāt ing pat′ ərn), *noun* Can repeat a motif, but change position; alter spacing between motifs or add a second motif

analogous colors (ə nal′ ə gəs kul′ ərs), *noun* Colors that sit side by side on the color wheel and have a common hue. Violet, blue-violet, blue, blue-green are examples of analogous colors.

appliqué (ap′ li kā), *noun* Decoration made from cloth cutouts and applied, usually through embroidery, onto a background cloth

approximate symmetry (ə 'präk sə mət sim′ i trē), *noun* A type of formal balance that is almost symmetrical but small differences in the artwork make it more interesting

armature (är′ mə chər), *noun* A framework for supporting material used in sculpting

assemblage (ä säm bläzh′), *noun* A sculpture technique in which a variety of objects is assembled to create one complete piece

asymmetrical balance (ā sim′ i tri cəl bal′ əns), *noun* Another name for informal balance

atmospheric perspective (ət mos fer ik per spek′ tiv), *noun* The effects air and light have on how we perceive an object

B

background (bak′ ground′), *noun* The area of the picture plane farthest from the viewer

balance (bal′ əns), *noun* The principle of design that deals with visual weight in an artwork

blending (blen ding), *noun* A shading technique that creates a gradual change from light to dark or dark to light

body proportion (bod′ ē prə pôr shən), *noun* The size relationship of one part of the body to another

C

central axis (sen′ trəl ak′ sis), *noun* A real or imaginary dividing line which can run in two directions, vertically and horizontally

collage (kō läzh), *noun* A two-dimensional work of art made up of pieces of paper and/or fabric to create the image.

collograph (kə lō graf), *noun* A printmaking technique where cut papers or thin boards are arranged to create an image on a stiff printing plate.

color (kul′ ər), *noun* 1. The art element that is derived from reflected light; 2. In balance: a brighter color has more visual weight than a dull color; 3. In perspective: bright-colored objects seem closer, while dull or pale objects appear farther away.

258 Glossary

color scheme (kul' ər skēm'), *noun* A plan for organizing the colors used in an artwork

color spectrum (kul' ər spek' trum), *noun* The effect that occurs when light passes through a prism and separates into a band of colors in the order of red, orange, yellow, green, blue, and violet

color wheel (kul' ər 'wēl), *noun* Shows the color spectrum bent into a circle

complementary colors (kom' plə men tə rē kul' ərz), *noun* Colors that are opposite each other on the color wheel

complex geometric shapes (kom' pleks jē' ə met' rik shāps), *noun* Combined basic geometric shapes: a pentagon or hexagon

contour line (kon' tür līn), *noun* Defines the edges and surface ridges of an object

contrast (kon' trast), *noun* 1. A technique for creating a focal point or area of interest in a work of art using differences in elements; 2. In emphasis: contrast occurs when one element stands out from the rest of the work.

converging lines (kən vərg ing līnz), *noun* One of the six perspective techniques. Parallel lines seem to converge or move toward the same point as they move away from you.

cool colors (kül kul' erz), *noun* Green, violet, and blue. They suggest coolness and move away from the viewer.

cross-hatching (krôs hach' ing), *noun* A shading technique created when sets of parallel lines cross or intersect

curved (kûrvd), *adj.* A line that bends and changes gradually or turns inward to form spirals

D

detail (dē tāl), *noun* One of the six perspective techniques. Objects with fuzzy, blurred edges appear farther away than those with clear sharp edges.

diagonal (dī ag' ə nəl), *noun (adj.)* A line that moves on a slant

directional lines (di rekt' shən' al līnz), *noun* How a line moves: diagonally, vertically, or horizontally

distortion (di stôr shən), *noun* A deviation from normal or expected proportions

E

elongate (ē' lôn gāt), *verb* To stretch out or make long

embroidery (im broi də rē), *noun* The art of decorating designs with needle and thread

emphasis (em' fə sis), *noun* The principle of design that stresses one area in an art work over another area

exaggeration (eg zaj' ə rā' shən), *noun* To increase or enlarge beyond what is expected or normal

F

facial proportions (fā' shəl prə pôr shənz), *noun* The relationship of one feature of a face to another feature

focal point (fo' kəl point'), *noun* The point which the receding lines meet. It is the first part of a composition to attract the viewer's attention.

foreground (fôr' ground'), *noun* The area of the picture plane that is closest to the viewer

form (form), *noun* A three-dimensional object that is measured by height, width, and depth

formal balance (fôr' mel bal' əns), *noun* Occurs when equal or similar elements are placed on opposite sides of a central axis

free-form forms (frē' fôrm' fôrmz), *noun* Three-dimensional forms with irregular edges often found in nature

free-form shapes (frē' fôrm' shāps), *noun* Two-dimensional images made of straight or curved lines or a combination of both

freestanding sculpture (frē stan' ding skulp' chər), *noun* A three-dimensional work of art that can be viewed on all sides because it is surrounded by space

frontal proportions (frən' təl prə pôr' shənz), *noun* A front view of the head that is divided by three horizontal lines across the central axis

futurists (fyü' chə' rists), *noun* A group of Italian artists during the early twentieth-century who repeated and overlapped shapes and lines, to create the illusion of movement

G

geometric forms (je' ə met' rik fôrmz), *noun* Mathematically precise forms based on geometric shapes

geometric shapes (je' ə met' rik shāps), *noun* Mathematically precise shapes: circle, square, and triangle

gesture drawings (jes' chər drô' ing), *noun* Quick drawings used to capture the position or pose of the body

H

harmony (här' mə nē), *noun* The principle of art which creates unity by stressing similarities of separate but related parts

hatching (hach' ing), *noun* A shading technique that looks like a series of parallel lines

high-intensity color (hī in ten' si te kul' ər), *noun* A pure hue such as red

horizontal (hôr' ə zon təl), *noun* A line that moves from side to side

hue (hū), *noun* Another name for color

I

informal balance (in fôr'məl bal' əns), *noun* A way of organizing parts of a design so that unlike objects have equal visual weight

installation (in stäl ā shən), *noun* An artwork which was created for a specific place, such as a gallery or outdoor location

intensity (in ten' si te), *noun* The brightness or dullness of a color

intermediate colors (in' tər m' de it kul' ərs), *noun* Yellow-green, red-orange, blue-green; made by combining a primary with either of the secondary colors that are adjacent on the color wheel

isolation (ī' sə lā' shən), *noun* An object is emphasized by its placement apart from other objects.

K

kinetic movement (kin' e tic müv' mənt), *noun* Actual or real movement

kinetic sculpture (kin' e tic skulp' chər) *noun* A three-dimensional form that actually moves in space

260 Glossary

L

line (līn), *noun* The path of a moving point through space

linear perspective (lin ē' ər pər spek' tiv), *noun* A system used to create the illusion of depth on a flat surface

location (lō cā' shən), *noun* Artists can emphasize an object by placing it closer to the center of the piece.

low-intensity color (lō in ten' si te kul' ər), *noun* A dull hue made by mixing a color with its complement

M

maquette (ma' ket), *noun* A small model for a larger sculpture

middle ground (mid' əl ground'), *noun* The area of the picture plane that is usually toward the center

mixed-media (mikst mē dē' ə), *noun* An art object that has been created from an assortment of media or materials

mobile (mō bēl), *noun* A moving sculpture in which shapes are balanced and arranged on wire arms and suspended from the ceiling to move freely in the air currents

monochromatic (mon' ə kro mat' ik), *adj.* A color scheme that is made up of one hue and the tints and shade of that hue

monumental sculptures (mon ū' men' təl skulp' chərz), *noun* Sculptures that are larger than human forms

motif (mō tēf), *noun* A unit that is made up of objects or art elements which can be repeated

movement (müv' mənt), *noun* The principle of art that leads a viewer's eyes throughout a work of art

N

negative space (neg' ə tiv spas'), *noun* The empty space that surrounds objects, shapes, and forms

neutral colors (nü trəl kul' ərz), *noun* Black, white, and gray; give hues a range of values

nonobjective (non' əb jek' tiv), *adj.* Art that has no recognizable subject matter

O

one-point linear perspective (wun' point lin ē' ər pər spek' tiv), *noun* A system used to create the illusion of depth on a flat surface where all receding lines meet at one point

overlapping (o' vər lap ing), *noun* 1. One object covers a portion of another object. 2. In perspective: one of the six perspective techniques; the object covering another will appear closer to the viewer, creating a feeling of depth.

P

parallel lines (per ə lel līnz), *noun* Lines that move in the same direction and always stay the same distance apart

pattern (pat' ərn), *noun* A repeated surface decoration

perspective techniques (pər spek' tiv tek neks'), *noun* The six techniques an artist uses to create the illusion of depth in two-dimensional art: overlapping, size, placement, detail, color, converging lines

picture plane (pik' chər plān'), *noun* The surface of a drawing or painting

Glossary **261**

placement (plās ment), *noun* One of the six perspective techniques. Objects placed lower in the picture plane appear to be closer than those placed near eye level. There are three areas on a picture plane: foreground, middle ground, and background.

portrait (por trət), *noun* A two or three-dimensional artwork created in the image of a person or animal

position (pə zish' ən), *noun* In balance: a larger, positive shape and a small, negative space can be balanced by a small, positive shape and a large, negative space.

positive space (poz' i tiv spas'), *noun* Refers to any object, shape, or form in two- and three-dimensional art

primary hues (pri' mer ē hūz), *noun* Red, yellow, and blue, used to mix the other hues on the color wheel

printing plate (print ing plāt), *noun* A plate that holds the image that will be used to create a print

prism (pri' zm), *noun* A wedge-shaped piece of glass that bends light as it passes through

profile (prō fīl), *noun* A side view of a person or animal

profile proportions (prō fīl prə pôr' shənz), *noun* A side view of the head that is divided by three horizontal lines

proportion (prə pôr' shən), *noun* The principle of art that is concerned with the size relationship of one part to another

R

radial balance (rā' dē əl bal' əns), *noun* A type of balance that occurs when the art elements come out, or radiate, from a central point

random pattern (ran' dəm pat' ərn), *noun* Occurs when the motif is repeated in no apparent order

realistic scale (rē ə lis' tik skāl), *noun* When an artist creates a work of art where everything fits together and makes sense in size relation

regular pattern (reg' yə lər pat' ərn), *noun* Occurs when identical motifs are repeated with an equal amount of space between them

rhythm (rith' əm), *noun* The principle of design that organizes the elements in a work of art by repeating elements and/or objects

S

scale (skāl), *noun* Size as measured against a standard reference

score (skōr), *verb* The repeated scratching of the clay surface at the area that another scored piece will be attached

sculpture model (skulp' chər mo' dəl), *noun* The study or detailed example of what the sculpture will look like when completed

secondary hues (sek' ən der' ē hūz), *noun* Orange, green and violet; the result of mixing two primary hues

self-portrait (self por trət), *noun* A two or three-dimensional artwork that an artist makes of him or herself

shade (shād), *noun* Any hue blended with black

shape (shāp) *noun* A two-dimensional area that is measured by height and width

simulated texture (sim' u la' təd teks chər), *noun* Imitates real textures, see also visual texture

size (sīz), *noun* 1. in perspective: objects that are closer look larger than objects that are farther away; 2. In balance: a large shape or form will appear to be heavier than a small shape, and several small shapes can balance one large shape.

slip (slip), *noun* A mixture of clay and water that is creamy to the touch and is used to attach two scored pieces of clay together

space (spās), *noun* The art element that refers to the areas above, below, between, within, and around an object

still life (stil' līf'), *noun* The arrangement of common inanimate objects from which artists draw or paint

stippling (stip' ling), *noun* A shading technique using dots to show value

surrealism (sə' rē' əl izəm), *noun* An art movement that emphasized art in which dreams, fantasy, and the subconscious served as inspiration for artists

symmetry (sim' i trē), *noun* A type of formal balance in which two halves of a balanced artwork are identical, mirror images of each other

T

tactile texture (tak' təl teks' chər), *noun* Actual texture, texture that can really be felt

texture (teks' chər), *noun* 1. The art element that refers to the way something feels; 2. In balance: a rough texture has an uneven pattern of highlights and shadows. For this reason, a rough surface attracts the viewer's eyes more easily than a smooth, even surface.

three-dimensional patterns (thrē di men' shə nəl pat' ərnz), *noun* Patterns that have depth and are formed on the surface of a sculptural form

tint (tint), *noun* Any hue blended with white

two-dimensional decoration (tü' di men' shən nəl dek ə' rā shən), *noun* Flat decoration produced on the surface of a work of art

U

unity (ū' ni tē), *noun* The feeling of wholeness or oneness that is achieved by properly using the elements and principles in art

unrealistic scale (un' rē ə lis' tik skāl), *noun* When an artist makes size relationships that do not make sense

V

value (val' ū), *noun* The lightness or darkness of a hue

variety (və ri' ə tē), *noun* The principle of art which is concerned with difference or contrast

vertical (vür' tə kəl), *noun (adj.)* A line that moves from top to bottom

visual movement (vizh' ü əl müv' mənt), *noun* Created by repeating an art element or object in a work of art

visual texture (vizh' ü əl teks' chər), *noun* Or simulated texture, imitates real texture. It is the illusion of a three-dimensional surface.

W

warm colors (wōrm' kul' ərz), *noun* Red, yellow, and orange. They suggest warmth and come forward toward the viewer.

Z

zigzag (zig' zag) *noun (adj.)* A line that is made by joining diagonal lines

Index

A

African American art, 164, 165
akrafokonmu, 138
Akrafokonmu (Soul Discs) (Unknown), 139
alternating pattern, 102, 106
analogous color scheme, 80
Andrews, Benny, 210
Animals in a Landscape (Marc), 108
animation, 62
Anna and David (Schapiro), 66
Apollinaire, Guillaume, 56, 57
approximate symmetry, 130–133
archivists, 122
area, 146–149
Armor of George Clifford, Third Earl of Cumberland (Royal Workshops), 160
Asante people, 138
assemblages, 200
atmospheric perspective, 54
axis, 128, 158

B

background, 54
balance, 126–129, 134–141, 153
Baliker, Paul A., 48
Basket (Keyser), 202
Bates, David, 56
Bellows, George Wesley, 60
Bennion, Lee, 187
Bishop, Isabel, 156
Blanco, Teodora, 104
blending, 72
Bo Bo Festival Series 3 (Bustion), 186
book designers, 182
Botero, Fernando, 168, 169
Bottom of the Ravine (Cézanne), 113
Brach, Paul, 191
Braque, Georges, 78, 79, 94
The Brooding Woman (Gauguin), 184
buildings, 126–129
Bull's Eye Quilt (Herb), 138
Bustion, Nathaniel, 186

C

Cabin Fever (Rothenberg), 142
Café Terrace at Night (van Gogh), 53
Calder, Alexander, 116, 118
careers, 62, 122, 182
Carved Animals (Unknown), 105
Cassatt, Mary, 90, 134, 135
central axis, 128, 158
Ceramic Figures (Blanco), 104
Ceremonial Hanging (Unknown), 203
Ceremonial Skirt (Unknown), 37
Cézanne, Paul, 112, 113
Chardin, Jean-Baptiste Simeon, 82, 83
chiaroscuro, 124
Chicago Picasso (Picasso), 177
Chinese Restaurant (Weber), 94
chromolithography, 142
Chuska (Brach), 191
circle, 46
City Square (Giacometti), 168
Cliff Dwellers (Bellows), 60
coiling, 202
colors
    analogous, 80
    complementary, 76, 78
    cool, 80
    in dance, 93
    and informal balance, 136
    neutral, 72
    and perspective, 54
    and texture, 64–65
    using, 66–69
    and variety, 186–189
    warm, 80
color schemes, 78–81
Coming of Age Hat (Unknown), 86, 87
complementary colors, 76, 78
Conception Synchromy (Stanton), 67
cone, 46
conservators, 122
contour lines, 38
contrast, 148, 190–193
converging lines, 54
Conversation Piece (Muñoz), 147

Copley, John Singleton, 157
Cow's Skull: Red White and Blue (O'Keeffe), 130
cropping, 134
cross-hatching, 72
cube, 46
cubism, 78, 94
Cubi XVII (Smith), 44
curators, 122

D

Dalí, Salvador, 176
Dallas Museum of Art, 212
dance, 93, 153, 183, 213
Dancing in Colombia (Botero), 169
Dancing Lady (Unknown), 160, 161
Dark Snapper (Warren), 48, 49
da Vinci, Leonardo, 180
degikup, 202
depth, 53
Derain, André, 74
Die Erfüllung (Fulfillment) (Klimt), 34
distortion, 155, 164–171, 183
Double Pan Swoosh (Rose), 116, 117
Down Eighteenth Street (Thiebaud), 120

E

Eagle Eye (Paik), 206
Egungun from Ogbomoso (Unknown), 96, 97
Eiffel Tower (Eiffel), 126, 127
Ellett, Randy, 198, 199
embroidery, 36
emphasis, 142–149
Ensor, James, 78
Evans, Minnie, 100, 101
exaggeration, 170
Exotic Landscape (Rousseau), 112

F

face distortion, 164–167
Face Jugs (Unknown), 165
Face Mask of Kumugwe' (Unknown), 96
face proportions, 156–159

figure distortion, 168–171
figure proportion, 160–163
Fireworks (Ensor), 78
Fishing Boats (Braque), 79
Fish Story (Baliker), 48
focal point, 140, 148
folk art, 104
font designers, 182
foreground, 54
form, 35, 44–51, 62
formal balance, 126–129
free-form form, 48–51
free-form shapes, 40–43
Frieda y Diego Rivera (Kahlo), 154
frontal proportion, 158
futurists, 118

G

Gauguin, Paul, 184, 185
geometric forms, 44–47, 50
geometric shapes, 40–43, 40–43
Ginevra de' Benci (da Vinci), 180
Giacometti, Alberto, 168
Grandma Moses [Anna Mary Robertson Moses], 194
Grandmother's Dinner (Andrews), 210
Great Water Lily of America (Sharp), 143

H

Habitat (Safdie), 172
harmony, 185, 194–201, 213
Hart, George, 45
Hartley, Marsden, 100
Hartmann, William, 176
hatching, 72
Henry Pelham (Boy with a Squirrel) (Copley), 157
Herb, Alverda, 138
hexagon, 42
Hodler, Ferdinand, 130, 131
Hokusai, Katsushika, 134
hues, 66–69. *See also* colors

I

impressionism, 112, 134
Indian Fantasy (Hartley), 100
informal balance, 134–137
intensity, 74–77
intermediate colors, 68
isolation, 148

J

James Vibert, Sculptor (Hodler), 131
jewelry, 206–207

K

Kahlo, Frida, 154, 155
Keyser, Louisa (Dat So La Lee), 202
kinetic movement, 116–119
King (Evans), 101
King's Crown (Unknown), 86
Klimt, Gustav, 34, 35

L

layout artists, 62
Lemon, Christina, 206, 207
Leonardo da Vinci Chair (Russell), 173
LeVan, Susan, 82
Li Bai (Hokusai), 134
linear perspective, 54
lines, 35, 36–39, 54, 62, 186–189
lithography, 142
Lobster Trap and Fish Tail (Calder), 116
location, 148
Loneliness (Neel), 150

M

MacDonald-Wright, Stanton, 67
Marc, Franz, 108
Mask Brooch (Lemon), 207
Matisse, Henri, 36
matte surface, 88
middle ground, 54
mobiles, 116–117, 119

Moses, Anna Mary Robertson, 194
Mother and Child (Cassatt), 90
motif(s), 96–99, 106
movement, 95, 112–119
Mt. Nebo on the Hill (Moses), 194
Munch, Edvard, 164
Muñoz, Juan, 147
museums, 92, 152, 212
music, 62

N

National Parts (Ellett), 199
Neel, Alice, 150
negative space, 56–59
neutral color scheme, 72
Nevelson, Louise, 198
Norton Simon Museum, 152

O

Oaxacan sculpture, 104
octagon, 42
O'Keeffe, Georgia, 130
overlapping, 54

P

packaging designers, 182
Paik, Nam June, 206
palepai, 202
Pannini, Giovanni Paolo, 52
parallelogram, 42
Pas de Deux (Ragans), 190
pattern, 95, 96–107
pentagon, 42
Persistence of Memory (Dali), 176
perspective, 52–55
Picasso, Pablo, 56, 57, 94, 109, 176, 177
Pictorial Quilt (Powers), 41
The Picture Gallery of Cardinal Silvio Valenti Gonzaga (Pannini), 52
Pilobolus Dance Company, 153
placement, 54
Plate 24 from Poésies (Matisse), 36
Portrait of a Young Girl in Black (Derain), 74

Portrait of Dora Maar (Picasso), 109
Portrait of Emy (Schmidt-Rottluff), 74, 75
Portrait of Joseph Roulin (van Gogh), 70
Portrait of Rembrandt (van Rijn), 124
position, 136
positive space, 56–59
Powers, Harriet, 41
primary colors, 68
prism, 68
profile proportion, 158
proportion, 155–163, 183
Proposal for a Monument to Apollinaire (Picasso), 57
pyramid, 46

Q

Quilt (Unknown), 40

R

radial balance, 138–141
Ragans, Rosalind, 190
random pattern, 102, 106
ratio, 162
realistic scale, 172–175
regular pattern, 102, 106
Rembrandt (van Rijn), 124, 125
Renoir, Pierre Auguste, 64, 65
rhythm, 95, 108–111
Roads Untaken (Hart), 45
Rose, Timothy, 116, 117
Rothenberg, Susan, 142
Rousseau, Henri, 112
Royal Workshops, 160
Russell, Julia, 172, 173

S

Safdie, Mosche, 172
scale, 155, 172–179, 183
Schapiro, Miriam, 66
Schmidt-Rottluff, Karl, 74, 75
The Scream (Munch), 164
Seated Man #4 (Bates), 56

secondary colors, 68
Segal, George, 146
shade, 72
shape(s), 35, 40–43, 62, 95, 110, 186–189
Sharp, William, 143
shiny surface, 88
simulated texture, 84
size, 54, 136
Smith, David, 44
Snow Queen, Portrait of Adah (Bennion), 187
Snow Scene (Twachtman), 70, 71
space, 35, 52–59, 62, 95, 110
special-effects technicians, 62
spectrum, 68
sphere, 46
square, 46
Still Life with the Attributes of the Arts (Chardin), 82, 83
stippling, 72
storyboard artists, 62
storytelling, 62
symmetry, 126–133
synchromy, 66

T

tactile texture, 86–89
The Tea (Cassatt), 134, 135
textiles, 194
texture, 64–65, 82–89, 93, 136
Thiebaud, Wayne, 120
three-dimensional art, 198–201, 206–209
three-dimensional space, 58
Three People on Four Park Benches (Segal), 146
tint, 72
trapezoid, 42
triangle, 46
Twachtman, John Henry, 70, 71
Two Birds in Hand (LeVan), 82
two-dimensional art, 194–197
Two Girls (Bishop), 156

U

United States Capitol, 126
unity, 185, 202–209, 213
unrealistic scale, 176–179

V

value, 70–73
van Gogh, Vincent, 53, 70
van Rijn, Rembrandt, 124, 125
variety, 185–189, 190–193, 213
visual movement, 112–115
visual texture, 82–85

W

Warren, John, 49
weaving, 202–205
Weber, Max, 94, 95
White Vertical Water (Nevelson), 198
The Whitney Museum, 92
Woman's Headcloth (Unknown), 195

Y

Young Spanish Woman with a Guitar (Renoir), 64

Acknowledgments

Grateful acknowledgment is given to the following publishers and copyright owners for permissions granted to reprint selections from their publications. All possible care has been taken to trace ownership and secure permission for each selection included. In case of any errors or omissions, the Publisher will be pleased to make suitable acknowledgments in future editions.

TE
Cover from GRANDFATHER'S JOURNEY by Allen Say. Jacket art copyright © 1993 by Allen Say. Reprinted by permission of Houghton Mifflin Company. All rights reserved.

Cover from BLACK AND WHITE by David Macaulay. Jacket art © 1990 by David Macaulay. Reprinted by permission of Houghton Mifflin Co. All rights reserved.

Cover from ZATHURA: A Space Adventure by Chris Van Allsburg. Jacket art copyright © 2002 by Chris Van Allsburg. Reprinted by permission of Houghton Mifflin Company. All rights reserved.

From N.C. WYETH'S PILGRIMS © 1991 by Robert San Souci. Illustrations © 1945 by Metropolitan Life Insurance Co. Used with permission of Chronicle Books LLC, San Francisco. Visit ChronicleBooks.com.

From TAR BEACH by Faith Ringgold, copyright © 1991 by Faith Ringgold. Used by permission of Crown Publishers, an imprint of Random House Children's Books, a division of Random House, Inc.

Jacket design from THE AMAZING BONE by William Steig. Copyright © 1976 by William Steig. Reprinted by permission of Farrar, Straus and Giroux, LLC.

Photo Credits

Cover Seattle Art Museum, Gift of John H. Hauberg. Photograph by Paul Macapia; 5 © AKG-Images; 6 National Gallery of Art, Washington, D.C. Ailsa Mellon Bruce Collection, Image © 2003 Board of Trustees, National Gallery of Art, Washington; 7 Purchase. Whitney Museum of American Art, New York. Photograph by Geoffrey Clements; 8 National Gallery of Art, Washington D.C. Widener Collection, Image © 2003 Board of Trustees, National Gallery of Art, Washington; 9 San Francisco Museum of Modern Art. © Banco de Mexico Diego Rivera & Frida Kahlo Museum Trust. Av. Cinco de Mayo No.2, Col. Centro, Del. Cuauhtemoc 06059, Mexico, D.F; 10 Worcester Art Museum. Worcester, Massachusetts, museum purchase; 12 (tl) Museum of Fine Arts, Boston: Bequest of John T. Spaulding 48.549, (tr) Hirshhorn Museum and Sculpture Garden, Smithsonian Institution, Gift of Joseph H. Hirshhorn, 1966, (bl) Dallas Museum of Art, Dallas, Texas, (br) © Philip Hayson/Photo Researchers Inc; 13 (tl) Honolulu Academy of Art. Honolulu, Hawaii. Gift of James A. Michener, 1955 (13,694), (tr) Purchased with funds provided by the Smithsonian Collections Acquisition Program. Photograph by Frank Khoury. National Museum of African Art, Smithsonian Institution, Washington D.C., (bl) Image no.EEPA 1474. Eliot Elisofon Photographic Archives, National Museum of African Art, Smithsonian Institution, Washington, D.C., (br) Royal British Columbia Museum, Victoria, Canada; 15 (tl) The Ogden Museum of Southern Art, University of New Orleans, Gift of the Benny Andrews Foundation, (tr) Amon Carter Museum, Fort Worth, Texas. 1999.33.E; 15 (bl) From the Girard Foundation Collection, in the Museum of International Folk Art, a unit of the Museum of New Mexico, Santa Fe, New Mexico. Photographer: Michel Monteaux, (br) © Carl & Ann Purcell/CORBIS; 16 Helen Birch Bartlett Memorial Collection, 1926.252. Photograph © 2001, The Art Institute of Chicago, All Rights Reserved; 17 © Northwest Museum of Arts & Culture. Photo by David Anderson; 18 Wadsworth Atheneum, Hartford. The Ella Gallup Sumner and Mary Catlin Sumner Collection Fund; 19 (t) Dallas Museum of Art, Dallas, Texas, (b) Smithsonian American Art Museum, Washington, DC/Art Resource, NY. © Elizabeth Catlett/Licensed By VAGA, New York, New York; 20 National Gallery, London/Art Resource, NY. Erich Lessing, photographer; 22 (t, tcl, tcr, br, bcr) © Photodisc/Getty Images, Inc, (bcl, bl) © Digital Vision/Getty Images, Inc; 23 (t) © Corbis, (tcl, tcr, bl, bcl, bc) © Photodisc/Getty Images, Inc, (br) © Index Stock Inc; 24, 26, 28, 30 San Francisco Museum of Modern Art. © Banco de Mexico Diego Rivera & Frida Kahlo Museum Trust. Av. Cinco de Mayo No.2, Col. Centro, Del. Cuauhtemoc 06059, Mexico, D.F; 32-33 (t) © Aaron Haupt; 34 © AKG-Images; 35 © Bildarchiv, Österreichische Nationalbibliothek/Sté Nlle des Editions du Chêne; 36 Digital Image © The Museum of Modern Art/Licensed by Scala/Art Resource, NY. © 2004 Succession H. Matisse, Paris/Artists Rights Society (ARS), New York; 37 Dallas Museum of Art; 38 © Eclipse Studios; 39 Randy Ellett; 40 International Folk Art Foundation Collection. Museum of International Folk Art. Santa Fe, New Mexico. Photo by: Pat Pollard; 41 Museum of Fine Arts, Boston: Bequest of Maxim Karolik 64.619; 42 © Eclipse Studios; 43 Randy Ellett; 44 Dallas Museum of Art, Dallas, Texas. Art © Estate of David Smith/Licensed by VAGA, New York, New York; 45 © George Hart; 46 © Eclipse Studios; 47 Randy Ellett; 48 © Paul Baliker; 49 © John Warren; 50 (tl, tc, tr) Photodisc/Getty Images, Inc, (b) © Eclipse Studios; 51 Randy Ellett; 52 Wadsworth Atheneum, Hartford. The Ella Gallup Sumner and Mary Catlin Sumner Collection Fund; 53 © Rijksmuseum Kroller-Muller, Otterlo, Netherlands/Bridgeman Art Library; 54 © Eclipse Studios; 55 Randy Ellett; 56 Dallas Museum of Art, Dallas, Texas; 57 Photo: B. Hatala. Musee Picasso, Paris, France. © Reunion des Musees Nationaux/Art Resource, NY. © 2001 Estate of Pablo Picasso/Artists Rights Society (ARS), New York; 58 © Eclipse Studios; 59 Randy Ellett; 60 Los Angeles County Museum of Art, Los Angeles County Fund; 62 Jeff Kaufman/Taxi/Getty Images, Inc; 63 David Cooper, Vancouver, CANADA; 64 National Gallery of Art, Washington, D.C. Ailsa Mellon Bruce Collection, Image © 2003 Board of Trustees, National Gallery of Art, Washington; 65 © Bettmann/Corbis; 66 © 1997 Miriam Schapiro; 67 Hirshhorn Museum and Sculpture Garden, Smithsonian Institution, Gift of Joseph H. Hirshhorn, 1966; 68 © Eclipse Studios; 69 Randy Ellett; 70 Courtesy of the J. Paul Getty Museum; 71 © Cincinnati Art Museum. Photo by Tony Walsh, 2002; 72 © Eclipse Studios; 73 Randy Ellett; 74 © Hermitage, St. Petersburg, Russia/Bridgeman Art Library; 75 North Carolina Museum of Art, Raleigh, North Carolina. Bequest of W.R. Valentiner. G.65.10.58. © 2004 Artists Rights Society (ARS), New York/VG Bild-Kunst, Bonn; 76 © Eclipse Studios; 77 Randy Ellett; 78 Albright-Knox Art Gallery, Buffalo, New York, George B. and Jenny R. Mathews Fund, 1970. © 2004 Artists Rights Society (ARS), New York/SABAM, Brussels; 79 Museum of Fine Arts, Houston; Gift of Audrey Jones Beck © 2004 Artists Rights Society (ARS), New York/ADAGP, Paris; 80 © Eclipse Studios; 81 Randy Ellett; 82 Bruck and Moss Gallery; 83 © Erich Lessing/Art Resource, NY; 84 (tl, tr, tcl, tcr) Photodisc/Getty Images, Inc, (b) © Eclipse Studios; 87 St. Louis Museum of Art. Museum Shop Fund; 88 (t, tc) Photodisc/Getty Images, Inc, (cl, cr) Getty Images, Inc, (cr) Getty Images, Inc, (b) Eclipse Studios; 89 Randy Ellett; 90 The Roland P. Murdock Collection, Wichita Art Museum, Wichita, Kansas; 92 © Bettmann/Corbis; 93 Craig Schwartz; 94 Purchase. Whitney Museum of American Art, New York. Photograph by Geoffrey Clements; 96 Seattle Art Museum, Gift of John H. Hauberg. Photograph by Paul Macapia; 97 North Carolina Museum of Art, Purchased with funds provided through a bequest from Lucile E. Moorman; 98 © Eclipse Studios; 99 Ko Yoshida; 100 North Carolina Museum of Art, Purchased with funds from the North Carolina Museum of Art; 101 North Carolina Museum of Art, Gift of Mr. and Mrs. D. H. McCollough and the North Carolina Art Society. Robert F. Phifer Bequest; 102 (t, tc) Photodisc/Getty Images, Inc, (b) © Eclipse Studios, (bc) © Royalty-Free/Corbis; 103 Photo by Ko Yoshida; 104 The Nelson A. Rockefeller Collection. San Antonio Museum of Art; 105 Photo by Frank Fortune; 106 (tl) Photodisc/Getty Images, Inc, (tr, b) © Eclipse Studios; 107 Randy Ellett; 108 Detroit Institute of Arts. The Bridgeman Art Library; 109 Hirshhorn Museum and Sculpture Garden, Smithsonian Institution, Gift of Joseph H. Hirshhorn, 1966. © 2004 Estate of Pablo Picasso/Artists Rights Society(ARS), New York; 110 (tl, tr) Photodisc/Getty Images, Inc, (b) © Eclipse Studios; 112 © 2004 The Norton Simon Foundation; 113 Museum of Fine Arts, Houston; Gift of Audrey Jones Beck; 114 (tl) Michael Nicholson/Corbis, (tr) George Grall/National Geographic Society/Getty Images, Inc, (b) © Eclipse Studio; 115 Randy Ellett; 116 Digital Image © The Museum of Modern Art/Licensed by SCALA/Art Resource, NY. © 2004 Estate of Alexander Calder/Artists Rights Society (ARS), New York; 117 © Timothy Rose Artist, www.mobilesculpture.com; 118 (tl, tr) Photodisc/Getty Images, Inc, (b) © Eclipse Studios; 120 Hirshhorn Museum and Sculpture Garden, Smithsonian Institution, Museum Purchase with funds donated by Edward R. Downe, Jr., 1980; 122 Ed Lallo/Index Stock Imagery; 123 Courtesy of African American Dance Ensemble; 124 National Gallery of Art, Washington D.C. Widener Collection, Image © 2003 Board of Trustees, National Gallery of Art, Washington; 125 © Kevin Fleming/Corbis; 126 © Ferrell McCollough/SuperStock; 127 © Art on File/Corbis; 128 Eclipse Studios; 129 Mike Ramsey; 130 The Metropolitan Museum of Art, Alfred Stieglitz Collection, 1952. (52.203) Photograph © 1994 The Metropolitan Museum of Art. © 2004 The Georgia O'Keeffe Foundation/Artists Rights Society (ARS), New York; 131 Helen Borch Bartlett Memorial Collection, 1926.212 Photograph by Bob Hashimoto. Image © The Art Institute of Chicago; 132 © Eclipse Studios; 133 Randy Ellett; 134 Honolulu Academy of Art, Honolulu, Hawaii. Gift of James A. Michener, 1969 (21,892); 135 Museum of Fine Arts, Boston, Massachusetts; 136 © Eclipse Studios; 137 Randy Ellett; 138 Collection American Folk Art Museum, New York. Gift of Jackie and Stanley Schneider. 1980.31.2. Photo Matt Hoebermann; 139 The Museum of Fine Arts, Houston; The Glassell Collection of African Gold; gift of Alfred C. Glassell, Jr.; 140 © Eclipse Studios; 141 Randy Ellett; 142 Collection of the Modern Art Museum of Fort Worth, Museum Purchase, Sid W. Richardson Foundation Endowment Fund and an Anonymous Donor. © 2004 Susan Rothenberg/Artists Rights Society (ARS), New York; 143 Amon Carter Museum, Fort Worth, Texas. 1999.33.E; 144 © Eclipse Studios; 145 Mike Ramsey; 146 New Orleans Museum of Art: Gift of the Sydney and Walda Besthoff Foundation. © George Segal/Licensed by VAGA, New York, New York; 147 Hirshhorn Museum and Sculpture Garden, Smithsonian Institution, Museum Purchase, 1995; 148 © Eclipse Studios; 149 Randy Ellett; 150 National Gallery of Art, Washington D.C. Gift of Arthur M. Bullowa, in Honor of the 50th Anniversary of the National Gallery of Art; 152 Gibson Stock Photography; 153 Courtesy of Pilobolus Dance Theatre; 154 San Francisco Museum of Modern Art. © Banco de Mexico Diego Rivera & Frida Kahlo Museum Trust. Av. Cinco de Mayo No.2, Col. Centro, Del. Cuauhtemoc 06059, Mexico, D.F; 155 © Bettmann/Corbis; 156 The Metropolitan Museum of Art, Arthur Hoppock Hearn Fund, 1936. Photograph © 1987 The Metropolitan Museum of Art; 157 Museum of Fine Arts, Boston, Massachusetts; 158 © Eclipse Studios; 159 Randy Ellett; 160 The Metropolitan Museum of Art, Munsey Fund, 1932. Photography © 1991 The Metropolitan Museum of Art; 161 Cleveland Museum of Art, Cleveland, Ohio; 162 © Eclipse Studios; 163 Randy Ellett; 164 © SuperStock. © 2004 Artists Rights Society (ARS), New York/ADAGP, Paris; 165 Rosalind Ragans; 166 © Eclipse Studios; 167 Randy Ellett; 168 Digital Image © The Museum of Modern Art, New York/Licensed by Art Resource, NY. © 2004 Artists Rights Society (ARS), New York/ADAGP, Paris; 169 The Metropolitan Museum of Art, Anonymous Gift, 1983. Photograph © 1983 The Metropolitan Museum of Art; 170 © Eclipse Studios; 171 Randy Ellett; 172 © Carl & Ann Purcell/CORBIS; 173 Frank Fortune; 174 © Eclipse Studios; 175 Mike Ramsey; 176 © Digital Image © The Museum of Modern Art, New York/Licensed by Art Resource, NY. © 2004 Salvador Dali, Gala-Salvador Dali Foundation/Artists Rights Society (ARS), New York/ADAGP. Paris; 177 © City of Chicago; Graphics and Reproduction Center © 2004 Estate of Pablo Picasso/Artists Rights Society (ARS), New York; 178 © Eclipse Studios; 179 Randy Ellett; 180 National Gallery of Art, Washington D.C. Ailsa Mellon Bruce Fund, Image © 2003 Board of Trustees, National Gallery of Art, Washington; 182 Peter Beavis/Taxi/Getty, Inc; 183 Craig Schwartz © 1999; 184 Worcester Art Museum. Worcester, Massachusetts, museum purchase; 185 © Bettmann/Corbis; 187 Lee Udall Bennion/Springville Museum of Art; 188 © Eclipse Studios; 189 Ko Yoshida; 191 © Paul Brach; 192 (t) Photodisc/Getty Images, Inc, (b) © Eclipse Studios; 193 Randy Ellett; 194 © Grandma Moses Properties; 195 Dallas Museum of Art, the Patsy R. and Raymond D. Nasher Collection of Maya Textiles from Guatemala, gift of Patsy R. and Raymond D. Nasher; 196 © Eclipse Studios; 197 Randy Ellett; 198 Solomon R. Guggenheim Museum, New York. Gift, Mr. and Mrs. James J. Shapiro, 1985 85.3266. Photograph by Myles Aronowitz@SRGF, NY. © 2004 Estate of Louise Nevelson/Artists Rights Society (ARS), New York; 199 Photograph by Randy Ellet; 200 (t) Richard Gross/Corbis, (b) © Eclipse Studios; 201 Randy Ellett; 202 The Philbrook Museum of Art, Tulsa, Oklahoma. Gift of Clark Field; 203 Dallas Museum of Art, the Steven G. Alpert Collection of Indonesian Textiles, gift of the McDermott Foundation; 204 © Eclipse Studios; 205 Randy Ellett; 206 Ackland Art Museum, The University of North Carolina at Chapel Hill, Ackland Fund; 208 (l) Tomas Schmitt/Image Bank/Getty Images, Inc, (r) Photodisc/Getty Images, Inc, (b) © Eclipse Studios; 209 Randy Ellett; 210 The Ogden Museum of Southern Art, University of New Orleans, Gift of the Benny Andrews Foundation; 212 Dallas Museum of Art; 213 Craig Schwartz © 1997; 230-234 © Eclipse Studios; 235 (t) © Matt Meadows, (b) © Eclipse Studios; 236-238 © Eclipse Studios; 239 (t) © Eclipse Studios, (b) © Matt Meadows; 240-242 © Eclipse Studios; 243 (t) © Eclipse Studios, (b) © Matt Meadows; 244-247 © Eclipse Studios.

Notes

Notes

Teacher's Handbook

Table of Contents

The Elementary Art Curriculum T2
About Aesthetic Perception T3
Introduction to Art History T4
Art Criticism T6
Meeting National and State Standards for Art Education T7
The Development of Children's Art T8
Brain-Based Learning T9
Classroom Management and Motivation
Strategies for Teaching Elementary Art T10
Art Instruction for Students with Disabilities T11
Safe Use of Art Materials T12
The Community as a Resource for Art Materials T13
Displaying Students' Art T14
Art Assessments T15
Art and Cross-Curricular Connections T16
Integrating the Four Art Forms T17
The Creative Process and Problem Solving T18
Using Writing to Enhance Your Art Curriculum T19
The Importance of Cultural Diversity Through
Art in the Elementary Classroom T20
Museum Education T21
United States Museum Resources T22
World Museum Resources T26
Program Scope and Sequence T30
Program Glossary T34
Program Index T40

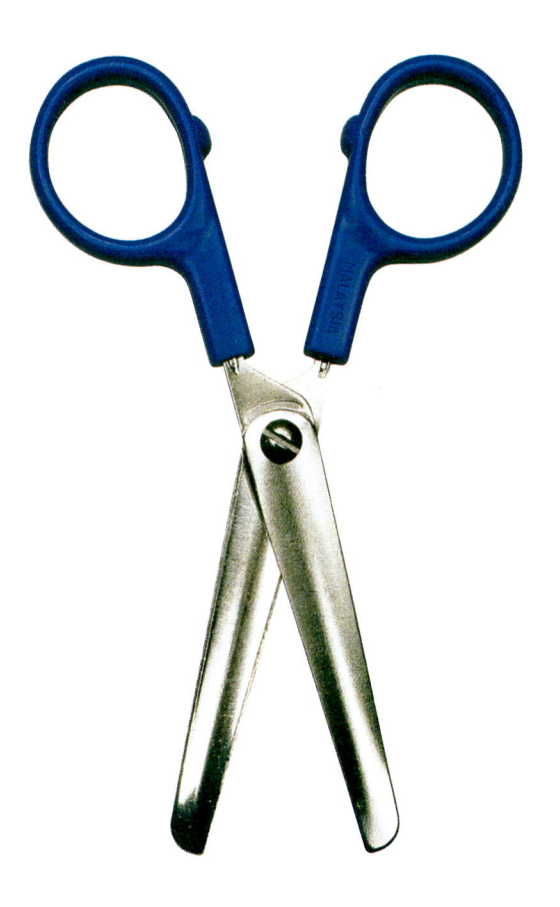

The Elementary Art Curriculum

Rosalind Ragans, Ph.D., Associate Professor Emerita, Georgia Southern University

Art education is for all students. It provides learning opportunities for the artistically talented few, as well as the many students who may never produce art outside the classroom.

A strong elementary visual arts curriculum teaches students that they can communicate a variety of ideas and emotions in many different ways. Students learn that some problems have many different solutions, and they will not be afraid to use divergent-thinking strategies. They will learn concepts and techniques that will give them control of the visual images they produce.

A strong elementary art curriculum also enables students to expand their perceptive, interpretive, and analytical abilities. They learn to find meaning in visual images, and they learn to identify aesthetic qualities in a variety of works of art and in the environment. They begin to develop the ability to make aesthetic judgments.

The visual arts have always been an integral component in the history of humanity, and through the study of art history, students will develop a better understanding of beliefs and ideas that are different from their own.

The four components of a quality art program are Aesthetic Perception, Art Criticism, Art History and Culture, and Art Production and Creative Expression.

Aesthetic Perception

Aesthetics is a branch of philosophy. In visual art, aesthetics becomes the study of the nature of beauty and art. Aesthetics is concerned with the question "What is art?" In the past, aesthetics was defined as the study of beauty because the creation of beauty was thought to be the purpose of art. Today, some aestheticians still believe that the purpose of art is to create beauty or beautifully organized arrangements of the elements of art. Some believe that art must imitate reality. Others think of art as a strong means to communicate ideas and emotions.

Aesthetic concepts are the core of the *Art Connections* curriculum. They are the framework upon which all aspects of art learning are constructed. The **About Aesthetic Perception** section in the *Student Edition* and *Teacher Edition* offers concrete methods for introducing students to aesthetics.

Art Criticism

Works of art are the focus of every lesson. Art criticism is the sequential process used in this textbook to guide students through the procedures needed to learn from these works of art. Art criticism enables students to learn from works of art that have been created by artists from many cultures and time periods. Art criticism also provides a procedure that students can use to objectively study their own art products.

The four-step process of art criticism will help students expand their perceptive, analytical, interpretive, and aesthetic valuing abilities. The sequential steps of art criticism are similar to those used in the scientific method. During the first two steps, **Describe** and **Analyze**, students are asked to collect data objectively. During the third step, **Interpret,** students speculate about the meaning of the work based on the data collected: they make a hypothesis abut the idea, emotion, or mood expressed by the artist. During the fourth step, **Decide,** or aesthetic judgment, the students offer their conclusions about the work of art.

Art criticism helps students study a work of art before making an aesthetic judgment. Too often, beginners look at a work of art briefly and immediately make a value judgment. The sequential procedures in art criticism force the students to postpone judgment while becoming immersed in the image.

In this program art criticism is used as a higher-level method of thinking about the concepts taught in each unit. One work of art has been selected that emphasizes the elements or principles that were the focus of the lesson. Art criticism is also used to help students make a personal assessment of the artwork produced during the Creative Expression activities. The questions offered are neutral and avoid judgments involving likes and dislikes. This avoids embarrassing moments when discussing works in front of peers.

Art History and Culture

Art Connections is not an art history text, but any study of art should begin with learning something about the history of world art and the people who created it. Information about art history related to the featured work of art in each lesson is provided for the students throughout the text. The **About Art History and Culture** section provides an overview of how to include art history information in classroom instruction. Additional information is provided for the teacher in each lesson and in ancillary materials such as the *Artist Profiles* books and on the backs of the *Large Prints.* The *Art Around the World* collection and *The National Museum of Women in the Arts Collection* contain works of art from many countries and provide additional historical and cultural information.

Art Production and Creative Expression

Each lesson includes an art production activity identified as **Practice** and **Creative Expression** in the *Student Edition.* This is the place for each student to creatively explore the lesson concept. Hands-on activities are often the most enjoyable aspect of art learning. The student integrates and internalizes the verbal and visual concepts of the lesson during the creative manipulation of art materials. While every component in the art program is equally important, every component does not need equal time. Art production requires the longest amount of time.

Do not skip the self-assessment section of the lesson. Most students would be embarrassed to offer subjective statements about their own work or the work of classmates. The four steps of art criticism offer an objective procedure for thinking about the concepts and technical procedures used during the creation of art.

Art Magazine Resources for Teachers

American Artist	ARTnews	Crayola Kids
Art Education	Arts and Activities	Scholastic Art
Art to Zoo	Arts Education Policy Review	School Arts

T2 TEACHER'S HANDBOOK • Professional Development

Teacher's Handbook

About Aesthetic Perception

Richard W. Burrows, Executive Director, Institute for Arts Education, San Diego, California

> The Association of Institutes for Aesthetic Education promotes and fosters aesthetic education principles and practices through professional and institutional development. The Association provides policy and program leadership to the arts and education field at the national, state, and local levels.

Aesthetics has been defined as the branch of philosophy that focuses on the nature of beauty, the nature and value of art, and the inquiry processes and human responses associated with those topics.

Aesthetic perception can be most simply defined as an educational approach designed to enhance understanding of artistic expression. Aesthetic perception requires two primary elements to exist: a work of art and a viewer to perceive it. An aesthetic perception approach to viewing works of art is predicated on the belief that the arts can be studied in an active, experiential way. The focus is on developing skills of perception by using works of art as a "textbook" or a focus for study. The instruction delivered by teachers is in partnership with the work of art.

Aesthetic perception provides opportunities to heighten perception and understanding through direct encounters with a broad spectrum of works of art. Students and teachers become actively involved with the artwork—observing, listening to and discussing works of art, and exploring their perceptions of these works through participatory activities. The focus is on developing skills of perception through greater understanding of art forms, of how artists make aesthetic choices, and of how these understandings relate to other aspects of life.

Misconceptions About Aesthetic Perception

As aesthetic perception approaches have become more widely used, a number of misconceptions have developed about the purpose of aesthetic perception education in the understanding of works of art.

Multidisciplinary Versus Interdisciplinary

The purpose of aesthetic perception is not to explore the commonalities among works of art. Each work of art must be studied separately first; connections should be made after an in-depth understanding of that particular work. Every work of art has a separate intention and different meaning. If aesthetic perception is to develop a thinking- or meaning-based understanding of the work of art, then activities must reflect that point of view.

You Cannot Teach What You Do Not Like

A strong "personal" negative reaction to a work of art does not invalidate it as an object of study for students.

Arts Integration

While arts experiences must integrate with all other areas of the curriculum, it is important to understand the separate language that the arts have and acknowledge the connections with other cross-curricular areas as they arise.

The Therapeutic Value of Aesthetic Perception

Very often students and teachers will comment on the therapeutic value of aesthetic perception—it seems separate from the actual art-making processes. This is often a side effect of active engagement in artistic creation and perception. This is not the purpose of aesthetic perception, which should be seen as an alternative way of viewing the work of art and the world in which it is created.

Using Aesthetic Perception

Below are some guidelines for using an aesthetic-perception approach to education.

Deciding What to Teach

It would not be appropriate to teach the same elements over and over in connection with each work of art. Instead, knowledge of all of the elements within a given art discipline should provide the background knowledge for making a decision about what aesthetic perception experiences to design. These decisions should be based on the most predominant elements in the work of art—the responses and the backgrounds of the students.

Creating a Safe Space and Adopting a Critical Stance

It is important to create a working and learning environment with both students and teachers in which they feel comfortable taking risks and trying out new ideas. This does not mean, however, that everything that occurs in aesthetic perception has to be met with uncritical approval. Instead, experiences can be structured so that participants receive feedback on their aesthetic choices and are given an opportunity to revise and improve their solutions to problems.

Documenting the Experience

Various types of documentation serve as a way of recording the aesthetic perception events as they occur or are revisited. This documentation should include written observations, interviews, journals, and student projects. It is important in any case to record this work in order to be able to see the "habits of mind" that reveal themselves in this complex and rich way of thinking and knowing.

Aesthetic perception is a long-term undertaking and requires a patient conviction that the arts and aesthetic perception should be a part of the learning experience of young people. It requires flexibility, stamina, ingenuity, and perseverance. The rewards are astronomical in terms of student response, content understanding, and classroom relationships.

Introduction to Art History

Gene A. Mittler, Ph.D., Professor Emeritus, Texas Tech University

> "The art of the Greeks, of the Egyptians, of the great painters who lived in other times, is not an art of the past; perhaps it is more alive today than it ever was. Art does not evolve by itself; the ideas of people change and with them their mode of expression." —Pablo Picasso

One of the primary goals of education in the visual arts is to prepare students to make and support intelligent and sensitive decisions about works of art. In order to make those kinds of decisions students can employ two ways of examining and responding knowledgeably to visual art forms. One of these ways, art criticism, involves them in learning *from* works of art. Another approach is art history, which enables students to learn *about* works of art and the artists who created them.

The Art History Approach to Learning about Art and Artists

Art historians contend that no work of art can be fully understood unless it is viewed in relation to the circumstances in which it was created. Every artwork is created in a particular place at a particular time in history and to some degree is bound to reflect the prevailing conditions of that time and place. For example, an art history approach to the study of a painting by Rembrandt would include an examination of seventeenth century Holland—the time and place in which that particular artist lived and worked. Adhering to this approach would require that students focus attention on the social, religious, and economic conditions that existed in the republic at that time in history before focusing attention on the painter and his work. All these conditions would have impacted Rembrandt's choice of subject matter, medium, his way of handling materials, and the visual language he chose to use in expressing his ideas and feelings.

Art history, then, involves a study of the visual arts in relation to the times and places from which they sprang. This study will provide students with a richer, broader, and deeper understanding of the specific art objects selected for study and the world as it existed when those art objects were created. However, to determine the significance of the place of a particular work, such as a picture by Rembrandt, involves more than just an examination of the world conditions at the time that artist lived. It also requires a study of what went on in the world *before* and *after* Rembrandt painted his picture. A study of this kind will show students that Rembrandt, like all artists, took into account the works of other artists, selecting some ideas and techniques to use in his own painting while rejecting other ideas and techniques. This is a valuable lesson that students can apply to their own efforts to create art.

Consequently, a historical examination of a painting by Rembrandt would include the identification of any artists who may have influenced his style of painting. The most important of these artists was the Italian painter Caravaggio, whose paintings Rembrandt never saw, but without which his own work would not have taken on certain stylistic innovations. However, to understand Caravaggio, students would have to become acquainted with the artists *he* admired as well as the ones he rejected while arriving at his own revolutionary painting style. Thus, students adhering to an art history approach will find themselves involved in a fascinating learning process not unlike a game of dominoes, in which an entire row of game pieces is seen to collapse by upsetting the first domino in that row. The very last "domino" to fall in this comparison of art history to dominoes would be the very first visual image ever created—perhaps an image scratched on the rough wall of a cave by the very first prehistoric artist.

The Use of Historical Periods

For convenience, art historians divide the history of art into more or less artificial periods such as Medieval, Renaissance, Baroque, and Rococo. Doing so does no harm as long as students are reminded that the changes in art history identified by these labels, like changes of the seasons, are gradual. Each historical period passes into the next as smoothly as spring passes into summer.

If it can be assumed that an understanding of the present can be illuminated by a study of the past, then a chronological ordering of art history periods can be most helpful. By beginning at the beginning and observing the changes in art created from one year, decade, or century to the next, students will find it easier to understand how the art produced today has its roots in the art produced in the past. If students are to gain an understanding of art history, they should be afforded opportunities to see and learn about art examples from every corner of the world representing every historical period, not just those created by Western artists.

In every art history period students will encounter artists whose works preserve the traditional values of earlier artists, artists who chose to build upon current art trends, and still other artists who opted to explore revolutionary ways of expressing themselves through their art. Art history is filled with the stories of artists who accepted or rejected, endorsed or protested, conformed or reformed, contrasted or destroyed, dreamed of the past or conjured up visions of the future—but every one of those artists did so from the springboard of his or her own time and place, be that tenth-century China or twentieth-century America.

Art History as a Means of Understanding Each Other

Through art history students learn that a painting, a statue, or a temple is a consequence of how imaginative, sensitive members of any given society viewed and responded to the world around them. Art history also encourages students to regard works of art as more than objects that are pleasing to the eye, more than splendid and original products of human skill and inventiveness. Works of art also represent springboards for learning, revealing how differently people thought and acted at different times and in different geographical locations throughout the long history of humankind. A work of art reveals not only the customs, social habits, architecture, and technical achievements of its time and place; it also reflects the prevailing fears, beliefs, superstitions, desires, and values of people living in different ages at different geographic locations. Art history, then, is a vital part of the history of the human race.

Art History and Changing Tastes

As they study art history, students will discover that, over time, works of art do not always look the same to the people viewing them. This happens because people from different times and places look at art from different points of view. Cultures vary and change and so do tastes. Take any great artist or any great work of art from a bygone era and note how there have been periods in which that artist or work has been highly regarded, treated with indifference, or even ridiculed. For example, few today would venture a negative judgment of a painting created by Rembrandt, who is universally regarded as one of the greatest artists of all time. Yet, over the years, this Dutch master has not always been understood or appreciated. Indeed, when Italian artists first viewed a painting by Rembrandt they were puzzled and disappointed. They failed to understand why this artist was so highly regarded. His style, they concluded, was most peculiar because it made use of large areas of dark values and made no use of outlines favored by Italian artists.

Students must learn that art is a two-way process involving *both* artist and viewer. If students are to grasp more than the superficial appearance of a work of art, they must be prepared to learn its purpose, its *contemporary* meaning within the society in which it was produced, and its place in the historical process. No work of art is created in a vacuum. If students are to share in the ideas and feelings that contributed to the creation of a work of art, they must recognize the concepts, desires, and expectations of the person expressing those ideas and feelings at a particular point in time. This will result in a richer, broader, deeper understanding of both the artwork and the culture that witnessed its creation.

The Art History Operations

The study of art history is made easier for students if a plan of action is offered. One such plan makes use of four steps, or operations, that bear the same labels used to describe the four steps used in art criticism. These operations are description, analysis, interpretation, and decision. However, while these operations enable students to gain information from works of art during art criticism, they also are used to help students gather information about those works during art history. Briefly, the four art history operations are:

Description During this first operation, students seek to discover when, where, and by whom the work was created. In other words, they determine the period in which the work was created, the place where the artist lived, and, assuming it is known, the name of the artist.

Analysis This operation requires students to identify the unique features in a work of art that determine its artistic style. In the visual arts, style has come to mean the personal and unique way in which the artist uses the elements and principles of art to express ideas and feelings. For example, one artist may choose to delineate shapes in his painting by surrounding them with a heavy dark outline. Another painter might ignore the use of an outline and suggest shapes by creating areas of bright hues that contrast with the dull hues surrounding them.

> "Art historians contend that no work of art can be fully understood unless it is viewed in relation to the circumstances in which it was created."

Interpretation When interpreting a work of art, students take into account the impact of time and place upon the artist. It is during this operation that they learn that pictures of the same subject painted at the same time but in different geographic locations typically differ in appearance because they reflect different traditions and values. A landscape painted in fifteenth-century Italy will differ dramatically from a landscape painted at the same time in Japan. Moreover, a work of art created in the same country but at different times may also bear few stylistic similarities. A landscape painted by a French artist living and working in the late nineteenth century would have little in common with a landscape done by a French artist living and working at the beginning of the same century.

In an effort to express themselves in visual terms, artists make use of the materials and processes placed in their hands by the circumstances of time and place. Thus, a nineteenth-century African artist might have carved a figure from a piece of wood to serve as a dwelling place for a departed spirit, while a seventeenth-century artist applied his brush to canvas to paint a lifelike portrait of his king. In the spotlight of history, the efforts of both artists are magnified or diminished, honored or dismissed by forces that neither could predict or control but that had little to do with the values the artists sought to express in their work. It is the desire to discover those values that motivates students when interpreting artists' works.

Decision The final art history operation requires that students make a decision about the historical importance of a work of art. They will discover that some works are more important than others because they were the first examples of a new, revolutionary style. Others are found to be significant because they are the most accomplished and successful examples of a particular style. As their knowledge and understanding of art grows, students will find themselves liking a great many more works of art than they thought possible at the start. Gradually they will gain confidence in their historical judgments and exercise skill in defending those judgments.

Art history is a fascinating, provocative learning experience affording students the opportunity to travel through time and space. It provides them with access to the inner lives of many kinds of people and offers clues to where we come from and who we are. Finally, art history reveals that artists and their art have succeeded in helping people communicate with each other in a manner we cannot express in any other way.

Art Criticism

Rosalind Ragans, Ph.D., Associate Professor Emerita, Georgia Southern University

Art criticism is organized discussion about art. The art criticism procedures used in this program were developed by Edmund B. Feldman based on his analysis of the writings of professional art critics. He organized the elaborate procedures followed by critics and summarized them into four steps. The purpose of these four steps is to delay impulse judgments of visual images and to involve the viewer in a complex interaction with the image that can result in a truly aesthetic experience.

Art criticism involves the use of high-level thinking skills. The viewer translates the visual language of the image created by an artist into everyday words. To have a truly aesthetic experience the viewer must go beyond simple identification and recognition to the types of thinking required to analyze, interpret, and judge visual clues.

Anyone can do art criticism. All that is needed are eyes to see the image and a brain to think about what is seen. Art criticism gives a viewer of any age the confidence to discuss a work of art without worrying about what other people have said about it. One does not need to know anything about the artist, the style, or the time when the work was made to get involved with the work. After the steps of art criticism have been followed in a school setting, students are usually so interested in the art that they want to know more about the who, what, where, when, and how of the work. In other words, the students are ready to learn about art history and culture.

Description

The first step of art criticism is a clue-collecting step. The purpose of this step is to get to know the work as intimately and deeply as one can. All the information from the credit line should be noted. It is important for the viewer to know whether the artwork is 20 × 30 inches or 20 × 30 feet. The medium with which the work is made is also important. Whether a piece of sculpture is modeled with clay or carved from stone affects the viewer's impression. Then the observer names everything that is seen in the image. During description the observer must remain objective. All the descriptive terms must be neutral, value-free words.

Analysis

This is an advanced form of description. It is also an objective, clue-collecting step. During this stage the viewer studies the elements of art and the principles that have been used to organize those elements. It is during this step that the viewer begins to discover how the artist has organized the formal qualities of the work to create the content or meaning. In this program you will see how the art criticism lesson at the end of each unit is used to reinforce the concepts taught during each unit. Works of art have been selected that will help the student comprehend the artist's use of the specific elements or principles that were introduced in that unit.

Interpretation

This is the most important part of art criticism. It is during this step that the viewer pulls together all the descriptive and analytical observations to make sense of the work. The viewer makes inferences about the mood, meaning, or message being conveyed by the work. This step goes beyond narration to a generalization about life. The viewer makes guesses, but these ideas must be supported by the clues collected during the first two steps. This can be the most difficult step because it requires imagination and courage. Every interpretation can be different because each is based on the feelings and life experiences of the viewer. No one individual has done or seen exactly the same things as the next person. The viewer may see ideas in a work of art that were never dreamed of by the artist. That is not wrong. It simply means that the work is so powerful that it carries special meanings for everyone.

A good interpretation goes beyond answering "What is happening?" to answering "What does it mean?"

Decision (Judgment)

This is the step where a professional critic will decide the quality of a work. Is this as good as the rest of the works by this artist? How does it measure up to the works of other artists in the same group? The students who are using this program do not have enough experience to make that level of decision, so the works of art in *Art Connections* have been selected because they have already been judged to be outstanding examples of art.

The students are asked to make personal decisions. There are two levels of judgment to be made. The first is "Do you like the work?" This opinion may be embarrassing for students to share in front of classmates, and it is best left unspoken. No one can ever tell someone else what they should like or dislike.

The second level of judgment is also subjective. We ask the student to decide why the work is successful, and we use aesthetic theories to help each individual make decisions about the work. The three aesthetic theories that we employ are the most common theories: imitationalism/realism, formalism/composition, and emotionalism/expressionism. More than one theory can be used to judge a work of art.

- Some critics think the most important thing about a work of art is the realistic presentations of the subject matter. People with this point of view think that an artwork should imitate life. This theory, called **imitationalism** or **realism,** focuses on realistic representation.
- Other critics think that composition is the most important factor in a work of art. This aesthetic theory, called **formalism** or **composition,** places emphasis on the design qualities, the arrangement of the elements of art using the principles of art.
- **Emotionalism** or **expressionism** is the theory concerned with the content or meaning of the work. This theory requires that a work of art convey a message. It must arouse a response of feelings, moods, or emotions in the viewer.

In this program we provide leading questions to help the teacher and student delve into a work of art by using the steps of art criticism. These are not all the questions that can be addressed in viewing a work, and teachers are encouraged to go beyond what is presented on the pages of these books.

Teacher's Handbook

Meeting National and State Standards for Art Education

Nan Yoshida

Art Connections has been carefully designed to help educators meet the standards of state and national art curriculum guidelines.

The *National Standards for Arts Education* are part of Goals 2000, the overarching plan for improving American education. Approved by the United States Congress in 1994, the standards describe what every young American student should know and be able to do in the arts.

In addition to the national standards, individual states have curriculum documents that set forth guidelines and requirements in subject areas. For example, both the *Texas Essential Knowledge and Skills for Art* and the *Visual and Performing Arts Framework for California Public Schools, Kindergarten through Grade Twelve* discuss four components of visual arts education common to most other state guidelines.

Placing the national standards side by side with the Texas and California standards, one can readily see that the documents match in their expectations of what students should know and be able to do in the visual arts.

Art Connections has been developed with these national and state expectations in mind. Every lesson in the program was designed to address the components of art education in Aesthetic Perception, Art History and Culture, Creative Expression, and Art Criticism.

Aesthetic Perception
(Artistic Perception)

Each lesson begins with Activate Prior Knowledge, which asks students to recall and visualize an image from personal experience that will help them take a purposeful look at the artwork.

Introduce the Art focuses students' attention on specific attributes of the artwork, design elements and principles, underlying structures, and functions. As students answer the questions about the work of art, they develop critical *observation* skills.

Aesthetic Perception directs students to extend their artistic perception to their environment and objects in the environment. The transition is made to use keen visual and tactile perception of formal art objects in everyday life (lifelong learning).

> "In *Art Connections* students are exposed to a variety of types and styles of art from many cultures and historical periods."

Art History and Culture
(Cultural Context)

In *Art Connections* students are exposed to a variety of types and styles of art from many cultures and historical periods. Students study art from Africa; Asia; Australia; Europe; and North, Central, and South America. They learn about the role of the artist in societies. They develop appreciation for paintings, drawings, prints, photographs, sculptures, textiles, and architecture. They relate to folk, decorative, functional, and formal arts.

While information about the works of art and the artist is necessarily brief in the *Student Edition*, teachers are encouraged to use the Art History and Culture feature of the *Teacher Edition* and the *Artist Profiles* books to provide students with enriching information about the artists, the periods of art history, and cultural perspectives.

Creative Expression
(Art Production)

Creative expression is fundamental to every art lesson. The Practice activity provides a structure for students to apply lesson concepts in meaningful practice. In the Creative Expression activity, students refine their new knowledge and skills by producing original artwork based on their personal visions. The lessons throughout the program introduce a variety of art media and techniques.

Art Criticism
(Aesthetic Valuing)

Reflection and self-assessment are inherent in the art-making process. Upon completion of the Creative Expression activity, students evaluate their own work using the four steps of art criticism: Describe, Analyze, Interpret, and Decide. These four steps of art criticism are a method for making an informed critique of others' artwork as well.

Arts Integration

In addition to the high priority placed on teaching the visual arts as a unique discipline, both national and state standards recommend the appropriate integration or interrelation of the visual arts with the other arts disciplines of music, dance, and theatre. Toward this goal, every unit in *Art Connections* culminates with a lesson integrating one of these performing arts. In addition, connections are made to music and movement/dance in every lesson of the *Teacher Edition*.

Curriculum Integration

The *Teacher Edition* has an Art Across the Curriculum section that ties art concepts to other curriculum areas. Every lesson has a connection to Reading/Language Arts, Math, Science, Social Studies, and Technology.

National Standards for Arts Education © 1994

1. Understand and apply media, techniques, and processes.
2. Use knowledge of structures and functions.
3. Choose and evaluate a range of subject matter, symbols, and ideas.
4. Understand the visual arts in relation to history and cultures.
5. Reflect upon and assess the characteristics and merits of their work and the work of others.
6. Make connections between the visual arts and other disciplines.

The Development of Children's Art

Rosalind Ragans, Ph.D.

A child's ability to make and understand art develops along with his or her cognitive, social, emotional, and physical development. In 1947 Victor Lowenfeld was the first to identify and label the sequential stages that students move through as they create images. Since then many others have continued to study the development of children's visual images.

Understanding these stages will help you recognize what your students are doing; however, you must also understand that these stages describe untutored progression through the making of images. There are many outside influences on students, and these will show in their work. A well-meaning adult might teach a child to make stick figures, and because they are so easy to make, the child adopts this symbol.

Just as reading levels vary widely within one class, so do art abilities. Just as you teach students to appreciate differences in ability in other subject areas, you must help them understand that not everyone will have the same art abilities at the same time.

There are many different versions of the developmental stages; here we present a three-step version of art development. The stages of artistic development are useful norms that can help you, but they are **not** rules that must be followed.

The Manipulative Stage
Ages 2–5 (Grade K)

This has been called the scribble stage, and it is usually seen in children from two to five years old. During the early part of this stage, the child makes random, disordered scribbles. Making art at this stage is such a sensory experience that the child may hold crayons in both hands. Children who have opportunities to scribble produce a wide variety of lines, marks, dots, and shapes. The child who develops a variety of graphic marks during the scribble years will use them to produce complex symbolic drawings as he or she matures. Children who rarely scribble will have a more limited range of expression, and they will need a great deal of encouragement to continue drawing.

As the random scribbles become more controlled, the child starts to pull the marks into circular patterns until a mandala, or rough circle, is created. Rhoda Kellogg, who studied thousands of children's drawings from all over the world, found that the mandala appears as the final stage between random scribbling and representation. This controlled scribble becomes a named scribble. Expressive concepts develop as children recognize the relationship between their marks and the visual outcome.

The Symbol-Making Stage
Ages 4–9 (Grades 1–4)

When a child makes the connection between images and an idea, a shape becomes a symbol. During this stage children develop a series of distinct images that stand for objects in their experiences. These symbols are eventually related to an environment within the drawing. The first representation of a person is a mandala. This can represent anyone the child wants it to be. Although this shape appears to be just a head, it represents the entire person. Soon the child adds a line and two marks, which represent a person with a mouth and two eyes. Then two lines are added to the shape to represent legs, two lines for arms, and a scribble for hair. The child is drawing what he or she knows, not what he or she sees. As children develop from the early symbolic stage into the symbol-making stage, they start to add more details and develop a symbol that includes all the body parts.

At first, space is not a consideration, and the size of symbols in a work is related to importance. Objects and people seem to float. Eventually the child wants to make people and objects stand up and will line things up on the bottom of the paper or on a baseline. Along with a baseline, the child starts to represent the sky with a strip of color across the top of the paper that includes a round symbol with radiating lines for the sun. As far as the child is concerned, the space between the sky and the baseline is air. The sky will not touch the earth until the child develops a more mature sense of perception, usually the result of sensitive art instruction.

Another spatial problem is overlap. Children realize that two objects cannot occupy the same space at the same time, and they avoid overlapping. As the environments they depict become more complex, children may use a bird's-eye view, a foldover view, or multiple views to represent space.

Children in this stage develop their own schema, or image, that resembles an actual object. Once a schema has been invented it will be used over and over. As the child continues to make art, the schema will become more detailed and sophisticated.

Giving a child this age coloring books may lead to self-doubt because of the conflict between the child's schema and the adult image. After coloring a seated dog in a coloring book, the child may become frustrated when his or her own drawing of a dog does not measure up to his or her memory of the adult image. Because children are exposed to so many adult images, many of which have low artistic quality, it is helpful for the teacher to expose children to the many high-quality works of art available in this program.

The Preadolescent Stage
Ages 8–13 (Grades 3–8)

Preadolescent children are still naturally inquisitive and creative, but they have learned to be more cautious. They have become very sensitive to peer opinion. They have reached a "crisis of confidence" regarding the images they make. If a work doesn't look exactly the way they think it should, or if it looks childlike, they reject the art product. This is the time when many children become frustrated and stop making art.

This is a critical time in students' visual development. They need to be taught to work slowly and with patience. They need to be taught drawing skills such as perspective and human proportions. They need to master the language of art and the use of design principles. They need the technical skills to master the various media such as painting, printmaking, ceramics, and sculpture.

Students need to see how different artists in the past have solved problems, and to observe what contemporary artists are doing today. Artists solve problems differently, and young people need to be exposed to many different ideas as they try to create their own solutions to visual problems.

The strong art teacher will lead students over this perilous bridge of doubt by gently stretching their minds to help them see more so that they can do more. At every stage in the child's visual development, a strong, understanding teacher can help the child move forward.

Teacher's Handbook

Brain-Based Learning

Jamye Ivey, K–12 Art Supervisor, Dougherty County School System, Georgia

At the end of the school day, teachers often face many unanswered questions concerning the young people whose education is their responsibility. Educators cannot help but wonder why students fail to respond to instructional strategies that were successful in their own experiences. Why is today's student so different?

Brain Research

Neuroscientists are now able to supply some of the answers that have plagued educators for years. The amazing, constantly changing world of technology has unlocked for researchers a new realm of understanding of the human brain. With the aid of advanced medical techniques and strategies using equipment such as MRI, FMRI, CAT, and PET scans, the working brain can be observed. Translating these new and often startling medical findings into the educational arena has provided the classroom teacher with practical methodologies and a better understanding of how, why, and when students learn best.

The brain is the most powerful organ in the body. Researchers have discovered that today's brains grow better in the real world than in artificial learning environments. Students must be able to connect their learning to previous experience in order for new learning to occur. For years teachers have designed and taught units with the activities culminating in field trips. When we consider these recent findings, we realize this procedure should be reversed. The field trip provides the student relevance that would facilitate learning. Without a related experience in the memory bank of past experiences, the learner finds no significance in the new material.

It is also important to note that synapses in the brain are formed, strengthened, and maintained by interaction with experience. The stronger the synapses, the faster the messaging travels and the greater the number of neural pathways that are created in the brain. This enables a person to be capable of creating more flexible thought processing and better memory.

Research confirms that environments shape brains. Teachers should create an environment that provides the best opportunities for this generation of young people to learn. Students of today need to move, talk, and touch more than previous learners did. Eric Jensen explains that the part of the brain that processes movement is the same part that processes learning. Thus, there needs to be movement in the classroom.

Today, we know that lecturing is the poorest way to present new learning. Only about fifty percent of the audience is actively listening in any given oral presentation. Students learn the most at the beginning of a presentation, the second-most at the end, and the least in the middle. Learners need breaks during teacher talk sessions. The attention span of a preadolescent is ten to twelve minutes.

This generation of children has more trouble organizing thoughts and learns on a more global scale. Expect students to want to understand the big picture before dealing with the details. One way to accomplish this is to let the class spend a few minutes looking through the whole chapter before focusing on the first page.

We know now that students cannot learn if they feel threatened or stressed. If a teacher shouts at a student, it takes fifteen minutes for the adrenaline levels to subside in all the students in the class. The glucose needed for cognitive functioning is redirected to combat stress, so all learning is governed to some extent by emotions. The constant threat of failure needs to be removed and recognition should be placed on individual performance, experience, and interest. Pressure, tension, and stress slow down or eliminate learning.

Brain-Based Learning and the Arts

Art teachers are known for using creative methods to capture the imaginations of their students. Need, novelty, meaning, and emotion are four ways to gain a student's attention, and using humor during instruction increases attention by fifty percent. A happy classroom is a more brain-compatible classroom.

The arts are an important part of effective teaching and an essential component of brain-compatible instruction. There is evidence that art-making has been around for over one million years. Brain research documents the arts as basic to the brain. Every culture in human history has one common thread: all had the arts. Stable art, music, and dance experiences not only enhance the aesthetic life of the learner, but they also provide important activity for the growing neurological system.

For both teacher and student, the most encouraging summation from recent research is that we continue to grow brain cells regardless of our age. Noted neuroscientist Marion Diamond explains that it is best to keep the brain curious and active. In her opinion the most significant finding of her career has been that the brain can learn at any age. Be a lifelong learner and engage in physical activities, which also helps build brain cells. Stay curious and stay active. How affirming this is for art educators because the successful teaching of art daily demands both creative curiosity and physical endurance.

References

Sousa, David A. (2002). *How the Brain Learns, Second Edition.* Corwin Press.

Sylwester, Robert (1995). *A Celebration of Neurons, an Educator's Guide to the Brain.* Alexandria, VA: Association for Supervision and Curriculum Development.

Eric Jensen (2001). *Arts With the Brain in Mind.* Alexandria, VA: Association for Supervision and Curriculum Development.

Sprenger, Marilee (1999). *Learning & Memory-The Brain in Action.* Alexandria, VA: Association for Supervision and Curriculum Development.

Armstrong, Thomas (1987). *In Their Own Way.* G.P. Putnam's Sons.

Armstrong, Thomas (1991). *Awakening Your Child's Natural Genius.* G.P. Putnam's Sons.

Classroom Management and Motivation Strategies for Teaching Elementary Art

Bunyan Morris, Art Teacher, Effingham County School System, Georgia

While motivating students to express themselves visually through creative means, the elementary art teacher is challenged with the task of maintaining proper classroom management. The purpose of this article is to provide some practical methods of motivating creative thought and action under the guidance of successful classroom management. Combine these methods with your own to give students the best learning experience possible.

Be Prepared. Begin the lesson excited and ready. Students will pick up on your mood the moment they walk into the room. If you set the tone at the beginning and grasp immediate control, it will be much easier to keep it throughout the lesson. It is important to have art prints and demonstration materials ready and in place for the initial focus. Practice an activity before demonstrating it if it is the first time that it has been taught. Something might happen that could not be foreseen; prepare for the best and the worst. Also, it might be a good idea to practice a concept or an activity that has not been taught in a long time. Even classroom veterans forget things.

Focus. For the initial focus of the lesson, gather the students into a group on the floor, in chairs, or on benches in an area of the room that is ready for discussion and demonstration. By gathering the students into a compact group, it is easier to make eye contact and to keep the attention of all learners. If there is no room for a separate demonstration and discussion spot, gather the tables or desks into a closer group so that no one is "out of reach."

Introduce the Art. Always introduce a lesson with a work of art that relates to what the students will be learning. Students get excited playing detective. Finding clues and ideas in a painting or sculpture allows them to make their own interpretations and assessments about art. They will in turn learn to apply this to their own work. The students don't have to know that this activity has a lofty term called *art criticism* to gain from its purpose. Encouraging them to ask questions and share ideas about a master work will give the students motivation and fresh ideas to take into the Creative Expression portion of the lesson.

Moving to Art Production. Always control the manner in which students move to the Creative Expression area from the Demonstration/Discussion center. Release students in a manner that will keep order but not quell their enthusiasm about the lesson. Use positive reinforcement by complimenting those who are sitting quietly, and send them first. It will not take long for the others to catch on. After time most of the students will become conditioned to this expectation. Even if they've been involved in a lively discussion, they will automatically become settled as this transitional period approaches.

Classroom Design. Not only should the students be orderly, but the classroom must also be organized and conducive to the movement of the teacher and students. The Creative Expression stations should have enough space between them for the teacher to reach every student. There should be enough space in traffic areas for student movement. Children need easy access to supply shelves and sinks, and should be able to move from one Creative Expression station to another unencumbered. The supplies should be organized on leveled shelves so that the students will return them to their proper places. If the teacher keeps the room and supplies organized, hopefully the students will too.

As well as keeping the room and supplies organized, the rest of the room should be visually pleasing. Display student art with master prints. This builds self-esteem. When possible, display every child's work. Make learning centers organized and interesting. Keep interesting objects around the room for visual reference. These objects might include plants, pottery, old bottles, discarded sports equipment, old toys, or anything that might capture the attention and interest of your students. Use these objects in still lifes and as objects of visual reference for lines, shapes, and other elements and principles of art.

When moving about the room assisting students, it is important to keep the senses alive and be aware of what is happening with the other students. See and hear what they think you can't.

Closing the Lesson. Normally one should try to close the class with a review of the lesson's objectives. This should be short and interesting. This is also the time to reward the students for good behavior. The art teacher must set the criteria for earning the award. Do not give the award if it is not earned. Of course, the students must be aware of the opportunity to earn an award ahead of time.

One method that works is to award the students with a "Super Behavior Card." This is simply a colorful card that can be given to the class to take back to their classroom teacher for having good behavior during art. This requires the cooperation of the classroom teacher to award the students in some manner for collecting a certain number of Super Behavior Cards. Awards might include a popcorn party or extra time at recess. If the classroom teacher is unwilling, you will have to provide the award in your class. Awarding of the Super Behavior Card can be coordinated with cleanup at the end of the period. Choose one student at the table who cleans up most thoroughly and quietly to carry the Super Behavior Card back to the classroom teacher. The students at each table will work together to earn the Super Behavior Card.

Hopefully these ideas and suggestions will reduce the challenge of maintaining classroom control and motivating students. The individual teacher must decide what works best for each situation. All of the motivation and management techniques suggested here have been tried and have been proven to work. Combined with each teacher's individual strategies, they will increase the probability of success in the art classroom.

A Sampling of Art Games for Home or School

Art Lotto: National Gallery of Art. Safari Limited, Miami, Florida.

ARTDECK. Aristoplay, Ann Arbor, Michigan.

The Fine Art Game. Piatnik, Wiener Spielkartenfabrik, Ferd. PIATNIK & Söhne.

Where Art Thou? WJ Fantasy, Inc., Bridgeport, Connecticut.

Teacher's Handbook

Art Instruction for Students with Disabilities

Mandy Yeager, Art Educator, Ph.D. Student, The University of North Texas, Denton, Texas

Art education empowers all students to look at, respond to, create, and enjoy works of art. Students who are disabled are no exception to this privilege. The arts have often been understood as an equalizing force in the education of students with disabilities; often these students experience discrimination from peers and adults because of their disability. This discrimination often manifests itself in avoidance of or lowered expectations for these students. Stereotypes of persons with disabilities cast them as helpless, unintelligent, dangerous, or contemptible. These stereotypes are maintained by a lack of knowledge or personal experiences with persons who are disabled.

The visual arts, because they use images to express ideas about the human experience, play a vital role in challenging and eliminating many of these stereotypes. The current emphasis of art education upon visual literacy allows students to examine and transform stereotypes that exist in the media regarding all types of differences (including age, race, class, gender, and ability). Artists throughout time have engaged in this process of recording and seeking to transform societal injustices through visual imagery.

The benefits of art for students with disabilities cannot be underestimated. The skills gained in visual arts often result in increased confidence and ability in other academic subjects. Arts-based learning is often effective because of the ways it engages the multiple senses and abilities of students.

The arts also give students opportunities to explore, express, and celebrate their identities. Teachers who include the work of artists with disabilities in their art curriculum help all students realize that disability is a part of the human experience and does not prevent anyone from being a creator of art.

Resources to Assist Art Educators

The first step to developing competence is to develop an understanding of the child's disability. There are a number of resources to assist the art teacher in this regard.

Resources at the School Level

Resources at the school level include special-education staff and related service providers who have contact with the child such as occupational and physical therapists. All of these staff members can provide the art teacher with insight into the child's learning strengths and needs and his or her physical and emotional development. They can also provide helpful suggestions for how a particular art medium or tool can be made accessible to a particular student.

Another valuable resource for the art teacher is the student's Individualized Education Plan (IEP). This plan exists for every student receiving special education services and provides information about learning styles, needs, and modifications. The *Individuals with Disabilities Education Act* (IDEA) requires that all regular education teachers of students with disabilities have access to the child's IEP and are provided support in implementing modifications to the general curriculum.

Art educators can design their art curricula to meet students' annual IEP goals. For instance, art criticism activities have the potential to enhance students' expressive language skills. Cooperative learning activities such as mural painting can foster social skills. Art production often produces self-efficacy in students with disabilities as they learn to trust their ability to achieve success. Art teachers who engage in this process of reviewing a child's IEP and delineating the ways that art curricula can address annual goals become more confident in their abilities to successfully instruct students with disabilities.

Art Education and Disability Organizations

VSA arts has been designated by the U.S. Congress as the National Coordinating Agency of Arts in Learning for Persons with Disabilities. The agency fulfills this role through a vast network of state affiliates. VSA arts produces art and disability awareness curricula and showcases the work of students with disabilities by regularly sponsoring national calls for art. It also provides access to the work of artists with disabilities.

The Special Needs Interest Group of the National Art Education Association (NAEA) meets annually at the NAEA convention to discuss best practices in art education and disability. This group publishes a column in the bimonthly publication *NAEA News*.

Adapting the Art Experience for Students with Disabilities

It is often necessary to adapt some aspect of the art experience for students with disabilities. Adaptations ensure that learning is accessible to every child; as such, adaptation is a principle of good instruction.

Adapting the art experience is essentially a creative activity, as many different combinations of students, media, and processes coalesce in one semester of art instruction. Accordingly, effective adaptations are individualized and begin with knowledge of a particular student's learning strengths and needs. Teachers may choose to adapt art media, instructional strategies, and/or physical space, depending upon the situation. This process of adaptation often begins by observation of students in an introductory art-making experience. If a student is having difficulty with an art task, try to determine the source of the difficulty. Consult with other school staff and use some of the resources listed below to determine what is most appropriate for the student and situation.

The adaptations accompanying every lesson in this text are provided as suggestions only, because learning needs and strengths vary with each child, medium, and project. It is hoped that art educators, upon reading this article, will feel equipped to utilize available resources to design and implement empowering learning experiences for all students.

Resources

Disability Education Organizations

National Dissemination Center for Children with Disabilities (NICHCY), www.nichy.org/index.html

The Council for Exceptional Children, www.cec.sped.org/

ERIC Clearinghouse on Disability and Gifted Education, http://ericec.org

Art and Disability Organizations and Resources

VSA arts, www.vsarts.org

Art, Disability and Expression Online Exhibit, www.vsarts.org/showcase/exhibits/disability/index.html

The National Art Education Association Special Needs Interest Group

EDGE: Education for Disability and Gender Equity, www.disabilityhistory.org/dwa/edge/curriculum/index-netscape.htm

National Arts and Disability Center (NADC), http://nadc.ucla.edu/

Safe Use of Art Materials

Mary Ann Boykin, Director, The Art School for Children and Young Adults
University of Houston–Clear Lake, Texas

Elementary art teachers need to be aware of safety issues that can affect the well-being of the children they teach, as well as themselves. Follow the guidelines established by the Center for Safety in the Arts to assure that neither students nor teachers are injured by the unsafe use of art materials.

Elementary teachers should do two things to prevent problems. The first is to keep all toxic and hazardous substances out of the classroom. The second is to know how to use the materials safely, because any materials can become hazardous when used inappropriately.

Toxic Substances

A toxic substance is defined by the Center for Occupational Hazards as "a poison which can damage your body's organ systems when you are overexposed to it." This harm can be immediate or can be the result of repeated exposure over time. Toxic substances can enter the body in three ways:

1. absorption through the skin
2. inhalation through the nose or mouth
3. ingestion through eating or drinking in the area where toxic materials are being used

It is up to the teacher to make sure toxic substances do not enter the classroom and that all materials are used safely to avoid problems.

Pregnant women and those who are nursing must be especially careful to prevent exposure to toxic substances. Fumes, sprays, dusts, and powders present a real hazard to the fetus, can be transferred to the infant through the mother's milk, and can be carried home to the infant or young child through dusts and residue picked up by clothing and hair. The safe path is to completely avoid exposure to any toxin by carefully reading labels and applying common sense to the situation. For example, if you plan to mix powdered tempera paint or work with chalks or clay, the safe method would include use of a respirator mask, which would prevent inhalation of these substances.

Children and Safe Art Materials

Preschool and elementary children are particularly vulnerable to unsafe art materials for a variety of reasons. Their lower body weight allows a toxic substance to become more concentrated in their bodies. Because children have a more rapid metabolism than adults, toxic substances are more quickly absorbed into their bodies. Children also tend to have more hand-to-mouth contact than adults, which allows ingestion of toxic materials. Furthermore, children are easily distracted from safety warnings regarding materials as they become involved in the art process. The tendency of children to have cuts and scratches also allows for ready entry of toxins into their bodies.

What the Labels Mean

Since 1990 our government has required the labeling of all hazardous materials. Any product labeled as hazardous is totally inappropriate for the elementary school. Safe art materials carry the statement that the material "Conforms to ASTMD-4236." A simple "nontoxic" statement on a product is not adequate.

The Arts and Crafts Materials institute developed a voluntary program to provide a safe standard for materials used by children. Products bearing the labels AP (Approved Product) or CP (Certified Product) have been tested by toxicologists in major universities and have been deemed safe for children to use. The HL (Health Label) on art products indicates that these products are appropriate to use with children 12 years old or older under the supervision of an art teacher. Products with HL labels are not safe for elementary children.

Safe Art Materials

The following are guidelines for choosing and using basic art materials in a safe manner.

Drawing Materials

- Use only water-soluble AP- or CP-designated markers. Permanent markers are extremely dangerous and can cause lung and liver damage if inhaled. Never use permanent markers in the elementary classroom.
- Do not use scented markers. This teaches children to sniff or smell materials.
- Use only dustless chalk. The amount of dust created in a classroom by twenty children wiping and blowing chalk can be irritating to those who suffer from allergies, asthma, and other respiratory problems.
- Use oil pastels; the colors are richer than crayons and the satisfaction is greater! Crayons should also bear the AP or CP label to ensure that no lead is present in these materials.

Painting Materials

- Use only liquid tempera and/or watercolor paints. If you must use powdered tempera paints, mix these outside and have the paints ready before children enter the classroom. Avoid inhaling the powders of tempera paints.
- Do not use any spray paints or fixatives. These are extremely dangerous.

Printmaking Materials

- Use only water-soluble printers' inks. Do not use any solvent-based inks.
- Use pencils to carve into unused foam trays for printing blocks. Do not use mat knives or other sharp instruments.

Collage Materials

- Sharp scissors should not be used by young children; blunt points are safe. Fourth- and fifth-graders may use rounded points with teacher supervision.
- Use only school paste or white glue for adhering papers. Do not use rubber cement unless it bears the AP or CP label. Do not use any solvent-based glues.

Sculpture and Three-Dimensional Materials

- Use premixed, moist clay for sculpture and pottery. Do not allow students to take home any unfired clay.
- Remind students to wash their hands thoroughly after using clay. The residual dust can be harmful and irritating if inhaled.
- Paint clay pieces with tempera or watercolor paints. Do not use glazes. Some have the approved labels, but they are not recommended for elementary use.
- Use pencils, craft sticks, or other blunt tools to carve clay. Soapstone should not be used for carving in a closed environment.
- Read labels carefully on pastes used for papier-mâché, because some pastes contain pesticides or preservatives that are extremely harmful.

Stitchery, Weaving, and Fiber Materials

- Use blunt plastic needles and loosely woven fabrics such as burlap for stitchery. Blunt metal tapestry needles are safe if their use is supervised.
- Young children will have trouble cutting fabric and yarn with their scissors. Precut lengths of fabric and yarn prior to introducing a task.

Teacher's Handbook

The Community as a Resource for Art Materials

Willis "Bing" Davis, Associate Professor Emeritus, Central State University, Ohio
President and Founder of SHANGO: The Center for the Study of African American Art & Culture

Ingenuity, resourcefulness, and creative survival have always been important to most successful art and classroom teachers when it comes to providing meaningful arts experiences for students. We are known as collectors who almost never throw anything away. Some art and classroom teachers will need to acquire the skill of always being on the lookout for resources, materials, and supplies that can supplement art materials in the classroom. It can be fun; plus, it stimulates the imagination and creative impulse. This is also a great way to build bridges and advocates for arts education.

Think of all the things you use in the art room. How many can be found locally? Safe, usable materials or supplies that can be found free or reduced in price leave more of the art budget to buy the things that have to be purchased. There are different forms of searching for inexpensive and free materials for art activities. The following are a few tried and proven ways to acquire materials, supplies, and resources that can be used for art and other educational activities.

Materials in the School Building

- Leftover wood or metal from a shop class
- Clean, empty food containers from the food-service area
- Cardboard tubes from the food-service area or copy machine
- Scrap paper from copy machines

Annual Open-House Night Resources

Open house is a great time to post a small list of hand tools needed for the art program. You would be surprised by how many extra hammers, pliers, screwdrivers, bent forks, and so on are in garages and basements. Many parents or caregivers also work at places that have by-products that could supplement the art materials in the art program.

Local Business Material Sources

- *Wood* Lumberyards are usually willing to let teachers collect boxes of scrap wood for art production. Some lumberyards will even let you leave a box with your school's name on it.
- *Wallpaper* Ask for discontinued wallpaper design sample books from paint stores.
- *Paper* Large quantities of damaged paper may be available from local paper or paper distribution companies.

> "Many local service organizations have an interest and commitment to youth and the arts."

Community Resources

- Many communities participate in the popular "Take a Child to Work" programs that allow children to see and experience where their parents or caregivers work. Almost every school also has a career day when many professional individuals visit schools to talk to students about potential careers. Both programs put schools, students, and teachers into direct contact with local businesses.
- Teachers may find that companies with national headquarters in their communities often have a strong commitment to those communities and their educational systems. Teachers can assist these companies in reaching their community commitment goals by suggesting ways to assist the school art program. Local businesses may want to sponsor the visit of a local artist or donate materials.
- Many local service organizations have an interest and commitment to youth and the arts. They often look for art and cultural events and activities to which they can contribute. Find out how they want to contribute and help them reach their goal. These events could be funding an exhibit, hosting an art reception, donating materials and supplies, framing student artwork for display in the hallways, sponsoring a local or major art field trip, and so on.

Artist Resources

- Local and regional emerging artists live in every community and can make meaningful contributions to the school art program. Artists from the community or region offer a "realness" to the program from knowing and living in the area.
- Some artists do a good job at demonstrating, some do a good slide lecture, some are more effective in large or small groups, some do great critique sessions, and some may be better mentoring one-on-one. Each individual teacher or school district can develop an annotated artist directory listing the artists' strong points for reference.
- Most communities also have one or more local arts groups or arts organizations that can assist schools in identifying and securing the services of local artists. A local arts group may be willing to do a series of Member Art Demos over the course of the year in your school.
- Another great source of local and regional artists can be found in the colleges and universities in your area. The college or university art program can show your students some of the quality art teachers students might be working with in the future. This is a great source of judges for student competitions.

Art Agencies at Local and State Levels

While everyone is aware of the existence of the National Endowment for the Arts in Washington, D.C., many may not be aware that there are state arts agencies and many community-based arts councils that can be an important resource for your art program. Find ways to let everyone in the community help your art program to be the best it can be.

TEACHER'S HANDBOOK • Professional Development T13

Displaying Students' Art

Jackie Ellett

"My picture is hanging in the hall!" exclaims an excited second-grader. Yes, having one's work displayed is exciting. When you display a child's artwork, you are communicating two things to that child: you value what he or she has created *and* you value the child.

Why Display Students' Art?

Students are intrigued by the work their peers produce and are eager to join in any discussion that arises from the shared experiences of the work. They often compare what they have created to the work made by their peers. A natural aesthetic experience occurs, and questions and comparisons arise. These are either verbalized or internalized, depending on the circumstance of the viewing. "Why did Erin paint that flower large and the others small?" "I like the details of the seeds that Galvin added to his painting; I'll do more details next time." These are examples of questions, comments, or thoughts that may arise when students are viewing a display. Not only do displays allow students to appreciate their completed projects, but they also allow students to aspire to better art endeavors.

A class display allows students the opportunity to stand back and critique their work. A teacher-led critique is best. Students are able to evaluate their work, gain insight into things they may not have thought about, and may learn a new solution to a problem they have encountered. Discussing their works as you would a fine-art print validates the importance of what they have created. Art is so personal that a discussion can become quite insightful.

Preschool and early elementary-aged students are eager to take their works of art home to show their parents what they have created. You should ask permission of all students to display their work. By asking permission you are showing respect for their work, and for those students as individuals.

Displays are also a good way to show administrators, parents, and the community what students are learning.

Where to Display Students' Art

Many art educators believe that the farther away from the classroom the display, the more selective the images need to be. In the classroom, every student's art may be displayed. This area can be controlled by the teacher, students, or both. Students can be allowed to change their own work when they decide to.

Outside of the classroom there is usually an assigned area for each class to display its work. Bulletin boards made of composition board are the most desirable of all surfaces for two-dimensional art. Artwork is easily attached using staples, and the walls are protected from any damage.

Setting up a school gallery of permanent or rotating student art is wonderful for promoting the art program within a school. This should be housed in a high-traffic area where parents, administrators, and visitors can view students' art. In "Leadership and the Elementary Art Specialist: Twenty Ways to Improve Your Program's Position in the Educational System," Phillip Dunn recommends establishing a "Principal's Permanent Art Collection." Having a gallery within the school with professionally matted and framed student art communicates that students' works and the art program are valued. In an era where budget cuts are customary, promoting the work of students is very important to the survival of art programs.

Displays in local businesses, civic centers, or art centers help educate the public about the work being done within their schools. These exhibits contain a mix of student art that has gone through a selection process. Depending on the guidelines and formality of the display, the works can be mounted, matted, or framed, with three-dimensional works displayed in sculpture cases or on sculpture stands.

How to Display Students' Art

Student art can be displayed in a variety of ways. Some teachers take digital photos of their students in the process of creating a work of art and critiquing their work, and then take a photo of the finished art itself. These images can be posted on a school Web site with descriptions of the activity. Digital images are sometimes used as screen savers on the school's computer system and highlighted on closed-circuit TVs in the classrooms. The most common method of display, however, is the bulletin board. These have evolved from simple displays to elaborate descriptions of the process and documentation of student learning. Teacher-focused bulletin boards have given way to student-focused displays that often include student reflections and interpretations. Including descriptions of the process and background information adds to better understanding of the learning that has taken place.

Two-dimensional works of art should be mounted on larger contrasting or neutral-toned paper. The top and sides are usually of equal width with the bottom larger, unless the work is square, in which case all four sides are equal in width. When matting art, a two- to three-inch mat is standard, with the bottom being an inch wider than the top and sides. The mat acts as a resting place, so when arranging mounted or matted art, the works should not overlap.

A sheet of butcher paper or bulletin-board paper can be attached to a wall to define a display area and unify the works of art. Poster board or construction paper cut wider on all sides than the largest paper used by a class can be attached to the wall as an area for mounting individual students' work. Glue a clothespin to the top of the mounted paper so students can easily change their artwork. The background papers are usually in neutral colors, although primary colors may be used in classrooms for younger children. Each background paper is individually identified by placing the child's name in large print on a label.

Three-dimensional works look best in sculpture cases or on sculpture stands. Not every school can afford these. Arranging sturdy boxes of varying heights and covering them with complementary cloths allow sculptures to be equally viewed. If sculptures are of varying sizes, the largest should always be placed toward the back and the small works in front. Arranging works in odd numbers creates interest as well.

Mobiles and kites are best displayed from the ceiling. Make certain that all materials are well attached and that the items hung from the ceiling are secure so they do not fall or set off sensor alarms. As with all displays, it is important to know your school's policies about the types of adhesives allowed. Hot glue has a tendency to peel paint, low-temperature glue guns may not work on some surfaces, and double-sided tape can leave a residue. Humidity and the wall's surface both affect what will and will not work. Reusable tacky putty sticks to most surfaces and leaves few marks.

Displays do much to enhance and rejuvenate students' spirits and allow students to communicate in a way that is neither mathematical nor verbal. The art that students make is very personal and deserves careful attention when being displayed.

Teacher's Handbook

Art Assessments

Assessment in art can be problematic for a variety of reasons. Many educators are reluctant to evaluate a student's creative expression as good or bad. Because there are often no right or wrong answers, students and their parents could challenge a teacher's subjective opinion of a work if it is reflected in a letter grade. Furthermore, many teachers without a strong art background do not feel qualified to grade student artwork. In addition, teachers do not want to discourage creative expression by giving a low grade or an undeserved grade. Many people also often feel that talented students have the advantage in art class and that students should not be evaluated on how talented they are, but rather on how much effort they put into their work and how much progress they make.

All of these assessment difficulties stem from the focus on art production in the art classroom, rather than a reflection of art history and culture, aesthetics, or art criticism. A broader focus in the art classroom and a variety of assessment options may help in more effective art assessment.

Assessment of Lesson Objectives

Instead of subjective opinions of whether or not one likes a student's artwork, students can be evaluated on whether or not they meet the art lesson objectives or demonstrate the knowledge and skills introduced in the lesson. In a quality art program, there are objectives for aesthetic perception, art history, and art criticism, as well as for demonstrating understanding of the elements and principles of art in art production.

In *Art Connections,* every lesson has four clear, measurable objectives. At the end of each lesson, a rubric provides evaluation criteria for each objective.

Art Production: Evaluating Student Artwork

Art teachers frequently evaluate student artwork on the basis of how well it reflects the elements and principles of art that are being stressed in the lesson and how well the student meets the criteria for the artwork. Some teachers can construct rubrics or standards for the artwork beforehand and tell students how their work will be evaluated at the time it is assigned. Other teachers use written or mental checklists of their standards as they look at student artwork. Teachers may use this form of evaluation as an opportunity to discuss the work with a student and find out whether the student thought he or she met the objectives for the artwork.

In *Art Connections,* teachers can also use the Assessment Masters in the *Assessment* book to get an idea of whether a student understands the elements or principle of art for a lesson.

Art Criticism and Aesthetic Perception: Self- and Peer-Assessment

The four-step process of art criticism (Describe, Analyze, Interpret, Decide) provides a procedure that students can use to objectively study their own art products, as well as the works of others. The sequential steps of art criticism are similar to those used in the scientific method. During the first two steps, Describe and Analyze, students are asked to collect data objectively. During the third step, Interpret, students speculate about the meaning of the work based on the data collected: they make a hypothesis about the idea, emotion, or mood expressed by the artist. During the fourth step, Decide, students offer their aesthetic judgment about the work of art. The sequential procedures in art criticism force students to postpone judgment while becoming immersed in the image. It forces them to have a fully funded visual experience before drawing conclusions about a work.

Art Connections includes art criticism questions for every Creative Expression activity. Additionally, the Aesthetic Perception feature in every lesson of the *Student Edition* provides students with an opportunity to evaluate their developing aesthetic perception.

Art History and Culture

Art is a visual record of history and diverse cultures. The goals for elementary art education are that students understand and appreciate different historical periods, cultures, and artistic styles and develop respect for the traditions and contributions of diverse societies.

In *Art Connections* every lesson introduces a work of art from a particular culture, time, and style. In the Introduce the Art strategies, teachers are encouraged to compare, contrast, and share the Art History and Culture information as well as the information provided in *Artist Profiles* to help students develop an understanding of the visual arts in relation to history and cultures. Through discussion and elements in students' own artwork, teachers can evaluate students' awareness in this area.

Portfolio Assessment

Art educators could claim to have inspired the growing use of portfolio assessment in other subject areas. Many art teachers collect the best examples of a student's work and look at the progress over time. They display it and discuss it with students and parents. Student art journals with ideas, drawings, and sketches also provide an opportunity for portfolio assessment.

In *Art Connections* students are encouraged to keep their best work in a Student Portfolio and to maintain an Art Journal. Reminders of these types of portfolio assessments appear in the *Teacher Edition.*

Performance Assessment

Unlike other subject areas, art education has a long tradition of performance assessment. In art class students make things to demonstrate what they can do. In quality art programs, teachers use performance descriptions not only for art production, but also for art criticism, art history and culture, and aesthetic perception to aid them in evaluating student demonstrations of their knowledge and skills in art.

In *Art Connections,* every work of art a student produces can be considered for performance assessment of the lesson concept. Performance assessments can also involve discussions about the works of art to introduce the lesson concept and art criticism questions.

Art not only enables teachers to evaluate student knowledge and skills in art each year, but it also provides a wonderful opportunity to assess students' growth and development over time. Students and parents are often reluctant to discard artwork and fondly review it from time to time to see how children's ideas and skills have changed. Schools often keep examples of student artwork in student portfolios from year to year.

A thoughtful and fair art assessment program enables teachers to really see how much their students are capable of accomplishing.

Art and Cross-Curricular Connections
Tina Farrell

The study and production of artwork enhances learning in all areas of the curriculum. When teachers and students connect art to other subjects, learning occurs in the natural and interrelated way that it exists in the real world. We know from experience that learning is most meaningful when it is interconnected, not isolated. Therefore, making the natural connections that exist within each discipline of study, art including, enhances total understanding and brings meaning to fragmented information.

Below are a few of the ways that art education can impact the study of other subjects.

Reading/Language Arts In the viewing and analysis of a work of art, students develop oral and written communication skills. Teachers can enhance the language process by writing art terms and concepts on the board, having students generate lists of adjectives and adverbs to describe works of art, encouraging reflective inquiry into art, having students read about art and artists, and having students use works of art as stimuli for all forms of writing.

Mathematics Mathematics concepts are enhanced through art. When math concepts are presented or expressed in a visual or manipulative manner, students can more easily grasp them. The comparison and development of shapes and forms, visual-spatial relationships, measurement, proportion, estimation, and grids and graphs, for example, all are best explained through art.

> "We know from experience that learning is most meaningful when it is interconnected—not isolated."

Science In the art-making process, children learn that multiple ways to solve problems exist. They learn to discover, imagine, try new materials and techniques, experiment, develop and test hypotheses, and observe and record visual data. These are many of the skills, objectives, and habits of mind taught in science.

Social Studies The history of the world is reflected in the functional and aesthetic works of art produced by the peoples of the world. Children can gain great insights about near and distant cultures through the study of art, artifacts, and architecture.

The Arts The arts all complement each other in the skills, elements, principles, and beliefs that are emphasized in each one. Each discipline presents a unique way to express ideas and transform emotions into song, dance, interactions, words, or images. Visual artists research, develop rough drafts (sketches), plan, develop ideas, produce completed visual ideas, and sign and title their works. These are the processes that authors, writers, dancers, composers, actors, and poets also employ.

Life Skills In art, children develop craftsmanship, self-discipline, dedication to a task, skills for working both individually and cooperatively, and pride in one's work. These skills are necessary for success in all areas of their lives.

Critical-Thinking Skills Studying the visual arts develops higher-level thinking skills as studenst analyze, compare, interpret, synthesize, and make inferences and judgments about works of art.

Art is a great integrating subject because art, first and foremost, is a form of human communication. Art is one of the first forms of communication for children. Children often express complex ideas through visual symbols that represent their beginning language systems. Art is a vehicle for children to learn about the world around them and to organize the information in a comprehensive format. As young children draw, they take textures, shapes, and colors from a complex world and form them into coherent visual images. This visual cognition, a powerful way for children to process information, is the basis for learning in and through art.

A Sampling of Art Program Resources for Schools

The California Arts Project
 (http://www.ucop.edu/tcap/aeol.html)
Getty Education Institute for the Arts
 (http://www.artsednet.getty.edu)
The Kennedy Center ArtsEdge
 (http://artsedge.kennedy-center.org)
The Metropolitan Museum of Art
 (http://www.metmuseum.org/explore/index.asp)
The Educator's Reference Desk
 (http://www.eduref.org/cgi-bin/res.cgi/Subjects/Arts)

Teacher's Handbook

Integrating the Four Art Forms

Susan Cambigue-Tracey, Education Division, The Music Center of Los Angeles County

Albert Einstein said, "Imagination is more important than knowledge." Without exercising the imagination, knowledge is stored in the individual containers of the mind, but connections are not made. When students are taught to use the elements, skills, and content of the visual and performing arts the possibilities for synthesizing and applying what they know are multiplied. Teachers need to ensure that imagination and creativity are always nourishing the roots of learning.

The importance of artistic activity for all students goes beyond the intrinsic value of each art form in itself. Real arts investigation requires the rigor of being able to focus, make decisions, develop discipline, promote originality, and undertake research, study, and practice. Helping students to experience new ways of thinking and seeing allows them to construct personal meaning from what they experience and to build confidence and motivation.

Each art form is a discrete discipline with its own elements, vocabulary, and strategies. However, it is interesting to see connections among them where there are fundamental concepts shared across the arts and other subjects. For example, lines in art are the marks used to create images. Line in dance is the path of gestures and traveling movements, as well as body design. Line in music is a melody and also the lyrics of a song, while lines in theatre are the words that the actors speak.

A common core of knowledge is built through the arts. The principles of visual art, such as emphasis, variety, harmony, unity, and contrast, are the underlying principles used to creating anything—an architectural structure, a musical composition, a piece of literature, a dance, or a play.

It is easy to find ways to integrate one or more of the art forms and still make connections that are viable and authentic. For example, when viewing and discussing a work of art from a particular time period or culture, select music from that same time period or culture. Aztec art will have more relevance when Aztec-inspired music is played or students can view an Aztec dance and see the colors and design of the costumes. A style of music might also inspire art. Matisse did a jazz series that begs for jazz music and dance. Students can then see and hear the structural and improvisational aspects of this style in three different art forms.

When viewing or painting family scenes in art, challenge students to think of family activities that can be portrayed in a tableau, or live, frozen picture. When viewing or creating sculpture, pair students and have one person become the "clay" and the other the "sculptor" who shapes the clay with respect and cooperation. This can extend into dance by directing the sculpted person (clay) to develop a movement idea lasting eight counts that starts and ends with the sculpted pose or form. Two people in contrasting sculptural poses can have eight counts to slowly transform from one into the other.

Three-dimensional forms in art can inspire counterbalanced (push, pull, leaning) designs made by small groups. A story, such as "The Two Skyscrapers Who Wanted to Have a Child" by Carl Sandburg, could be retold using story theatre or be portrayed in tableaux or as dramatized scenes. Students could also research musical selections to accompany their work.

> "Imagination is more important than Knowledge."
> –Albert Einstein

Students will be better able to express emotions in their visual artwork if they first work with them through drama, music, and dance. Students can begin by showing a variety of emotions in the face, hands, and feet and then move toward portraying these emotions in postures such as sitting, standing, and walking. Everyday activities such as cooking or brushing teeth can be done with different emotional motivations. Students can also create short musical pieces depicting an emotion or mood or find music that expresses specific feelings or moods.

All four performing arts can become a powerful component of integrated learning. For example, during a fifth-grade project focused on the Lewis and Clark expedition, students did research in books and on the Internet to collect historical, scientific, geographical, and cultural content. This information served as the basis for group projects in music, dance, theatre, visual arts, technology, and language.

Challenged by well-designed tasks, students discussed what they knew and selected different aspects to explore through dance, music, theatre, and visual art. They learned songs of the times, listened to traditional fiddle music, and learned a rhythmic chant that was used to measure the depth of rivers. In dances, they captured the sense of traveling through "boundless space"; portrayed animals encountered during the expedition; created weather conditions such as storms; and showed the struggles in navigating rivers, waterfalls, and mountains. In theatre, students drew upon the historical characters, interpreted various scenarios, and read journal entries of Lewis and Clark. Visual art classes focused on observation drawings of plants and wild animals.

Students also created journals in which they recorded their feelings, observations, sketches, and discoveries. They were able to make connections between their own journeys and that of the Corps of Discovery. Finally, the students shared what they had learned about this epic journey in a multi-arts culmination.

The arts bring accessibility and vitality to learning, empowering students to construct meaning that has relevance for their lives. When children learn to draw, they learn to see. When children learn to act, they learn how it feels to be in different roles, cultures, and circumstances. When children learn to dance, they learn to feel comfortable in their bodies and to use movement expressively. When children learn to play an instrument, they learn perseverance and the rewards of expression through music. When children learn to sing, they release their voices and are empowered to harmonize. When children learn to write a play, they learn to observe life by thinking, reflecting, and writing. When creativity and imagination are nurtured, children learn how to use all of their resources to solve problems, to dream, and build on the ideas of others.

The Creative Process and Problem Solving

Bunyan Morris, Art Teacher, Effingham County School System, Georgia

There is great reward in watching the artistic growth of a child. Simply providing the media and the time for creating is not enough. The student's natural curiosity and desire to create must be nurtured, encouraged, and challenged. Even the brightest and most talented students need a teacher's guidance in developing the critical-thinking skills necessary for creative problem solving. The intention of this article is to provide ideas and methods for fostering creativity by developing and encouraging divergent problem solving and critical-thinking skills in elementary school art students.

Classroom Management

Fostering creativity in the art classroom is possibly an art teacher's most important skill. In order to encourage creativity, a teacher must be able to relate to students at their thinking level and then guide them to a higher level of cognitive reasoning. Classroom and behavior management are essential. There cannot be an atmosphere of creativity in a room with chaos. That is not to say that one must be a firm authoritarian. A good art teacher will learn how to walk the fine line between maintaining order and maximizing creative energy among students. Although some may not admit it, all students prefer an educational environment that is free from annoying distractions created by other students. Therefore, good behavior management is a must for maintaining a creative environment.

Visual References

Introducing a lesson with a work of art and going through the art criticism process is a tried and true method of encouraging creativity. It is important to discuss works of art that are related to the objectives of the lesson. Working strictly from imagination and memory is usually not effective. Students must have visual references from which to gather ideas.

Picture files, reference books, and the Internet are just a few sources for visual images. Photographs of people and various natural and humanmade objects provide ideas and references for drawing. Images can be collected from magazines and calendars or unwanted photographs. The image file should be organized according to subject matter or theme.

Reference books filled with images related to the lesson should be available to students. They may be checked out of the media center and kept in the room, or they may belong to the classroom. Some media specialists are willing to search for and reserve books that a teacher may need for an upcoming lesson.

An image search on the Internet is one method to help students access a visual reference that may not be available in the classroom's image file, reference books, or the school's media center.

Art Journals

Students who keep art journals maintain handy reference tools. An art journal is the best way to record ideas through sketching and writing. If art journals and writing tools are kept handy, students can jot down ideas or make sketches to save for future use. Ideas can come to mind any place or any time such as in the cafeteria, on the playground, or at the bus stop. The method or tool doesn't really matter that much. It is just important that students have a way of practicing and recording creative ideas.

Exercising the Brain

Reading should be encouraged. Students who like to read perform better in all subjects. Descriptive language stimulates the imagination. Reading a passage about the beauty of a tree or the sound of a waterfall creates a visual image in the brain. This visual image can be stored in the sketchbook and later rendered as a sculpture, painting, or drawing. Encouraging reading encourages creativity. Teachers and schools should encourage parents to limit their children's time watching television because this takes away from reading and creative play time.

Resting the Brain

Teachers should be tolerant of students taking small breaks. Sometimes students need down time to regenerate their mental energy. This down time can take the form of daydreaming or play. Both are important to the creative process. Common sense and good judgment is used to determine when a student is using time for thinking as opposed to just wasting time. Students should be reminded to get a good night's sleep every night. This is not something teachers can control, but it should be encouraged. We all know that brains function better after a good night's rest.

> "Fostering creativity in the art classroom is possibly an art teacher's most important skill."

Enriching Observation Skills

Enriched observation skills lead to more focused experimentation in art. Artists are naturally observant, but teachers know that most students are not born with natural talent. Through practice, all students can enrich their observation and critical-thinking skills. It is important to get students to slow down and see what they might not otherwise observe. One way to do this is to play an observation game. With the students' help, the teacher can set up a still life in the room. A fun game similar to "I Spy" can be played once the still life is ready. The students describe textures, lines, shapes, colors, and other elements and principles of art found within the real-life objects. The teacher writes the observations and descriptions on the board. Once the game is over and students move to the project portion of the lesson, they will be better equipped with enriched observation skills and more focused critical-thinking skills as they create.

In order to gain more focused and creative experimentation from students, an important goal of every art teacher should be to encourage creativity and divergent problem solving and critical thinking. Hopefully, teachers will find value in the ideas shared in this article and combine them with their own ideas to encourage creativity in their students.

Teacher's Handbook

Using Writing to Enhance Your Art Curriculum

Mary Lazzari, Ed.S., Elementary Art Teacher, Clarke County School District, Athens, Georgia

In recent decades, art teachers have expanded their area of expertise from art production to lessons that include art criticism, art history, and aesthetics. Art is being used as a vehicle not only for increasing creativity but also for developing thinking skills. One way to broaden the art experience and enhance these skills is through guided, interactive writing techniques. Writing about art is an essential component of a well-rounded art curriculum because it provides students with the opportunity to transform thoughts and feelings into words and images. It can also provide the art teacher a more personalized format for communicating with a large student population and assist art teachers in meeting the increased demand to qualify and quantify their students' learning.

> "Art is being used as a vehicle not only for increasing creativity but also for developing thinking skills."

A visual arts curriculum rich in written language activities can facilitate the development of higher-order thinking skills, such as the ability to analyze, defend, and interpret. The use of written statements can help students slow down and refine their thoughts about their own art and the art of others. Words can become the voice for a shy or inarticulate student. With writing as a means of self-expression, art educators can be more in tune with their students' inner thoughts. Some art teachers may be reluctant to incorporate writing into their curriculum because they fear a less than enthusiastic response from their students. Here are a variety of suggestions that can help motivate elementary students to write about art.

Journals

Whether it is a few sheets of paper stapled together or a spiral notebook, students enjoy having a place to write their private thoughts and feelings. Journals can be used to record the thought process from the beginning to the end of a project. It can also be a place to brainstorm ideas or vent frustrations. Art teachers can give written feedback and encouragement to each student in his or her journal.

Titles

Materials: Selected works of art, pencil and paper

At the completion of a project, students can write descriptive titles for their works of art. A title can inform, challenge, or even surprise a viewer. Younger children or students with a language deficit can dictate the title as the teacher writes. Include the student's title when displaying the artwork. Students can also think of a new title for a famous work of art. Compare it to the artist's original title and discuss the similarities and differences.

Acrostic Poems

Materials: Selected works of art, pencil and paper (for individual writings), or dry/wipe board (for group writing)

Select an artist's name or art topic and write the letters vertically. Instruct students to think of words that describe the artist or topic. Students should think of a decriptive word for each letter in the artist's name or art topic. Descriptive words can start, end, or have the letter anywhere in the selected word. Display acrostic poems with the art work that inspired them.

Venn Diagrams

Materials: Individual sheets of Venn diagrams (or draw a large diagram on the board for a whole group discussion); a set of art postcards

Place an image in each of the two outer circles of the Venn diagram. Students describe qualities they see in each of the two works of art. Qualities that are unique to each image are written in the circle that contains the image. Qualities that they have in common are written in the center of the diagram where the two circles overlap. Invite individuals or groups to share their observations. Mount and display Venn diagrams with student artwork.

Artist Statements

Materials: Pencil and paper

Direct students to write three to five sentences about their artwork. Have the students consider these questions: What did I study? What did I create? What did I learn? Display the artist statements with the completed artwork.

Writing Buddies

If you have students who are reluctant or unmotivated to write during art class, have them work in groups. Ask for a student volunteer to be the group secretary. This student is responsible for writing down the group's thoughts and ideas. Students who are not strong in written expression will still feel success in sharing their ideas and opinions.

Brainstorming Ideas

Incorporate writing at the beginning of a lesson by having students use writing devices such as webs. The main topic is placed on the center of the page and ideas that support or expand it are written on the sides.

Vocabulary

Incorporate vocabulary into the art room. Post the "Word of the Day" on a chart or bulletin board display. Build a "Word Wall" with art vocabulary that is added throughout the year. Use word labels on art materials and equipment around the room. Create art flash cards with art words or concepts printed on them. Use the flash cards to find elements such as line, shape, and color in works of art or to review these concepts at the beginning or end of a lesson.

Try writing yourself!

Post statements about projects when displaying your students' works of art. Describe the learning objects and concepts in your statement. Use the display to inform parents, teachers and administrators about the rich and interesting learning that is taking place in your art class. Include articles about lessons, projects, and student achievements in your school or district newsletter.

Writing is an important means of creative expression. It is as valid and essential to the art curriculum as drawing or painting. Using writing to augment the art curriculum not only improves the students' ability to express ideas, it helps the art teacher communicate more effectively with every student. When art teachers integrate art instruction and writing about art, the entire curriculum is enhanced. By pairing art production, a realization of students' thoughts and ideas, with writing, a reflective way to understand and validate their opinions and feelings, art teachers can broaden the scope of the art experience. At the same time, the art teacher will develop a critical means to record and assess student learning.

The Importance of Cultural Diversity Through Art in the Elementary Classroom

Jane Rhoades Hudak, Ph.D., Professor of Art, Georgia Southern University

Culture is learned. People acquire information about the world and how to deal with it as members of a society. Individuals do not learn about their culture by themselves. Children learn about the art of their own culture and other cultures through family and friends, through the mass media, and through the Internet. The information learned this way is often valuable, but it cannot be relied upon to always give adequate and correct information. Schools are often the most effective place for giving students the opportunity to learn about the art of their culture and other cultures.

Our view of the nature of the world and our place in it is expressed and communicated culturally. Every society has institutions that teach culture—family and school are two of the best examples in our society. All societies have religions, which are bodies of cultural knowledge and practices. We also have rituals for birth and death. All cultures have objects that are used for everyday living. We express our world and views through dance, drama, music, and art. We decorate our world and our bodies. We paint our faces and the walls of our houses. We make music with instruments and our voices. All this activity is shaped by our participation in a cultural tradition.

A quality elementary art program provides a wonderful opportunity for teachers to expose students to a variety of cultures as well as their own and to help them to become culturally aware. Following are several of the areas such a program can enhance.

Art Promotes Intracultural Understanding

Through a culturally diverse art program, students begin to understand the role and function that art and artists play in society. Through learning about the art of other cultures, they have the opportunity to identify similarities and differences among their culture and others. They learn that art reflects the religion, politics, economics, and other aspects of a culture.

Through a quality art program, students can address issues of ethnocentrism, bias, stereotyping, prejudice, discrimination, and racism. Students can learn that no one racial, cultural, or national group is superior to another and that no one group's art is better than another.

Art Teaches Self-Esteem Through Diversity

Through a quality art program, students learn to recognize, acknowledge, and celebrate racial and cultural diversity through art within their own society. A good program helps promote the enhancement and affirmation of their self-esteem and encourages pride in their heritage. Personal expression is encouraged, and the result is often a statement in visual form that is both inventive and filled with personal meaning.

Art Teaches Effective Communication

When a quality art program is implemented, students are encouraged to increase their visual literacy skills. Students begin to understand that artists transmit information that cannot be disclosed through other modes of communication. Students learn visual literacy by looking, understanding, talking, writing, and making images. They learn that each society has its own way of communicating through image. Through a culturally sensitive art program, students will be able to discuss and compare art from other societies.

Art Teaches about the Past

Through a quality art program, students develop sensitivity and understanding for the history of humankind. For many periods in history, it is only through visual remains or material culture that societies' cultures can be pieced together. Experiences that students have with these art objects from the past teach them respect for others, challenge their minds, and stimulate not only their intellect but also their imagination.

Art Teaches Critical Thinking

A culturally sensitive art program encourages a variety of critical thinking skills. When students look at art from other cultures, they make critical judgments and develop their own opinions. Students are asked to identify and recall information; to organize selected facts and ideas; to use particular facts, rules, and principles; to figure out component parts or to classify; and to combine ideas and form a new whole.

Art Teaches Perceptual Sensitivity and Aesthetic Awareness

As a result of a quality art program, students develop a keen sense of awareness and an appreciation for beauty. They learn that each culture has its own criteria for beauty. Art experiences help cultivate an aesthetic sensitivity and respect for the natural and humanmade environment. Art classes are the only place in the school curriculum where students learn about what constitutes quality visual design—about harmony, order, organization, and specific design qualities such as balance, movement, and unity.

Art Teaches Creativity

When a culturally sensitive art program is implemented, creativity in all students is stimulated and nurtured. Students learn to solve problems creatively. They learn that every society has some form of creative expression. In some societies, no one special person is called an artist—everyone in the culture makes "art" objects.

Teachers can help prevent students from having a simplistic view of other cultures and help them understand the cultural context of how and why works of art are created. *Art Connections* has been carefully constructed so that students will be exposed to works of art that represent a wide variety of cultures. Questions and strategies are designed to help teachers put art in a cultural context for students. The Art History and Culture feature in the *Teacher Edition* and the *Artist Profiles* book provide additional information about the works of art and the artists.

As a teacher, you are a cultural transmitter. A quality art program taught by a culturally sensitive teacher benefits every student. When educators teach in a systematic, meaningful way, students acquire knowledge about art and cultures that will benefit them throughout their lives.

Museum Education

Marilyn J.S. Goodman, Director of Education, Solomon R. Guggenheim Museum

Museums are truly magnificent places. In recent years, these bastions of culture have taken tremendous strides toward making their collections accessible to a broader audience. Museum educators are usually eager to share new information and ideas and are delighted to assist school educators with programs and materials that can easily be incorporated into the classroom. Museums contain a wealth of treasures that offer extraordinary resources for teachers and students, and which will undoubtedly enrich the overall classroom experience.

Getting acquainted with museums in your region can be a real eye-opener. Museums collect objects that document human achievement, both in our own and in other cultures. A local historical society or farm museum might contain a variety of clothing and tools that can bring history to life. A science museum may offer interactive exhibits about phenomena in the natural or physical sciences, sensory perception, new technologies, or space exploration. A children's museum will offer hands-on displays specially designed to motivate young children to learn by doing. Art museums contain visually stunning works that reflect the diversity of human thought and experience.

Museums do not supplant classroom instruction. They enhance and reinforce what is taught by providing raw materials in the forms of objects, artifacts, and exhibits. Museums give students the chance to see and sometimes handle the real thing. It is one thing to talk about Egypt's role in the history of civilization; it is another thing entirely to see the wrappings on a cat mummy, discover hieroglyphs on a sarcophagus, or be overwhelmed by the power and grandeur of large stone sculptures of kings and queens.

When students have the chance to look at portraits, still lifes, landscapes, genre scenes, furniture, clothing, and artifacts, they learn more than by just seeing a picture of a person, place, or thing. They learn how to "read" a culture. Perhaps more importantly, they learn to develop their own process of investigation and critical inquiry. What was this person's life really like? What can one learn about the class structure of this society? What can we tell about craftspeople, available materials, or the objects this society valued? What does the clothing tell us about the climate of the region? What can we learn about the geography, topography, and vegetation? What did people eat? How did they spend leisure time? What were their religious beliefs? Is there any evidence of trade and communication with other regions? What scientific inventions were present at the time? Can one tell if they communicated through language or by writing? Because children are naturally curious, objects will motivate them to think, research, and learn.

> "A visit to a museum will make the curriculum come alive as students begin to explore objects and learn about their meanings."

A visit to a museum will make the curriculum come alive as students begin to explore objects and learn about their meanings. Museum objects give us information in a way that is very different from reading about the objects. Students must think critically to determine both the questions and answers for themselves. A first-hand, visual investigation of an object's style, material, subject matter, and physical characteristics offers preliminary clues to deciphering its meaning. When the exploration is combined with other knowledge, such as the geography and natural resources of a region; the historical context; the social, political, and economic structure of a culture; or even advances in science and technology, students can be engaged in a type of learning that is truly multidisciplinary and may lead them into other areas of study. Moreover, methods for gathering information go far beyond what people see. Exploring objects and works of art allows students to use all of their senses, combining intellect with intuition. The opportunity for experiential, emotional, and intellectual learning is always present.

Museum objects present different historical and cultural perspectives. Students can gather information about people, culture, belief systems, values, and the ways people lived in the past. Museum visits encourage students to see things from broader global and intellectual points of view, developing respect for the work, lives, and points of view of others. Students are encouraged to respond in a variety of ways and on different levels. Most importantly, students are invited to formulate and express their ideas and then discuss them with others.

To learn about museum resources, teachers can contact the education departments of museums in their region. If teachers explain the level of their students, the subjects they are studying, and the specific aspects of the curriculum they would like to supplement, the museum's education department can help to tailor the resources to the class. In addition to guided tours and workshops, the museum education department may offer materials for loan, including slides, pamphlets, posters, postcards, kits, and other printed materials. Some museums have teacher resource rooms filled with books, films, videos, CD-ROMs, and computer databases geared toward educators. Trained staff is available to answer questions or to help teachers develop a complete learning unit that can integrate museum objects with classroom studies.

Using museums is an excellent way to enrich and enliven the classroom experience. Educators can take the first step by learning all they can about the rich and diverse resources available to them and their students.

U.S. Museum Resources

Alabama

1 Birmingham Museum of Art
2000 8th Avenue North, Birmingham
http://www.ARTSbma.org

2 Mobile Museum of Art
4850 Museum Drive, Mobile
http://www.mobilemuseumofart.com

3 Montgomery Museum of Fine Arts
1 Museum Drive, Montgomery
http://www.mmfa.org

Alaska

4 Alaska State Museum
395 Whittier Street, Juneau
http://www.museums.state.ak.us/asmhome.html

5 Anchorage Heritage Library Museum
301 West Northern Lights Boulevard, Anchorage
http://www.wellsfargohistory.com/museums/alaska.ht

6 Anchorage Museum of History and Art
121 West 7th Avenue, Anchorage
http://www.anchoragemuseum.org

Arizona

7 Heard Museum
2301 N Central Avenue, Phoenix
http://www.heard.org/

8 Phoenix Art Museum
1625 North Central Avenue, Phoenix
http://www.phxart.org

9 Scottsdale Museum of Contemporary Art - (SMOCA)
7380 E 2nd St, Scottsdale
http://www.scottsdalearts.org

Arkansas

10 Arkansas State University Museum
Jonesboro, AR 72467
http://museumastate.edu

11 Historic Arkansas Museum
200 East 3rd Street, Little Rock
http://www.arkansashistory.com/

12 Old State House Museum
300 West Markham Street, Little Rock
http://www.oldstatehouse.com

California

13 Asian Art Museum of San Francisco
Golden Gate Park, San Francisco
http://www.asianart.org

14 Berkeley Art Museum and Pacific Film Archive
2625 Durant Avenue, Berkeley
http://www.bampfa.berkeley.edu

15 El Museo Mexicano - Mexican Museum
Fort Mason Center, Building D, San Francisco
http://www.mexicanmuseum.org

16 J Paul Getty Center Museum
1200 Getty Center Drive, Los Angeles, CA
http://www.getty.edu

17 Japanese American National Museum
369 East 1st Street, Los Angeles
http://www.janm.org

18 Korean American Museum
3780 Wilshire Boulevard # 220, Los Angeles
http://www.kamuseum.org

19 L A County Museum of Art
5905 Wilshire Boulevard, Los Angeles
http://www.lacma.org

20 San Francisco Museum of Modern Art
151 3rd Street Building A, San Francisco
http://www.sfmoma.org/

21 Santa Barbara Museum of Art
1130 State Street, Santa Barbara
http://www.sbmuseart.org

22 Southwest Museum
234 Museum Drive, Los Angeles
http://www.southwestmuseum.org/

Colorado

23 Aspen Art Museum
590 North Mill Street, Aspen
http://www.aspenartmuseum.org

24 Boulder Museum of Contemporary Art
1750 Thirteenth Street, Boulder
http://www.bmoca.org/

25 Denver Art Museum
100 West 14th Avenue, Denver
http://www.denverartmuseum.org

Connecticut

26 New Britain Museum of American Art
56 Lexington Street, New Britain
http://www.nbmaa.org

27 Norwalk Museum
41 North Main Street, Norwalk
http://www.norwalkct.org/norwalkmuseum/index.htm

28 Wadsworth Atheneum Museum of Art
600 Main Street, Hartford
http://www.wadsworthatheneum.org/

Delaware

29 Delaware Art Museum
800 S Madison Street Suite B, Wilmington
http://www.delart.org

30 Sewell C Biggs Museum of American Art
406 Federal Street, Dover
http://www.biggsmuseum.org

31 Winterthur Museum
Route 52, Winterthur
http://www.winterthur.org/

Florida

32 Bass Museum of Art
2121 Park Ave, Miami
http://www.bassmuseum.org/

33 Key West Art and Historical Society
281 Front Street, Key West
http://www.kwahs.com

34 Lowe Art Museum
1301 Stanford Drive, Miami
http://www.lowemuseum.com/

35 Miami Art Museum
101 West Flagler Street, Miami
http://www.miamiartmuseum.org/

36 Museum of Fine Arts, St Petersburg
255 Beach Drive Northeast, St Petersburg
http://www.fine-arts.org

37 Salvador Dali Museum
1000 3rd Street South, St Petersburg
http://www.salvadordalimuseum.org

Georgia

38 Albany Museum of Art
311 Meadowlark Drive, Albany
http://www.albanymuseum.com/

39 High Museum of Art
1280 Peachtree Street Northeast, Atlanta, GA
http://www.high.org

40 Morris Museum of Art
1 10th Street, Augusta
http://www.themorris.org

Hawaii

41 Contemporary Museum, Honolulu
2411 Makiki Heights Drive, Honolulu
http://www.tcmhi.org

42 Kauai Museum
4428 Rice Street, Lihue
http://www.kauaimuseum.org

43 University of Hawaii at Manoa Art Gallery
University of Hawaii at Manoa, Honolulu
http://www.hawaii.edu/artgallery

Idaho

44 Boise Art Museum
670 Julia Davis Drive, Boise
http://www.boiseartmuseum.org

45 Eagle Rock Art Museum and Education Center, Inc.
300 S Capital Avenue, Idaho Falls
http://www.eaglerockartmuseum.org

Illinois

46 Art Institute of Chicago
111 South Michigan Avenue, Chicago
http://www.artic.edu/aic/

47 Krannert Art Museum
500 East Peabody Drive, Champaign
http://www.kam.uiuc.edu

48 Martin D'Arcy Museum of Art
6525 N Sheridan Road, Chicago
http://darcy.luc.edu

49 Mitchell Museum of the American Indian
2600 Central Park Ave, Evanston
http://www.mitchellmuseum.org/

50 Museum of Contemporary Art
220 East Chicago Avenue, Chicago
http://www.mcachicago.org

51 Smart Museum of Art
5550 South Greenwood Avenue, Chicago
http://smartmuseum.uchicago.edu/

Indiana

52 Brauer Museum of Art
Valparaiso University Center for the Arts, Valparaiso
http://wwwstage.valpo.edu/artmuseum/index.html

53 Eiteljorg Museum of American Indian and Western Art
500 West Washington Street, Indianapolis
http://www.eiteljorg.org

54 Indianapolis Museum of Art
1200 West 38th Street, Indianapolis
http://www.ima-art.org

T22 TEACHER'S HANDBOOK • Resources

Teacher's Handbook

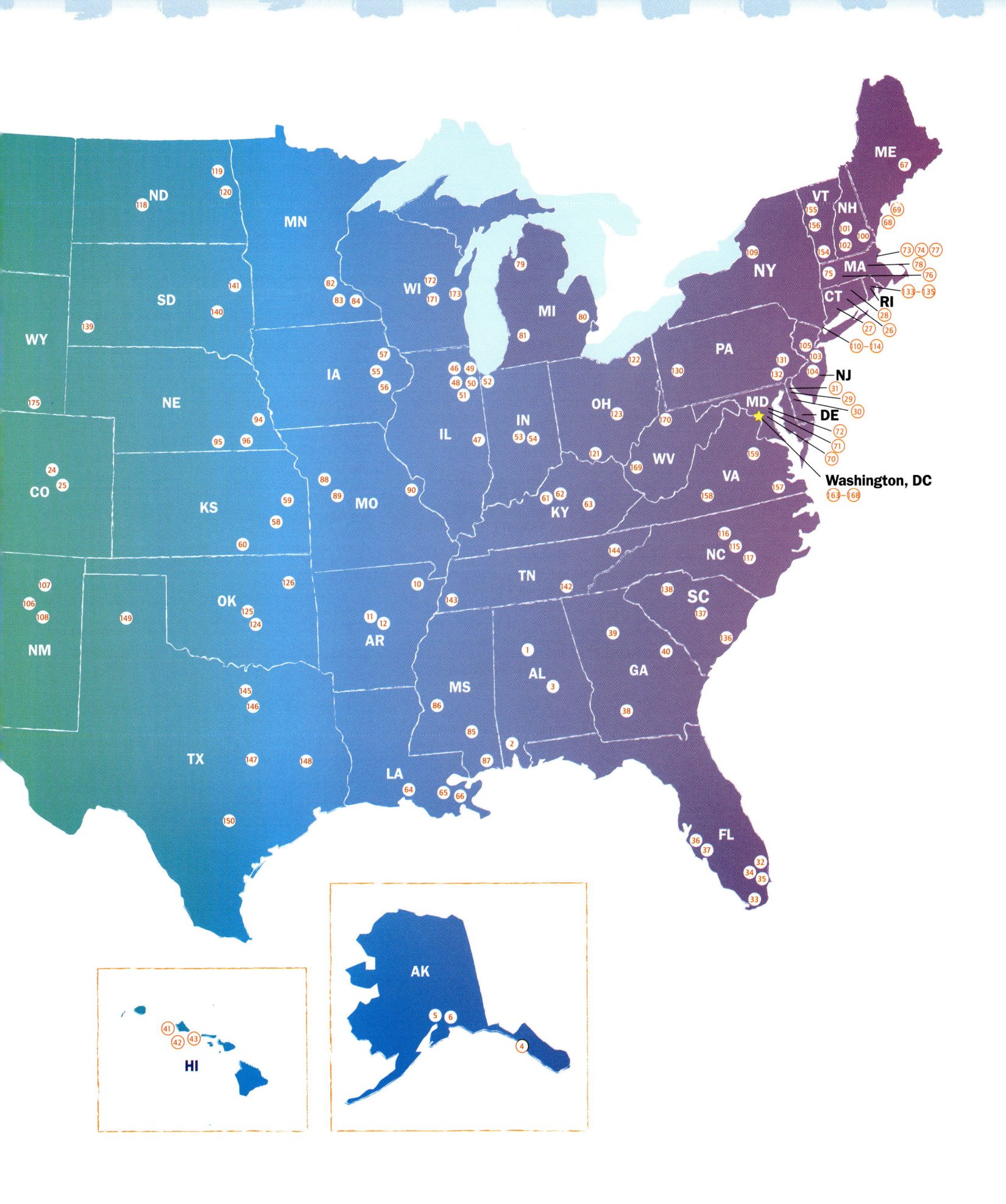

TEACHER'S HANDBOOK • Resources   T23

U.S. Museum Resources (continued)

Iowa

55 Cedar Rapids
Museum of Art
*410 3rd Avenue Southeast,
Cedar Rapids*
http://www.crma.org

56 Davenport Museum of Art
*1737 West 12th Street,
Davenport*
http://www.art-dma.org

57 Dubuque Museum of Art
36 East 8th Street, Dubuque
http://www.dbqart.com

Kansas

58 Coutts Memorial Museum
*110 North Main Street,
El Dorado*
http://skyways.lib.ks.us/kansas/museums/coutts/ind

59 Spencer Museum of Art
*1301 Mississippi Street,
Lawrence*
http://www.ukans.edu/~sma/

60 Wichita Art Museum
*West Museum Boulevard,
Wichita*
http://www.wichitaartmuseum.org

Kentucky

61 Kentucky Museum
of Arts + Design
609 West Main Street, Louisville
http://www.kentuckycrafts.org

62 Speed Art Museum, the
2035 South Third St., Louisville
http://www.speedmuseum.org

63 University of Kentucky
Art Museum
*Rose and Euclid Avenue,
Lexington*
http://www.uky.edu/ArtMuseum/

Louisiana

64 African-American Museum
*125 New Market Street,
St Martinville*
http://stmartinparish-la.org/tourism_africanmuseum

65 Louisiana State Museum
751 Chartres Street, New Orleans
http://lsm.crt.state.la.us/

66 New Orleans
Museum of Art
*City Park 1 Collins Diboll Circle,
New Orleans*
http://www.noma.org

Maine

67 Farnsworth Art Museum
*352 Main Street, Box 466,
Rockland*
http://farnsworthmuseum.org/

68 Ogunquit Museum
of American Art
Shore Road, Ogunquit
http://www.ogunquitmuseum.org

69 Portland
Museum of Art
7 Congress Square, Portland
http://www.portlandmuseum.org

Maryland

70 African Art
Museum of Maryland
*5430 Vantage Point Road,
Columbia*
http://www.Africanartmuseum.org

71 Baltimore
Museum of Art
10 Art Museum Drive, Baltimore
http://www.artbma.org/

72 Walters Art Museum
*600 North Charles Street,
Baltimore*
http://www.thewalters.org

Massachusetts

73 Harvard University
Art Museums
32 Quincy Street, Cambridge
http://www.artmuseums.harvard.edu/

74 Institute of Contemporary
Art
955 Boylston Street, Boston
http://www.icaboston.org

75 MASS MoCA -
Massachusetts Museum
of Contemporary Art
87 Marshall Street, North Adams
http://www.massmoca.org

76 Mead Art Museum
*Amherst College, PO Box 5000,
Amherst*
http://www.amherst.edu/~mead/

77 Museum of Fine Arts
Boston
465 Huntington Avenue, Boston
http://www.mfa.org/

78 Worcester Art Museum
55 Salisbury Street, Worcester
http://www.worcesterart.òrg

Michigan

79 Cranbrook Art Museum
*39221 Woodward Avenue,
PO Box 801, Bloomfield Hills*
http://www.cranbrook.edu/art/museum/

80 Detroit Institute of Arts
*5200 Woodward Avenue,
Detroit*
http://www.dia.org

81 Grand Rapids
Art Museum
55 Division Ave N, Grand Rapids
http://www.gramonline.org

Minnesota

82 Frederick R Weisman
Art Museum
*333 East River Road # 200,
Minneapolis*
http://hudson.acad.umn.edu/

83 Minnesota Museum
of American Art
*Landmark Center 75 West 5th
Street West, St Paul*
http://www.mmaa.org

84 Walker Art Center
*725 Vineland Place,
Minneapolis*
http://www.walkerart.org

Mississippi

85 Lauren Rogers
Museum of Art
*5th Avenue and 7th Street,
Laurel*
http://www.lrma.org/

86 Mississippi Museum
of Art
*201 E Pascagoula St
Ste 103, Jackson*
http://www.msmuseumart.org/

87 Walter Anderson
Museum of Art
*510 Washington Avenue,
Ocean Springs*
http://www.walterandersonmuseum.org/

Missouri

88 Albrecht-Kemper Art Museum
2818 Frederick Avenue, St Joseph
http://www.albrecht-kemper.org/

89 Nelson-Atkins
Museum of Art
4525 Oak Street, Kansas City
http://www.nelson-atkins.org/

90 St Louis Art Museum
1 Fine Arts Drive, St Louis
http://www.slam.org

Montana

91 Art Museum of Missoula
*335 North Pattee Street,
Missoula*
http://www.artmissoula.org/

92 Hockaday Museum
of Art
*2nd Avenue East at
Third Street, Kalispell*
http://www.hockadayartmuseum.org/

93 Montana Museum
of Art and Culture
University of Montana, Missoula
http://www.umt.edu/partv/famus/

Nebraska

94 Joslyn Art Museum
2200 Dodge St., Omaha
http://www.joslyn.org

95 Museum of Nebraska Art
(MONA)
2401 Central Avenue, Kearney
http://monet.unk.edu/mona/

96 Sheldon Memorial
Art Gallery and
Sculpture Garden
*University of Nebraska-Lincoln,
12th and R Streets, Lincoln*
http://sheldon.unl.edu/

Nevada

97 Las Vegas Art Museum
*9600 West Sahara Avenue,
Las Vegas*
http://www.lvam.com

98 Nevada Museum of Art
160 West Liberty Street, Reno
http://www.nevadaart.org

99 Walker African-American
Museum and Research Center
*705 W Van Buren Ave,
Las Vegas*
http://members.aol.com/Bigbrwnsis/

New Hampshire

100 Currier Museum of Art
201 Myrtle Way, Manchester
http://www.currier.org

101 Hood Museum of Art
Wheelock Street, Hanover
http://web.dartmouth.edu/~hood/

102 Mariposa Museum
26 Main Street, Peterborough
http://www.mariposamuseum.org

New Jersey

103 Jane Voorhees
Zimmerli Art Museum
*71 Hamilton St, Rutgers
University, New Brunswick*
http://www.zimmerlimuseum.rutgers.edu

104 Jersey City Museum
*350 Montgomery Street,
Jersey City*
http://www.jerseycitymuseum.org/

105 Princeton University
Art Museum
Princeton University, Princeton
http://www.princetonartmuseum.org/

New Mexico

106 Georgia O'Keeffe Museum
217 Johnson Street, Santa Fe
http://www.okeeffemuseum.org

107 Harwood Museum of Art
*238 Ledoux Street, 4080
NDCBU, Taos*
http://www.harwoodmuseum.org

108 Institute of American
Indian Arts Museum
Cathedral Place, Santa Fe
http://www.iaiancad.org

New York

109 Albright-Knox
Art Gallery
1285 Elmwood Avenue, Buffalo
http://www.albrightknox.org

110 Metropolitan Museum
of Art
*6626 Metropolitan Avenue
FL 2, Flushing*
http://www.Metmuseum.org/

111 Museum of Modern Art
MoMA
11 West 53 Street, New York
http://www.moma.org/

112 New Museum
of Contemporary Art
583 Broadway, New York
http://www.newmuseum.org/

113 Solomon R Guggenheim
Museum, New York
1071 5th Ave at 89th, New York
http://www.guggenheim.org/new_york_index.html

114 Whitney Museum
of American Art
*945 Madison Avenue FL 5,
New York*
http://www.whitney.org

North Carolina

115 Ackland Art Museum
*Columbia and Franklin Street,
Chapel Hill*
http://www.ackland.org

116 Duke University
Museum of Art
*Buchanan Blvd-Trinity Avenue,
Durham*
http://www.duke.edu/web/duma/

117 North Carolina Museum
of Art
2110 Blue Ridge Road, Raleigh
http://www.ncartmuseum.org/

North Dakota

118 North Heritage Center of
the State Historical Society of
North Dakota, Bismarck
http://www.state.nd.us/hist/index.html

119 North Dakota
Museum of Art
Centennial Drive, Grand Forks
http://www.ndmoa.com

120 Plains Art Museum
219 7th Street South, Fargo
http://www.plainsart.org/

Ohio

121 Cincinnati Art Museum
953 Eden Park Drive, Cincinnati
http://www.cincinnatiartmuseum.com/

122 Cleveland Museum of Art
11150 East Boulevard, Cleveland
http://www.clemusart.com/

123 Columbus Museum of Art
480 East Broad Street, Columbus
http://www.columbusmuseum.org

Teacher's Handbook

Oklahoma

124 Fred Jones Jr Museum of Art
410 West Boyd Street, University of Oklahoma, Norman
http://www.ou.edu/fjjma/

125 Oklahoma City Art Museum
3113 Pershing Boulevard, Oklahoma City
http://www.okcartmuseum.com/

126 Philbrook Museum of Art
2727 South Rockford Road, Tulsa, OK
http://www.philbrook.org/

Oregon

127 Coos Art Museum
235 Anderson Avenue, Coos Bay
http://www.coosart.org

128 Portland Art Museum
1219 SW Park Ave., Portland
http://www.pam.org

129 University of Oregon Museum of Art
1223 University of Oregon, Eugene
http://uoma.uoregon.edu/

Pennsylvania

130 The Andy Warhol Museum
117 Sandusky Street, Pittsburgh
http://www.clpgh.org/warhol/

131 The Palmer Museum of Art
Curtin Rd, The Pennsylvania State University, University Park
http://www.psu.edu/dept/palmermuseum/

132 Philadelphia Museum of Art
26th Street and the Benjamin Franklin Parkway, Philadelphia
http://pma.libertynet.org/

Rhode Island

133 Museum of Art, Rhode Island School of Design
224 Benefit Street, Providence
http://www.risd.edu/

134 Museum Of Primitive Art & Culture
1058 Kingstown Road, South Kingstown

135 National Museum of American Illustration
Vernon Court 492 Bellevue Avenue, Newport
http://www.americanillustration.org

South Carolina

136 Gibbes Museum of Art
135 Meeting Street, Charleston
http://www.gibbes.com/

137 Columbia Museum of Art
Main and Hampton Streets, Columbia
http://www.colmusart.org/

138 The Spartanburg County Museum of Art
385 S Spring St., Spartanburg
http://www.sparklenet.com/museumofart

South Dakota

139 Journey Museum
222 New York Street, Rapid City
http://www.journeymuseum.org

140 Oscar Howe Art Center and Middle Border Museum
1300 E University Street P.O Box 1071 Mitchell
http://www.oscarhowe.com/index.htm

141 South Dakota Art Museum
P.O. Box 2250, Brookings
http://web.sdstate.edu/sites/artmuseum/

Tennessee

142 Hunter Museum of Art
10 Bluff View, Chattanooga
http://www.huntermuseum.org/

143 Institute of Egyptian Art and Archaeology
The University of Memphis, Memphis
http://www.memst.edu/egypt/about.html

144 Knoxville Museum of Art
1050 Worlds Fair Park Drive, Knoxville
http://www.knoxart.org

Texas

145 Dallas Museum of Art
1717 North Harwood, Dallas
http://dm-art.org/

146 Kimbell Art Museum
3333 Camp Bowie Blvd., Fort Worth
http://kimbellart.org/

147 Mexic-Arte Museum
419 Congress Avenue, Austin
http://www.mexic-artemuseum.org

148 The Museum of Fine Arts
1001 Bissonnet, Houston
http://mfah.org/

149 Panhandle-Plains Historical Museum,
West Texas A&M University 2401 4th Ave., Canyon
http://www.wtamu.edu/museum/

150 San Antonio Museum of Art
200 West Jones Avenue, San Antonio
http://www.sa-museum.org

Utah

151 BYU Museum of Art
Brigham Young University, Provo
http://www.byu.edu/moa/

152 St George Art Museum
175 East 200 North, St George
http://www.ci.st-george.ut.us/arts/artmuseum.php

153 Utah Museum of Fine Arts, University of Utah
370 South 1530 East University of Utah, Salt Lake City
http://www.utah.edu/umfa/

Vermont

154 The Bennington Museum
West Main St., Bennington
http://www.benningtonmuseum.com

155 Robert Hull Fleming Museum
Colchester Avenue, Burlington
http://www.uvm.edu/~fleming/home/

156 Shelburne Museum
US Route 7, PO Box 10, Shelburne
http://www.shelburnemuseum.org

Virginia

157 Chrysler Museum of Art
245 West Olney Rd., Norfolk
http://www.chrysler.org/

158 Maier Museum of Art
2500 Rivermont Avenue, Lynchburg
http://www.rmwc.edu/Maier/

159 Virginia Museum of Fine Arts
2800 Grove Ave., Richmond
http://www.vmfa.state.va.us/

Washington

160 Frye Art Museum
704 Terry Ave., Seattle
http://fryeart.org/

161 Jundt Art Museum
502 East Boone Avenue, Spokane
http://www.gonzaga.edu/Campus+Resources/Museums+an

162 Seattle Art Museum
100 University St., Seattle
http://seattleartmuseum.org/

Washington, D.C.

163 Arthur M Sackler Gallery and the Freer Gallery of Art
1050 Independence Avenue, SW
http://www.asia.si.edu/default.htm

164 Corcoran Gallery of Art
500 17th Street Northwest
http://www.corcoran.org/

165 Hirshhorn Museum and Sculpture Garden
Independence Avenue and 7th Street Southwest
http://hirshhorn.si.edu/

166 National Gallery of Art
http://www.nga.gov/

167 The National Museum of Women in the Arts
1250 New York Ave., NW
http://www.nmwa.org/

168 Smithsonian Museums
Smithsonian Institution
http://www.si.edu/

West Virginia

169 Huntington Museum of Art
2033 McCoy Rd., Huntington
http://www.hmoa.org/

170 Oglebay Institute: Mansion Museum and Glass Museum
Burton Center, Wheeling
http://www.oionline.com/

Wisconsin

171 Elvehjem Museum of Art
800 University Avenue, Madison
http://www.lvm.wisc.edu

172 Leigh Yawkey Woodson Art Museum
700 North Twelfth St, Wausau
http://www.lywam.org/

173 Milwaukee Art Museum
750 North Lincoln Memorial Dr., Milwaukee
http://www.mam.org/

Wyoming

174 National Museum of Wildlife Art
2820 Rungius Road, Jackson
http://www.wildlifeart.org

175 University of Wyoming Art Museum
2111 Willett Dr., Laramie
http://uwadmnweb.uwyo.edu/artmuseum/

World Museum Resources

Argentina
1 Fundacion Federico Klemm
Buenos Aires, Argentina
www.fundacionfjklemm.org

Australia
2 Art Gallery of New South Wales
Sydney, Australia
www.artgallery.nsw.gov.au/

3 Australian National Art Gallery
Canberra, Australia
www.nga.gov.au/Home/index.cfm

4 Museum of Contemporary Art
Sydney, Australia
www.mca.com.au/

Austria
5 Kunsthistorisches Museum Wien
Vienna, Austria
www.khm.at/

Bahrain
6 Al Hayat Museum
Manama, Bahrain
www.beitalquran.com/

Brazil
7 Museu Historico Nacional
Rio de Janeiro, Brazil
www.museuhistoriconacional.com.br/ingles/index.htm

Canada
8 Art Gallery of Calgary
Calgary, Canada
www.artgallerycalgary.com/

9 Morris and Helen Belkin Art Gallery, University of British Columbia
Vancouver, Canada
www.belkin-gallery.ubc.ca/

10 Art Gallery of Newfoundland and Labrador
St. Johns, Canada
www.mun.ca/agnl/main.html

11 Art Gallery of Nova Scotia
Halifax, Canada
www.agns.gov.ns.ca/

12 Art Gallery of Ontario
Toronto, Canada
www.ago.net/navigation/flash/index.cfm

13 National Gallery of Canada
Ottawa, Canada
www.national.gallery.ca

14 The Montreal Museum of Fine Arts
Quebec, Canada
www.mmfa.qc.ca/en/index.html

15 McMichael Canadian Art Collection
Toronto, Canada
www.mcmichael.com/

16 Winnipeg Art Gallery
Winnipeg, Canada
www.wag.mb.ca/

T26 TEACHER'S HANDBOOK • Resources

Teacher's Handbook

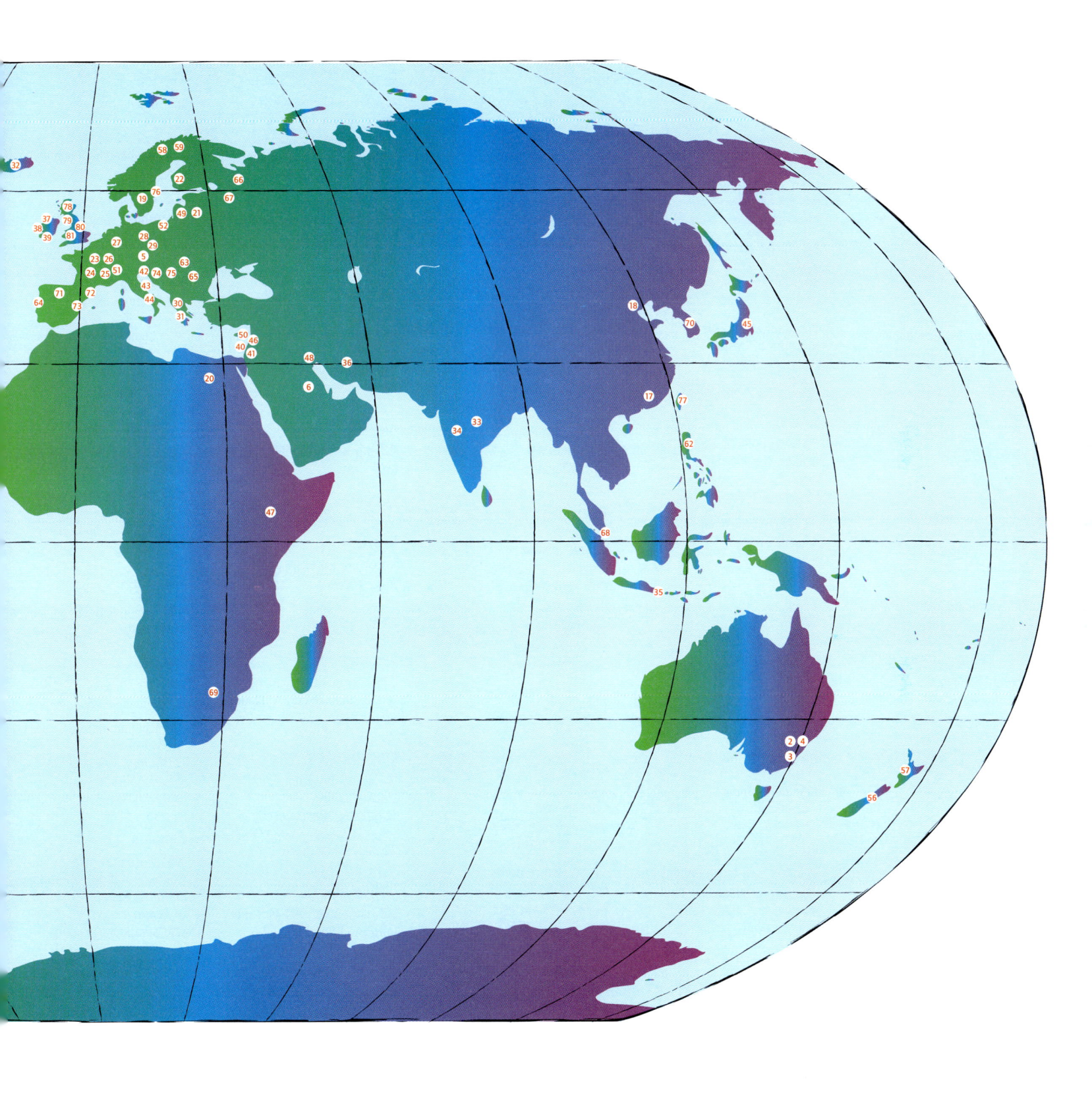

TEACHER'S HANDBOOK • Resources T27

World Museum Resources

China
17 Hong Kong Museum of Art
Hong Kong, China
www.lcsd.gov.hk/CE/Museum/Arts/english/intro/eintro.html

18 Palace Museum
Beijing, China
www.dpm.org.cn/

Denmark
19 National Museum
Copenhagen, Denmark
www.natmus.dk/sw1413.asp

Egypt
20 The Egyptian Museum
Cairo, Egypt
www.egyptianmuseum.gov.eg/

Estonia
21 Estonian National Museum
Tartu, Estonia
www.erm.ee/?lang=ENG

Finland
22 The Finnish National Gallery
Helsinki, Finland
www.fng.fi/fng/rootnew/en/vtm/etusivu.htm

France
23 The Louvre
Paris, France
www.louvre.fr/louvrea.htm

24 Musee d'Orsay,
Paris, France
www.musee-orsay.fr/

25 Centre Georges Pompidou
Paris, France
www.cnac-gp.fr/Pompidou/Accueil.nsf/tunnel?OpenForm

Germany
26 Neues Museum
Nuremberg, Germany
www.nmn.de/

27 Hamburg Kunsthalle
Hamburg, Germany
www.hamburger-kunsthalle.de/

28 Alte National Galerie
Berlin, Germany
www.alte-nationalgalerie.de/

29 Bauhaus Archiv Museum of Design
Berlin, Germany
www.bauhaus.de/english/

Greece
30 Acropolis Museum
Athens, Greece
www.culture.gr/2/21/211/21101m/e211am01.html

31 Benaki Museum
Athens, Greece
www.benaki.gr/index-en.htm

Iceland
32 Living Art Museum
Reykjavik, Iceland
www.nylo.is/English/index.html

India
33 National Museum of India
New Delhi, India
www.nationalmuseumindia.org/index.html

34 Chhatrapati Shivaji Maharaj Vastu Sangrahalaya
(Formerly the Prince of Wales Museum of Western India)
Mumbai (Bombay), India
www.bombaymuseum.org/

Indonesia
35 Agung Rai Museum of Art
Ubud, Bali, Indonesia
www.nusantara.com/arma/

Iran
36 National Museum of Iran
Tehran, Iran
www.nationalmuseumofiran.com/

Ireland
37 Hunt Museum
Limerick, Ireland
www.huntmuseum.com/

38 Irish Museum of Modern Art
Dublin, Ireland
www.modernart.ie/

39 National Gallery of Ireland
Dublin, Ireland
www.nationalgallery.ie/

Israel
40 The Israel Museum
Jerusalem, Israel
www.imj.org.il/

41 Tel Aviv Museum of Art
Tel Aviv, Israel
www.tamuseum.com/

Italy
42 Uffizi Gallery
Florence, Italy
www.uffizi.firenze.it/welcomeE.html

43 Museo di Roma
Rome, Italy
www.museodiroma.comune.roma.it/PalazzoBraschi/inizio.mostra

44 Vatican Museum
Vatican City
http://mv.vatican.va/3_EN/pages/MV_Home.html

Japan
45 Kyoto National Museum
Tokyo, Japan
www.kyohaku.go.jp/indexe.htm

Jordan
46 Darat al Funun Home for the Arts
Amman, Jordan
www.daratalfunun.org/

Kenya
47 National Museum of Kenya
Nairobi, Kenya
www.museums.or.ke/

Kuwait
48 Kuwait National Museum
Kuwait City, Kuwait
www.kmia.org.kw

Latvia
49 State Museum of Art
Riga, Latvia
www.vmm.lv/en/muzejs.html

Lebanon
50 American University of Beirut Archaeology Museum
Beirut, Lebanon

Liechtenstein
51 Kunstmuseum Liechtenstein
Vaduz, Liechtenstein
www.kunstmuseum.li/web2306e/index.html

Lithuania
52 Lithuanian Art Museum
Vilnius, Lithuania
www.ldm.lt/ldm_en.htm

Mexico
53 Museo de Arte Moderno
Mexico City, Mexico
www.arts-history.mx/museos/mam/home2.html

54 National Museum of Anthropology
Mexico City, Mexico
www.mna.inah.gob.mx/

55 Museo de Arte Contemporaneo de Oaxaca
Oaxaca, Mexico
www.arts-history.mx/museos/maco/home.html

New Zealand
56 Centre of Contemporary Art
Christchurch, New Zealand
www.coca.org.nz/

57 Auckland Art Gallery
Auckland, New Zealand
www.aucklandartgallery.govt.nz/

Norway
58 National Gallery of Norway
Oslo, Norway
www.museumsnett.no/nasjonalgalleriet/flash_versjon_engelsk/

59 Lillehammer Art Museum
Lillehammer, Norway
www.lillehammerartmuseum.com/

Panama
60 Museo de Arte Contemporaneo de Panama
Panama, Republic of Panama
www.macpanama.org/

Peru

61 Museo Arqueologico Rafael Larco Herrera
Lima, Peru
museolarco.perucultural.org.pe/

Philippines

62 Philippine National Museum
Manila, Philippines
http://nmuseum.tripod.com/

Poland

63 Polish National Museum
Warsaw, Poland
www.mnw.art.pl/

Portugal

64 Museu Calouste Gulbenkian
Lisbon, Portugal
www.gulbenkian.pt/

Romania

65 The National Museum of Art of Romania
Bucharest, Romania
http://art.museum.ro/museum.html

Russia

66 The State Hermitage Museum
St. Petersburg, Russia
www.hermitagemuseum.org/

67 Pushkin Museum of Fine Arts
Moscow, Russia
www.museum.ru/gmii/

Singapore

68 Singapore Art Museum
Singapore, Republic of Singapore
www.nhb.gov.sg/SAM/sam.shtml

South Africa

69 Pretoria Art Museum
Pretoria, South Africa
www.pretoriaartmuseum.co.za/

South Korea

70 Seoul Metropolitan Museum of Art
Seoul, South Korea
www.metro.seoul.kr/muse/eng/

Spain

71 Guggenheim Bilbao Museum
Bilbao, Spain
www.guggenheim-bilbao.es/idioma.htm

72 Museu d'Art Contemporani
Barcelona, Spain
www.macba.es/home.php

73 Valencian Institute of Modern Art
Valencia, Spain
www.ivam.es/

Switzerland

74 Kunstmuseum Basel
Basel, Switzerland
www.kunstmuseumbasel.ch/de/

75 Kunsthaus
Zurich, Switzerland
www.kunsthaus.ch/

Sweden

76 National Museum
Stockholm, Sweden
www.nationalmuseum.se/

Taiwan

77 National Palace Museum
T'aipei, Taiwan
www.npm.gov.tw/english/index-e.htm

United Kingdom

78 National Gallery of London
London, England
www.nationalgallery.org.uk/

79 British Museum
London, England
www.thebritishmuseum.ac.uk/

80 Tate Gallery
London, England
www.tate.org.uk/home/default.htm

81 Victoria and Albert Museum
London, England
www.vam.ac.uk/

Uruguay

82 Museo Nacianal de Artes Visuales
Montevideo, Uruguay
www.mnav.gub.uy/

Elements and Principles of Art

Scope and Sequence

Elements of Art	Level K u1	u2	u3	u4	u5	u6	Level 1 u1	u2	u3	u4	u5	u6	Level 2 u1	u2	u3	u4	u5	u6	Level 3 u1	u2	u3	u4	u5	u6
Line	1–6						1–6	1					1–4						1–2					
Shape		1–6				6		1–6		1			5–6						2, 4	3–6				
Color			1–6						1–6				1–3			1, 3			1–6					
Value																4–6				1				
Space			1, 3							2, 5, 6				5–6					1–3					
Form			2–6	5						1–4		4	1–4			2, 4	4–6							
Texture					1–6						1–3						5–6						5–6	

Principles of Art	Level K u1	u2	u3	u4	u5	u6	Level 1 u1	u2	u3	u4	u5	u6	Level 2 u1	u2	u3	u4	u5	u6	Level 3 u1	u2	u3	u4	u5	u6
Pattern						1				4–5			1–2										1–3	
Rhythm						2						6			3–6								4–6	
Balance					3–4						1–2				1–2							1–4		
Proportion																								
Emphasis											3–4					3–4								3–4
Variety																	3–4							2
Harmony																1–2								1
Unity						5–6						5–6						5–6						5–6

*Numbers indicate lesson numbers within a given unit.

T30 TEACHER'S HANDBOOK • Scope and Sequence

Teacher's Handbook

Level 4						Level 5						Level 6						Level 7	Level 8
U1	U2	U3	U4	U5	U6	U1	U2	U3	U4	U5	U6	U1	U2	U3	U4	U5	U6	Exploring Art	Understanding Art
1–6						1–2						1						Chapter 2, 6, 7, 8, 9, 10, 11	Chapter 2, 6, 8, 9, 12, 15, 16
	1–2							3	1				2					Chapter 2, 6, 8, 9, 10, 11	Chapter 2, 3, 5, 8, 9, 13, 14, 16, 17
		1–4								1–4				1–4				Chapter 2, 4, 8, 9, 11, 13	Chapter 2, 3, 4, 8, 11, 12, 14–17
		5–6							4–6				2–3					Chapter 14	Chapter 13, 14, 15
				1–3				1–3								5–6		Chapter 2, 4, 10, 12	Chapter 6, 7, 13, 15
			1–3							4–6					3–4			Chapter 2, 6, 11, 12, 13	Chapter 6, 14, 15
					4–5						1					5–6		Chapter 2, 14	Chapter 3, 5, 6, 11–16

Level 4						Level 5						Level 6						Level 7	Level 8
U1	U2	U3	U4	U5	U6	U1	U2	U3	U4	U5	U6	U1	U2	U3	U4	U5	U6	Exploring Art	Understanding Art
	3									5–6			1–3					Chapter 3, 6	Chapter 7, 8, 10, 15, 17
	4–6								2–3				4–6					Chapter 3, 4, 7	
			1–3							4–6					1–4			Chapter 3, 11, 12	Chapter 5, 7, 9, 10, 11, 13
		4–6					1–6										1–6	Chapter 3, 11, 14	Chapter 5, 11, 12
				6					5						3–4			Chapter 3, 11	Chapter 5, 10, 11, 12, 16
									5					2			1–2	Chapter 3, 6, 13	Chapter 3, 4, 5, 10, 15
									4							1	3–4	Chapter 3, 6, 7	Chapter 4, 5, 7, 12, 16
									6							5–6	5–6	Chapter 3	Chapter 7

TEACHER'S HANDBOOK • Scope and Sequence   T31

Media

Scope and Sequence

Media	Level K U1	U2	U3	U4	U5	U6	Level 1 U1	U2	U3	U4	U5	U6	Level 2 U1	U2	U3	U4	U5	U6	Level 3 U1	U2	U3	U4	U5	U6
Collage	6	2	2, 3		1	3	3		5			3, 4	5	5					4					
Drawing	2, 4, 5	4, 5	1, 4, 5	1	2	1, 2	1	1-3, 5	1, 4		2, 6	1, 5			2, 3	2-4, 6	4		1, 2, 5, 6	3	1	1	3, 5	6
Fiber Arts				4, 6							5						5						6	2
Mixed Media		6		3, 4	3		5			5	1	2	2, 6	2		2, 3	6			6	4, 6			4
Painting	1		6				1, 2, 4	4	3, 6	6			3, 4	6	1, 4-6			1, 3	3	2	2, 3, 5	4		
Photography																								
Printmaking		3								4					1				1				1	
Three-Dimensional Forms				2, 5, 6	5	4, 6			1-4	3	6	1	1, 3, 4		4	1	5		4, 5		2, 3	4, 6	1, 5	
Technology	3	1				5	6	6	2						5		2, 6				5	2	3	

*Numbers indicate lesson numbers within a given unit.

Teacher's Handbook

Level 4							Level 5							Level 6							Level 7	Level 8
u1	u2	u3	u4	u5	u6	u1	u2	u3	u4	u5	u6	u1	u2	u3	u4	u5	u6	Exploring Art	Understanding Art
	6	3				1		4	2		5	6					1	Chapter 1, 6, 10	Chapter 10
1–6	3, 4	2		1, 2, 4, 5		2, 4, 5	1, 4	1, 5	1, 4	3	2	1	3	1, 2, 4	3–5	1, 2, 5		Chapter 2, 7, 11, 14	Chapter 3, 15, 16
					3, 6					2	4	2					3, 5	Chapter 1, 2, 3, 13	Chapter 7, 8, 10, 12
	1, 5		4, 5		1, 4				1				6			6	4	Chapter 5, 13	Chapter 2, 3
		4–6		2, 5		2, 3	3	3	4, 5	1		5	1, 2, 4		5	1		Chapter 2, 3, 4, 5, 6, 9, 11, 14	Chapter 1–8, 10, 11, 13–17
				3		6											2	Chapter 10	Chapter 1, 17
										3								Chapter 3, 4, 8	Chapter 1, 3, 6, 8, 14–17
		1–3				5, 6	6	5, 6		6	3, 4		3, 6	6	3		6	Chapter 2, 3, 4, 5, 7, 12, 13	Chapter 1, 2, 3, 5–13, 15–17
	2	1	6	6		3		2			6		5			2	4	Chapter 4, 11, 15	Chapter 3, 17

TEACHER'S HANDBOOK • Scope and Sequence **T33**

Program Glossary

A

active lines *noun* Lines that show action and add energy and movement to a work of art. Diagonal, zigzag, and curved lines are examples of active lines.

additive sculpture *noun* When something is added to either relief or freestanding sculpture

alternating pattern *noun* Can repeat a motif, but change position; alter spacing between motifs or add a second motif

analogous color scheme *noun* Uses colors that are side by side on the color wheel and have a common color

analogous colors *noun* Colors that sit side by side on the color wheel and have a common hue. Violet, blue-violet, blue, blue-green are examples of analogous colors.

angle *noun* A shape formed when two lines extend in different directions from the same point

animal forms *noun* A three-dimensional representation of an animal

ant's view *noun* Viewers feel they are looking up, toward an object or figure.

appliqué *noun* An art form in which cutout fabrics are attached to a larger surface

approximate symmetry *noun* A special kind of formal balance where both sides of a design are almost exactly the same. One example is the human face: each side is almost the same as the other.

arc *noun* Any portion of a curved line from a circle

architects *noun* Artists who design buildings, cities, and bridges using three-dimensional forms

architecture *noun* The art of designing and planning buildings, cities, and bridges

armature *noun* A framework for supporting material used in sculpting

art form *noun* A type of art

assemblage *noun* A sculpture technique in which a variety of objects is assembled to create one complete piece

asymmetrical balance *noun* Another name for informal balance

asymmetry *noun* Another name for informal balance. Something asymmetrical looks balanced even if it is not the same on both sides.

atmospheric perspective *noun* The effects air and light have on how we perceive an object

axis *noun* A real or imaginary line across the center of a work of art

B

background *noun* The area of the picture plane farthest from the viewer

balance *noun* The principle of design that deals with visual weight in an artwork

bird's-eye view *noun* Or aerial view; viewers feel they are looking down on a scene.

black

blending *noun* A shading technique that creates a gradual change from light to dark or dark to light

blind contour drawing *noun* A drawing that is made by looking at the object being drawn, not at the paper.

blob *noun* A type of free-form shape

body forms *noun* Three-dimensional representations of a person

body proportions *noun* The size relationship of one part of the body to another

brass *noun* A metal made by combining copper and zinc

bright colors *noun* colors that appear to reflect light

broken (line) *noun* A line that is made of a series of dashes, not solid

building *noun* a structure where we live, work, meet, or play

C

calm lines *noun* Lines that give a work of art a quiet and peaceful mood. Horizontal and vertical lines are calm lines.

carving *noun* Art made by cutting into the surface of the medium.

central axis *noun* A real or imaginary dividing line that can run in two directions, vertically and horizontally

circle *noun* A round, geometric shape made when all points are placed the same distance from a center point.

close-up view *noun* Viewers feel they are right next to an object, or are a part of the action in a picture.

coil *noun* A long roll of clay joined into a circle or spiral. Clay coils are used to make pottery.

collage *noun* A two-dimensional work of art made up of pieces of paper and/or fabric to create the image.

collograph *noun* A printmaking technique where cut papers or thin boards are arranged to create an image on a stiff printing plate.

color *noun* 1. The art element that is created from reflected light; 2. In balance: a brighter color has more visual weight than a dull color; 3. In perspective: bright-colored objects seem closer, while dull or pale objects appear farther away.

color intensity *noun* The brightness or dullness of a color

color scheme *noun* A plan for organizing the colors used in an artwork

color spectrum *noun* The effect that occurs when light passes through a prism and separates into a band of colors in the order of red, orange, yellow, green, blue, and violet.

color wheel *noun* Shows the color spectrum bent into a circle

column *noun* A supporting pillar on a building

T34 TEACHER'S HANDBOOK • Glossary

Teacher's Handbook

complementary color scheme *noun* Uses one set of complementary colors; for example, red and green, blue and orange, and yellow and violet

complementary colors *noun* Colors that are opposite each other on the color wheel

complex geometric shapes *noun* Shapes made by combining simple geometric shapes such as triangles, squares, and rectangles. Some examples of complex geometric shapes are diamonds, pentagons, trapezoids, hexagons, parallelograms, and octagons.

contour *noun* The edges and surface ridges of an object

contour hatching *noun* A shading technique that follows the form of an object

contour lines *noun* Continuous, unbroken lines that show the edges and surface ridges of an object or figure

contrast *noun* 1. A technique for creating a focal point or area of interest in a work of art using differences in elements; 2. In emphasis: contrast occurs when one element stands out from the rest of the work; 3. showing differences between things

converging *adj.* (*verb*) Coming together at one point or place

converging lines *noun* One of the six perspective techniques. Parallel lines seem to converge or move toward the same point as they move away from you.

cool colors *noun* Green, violet, and blue. They suggest coolness and move away from the viewer.

cool hues *noun* Blue, green, and violet. Cool hues are associated with cool things like snow, water, and grass.

cross-hatching *noun* A shading technique created when sets of parallel lines cross or intersect

culture *noun* Another word for custom

curling *verb* Hold one end of a long strip of paper. Grip the middle of the paper strip next to the side of a pencil. With a quick motion, pull the strip firmly across the pencil.

curved *adj.* Lines that bend and change gradually or turn inward to form spirals

curved (line) *noun* A line that changes directions slowly and bends in arcs

curving movement *verb* Using curved lines to move the viewer's eyes through a work of art and make the viewer feel that objects in the work of art are moving along curves

D

dark lines *noun* Created by using less water for watercolor paints

dark value *noun* A value that has more black added to it

decorative *adj.* Serving to make more beautiful; to adorn with ornaments

depth *noun* 1. The appearance of distance; 2. How far something extends toward or away from the viewer.

detail *noun* One of the six perspective techniques. Objects with fuzzy, blurred edges appear farther away than those with clear sharp edges.

diagonal *noun* (*adj.*) Lines that are slanted. They look as if they are falling or rising. They make things look active.

diagonal movement *verb* Using diagonal lines to move the viewer's eyes through a work of art and make the viewer feel that objects in the work of art are moving along diagonals

dimension *noun* A measurement of the amount of space an object takes up in one direction

diorama *noun* A display of a scene using sculpted, miniature figurines

directional lines *noun* How a line moves: diagonally, vertically, or horizontally

distortion *noun* A deviation from normal or expected proportions

dominant *noun* (*adj.*) The part of the work of art that seems more important to the viewer. Dominant elements have been emphasized.

dominant element *noun* The element in a work of art that is noticed first.

dull colors Colors that are not bright

E

earthenware *noun* Ceramics made out of clay and fired at a low heat

elongate *verb* To stretch out or make long

embroidery *noun* The art of decorating designs with needle and thread

emphasis *noun* The principle of design that stresses one area in an art work over another area

even balance *adj.* Both halves are equal. Left side and right side are the same.

exaggerate *verb* To make much larger than actual size

exaggeration *noun* To increase or enlarge beyond what is expected or normal

F

facial proportions *noun* The relationship of one feature of a face to another feature

faraway view *noun* Or eye-level view; viewers feel they are standing far away from the scene.

fiber *noun* A material used to make baskets and cloth. Grass, yarn, and straw are kinds of fibers.

flowing lines *noun* Create a feeling of calm and gracefulness. Flowing lines are fluid; they change direction and size.

flowing rhythm *noun* Created when curved lines or shapes are repeated

focal point *noun* The point where the receding lines meet. It is the first part of a composition to attract the viewer's attention.

foreground *noun* The area of the picture plane that is closest to the viewer

form *noun* A three-dimensional object that is measured by height, width, and depth

formal balance *noun* Occurs when equal or similar elements are placed on opposite sides of a central axis

TEACHER'S HANDBOOK • Glossary   T35

Program Glossary (continued)

free-form forms *noun* Three-dimensional forms with irregular edges often found in nature

free-form shapes *noun* Two-dimensional images made of straight or curved lines or a combination of both

freestanding *noun* Forms that can be seen from all around

freestanding sculpture *noun* A three-dimensional work of art that can be viewed on all sides because it is surrounded by space

fringing *verb* Make parallel straight cuts along the edge of a piece of paper to create a ruffled look.

frontal proportions *noun* A front view of the head that is divided by three horizontal lines across the central axis

futurists *noun* A group of Italian artists during the early twentieth-century who repeated and overlapped shapes and lines to create the illusion of movement

G

geometric forms *noun* Mathematically precise forms based on geometric shapes

geometric shapes *noun* Mathematically precise shapes: circle, square, and triangle

gesture *noun* An expressive movement

gesture drawings *noun* Quick drawings used to capture the position or pose of the body

gesture lines *noun* Lines drawn to capture the movement of a person, an animal, or an object in a painting or drawing

gesture sketch *noun* Quick drawings used to capture the position or movement of the body

guide lines *noun* Lines used by artists to create both full-face and profile portraits more accurately

H

hand tools *noun* Simple instruments for carving or sculpting

harmony *noun* The principle of art that creates unity by stressing similarities of separate but related parts

hatching *noun* A shading technique that looks like a series of parallel lines

height *noun* A vertical measurement, or how tall something is

high-intensity color *noun* A pure hue such as red

highlights *noun* Small areas of white or light value to show the brightest spots

horizon line *noun* The point at which the earth and sky meet. The horizon line is always at the viewer's eye level.

horizontal *noun* (*adj.*) A line that moves from side to side

hues *noun* The spectral colors, or colors of the rainbow. Hues do not include black or white. Hues are red, orange, yellow, green, blue, and violet.

I

informal balance *noun* A way of organizing parts of a design so that unlike objects have equal visual weight

installation *noun* An artwork that was created for a specific place, such as a gallery or outdoor location

intensity *noun* The brightness or dullness of a color

interior designers *noun* Artists who decorate the inside of a building

intermediate colors *noun* Colors made by mixing a primary color and a secondary color. There are six intermediate colors—red-orange, yellow-orange, yellow-green, blue-green, blue-violet, and red-violet.

intermediate hues *noun* Yellow-green, red-orange, blue-green, made by combining a primary hue with either of the secondary hues that are adjacent on the color wheel

invented texture *noun* Created when an artist uses lines or other elements to make a textural look without any specific texture in mind

irregular *adj.* Does not follow a rule or pattern

isolation *noun* An object is emphasized by its placement apart from other objects.

J

jeweler *noun* An artist who designs and makes jewelry

jewelry *noun* Three-dimensional artwork that is made for people to wear

K

kinetic movement *noun* Actual or real movement

kinetic sculpture *noun* A three-dimensional form that actually moves in space

L

landscape *noun* a picture of the outdoors

light lines *noun* Created by adding more water to watercolor paints

light value *noun* A value that has more white added to it

line *noun* A mark drawn by a tool such as a pencil, pen, or paintbrush as it moves across a surface

line variety *noun* The different possibilities in the character of lines. For example, lines can be long or short, thick or thin, rough or smooth, and broken or solid.

linear perspective *noun* A system used to create the illusion of depth on a flat surface

lines *noun* One of the six perspective techniques. Parallel lines seem to converge or move toward the same point as they move away from the viewer.

location *noun* Artists can emphasize an object by placing it closer to the center of the piece.

low-intensity color *noun* A dull hue made by mixing a color with its complement

M

mandala *noun* A radial design divided into sections or wedges, each of which contains a different image

maquette *noun* A small model for a larger sculpture

mask *noun* A three-dimensional art form of sculpted faces

matte *noun* A dull, sometimes rough finish

medium *noun* The supply an artist uses to create art. Some media are clay, paint, or wood.

middle ground *noun* The area of the picture plane that is usually toward the center

minimal details *noun* Used in gesture sketches to complete the drawing

mix a neutral color *verb* Mix a neutral color with another color to change its value

mixed-media *noun* An art object that has been created from an assortment of media or materials

mobile *noun* A moving sculpture in which shapes are balanced and arranged on wire arms and suspended from the ceiling to move freely in the air currents

monochromatic *adj.* A color scheme that is made up of one color and the tints and shade of that color

monochromatic color scheme *noun* Uses only one color and the values of that color

monotonous *adj.* Lack of variety; boring

monumental sculptures *noun* Sculptures that are larger than human forms

motif *noun* A unit that is made up of objects or art elements that can be repeated

movement *noun* The principle of art that leads a viewer's eyes throughout a work of art

mural *noun* A painting done on a wall

N

negative space *noun* The empty space that surrounds objects, shapes, and forms

neon *noun* A special kind of light that can be made to be many bright colors

neutral color scheme *noun* Uses black, white, and a variety of grays

neutral colors *noun* Black, white, and gray; give hues a range of values

nonobjective *adj.* Art that has no recognizable subject matter

O

one-point linear perspective *noun* A system used to create the illusion of depth on a flat surface where all receding lines meet at one point

opaque *adj.* Does not let light through

outline *noun* a line drawn around the edge of an object

overlap *verb* To place one object on top of another object and partially cover the first object up

overlapping *noun* 1. One object covers a portion of another object. 2. In perspective: one of the six perspective techniques; the object covering another will appear closer to the viewer, creating a feeling of depth.

P

painting *noun* An art form using paint on a flat surface

paper sculpting techniques *noun* Six different techniques used to create paper sculptures: scoring a straight line, scoring a curve, pleating, curling, fringing, tab and slot.

parallel lines *noun* Lines that move in the same direction and always stay the same distance apart

pattern *noun* A repeated surface decoration

perception drawing *verb* Looking at something carefully and thinking deeply about what you see as you draw

perspective *noun* The method used to create the illusion of depth in two-dimensional art: overlapping, size, placement, detail, color, converging lines

perspective techniques *noun* The six techniques an artist uses to create the illusion of depth in two-dimensional art: overlapping, size, placement, detail, color, converging lines

photograph *noun* A picture taken using light-sensitive film and a camera

picture plane *noun* The surface of a drawing or painting

Teacher's Handbook

placement *noun* One of the six perspective techniques. Objects placed lower in the picture appear to be closer than those placed near eye level. There are three areas on a picture plane: foreground, middle ground, and background.

pleating *verb* Fold piece of paper from edge to edge. Then fold the same amount of paper in the other direction. Continue folding the paper back and forth in this manner.

point of view *noun* The angle at which the viewer sees an object

portrait *noun* A two- or three-dimensional artwork created in the image of a person or animal

posed *verb* Arranged in a special way

position *noun* In balance: a larger, positive shape and a small, negative space can be balanced by a small, positive shape and a large, negative space.

positive space *noun* Refers to any object, shape, or form in two- and three-dimensional art

primary colors *noun* Red, yellow, and blue. They cannot be made by mixing colors.

primary hues *noun* Red, yellow, and blue, used to mix the other hues on the color wheel

print *noun* An image created by using a stamp or printing plate. When artists make prints, they can make many identical images.

printing *verb* Pressing a shape from one thing to another many times

printing plate *noun* A plate that holds the image that will be used to create a print

prism *noun* A wedge-shaped piece of glass that bends light as it passes through

profile *noun* A side view of a person or animal

profile proportions *noun* A side view of the head that is divided by three horizontal lines

proportion *noun* The principle of art that is concerned with the size relationship of one part to another

TEACHER'S HANDBOOK • Glossary **T37**

Program Glossary (continued)

R

radial balance *noun* A type of balance that occurs when the art elements come out, or radiate, from a central point

rainbow *noun* An arc of spectral colors, usually identified as red, orange, yellow, green, blue, indigo, and violet, that appears in the sky opposite the sun

random pattern *noun* Occurs when the motif is repeated in no apparent order

ratio *noun* A comparison of size between two things

real texture *noun* Texture you can feel

realistic scale *noun* When an artist creates a work of art where everything fits together and makes sense in size relation

rectangle *noun* A four-sided geometric shape made of all right angles and whose opposite sides are equal in length.

regular pattern *noun* Occurs when identical motifs are repeated with an equal amount of space between them

relief *noun* A type of sculpture where forms project from a flat background

relief sculpture *noun* A sculpture in which objects stick out from a flat surface

repeated lines *noun* Used to give the feeling of movement or motion in a gesture drawing

repetition *noun* Lines, shapes, colors, or textures that are repeated throughout an artwork

rest *noun* The negative space between repetitions of the motif

rhythm *noun* The principle of design that organizes the elements in a work of art by repeating elements and/or objects

rough *noun* (*adj.*) A surface that has ridges; not smooth

rough (line) *noun* A line that has jagged, uneven edges

S

sail *noun* A type of free-form shape

scale *noun* Size as measured against a standard reference

score *verb* The repeated scratching of the clay surface at the area that another scored piece will be attached

scoring a curve *verb* Gradually cut bending curves in the paper with the point of the scissors

scoring a straight line *verb* Hold a ruler in the center of a piece of paper. Run the point of the scissors along the edge of the ruler to cut the paper in a straight line.

sculpture *noun* Three-dimensional art

sculpture model *noun* The study or detailed example of what the sculpture will look like when completed

secondary colors *noun* Orange, green, and violet. These colors are made by mixing two primary colors.

secondary hues *noun* Orange, green, and violet; the result of mixing two primary hues

self-portrait *noun* A two- or three-dimensional artwork that an artist makes of him or herself

sets of complementary colors *noun* There are three sets on the color wheel: red and green, blue and orange, and yellow and violet.

shade *noun* Any hue blended with black

shading *noun* A technique for creating dark values or darkening an area by repeating marks such as lines or dots

shadows *noun* Shaded areas in a painting or drawing

shape *noun* A two-dimensional area that is measured by height and width

shape reversal *noun* Occurs when an object, shape, or form is positive space in one image and then in another image becomes negative space

shiny *noun* Bright from reflected light

silhouette *noun* The shape of a shadow

simulated texture *noun* Imitates real texture, see also visual texture

size *noun* 1. in perspective: objects that are closer look larger than objects that are farther away; 2. In balance: a large shape or form will appear to be heavier than a small shape, and several small shapes can balance one large shape.

slip *noun* A mixture of clay and water that is creamy to the touch and is used to attach two scored pieces of clay together

smooth *noun* A surface free from roughness; even

smooth (line) *noun* A line that has even edges

solid (line) *noun* A line that has no breaks, gaps, or holes

space *noun* The art element that refers to the areas above, below, between, within, and around an object

spectral color scheme *noun* Uses all the colors of the rainbow: red, orange, yellow, green, blue, and violet

spectral colors *noun* The colors of the light spectrum: red, orange, yellow, green, blue, and violet

spectrum *noun* The range of colors that it is possible to see; the rainbow

splash *noun* A type of free-form shape

square *noun* A four-sided geometric shape where all sides are the same length and all angles are right angles

statue *noun* Three-dimensional art that is a body form

still life *noun* The arrangement of common inanimate objects from which artists draw or paint

stippling *noun* A shading technique using dots to show value

stitchery *noun* Art made with yarn on cloth

storyteller doll *noun* A Native American sculpture that shows one person relating the history of the culture to many children

style *noun* A unique quality of an object

subordinate *noun* The parts of the artwork that seem less important. Subordinate objects are not emphasized.

subtractive sculpture *noun* When an artist carves pieces away from a form

surrealism *noun* An art movement that emphasized art in which dreams, fantasy, and the subconscious served as inspiration for artists

symmetrical When two sides of a work of art are mirror images of each other

symmetry *noun* A type of formal balance in which two halves of a balanced artwork are identical, mirror images of each other

Teacher's Handbook

T

tactile texture *noun* The texture that can be felt

texture *noun* 1. The art element that refers to the way something feels; 2. In balance: a rough texture has an uneven pattern of highlights and shadows. For this reason, a rough surface attracts the viewer's eyes more easily than a smooth, even surface.

thick (line) *adj.* Wide

thick line *noun* Created by beginning with a thin line and gradually pressing the brush down

thin (line) *adj.* Narrow

thin line *noun* Created when a brush is held vertically to paper and touched lightly with the tip of the brush

three-dimensional *adj.* Has measurements in three directions: height, width, and depth

three-dimensional patterns *noun* Patterns that have depth and are formed on the surface of a sculptural form

three-dimensional rhythm *noun* A principle of design that indicates movement by the repetition of elements in a form

tint *noun* Any hue blended with white

transparent *adj.* Allows light to pass through so objects on the other side can be seen

triangle *noun* A three-sided geometric shape

two-dimensional *adj.* Shapes that are flat and can be measured by length and width

two-dimensional decoration *noun* Flat decoration produced on the surface of a work of art

U

unity *noun* The feeling of wholeness in a work of art. Artists use repetition and grouping to show that different parts of a work belong together.

unrealistic scale *noun* When an artist makes size relationships that do not make sense

V

value *noun* The lightness or darkness of a hue

value contrast *noun* The lightness or darkness stands out from the value that surrounds it

vanishing point *noun* The point on the horizon line where all parallel receding lines meet

variety *noun* The principle of art which is concerned with difference or contrast

vertical *noun* (*adj.*) Lines that move straight up and down. They make things look tall, steady, and calm.

visual movement *noun* Occurs when the eye is pulled through a work of art by a rhythm of beats and rests

visual rhythm *noun* The feeling of movement created when artists repeat colors, shapes, lines, and textures to lead the viewer's eyes through a work of art

visual texture *noun* Or simulated texture, imitates real texture. It is the illusion of a three-dimensional surface.

visual weight *noun* cannot be measured on a scale; it is measured by which objects the viewer's eyes see first.

W

warm colors *noun* Red, yellow, and orange. They suggest warmth and come toward the viewer.

warm hues *noun* Red, orange, and yellow. Warm hues are associated with warm things such as fire or sunshine.

weave *verb* To interlace or interweave strips or strands of material

width *noun* A horizontal measurement, or how long across something is

Z

zigzag *noun* (*adj.*) A line that is made by joining diagonal lines

TEACHER'S HANDBOOK • Glossary **T39**

Program Index

A

About Me, **L3** 138; **L4** 74
Abrasha, **L3** 169
abstract art, **L1** 36, 82; **L3** 96, 97; **L4** 34, 71
Abstract Art in Five Tones and Complementaries (Torres Garcia), **L4** 67
Adams, Ansel, **L2** 109; **L5** 57
additive sculpture, **L4** 130–133
advertisers, **L3** 62
advertising photographers, **L4** 92
Aesthetic Perception
 balance, **LK** 195, 199; **L1** 187, 191; **L2** 157, 161; **L3** 127, 131; **L4** 187, 191, 195; **L5** 169, 177, **L6** 135, 139
 blending, **L5** 53
 buildings, **L1** 143
 colors, **LK** 97, 101, 105, 109, 113, 117; **L1** 97, 101, 105, 109, 113, 117; **L2** 97, 101, 105, 187; **L3** 97, 101, 105, 109, 113, 117; **L4** 97, 101, 105, 109, 117; **L5** 97, 101, 105, 109; **L6** 79
 contrast, **L5** 57
 depth, **L3** 71
 distortion, **L4** 177; **L5** 139, 143, **L6** 165, 169
 emphasis, **L1** 195, 199; **L2** 165, 169; **L3** 195, 199; **L4** 145B; **L5** 196, 199; **L6** 143, 147
 foreground, middle ground, and background, **L4** 157
 form, **L1** 131, 135, 139; **L2** 67, 71, 75, 79; **L3** 79; **L4** 125B; **L5** 83, 87; **L6** 45, 49
 harmony, **L2** 191; **L3** 187; **L4** 199; **L5** 187; **L6** 195, 199
 hatching, **L5** 49
 hues, **L6** 67
 intensity, **L6** 75
 lines, **LK** 37, 41, 45, 49, 53, 57, 60; **L1** 37, 41, 45, 49, 53, 57, 61; **L2** 37, 41, 45, 49; **L3** 37, 41; **L4** 37, 41, 49, 53; **L5** 37; **L6** 37
 motif, **L6** 97
 movement, **L2** 143, 147; **L6** 113, 117
 observation drawings, **L4** 45
 overlapping, **L3** 75
 pattern, **LK** 187; **L1** 169, 173; **L2** 127, 131; **L3** 157, 161, 165; **L4** 75; **L5** 113, 117; **L6** 101, 105
 perception drawing, **L5** 41
 perspective, **L4** 161; **L5** 75; **L6** 53
 point of view, **L4** 165
 proportion, **L4** 169, 173; **L5** 127, 135, 147; **L6** 157, 161

rhythm, **LK** 191; **L1** 177; **L2** 135, 139; **L3** 169, 173, 177; **L4** 79, 82, 87; **L5** 161, 165; **L6** 109
 scale, **L5** 131; **L6** 173, 177
 sculpture, **L3** 83; **L4** 131, 135
 shading, **L4** 57, 113; **L5** 79
 shapes, **LK** 67, 71, 75, 79, 83, 87; **L1** 67, 71, 75, 79, 83, 87, 91, 127; **L2** 53, 57; **L3** 45, 49, 53, 57; **L4** 67, 71; **L5** 45, 67, 71; **L6** 41
 space, **L1** 147, **L2** 83, 87, **L3** 67, **L6** 57
 symmetry, **L3** 135, 139; **L6** 127, 131
 texture, **L1** 157, 161, 165; **L2** 173, 177, **L3** 143, 147; **L4** 139, 143; **L5** 157; **L6** 83, 87
 three-dimensional art, **L3** 87
 unity, **LK** 203, 207; **L1** 203, 207; **L2** 203, 207; **L3** 203, 207; **L4** 207; **L5** 201B, 207; **L6** 203, 207
 value, **L2** 109, 113, 117; **L6** 71
 variety, **L2** 195, 199; **L3** 191; **L4** 203; **L5** 191; **L6** 187, 191
African American art, **L6** 164, 165
African American Dance Ensemble, **L3** 123; **L6** 123
African Americans, **LK** 82–83
akrafokonmu, **L6** 138
Akrafokonmu (Soul Discs) (Unknown), **L6** 139
Alanda's Dream Tree (Scott), **L2** 40
Aliki, **L3** 125A
'Ali, Mir Sayyid, **L3** 180
alternating pattern, **L3** 164–167; **L4** 76; **L5** 118; **L6** 102, 106
AMAN International Folk Ensemble, **LK** 93; **L4** 63
America
 demographics, **L5** 193
 economics, **L5** 43
 Harlem Renaissance, **L5** 189
 history and culture, **LK** 111, 198; **L1** 116; **L5** 51, 96
 Native Americans, **LK** 36; **L1** 156; **L2** 74
 patriotism, **L5** 209
 society, **L4** 206
American Collectors (Hockney), **LK** 41
American Express Train (Currier and Ives), **LK** 91
American Gothic (Wood), **LK** 64
American Indian Dance Theatre, **L3** 63
Americanoom (Chyrssa), **L4** 143
Amour (Herbin), **L2** 52
analogous color scheme, **L4** 118; **L5** 100–103; **L6** 80
Ancestral Spirit Dance #187 (Davis Bing), **L5** 105

Ancestral Spirit Dance (Davis), **L3** 206
Ancient Civilizations, **L2** 70; **L5** 179; **L6** 86, 103
Ancient Egyptian Hippo "William" (Unknown), **LK** 142–145
Anderson, N., **L5** 177
Andrews, Benny, **L4** 48; **L6** 210
Anguissola, Sofonisba, **L5** 172
animals
 in art, **L5** 206
 and balance, **LK** 194–97
 body shapes, **LK** 89
 coloration, **LK** 103
 ecology, **L1** 77
 and form, **LK** 142–145; **L2** 78–81
 habitats, **LK** 119
 and harmony, **L2** 190
 and lines, **LK** 47; **L1** 66–68
 in Native American art, **L3** 63
 and pattern, **L2** 130
 and texture, **LK** 52
 and variety, **L2** 198
Animals in a Landscape (Marc), **L6** 108
animation, **L3** 93; **L6** 62
animators, **LK** 152; **L2** 152
Anna and David (Schapiro), **L6** 66
Anno, Mitsumasa, **LK** 125A
Apollinaire, Guillaume, **L6** 56, 57
Appalachian Basket (Unknown), **LK** 168
Appalachian Big Circle Dance, **LK** 93; **L4** 63
Appalachian Folk Music and Dance, **LK** 93
appliqué, **L3** 66, 148
appraisers, **L5** 152
approximate symmetry, **L3** 138–141; **L6** 130–133
Arapaho Man's Shirt, **L1** 187
Archaeology, **L1** 164; **L4** 137; **L6** 103
architects, **LK** 138, 186; **L1** 152; **L2** 208, 212; **L3** 54, 92, 148
architectural graphic designers, **L3** 182
Architecture, **L2** 206–209; **L3** 52–55; **L4** 186, **L5** 86–89, 126; **L6** 126
archivists, **L6** 119A, 122
area, **L6** 146–149
Armor of George Clifford, Third Earl of Cumberland (Royal Workshops), **L6** 160
Around the Cake (Thiebaud), **L4** 112
art directors, **L3** 62
The Art Institute of Chicago, **L5** 62
Artist's Sisters Playing Chess and Their Governess (Anguissola), **L5** 172
art photography, **L4** 92
art teachers, **L1** 212
Art Teacher (Surowiec), **L5** 190

Aruego, José, **L1** 185A
Asante Paramount Chief Nana Akyanfuo Akowuah Dateh II, Akwamuhene of Kumase (Elisofon), **L4** 75
Asante people, **L6** 138
Ashanti people, **LK** 172; **L1** 172
Ashoona, Kiawak, **L2** 75
Aspens, Northern New Mexico (Adams), **L5** 57
assemblages, **L4** 200; **L6** 200
Astronomy, **L1** 69, 130; **L3** 39; **L5** 69, 78, 81; **L6** 81
asymmetry, **L4** 192
atmospheric perspective, **L6** 54
Audubon, John James, **L2** 131, 198; **L3** 154, 155
Au Printemps, Springtime (Hofmann), **L1** 120
Autumn Leaves-Lake George (O'Keeffe), **LK** 75
Avery, Milton, **L3** 108, 109; **L4** 100
axis, **L2** 158, 162; **L3** 136; **L5** 170; **L6** 128, 158

B

background, **L3** 72; **L4** 158; **L6** 54
back view, **L4** 166
Bactrian Camel (Unknown), **LK** 142–145
Baird Trogon (Lostutter), **L2** 96
Bakula, Stanistawa, **L3** 67
balance
 creating, **L4** 185
 in dance, **L6** 153
 defined, **LK** 194–197; **L1** 185–189; **L5** 155
 formal, **L3** 126–129; **L4** 186–189; **L5** 168–171; **L6** 126–129
 informal, **L4** 190–193; **L5** 172–175; **L6** 134–137
 in masks, **L1** 190–193
 and people, **L2** 155–163
 radial, **L4** 194–197; **L5** 176–179; **L6** 138–141
 and sculpture, **LK** 198–201
 in stories, **L1** 213
 and symmetry, **L3** 134–137
 and texture, **L3** 124–125
Baliker, Paul A., **L6** 48
Ballerinas (Degas), **L5** 40
Ballet Dancers (Scott), **L2** 164
Ballet Folklórico de México, **L4** 213
Ballet Scene (Degas), **L2** 143
Bang, Molly, **LK** 155A
Baranoff-Rossine, Vladimir, **L4** 198
Bareback Riders (Brown), **LK** 42
Bartlett, Jennifer, **L5** 164
Basket (Keyser), **L6** 202
baskets, **LK** 168–171; **L4** 206

Basket (Unknown), **L4** 207
Bates, David, **L6** 56
Bearden, Romare, **LK** 87; **L4** 138
Beaux, Cecilia, **L2** 165
Begay, Harrison, **L1** 56, 57
Bell, John, **L2** 78
Bellows, George Wesley, **L6** 60
Bennion, Lee, **L6** 187
Benton, Thomas Hart, **L1** 116; **L2** 142; **L5** 186
Berenstain, Stan and Jan, **L2** 65A
Bernadita (Henri), **L4** 169
Berry, Martha, **L1** 173
Between the Clock and the Bed (Johns), **L1** 44
Bible Quilt, Detail: Dark Day of May 19, 1817 (Powers), **LK** 176
The Bicycle Race (Ruíz), **L4** 161
Big Blues Man II (Twiggs), **LK** 90
Biggers, John, **L4** 66, 93
Billy the Kid, **L3** 213; **L5** 183
Bird Watchers (Tooker), **L5** 127
Birthday (Chagall), **L1** 195
The Birthplace of Herbert Hoover, West Branch, Iowa (Wood), **L4** 160
Bishop, Isabel, **L1** 79; **L5** 210; **L6** 156
Black Bear Storyteller figurine with Six Cubs (Naranjo), **L2** 138
Blake, William, **LK** 48
Blanco, Teodora, **L4** 131; **L6** 104
The Blank Signature [Carte Blanche] (Magritte), **L3** 90
blending, **L5** 52–55, 80; **L6** 72
blind contour drawing, **L4** 50
Blue and Green Music (O'Keeffe), **L4** 116
Blueberry Eyes (Kline), **L2** 40, 41
Blue Dome-House Blessing (Anderson), **L5** 177
Bo Bo Festival Series #30 (Bustion), **L6** 186
body forms, **L2** 74–77
body proportions, **L5** 138–141
Bonheur, Rosa, **L3** 168
Bonnard, Pierre, **L1** 90
book designers, **L6** 182
Borofsky, Jonathan, **L3** 41
Botero, Fernando, **L5** 138; **L6** 168, 169
Bottom of the Ravine (Cézanne), **L6** 113
Bouguereau, William Adolphe, **L5** 71
Bowl (Unknown), **LK** 147; **L5** 116
Boy Juggling Shells (Hokusai), **LK** 49
Boy's day (Russell), **L3** 96
The Boy Who Wanted to Talk to Whales, **L6** 63
The Boy Who Wnated to Talk to Whales, **L4** 123

T40 TEACHER'S HANDBOOK • Program Index

Boy with a Flute (Hokusai), **L4** 53
Brach, Paul, **L6** 191
Branch, Paul, **L2** 191
Braque, Georges, **L5** 44; **L6** 78, 79, 94
The Brass Ring, **L6** 153
The Breakfast Room (Bonnard), **L4** 90
Brett, Jan, **L5** 125A
Bridal Bed Cover (Unknown), **L1** 48, 49
Brilliant as the Sun Upon the World (Jones), **L3** 105
British Museum Memoir (Spitzmueller), **L3** 198, 199
Broadway Boogie Woogie (Piet), **L1** 100
The Brooding Woman (Gauguin), **L6** 184
The Brooklyn Bridge: Variations on an Old Theme (Stella), **LK** 210
Brosen, Frederick, **L5** 75
Brother Sun, Sister Moon, **LK** 213
Brown, Roger, **L5** 78
Brown, W. H., **LK** 42, 44
Bruegel, Pieter (the Elder), **L4** 44
Bryan, Ashley, **L1** 35A
Builders No. 1 (Lawrence), **L3** 60
Builders Red and Green Ball (Lawrence), **L1** 82
buildings. *See also* Architecture
 and form, **LK** 138–141
 and formal balance, **L6** 126–129
 and lines, **L1** 52–55
 and pattern, **LK** 186–189
 and shapes, **L3** 52–55
 and space, **L1** 142–145
Bull's Eye Quilt (Herb), **L6** 138
Burton, Virginia Lee, **L2** 95A
Bustion, Nathaniel, **L6** 186
Butterfield, Deborah, **L1** 66, 67; **L4** 199
Butterfly (Unknown), **LK** 194
Button Robe-Orca Whale Design (Yeiltzatzie), **LK** 195

C

Cabin Fever (Rothenberg), **L6** 142
Café Terrace at Night (van Gogh), **L6** 53
Caged Pie (Thiebaud), **LK** 71
Cai, Lily, **L1** 123
Caillebotte, Gustave, **L3** 142
Calder, Alexander, **L1** 126; **L6** 116, 118
Camillus (Unknown), **LK** 131
Canal, Giovanni Antonio, **L3** 53
Candelabra (Flores), **L3** 134, 135
Canister (Unknown), **L4** 105
careers
 advertisers, **L3** 62
 animators, **LK** 152; **L6** 62
 architects, **LK** 138, 186; **L1** 152; **L2** 208; **L3** 148
 in architecture, **L3** 92, 182; **L5** 92

in art history, **L6** 122
in art photography, **L4** 92
art teachers, **L2** 212
botanical curators, **L2** 92
in computers, **L4** 152
designers, **L6** 182
fabric and fashion designers, **L1** 92
illustrators, **LK** 74, 92; **L4** 212
interior designers, **L3** 148
in jewelry making, **L3** 88; **L5** 152
make-up artists, **LK** 152
in movies, **L2** 152
museum guides, **L1** 212
painters, **LK** 212
sculptors, **LK** 212
toy designers, **L5** 212
Carle, Eric, **L1** 95A
Carolina Parrot (Audubon), **L2** 131
Carousel Rabbit (Dentzel Company), **L2** 203
Carr, Emily, **L4** 60
Carved Animals (Unknown), **L6** 105
carving, **L1** 166; **L2** 172
Case with Five Balusters (Nevelson), **L3** 176, 177
Cassatt, Mary, **L1** 94, 95; **L6** 90, 134, 135
Catlett, Elizabeth, **L5** 48, 134
Catlin, George, **L2** 177; **L5** 157
Cattleya Orchid and Three Brazilian Hummingbirds (Heade), **L4** 202, 203
central axis, **L3** 136; **L5** 170; **L6** 128, 158
Ceramic Figures (Blanco), **L6** 104
Ceremonial Hanging (Unknown), **L6** 203
Ceremonial Shield (Unknown), **L4** 108
Ceremonial Skirt (Unknown), **L6** 37
Cézanne, Paul, **L1** 86; **L2** 87; **L5** 45, 120; **L6** 112, 113
CGI animators, **L2** 152
Chagall, Marc, **LK** 57, 104; **L1** 195; **L4** 177; **L5** 150
Chapelle de Notre-Dame du Haut (Le Corbusier), **L5** 86
Chardin, Jean-Baptiste Simeon, **L6** 82, 83
Charlip, Remy, **L2** 183
Cherry, Lynne, **L4** 125A
chiaroscuro, **L6** 124
Chicago Picasso (Picasso), **L6** 177
Chief Black Hawk, **L4** 78
Children at Play (Lawrence), **L1** 56
Children's Games (Bruegel), **L4** 44
Children's Theatre Company, **L1** 93; **L3** 123
Child's Beaded Shirt (Unknown), **L3** 190
Child with Ball (Münter), **LK** 160
Chinese Children's Slippers (Unknown), **L1** 198
Chinese Restaurant (Weber), **L6** 94
chromolithography, **L6** 142
Chryssa, **L2** 154, 155; **L4** 143
Church (Mendoza), **L2** 36
Chuska (Brach), **L6** 191

cinematographers, **L2** 152
circle, **LK** 72; **L1** 72; **L3** 46; **L4** 68, 128; **L5** 88; **L6** 46
The City (Hopper), **L3** 52
city planners, **L3** 92
City Square (Giacometti), **L6** 168
Classic Serape Style Wearing Blanket (Unknown), **LK** 36
Cliff Dwellers (Bellows), **L6** 60
The Cliff, Etretat, Sunset (Monet), **L2** 195
The Clock Tower in the Piazza San Marco (Canaletto), **L3** 53
cloth, **LK** 176–179
The Cocktail Party (Skoglund), **L4** 142
coiling, **L6** 202
Cole, Allen E., **L3** 56
collages, **LK** 107, 159; **L5** 39
Collar (Unknown), **L3** 164, 165
colors
 analogous, **L5** 100–103; **L6** 80
 and balance, **L3** 127; **L5** 174
 complementary, **L4** 104–107; **L5** 104–107; **L6** 76, 78
 and contrast, **L3** 116–119; **L4** 106
 cool, **L3** 108–111, 118; **L5** 108–111; **L6** 80
 and dance, **L1** 123; **L4** 123; **L6** 93
 and feelings, **LK** 112–115
 green, **L1** 108–111
 and harmony, **L2** 186–189; **L3** 188; **L4** 200; **L5** 188
 and hues, **L2** 96–107
 and informal balance, **L6** 136
 intermediate, **L3** 100–103, 118
 light and dark, **LK** 116–119
 low-intensity, **L4** 108–111
 monochromatic, **L5** 96–99
 and mood, **L4** 116–119
 neutral, **L4** 100–103; **L6** 72
 of objects, **LK** 100–105
 orange, **L1** 104–107
 and pattern, **L5** 94–95
 and perspective, **L4** 162; **L5** 72; **L6** 54
 primary, **L1** 100–103; **L3** 98, 102; **LK** 108–111
 of the rainbow, **L1** 96–99
 secondary, **L1** 106, 110, 114; **L3** 98, 102
 spectrum, **L3** 106
 and texture, **L6** 64–65
 in theater, **L5** 123
 tint and shade, **L4** 112–115
 and unity, **LK** 208; **L3** 202–205
 using, **LK** 106; **L6** 66–69
 and value, **L3** 94–95, 123; **L4** 94–95, 102, 114
 and variety, **L3** 192; **L6** 186–189
 variety of, **LK** 96–99
 violet, **L1** 112–115
 and visual weight, **L4** 192
 warm, **L3** 112–115, 118; **L5** 108–111; **L6** 80
color schemes, **L4** 118; **L5** 102; **L6** 78–81
color wheel, **L1** 98; **L2** 98, 102, 106; **L3** 102, 104–107; **L4** 96–99; **L5** 102
columns, **L2** 206

Coming of Age Hat (Unknown), **L6** 86, 87
Coming of Age (Houser), **L4** 86
Communication
 In art, **L4** 70
 cooperation, **L1** 82
 feelings, **LK** 82, 112; **L2** 116; **L5** 48; **L6** 74, 190
 masks, **L3** 130
 portraits, **L2** 176
 types of, **L5** 134
complementary colors, **L4** 104–107; **L5** 104–107; **L6** 76, 78
complementary color scheme, **L4** 118
Composition 8 (Wassily), **L1** 37
Composition (Davis), **L4** 64
Composition on the Word "Vie" 2 (Herbin), **LK** 70
Composition VI (Kandinsky), **L2** 48
Composition V (Piet), **L1** 41
Composition (Vytlacil), **L3** 45
computer game developers, **L4** 152
computer graphics designers, **L4** 152
Conception Synchromy (Stanton), **L6** 67
The Concert (Leyster), **L4** 184
The Concert (Vermeer), **L5** 64
Conchero Pull Toys (Unknown), **LK** 164–167
cone, **L3** 80–81; **L5** 88; **L6** 46
conservators, **L6** 122
contour hatching, **L4** 58
contour lines, **L4** 48–51, 53, 192; **L5** 42; **L6** 38
contrast, **L2** 168–171; **L3** 116–119, 196; **L4** 106; **L5** 56–59; **L6** 148, 190–193
Control Chair (Greenblat), **LK** 120
Convergence (Pollock), **L5** 36, 37
converging lines, **L5** 72; **L6** 54
Conversation Piece (Muñoz), **L6** 147
cool hues, **L5** 108–111
Cooney, Barbara, **L1** 125A
Cooperation
 and colors, **L5** 52, 108
 communication, **L1** 82
 community, **LK** 206; **L1** 36
 competition, **L4** 78; **L5** 36
 harmony, **L4** 198; **L6** 198
 and pattern, **L5** 112
 in school, **LK** 44
Cooper, Floyd, **L3** 65A
Copley, John Singleton, **L1** 160; **L4** 154, 155; **L6** 157
Le Corbusier, **L5** 86
Corn Palace (Unknown), **L1** 142–145
Cote d'Ivoire (Unknown), **L3** 87
Cottingham, Robert, **L3** 195
Country Dance (Benton), **L2** 142
Country Life, **L4** 141, 156; **L5** 129
Courage, **L6** 176
Covered Jar (Unknown), **L3** 116, 117
Cover of Armenian Book (Unknown), **L3** 198
Cow's Skull: Red White and Blue (O'Keefe), **L6** 130

Coyote Koshare (Fonseca), **L1** 176
Crews, Donald, **L2** 155A
Crite, Allan Rohan, **LK** 78
cropping, **L6** 134
cross hatching, **L4** 58; **L5** 50, 58, 80; **L6** 72
Crow Men in Ceremonial Dress (Chief Black Hawk), **L4** 78
cube, **L4** 128; **L5** 88; **L6** 46
cubism, **L3** 35; **L6** 78, 94
Cubi XVIII (Smith), **L2** 66; **L6** 44
Cultural Diversity
 discuss, **L2** 126; **L3** 66; **L5** 104
 families, **LK** 86
 history, **L4** 104
 Native Americans, **LK** 36; **L1** 156; **L2** 74; **L3** 146
 and student experience, **LK** 89
culture, **L3** 132
Cups 4 Picasso (Johns), **L5** 66, 67
curators, **L2** 92; **L6** 122
curling, **L5** 84
Currier and Ives, **LK** 53, 191
Curry, John Steuart, **L5** 126
cylinder, **L3** 80–81

D

Dali, Salvador, **L4** 176
Dali, Salvador, **L6** 176
Dallas Museum of Art, **L6** 212
dance, **LK** 183; **L1** 123, 183; **L2** 212; **L4** 63, 123; **L6** 93, 153, 183, 213
Dance at El Jardin (Garza), **LK** 203
Dance By Numbers Bandolier Bag (Berry), **L1** 173
Dancing in Colombia (Botero), **L6** 169
Dancing Lady (Unknown), **L6** 160, 161
Danza de Reata & Jarabe del Amor Ranchero, **L4** 213
Dark Snapper (Warren), **L6** 48, 49
The Daughters of Edward Darley Boit (Sargent), **L4** 191
David (del Verrocchio), **L4** 172
da Vinci, Leonardo, **L1** 184, 185; **L6** 180
Davis, Stuart, **L1** 202, **L4** 64, 65, 97
Davis, Willis Bing, **L3** 206
Davis, Willis Bing, **L5** 105
Dawn (Nevelson), **L2** 124
On the Day You Were Born, **L5** 123
Dead as a Dodo & Save the Forests, Save the Trees, **L1** 63; **L5** 93
decoration, **L3** 200–201; **L5** 116–119
Deep Dish/Spain/from Valencia (Unknown), **L5** 176
Degas, Edgar, **L2** 143; **L3** 64, 65; **L5** 40
degikup, **L6** 202
Delaunay, Robert, **L2** 97
Delaware Shoulder Bag (Unknown), **L2** 126
del Verrocchio, Andrea, **L4** 172

Program Index (continued)

Dentzel Company, **L2** 203
depth, **L2** 88–89; **L3** 70–77; **L4** 155; **L6** 53
Derain, André, **L6** 74
design, **LK** 164–167
Design Made at Airlie Gardens (Evans), **L4** 70
DesJarlait, Patrick, **L2** 100
detail, **L4** 162; **L5** 72
Dhon Dholak Cholam, **L5** 213; **LK** 153
diamond, **L3** 50
Díaz, David, **LK** 95A
Dick, Beau, **LK** 154, 155
Dido (Hartigan), **L1** 112
Diebenkorn, Richard, **L2** 44
Die Brücke, **L6** 75
Die Erfüllung (Fulfillment) (Klimt), **L6** 34
digital filmmakers, **L4** 152
Dillon, Diane and Leo, **L3** 155A
The Diner (Segal), **LK** 150
Display Rows (Thiebaud), **L3** 120
distortion, **L4** 176–179; **L5** 124–125, 138–145; **L6** 155, 164–171, 183
Djanbazian Dance Company, **L6** 93
Djukulul, Dorothy, **L3** 161
dominant element, **L2** 166; **L4** 204
Double Pan Swoosh (Rose), **L6** 116, 117
Double Saddlebag (Unknown), **L3** 48
Dove, Arthur, **L5** 194
Down Eighteenth Street (Thiebaud), **L6** 120
Drouet (Whistler), **L4** 56
Dr. Seuss, **L2** 35A
Dufy, Raoul, **LK** 126; **L5** 60, 108
Duke, Jerry, **LK** 93; **L4** 63
Dürer, Albrecht, **L1** 34, 35
The Dwell House (Central Office of Architecture, LA, CA), **L1** 143

E

Eagle and Salmon (Hoover), **LK** 157
Eagle Dance, **L3** 63
Eagle Eye (Paik), **L6** 206
Eagle's Song (Naranjo), **L4** 164–165
Early Sunday Morning (Hopper), **L2** 53
Early Sunday Morning, Merced River, Yosemite Valley, CA (Adams), **L2** 108, 109
earthenware, **L2** 78
Earth Song (Houser), **LK** 124
Easy Chair (Gardner), **L3** 157
Ecology
 animals, **L1** 77
 economics, **L1** 103
 environment, **LK** 116; **L1** 108, 197; **L4** 100
 form, **L1** 134
 fossils, **L1** 164
 habitats, **LK** 119
 insects, **L1** 168
 lines, **L1** 44
 and the outdoors, **L5** 70
 plants, **LK** 96, 99; **L1** 74; **L2** 134; **L4** 202
 recycling, **L1** 159
Edenshaw, Charles, **L4** 187
Egungun from Ogbomoso (Unknown), **L6** 96, 97
Egyptian Cat (Unknown), **L4** 135
Eiffel Tower (Eiffel), **L6** 126, 127
element, **L5** 194–197
The Elephants (Dali), **L4** 176
Elevator Grill (Sullivan), **L5** 117
Elisofon, Eliot, **L4** 75
Ellett, Randy, **L6** 198, 199
The Elm Tree (Summer) (Mangold), **L1** 45
Embroidered Pillow (Unknown), **LK** 176
embroidery, **L6** 36
The Emergence of the Clowns (Swentzell), **L2** 74
Emperor Shah Jahan, **L5** 130
Emperor Shah Jahan and His Son, Suja (Nanha), **L5** 131
emphasis
 of area, **L6** 146–149
 creating, **L2** 164–171; **L3** 196–197; **L4** 146–149; **L5** 185
 and decoration, **L3** 200–201
 defined, **L1** 185; **L3** 185
 of an element, **L5** 194–197; **L6** 142–145
 in forms, **L1** 198–201
 in paintings, **L1** 194–197
 through placement, **L5** 198–201
 and variety, **L4** 202–205
The Empire of Lights (Magritte), **L2** 169
Endangered Species (Goodnight), **L4** 44, 45
Energy Apples (Flack), **LK** 100
Ensor, James, **L6** 78
The Equatorial Jungle (Rousseau), **L1** 74
Ernesta (Child with Nurse) (Beaux), **L2** 165
Escobar, Marisol, **L5** 90
Esquisse for Ode to Kinshasa (Jones), **L1** 64
Estes, Richard, **L3** 142, 143
Eth-Noh-Tec, **L2** 92, 93; **L4** 93
Evans, Minnie, **L4** 70; **L6** 100, 101
even balance, **LK** 196–197
Evergood, Philip, **L3** 139
Every Picture Tells a Story, **L3** 93; **L6** 213
exaggerated features, **L3** 132; **L5** 144; **L6** 170
Exotic Landscape (Rousseau), **L6** 112
expression, **L5** 36–39
Eyre, Ivan, **L1** 108; **L2** 187

F

Faaturuma [Melancholic] (Gauguin), **L4** 120
fabric designers, **L1** 92
face distortion, **L6** 164–167
Face Jugs (Unknown), **L6** 165
Face Mask of Kumugwe' (Unknown), **L6** 96
face proportions, **L5** 134–137, 142–145; **L6** 156–159
False Face Mask (Webster), **L5** 142
Families, **L5** 130
The Family (Escobar), **L5** 90
Family Group (Moore), **L2** 64
Family Portrait (Frey), **L4** 210
fashion designers, **L1** 92
fashion photographers, **L4** 92
Father and Daughter (Schapiro), **LK** 86
Faust, Robert, **L2** 63; **L3** 153; **L5** 63; **L6** 183
Fauves, **L1** 112
Featherwork Neckpiece (Unknown), **L5** 104
Feeding Caitlin (Fish), **LK** 112
Feline Felicity (Sheeler), **L5** 52
Fenetre Ouverte Devant la Mer (Dufy), **L5** 108
fiber textures, **LK** 168–171
fiber works of art, **L4** 74
Figure: Churinga (Hepworth), **L1** 135
figure distortion, **L6** 168–171
Figure from House Post (Unknown), **L4** 186
Figure (Lipchitz), **L1** 131
Figure of a Lion (Bell), **L2** 78
figure proportion, **L6** 160–163
Fireworks (Ensor), **L6** 78
The First Aeroplane (Town), **L2** 117
Fish, Gold Weight (Unknown), **LK** 172
Fishing Boats (Braque), **L6** 79
Fish, Janet, **LK** 112; **L1** 82; **L3** 44
Fish Story (Baliker), **L6** 48
Flack, Audrey, **LK** 100; **L3** 124, 125; **L4** 40
The Flatiron (Steichen), **L2** 108
Flores, Aurelio and Francisco, **L3** 135
florists, **L2** 92
Flower Day (Rivera), **L5** 169
Flowers (Warhol), **L5** 202
flowing contour lines, **L4** 53
The Fly (Blake), **LK** 48
Flying Goddess, **L1** 123
focal point, **L2** 166, 170; **L3** 196; **L4** 148; **L5** 200; **L6** 140, 148
folk art, **L6** 104
Fonseca, Harry, **L1** 176
Fontana, Lavinia, **L5** 94, 95
font designers, **L6** 182
Football Player (Hanson), **L5** 147
The Football Players (Rousseau), **L2** 150; **L3** 150
foreground, **L3** 72; **L4** 158; **L6** 54
form
 and animals, **LK** 142–145; **L2** 78–81
 in animation, **L3** 93
 in architecture, **L5** 86–89
 body, **L2** 74–77
 and buildings, **LK** 138–141
 defined, **L2** 64–65
 and emphasis, **L1** 198–201
 free form, **L6** 48–51
 geometric, **L1** 136;
L2 66–69; **L6** 44–47
 and harmony, **L2** 192–193
 in music, **LK** 153; **L6** 62
 and people, **L1** 138–141
 and real texture, **LK** 172–175
 and rhythm, **L2** 138–142
 and sculpture, **LK** 130–137, 144; **L4** 130–133
 and shapes, **L1** 126–129; **L3** 78–81; **L4** 128
 in song writing, **L5** 93
 and space, **LK** 124–125, 134–138; **L1** 125, 130–133; **L3** 64–65; **L5** 64–65
 and theater, **L2** 93
 three-dimensional, **L2** 68
 and unity, **LK** 208
 using, **LK** 146–149; **L5** 82–85
 and variety, **L2** 198–201
 formal balance, **L3** 126–137; **L4** 186–189; **L5** 168–171; **L6** 126–129
La Fortune (Ray), **L3** 104
At Four and a Half (Twiggs), **L2** 49
Four by Four (Loeser), **L3** 160
Four Ladies of the Court Playing Polo (Unknown), **LK** 207
The Four Seasons (Chagall), **LK** 57
Francesco Sasetti and His Son Teodoro (Ghirlandaio), **L5** 130
Frances Lehman Loeb Art Center, **L1** 122
Free Fall (Wiesner), **LK** 74
free-form forms, **L2** 70–73; **L6** 48–51
free-form shapes, **LK** 74–81, 83–84; **L1** 74–77, 85, 88, 134–137; **L2** 56–59; **L3** 46, 54, 58, 80; **L4** 70–73, 128; **L5** 44–47, 88; **L6** 40–43
freestanding sculpture, **L3** 84; **L4** 132
Frey, Viola, **L4** 210; **L5** 124, 125
Frieda y Diego Rivera (Kahlo), **L6** 154
Friendship, **L6** 156
Friesen, Eugene, **L3** 153; **L5** 63
fringing, **L5** 84
frontal proportion, **L6** 158
front view, **L4** 166
Full Fathoms Five, Turbo Power, Spirit of the Landscape, **L3** 93; **L6** 213
futurists, **L6** 118

G

Gainsborough, Thomas, **L3** 57
Games, **LK** 48; **L1** 56, 186; **L2** 202; **L3** 96; **L5** 172
Garden at Vaucresson (Vuillard), **LK** 97
In the Garden (Cassatt), **L1** 94
Garden Landscape and Fountain (Tiffany), **LK** 56
Gardner, Caleb, **L3** 157
Garrison, Elizabeth, **L5** 203
Garrowby Hill (Hockney), **L2** 147
Garza, Carmen Lomas, **LK** 203; **L1** 78; **L2** 125A
The Gates to Times Square (Chryssa), **L2** 154, 155
Gathering Wild Rice (DesJarlait), **L2** 100
Gauguin, Paul, **L4** 120; **L5** 160; **L6** 184, 185
Gay, Jacob, **L2** 172
Geisel, Theodore Seuss, **L2** 35A
genre paintings, **L1** 116
geometric forms, **L1** 136; **L2** 66–69; **L6** 44–47, 50
geometric shapes, **LK** 70–73, 78–81; **L1** 70–73, 88; **L2** 52–55; **L3** 46, 48–51, 58; **L4** 66–69; **L5** 44–47; **L6** 40–43, 40–43
Georgia (Garrison), **L5** 203
Georgia Stele (Moroles), **L2** 67
gesture art, **L5** 42
gesture drawings, **L4** 40–44
Ghirlandaio, Domenico, **L5** 130
Gift Basket (Unknown), **LK** 168–171
Gile, Seldon Conner, **L1** 101
Gilles, Joseph-Jean, **L3** 74, 75
Ginevra de' Benci (da Vinci), **L6** 180
Gin Matsuba (Kudo), **L3** 202, 203
Girl in a Boat with Geese (Morisot), **L4** 157
The Girl on the Rock, **LK** 123
The Girl With the Red Hat (Vermeer), **L2** 176
Glacometti, Alberto, **L6** 168
A Glimpse of Notre Dame in the Late Afternoon (Matisse), **L1** 113
Going West, **L2** 112; **L5** 100
goldsmiths, **L5** 152
Goncharova, Natalia, **L4** 34, 35
Goodnight, Paul, **L4** 45
Gottlieb, Adolph, **L2** 116
Gracehoper (Smith), **L5** 83
Graham, Martha, **L5** 153
Grandma Moses [Anna Mary Robertson Moses], **L6** 194
Grandmother's Dinner (Andrews), **L6** 210
Grandmother Series: July Cone Hat (Frey), **L5** 124
Granite Weaving (Moroles), **L1** 154
graphic designers, **L3** 182
Great Blue Heron (Audubon), **L3** 154
Great Water Lily of America (Sharp), **L6** 143
The Great Wave Off Kanagawa (Hokusai), **LK** 34
green, **L1** 108–111
Greenblat, Rodney Alan, **LK** 120
The Green House (Skoglund), **LK** 206
Guevara, Susan, **L4** 65A
guide lines, **L5** 136
Gui Ritual Food Container, **L2** 156

H

Habitat (Safdie), **L6** 172
Hairdresser's Window (Sloan), **L3** 194

Haitian Landscape (Jean Gilles), **L3** 74, 75
Hand Puppets (Unknown), **LK** 164
Hannukka Menorah (Abrasha), **L3** 168, 169
Hanson, Duane, **LK** 135; **L2** 160; **L4** 173; **L5** 147
harmony
 of color, **L2** 186–189
 creating, **L3** 188–189; **L4** 185, 198–201; **L5** 185–189; **L6** 185
 in dance, **L2** 212; **L6** 213
 defined, **L2** 185; **L3** 185
 of shape and form, **L2** 192–193
 in three-dimensional art, **L6** 198–201
 in two-dimensional art, **L6** 194–197
Harriet Tubman Series #4 (Lawrence), **LK** 83
Harris, Lawren S., **L1** 52
Hart, George, **L6** 45
Hartigan, Grace, **L1** 112
Hartley, Marsden, **L6** 100
Hartmann, William, **L6** 176
Hassam, Childe, **L5** 74
Hat: Birds and Geometric Patterns (Unknown), **L3** 100
hatching, **L4** 58; **L5** 48–51, 58, 80; **L6** 72
Headdress for Epa Masquerade (Yoruba People), **L2** 90
Heade, Martin Johnson, **L4** 203
Health
 human body, **LK** 69, 73, 85; **L1** 78, 137, 190; **L4** 172; **L6** 168
 nutrition, **LK** 100; **L1** 86; **L2** 86; **L3** 44; **L4** 112
 safety, **LK** 47, 81; **L1** 70, 85, 194
In the Heart of the Beast Puppet and Mask Theatre, **L1** 153; **L5** 123
Held, Al, **L3** 97
Helder, Z. Vanessa, **L4** 101
Henkes, Kevin, **L2** 185A
Henri, Robert, **L4** 169; **L5** 135
Henry Pelham (Boy with a Squirrel) (Copley), **L6** 157
Hepworth, Barbara, **L1** 135
Herb, Alverda, **L6** 138
Herbin, Auguste, **LK** 70; **L1** 70; **L2** 52
Here Look at Mine (Robinson), **L5** 191
The Hermitage at Pontoise (Pissaro), **L4** 156
Heroes, **L2** 160
hexagon, **L3** 50; **L5** 46; **L6** 42
highlights, **L3** 144
High School Student (Hanson), **L4** 173
Hirondelle/Amour (Miro), **L5** 161
Hmong Story Cloth (Unknown), **L1** 180
Hoban, Tana, **LK** 65A
Hockney, David, **LK** 41; **L1** 97; **L2** 147; **L4** 96
Hodges, Margaret, **LK** 35A
Hodler, Ferdinand, **L6** 130, 131
Hofmann, Hans, **L1** 120
Hokusai, Katsushika, **LK** 34,
35, 49, 117; **L4** 53, 87; **L6** 134
Holidays, **L3** 134
Hollywood Hills House (Hockney), **L1** 97
Homer, Winslow, **L1** 161; **L5** 70
Homes
 buildings, **L1** 142
 families, **LK** 86; **L1** 48; **L2** 82
 geography, **L3** 55
 imagination, **L3** 160
 location, **L2** 104
 objects in, **L1** 146; **L5** 176; **L6** 172
Homesick Proof Space Station (Brown), **L5** 78
Hong Shancha: Red Camellia (Liu), **L1** 75
Hoop Dance, **L3** 63
Hoover, John, **LK** 157; **L3** 176
Hopper, Edward, **LK** 126, 127; **L2** 53; **L3** 52
house posts, **LK** 198, 201
House Post (Unknown), **LK** 199
Houser, Allan, **LK** 124, 125; **L4** 86
Houses at Auvers (van Gogh), **L5** 154
Hudson River Quilters, **L5** 202
The Hudson River Quilt (Miller), **L5** 202
hues, **L2** 94, 96–99, 100–107, 114, 186–189; **L3** 98; **L4** 98; **L5** 98; **L6** 66–69. *See also* colors
Huichol Bead Mask (Unknown), **L5** 199
Huipil Weaving (Unknown), **L5** 36
Humpty Dumpty Circus (Schoenhut), **LK** 44, 45
Hunting Scene on Handle from a Large Bowl (Unknown), **L3** 83
Hyman, Trina Schart, **L3** 35A

I

Ice Cream Cones (Bishop), **L1** 79
illustrators, **LK** 35A, 65A, 74, 92, 95A, 125A, 155A, 185A ; **L1** 35A, 65A, 95A, 125A, 155A, 185A; **L2** 35A, 65A, 95A, 125A, 155A, 185A; **L3** 35A, 65A, 95A, 125A, 155A, 185A; **L4** 35A, 65A, 95A, 125A, 155A, 185A, 212; **L5** 35A, 65A, 95A, 125A; **L6** 35A, 65A, 95A, 125A, 155A, 185A
Imagination
 artists, **L3** 40; **L4** 116
 communication, **L5** 138
 creativity, **L6** 56
 homes, **L3** 160
 inventions, **L1** 129
 lines, **L2** 40
 stories, **LK** 66; **L3** 82
 texture, **L1** 160
impressionism, **L6** 112, 134
Impressions #2, **LK** 63
Improvisation No. 27 (Kandinsky), **L3** 40
Indian Fantasy (Hartley), **L6** 100
Indonesian Shadow Puppet (Unknown), **L2** 56
informal balance, **L4** 190–193; **L5** 172–175; **L6** 134–137

intensity, **L4** 108–111; **L6** 74–77
interior designers, **L2** 212; **L3** 148; **L5** 92
intermediate colors, **L3** 100–103, 118; **L4** 98; **L5** 102; **L6** 68
invented texture, **L4** 140
Isa, Ustad, **LK** 139
Isicathulo, **L3** 123; **L6** 123
isolation, **L5** 200; **L6** 148

J

Jackson, Mary A., **L4** 206
Jacquette, Yvonne, **L2** 210
Jaguar (Unknown), **L4** 134
James, Charlie, **L5** 142
James Vilbert, Sculptor (Hodler), **L6** 131
Jane's Remington (Cottingham), **L3** 194, 195
Japanese Bridge over a Pool of Water Lilies (Monet), **L3** 36
Japanese prints, **LK** 116
Jar (Unknown), **L3** 126, 127, 186
jewelers, **L3** 88
jewelry, **L3** 86–89; **L5** 152; **L6** 206–207
Jitterbugs [II] (Johnson), **L2** 60
Joffrey Ballet, **L1** 183
The Joffrey Ballet of Chicago, **L4** 153
John, Isabel, **L3** 191
Johns, Jasper, **L1** 44; **L5** 66, 67, 97
Johnson, Joshua, **L4** 190
Johnson, Willam H., **LK** 82; **L2** 60
Johnson, William, **L4** 195
Jonathan Buttall: The Blue Boy (Gainsborough), **L3** 57
Jones, Ben, **L5** 96
Jones, Calvin, **L3** 104, 105
Jones, Loïs Mailou, **L1** 64, 65
Joropo Azul, **L4** 183
Journeys, **L2** 146, 172; **L5** 198; **L6** 146, 160, 186
July Hay (Benton), **L1** 116
Jump (Fish), **L1** 83
Jungle Tales (Shannon), **L2** 82

K

Kabotie, Fred, **L3** 173
Kahlo, Frida, **L5** 180; **L6** 154, 155
Kahng-Gang-Sool-Le, **L2** 213
Kahn, Wolf, **L1** 40
Kandinsky, Wassily, **L1** 37; **L2** 48; **L3** 40; **L4** 36, 37
Keams, Geri, **L2** 153
Keats, Ezra Jack, **L3** 95A
Kelly, Ellsworth, **L1** 96
Kensett, John Frederick, **L2** 105
Kente Cloth (Unknown), **L1** 172
Keyser, Louisa (Dat So La Lee), **L6** 202
Kimbell Art Museum, **L1** 182
kinetic movement, **L6** 116–119
King (Evans), **L6** 101
King Family (Jones), **L5** 96
King's Crown (Unknown), **L6** 86
Kirifuri Waterfall on Mount Kurokami in Shimotsuke Province (Hokusai), **LK** 117
Klee, Paul, **L2** 186; **L3** 112; **L4** 108, 109
Klimt, Gustav, **L6** 34, 35
Kline, Franz, **L2** 41
Kneeling Child on Yellow Background (Rivera), **L3** 94
Kohlmeyer, Ida, **L1** 202, 203
Korean Classical Music and Dance Company, **LK** 183; **L2** 213
Krasle, Elizabeth Paulos, **L5** 207
Krasner, Lee, **L4** 138, 139
Kudo, Lundin, **L3** 203
Kurelek, William, **L2** 180
Kwele Face Mask (Unknown), **L5** 143

L

Lai Haraoba, **L2** 123
Lamentation, **L5** 153
landscape architects, **L1** 152; **L3** 92
landscape paintings, **L4** 100, 101, 156–157
landscapes, **L1** 108
Language Arts and Reading Art Connections
 Descriptive Writing, **LK** 39, 69, 103, 107, 193; **L1** 43, 69, 115, 133, 159, 201; **L2** 43, 55, 89, 99, 175, 197; **L4** 47, 73, 99, 133, 159, 205; **L5** 47, 51, 59, 77, 145, 171, 175; **L6** 59, 77, 85, 89, 115, 145, 167, 189
 Expository Writing, **LK** 59, 81, 99, 201; **L1** 39, 89, 107, 129, 175, 193; **L2** 51, 77, 107, 119, 129, 137, 163, 193; **L4** 55, 69, 111, 129, 179, 197; **L5** 85, 103, 129, 209; **L6** 47, 73, 99, 141, 171, 197
 Narrative Writing, **LK** 47, 77, 89, 115, 197, 209; **L1** 59, 85, 99, 137, 167, 189; **L2** 59, 73, 103, 141, 159, 201; **L3** 39, 43, 47, 51, 55, 59, 69, 73, 77, 81, 85, 89, 99, 107, 133, 137, 141, 145; **L4** 43, 85, 119, 145, 163, 193, 209; **L5** 39, 69, 99, 115, 119, 137, 149, 205; **L6** 39, 43, 51, 107, 133, 137, 159, 209
 Personal Writing and Poetry, **LK** 51, 119, 189, 205; **L1** 47, 55, 73, 77, 103, 111, 141, 145, 163, 171, 197, 209; **L2** 39, 47, 69, 81, 85, 111, 115, 133, 145, 149, 167, 189, 209; **L4** 51, 59, 77, 81, 103, 115, 137, 149, 167, 171, 189; **L5** 43, 55, 81, 107, 133, 141, 159, 167, 179, 189, 197, 201; **L6** 69, 103, 111, 129, 149, 175, 179, 193, 205
 Persuasive Writing, **LK** 43, 55, 73, 85, 111; **L1** 51, 81, 119, 149, 179, 205; **L2** 171; **L4** 39, 89, 107, 141, 175, 201; **L5** 73, 89, 111, 163, 193; **L6** 55, 81, 119,
163, 201
Large Eagle (Schimmel), **L2** 199
Large Interior Los Angeles (Hockney), **L4** 96
Las Meninas (The Maids of Honor) (Velazquez), **L2** 184, 185
Lawrence, Jacob, **LK** 83, 101; **L1** 56, 82; **L2** 35; **L3** 60,172; **L4** 180
layout artists, **L3** 62; **L6** 62
Lazzell, Blanche, **L1** 53
Leger, Fernand, **L3** 78
Lemon, Christina, **L6** 206, 207
Leonardo da Vinci Chair (Russell), **L6** 173
Leopard Aquamanile (Unknown), **L2** 79
Letter Holder or Book Cover (Mimac People, Nova Scotia) (Unknown), **L1** 157
Let Them Eat Books, **L1** 213
LeVan, Susan, **L6** 82
Lewitzky Dance Company, **LK** 63
Leyster, Judith, **L4** 184, 185
L'Hiver: Chat sur un Coussin (Winter: Cat on a Cushion) (Steinlen), **LK** 52
Li Bai (Hokusai), **L6** 134
light, **LK** 40; **L2** 178
Lighted City (Thiebaud), **L3** 108
The Lighthouse at Two Lights (Hopper), **LK** 127
Lilac-colored Landscape (Kahn), **L1** 40
Li'l Sis (Johnson), **LK** 82
linear perspective, **L5** 74–77; **L6** 54
lines
 active, **L2** 48–51
 broken, **LK** 56–59
 in buildings, **L1** 52–55
 calm, **L1** 40–43; **L2** 44–47
 contour, **L4** 48–51
 converging, **L5** 72; **L6** 54
 curved, **LK** 48–50; **L1** 48–51, 58
 in dance, **L4** 63
 diagonal, **LK** 45–47; **L1** 44–47, 58
 expressive, **L3** 34–39; **L5** 36–39
 finding, **L1** 34–39
 flowing, **L4** 52–55
 and harmony, **L3** 188; **L5** 188
 horizontal, **LK** 40–43; **L5** 76
 and movement, **L1** 56–59; **L2** 48–51; **L4** 41–43
 in music, **L6** 62
 perspective, **L4** 162
 qualities of, **L6** 36–39
 rough, **LK** 52–55
 and shape, **L1** 65
 smooth, **LK** 52–55
 in song writing, **L1** 63
 in theatre, **L5** 63
 thick, **LK** 36–39
 thin, **LK** 36–39
 types of, **L2** 40–43; **L3** 40–43; **L4** 36–39
 using, **L2** 34–39; **L6** 35
 and variety, **L3** 192; **L6** 186–189
 vertical, **LK** 40–43
 and visual weight, **L4** 192
 zigzag, **LK** 45–47; **L1** 46, 58
Lionni, Leo, **LK** 185A; **L2** 194

TEACHER'S HANDBOOK • Program Index **T43**

Program Index (continued)

The Lion on the Path, **LK** 123
Liotard, Jean Etienne, **LK** 161
Lipchitz, Jacques, **L1** 131; **L4** 126, 127
Lismer, Arthur, **L3** 37
Literature, **LK** 35A
Literature and Art Video
  Abeula, **L3** 155A
  Bridge to Terabithia (Paterson), **L6** 65A
  Call it Courage (Sperry), **L6** 35A
  A Chair for My Mother (Williams), **L2** 155A
  At the Crossroads, **L4** 155A
  The Dancing Skeleton, **L4** 35A
  Diego, **L3** 95A
  Ernst, **L1** 95A
  Eskimo Art, **L4** 125A
  Follow the Drinking Gourd, **L5** 185A
  The Forest Dwellers: Native American Arts of the Pacific Northwest, **L3** 125A
  Free Fall (Wiesner), **LK** 65A
  The Girl Who Loved Wild Horses (Goble), **L6** 95A
  The Great Kapok Tree (Cherry), **LK** 95A
  The Grey Lady and the Strawberry Snatcher (Bang), **L6** 155A
  Heckedy Peg (Wood), **L2** 65A
  Henry and Mudge Under the Yellow Moon (Rylant), **LK** 125A
  Hiawatha's Childhood, **L4** 95A
  The Hundred Penny Box (Mathis), **L6** 185A
  It Could Always Be Worse (Zemach), **L2** 185A
  Jumanji, **L5** 35A
  Kachina Spirit, **L4** 65A
  King Bidgood's in the Bathtub, **L4** 185A
  The Little Band, **L1** 185A
  The Maestro Plays (Martin), **LK** 185A
  Mama Don't Allow, **L1** 35A
  Meet Leo Lionni, **L3** 185A
  Meet the Caldecott Illustrator: Jerry Pinkney, **L5** 95A
  Monster Mama, **L1** 155A
  Narrative Writing, **L3** 129
  Old Henry, **L3** 35A
  Paper Crane, **L1** 125A
  The Pig's Picnic (Kasza), **LK** 155A
  The Polar Express (Van Allsburg), **L2** 95A
  The Relatives Came, **L1** 65A
  Rumpelstiltskin, **L5** 155A
  Saint George and the Dragon (Hodges), **LK** 35A
  Song and Dance Man (Ackerman), **L2** 125A
  The Talking Eggs (San Souci), **L2** 65A
  Tuesday (Weisner), **L6** 125A
  When I Was Young in the Mountains, **L3** 65A
  Yonder, **L5** 65A
lithography, **L6** 142
Little Dancer, Aged Fourteen (Degas), **L3** 64

Little Painting with Yellow (Improvisation) (Kandinsky), **L4** 37
Liu, Hung, **L1** 75
Lobel, Arnold, **L3** 185A
Lobster Trap and Fish Tail (Calder), **L6** 116
location, **L5** 200; **L6** 148
The Locust Trees with Maple (Mangold), **L3** 74
Loeser, Tom, **L3** 160
Loneliness (Neel), **L6** 150
Long Haired Girl, **L2** 92; **L4** 93
Long, Sylvia, **LK** 37
Look Again, **L2** 48; **L5** 116; **L6** 82, 130
The Lookout—"All's Well" (Homer), **L1** 161
Loomings 3X (Stella), **L1** 127
Looner Eclipse (Hoover), **L3** 176
Loring, Eugene, **L3** 213; **L5** 183
Lostutter, Robert, **L2** 96
Lovebird Token (Johnson), **L4** 195
Low Basket with Handle (Jackson), **L4** 206
Lower Manhattan (View Down Broad Street) (Hassam), **L5** 74
low-intensity colors, **L4** 108–111
Lyons, Mitch, **L5** 195

M

Mabe, Manabu, **L5** 109
Macaulay, David, **L6** 65A
MacDonald-Wright, Stanton, **L6** 67
Madame Thadée Natanson at the Theater, **L5** 41
The Magic Room (Valdez), **L4** 82
Magritte, Rene, **L1** 194; **L2** 169; **L3** 90
Mah-To-Toh-Pa, Four Bears, Second Chief (Catlin), **L5** 157
Maison Carree, Nimes, France (Unknown), **L2** 206
"Ma Jolie" (Woman with a Zither or Guitar) (Picasso), **L5** 165
make-up artists, **LK** 152
Mangold, Sylvia Plimack, **L1** 45; **L3** 74
Manguin, Henri-Charles, **LK** 60
Manitoba Party (Kurelek), **L2** 180
Man's Headband of Toucan Feathers (Unknown), **L1** 104
Man (Trujillo), **LK** 130
Map (Johns), **L5** 96, 97
Map Quilt (Unknown), **L2** 173
Maquillage (Goncharova), **L4** 34
Marc, Franz, **L6** 108
marine architects, **L5** 92
marine illustrators, **L4** 212
Marquet, Albert, **L1** 71
Martínez, Maria, **LK** 184, 185
Mask Brooch (Lemon), **L6** 207
Mask Communion

(Mazloomi), **L4** 74
The Mask Messenger, **L2** 63; **L6** 183
Mask of Fear (Klee), **L4** 109
Mask of the Moon (Seaweed), **L1** 191
masks, **L1** 190–193; **L2** 63; **L3** 130–133
Masks: A World of Diversity, **L5** 125A
Mask (Unknown), **L5** 143
Mask with Seal or Sea Otter Spirit (Unknown), **L3** 130, 131
materials, **L2** 66
Mathematics Art Connections
  Geometry, **LK** 43, 47, 59, 73, 89, 189, 197, 201, 209; **L1** 39, 43, 51, 73, 129, 137, 145, 159, 197; **L2** 47, 51, 55, 59, 69, 73, 141, 145, 159, 163; **L3** 39, 47, 51, 55, 77, 99, 137, 145; **L4** 39, 43, 47, 51, 55, 69, 73, 163, 167, 171, 201, 205; **L5** 47, 51, 55, 59, 69, 73, 81, 85, 89, 115, 141, 145, 171; **L6** 39, 43, 47, 55, 73, 77, 119, 149, 193, 197, 201
  Measurement, **LK** 55, 99; **L1** 111, 141, 149, 167, 209; **L2** 43, 107, 175, 193; **L3** 43, 141; **L4** 89, 103, 111, 129, 179, 197; **L5** 129, 197; **L6** 51, 59, 103, 115, 141, 167, 179, 205
  Numbers and Operations, **LK** 51, 69, 77, 81, 85, 103, 107, 111, 115, 119, 193, 205; **L1** 47, 55, 59, 69, 77, 81, 85, 89, 99, 103, 107, 115, 119, 133, 163, 171, 175, 179, 189, 193, 201, 205; **L2** 39, 77, 81, 85, 89, 99, 103, 111, 129, 137, 201, 209; **L3** 59, 69, 81, 89, 107; **L4** 59, 77, 81, 85, 99, 107, 115, 119, 133, 137, 141, 145, 149, 159, 175, 193, 209; **L5** 39, 43, 77, 99, 103, 107, 111, 119, 137, 149, 159, 163, 167, 175, 179, 189, 201, 205, 209; **L6** 69, 81, 89, 99, 107, 111, 129, 133, 145, 159, 163, 171
  Problem Solving, Reasoning, and Proof, **L3** 85; **L4** 189; **L5** 133, 193; **L6** 85, 137, 175, 189, 209
Matisse, Henri, **LK** 94, 95, 108; **L1** 112, 113; **L3** 207; **L4** 49; **L6** 36
matte surface, **L2** 178; **L6** 88
Mayer, Mercer, **LK** 67
Mazloomi, Carolyn, **L4** 74
McCall, Robert, **L5** 79
McCloskey, Robert, **LK** 35A
McCloskey, William H., **L2** 135
McIntosh, Harrison, **L1** 168
McIntyre, Chuna, **LK** 213
McKissack, Patricia C., **L5** 95A
media, **L5** 202–205
medical illustrators, **L4** 212
The Meeting of David and Abigail (Rubens), **L4** 146, 147
Mei, Gu, **L4** 52

Melancholy Metropolis (Mabe), **L5** 109
Memory Jar (Unknown), **L5** 156
Mendoza, Heron Martínez, **L2** 36
Merian, Maria Sibylla, **L2** 130
The Metropolitan Museum of Art, **L5** 122
Michelangelo, **L4** 124, 125
middle ground, **L4** 158; **L6** 54
Mihrab (Unknown), **L3** 49
Milkweed (Krasner), **L4** 139
Miller, Irene Preston, **L5** 202
The Mill (van Rijn), **L2** 168
Miró, Joan, **L5** 161
Miró, Joan, **L4** 79
Miss Liberty Celebration (Zeldis), **L4** 116, 117
mixed-media collages, **L5** 39
Miyawaki, Ayako, **L3** 146
mobiles, **L1** 126, 129; **L3** 81; **L6** 116–117, 119
Model Totem Pole (Edenshaw), **L4** 187
Modigliani, Amedeo, **L5** 139
Moillon, Louise, **L2** 86
Mola (Unknown), **L1** 186
Mona Lisa (da Vinci), **L1** 184
Mondrian, Piet, **L1** 41, 100
Monet, Claude, **LK** 40; **L2** 45, 195; **L3** 36
Money, **L1** 99, 167, 201; **L5** 56; **L6** 202, 206
monochromatic color scheme, **L4** 118; **L5** 96–99
The Monongahela at Morgantown (Lazzell), **L1** 53
Monument (Snowden), **L1** 206
mood, **L4** 116–119
Moore, Henry, **LK** 134; **L1** 208; **L2** 64, 65; **L4** 126
Morandi, Giorgio, **L4** 56, 57
Morisot, Berthe, **L4** 157; **L5** 184, 185
Moroles, Jesús, **L1** 154, 155
Mortlake Terrace (Turner), **L3** 71
mosaic, **LK** 56
Moses, Anna Mary Robertson, **L6** 194
Mother and Child (Cassatt), **L6** 90
Mother and Child (Picasso), **L3** 34
Mother of the Eagles (Unknown), **L5** 198
motif(s)
  and alternating pattern, **L3** 166
  and pattern, **L1** 174, 176–179; **L2** 126–129; **L3** 162; **L4** 76; **L5** 114; **L6** 96–99, 106
  and regular pattern, **L3** 155–159
motion pictures, **LK** 152
Moulthrop, Philip, **L3** 156
Mountain Man (Remington), **L3** 184
movement
  curving, **L2** 146–149
  defined, **L2** 125, **L3** 155
  diagonal, **L2** 142–145
  kinetic, **L6** 116–119
  and lines, **LK** 47–50;

L1 56–59; **L2** 48–51; **L4** 41–43
  and observation drawings, **L4** 45
  and rhythm, **LK** 190–193; **L4** 82–85; **L5** 164–167
  and shape, **L1** 82–85
  and theatre, **L4** 93
  using, **L5** 155
  visual, **L6** 112–115
  and visual rhythm, **L3** 174
Movement and Dance Arts Integration
  balance, **LK** 193B, 197B; **L1** 185B, 189B; **L2** 155B, 159B; **L3** 125B, 129B; **L4** 185B, 189B, 193B; **L5** 167B, 171B, 175B; **L6** 137B
  blending, **L5** 51B
  buildings, **L1** 141B
  colors, **LK** 95B, 99B, 103B, 107B, 111B, 115B; **L1** 95B, 99B, 103B, 107B, 111B, 115B; **L2** 95, 99B, 103B, 185B; **L3** 95B, 99B, 103B, 107B, 111B, 115B; **L4** 95B, 99B, 103B, 107B, 115B; **L5** 95B, 99B, 103B, 107B; **L6** 77B
  contrast, **L5** 55B
  depth, **L3** 69B
  distortion, **L4** 175B; **L5** 137B, 141B; **L6** 163B, 167B
  emphasis, **L1** 193B, 197B; **L2** 163B, 167B; **L3** 193B, 197B; **L4** 145B; **L5** 193B, 197B; **L6** 141B, 145B
  foreground, middle ground, and background, **L4** 155B
  form, **L1** 129B, 133B, 137B; **L2** 65B, 69B, 73B, 77B; **L3** 77B; **L4** 125B; **L5** 81B, 85B; **L6** 43B, 47B
  harmony, **L2** 189B; **L4** 197B; **L5** 185B; **L6** 193B, 197B
  hatching, **L5** 47B
  hues, **L6** 65B
  intensity, **L6** 73B
  lines, **LK** 35B, 39B, 43B, 47B, 51B, 55B; **L1** 35B, 39B, 43B, 47B, 51B, 55B; **L2** 35B, 39B, 43B, 47B; **L3** 35B, 39B; **L4** 35B, 39B, 47B, 51B; **L5** 35B; **L6** 35B
  motif, **L6** 95B
  movement, **L2** 141B, 145B; **L6** 111B, 115B
  observation drawings, **L4** 43B
  overlapping, **L3** 73B
  pattern, **LK** 185B; **L1** 167B, 171B; **L2** 125B, 129B; **L3** 155B, 159B, 163B; **L4** 73B; **L5** 111B, 115B; **L6** 99B, 103B
  perception drawing, **L5** 39B
  perspective, **L4** 159B; **L5** 73B; **L6** 51B
  point of view, **L4** 163B
  proportion, **L4** 167B, 171B; **L5** 125B, 133B, 145B; **L6** 155B, 159B
  rhythm, **LK** 189B; **L1** 175B; **L2** 133B, 137B; **L3** 167B, 171B, 175B; **L4** 77B, 81B, 85B; **L5** 159B, 163B;

L6 107B
scale, **L5** 129B; **L6** 171B, 175B
sculpture, **L3** 81B; **L4** 129B, 133B
shading, **L4** 55B, 111B; **L5** 77B
shapes, **LK** 65B, 69B, 73B, 77B, 81B, 85B ; **L1** 65B, 69B, 73B, 77B, 81B, 125B; **L2** 51B, 55B; **L3** 43B, 47B, 51B, 55B; **L4** 65B, 69B; **L5** 43B, 65B, 69B; **L6** 39B
space, **L1** 145B; **L2** 81B, 85B; **L3** 65B; **L6** 55B
symmetry, **L3** 133B, 137B; **L6** 125B, 129B
texture, **L1** 155B, 159B, 163B; **L2** 171B, 175B; **L3** 141B, 145B; **L4** 137B, 141B; **L5** 155B; **L6** 81B, 85B
three-dimensional art, **L3** 85B
unity, **LK** 201B, 205B; **L1** 201B, 205B; **L2** 201B, 205B; **L3** 201B, 205B; **L4** 205B; **L5** 201B, 205B; **L6** 201B, 205B
value, **L2** 107B, 111B, 115B; **L6** 69B
variety, **L2** 193B, 197B; **L3** 189B; **L4** 201B; **L5** 189B; **L6** 185B, 189B
Mrs. Ezekiel Goldthwait (Copley), **L1** 160
Mt. Nebo on the Hill (Moses), **L6** 194
Munch, Edvard, **L6** 164
Muniti Red Snapper (Puruntatameri), **L1** 66
Muñoz, Juan, **L6** 147
Münter, Gabriele, **LK** 160; **L1** 147
Murray, Elizabeth, **L4** 70, 71
museum guides, **L1** 212
The Museum of Fine Arts, Houston, Tx., **LK** 62; **L3** 122
The Museum of Modern Art, **L2** 122
museums, **LK** 62, 182; **L1** 62, 122, 182; **L2** 62, 122, 182; **L3** 122, 152, 212; **L4** 62, 122, 182; **L5** 62, 122, 182; **L6** 92, 152, 212
music
 dancing, **L2** 142
 harmony, **L5** 186, 189
 lines, **L4** 63; **L6** 62
 sharing, **LK** 108
 space, **LK** 153, 183; **L4** 183;
Music Arts Integration
 balance, **LK** 193B, 197B; **L1** 185B, 189B; **L2** 155B, 159B; **L3** 125B, 129B; **L4** 185B, 189B, 193B; **L5** 167B, 171B, 175B; **L6** 137B
 blending, **L5** 51B
 buildings, **L1** 141B
 colors, **LK** 95B, 99B, 103B, 107B, 111B, 115B; **L1** 95B, 99B, 103B, 107B, 111B, 115B; **L2** 95, 99B, 103B, 185B; **L3** 95B, 99B, 103B, 107B, 111B, 115B; **L4** 95B, 99B, 103B, 107B, 115B; **L5** 95B, 99B, 103B, 107B; **L6** 77B
 contrast, **L5** 55B
 depth, **L3** 69B
 distortion, **L4** 175B; **L5** 137B, 141B; **L6** 163B, 167B
 emphasis, **L1** 193B, 197B; **L2** 163B, 167B; **L3** 193B, 197B; **L4** 145B; **L5** 193B, 197B; **L6** 141B, 145B
 foreground, middle ground, and background, **L4** 155B
 form, **L1** 129B, 133B, 137B; **L2** 65B, 69B, 73B, 77B; **L3** 77B; **L4** 125B; **L5** 81B, 85B; **L6** 43B, 47B
 harmony, **L2** 189B; **L4** 197B; **L5** 185B; **L6** 193B, 197B
 hatching, **L5** 47B
 hues, **L6** 65B
 intensity, **L6** 73B
 lines, **LK** 35B, 39B, 43B, 47B, 51B, 55B; **L1** 35B, 39B, 43B, 47B, 51B, 55B; **L2** 35B, 39B, 43B, 47B; **L3** 35B, 39B; **L4** 35B, 39B, 47B, 51B; **L5** 35B; **L6** 35B;
 motif, **L6** 95B
 movement, **L2** 141B, 145B; **L6** 111B, 115B
 observation drawings, **L4** 43B
 overlapping, **L3** 73B
 pattern, **LK** 185B; **L1** 167B, 171B; **L2** 125B, 129B; **L3** 155B, 159B, 163B; **L4** 73B; **L5** 111B, 115B; **L6** 99B, 103B
 perception drawing, **L5** 39B
 perspective, **L4** 159B, **L5** 73B; **L6** 51B
 point of view, **L4** 163B
 proportion, **L4** 167B, 171B; **L5** 125B, 133B, 145B; **L6** 155B, 159B
 rhythm, **LK** 189B; **L1** 175B; **L2** 133B, 137B; **L3** 167B, 171B, 175B; **L4** 77B, 81B, 85B; **L5** 159B, 163B; **L6** 107B
 scale, **L5** 129B; **L6** 171B, 175B
 sculpture, **L3** 81B; **L4** 129B, 133B
 shading, **L4** 55B, 111B; **L5** 77B
 shapes, **LK** 65B, 69B, 73B, 77B, 81B, 85B; **L1** 65B, 69B, 73B, 77B, 81B,125B; **L2** 51B, 55B; **L3** 43B, 47B, 51B, 55B; **L4** 65B, 69B; **L5** 43B, 65B, 69B; **L6** 39B
 space, **L1** 145B; **L2** 81B, 85B; **L3** 65B; **L6** 55B
 symmetry, **L3** 133B, 137B; **L6** 125B, 129B
 texture, **L1** 155B, 159B, 163B; **L2** 171B, 175B; **L3** 141B, 145B; **L4** 137B, 141B; **L5** 155B; **L6** 81B, 85B
 three-dimensional art, **L3** 85B
 unity, **LK** 201B, 205B; **L1** 201B, 205B; **L2** 201B, 205B; **L3** 201B, 205B; **L4** 205B; **L5** 201B, 205B; **L6** 201B, 205B
 value, **L2** 107B, 111B, 115B; **L6** 69B
 variety, **L2** 193B, 197B; **L3** 189B; **L4** 201B; **L5** 189B; **L6** 185B, 189B
Music (Matisse), **LK** 108

My Dad's Violin (Zalucha), **LK** 180
My Little White Kittens into Mischief (Currier and Ives), **LK** 53

N

Nanha, **L5** 131
Naranjas (Oranges) (Garza), **L1** 78
Naranjo, Michael, **L4** 164–165
Naranjo, Virginia, **L2** 138
narrative painting, **L1** 176
National Gallery of Canada, **L2** 182
The National Museum of Women in the Arts, **L5** 182
National Parts (Ellett), **L6** 199
Native American art, **LK** 36; **L3** 63; **L4** 206
Native Americans, **L1** 156; **L2** 74; **L3** 146
nature, **LK** 36, 75; **L2** 130–133. *See also* Ecology
Navajo Blanket Eye Dazzler (Unknown), **L5** 101
Necklace (Unknown), **L3** 86
Neel, Alice, **L6** 150
negative space, **L2** 136; **L3** 66–70, 178; **L4** 136; **L5** 68; **L6** 56–59
Neighborhoods
 buildings, **L2** 168; **L3** 48, 52; **L5** 86
 community, **LK** 186; **L6** 194
 ecology, **L2** 108
 economy, **LK** 202; **L5** 74
 rhythm, **L1** 176
The Nelson Atkins Museum, **LK** 182
neon, **L2** 154
neutral colors, **L4** 100–103
neutral color scheme, **L4** 118; **L6** 72
Nevelson, Louise, **L2** 124, 125; **L3** 177; **L6** 198
New York City—Bird's-Eye View (Torres-García), **L1** 36
Ngady Ammmwaash (Mweel) Mask (Unknown), **L1** 190
Night Chant Ceremonial Hunt (Begay), **L1** 57
Night Raid (Teichert), **L2** 113
Nighttime in a Palace ('Ali), **L3** 180
Noah, Third Day (Bearden), **L4** 138
NO-HO-MUN-YA, One Who Gives No Attention (Catlin), **L2** 177
Nooning (Homer), **L5** 70
Norman, Joseph, **L1** 60
Norton Simon Museum, **L6** 152
The Nutcracker, "Waltz of the Flowers", **L4** 153
The Nut Gatherers (Bouguereau), **L5** 71

O

Oaxacan sculpture, **L6** 104
observation drawings, **L4** 44–47

Ocean Park #105 (Diebenkorn), **L2** 44
Oceans, **L1** 66; **L2** 44, 194; **L4** 197; **L6** 36, 48, 99
octagon, **L3** 50; **L5** 46; **L6** 42
Octopus Bag (Unknown), **LK** 108, 109
Offering (Shapiro), **L1** 210
O'Keeffe, Georgia, **LK** 75; **L1** 109; **L2** 94, 95; **L3** 113; **L4** 116, 202; **L5** 100; **L6** 130
Old Couple on a Bench (Hanson), **LK** 135
Oldenburg, Claes, **L1** 124, 125
Open Window (Dufy), **L5** 60
Opera House (Utzon), **L5** 87
orange, **L1** 104–107
Orchids and Rocks (Mei), **L4** 52
Ortiz, Alfredo Rolando, **L4** 183
outline, **LK** 66–69; **L1** 66–68
oval, **L3** 46; **L4** 68
Oval with Points (Moore), **L4** 126
overhead view, **L4** 166
overlapping, **L2** 82–85, 87; **L3** 74–77; **L4** 162; **L5** 72; **L6** 54

P

packaging designers, **L6** 182
Paik, Nam June, **L6** 206
Painted Storage Jar (Unknown), **LK** 146
painters, **LK** 212
Palazzo da Mula, Venice (Monet), **L2** 45
palepai, **L6** 202
Pannini, Giovanni Paolo, **L6** 52
Le Pantheon et Saint-Etienne-du-Mont (Dufy), **LK** 126
Papaw Tree (O'Keeffe), **L1** 109
paper designs, **LK** 194; **L3** 67
Parade (Lawrence), **L3** 172
parallelogram, **L3** 50; **L5** 46; **L6** 42
Paris Street, Rainy Day (Caillebotte), **L3** 142
Paris Through the Window (Chagall), **L4** 177
Parsons, Betty, **LK** 156
Pas de Deux (Ragans), **L6** 190
Pas de Deux (Schapiro), **L4** 94
Patriots (Andrews), **L4** 48
pattern
 alternating, **L3** 164–167
 and buildings, **LK** 186–189
 changing, **L1** 172–175
 and color, **L5** 94–95
 decorative, **L5** 112–119
 defined, **L1** 154; **L4** 65
 and motif, **L2** 126–129; **L3** 162; **L6** 96–99
 in nature, **L2** 130–133
 random, **L3** 158
 regular, **L3** 160–163
 and repetition, **L4** 74–78
 in theatre, **L5** 123
 three-dimensional, **L6** 104–107
 two-dimensional, **L6** 100–103
 using, **L1** 168–171
Peale, James, **L2** 161
Pectoral with the Name of Senwosret II (Unknown), **L2** 71
Peeters, Clara, **L4** 113
pentagon, **L3** 50; **L5** 46; **L6** 42
Peony Blooms IX (Zalucha), **L2** 134
people
 and approximate symmetry, **L3** 140
 in art, **LK** 86–89
 and balance, **L2** 160–163
 body proportion, **L4** 172–175; **L5** 128
 face proportion, **L4** 168–171; **L5** 134–137
 and form, **L2** 74–77
 and shape, **L1** 78–81; **L3** 56–59
 and space, **L2** 82–85
 perception drawing, **L5** 40–43
Persistence of Memory (Dali), **L6** 176
Personal Apperance (Schapiro), **L2** 120
perspective, **L4** 158–163; **L5** 72, 74–77; **L6** 52–55
The Philadelphia Museum of Art, **L3** 212
photographers, **L4** 92
photographs, **L2** 108–109
photojournalists, **L4** 92
Picasso, Pablo, **LK** 112, 113; **L1** 87; **L3** 34, 35; **L5** 165; **L6** 56, 57, 94, **L6** 109, 176, 177
Pictorial Quilt (Powers), **L6** 41
Pictorial Tapestry (John), **L3** 191
The Picture Gallery of Cardinal Silvio Valenti Gonzaga (Pannini), **L6** 52
picture plane, **L4** 158
Piero's Piazza (Held), **L3** 97
Pierrot and Harlequin (Cézanne), **L5** 120
Pietà (Michelangelo), **L4** 124
Pilobolus Dance Company, **L6** 153
Pinkney, Jerry, **LK** 92
Pippin, Horace, **L3** 126
Pissaro, Camille, **L4** 156
Pistia Kew (Weber), **L3** 116
placement, **L4** 162; **L5** 72, 198–201; **L6** 54
Plaque (Unknown), **L1** 164
Plate 24 from Poésies (Matisse), **L6** 36
Plate 2 (from "Dissertation in Insect Generations and Metamorphosis in Surinam (Merian), **L2** 130
Plate with Rams (Unknown), **L2** 70
pleating, **L5** 84
Plowing in Nivernais Region (Bonheur), **L3** 168
point of view, **L2** 164; **L4** 46, 164–167
Polacco, Patricia, **L4** 185A
Polar Bears and Cubs (Taqialuk), **L2** 190
Policeman (Hanson), **L2** 160
Pollock, Jackson, **L5** 36, 37
Le Pont Saint-Michel in Paris (Marquet), **L1** 70, 71
Poplars (Monet), **LK** 40
Portrait of a Boy (Unknown), **L3** 138
Portrait of a Noblewoman (Fontana), **L5** 94

TEACHER'S HANDBOOK • Program Index **T45**

Program Index (continued)

Portrait of a Polish Woman (Modigliani), **L5** 139
Portrait of a Woman with a Hood (Matisse), **L4** 49
Portrait of a Young Boy (Andre Berard) (Renoir), **L4** 168
Portrait of a Young Girl in Black (Derain), **L6** 74
Portrait of Dora Maar (Picasso), **L6** 109
Portrait of Emy (Schmidt-Rottluff), **L6** 74, 75
Portrait of Joseph Roulin (van Gogh), **L6** 70
Portrait of Marthe Marie Tronchin (Liotard), **LK** 161
Portrait of Rembrandt (van Rijn), **L6** 124
portraits, **L1** 160; **L2** 176; **L3** 140
Port Saint Tropez, le 14 Juillet (Manguin), **LK** 60
position, **L1** 84; **L6** 136
positive space, **L2** 136; **L3** 66–70; **L4** 136; **L5** 68; **L6** 56–59
Potawatomi Turban (Wisconsin, CIS 3146) (Unknown), **L1** 156
Potter, Beatrix, **LK** 35A
Pottery Vessels (Youngblood), **L3** 186, 187
Pousette-Dart, Richard, **L4** 83
Powder Horn (Gay), **L2** 172
Powers, Harriet, **L6** 41
Prendergast, Maurice, **L1** 117
Presentation of Captives to a Maya Ruler (Unknown), **L3** 82
primary colors, **LK** 108–111; **L1** 100–103, 116–119; **L3** 98, 102; **L4** 98; **L5** 98; **L6** 68
primary hues, **L2** 98
prism, **L6** 68
profile proportion, **L6** 158
proportion, **L2** 192; **L4** 168–175, 183; **L5** 124–129, 132, 134–149; **L6** 155–163, 183
Proposal for a Monument to Apollinaire (Picasso), **L6** 57
Pueblo Scene Corn Dance, Hopi (Kabotie), **L3** 172, **L3** 173
Pueblo Scene Corn Dancers and Church (Vigil Family), **L2** 139
Puff (Krasle), **L5** 207
puppets, **LK** 164–165; **L2** 56–59
Puruntatameri, Francesca, **L1** 66
pyramid, **L3** 80–81; **L4** 128; **L6** 46

Q

quilting, **LK** 176; **L5** 202–204
Quilt (Unknown), **L6** 40
The Quiltwork Girl, **L2** 153

R

radial balance, **L4** 194–197; **L5** 176–179; **L6** 138–141
Radio Dance, **L2** 183

Ragans, Rosalind, **L6** 190
rainbow colors, **L1** 96–99; **L2** 94
Rainbow (Smith), **L4** 36
raised texture, **L1** 164–167
Ramirez, John, **L3** 93; **L6** 213
random pattern, **L3** 158; **L4** 76; **L5** 114, 118; **L6** 102, 106
Ranganiketan Manipuri Cultural Arts, **LK** 153; **L2** 123, **L5** 213
ratio, **L5** 148; **L6** 162
Ray, Man, **L3** 104
realistic art, **L1** 82
realistic scale, **L5** 132; **L6** 172–175
real texture, **LK** 158–159, 172–175; **L1** 156–159
Reclining Figure (Moore), **LK** 134
Reclining Figure with Guitar (Lipchitz), **L4** 126, 127
rectangle, **LK** 72; **L1** 72; **L3** 46; **L4** 68; **L5** 88
Red and Pink Rocks and Teeth (O'Keeffe), **L5** 100
Red Canna (O'Keeffe), **L3** 113
The Red Foulard (Picasso), **L1** 87
The Red Horse (Chagall), **L5** 150
Red Horse Frieze (Branch), **L2** 191
The Red Poppy (O'Keeffe), **L2** 94
Red Rudder in the Air (Calder), **L1** 126
regular pattern, **L3** 160–163; **L4** 76; **L5** 118; **L6** 102, 106
relief art, **L3** 82–85; **L4** 132
reliefs, **L2** 70, 73
Rembrandt (van Rijn), **L2** 168; **L4** 146; **L6** 124, 125
Remedial Archaeology (Wiley), **L3** 101
Remington, Fredric, **L3** 184
Renoir, Pierre Auguste, **L2** 83; **L4** 168; **L6** 64, 65
repetition, **LK** 184–185; **L3** 206–209; **L4** 74–78
Report from Rockport (Davis), **L4** 97
rest, **L3** 170
Return from Bohemia (Wood), **LK** 65
Rex (Butterfield), **L1** 67
Rhinoceros (Dürer), **L1** 130
rhythm
  creating, **L5** 160–163
  and dance, **L1** 183
  defined, **L1** 154; **L2** 125; **L3** 155; **L4** 65
  flowing, **L4** 86–89
  and form, **L2** 138–142
  and motif, **L1** 176–179
  and movement, **LK** 190–193; **L4** 82–85; **L5** 164–167
  and repetition, **L5** 134–137
  and space, **L3** 168–171
  in theatre, **L4** 93
  three-dimensional, **L3** 176–179
  using, **L6** 95, 108–111
  visual, **L5** 172–175
Ringgold, Faith, **L3** 210; **L6** 95A
Riot (Butterfield), **L4** 199

Ritual Bell (Unknown), **LK** 198
Ritual Figure (Unknown), **L1** 138
Ritual Wine Container (Unknown), **LK** 173
Rivera, Diego, **LK** 202; **L3** 94, 95; **L5** 53, 169
Riverbank (Murray), **L4** 71
Roads Untaken (Hart), **L6** 45
The Robert Minden Ensemble, **L4** 123; **L6** 63
Robinson, John, **L5** 191
Rocks and Concrete (Helder), **L4** 101
Rodilla, Simon, **L2** 207
Within the Room (Pousette Dart), **L4** 82, 83
Rose, Timothy, **L6** 116, 117
Rotes Hause (Klee), **L3** 112
Rothenberg, Susan, **L6** 142
Rousseau, Henri, **L1** 74; **L2** 150; **L3** 150; **L6** 112
Royal Workshops, **L6** 160
Rubens, Peter Paul, **L4** 147
Ruben's Wife (Botero), **L5** 138
Ruíz, Antonio, **L1** 177; **L4** 161
Russell, Julia, **L6** 172, 173
Russell, Shirley Hopper Ximena, **L3** 96

S

Safdie, Mosche, **L6** 172
Saint George and the Dragon (Hodges), **LK** 35A
de Saint Phalle, Niki, **L3** 79
Sandburg, Carl, **L1** 213
The San Francisco Museum of Modern Art, **L4** 122
Sargent, John Singer, **L4** 191
Sarve Kashmir, **L6** 93
Satyric Festival Song, **L5** 153
Savitsky, Jack, **LK** 190
Savoy: Heel and Toe (Yard), **L5** 187
Say, Allen, **L6** 185A
scale, **L5** 130–133, 146–149; **L6** 155, 172–179, 183
Schapiro, Miriam, **LK** 86; **L1** 210; **L2** 120; **L6** 66
Schimmel, Wilhelm, **L2** 199
Schmidt-Rottluff, Karl, **L6** 74, 75
Schoenhut, Albert, **LK** 45
Scholl, John, **L4** 194
School, **L4** 171; **LK** 78
School Children on Parade (Ruíz), **L1** 177
School's Out (Crite), **LK** 78
Science Art Connections
  Earth Science, **LK** 81, 115; **L1** 69, 85, 119, 141, 145, 159, 175, 201; **L2** 43, 47, 55, 77, 89, 99, 103, 149; **L3** 39, 43, 89; **L4** 51, 89, 99, 103, 111, 119; **L5** 47, 69, 81, 111, 159, 179; **L6** 47, 59, 73, 77, 81, 89, 107, 129, 137, 163, 189
  Health, **LK** 43, 69, 73, 85; **L1** 137; **L3** 85; **L4** 43; **L5** 73, 209; **L6** 175
  Life Science, **LK** 47, 51, 55, 59, 77, 89, 99, 103, 111, 119, 189, 197, 205, 209; **L1**

43, 51, 59, 77, 89, 103, 111, 115, 149, 171, 179, 193, 197, 201, 209; **L2** 51, 73, 81, 85, 111, 115, 119, 133, 137, 163, 167, 171, 175, 197, 201; **L3** 47, 77; **L4** 39, 47, 55, 69, 73, 77, 81, 115, 133, 137, 141, 149, 159, 163, 167, 171, 179, 189, 197, 205; **L5** 39, 43, 59, 89, 99, 107, 115, 119, 129, 133, 141, 171, 189, 205; **L6** 39, 43, 51, 85, 99, 103, 115, 133, 145, 159, 167, 171, 193, 201, 205
  Physical Science, **LK** 107; **L1** 39, 47, 55, 73, 99, 107, 129, 133, 163, 189, 193, 205; **L2** 59, 69, 107, 159, 189; **L3** 51, 55, 59, 69, 73, 81, 137, 141; **L4** 59, 85, 107, 129, 145, 175, 193, 201, 209; **L5** 55, 77, 85, 103, 137, 145, 149, 163, 167, 175, 193; **L6** 55, 69, 119, 141, 149, 179, 197, 209
  Scientific Method, **L2** 39; **L5** 51, 197
scoring, **L5** 84
Scott, John T., **L2** 40
Scott, Lorenzo, **L2** 164
The Scream (Munch), **L6** 164
sculptors, **LK** 212
sculpture
  additive, **L4** 130–133
  and balance, **LK** 198–201
  earthenware, **L2** 78
  and form, **LK** 130–137, 144; **L3** 78–79
  and geometric form, **L2** 66–69
  positive and negative space, **L4** 136
  reliefs, **L3** 82–85
  and rhythm, **L2** 140
  and space, **L1** 131
  subtractive, **L4** 134–137
  techniques, **L5** 84
  and unity, **LK** 206–209; **L1** 206–209; **L2** 202–205
Sea Grasses and Blue Sea (Avery), **L3** 109
Seal Hunter (Ashoona), **L2** 74, 75
Seated Arhat (Unknown), **L1** 139
Seated Man #4 (Bates), **L6** 56
Seaweed, Joe, **L5** 191
secondary colors, **L1** 106, 110, 114, 116–119; **L3** 98, 102; **L4** 98; **L5** 98; **L6** 68
secondary hues, **L2** 98
Segal, George, **LK** 150; **L5** 146; **L6** 146
Selection from Swimmy (Lionni), **L2** 194
Self-Portrait (Catt), **L4** 60
Self-Portrait Dedicated to Leon Trotsky (Kahlo), **L5** 180
Self Portrait (Hokusai), **LK** 35
Self-Portrait (the Memory) (Flack), **L4** 40
Self Portrait with Big Ears (Learning to Be Free) (Borofsky), **L3** 41
Sendak, Maurice, **LK** 66;

L4 155A
Senufo Face Mask (Unknown), **L3** 130
September Gale, Georgian Bay (Lismer), **L3** 37
set builders, **L2** 152
Sewell, Leo, **L4** 150
Shacks (Harris), **L1** 52
shade, **L2** 118; **L3** 98; **L4** 112–115; **L5** 98; **L6** 72
shading, **L4** 56–59; **L5** 78–81
shadows, **L2** 56
Shadows, **L5** 66; 70
Shahn, Ben, **LK** 79
Shannon, James J., **L2** 82
shape reversal, **L5** 68
shape(s). *See also* form
  and action, **L1** 82–85
  in architecture, **L3** 52–55
  body, **LK** 82–83
  characteristics, **L1** 128
  free-form, **LK** 74–77, 78–81, 83–84; **L1** 74–77, 134–137; **L2** 56–59; **L3** 46, 54, 58; **L4** 70–73; **L6** 40–43
  geometric, **LK** 70–73, 78–81; **L1** 70–73; **L2** 52–55; **L3** 46, 48–51, 58; **L4** 66–69; **L5** 44–47; **L6** 40–43
  and harmony, **L2** 192–193; **L3** 188; **L5** 188
  irregular, **L2** 58
  and lines, **L1** 65; **L3** 34–39
  in music, **L6** 62
  and outline, **LK** 66–69; **L1** 66–68
  and people, **LK** 86–89; **L1** 78–81; **L3** 56–59
  and rhythm, **L6** 110
  in song writing, **L5** 93
  and space, **LK** 126–129; **L6** 95
  still life, **L1** 86–89
  and texture, **LK** 176–179
  in theatre, **L1** 93; **L4** 93; **L5** 63
  two-dimensional, **L2** 68, 128; **L3** 80; **L4** 68
  using, **L3** 44–47
  and variety, **L2** 198–201; **L3** 192; **L6** 186–189
  and visual weight, **L4** 192
Shapiro, Miriam, **L4** 94, 95
Sharecropper (Catlett), **L5** 48
Sharing Stories
  About Me, **L3** 138; **L4** 74
  families, **L5** 156
  feelings, **L4** 108, 168
  imagination, **L3** 82; **L5** 190
  journeys, **L5** 198
  music, **L5** 160
  storytelling, **L2** 138; **L3** 70; **L4** 66; **L5** 142
  Taking a Stand, **L4** 176
Sharp, William, **L6** 143
Sheeler, Charles, **L5** 52
Sheet of Studies for "The Martyrdom of Saint George" (Veronese), **L4** 40, 41
shiny surface, **L2** 178; **L6** 88
Shoestring Potatoes Spilling from a Bag (Oldenburg), **L1** 124
Shotguns Fourth Ward (Biggers), **L4** 66
side view, **L4** 166
Silas Johnson (Cole), **L3** 56

T46 TEACHER'S HANDBOOK • Program Index

silversmiths, **L5** 152
simplicity, **L3** 204; **L4** 204
simulated texture, **L4** 140; **L6** 84
Simultaneous Contrasts: Sun and Moon (Delaunay), **L2** 97
Singing Their Songs (Catlett), **L5** 134
Sioux Moccasins (Unknown), **L1** 199
Sir William Pepperrell and His Family (Copley), **L4** 154
The Sisters (Morisot), **L5** 184
size, **L4** 162; **L5** 72, 174; **L6** 54, 136
Skating in Central Park (Tait), **L1** 48
Skoglund, Sandy, **L4** 142; **LK** 206
Sleeveless Shirt (Unknown), **L3** 66
Slip Trail (Lyons), **L5** 195
Sloan, John, **L3** 194
Smith, David, **L2** 66; **L6** 44
Smith, Jaune Quick to See, **L4** 36; **L5** 34, 35
The Smithsonian Institution, **L4** 182
The Smithsonian Museum of American Art, **L2** 62
Smith, Tony, **L5** 83
Snowden, Gilda, **L1** 206
Snow Queen, Portrait of Adah (Bennion), **L6** 187
Snow Scene (Twachtman), **L6** 70, 71
Social Studies Art Connections
 Civics and Government, **LK** 43, 55, 73, 81, 103, 107, 189, 193, 197, 205, 209; **L1** 39, 51, 55, 85, 107, 115, 119, 145, 167, 171, 175, 197, 209; **L2** 47, 99, 111, 133, 167, 189, 193, 209; **L3** 39, 43, 51, 55, 69, 73, 81, 99, 133; **L4** 51, 77, 81, 103, 115, 119, 145, 167, 171, 201; **L5** 47, 59, 73, 77, 129, 171, 175, 209; **L6** 47, 69, 73, 77, 111, 129, 163, 171, 201, 209
 Economics, **LK** 99; **L1** 103, 189; **L5** 43, 119, 133, 197
 Geography, **LK** 39, 69, 77, 115, 119; **L1** 43, 47, 69, 77, 111, 133, 149, 159, 201; **L2** 39, 43, 55, 59, 69, 103, 107; **L3** 47, 89, 137; **L4** 39, 99, 159, 205; **L5** 39, 55, 69, 99, 103, 115, 141, 201, 205; **L6** 55, 59, 81, 141, 193, 205
 History and Culture, **LK** 36, 37, 40, 44, 45, 48, 49, 52, 56, 59, 60, 63, 85, 89, 111, 201; **L1** 59, 73, 81, 89, 99, 129, 141, 163, 179, 193, 205; **L2** 51, 73, 77, 81, 85, 89, 115, 129, 141, 145, 159, 163; **L3** 59, 75, 89, 129, 141; **L4** 43, 47, 55, 59, 69, 73, 85, 89, 107, 111, 129, 133, 137, 141, 149, 163, 175, 179, 189, 193, 197, 209; **L5** 51, 81, 85, 89, 107, 111, 145, 149, 159, 163, 167, 179, 189, 193; **L6** 39, 43, 51, 85, 89, 99, 103, 107, 115, 119, 133, 137, 145,

149, 159, 167, 175, 179, 189, 197
Solstice (Wilson), **L2** 112
song writing, **L1** 63; **L5** 93
The Sources of Country Music (Benton), **L5** 186
space
 in animation, **L3** 93
 and buildings, **L1** 142–145
 and depth, **L4** 155
 and form, **LK** 124–129, 134–138; **L1** 125, 130–133; **L3** 64–65; **L5** 64–65
 in music, **LK** 153; **L6** 62
 overlapping, **L2** 82–87
 and perspective, **L6** 52–55
 positive and negative, **L3** 66–70; **L5** 66–69
 and rhythm, **L2** 136; **L3** 168–171; **L6** 110
 and shape, **L6** 95
 in song writing, **L5** 93
 and still lifes, **L1** 146–149; **L2** 86–89
 and theatre, **L2** 93
 in three-dimensional art, **L6** 58
 in two-dimensional art, **L5** 70–73
 using, **L6** 35
Space Station #1 (McCall), **L5** 79
Spam (Smith), **L5** 34
Spanish Garden #IV (Norman), **L1** 60
special-effects technicians, **L6** 62
spectral color scheme, **L4** 118
Spectre of the Sea (Gottlieb), **L2** 116
spectrum, **L2** 94–95; **L3** 106; **L4** 98; **L6** 68
Spectrum III (Kelly), **L1** 96
Spectrum II (Kelly), **L1** 96
sphere, **L3** 80–81; **L4** 128; **L5** 88; **L6** 46
Spitzmueller, Pamela, **L3** 199
Spring Ice (Thomson), **L2** 104
Sprinkler Garden (Zalucha), **LK** 96
square, **LK** 72; **L1** 72; **L3** 46; **L4** 68, 128; **L5** 88; **L6** 46
Standing Ruler (Unknown), **L4** 130
Standing Youth (Unknown), **L1** 134
Starry Crown (Biggers), **L4** 90
The Starry Night (van Gogh), **LK** 63; **L2** 146
statues, **L2** 74–75
Stegosaurus (Sewell), **L4** 150
Steichen, Edward, **L2** 108
Steiglitz, Alfred, **L2** 95
Steig, William, **L6** 35A
Steinlen, Theophile-Alexandre, **LK** 52
Stella, Frank, **L1** 127; **L5** 82
Stella, Joseph, **LK** 210; **L2** 37
Steptoe, John, **L4** 95A
Still Life of Fish and Cat (Peeters), **L4** 113
Still Life on Red Tablecloth (Braque), **L5** 44
still lifes, **L1** 86–89, 146–149; **L2** 86–89; **L3** 44–45, 47
Still Life (Walker), **L1** 146
Still Life with Apples and Peaches (Cézanne), **L1** 86
Still Life with Apples and

Peaches (Lawrence), **LK** 101
Still Life with Apples (Cézanne), **L2** 87
Still Life with Basket of Apples (Cézanne), **L5** 45
Still Life with Cherries, Strawberries, and Gooseberries (Moillon), **L2** 86
Still Life with Coffee Pot (Morandi), **L4** 57
Still Life with Porcelain Dog (Münter), **L1** 147
Still Life with the Attributes of the Arts (Chardin), **L6** 82, 83
Still Life with Three Puppies (Gauguin), **L5** 160
stippling, **L5** 58, 80; **L6** 72
stitchery, **LK** 177; **L2** 172, 175
St. Michaels Counterguard (Frank), **L5** 82
Stockman House (Wright), **LK** 138
Stoneware Vase #661 (McIntosh), **L1** 168
stories, **L1** 213
storyboard artists, **L6** 62
The Story of Babar, the Little Elephant, **L1** 93
The Story ofo Babar, the Little Elephant, **L3** 123
The Story of the Nutcracker Ballet, **L4** 153
storytelling, **LK** 48; **L3** 132; **L6** 62
Strand, Paul, **L5** 56
Strawberry Tart Supreme (Flack), **L3** 124
Study for the Munich Olympic Games Poster (Lawrence), **L4** 180
Study for Time-Life Frieze (Moore), **L1** 208
Study of a Sleeping Woman (Rivera), **L5** 53
style, **LK** 96
subordinate part, **L2** 166
subtractive sculpture, **L4** 134–137
Subway Scene (Bishop), **L5** 210
Sugarman, George, **L1** 130
Suite of Appalachian Music & Dance, **LK** 93; **L4** 63
Sullivan Building (TK), **LK** 186
Sullivan, Louis, **L5** 117
Summer, New England (Prendergast), **L1** 117
Summer's Sunlight (Van Ness), **L2** 101
Sunburst (Scholl), **L4** 194
Sun (Dove), **L5** 194
The Sunflower Quilting Bee at Arles (Ringgold), **L3** 210
Sun God (de Saint Phalle), **L3** 78, 79
Sun Transformation Mask (James), **L5** 142
Surowiec, Judith, **L5** 190
Swentzell, Roxanne, **L2** 74
Swimmer Lost at Night (Bartlett), **L5** 164
symbols, **L1** 202–205
Symbols and Love Constellations of a Woman (Miró), **L4** 79
Symbols (Kohlmeyer), **L1** 203
Symmetrical View of a Totem Pole (Unknown), **L3** 134
symmetry, **L2** 156, 158, 162; **L3** 134–141; **L4** 188;

L6 126–133
Symphony Number 1 (Baranoff-Rossine), **L4** 198
synchromy, **L6** 66

T

tab and slot, **L5** 84
tactile texture, **L2** 173–174; **L3** 146–149; **L4** 142–145; **L5** 158; **L6** 86–89
Tait, Agnes, **L1** 48
Taj Mahal, **L5** 130
Taj Mahal (Isa), **LK** 139
Taking a Stand, **L4** 176; **L5** 82
The Tale of Peter Rabbit (Potter), **LK** 35A
Tamayo, Rufino, **L1** 104, 105
Taqialuk, Nuna, **L2** 190
The Tea (Cassatt), **L6** 134, 135
teachers, **L1** 212
technical illustrators, **L4** 212
Technology Art Connections
 balance, **L1** 189, 193; **L3** 129, 133; **L4** 189, 193, 197; **L5** 171, 175, 179; **L6** 137, 141
 blending, **L5** 55
 buildings, **L1** 145
 colors, **LK** 99, 103, 107, 111, 115, 119; **L1** 99, 103, 107, 111, 115, 119; **L2** 99, 103, 107; **L3** 99; **L4** 99, 103, 107, 111, 119; **L5** 99, 103, 107, 111; **L6** 81
 contrast, **L5** 59
 depth, **L3** 73
 distortion, **L4** 179; **L5** 141, 145; **L6** 167, 171
 emphasis, **L1** 197, 201; **L4** 149; **L5** 197, 201; **L6** 145, 149
 foreground, middle ground, and background, **L4** 159
 form, **L1** 129, 133, 137, 141; **L2** 69, 73, 77, 81; **L3** 81; **L4** 129; **L5** 85, 89; **L6** 51
 harmony, **L4** 201; **L5** 189; **L6** 197, 201
 hatching, **L5** 51
 hues, **L6** 69
 intensity, **L6** 77
 lines, **LK** 39, 47, 51, 55, 59; **L1** 39, 43, 47, 51, 55, 59; **L2** 39, 43, 47, 51; **L3** 39, 43; **L4** 39, 43, 51, 55; **L5** 39; **L6** 39, 43, 47
 motif, **L6** 99
 movement, **L2** 145, 149; **L6** 115, 119
 observation drawings, **L4** 47
 overlapping, **L3** 77
 pattern, **L1** 171, 175; **L2** 129, 133; **L4** 77; **L5** 115, 119; **L6** 103
 perception drawing, **L5** 43
 perspective, **L4** 163; **L5** 77; **L6** 55
 point of view, **L4** 167
 proportion, **L4** 171, 175; **L5** 129, 137, 149; **L6** 159, 163
 rhythm, **L1** 179; **L2** 137, 141; **L4** 81, 85, 89; **L5** 163, 167; **L6** 111
 scale, **L5** 133; **L6** 175, 179
 sculpture, **L3** 85; **L4** 133, 137

 shading, **L4** 59, 115; **L5** 81
 shapes, **LK** 69, 73, 77, 81, 85, 89; **L1** 69, 73, 77, 81, 85, 89; **L2** 55, 59; **L3** 47, 51, 55, 59; **L4** 69, 73; **L5** 47, 69, 73
 space, **L1** 149; **L2** 85, 89; **L3** 69; **L6** 59
 symmetry, **L3** 137, 141; **L6** 129, 133
 texture, **L1** 159, 163, 167; **L3** 145; **L4** 141, 145; **L5** 159; **L6** 85, 89
 three-dimensional art, **L3** 89
 unity, **L1** 205, 209; **L4** 209; **L5** 205, 209; **L6** 205, 209
 value, **L2** 111, 115, 119; **L6** 73
 variety, **L4** 205; **L5** 193; **L6** 189, 193
Teichert, Minerva, **L2** 113
Telfair Museum of Art, **L1** 62
Ten Little Rabbits (Long), **LK** 37
textiles, **L6** 194
texture
 and balance, **L3** 124–125; **L5** 174
 and color, **L6** 64–65
 creating, **L5** 155–159
 in dance, **LK** 154–155; **L1** 183; **L6** 93
 defined, **LK** 154–155; **L1** 154; **L2** 155
 and design, **LK** 164–167
 and fibers, **LK** 168–171
 and form, **LK** 172–175
 and informal balance, **L6** 136
 in music, **LK** 183
 real, **LK** 158–159, 172–175; **L1** 156–167
 and shape, **LK** 176–179
 tactile, **L2** 172–175; **L3** 146–149; **L4** 142–145; **L6** 86–89
 and touch, **LK** 156–159
 and variety, **L3** 192
 visual, **LK** 162–163; **L2** 176–179; **L3** 142–145; **L4** 138–141; **L6** 82–85
Thai Shadow Puppet (Unknown), **L2** 57
theatre, **L1** 93; **L2** 63, 93; **L4** 93; **L5** 63, 123
Theatre Arts Integration
 balance, **LK** 193B, 197B; **L1** 185B, 189B; **L2** 155B, 159B; **L3** 125B, 129B; **L4** 185B, 189B, 193B; **L5** 167B, 171B, 175B; **L6** 133B, 137B
 blending, **L5** 51B
 buildings, **L1** 141B
 colors, **LK** 95B, 99B, 103B, 107B, 111B, 115B; **L1** 95B, 99B, 103B, 107B, 111B, 115B; **L2** 95, 99B, 103B, 185B, 189B; **L3** 95B, 99B, 103B, 107B, 111B, 115B; **L4** 95B, 99B, 103B, 107B, 115B; **L5** 95B, 99B, 103B, 107B; **L6** 77B
 contrast, **L5** 55B
 depth, **L3** 69B
 distortion, **L4** 175B; **L5** 137B, 141B; **L6** 163B, 167B
 emphasis, **L1** 193B, 197B; **L2** 163B, 167B; **L3** 193B, 197B; **L4** 145B; **L5** 193B, 197B; **L6** 141B, 145B
 foreground, middle ground,

Program Index (continued)

and background, **L4** 155B
form, **L1** 129B, 133B, 137B;
  L2 65B, 69B, 73B, 77B; **L3**
  77B; **L4** 125B; **L5** 81B,
  85B; **L6** 43B, 47B
harmony, **L2** 189B; **L3**
  185B; **L4** 197B; **L5** 185B,
  L6 193B, 197B
hatching, **L5** 47B
hues, **L6** 65B
intensity, **L6** 73B
lines, **LK** 35B, 39B, 43B,
  47B, 51B, 55B; **L1** 35B,
  39B, 43B, 47B, 51B, 55B;
  L2 35B, 39B, 43B, 47B; **L3**
  35B, 39B; **L4** 35B, 39B,
  47B, 51B; **L5** 35B; **L6** 35B
motif, **L6** 95B
movement, **L2** 141B, 145B;
  L6 111B, 115B
observation drawings,
  L4 43B
overlapping, **L3** 73B
pattern, **LK** 185B; **L1** 167B,
  171B; **L2** 125B, 129B; **L3**
  155B, 159B, 163B; **L4** 73B;
  L5 111B, 115B; **L6** 99B,
  103B
perception drawing, **L5** 39B
perspective, **L4** 159B; **L5**
  73B; **L6** 51B
point of view, **L4** 163B
proportion, **L4** 167B, 171B;
  L5 125B, 133B, 145B;
  L6 155B, 159B
rhythm, **LK** 189B; **L1** 175B;
  L2 133B, 137B; **L3** 167B,
  171B, 175B; **L4** 77B, 81B,
  85B; **L5** 159B, 163B;
  L6 107B
scale, **L5** 129B; **L6** 171B, 175B
sculpture, **L3** 81B;
  L4 129B, 133B
shading, **L4** 55B, 111B;
  L5 77B
shapes, **LK** 65B, 69B, 73B,
  77B, 81B, 85B; **L1** 65B,
  69B, 73B, 77B, 81B, 125B;
  L2 51B, 55B; **L3** 43B, 47B,
  51B, 55B; **L4** 65B, 69B; **L5**
  43B, 65B, 69B; **L6** 39B
space, **L1** 145B; **L2** 81B,
  85B; **L3** 65B; **L6** 55B
symmetry, **L3** 133B, 137B;
  L6 125B, 129B
texture, **L1** 155B, 159B, 163B;
  L2 171B, 175B; **L3** 141B,
  145B; **L4** 137B, 141B; **L5**
  155B; **L6** 81B, 85B
three-dimensional art,
  L3 85B
unity, **LK** 201B, 205B; **L1**
  201B, 205B; **L2** 201B, 205B;
  L3 201B, 205B; **L4** 205B; **L5**
  201B, 205B; **L6** 201B, 205B
value, **L2** 107B, 111B,
  115B; **L6** 69B
variety, **L2** 193B, 197B; **L3**
  189B; **L4** 201B; **L5** 189B;
  L6 185B, 189B
theme, **L5** 206–209
*There's a Nightmare in My
  Closet* (Mayer), **LK** 67
Thiebaud, Wayne, **LK** 71, 104;
  L3 108, 120; **L4** 112; **L6** 120
The Thinker (Unknown), **L1** 150

Thomson, Tom, **L2** 104
three-dimensional art,
  L6 198–201, 206–209
three-dimensional forms,
  L1 138–141; **L2** 68, 140; **L3**
  80–81, 86–89; **L4** 128
three-dimensional rhythm,
  L3 176–179
three-dimensional shapes,
  L4 200
three-dimensional space,
  L6 58
Three Machines (Thiebaud),
  LK 104
*Three People on Four Park
  Benches* (Segal), **L6** 146
Thunderbird Shield
  (Unknown), **L3** 146, 147
Tiffany, Louis Comfort, **LK** 56
Tilly (Henri), **L5** 135
Time Transfixed (Magritte),
  L1 194
tint, **L2** 114; **L3** 98; **L4**
  112–115; **L5** 98; **L6** 72
Tissot, James, **L5** 173
Tlingit society, **L4** 104
Toast to the Sun (Tamayo),
  L1 105
Tooker, George, **L5** 127
Toraji Taryong **LK** 183
Tornado Over Kansas
  (Curry), **L5** 126
Torres-García, Joaquín, **L1** 36;
  L4 67
Tortilla Molds (Unknown),
  L1 165
Touchwood Hills (Eyre), **L1** 108
Toulouse-Lautrec, Henri de,
  L5 41
Town, Harold, **L2** 117
Town of Skowhegan, Maine
  (Jacquette), **L2** 210
Toy Banks (Unknown), **L5** 206
toy designers, **L5** 212
Tracey, Paul, **LK** 123; **L1** 63;
  L3 93; **L5** 93; **L6** 213
The Tragedy (Picasso), **LK** 113
Train in Coal Town
  (Savitsky), **LK** 190
trains, **LK** 190–193
Transportation, **LK** 190;
  L1 100; **L3** 39, 51
trapezoid, **L3** 50; **L5** 46; **L6** 42
The Tree of Houses (Klee),
  L2 186
Tree of Life (Bakula), **L3** 66, 67
triangle, **LK** 72; **L1** 72; **L3** 46;
  L4 68, 128; **L5** 88; **L6** 46
Trujillo, Felipa, **LK** 130
Tudor, Tasha, **L1** 155A
Tundra Swan (Audubon),
  L2 198
Tunic (Unknown), **L3** 164
Turner, Joseph Mallord
  William, **L3** 71
Twachtman, John Henry,
  LK 116; **L6** 70, 71
Twiggs, Leo, **LK** 90; **L2** 49
Two Birds in Hand (LeVan),
  L6 82
Two Black-on-Black Pots
  (Martínez), **LK** 184
two-dimensional art,
  L6 194–197
two-dimensional forms,
  L4 128

two-dimensional shapes,
  L2 68, 28; **L3** 80; **L4** 68
two-dimensional space,
  L5 70–73
Two Fishermen and a Boat
  (Gile), **L1** 101
Two Girls (Bishop), **L6** 156
Two Sisters (On the Terrace)
  (Renoir), **L2** 83

u

United States Capitol, **L6** 126
unity
  in architecture, **L2** 202–209
  and color, **L3** 202–205
  creating, **L4** 185, 206–209;
    L5 185; **L6** 185
  in dance, **L2** 212; **L6** 213
  defined, **LK** 202–209;
    L1 185; **L2** 185; **L3** 185
  and media, **L5** 202–205
  and repetition, **L3** 206–209
  in sculpture, **L1** 206–209
  in stories, **L1** 202–205, 213
  and theme, **L5** 206–209
  in three-dimensional art,
    L6 206–209
  in weaving, **L6** 202–205
unrealistic scale, **L5** 132;
  L6 176–179
urban design, **L5** 92
*Urban Raven/Urban Indian
  Transformation Mask*
  (Dick), **LK** 154
Utzon, Jørn Oberg, **L5** 87

v

Valdez, Patssi, **L4** 82
Valleyridge (Eyre), **L2** 187
value
  and blending, **L5** 52–55
  and color, **L3** 94–95, 123;
    L4 94–95, 102, 114
  and contrast, **L5** 56–59
  and dance, **L4** 123
  dark, **L2** 116–119
  defined, **L3** 98
  and hatching, **L5** 48–51
  light, **L2** 112–115
  in photographs, **L2** 108–109
  and shading, **L4** 58
  in theatre, **L5** 63
  using, **L6** 70–73
Van Allsburg, Chris, **L5** 155A
van Gogh, Vincent, **LK** 63;
  L2 146; **L5** 154, 155; **L6** 53, 70
vanishing point, **L5** 76
Van Ness, Beatrice Whitney,
  L2 101
van Rijn, Rembrandt, **L2**
  168; **L4** 146; **L6** 124, 125
variety
  of color, **L2** 194–197
  and contrast, **L6** 190–193
  creating, **L3** 190–193;
    L4 185; **L5** 185, 190–193;
    L6 185–189
  in dance, **L2** 212; **L6** 213
  defined, **L2** 185; **L3** 185
  and emphasis, **L4** 202–205
  of shape and form,
    L2 198–201
Various Fish (Miyawaki),
  L3 146
Velásquez, Diego, **L2** 184, 185
Vermeer, Jan, **L2** 176; **L5** 64, 65
Veronese, Paolo, **L4** 41
From the Viaduct, 125th St.
  (Strand), **L5** 56
Victorian Parlor (Pippin),
  L3 126
Vie No. 1 (Life No. 1)
  (Herbin), **L1** 70
A View of Mansfield Mountain
  (Kensett), **L2** 104, 105
Vigil Family, **L2** 139
violet, **L1** 112–115
Visa (Davis), **L1** 202
The Visitation (Rembrandt),
  L4 146
visual movement, **L4** 84;
  L5 166; **L6** 112–115
visual rhythm, **L3** 172–175;
  L4 78–81; **L5** 155, 162
visual texture, **LK** 162–163;
  L1 160–163; **L2** 176–179;
  L3 142–145; **L4** 138–141;
  L5 158; **L6** 82–85
visual weight, **L4** 192
*The Voice of the City of New
  York Interpreted...* (Stella),
  L2 37
Voice of the Wood, **L3** 153;
  L5 63
Vuillard, Edouard, **LK** 97
Vytlacil, Vaclav, **L3** 45

w

The Wadsworth Atheneum,
  L4 62
Walk Don't Walk (Segal),
  L5 146
The Walker Art Center, **L3** 152
Walker, Patricia, **L1** 146
The Walking Flower (Leger),
  L3 78
Warhol, Andy, **L3** 202
warm hues, **L5** 108–111
Warnyu (flying boxes)
  (Djukulul), **L3** 160, 161
Warren, John, **L6** 49
Washington at Yorktown
  (Peale), **L2** 161
Washington's Headquarters
  (Unknown), **L3** 70
watercolor, **L4** 54
Waterfall Blue Brook
  (Twachtman), **LK** 116
Watts Street (Brosen), **L5** 75
Watts Tower (Rodilla), **L2** 207
Weary (Whistler), **L5** 49
Weather
  changes, **L3** 36
  rainbow colors, **L1** 96
  seasons, **LK** 56; **L1** 40, 119; **L2**
    100; **L3** 74, 104; **L4** 99, 160
  shadows, **L5** 66; **L6** 70
  temperature, **LK** 40
  time, **L1** 112
  wind, **LK** 74; **L4** 86
weaving, **LK** 36, 170; **L1** 172;
  L6 202–205
Weber, Idelle, **L3** 116
Weber, Max, **L6** 94, 95
Webster, Elon, **L5** 142

L2 198–201
Various Fish (Miyawaki),
Wells, Rosemary, **L1** 65A
The Westwood Children
  (Johnson), **L4** 190
We Tell Stories, **L1** 213
Where the Wild Things Are
  (Sendak), **LK** 66
Whistler, James McNeill,
  L4 56; **L5** 49
White Pine Mosaic
  (Moulthrop), **L3** 156
White Vertical Water
  (Nevelson), **L6** 198
The White Wave (Avery), **L4** 100
The Whitney Museum, **L6** 92
Wiesner, David, **LK** 74; **L5** 185A
Wiley T, William, **L3** 101
Williams, Garth, **L5** 35A
Williams, Vera B., **L5** 155A
Wilson, Jane, **L2** 112
Winged Frog (Parsons), **LK** 156
Winter Loneliness (Hokusai),
  L4 87
Winxiang, Prince Yi
  (Unknown), **L5** 168
Woman (Blanco), **L4** 131
Woman in a Purple Coat
  (Matisse), **LK** 94
Woman in Blue (Matisse),
  L3 207
Woman's Headcloth
  (Unknown), **L6** 195
*Women of Paris: The Circus
  Lover* (Tissot), **L5** 173
Wood, Grant, **LK** 64, 65; **L4** 160
words, **L1** 202–205
Her World (Evergood),
  L3 138, 139
World's Greatest Comics
  (Shahn), **LK** 79
Wrapped Oranges
  (McCloskey), **L2** 135
Wright, Frank Lloyd, **LK** 138
Wyeth, N. C., **L6** 125A

y

The Yale University Gallery,
  LK 122
Yard, Richard, **L5** 187
Yeihl Nax'in Raven Screen
  (Unknown), **L4** 104
Yeiltatzie, John, **LK** 195
*Yellow Hickory Leaves with
  Daisy* (O'Keefe), **L4** 202
Yellow Pad (Fish), **L3** 44
Yellow Top (Sugarman), **L1** 130
Young, Ed, **L5** 65A
Youngblood, Nancy, **L3** 187
*Young Spanish Woman with
  a Guitar* (Renoir), **L6** 64

z

Zalucha, Peggy Flora, **LK** 96,
  180; **L2** 134
*Zandunga Tehuantepec
  Dance* (Rivera), **LK** 202
Zeldis, Malcah, **L4** 117
zigzag lines, **L1** 46, 58

T48 **TEACHER'S HANDBOOK** • Program Index